The **AA** **KEY**Guide
New Zealand

Contents

KEY TO SYMBOLS

- ✚ Map reference
- ✉ Address
- ☎ Telephone number
- 🕐 Opening times
- 💷 Admission prices
- 🚌 Bus number
- 🚆 Train station
- ⛴ Ferry/boat
- 🚗 Driving directions
- ℹ Tourist office
- 🎫 Tours
- 📖 Guidebook
- 🍴 Restaurant
- ☕ Café
- 🏬 Shop
- 🚻 Toilets
- 🛏 Number of rooms
- 🚭 No smoking
- ❄ Air conditioning
- 🏊 Swimming pool
- 🏋 Gym
- ❓ Other useful information
- 🛍 Shopping
- 🎭 Entertainment
- 🌙 Nightlife
- 🏃 Sports
- ⭐ Activities
- 💗 Health and beauty
- 👶 For children
- ▷ Cross reference
- ★ Walk/drive start point

HOW TO USE THIS BOOK

Understanding New Zealand is an introduction to the country, its geography, economy and people. **Living New Zealand** gives an insight into the country today, while the **Story of New Zealand** takes you through its past.

For detailed advice on getting to New Zealand—and getting around once you are there—turn to **On the Move**. For useful practical information, from weather forecasts to emergency services, turn to **Planning.**

Out and About gives you the chance to explore New Zealand through walks and drives.

The **Sights, What to Do** and **Eating and Staying** sections are divided geographically into six regions, which are shown on the map on the inside front cover. These regions always appear in the same order. Towns and places of interest are listed alphabetically within each region.

Map references for the **Sights** refer to the atlas section at the end of this book or to the individual town plans. For example, Wellington has the reference ✚ 318 J11, indicating the page on which the map is found (318) and the grid square in which Wellington sits (J11).

UNDERSTANDING
NEW ZEALAND

New Zealand took its place on the tourist map in 1880, when modish travellers included it on their route around the world. Although facilities were distinctly basic, visitors managed to fill several letters with enthusiastic reports of the countryside and its varied populations. These days, tourists can opt out of 'tent hotels' for world-class luxury, but New Zealand's beauty remains sublime. There are dozens of ways to experience it, too, from the high-adrenalin of jet-boats and bungy jumps to the serenity of walks, drives or alfresco dining. It is an easy country to enjoy—attractions, transport and Kiwi attitudes welcome more than 2 million visitors a year.

THE LANDSCAPE

New Zealand consists of three main islands—the North Island, the South Island and Stewart Island—with a handful of small, far-flung islands completing the family. The total land area is 270,500sq km (104,795 square miles).

Although compact in size, New Zealand's landscape is rich and varied, with glaciers, braided rivers, lakes, fiords, sounds (flooded riverbeds, found predominantly in the South Island), lowlands, alluvial plains, wetlands, large natural coastal harbours and a rash of offshore islands.

Because New Zealand is located at the meeting point of the Pacific and Indo-Australian tectonic plates, it also experiences frequent earthquakes. A string of volcanoes stretches from the currently active Whakaari/White Island in the Bay of Plenty to Mount Ruapehu in the heart of the North Island. The area also has numerous thermal features, including geysers, mineral springs, blowholes and mud pools, most of which can be found around Rotorua and Taupo.

The South Island is far more mountainous than the North and boasts the country's highest peak, Mount Cook/Aoraki (▷ 131). The country's longest river is the Waikato, which stretches 425km (264 miles) from Lake Taupo to the Tasman Sea.

Great stretches of these wonderful landscapes are unmarked by humans—no roads, no houses, no telegraph poles. Within an hour's drive from most main towns you can find the edge of habitation. Another hour or two in a chosen mode of transport—such as walking, horse-riding or kayaking—and you can be totally remote. While some outdoor areas are deservedly popular, like the tramping tracks of Fiordland, in plenty of other spots you can explore for miles without seeing another soul. Where else in the world can you do that without threat of a poisonous snake or spider?

PEOPLE AND POPULATION

The population of New Zealand currently stands at about 4 million: with just under 3 million in the

Milford Sound is one of the great sights of New Zealand, and the Milford Track is famous worldwide

North Island and just under 1 million in the South Island. Greater Auckland is home to just over 1 million people.

New Zealand is essentially a bicultural society made up of Maori and Europeans, with many other nationalities also present. Maori make up about 14 per cent of New Zealand's total population, with the vast majority living in the North Island. There are around 231,000 Pacific Islanders, with many living in greater Auckland. Asians make up three per cent of New Zealand's total population and are the fastest-growing minority group, again settled mainly in the greater Auckland area.

A number of distinctive personalities have made it big in national and local politics—Georgina Beyer, the world's first transsexual MP; Nandor Tanczos, the Rastafarian Green with waist-length dreadlocks; Tim Shadbolt, the flower-power activist turned mayor of Invercargill; and Dick Hubbard, breakfast cereal magnate and mayor of Auckland.

RELIGION

The dominant religion is Christianity, with Anglican, Presbyterian and Roman Catholic denominations being the most prominent. Minority religions include Hinduism, Islam,

Left, morning mist hangs above Lake Rotoaira; middle, ferns thrive in the wetlands of the southwest; right, natural steam-clouds at Wai-O-Tapu; below, traditional Maori moko (face decoration)

New Zealanders are famous for being the world's greatest travellers, and at any one time a large proportion of citizens are absent or living abroad. More than 400,000 live and work in Australia alone. Through their close trans-Tasman ties, Australian and New Zealand citizens are free to live and work in both countries.

MAORI CULTURE

A big draw for visitors is the vibrant culture of New Zealand's first inhabitants, the Maori. After being threatened with extinction at the turn of the last century, Maori society enjoyed a renaissance towards the end of the 1970s. Language, art and *kapa haka* (performance arts) are thriving. The most popular place for visitors to experience these is Rotorua.

POLITICS

Things change quickly in New Zealand. With its small population and triennial elections, it's sometimes seen as a social laboratory. Currently under the microscope is Mixed Member Proportional representation (MMP), an electoral system that has helped a wider range of MPs into parliament since it was introduced in 1996. As well as the two long-established parties, Labour and National, significant political stakes are held by the environmentally friendly Green Party, family-values oriented United Future and migrant-watching New Zealand First.

Judaism and Buddhism. The Maori developed two of their own minority Christian-based faiths, Ratana and Ringatu, both of which were formed in the late 19th to early 20th centuries. At least a quarter of the total population are atheists or have no religion, and this number is growing.

VISITING NEW ZEALAND

Many visitors from Asia experience New Zealand in three days flat—Auckland, Rotorua, Queenstown. These are great spots, but to get a feel for the country, its people and culture, you really need two weeks minimum. If your flight takes more than 12 hours, three weeks is preferable, simply because jet lag can spoil the first few days.

The easiest way to travel is by road. Coaches are inexpensive, reliable and connect most visitor areas, while campervans have become incredibly popular, providing flexible access to remote quarters with no worry of finding a bed for the night. Rail is limited, with some notable exceptions—the TranzAlpine trip from Christchurch to Greymouth is an attraction in its own right. If time is limited, a good way to see the highlights of both islands is to fly. If you have a contact, it's less expensive to book from within the country, and the earlier the better.

There are ample opportunities to try outdoor activities such as hiking, fishing, hunting and mountain biking. Just be aware that if you bring your own equipment, it must be scrupulously cleaned before you try to get it through customs. Most gear can be easily hired anyway, and the results are all but guaranteed if you use the services of an experienced guide.

LANGUAGE

See pages 308–309.

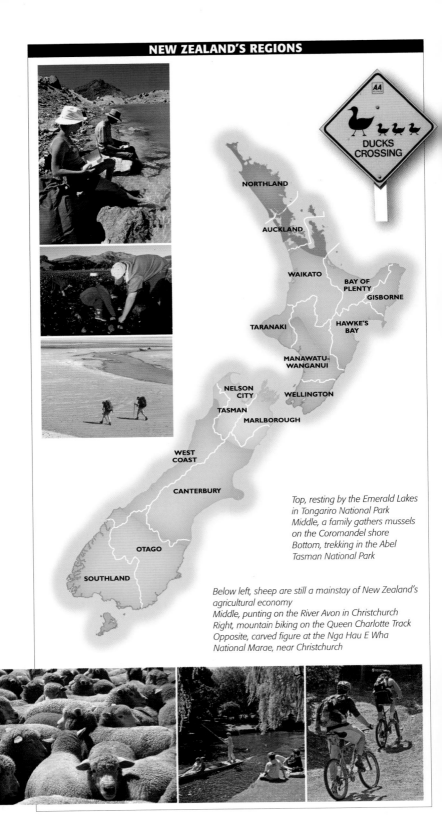

DUCKS CROSSING

NORTHLAND

AUCKLAND

WAIKATO

BAY OF PLENTY

GISBORNE

TARANAKI

HAWKE'S BAY

MANAWATU-WANGANUI

NELSON CITY

WELLINGTON

TASMAN

MARLBOROUGH

WEST COAST

CANTERBURY

OTAGO

SOUTHLAND

Top, resting by the Emerald Lakes in Tongariro National Park
Middle, a family gathers mussels on the Coromandel shore
Bottom, trekking in the Abel Tasman National Park

Below left, sheep are still a mainstay of New Zealand's agricultural economy
Middle, punting on the River Avon in Christchurch
Right, mountain biking on the Queen Charlotte Track
Opposite, carved figure at the Nga Hau E Wha National Marae, near Christchurch

AUCKLAND, NORTHLAND AND COROMANDEL

Auckland: New Zealand's commercial hub and largest city, with 1.2 million residents. Ferries give access to prettier areas such as Devonport and Waiheke Island, while the Sky Tower gives a 360-degree view of the city and its harbours.

Northland: Warm, humid and sparsely populated, with impressive coastal landscapes. North of Ninety Mile Beach is sacred Cape Reinga. The Waipoua Forest Sanctuary is home to New Zealand's largest kauri tree. The Bay of Islands, known for big-game fishing, has historic sites, including Waitangi National Reserve.

Coromandel: Conservationists and artisans now fiercely defend the sunny peninsula, once exploited for gold, coal and kauri.

CENTRAL NORTH ISLAND

Rotorua: Spectacular geothermal activity includes bubbling mud pools, geysers, steaming lakes and a welcoming spa complex. The tourist capital of Maori culture.

Lake Taupo: New Zealand's biggest lake. Its crystal waters are famed for trout fishing.

The Volcanic Plateau: Three volcanoes rise from an austere plain, including Mount Ruapehu, whose crater still simmers.

New Plymouth: Wedged between Mount Taranaki (Mount Egmont) and the Tasman Sea, the city gains an artistic edge from its cosmopolitan oil industry.

Napier: Destroyed by an earthquake in 1931, the city was rebuilt as an art deco delight.

SOUTHERN NORTH ISLAND

Wellington: The capital city looks a gem from the Botanic Garden's lookout, accessed by cable car. Home to national museum Te Papa, the Beehive parliament building and hundreds of excellent cafés.

The Wairarapa: Wine-making has brought boutique shopping and dining to villages like Martinborough and Greytown.

Kapiti Coast: Long white-sand beaches and a pleasant climate. Kapiti Island, 6km (4 miles) off the coast, is one of New Zealand's most important nature reserves.

Wanganui: The serene Whanganui River is rich in Maori history and legend. It is popular for jet-boating and kayaking.

NELSON AND MARLBOROUGH

Nelson: Warm, sandy beaches rival the best of the North Island's, while craggy mountains and rough rivers are distinctly South Island. Its many attractions include the vast stretch of Golden Bay and the easy-to-stroll Abel Tasman National Park.

Nelson City: The quality of local clay has attracted successful potters and other established artists. The town's creativity pulses through The World of Wearable Art and Classic Cars museum.

Marlborough: The first Marlborough wineries were instrumental in putting New Zealand on the world wine map. Now there are 44 within 15km (9 miles) of Blenheim, many also offering world-class cuisine.

CANTERBURY AND THE WEST COAST

Christchurch: Called the Garden City, the South Island's largest city has vast areas of parkland. Visitors can punt on the Avon, visit the landmark Anglican cathedral on Cathedral Square and explore the lively Arts Centre. The Port Hills and beaches make a delightful change to the city's flatness.

Canterbury: From the farms of the Canterbury Plains, the region suddenly rears up into the Southern Alps. Star of these great mountains is Aoraki (Mount Cook). Azure Lake Tekapo has a memorial to sheepdogs of the harsh McKenzie Country.

The West Coast: A thin strip of land between the Southern Alps and the ocean. Narrow State Highway 6 winds through dense rainforest, near Fox and Franz Josef Glaciers, and past Punakaiki Pancake Rocks. Evocative scenery is guaranteed, unlike the weather.

OTAGO AND THE FAR SOUTH

Dunedin: Victorian and Edwardian architecture beckon in Larnach Castle, Olveston and the railway station. The Otago Peninsula is home to the distinguished Royal Albatross Centre, plus many penguins and seals.

Otago: Queenstown is New Zealand's adventure capital, with world-renowned bungy jumping and jet-boating. Quieter but equally scenic towns include Wanaka and Arrowtown, with incredible mountains, lakes, rivers and autumn colour.

Fiordland: The wettest, wildest corner of New Zealand, consisting of mountains and water. Milford Sound is the most accessible of the fiords. Its photographic gems are Mitre Peak and the immense Bowen Falls.

THE BEST OF NEW ZEALAND

BEST PLACES TO STAY

Pukematu Lodge, Russell (▷ 275), a modern
B&B with great hospitality and fabulous views.
Huka Lodge, Taupo (▷ 278), the luxury lodge
where the stars go to be pampered.
The Lighthouse, Wellington (▷ 281), for
unusual accommodation in the capital.
Collingwood Homestead, Collingwood
(▷ 282) where Colonial comfort is the tops.
Corstorphine House, Dunedin (▷ 288), a
private hotel in a historic, stylish setting.

*Above, Collingwood Homestead
Left, Milford Sound, in Fiordland
National Park*

BEST ADRENALINE RUSHES

Bungy jump from Auckland's Sky Tower
(▷ 65, 167)—even watching it from the
viewing platform makes your stomach lurch!
Zorb at Rotorua (▷ 177)—but when
you've finished rolling downhill in an inflated ball you may
not recall which part of Down Under is down under!
Luge down a steep hill on little more than a tray, with
Skyline Skyrides near Rotorua (▷ 87)—take the
gondola up and the luge down.
Jet-boat on the Shotover River through
Skippers Canyon (▷ 147), with tours from
Queenstown (▷ 148)—after all, New
Zealanders developed the craft specially.
White-water raft on the Buller Gorge from Murchison
(▷ 117) or Westport (▷ 202), or join a
black-water rafting trip in the Waitomo cave
system (▷ 90, 179) if you're fearless.

*Above, bungy-jump
from the Sky Tower if
you dare…
Left, enjoy the thrills
of a jet-boat
Below, famed
Moeraki Beach*

BEST BEACHES

Ninety Mile Beach is an unequalled stretch of soft
white sands on the Aupouri Peninsula (▷ 57),
near the northern tip of the country, but don't be
tempted to drive on it yourself (for tours, ▷ 168).
Kaiteriteri, on the Abel Tasman coast of the South Island
(▷ 110), offers golden sands on a stunningly lovely bay.
Wharariki, on Farewell Spit (▷ 111), is a patch of golden sands
on a curving spit that harbours wading birds and fur seals.
Rabbit Island, by Nelson (▷ 114), offers seemingly endless
miles of volcanic grey sands backed by pine forest.
Moeraki beach (▷ 145) comes with the bonus of a bizarre clutch
of rounded boulders, a natural phenomenon well worth seeing.

*Above, surfing beaches abound,
but beware of rip-tides along
the coastline
Below, select your preferred
tipple or try new wines*

BEST PLACES FOR WINE TASTING

Martinborough's chief advantage (▷ 94, 181) is that there are
around 20 vineyards within strolling distance of its Wine
Centre—so no danger of drinking and driving as you sample
your way around.
Hawke's Bay is famous in international wine circles, and you can
compare some of the best at its annual wine festival (▷ 179).
Waiheke Island has a number of excellent vineyards—try
Stonyridge for its Cabernet Sauvignon (▷ 170), or join in the
annual winefest (▷ 171).
Napier is surrounded by extensive vineyards, including the venera-
ble Church Road winery (▷ 175), where you can also explore
the country's only wine museum.
Blenheim (▷ 111) is an otherwise unremarkable town at the
heart of the Marlborough/Wairau Valley wineries (▷ 119);
for some of the best wine in the South Island, head to Cloudy
Bay (▷ 189).

THE BEST OF NEW ZEALAND

*Above, a thermal mud pool
Right, the stylish White
restaurant*

BEST PLACES TO EAT

White, Auckland (▷ 253) for high-class dining in the City of Sails.
Chocolate Fish Café, Wellington (▷ 260), a relaxed waterfront hang-out frequented by the *Lord of the Rings* cast and crew.
Smokehouse Restaurant, Mapua (▷ 262) is the place for top-notch fish, close by Nelson.
C'est la Vie, Akaroa (▷ 264) for unusually intimate dining and French cuisine in this pretty settlement.
Saffron, Arrowtown (▷ 267) offers wild local ingredients perfectly combined, in a historic setting.

BEST LANDSCAPES

The Bay of Islands (▷ 68) offers some of the most outstanding coastal scenery in the North Island, and doubles as a popular watersports venue.
Rotorua's extensive geothermal landscape (▷ 84) is unrivalled, with stinking, steaming sulphur mud pools, spouting geysers of boiling water, and multi-hued lakes.
Abel Tasman National Park (▷ 109), with its sandy bays and azure sea, lush coastal vegetation and famous tramping trail, is a popular holiday destination for Kiwis.
Westland Tai Poutini National Park (▷ 134) boasts two of the great sights of New Zealand—the Franz Josef and Fox glaciers.
Fiordland National Park (▷ 141) takes in a spectacular landscape of steep forested peaks and drowned glaciated valleys, seen to advantage from the Milford Track (▷ 143).

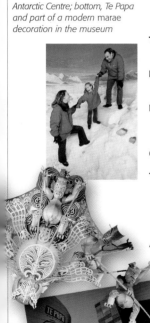

*Above,
volcanic
White Island, a
nature reserve;
left, penguins get
right of way in
Oamaru; below, fun at the
Antarctic Centre; bottom, Te Papa
and part of a modern marae
decoration in the museum*

BEST PLACES TO SEE WILDLIFE

Tiritiri Matangi Island (▷ 71) is an accessible haven in the Hauraki Gulf, just 35 minutes from Auckland, where endangered native birds such as takahe and little spotted kiwi thrive.
Pukaha Mount Bruce Wildlife Centre (▷ 95) is the Department of Conservation's flagship breeding centre, where you can see stitchbirds, wild eels and kaka parrots.
Kaikoura (▷ 113, 190) is known around the world for the success of its whale- and dolphin-watching tours, and you can also get up close (within smelling distance) to fur seals along this coast.
Oamaru (▷ 145) is the chosen home of little blue and yellow-eyed penguins, with opportunities to see both rare species.
The Otago Peninsula (▷ 147) stretches northeastwards from Dunedin and is home to the only mainland-based royal albatross colony in the world.

BEST BIG MUSEUMS AND GALLERIES

Auckland Museum Tamaki Paenga Hira (▷ 62), set in the Auckland Domain (park), has some of the finest collections of Maori and Pacific Island artefacts in the country.
Auckland Art Gallery (▷ 59) has what is probably the biggest and best collections of New Zealand art, including famous paintings by Goldie and Lindauer.
Te Papa Tongarewa-Museum of New Zealand (▷ 96), the national museum, set in an architecturally intriguing building on Wellington's harbourfront, opened in 1998 with highlights of a vast collection.
The International Antarctic Centre in Christchurch (▷ 128) is the public face of a lively, working campus, giving a great introduction to the science and history of south polar exploration.

BEST LOCAL MUSEUMS

The Matakohe Kauri Museum (▷ 69) celebrates a native New Zealand tree with creative displays about its value to early settlers, from ships' masts to the uses of its valuable gum resin.

The Museum of Caves at Waitomo (▷ 91) is a world-class introduction to the formation of limestone caves and the creatures and people who have used them.

The Museum of Wellington City and Sea (▷ 104) marks the maritime heritage of the 'windy city', with excellent displays of local exhibits.

The World of Wearable Art and Classic Cars (▷ 115) put Nelson firmly on the fashion map, with its wacky and outrageous costume designs and its light-hearted presentation—and the cars are pretty special, too.

Coaltown Museum at Westport (▷ 133) gives an insight into the heyday of mining on the west coast—both for coal and gold—with evocative items including the massive brake drum from the Denniston Incline.

TOP 10 EXPERIENCES

Go for a walk. The Kiwis call it tramping, and there's a huge choice of longer trails (▷ 246) and short strolls to get you closer to nature.

Eat a top-class meal of local delicacies (▷ 248–269). New Zealand lamb is hard to beat for taste and tenderness, the seafood is superb and the modern Pacific-influenced style of cooking is refreshing.

Learn about Maori culture. There are lots of opportunities in major towns to enjoy a Maori cultural event, partake of a *hangi* (▷ 251) or visit a *marae*—Rotorua offers some of the best (▷ 84–87).

Take to the water, even if it's only the Interislander ferry (▷ 52), and look for dolphins and seabirds. Sailing, kayaking and wildlife watching are just some of the options (▷ 151–212).

Ride on the TranzAlpine, the fabulous scenic rail route through the Southern Alps that links Christchurch and Greymouth (▷ 199).

Shop 'til you drop. There's much more to modern New Zealand fashion than the hard-working Swanndri (▷ 197), and the lively markets are a great way to source original souvenirs—try Aotea Square in Auckland (▷ 164), or Nelson (▷ 191), or Dunedin (▷ 205).

Watch sport and talk about it. It's probably the best way to blend in with the locals, whether you pick Ellerslie for racing (▷ 166), the Basin Reserve for cricket (▷ 185), Addington for trotting (▷ 198), or just about anywhere for rugby.

Sit in an outdoor thermal pool and experience natural reinvigoration. Rotorua (▷ 84–87) or Hanmer Springs (▷ 123) are the most obvious venues, but smaller places include Maruia Springs (▷ 130).

Fly over a glacier to experience a bird's-eye view of a moving snow-field—or better still, land on one and see it close up (▷ 200, 202)

Do something that sets your heart racing. New Zealand is becoming the world capital of adventure and adrenaline sports, and Queenstown (▷ 148–149) and Rotorua (▷ 84–87) are the main places, but you'll find opportunities everywhere. Go on—have a try!

Above, dolphin-spotting in the Bay of Islands; top, traditional Maori dancing; below, thermal bathing at Mount Maunganui

Above, tramping on the scenic Abel Tasman Coast Track
Left, Maori carving, Waitangi

Helicopter flights give thrilling access to remote landscapes

Living
New Zealand

Left, *Lord of the Rings* was the making of New Zealand tourism

Left, rainbow kiwi, Otorohanga; right, look smart with the Urban Stroller

New Zealand's
People

It's barely 200 years since European settlers moved into Aotearoa, the land they called New Zealand. In this short time, each city has developed an identity as distinctive as its new residents. Auckland's cosmopolitan citizens are known for their laptops, mobile phones and boating obsessions. Wellington is home to politicians, civil servants and cultured café society. Christchurch people, with their good manners and manicured gardens, are more English than the English. Dunedinites celebrate their Scottish heritage and the untamed freedoms of their wildlife and students. Beyond the cities, the farming folk are characterised by their bush-shirts, gumboots and staunched emotion.

The Maori maintain their cultural stronghold in places such as Rotorua and Gisborne, but their influence touches all parts of the country. Against all odds, Maori culture survived colonisation and continues to gain strength and standing. It is a highly regarded element of the national identity, for despite minor regional differences, the overriding belief is that New Zealanders—Kiwis—are one. They value a practical, down-to-earth approach, with nothing too frilly. They are great travellers who are unencumbered by tradition, and relish new ideas. They see themselves as 'laid back' but stand firm on issues they hold dear.

Retro chic: a restored Christchurch tram

Kiwi Ingenuity

New Zealanders reckon they can make just about anything with a good whack of No. 8 fencing wire. Their flair for lateral thinking has led to a disproportionate number of successful inventions—for example, the three-wheeled Mountain Buggy, developed by Allan Croad in his family garage from an old golf trundler bought for NZ$5 at a school gala in 1992. The company now exports to 16 countries and makes blokes proud to push the pram.

Classic Kiwi inventions include the tranquilliser dart gun, now exported from Timaru to zoologists, farmers and game-keepers worldwide, and the electric fence, brainchild of a Waikato farmer. Then there's the Hamilton jet-boat—which thrills visitors by speeding through mere centimetres of water—eartags for livestock, the electronic petrol pump, childproof bottle tops, spring-free trampolines and spreadable butter…

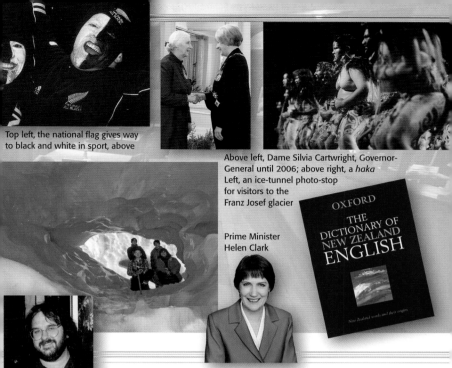

Top left, the national flag gives way to black and white in sport, above

Above left, Dame Silvia Cartwright, Governor-General until 2006; above right, a *haka*
Left, an ice-tunnel photo-stop for visitors to the Franz Josef glacier

Prime Minister Helen Clark

OXFORD

THE DICTIONARY OF NEW ZEALAND ENGLISH

New Zealand words and their origins

Scruffy Icon

New Zealand's devotion to Oscar-winning film-maker Peter Jackson is absolute.

Jackson has ticked every box on the Kiwi Hero scorecard. He was a DIY self-starter who made war films on his parents' back lawn, aged eight. His breakthrough movie, cult gorefest *Bad Taste*, was created with home-made equipment and a bunch of mates. He stuck by New Zealand when Hollywood offers flowed in, and insisted the *Lord of the Rings* trilogy should be made in his own backyard. New Zealanders love him just as he is...although there was a murmur of approval when, for a *King Kong* press launch, he was rumoured to have trimmed his hair.

The New Immigrants

The New Zealand government has worked hard to attract migrants with investment capital or much-needed job skills—such as trades people and medical specialists. The impact showed clearly in the 2001 census. The Asian population had doubled in 10 years, so for the first time their numbers (240,000) exceeded those of Pacific peoples (231,000). Those of European heritage decreased by 3 per cent to 80 per cent. Just over 14 per cent were Maori. The melting-pot effect is particularly noticeable in Auckland, which is home to two-thirds of Asian and Pacific peoples.

The total population tipped 4 million for the first time in 2003. This figure is always slightly skewed as at any one time an estimated half a million Kiwis are overseas. The majority live in Australia, thanks to the mutual absence of work restrictions.

Women's World

Despite New Zealand's macho history of farming and rugby, women have played a significant role in the nation's development. New Zealand was the first country in the world to give women the vote, in 1893; the first country where two women leaders fought in a general election, in 1999; and the first country to elect a transsexual MP. In the early 21st century women occupied all the top roles in the government—Head of State (Queen Elizabeth II), the Governor-General (Dame Silvia Cartwright, whose term finished in 2006), the Prime Minister (Helen Clark), the Chief Justice (Dame Sian Elias) and the Speaker of the House of Representatives (Margaret Wilson). In Parliament, 37 of the 121 MPs are women, including another party leader—Jeanette Fitzsimons, co-leader of the Green Party.

Local Lingo

The Dictionary of New Zealand English (OUP, 1997) contains 6,000 main entries and 9,300 sub-entries, proving that although the country's official language is English, a visitor should not expect to understand it all. Phrases like 'rattle your dags' (hurry up) reflect a farming background, while 'half pie' (not great) stems from the Maori word *pai* (good). *Jandals* (flip flops), *jaffas* (chocolate balls with an orange coating) and *pikelets* (hotcakes) are part of everyday life and language.

A strong New Zealand accent can be difficult to penetrate—it is similar to Australian, but the 'i' sound gives it away. Kiwis tend to turn it into a 'u' sound, as in 'fush and chups', while Australians say 'feesh and cheeps'. The accent is more-or-less consistent across the country except for Southland, where a rolled 'r' is common.

Above and left, the Coast to Coast endurance race; top right, river surfing; right, the calmer pursuits of mussel gathering and sea fishing

The Great
Outdoors

When Canadian country-pop star Shania Twain visited Central Otago, New Zealand was thrilled. When she decided to buy a slice of it in 2004, the reception was rather cooler. New Zealanders are strongly connected with their land and love to share it with visitors. But they became wary around 1998, when the world's super-rich started snapping up beauty spots at bargain prices. Land values shot up. Young farmers now struggle to get started and traditional *baches* (holiday cottages) are vanishing.

The most sensitive issue is public access to the land on the coast, under threat from developers, and the foreshore, where Maori customary rights and recently enacted Crown ownership don't always sit comfortably. In Twain's case, her company, Soho Properties, took out pastoral leases for Motatapu and Mount Soho Stations near Wanaka that were approved with stringent conservation and access conditions, some being suggested by Soho. Part of the agreement was the establishment of a walking track through both properties and the building of two new huts, funded by Soho Properties. Her land also hosts a walk/bicycle event, The Motatapu Icebreaker. So it's positive outcomes for all, as New Zealanders love being able to use and enjoy their countryside.

A Beautiful Game

Kiwi rugby fans were genuinely shocked that the All Blacks didn't make the final of the Rugby World Cup in 2003. After all, rugby is the national game. Since their victory at the inaugural World Cup in 1987 disappointment has dogged the All Blacks—in subsequent competitions they have made just one final and three semis. But the loyal fans are hoping that will change in the 2007 Rugby World Cup, in France. The All Blacks have led the International Rugby Board's world rankings continuously for nearly four years, so Kiwis are hopeful. What's more, New Zealand is the reigning champion in the under-21s and the under-19s, and the Black Ferns, the women's team, are three-time world champions.

Left, Doug Howlett takes the ball from French defenders at the 2003 Rugby World Cup

Bungy jumping—not a sport for the faint-hearted

Top, unwinding in Auckland; left, thrills and spills; below, not crazy golf but GolfCross, with inventor Burton Silver

Left, popular activities include sailing and mountain biking

Sailing Hopes

New Zealand is a nation of yachties—it's not for nothing that Auckland is known as the City of Sails, and at the Anniversary Day Regatta at the end of January the whole population seems to be out on the water. The whole country was swept up in the enthusiasm in 2000, when Team New Zealand became the first non-US syndicate to retain the America's Cup in 2000. This all fell to pieces in the next defence, in 2003, after star skipper Russell Coutts was lured to the Swiss Alinghi team, and the Kiwi team suffered a series of major equipment failures—the boat was swamped in one race, and the mast snapped in half in another. But hopes were riding high for the 2007 regatta in Valencia, Spain, with fans hopeful that Kiwi ingenuity and know-how would again prevail.

Crazy, But Smart

When A.J. Hackett jumped off the Eiffel Tower in a dinner suit in 1987, attached only to his prototype bungy cord, the world declared Kiwis crazy. Perhaps—but Hackett and co-founder Henry van Asch were on to something. Some 450,000 tourist jumps later, in 2004 a multimillion dollar Bungy Centre was opened at Kawarau Bridge in Queenstown by Prime Minister Helen Clark.

New buzzes are invented every year to enhance New Zealand's reputation as the adventure capital of the world, but bungy remains queen bee. There are now four A.J. Hackett bungy sites (and many non-Hacketts), offering something for everyone, including the original Kawarau site (43m/141ft) for history buffs, Auckland Harbour Bridge (40m/131ft) for those who like smart technology, or Nevis Highwire, near Queenstown (134m/440ft), for the truly brave.

Mountain Madness

Normal people take three hours to drive west-to-east across the South Island. But once a year, hardy souls do it the hard way, in the Speight's Coast to Coast multisport race from Kumara Beach, near Greymouth, to Sumner Beach, near Christchurch. The 243km (151-mile) course consists of 140km (87 miles) cycling, 67km (42 miles) kayaking and 36km (22 miles) running, including a 33km (20-mile) mountain stage across the Southern Alps. Competitors take anything from 10 hours 45 minutes (the course record) to 24 hours. The race's hero is Christchurch man Steve Gurney, who has competed 19 times and won 9 times since it began in 1983. More than 900 competitors from 18 countries vied for a place in the 2007 event, attracted by the promise of personal achievement and a free beer at the finishing line.

Don't Get Mad, Get Cross

It's not for purists, but anyone looking for a unique—yet sedate—outdoor experience in New Zealand couldn't do better than GolfCross. The game is much like golf but uses an oval ball and a large rubber tee. Players use regular clubs but the putter isn't required—instead of holes and greens, the ball is pitched into a triangular goal with a two-sided net.

Surprisingly, the oval ball is easier to control than a round one. How the ball is set on the tee determines whether it will fly straight, hook or slice. The game's creator, Wellington inventor and writer Burton Silver, says this encourages players to take greater risks. The four GolfCross courses are in beautiful farmland (complete with sheep) near Rotorua, Wanaka, Martinborough and Mount Cook/Aoraki.

Left, traditionally carved greenstone (*pounamu*) pendant

Above and below, inventive and quirky modern sculptures abound

Whale Rider threw young Keisha Castle-Hughes into the limelight

The Arts

The Next Precioussss

After starring as Middle Earth, New Zealand's next major film role was Narnia, under Kiwi director Andrew (*Shrek*) Adamson. Work on *The Lion, the Witch and the Wardrobe* began in Auckland in early 2004, the production's budget of over NZ$150 million nicely helping to fill the economic void left by the America's Cup. Later that year, filming moved to locations in the South Island, including high country, coast, alpine plateau, forests and mock English countryside. The only major hiccup was the Ministry for Agriculture and Forestry (MAF)'s refusal to let 14 American reindeer into the country in case they carried potentially deadly Q fever. It took six months to create a replacement team out of fibreglass and motors.

After suffering years of 'cultural cringe', New Zealanders are finding their own confident voice. Through the 1970s and 80s there was a perception that homegrown meant awful. Only accolades from abroad could guarantee artistic acceptance locally. High expectations perhaps had benefits—per head of population, New Zealand has a remarkable success rate. Literature had a good start with Katherine Mansfield (▷ 33) and the murder mysteries of Dame Ngaio Marsh (▷ 307). These days, children's fiction stands out, with Margaret Mahy, Joy Cowley and Lynley Dodd's *Hairy Maclary* selling millions of books worldwide.

Split Enz and Kiri Te Kanawa led the way into the international music scene in the 1980s; performers like Hayley Westenra and opera star Jonathan Lemalu now follow on. In the 1990s, a strong film industry emerged with *An Angel at my Table*, *Once Were Warriors*, *The Piano* and *Heavenly Creatures*. They laid the foundations for the proudest moment in the history of Kiwi arts: Peter Jackson, director of *The Lord of the Rings* trilogy, and Keisha Castle-Hughes, star of *Whale Rider*, together on the red carpet at the 2003 Academy Awards. Fabulous locations and tax breaks should keep the film-makers coming, but the greatest benefit is New Zealand's new pride in its cultural identity.

Mail boxes are an expression of folk art fun

hobbiton
movie set

Tour Booking Office
Tours Depart
9.30 / 10.45 / 12.00 / 1.15 / 2.30 / pm

Book here or
Phone 07 - 888 6838
www.hobbitontours.com

Rings Scenic
TOURS
MATAMATA · NEW ZEALAND

Maori carvings, above and below right

Singer Hayley
Westenra,
left; WOW,
below

Singing Belles

New Zealand's latest music export is Hayley Westenra (b.1987), young, gorgeous and acclaimed the world over. In 2004, 17-year-old Hayley's album *Pure* stormed into the UK pop chart at No. 8 and the classical chart at No. 1. In New Zealand, the album's 18-week stay at No. 1 made her the country's biggest-selling artist ever. Soon after, she was dovetailing exams at her Christchurch high school with international appearances alongside Pavarotti, José Carreras and Bryn Terfel. She has performed for the Queen, Tony Blair and President Bush.

For those who like something a little more Norah Jones, New Zealand offers Brooke Fraser. She was just 20 when she won 'Tuis' at the 2004 Vodafone New Zealand Music Awards for best female and breakthrough artist of the year.

Wow-wee!

The Montana World of Wearable Art (WOW) awards show is big and getting bigger. Sculptor Suzie Moncrieff started it in 1987 to promote her Nelson art gallery, and it quickly boomed into a two-hour theatrical extravaganza. The televised awards are held each September before an audience of thousands. Entrants, from overseas designers to first-time locals, submit fantastical costume creations in any materials: Stained glass, wood panelling, flax, car parts and dried sausage skins have featured. 2004 saw the awards' last night in Nelson; the show then moved to Wellington as part of an expansion plan. The ultimate vision is to stage events in different parts of the world and bring the winners to a grand final in New Zealand. The World of Wearable Art museum remains in Nelson (▷ 114–115).

Eeyore meets Michelangelo

What do you get when you cross a Portaloo with sounds of a braying donkey and a volcano? Some say groundbreaking art, others a shocking waste of taxpayers' money. For sure, it's an animated fracas when the work's creator is to represent New Zealand at the most important contemporary arts event in the world.

The 'Donkey Toilet' (real title *Rapture 2004*), created by a collective known as et al, caused a stink when exhibited at Wellington's City Gallery. But the stuff really hit the fan when CreativeNZ revealed that it provided NZ$500,000 to send et al's work to the 2005 Venice Biennale. It turned out the 'collective' was established artist Merilyn Tweedie, and her Venice installation would feature computer hardware rather than a noisy toilet—but Joe Kiwi remained staunchly unimpressed.

Frame and Mirror

One of New Zealand's literary giants was Janet Frame, and since her death in 2004 her life has been commemorated in a Heritage Trail in Oamaru (▷ 145). Born in 1924 in Dunedin, Frame grew up shy, poor and marked by a head of frizzy orange hair. A misdiagnosed schizophrenic, she passed most of her 20s in psychiatric institutions. Despite the fact she was intensely reclusive, readers knew her through her novels (especially *Owls Do Cry*) and her three-part autobiography: *To the Is-land*, *An Angel at My Table* and *The Envoy from Mirror City*. She became widely recognised in New Zealand after 1983, when her autobiographies brought international acclaim, and she was tipped for the Nobel Prize in 2003. The Janet Frame Heritage Trail in Oamaru includes the railway worker's house where she grew up, and places featured in her books.

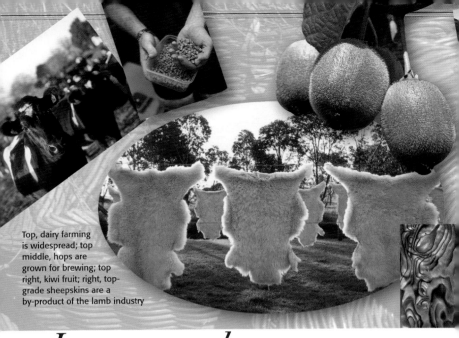

Top, dairy farming is widespread; top middle, hops are grown for brewing; top right, kiwi fruit; right, top-grade sheepskins are a by-product of the lamb industry

Income and
Industry

New Zealand is riding a wave of economic stability. The country's seventh successive year of growth was 2006, making this the strongest and longest period since the 1960s. The unemployment rate of 3.7 per cent is the lowest in 20 years. As ever, the country's largest industry is agriculture. It brings in over 60 per cent of export earnings, but national survival no longer depends on the population of 40 million sheep: the 5.2 million (and increasing) dairy and 4.4 million beef cattle are slowly changing the face of agriculture, creating wealth in regions such as Southland. Other industries such as forestry, fishing and deer farming have grown, each nurturing their niche products—such as mussels for the US and ice cream for Japan.

New Zealand's 'clean, green' image is ruthlessly exploited to market agriculture and the other big earner—tourism. More than 2 million visitors spend an estimated NZ$6 billion a year on unique Kiwi experiences. It's estimated that tourism accounts for one in ten jobs in New Zealand.

As prosperity has increased, so has the share price of Kiwi retail icon The Warehouse. The red sheds are 'where everyone gets a bargain', bulk discounting everything from sofas to face cream.

ORGANIC KIWIFRUIT. READY TO EAT. $2 Per bag

Roadside stalls are a regular sight in the major fruit-growing areas

Spreading the Web

The *Rings* trilogy shone the spotlight on New Zealand's IT industry, highlighting Kiwis' ability to combine creativity with computer genius. Gollum's parents at Weta Workshop continue to lead the way; aside from *King Kong*, their digital experts have been developing cost-effective animation for children's TV since 2003. Kiwis' other successful projects tend to be niche, such as web and email security, e-health systems, farming software, and the technology behind new-wave mobile phone services. It's hard going, though. Despite proven potential, the industry suffers from remoteness and lack of local investment capital. The story is all too common: Small development company is nurtured to world-class standing, then sold to US heavyweight who regrettably shuts the New Zealand office and makes the original staff redundant.

Sophisticated wine-making has become a top earner in New Zealand

Above, sheep outnumber citizens by 10 to 1; below, paua shell, used for souvenirs

Engineering feats: the Otira Viaduct (top right); Clyde hydro-electric dam (above); Tararua Wind Farm (right)

Deer Me!

France has Champagne; New Zealand has Cervena. This is top grade, trademarked venison—mild, tender, low in fat, and heavy on the clean, green imagery. With a national herd of 1.6 million, the industry is small fry compared to sheep and dairy. Nevertheless, it holds international significance as the world's number one source of farmed venison, exporting particularly to the US, Europe, Australia and Japan. Some 85 per cent of venison served in American restaurants comes from New Zealand. Deer velvet, known for its medicinal properties, is also in demand and earns around NZ$38 million a year. The deer population has grown 34 per cent since 1994, and the South Island herd by 70 per cent. The name Cervena comes from *cervidae*—Latin for deer—and venison.

Musseling In

What's so special about New Zealand mussels that makes them worth counterfeiting? The green-lipped mussel (*Perna canaliculus*) is native and unique to New Zealand. Its green-and-gold shell contains plump meat that is creamy white when male or apricot when female. Their size and taste give them a top reputation among mussel-buffs the world over, especially in the US, where inferior Chinese mussels (*Perna viridis*) have been sold in fake New Zealand packaging. The big concern—other than economic, as the industry is worth NZ$200 million a year—is that Chinese imposters are a potential health hazard. Mussels farmed under the New Zealand Greenshell trademark are grown under such stringent conditions they are safe to eat raw, but Chinese mussels are not. New Zealand's biggest mussel farms are in the Marlborough Sounds.

A Powerful Wind

New Zealand's geographical quirks aren't just for looks—they keep the country running. Mighty rivers like the Clutha and Waikato are dammed for hydro-electricity, which is the main source of power (61.4 per cent). Geothermal activity provides another 6.9 per cent, while gas, sourced particularly from the Taranaki offshore field, Maui, provides 24.4 per cent. But crisis looms. Drought in 2003 lowered lake levels so severely that the country was threatened with blackouts; and Maui reserves are expected to run out around 2015. The government aims to develop renewable energy to take up the slack. In 2004, Te Apiti wind farm was opened in the Manawatu. The country's fifth wind farm, it is expected to become the biggest in the southern hemisphere, with 55 turbines, each able to power 700 homes.

Top Tipple

Accessible and elegant, wine is perhaps the Kiwis' best-loved export. The industry burgeoned from a historical fondness for beer and sherry, surprising the world in 1988 when it was highly featured at the London Wine Trade Fair. Export earnings have rocketed from NZ$18 million in 1990 to NZ$600 million in 2006: more New Zealand wine is drunk overseas than domestically. New Zealand Sauvignon blanc is a reliable award-winner and has become the world's benchmark. Chardonnay, Pinot noir and Cabernet/Merlot blends are also gaining recognition.

New Zealand has 10 main wine-growing areas from Northland to Central Otago, the most established being Gisborne, Hawke's Bay and Marlborough. Many vineyards rate highly on the tourist trail, offering exceptional cuisine to complement tastings.

INCOME AND INDUSTRY 19

Right, the problematic possum

Right, a seahorse farm at Napier; below, autumn colour on the Kapiti Coast

Left, a frosty fern; right, cuddling a tuatara

Nature and Wildlife

Even as they step off the plane, visitors discover how serious New Zealand is about protecting its environment. No foreign plant or animal matter slips easily across the border; and a forgotten apple earns a NZ$250 spot fine.

Vigilance has been learned the hard way. Before man's arrival the country's only mammals were bats. The bush was thick with birds, many of which safely evolved as ground-dwellers—including the moa, kakapo and kiwi. The meaty moa was hunted to extinction by the Maori, and with the arrival of Europeans, hundreds more species vanished as their habitats were destroyed. Introduced animals compounded the disaster. With no natural predators, possums, cats, dogs, stoats, ferrets and rats ran rampant and are still a severe menace to native birds.

What's truly remarkable is that in spite of all the losses, wildlife remains one of New Zealand's greatest marvels. Native flora and fauna flourish in wilderness pockets all over the country, as well as a few inner-city areas such as Karori Wildlife Sanctuary in Wellington, where populations of rare kiwis, saddlebacks and kereru thrive. Much can be attributed to the expertise of local conservationists, who are in hot demand as far away as Indonesia and Madagascar.

The emblematic ponga, or black tree fern (*cyathea medullaris*)

Super Bugs

The giant weta is a heavyweight of the insect world. It can grow 9cm (3.5 inches) long, excluding antennae, and weigh up to 80g (3oz)—the same as four average mice. Even so, it is the sweetest-looking of New Zealand's five types of weta and by far the rarest. These nocturnal super-bugs evolved good defences against their natural enemies—birds—but are poor jumpers and no match for hungry stoats, rats or weasels. However, weta breed well in captivity and their track record for survival is good—in evolutionary terms they are older than dinosaurs. The mountain rock weta of the Southern Alps is the largest insect known to tolerate being frozen solid in winter. Most weta eat foliage or animal remains, but will try a human finger if threatened.

Right, bottlenose dolphins off the Nelson coast; left, flora in Wellington Zoo

Below, yellow-eyed penguin; right, a basking New Zealand fur seal

Below, familiar New Zealand birds include the kiwi, the kea (a parrot), the flightless weka, the New Zealand robin and the royal albatross

Keeping the Balance

When Penguin Place on the Otago Peninsula opened to visitors in 1984, there were eight pairs of rare yellow-eyed penguins on the reserve. By 2004 that number had tripled. The attraction now runs programmes for scientific research, native reforestation, predator control and an ornithological hospital. It's cost thousands, but every project was funded with tourist dollars. Eco-tourism creates a win-win situation—if the operators create the best environment possible, wildlife thrives, creating an even more attractive tourist destination. In exchange for their dollars, tourists access a unique, hands-on experience. Top eco-friendly activities include spotting endangered Hector's dolphins near Christchurch, the Waimangu valley near Taupo, and guided nature walks around Queenstown.

Threatened Identity

Human Kiwis were shocked in the 1980s to realise their feathered namesake was in serious trouble. Despite urgent action, the numbers continued to decline by up to five per cent a year. The current total population across six varieties is estimated at 70,000.

However, the Bank of New Zealand Kiwi Recovery Trust is striking back. Operation Nest Egg (ONE) increases chicks' chances of reaching adulthood from five per cent to forty, at which point they can defend themselves. The enormous egg is taken from the sitting adult, and the chick is hatched and reared in captivity. Kiwi chicks fend for themselves once hatched, so in some situations the parents can be left undisturbed and the newly hatched chick removed to a predator proof 'kiwi crèche' within its wild habitat.

The Problem with Possums

One feature of every New Zealand highway is the squashed possum. Never mind, there's plenty more. An estimated 70 million Australian brushtail possums (introduced in 1837) are stripping native forests in 98 per cent of the country, often decimating prized trees such as rata for miles around. Their main food is young tree foliage, but they tuck into flowers, fruit, berries and insects if available. It was originally thought their impact on native birdlife was indirect, but time-lapse video has caught them eating eggs, chicks and adult birds. The NZ$60 million spent each year on possum control is not working. Current hopes lie in a contraceptive vaccine. A fur trade makes a tiny dint in the population, with luxury products like Merinomink (possum/fine wool) clothing, bedspreads, gloves and...nipple warmers.

Treasure or Traitor?

A unique conservation debate was highlighted in June 2004, when the Department of Conservation (DoC) dropped 55 tonnes of rat poison on Little Barrier Island in the Hauraki Gulf. It was the first stage of a NZ$700,000 operation to wipe out the kiore, or Polynesian rat, from New Zealand's oldest nature reserve. The issue was sensitive because some Maori tribes consider the kiore a *taonga*, or treasure. It has probably been in New Zealand as long as the Maori, having arrived with the early canoes, and was once important for food and cloak-making. However, it's a predatory rodent and considered a threat to native weta, frogs, skinks, birds and other wildlife. Although kiore are common in the southwestern Pacific and on some of New Zealand's offshore islands, they are rare on the mainland.

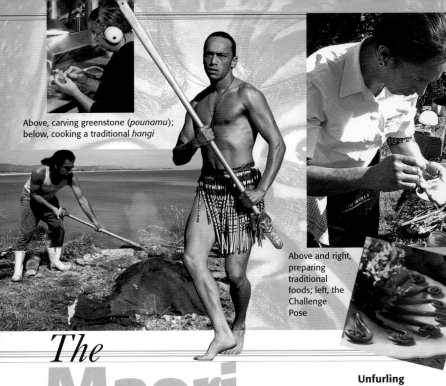

Above, carving greenstone (*pounamu*); below, cooking a traditional *hangi*

Above and right, preparing traditional foods; left, the Challenge Pose

The Maori

The Big Issue

Does the Crown own New Zealand's foreshore and seabed? In 1997 the Ngati Apa tribe of Marlborough asked the court. In 2003 the Court of Appeal ruled it was Maori customary land. As no laws had been made to change this, the foreshore and seabed did not belong to the Crown absolutely. Kiwis prize nothing more than a day at the beach, so the Government leaped to legislate in 2004, giving ownership of the foreshore and seabed to the state. Their principles were that these areas should be public domain, with open access for all New Zealanders, but the customary interests of Maori would be protected. Maori—and the Waitangi Tribunal—called the ruling discriminatory because it abolished Maori property rights while apparently protecting everyone else's.

Far from dying out, as predicted by colonists, Maori culture is an integrated component of everyday New Zealand. Te Reo (Maori language) is taught in schools and culturally specific words like *iwi* (tribe), *taonga* (treasure), *whanau* (family) and *tapu* (sacred) are commonly used without elaboration. A Maori television channel was launched in 2003, the same year as the Maori Party in politics. Understanding and value of New Zealand's Maori heritage continues to grow; it's part of what makes the country unique. Indeed, when cyclist Sarah Ulmer won gold at the 2004 Athens Olympics, it was her supporters' spontaneous *haka*, not the medal ceremony, that touched her most.

Ka mate, Ka mate!

Haka were around long before the All Blacks, but the rugby team certainly helped to cement the dance in Kiwi culture. Traditionally *haka* could refer to all Maori dance, but now it implies a vigorous posture dance. Men and women both perform *haka* but the men have the more spirited role, slapping thighs and chests, enlarging their eyes and sticking out their tongues. Haka can intimidate first-time spectators but they are not necessarily war dances—they are also performed at times of welcome, success or strong emotion.

Unfurling Economy

The emerging phrase 'Maori economy' describes enterprises run in line with Maori cultural values, such as *whanaugatanga* (kinship), *kotahitanga* (unity), *kaitiakitanga* (guardianship) and *mana whenua* (control of land). The end product doesn't need a particularly Maori flavour to qualify—Maori exports largely consist of fisheries, beef cattle, sheep meat, wool and forest products. But in some cases the Maori-ness is the product's selling point. Entrepreneurial chef Charles Royal has developed a demand for *pikopiko* (delicately unfurling fern fronds), a traditional Maori food that can be poached, grilled, barbecued or stir-fried. Under the label Kinaki Wild Herbs, he also produces medicinal body rubs containing *horopito* (bush pepper), a traditional aid to skin repair, and *kawakawa*, considered a blood purifier.

The Story of New Zealand

New Land, New People

New Zealand was 680 million years in the making. Humans arrived on its shores perhaps a thousand years ago—hardly a tick on the geological clock—but their effect was profound and irreversible. The first settlers from East Polynesia probably numbered between one and two hundred, but within a century several species of bird were extinct, seals and other seabirds were all but eradicated from the main islands and large tracts of land were destroyed by fire. The easy pickings from New Zealand's great natural store cupboard had gone and the settlers were forced into more considered methods of survival. This marked the transition from the 'archaic' era of Maori settlement to the 'classic'.

Groups became more settled as they developed sustainable food production such as gardening. The tubers of their kumara (sweet potato) became more valuable and had to be protected, giving rise to *pa* (fortified villages). By the 16th century a tribal system had developed. Now fully adjusted to the challenges of their environment, settlers could keep warm, build appropriate shelters and grow food. The focus moved to building social and cultural systems based on the old ways, but suited to their new country. They were no longer immigrants from Polynesia, but Maori.

In the Beginning

There are two quite different Maori myths about New Zealand's origins. One concerns Maui, the heroic trickster, who hauled up the North Island while he was out fishing.

The other is of Papatuanuku (the Earth Mother) and Ranginui (the Sky Father), who embraced each other so tightly their 70 sons were squashed between them. After much discussion, all the sons except one agreed their parents should be prized apart. Tanemahuta stood on his shoulders and pushed up the sky with his feet. He then clothed Papa with the green of the forest and adorned Rangi with the sun and stars, but still they wept for each other, creating rain and mist. Tawhiri-matea, the son who objected to his parents' separation, angrily followed Rangi into the sky and created wind and storms.

The myth of fisherman Maui, whose anchor formed Stewart Island (Rakiura), is celebrated with a massive chain sculpture in Lee Bay

1000

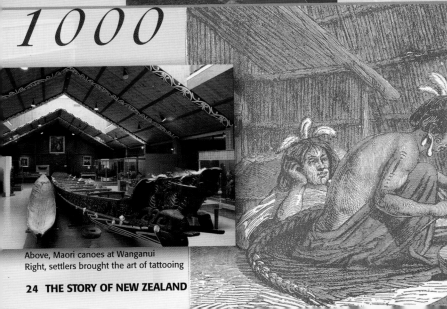

Above, Maori canoes at Wanganui
Right, settlers brought the art of tattooing

Man Becomes Myth

Until recently, Maori arrival in New Zealand was neatly tied up: in AD950, a Polynesian navigator, Kupe, left Hawaiki (Tahiti) with his family and crew. Eventually, he sighted a white cloud (*aotea*), which revealed a bush-covered land. He called it Aotearoa—Land of the Long White Cloud. In 1350, a 'Great Fleet' of seven canoes followed in his wake.

However, 1970s research found these 'truths' were not authenticated by Maori sources but had been cobbled together by a European scholar.

What we do know for sure is the Maori came from East Polynesia, a race of seafarers with the sophisticated navigation needed to complete the 3,000km (1,860-mile) journey and return home. It seems likely that after initial voyages of discovery, men and women came in several canoes, equipped for settlement, during the 13th century.

Hunted Down

Maori settlers walked into a teeming store cupboard. The moa was not the only ground-dwelling bird with little fear of predators, but it remains the most distinctive. It looked like a chunky ostrich, or an enormous kiwi with a long neck. At around 3m (10ft), the giant moa was the world's tallest bird, with drumsticks equivalent to a leg of beef. Even the smaller bush moa were as big as turkeys. They were zealously rounded up and killed in their thousands until, in little more than 100 years, they were gone. Archaeologists have found traces of massive fires that destroyed forests, especially in Hawke's Bay and on the east coast of the South Island—these may have been started as a last-ditch effort to flush out the last of the species.

Codes of Conduct

As Maori culture developed into the tribally organised 'classic' phase, common values emerged. Links between tribes were strong enough for these values to be shared by all, just like the language. For example, it was accepted that people were either *rangatira* (aristocrats) or *tutua* (commoners). *Rangatira* had more *mana* (honour), but anyone could gain or lose *mana* according to their skills and achievements. Another common concept was *utu*. This idea of reciprocation could be positive or destructive, in response to a favour or an insult. It could sweeten relationships between tribes or families—one could gift basalt while the other returned with fish, raising the *mana* of both parties. Or it could mean war, as one tribe rectified another tribe's misdeed, which could have occurred days or decades before.

The first settlers soon hunted the flightless moa to extinction

A Race Wronged

The Moriori came from East Polynesia and settled in the Chatham Islands (Rekohu). They shared the same genes as the Maori and travelled at around the same time, but away from the mainland they developed cultural differences: a society without hierarchy, their own dialect and a covenant to settle disputes by one-on-one combat, rather than warfare. During the 20th century historians portrayed Moriori as an inferior race exterminated by the Maori—a useful justification for European colonisation. Moriori numbers were indeed decimated by the 1835 invasion of two Maori tribes, but descendants survived. However, most kept their heritage quiet until these presumptions were challenged in the late 20th century. In 2004, three Moriori groups signed terms with the Government under the Treaty of Waitangi, and three more were expected to follow suit.

1769

Early settlers (above, below) challenged and saw off Abel Tasman's curious crew in 1642 at Murderers' Bay (left)

Trading
Goods and Lives

New Zealand's appearance on the world map did not suddenly change life for the Maori. English navigator Captain James Cook came and went in 1769, and the next 70 years brought an odd assortment of Europeans who settled around the edges of Maoridom. Many coastal tribes happily adopted individual missionaries or traders—it was a boost to *mana*, having one's own white man. Similarly, they adopted the goods that suited them best and discarded the rest. Maori bred pigs and grew flax, fruit and vegetables—especially the new white potatoes—specifically to barter with the Europeans. Europeans depended on this trade for survival; Maori came to depend on it for muskets.

By the 1830s the entire country was consumed by a bloody carnage known as the Musket Wars. Trade intensified as the acquisition of guns became obsessive. Traditional power balances were abolished as tribes such as Ngapuhi and Ngati Toa swept across vast sections of the country, annihilating rival tribes on the way. Men, women and children were all game. During 3,000 or so battles that took place from 1818 to 1840, an estimated 30,000 of the total 100,000 Maori population was killed by warfare, disease, starvation, slavery or in the cannibal feasts of victory.

A Floating Laboratory

The first map of New Zealand represented disappointment. Captain James Cook's 1769 circumnavigation proved the country was not the hoped-for corner of a Southern Continent, as suggested by Dutch explorer Abel Tasman in 1642. But Cook's scientific expedition had many successes. He observed the transit of Venus across the sun from Tahiti as directed by London's Royal Society, providing vital data to map the solar system. He proved that regular doses of sauerkraut (rich in vitamin C) prevented sailors from dying of scurvy. And with naturalists headed by Joseph Banks, hundreds of plant and animal specimens were collected.

Deadly muskets replaced traditional Maori weapons carved from wood or stone

James Cook
(1728–79)

1769

Above, the first Europeans were keen to map the coastline and exploit whaling resources, right; left, portrait of Te Pehi Kupe in Western dress, c.1826; far right, signing the Treaty of Waitangi

Pakeha Maori

New Zealand's early Europeans were a diverse group. Among the sealers, whalers and missionaries was a small group known as Pakeha Maori—people like Barnet Burns, a trader who came in 1830 and went native. He lived in Mahia, south of Gisborne, under the protectorate of a chief he called 'Awhawee'. He married the chief's daughter, Amotawa, with whom he had three children. Over three intensive years he was abducted by rival tribesmen, escaped, led two major battles and claimed to have been made chief of a tribe of 600. He sailed to England on business in 1835 and gave a series of lectures—resplendent in full Maori dress and *moko* (facial and body tattoos). He never returned to New Zealand, but numerous descendants still live on the East Coast.

Men of influence: right, Samuel Marsden and far right, William Hobson

God and Grammar

Christianity came to the Maori in 1814. Anglican chaplain Samuel Marsden planted three lay workers at Rangihoua, in the Bay of Islands. One, Thomas Kendall, approached his task by immersing himself in Maori culture and language. To his dismay, he nearly converted himself to heathen ways long before any Maori turned Christian. Marsden eventually dismissed him for misdemeanors including adultery, but not before Kendall could accompany his friend chief Hongi Hika and a younger chief, Waikato, to England in 1820. There, Hongi Hika (a fearsome figure of the Musket Wars) had an audience with George IV. The threesome worked with a Cambridge linguist to produce the foundations of written Maori. The conversion rate stayed on zero until the late 1820s, when Christian peace gave an alternative to the bloodshed of the Musket Wars.

The Treaty of Waitangi

In 1839, naval officer William Hobson was sent from London to formally establish New Zealand as a British colony. He invited chiefs from the North Island to sign a treaty at Waitangi on 5 February 1840. The government provided no draft document, so, with no legal training, Hobson and his officials hurriedly prepared the treaty in the four days preceding. Most inter-racial communication occurred in Maori, so it was also translated the night before. Forty-five chiefs signed after extended deliberations on 6 February; by September over 500 had signed. The question was—and still is—what did they agree to? Discrepancies between British and Maori understandings were quickly realised but not easily rectified. Despite good intentions, the Treaty of Waitangi became the most contentious issue in New Zealand's history.

Names for Faces

The word Maori means ordinary. It was widely used by Maori to describe themselves by the 1830s, although to most Europeans they were simply 'New Zealanders'. The Maori version of the Treaty of Waitangi uses the phrase *tangata maori*—ordinary people. As for Europeans, Maori had used the word *Pakeha* since at least 1814, when missionary William Hall recorded he had been referred to as a 'rungateeda pakehaa' (*rangatira pakeha*), meaning a European gentleman. By the 1830s the word's usage among Maori was widespread. Europeans still described themselves according to their home countries, such as British. Pakeha probably originates from *pakepakeha*, an imaginary light-skinned being. The word's use was purely descriptive rather than derogatory, although it was also used for turnip (because of its white flesh) and flea.

1840

A botanical illustration from Cook's first voyage, 1768–71

A Surge of Settlers

The year 1840 marked the start of mass migration to New Zealand. The imminent tide of settlers was one reason Hobson needed to push through the Treaty of Waitangi—the Crown's right to purchase land had to be secured before private enterprise companies (notably the New Zealand Company) could steal the march. The next 20 years passed in relative peace, as Maori and Pakeha traded goods and land, but shady deals sowed seeds for future discontent. Maori land was communally owned, and wide consultation was required for a valid sale. New Zealand Company agents in Wellington, Nelson and Wanganui often found it easier to skip difficult owners and close a quick deal, while some Maori found their land had been 'sold' from under them by rivals.

In 1840 there were just over 2,000 Pakeha settlers. By 1858 there were 59,000—3,000 more than there were Maori. As the numbers changed, so did the countryside; settlers made it more homely. Hundreds of plants, birds and animals were introduced, including 1.5 million sheep. The land was surveyed and mapped. Mountains, lakes and rivers known by the Maori for generations were 'discovered' and given European names. New Zealand was becoming 'the Britain of the South'.

Primitive settlers' houses with tin chimneys were replaced by cob, brick and weatherboard

1840

End of an Empire

The most powerful man in 1840 was Te Rauparaha—warrior chief, strategist and entrepreneur. Kicked out of his Kawhia homeland by Waikato relatives, Te Rauparaha and his Ngati Toa tribe conquered Horowhenua with guns in 1823. From his stronghold on Kapiti Island he led murderous raids as far south as Banks Peninsula, and soon dominated the lower North Island and upper South Island. Wellington and Nelson were established only with his permission in the 1840s, but disputes later arose over which areas he actually sold. In 1843 a confrontation over land on the Wairau Plains, north of Blenheim, ended violently and settlers became nervous. Governor George Grey decided Te Rauparaha could not be trusted and arrested him in 1846. During 10 months in prison his *mana* waned. Te Rauparaha died in 1849.

Powerful rivals: Te Ruaparaha and Governor George Grey

Above, Maori chief Hone Heke defied authorities, sparking the Northern War, in 1845; right, Auckland's Queen Street *c.*1853

Maori Monarchy

As Maori felt their land and culture slipping away, they looked for strength in unity. Tribes around Waikato, Taranaki and the central North Island acted by selecting the first Maori king: the Waikato chief Te Wherowhero. In 1858, he took his seat at Ngaruawahia, north of Hamilton, in the district now known as the King Country. Maori intended their monarchy to complement the British Crown—the Maori king and Queen Victoria would be joined in accord. They hoped this unity would give Maori a chance against the confident and cohesive settlers. Instead, it aggravated the colonists, who thought it showed disloyalty to the Queen. It was also seen as a stumbling block to further land sales, and fuelled the idea that Maori were getting too big for their boots.

Dreams for Sale

For the equivalent of NZ$101, the New Zealand Company sold investors one town acre (0.4ha) and 100 country acres (40ha). Not that the company had any land to sell—the ships containing buyers and surveyors scooted into Port Nicholson (Wellington) just 18 days before 1,000 unsuspecting migrants. They found no sign of the undulating plains promised in company propaganda, described as perfect for grapevines, wheat, olives and bananas—only swamp, forest, steep hills and sand hummocks. The plan of 1,100 one-acre sections simply wouldn't fit into the proposed Hutt Valley site. Migrants camped on the Petone foreshore, with possessions from beds to pianos heaped around them. At least they wouldn't starve: From the moment they stepped off the boat, they started shooting birds.

Great Shakes

As if the Wellington settlers hadn't enough to contend with, their fledgling town was struck by the country's biggest recorded earthquake in January 1855. It measured 8 on the Richter scale—the 1999 Taiwan quake that claimed 2,330 lives was 7.6. In this case, one person died in Wellington and three in Wairarapa. But it wasn't all bad. The shoreline rose 1m (3ft) on average, leaving Lambton Quay high and dry—it is now a main shopping street. Plans for a new dock had to be shelved (the area is now Basin Reserve cricket ground, ▷ 104), but there was suddenly space for a road to link Wellington with the Hutt Valley, reclaimable land around the harbour and another 100m (110 yards) of beach at Petone. Wooden buildings were proved safer than brick, and carpenters rejoiced.

Heaven or Hell?

The primitive conditions of New Zealand shocked new arrival Georgiana Bowen. She wrote to her sister in 1851: 'It is only Colonists who can have any idea of what roughing it is, and it is ill suited for any but the young, strong and active…We are now in wooden shanties or tents of which perhaps you can form no idea.' Maria Richmond, on the other hand, was smitten after just six months. In 1853 she wrote: 'I have never felt so wide awake as I have done since I landed in New Zealand…the feeling of coming home, as it were, to a country wanting you, asking for people to enjoy and use it, with a climate to suit you, a beauty to satisfy and delight, and with such possibilities for the future.'

Land was cleared of spear grass and matagouri to make way for sheep

1860

Below, the *Randolph* was one of four ships that brought colonists to the Canterbury settlement in 1850; above left, mail home encouraged more to follow

The Colony Gains
Confidence

The colony entered an unsettled time of change. Rapid growth put pressure on towns like Auckland and New Plymouth, which in turn put pressure on Maori to sell more land. Discontent on both sides sparked a series of land wars, which ripped through the North Island from 1860 to 1872. Colonial forces fought Maori and Maori fought each other. By the turn of the century, Maori were considered a dying race. Many tribes had lost their livelihoods and their morale with the confiscation of millions of hectares of land. They were also ravaged by influenza, measles, whooping cough and dysentery.

Meanwhile, the European population boomed. Premier Julius Vogel borrowed a staggering amount of money on the London capital market during the 1870s to put in thousands of kilometres of roads, railways and telegraph lines, and to assist another 100,000 settlers into the country. It was not enough to protect New Zealand from worldwide recession, which lasted into the 1890s, but the advent of refrigeration brought new hope. The first successful shipment of frozen lamb and mutton to England in 1882 granted the country a major new export earner.

Out of enforced bachelor life emerged the Kiwi spirit of self-reliance and mateship

The Bachelor Life

In 1871, men outnumbered women two to one. With no prospect of marrying, many vanished into a men's world of shearing, farm work, timber milling, mining or public works. Once in the back blocks, they would live in shanty camps for years. It was the start of New Zealand's 'bloke' culture, where hard work, honesty, camaraderie, sense of humour and mateship were highly valued. The government aimed to boost the population by offering free passage to single British women. Many obliged; domestic servants could earn more than in England. Even so, mistresses had to bargain hard to keep their staff, and domestics with an apparent impediment to matrimony— such as Gaelic speakers— were preferred. Twenty years later, the sex ratios were nearly balanced.

1860

Above, Gottfried Lindauer's portrait of Ana Rupene and child, c.1880; above right, fighting in the land wars

Chinatown

Gold in Otago and Westland brought a new wave of immigrants—the Chinese. They made up 6 per cent of the Otago population in 1871, virtually all men who lived on the breadline to send money back to their wives and families. Isolated by appearance and culture, they stuck together and were treated with suspicion by Europeans. Their greatest success story was Choie Sew Hoy, whose pioneer gold dredge enabled miners to winkle sand out of river flats as well as the river bed. Hoy established a store in Dunedin importing Chinese goods and became a mentor for other Chinese in the area. Unlike his compatriots, he opted to stay in New Zealand and married locally. By 1880 he was the best-known Chinese figure in Dunedin. Sew Hoy's Dunedin store still trades on Stafford Street.

A Great Explosion

On 10 June 1886, the ground south of Rotorua shook violently as Mount Tarawera split open, sending a column of fire into the night sky. Tourists staying at the Rotomahana Hotel fled to the *whare* of Sophia, a Maori guide. Her small house sheltered 60 people through the night and was one of only two buildings in Wairoa village to survive the eruption. The rest were buried under tonnes of mud, rock and ash. An estimated 153 people were killed, including the school teacher and five of his children. His wife was later pulled from the mud alive. Lake Rotomahana is now 30m (98ft) higher than before the eruption. The blasted face of Mount Tarawera still tells a tale, and destroyed the famous pink-and-white terraces (▷ 87).

Taking the Lead

Two remarkable world firsts passed into law under Richard ('King Dick') Seddon's Liberal government: old-age pensions (1898) and universal suffrage. Winning the world's first national votes for women took a good deal of hard graft by Kate Sheppard, temperance supporter, writer, speaker and early feminist. She liked women to be 'hearty and hale', and rode a bike around Christchurch when women were considered too fragile for such activity. But she also had the tact, intellect and determination to win allies and advance her battle. Her first petition in 1891 contained 9,000 signatures. Her second, a year later, had 19,000. Her final petition was signed by nearly 32,000 women—around a third of the female population. The Women's Suffrage Bill passed by two votes in 1893.

Blowing the Whistle

New Zealand stamped its first mark on rugby in 1884, when referee W.H. Atack of Canterbury got sick of shouting himself hoarse at two marauding teams. According to the official historian of the NZ Rugby Football Union, Atack was mulling over the problem when his fingers strayed to a waistcoat pocket. There, they encountered a dog whistle. With a flash of inspiration, he realised it would be a perfect way to stop the game. The next time he refereed, he called the teams together and they agreed to play to the whistle. It was a great success and was adopted all over the country. New Zealand's first national rugby team toured the UK in 1888–89 as the New Zealand Native Team— they weren't called the All Blacks until 1905.

Left, gold miners take a break at Monteith's Brewery, Greymouth
Below, Cardrona started as a gold-rush town and retains a frontier feel

Richard 'King Dick' Seddon (1845–1906)

1900

Below, some gold hunters joined the coal mines
Left, Mount Tarawera, 1886

A Nation
Goes Forth

There was no doubt New Zealand would fight alongside Mother England when World War I broke out. After a period of relative peace and prosperity, young men jumped at the chance to take part—both Pakeha and Maori. It was exciting, patriotic, a chance for blokes to get together and see the world. They would fight alongside Australians as the Australia and New Zealand Army Corps—ANZACs.

But euphoria vanished when 3,000 New Zealanders landed at Gallipoli on the Turkish Coast on 25 April 1915. The campaign was a disaster from the outset—troops were landed 3km (2 miles) from the intended beach and faced a wall of cliffs. One soldier in five was mown down on the first day. For eight months, they existed in trenches metres away from the Turkish troops, prey to disease, heat, blizzards, snipers and the stench of irretrievable bodies.

Despite valiant attempts to claim the peninsula, the attack was an utter failure. When the troops were finally pulled out in mid-December, the casualty rate stood at 88 per cent. New Zealanders went on to fight at the Western Front and in the Middle East but Gallipoli is still the campaign most remembered. April 25 is ANZAC Day, a national day of commemoration.

Welfare For All

Few prime ministers have their photos hung over the mantelpiece, but Michael Joseph Savage was different. He was the benign face of the Labour government that stormed to victory in 1935, just as the Great Depression was tailing off. Their mission to look after New Zealanders 'from the cradle to the grave' had a positive effect—a free hospital system, universal super-annuation at 65, a 40-hour working week and a basic wage considered enough to keep a man, wife and three children comfortably. In three years, 3,500 state houses were built with modern kitchens and the luxury of an indoor toilet.

Michael Joseph Savage (1872–1940)

Recruiting poster for World War II—New Zealand regiments fought with distinction in Crete and the Middle East

1900

Above, pioneer aviator Jean Batten (1909–82); right, Gallipoli; far right, war memorials are a familiar sight

Taking Off

When does 'powered flight' become 'controlled'? If you can land in a river and still be 'controlled', then Richard Pearse was a world-class achiever. And even if you can't, his 1902 aircraft still flew 21 months before the Wright brothers'. The South Canterbury farmer created a plane with a two-cylinder engine, vertical rudder, tricycle undercarriage and propeller. Eyewitnesses say that on 31 March 1902 this craft took off from a farm paddock, climbed slowly, turned right and flew 1,200m (3,963ft) before landing in a river. A modified version flew 50m (164ft) one year later before colliding with a gorse bush. Pearse patented ailerons—flaps that give planes vertical control—in 1906, but he let the patent lapse in 1910 because he didn't see much prospect of selling planes in New Zealand.

Deadly Virus

On 11 October 1918, the passenger liner *Niagara* was permitted to dock in Auckland harbour, despite radioed warnings that Spanish influenza was on board. Why wasn't the ship quarantined? Among the passengers were Prime Minister William Massey and his Minister of Finance, anxious to return to work after meetings in Britain and Europe. It's not known if they influenced the decision to let passengers disembark, but by 3 November, 120 cases of flu were admitted to Auckland Public Hospital. There was no cure. The disease quickly spread south, shutting schools, shops and pubs and disrupting industry. More than 6,700 New Zealanders died, including an estimated 2,160 Maori.

Literary Talent

Katherine Mansfield is New Zealand's best-known writer. Even though she was 'ashamed' of her young country's stifling lack of creativity, her childhood memories gave richness to her masterful short stories. She was born in 1888 to a socialite Wellington family. At the age of 14 she went to England for three years of schooling, and on returning home found she couldn't wait to get back to London. 'It is Life,' she wrote. Her avid pursuit of 'Life' took her back to London in 1908, where she mingled with the intellectual Bloomsbury group of writers. After passionate affairs, an inexplicable marriage and a last-ditch hunt for inner peace, she died of tuberculosis near Paris in 1923, aged 34. She was the first New Zealand-born writer to earn international recognition.

Maoris Enter Politics

By the start of the 20th century, a group of well-educated leaders emerged to fight the Maori cause through politics: Maui Pomare, James Carroll and Apirana Ngata.

Less conventional was Tahupotiki Wiremu Ratana. The ploughman's journey began in 1918, when he heard the voice of God telling him that Maori were God's chosen people, and that he should unite Maori and turn them towards God. Ratana began faith healing and was so successful that a settlement grew around his house, south of Wanganui (it is now called Ratana). Ratana MPs held all four Maori parliamentary seats by 1943 and provided Labour with a vital alliance during 1946 to 1949. Attention to Maori land development, schooling, housing and unemployment brought a marked improvement to Maori conditions. The Ratana church now has over 49,000 members.

Architectural confidence in Dunedin's railway station, 1906

Katherine Mansfield (1888–1923)

1945

A replica of Richard Pearse's aeroplane at MOTAT

Age of Assertion

Mother England gently loosened the apron strings in 1931 by proclaiming her Dominions autonomous. New Zealand remained in denial, even as she backed out of their stifling economic relationship in preference for Europe.

In 1984, a new Labour government showed the first signs of the rebellious teenager. It was led by quick-witted barrister David Lange, who soon had to grasp the prickly end of Labour's anti-nuclear stance. When the US ship *Buchanan* refused to confirm or deny its nuclear capabilities, Lange denied it entry. This signalled the effective end of ANZUS, a key defence treaty with Australia and America. The US's subsequent bullying did not impress the public, but on 10 July 1985 the Kiwis' nuke-free stance turned absolute. That night, the Greenpeace ship *Rainbow Warrior* was blown up in Auckland harbour, killing one crew member. The ship was about to sail to Mururoa atoll in the Pacific to protest against French nuclear tests. In a matter of days the New Zealand police caught those responsible—two French agents. The leaders of the US, Britain and Australia barely said a word against it. New Zealanders were outraged, and determined to stand by their principles. The agents were later decorated by the French government.

Then and now: the *Rainbow Warrior* (bottom) is now a dive site (right)

1945

Land Rights to the Fore

The government continued to take Maori land in the 1970s but there was a difference—Maori numbers, awareness and anger had grown. In 1975, a march from Northland ended in Wellington with 50,000 supporters asking the government to guarantee that not one more hectare of Maori land would be lost. The government did not commit. Rather, in 1976, it decided to sell land at Bastion Point, which originally belonged to Ngati Whatua. The tribe had reserved it nearly 100 years before, after selling thousands of hectares for Auckland development. Over time, pockets were lost—much of it to compulsory Crown acquisition. Maori patience ran out when the government tried to sell the land for high-priced housing—protesters occupied the site for 17 months before being arrested in May 1978.

Top, anti-nuclear Prime Minister David Lange, 1986
Right, Waitangi protesters

The Open Market

The Labour government created the welfare state in 1935; in 1984 they took most of it away. With the over-protected economy verging on bankruptcy, finance minister Roger Douglas opened New Zealand to the ravages of the free market. The changes were abrupt, unexpected and painful. Agriculture subsidies were phased out; farmers walked off the land. The dollar was devalued and later floated on the international market. Government enterprises such as the Post Office and New Zealand Steel became State Owned Enterprises and were expected to turn a profit. Thousands of public servants were made redundant and unions reeled as their power base was chipped away. 'Rogernomics' changed New Zealand's fundamental economic values forever.

Divided Fans

Could any other country be so divided by rugby? In 1981, the New Zealand Rugby Union invited the South African Springboks to play three test matches against the All Blacks. Prime Minister Rob Muldoon refused to intervene even though he had signed the Gleneagles Agreement, discouraging sporting contact with apartheid South Africa. It sparked an unofficial civil war—barbed-wire fences, street blockades and riot police became as common as street marches. The first match in Hamilton was abandoned when 300 protestors sat on the pitch, tempting the wrath of 27,000 fans. The violence peaked at the final match in Auckland. Protesters made 362 complaints against the police; 75 were eventually upheld. In all, 2,000 arrests were made and tour defence cost the country NZ$7.2 million.

Running the Race

Ever been for a jog? Thank Aucklander Arthur Lydiard, who formed the world's first jogging group. In 1944, at the age of 27, he struggled to run 10km (6 miles) with a friend. The training method of the day—speeding round a track to point of collapse—didn't work for him. Instead, he devised a programme of gradual build-up. By his early 30s he was New Zealand's top marathon runner, and his times over shorter distances had also improved. A group of younger runners started training under his guidance. Two became stars of the 1960 Rome Olympics—Murray Halberg, who won the 5,000m gold, and Peter Snell, who won the 800m and smashed the Olympic record by 1.4 seconds. Lydiard later applied his principles to fitness for the general public and invented 'jogging'.

Homegrown Supermodel

When everyone was talking about the supermodels of Britain, the US and Europe, New Zealand was surprised to realise it had one too. Rachel Hunter (born in Auckland in 1969) started modelling at the age of 17. After starring as 'the Trumpet girl' in an ice cream advertisement on TV, she leapt to the pages of *Sports Illustrated*—the magazine famed for making models famous. She appeared on thousands of covers worldwide, including *Cosmopolitan* and *Vogue*. Not only that, but by 1990 Hunter had married Rockin' Rod Stewart—the British crooner 24 years her senior. For a while she was the ultimate home girl made good—she even brought Rod and her two children home for holidays. In 1999 the pair split but Rachel continued to dominate magazine headlines. She now lives in the US.

Jogging owes its origins to Aucklander Arthur Lydiard

Rugby became a political issue in 1981

1999

Above, Kiwi Edmund Hillary conquered Mount Everest in 1953; left, supermodel Rachel Hunter

Into the New Millennium

New Zealand's taste for independence has grown to a hearty appetite and the country has bravely adopted its new position as a Pacific nation, closer to Asia than Europe. In trade, the country gradually recovered to establish healthy relationships with countries other than Britain, particularly Australia, the US, Europe, Japan and China. Agricultural products like meat and dairy remained substantial export earners, but tourism, forestry and fisheries widened the economic base. The surprise boon of the new century was film-making. By 2004, nine big-budget Hollywood films had been released or were in production, including the Oscar-sweeping *Lord of the Rings*.

Competitive Spirit

Kiwis were devastated to lose the America's Cup in 2003, and appalled to see England crowned rugby world champions in the same year. The Athens Olympics of 2004 gave them a much-needed boost, as cyclist Sarah Ulmer ripped six seconds off her own world record, and triathletes Hamish Carter and Bevan Docherty won gold and silver. Gold was also won by sculling twins Caroline and Georgina Evers-Swindell.

Race Relations

The Waitangi Tribunal was created in 1975 to inquire into Maori grievances against the Crown but grew teeth only in 1985, when it was able to consider claims dating back to 1840. In October 2000, 870 claims had been registered with the Tribunal. Claims could be historical, such as compensation for confiscated land, or contemporary, if current government actions were thought to breach treaty principles. Apart from tribal land, claims have been made about sharing resources as diverse as the airwaves, oil, fisheries, airspace and, in 2004–5, the foreshore and seabed. Successful claimants, such as Ngai Tahu in the South Island, who settled on a NZ$170 million compensation package, have generated business success and morale. The Tribunal expects to report on all claims by 2012.

Governor-general Anand Satyanand

War Against Terror

After September 11, New Zealand joined the United Nations in disagreeing with the need to invade Iraq. Prime Minister Helen Clark clearly believed the US was wrong to proceed without UN backing. After the invasion, nearly 70 per cent of New Zealanders approved of her Labour government's opposition to the war. The stand was principled but it wasn't easy, especially as New Zealand had high hopes of jumping on Australia's free trade deal with the US. Clark's widely reported comment that the war would never have happened if Al Gore was president was considered by some a major gaffe. In 2003, 61 army engineers and support staff were sent to contribute to reconstruction and humanitarian tasks in southern Iraq. Their deployment ended in October 2004.

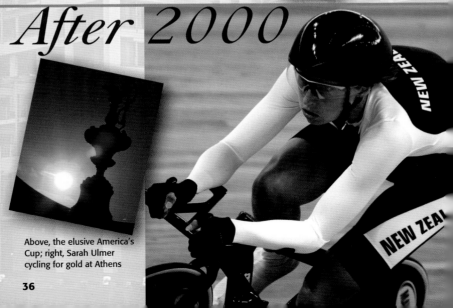

After 2000

Above, the elusive America's Cup; right, Sarah Ulmer cycling for gold at Athens

On the Move

ARRIVING

Arriving By Air

The vast majority of visitors to New Zealand arrive by air. The three main international airports are Auckland, Christchurch and Wellington, with Auckland being the principal entry point. Palmerston North and Hamilton in North Island and Christchurch, Dunedin and Queenstown in South Island all offer regular air services to eastern Australia.

ON THE MOVE

Auckland International Airport

Auckland airport, a relatively small, modern gateway to the nation, is 21km (13 miles) south of the city's central business district. The airport has two terminals—international and domestic. A free transit shuttle operates between them every 20 minutes from 6am to 10.30pm, and there is a connecting walkway.

- At the i-SITE visitor information office on the ground floor of the Arrivals hall you can book hotels, check transport details and store luggage. Hospitality ambassadors, dressed in bright blue jackets, or customer service officers, dressed in red jackets, are available for assistance.
- Shops, food outlets, mail boxes, internet access, crèche, free showers (towels are rented out from the florist on the ground floor for a small fee plus deposit) and phones are all available at the airport.
- Additional services include dayrooms containing a bed, desk, TV, coffee, tea and shower, which can be rented from NZ$30 for four hours. There are banks with currency exchange facilities

throughout Departures and Arrivals in the International Terminal. ATMs can be found in various locations in the International Terminal. A medical facility operates just outside the International Terminal.

- All the well-known rental car operators (▷ 41) are represented at both terminals on the ground floor.

Wellington International Airport

Wellington airport, in the suburb of Rongotai, 6km (3 miles) south of the heart of the city, handles both international and domestic flights from one terminal. Take-offs and landings along its short runway are particularly memorable.

AIRPORT CONTACTS		
North Island		
Auckland	tel 09-276 8899	www.auckland-airport.co.nz
Wellington	tel 04-388 9900	www.wellington-airport.co.nz
Palmerston North	tel 06-351 4415	www.pnairport.co.nz
Hamilton	tel 07-848 9027	www.hamiltonairport.co.nz
South Island		
Christchurch	tel 03-358 5029	www.christchurch-airport.co.nz
Dunedin	tel 03-486 2879	www.dnairport.co.nz
Queenstown	tel 03-442 3505	www.queenstownairport.co.nz

- Although there are dozens of Trans-Tasman and Pacific Island flights per week, Wellington primarily operates a busy domestic schedule, with regular daily flights to most principal cities. Air New Zealand and Qantas are the main carriers, but a number of smaller operators fly to upper South Island destinations. These include Sounds Air, who offer flights to Picton, Nelson and Blenheim for relatively low fares.
- The terminal has all the usual facilities, including food outlets, shops, luggage deposit and an information office.
- All the major car rental companies (▷ 41) are represented at the airport. Both shuttles and taxis depart from directly outside the baggage claim area.

Christchurch International Airport

Christchurch airport is 12km (7 miles) northwest of the city. The international and domestic terminals are housed in one building; domestic transfer check-in counters are in the international arrivals hall. The terminal is open for all flight

Air pockets and strong winds enliven flights into Wellington

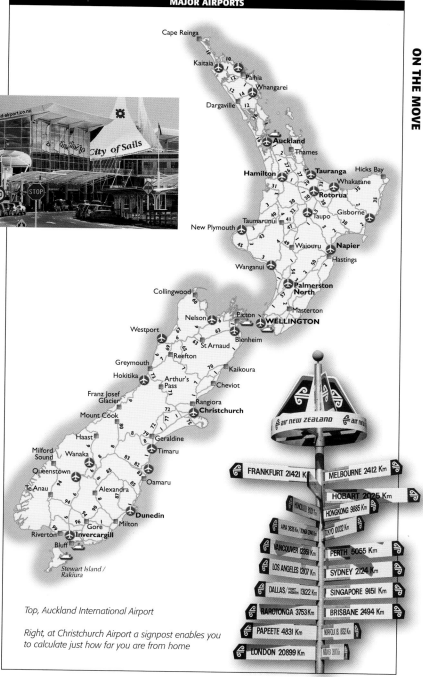

Top, Auckland International Airport

Right, at Christchurch Airport a signpost enables you to calculate just how far you are from home arrivals and departures, while the domestic terminal is open from 7.30am to 8pm.

● The international terminal has direct links with Australia, Singapore and Japan.

● There are bars and restaurants in both terminals. The International Atrium has duty-free shopping and other shops, including clothes stores in the departures hall. A smaller variety of shops is available in the domestic terminal. ATMs are found in both terminals.

● Information desks in both the domestic terminal and international arrivals hall can make reservations for local hotels and tours, provide full travel agency services and arrange any further international or domestic travel plans.

Top, Air New Zealand is the national airline; below, many visitors use minivans to get to top locations

NEW ZEALAND INTERNATIONAL AIRLINES
Air New Zealand tel 0800-352 266 www.airnz.co.nz
Freedom Air International tel 0800-600 500 www.freedomair.com

Foreign Airlines Operating to New Zealand

Aerolineas Argentinas tel 0800 0969 747 (UK), 800-333 0276 (US) www.aerolineas.com.ar

Air Pacific tel 0845-774 7767 (UK), 800-227 4446 (US) www.airpacific.com

British Airways tel 0870-850 9850 (UK), 800-AIRWAYS (US) www.british-airways.com

Cathay Pacific tel 020-8834 8888 (UK), 800-233 2742 (US) www.cathaypacific.com

Emirates tel 0870 243 2222 (UK), 800-777 3999 (US) www.emirates.com

Garuda Indonesia tel 020-7467 8600 (UK), 800-3 GARUDA (US) www.garuda-indonesia.com

Japan Airlines tel 0845 774 7700 (UK), 800-525 3663 (US) www.jal.com

Jetstar tel 866-397 8170 (US) www.jetstar.com

Korean Air tel 0800 413 000 (UK), 800-438 5000 (US) www.koreanair.com

Malaysia Airlines tel 0870 607 9090 (UK), 800-552 9264 (US) www.malaysiaairlines.com

Pacific Blue tel 13 1645 (Australia) www.flypacificblue.com

Qantas Airways tel 0845 774 7767 (UK), 800-227 4500 (US) www.qantas.com.au

Singapore Airlines tel 0844 800 2380 (UK), 800-742 3333 (US) www.singaporeair.com

Thai Airways International tel 0870 606 0911 (UK), 800-426 5204 (US) www.thaiair.com

GETTING AROUND
Vehicle Rental

Car
All the major car rental firms have offices at the airports and in cities and provincial towns. There are also many local operators. Shop around, and always read the small print before you sign. Some of the less expensive companies have an insurance excess of NZ$700 even on minor repairs.

● Always go over the car with a company representative and ask for a list of any dents or scratches that you see on the vehicle.

● If you have a digital camera take a few pictures of your own.

● If you do not have a credit card you may have to leave a substantial cash deposit of between NZ$500 and NZ$1,000.

● You must be over 21 and have a valid driver's licence to rent a vehicle; insurance premiums for the under-25s can be high.

● Small, older and, typically, Japanese cars (1,600cc) start at about NZ$80 per day but rates vary depending on season, kilometres covered and the length of time you have the car. A medium-size new car costs around NZ$100 per day with unlimited kilometres. Without unlimited kilometres the cost is about NZ$0.30 per kilometre.

● You can rent a vehicle in one city and drop it off at another. This will almost certainly involve a drop-off fee of around NZ$120–NZ$150. In the summer, if you are returning to Auckland, it is worth shopping around and trying to strike a bargain, since many operators have a glut of cars needing to be driven back north.

● Insurance is not compulsory but highly recommended. Note that you may not be covered on certain roads. You will certainly not be covered if you venture onto any of the 'sand highways' on the coast, such as Ninety Mile Beach (▷ 57), and many companies do not provide cover in the Catlins (▷ 137).

Motorcycle
Motorcycle rental is not an inexpensive option, but it can be a superb way to see the country.

● Depending on the model and package, renting a motorcycle for a week can cost anything between NZ$80 and NZ$1,000. To ride a Harley Davidson expect to pay around NZ$250 a day.

● Website links to motorcycle rental companies are listed on www.piperpat.co.nz.

Campervan (RV)
Campsites are readily available even in the more remote places. Parking in a powered site costs around NZ$10–NZ$15 per night. Note that lay-by (turnout) parking is illegal.

● Like car rental rates, campervan rates vary and are seasonal. Costs are rated on a sliding scale according to model, season and number of days of use. The average daily charge for a basic two-berth/six-berth for rent over 28 days, including insurance, is around NZ$195/NZ$295 in the high season and NZ$90/NZ$140 in the low season.

● The same general rules apply as with car rental. For estimating costs, fuel usage for the average campervan works out at around 14–16L (4gal) per 100km (62 miles).

● Website links to campervan/RV rental companies are listed on www.piperpat.co.nz.

RENTAL CONTACTS

Car Rental Contacts

About New Zealand tel 0800-455 565 www.rentalcar.co.nz
Ace Rental Cars tel 09-303 3112 www.acerentals.co.nz
Avis tel 0800-655 111 www.avis.com
Budget tel 0800-283 438 www.budget.co.nz
Car Rental Centre (cooperative group of rental companies) tel 0800-746 378 www.carhire.co.nz
Hertz tel 0800-654 321 www.hertz.com

Motorcycle Rental Contacts

Adventure Motorcycles tel 0508 RIDE BMW www.adventuremotorcycles.co.nz
Adventure Trailrides tel 0274 510 584 www.adventureride.co.nz
New Zealand Motorcycle Rentals & Tours tel 0800-917 3941 (UK), 866-490 7940 (US) www.nzbike.com
South Pacific Motorcycle Tours tel 03 312 0444 www.motorcycletours.co.nz
Te Waipounamu Motorcycle Hire and Tours tel 03-372 3537 www.motorcycle-hire.co.nz

Bicycle Rental Contacts

Bicycle Rentals tel 0800 444 144 www.bicyclerentals.co.nz (throughout New Zealand)
City Cycle Hire (Christchurch) tel 03-339 4020 www.cyclehire-tours.co.nz
Hedgehog Bikes (Auckland) tel 09 486 6559 www.hedgehog.co.nz

Campervan Rental Contacts

Britz tel 0800-831 900 www.britz.co.nz
Kea Campers tel 09-441 7833 www.kea.co.nz
Kiwi Campers tel 0800 549 44, www.nzcampers.com
Maui tel 09-275 3013/0800 651 080 www.maui.co.nz

Getting Around in Auckland

Auckland's public transportation system has been overhauled to provide a more consistent service between buses, ferries and trains. Information on all types of transport is available from MAXX (see Useful Contacts, below).

The handiest way to travel in the city is by bus. Several travel pass schemes are available: the Auckland Discovery Day Pass gives unlimited travel on the five major bus companies, suburban trains and inner port ferries between 5am on the day of purchase and 4.59am the following morning. Auckland Pass gives one day's unlimited travel on North Star and Stagecoach Auckland buses (including the Link; see below) and includes travel on ferry services to the North Shore. A similar deal is offered by the Three-Day Rover, but for three consecutive days.

BUS

● Most central and suburban buses stop at the Britomart Transport Centre, between Customs and Quay streets, near the waterfront.
● An Auckland Busabout Guide is available from the bus terminal and all major tourist information offices, showing routes and departure points for the main attractions. Fares are on a staged system, 1–8 (NZ$1.60–NZ$9.70).
● City Circuit is a red bus providing a free service around the city's heart every 10 minutes, daily 8–6.
● The Link bus has a flat fare of $1.60 and runs every 10 minutes 6am–7pm weekdays, 7am–6pm Saturdays, every 15 minutes evenings and Sundays. The route is Britomart–Quay Park–Parnell–Museum–Domain–Newmarket–Hospital–University–AUT–Library–Karangahape Road–Ponsonby–Victoria Park–SKYCITY–Queen Street–Britomart.
● The double-decker Auckland Explorer bus has all-day sightseeing with commentary (NZ$30 day pass).

The Britomart Transport Centre, a hub for travel information

GREEN TRAVEL

Walking is a good way of getting to know the cities. Wellington and Christchurch are compact enough to walk to most central attractions, while Auckland's Link and City Circuit buses connect the main areas. Wellington's electric trolleybuses, Auckland's free hybrid electric City Circuit and Christchurch's City Shuttle buses all help minimise effects on the environment.

TRAIN

● Local and intercity trains arrive and depart from the Britomart Transport Centre, near the waterfront.
● Two main commuter lines run west to Waitakere and south to Papakura. Contact MAXX.

FERRY AND WATER TAXI

● Almost all ferries depart from around the Ferry Buildings on the waterfront, at Quay Street. Commuter service is expanding.
● The main ferry company is Fullers, with an information office on the ground floor of the Ferry Building, tel 09-367 9111, www.fullers.co.nz.
● Water taxis sail from the North Shore, tel 0800 111 616, www.watertaxi.co.nz.

TAXI

● Taxis are generally widely available and can be flagged down, ordered by phone or picked up at ranks.
● All Auckland taxi drivers are required to belong to a registered taxi company. Meters are usually based on time, not distance, so it often pays to get an estimate first.

USEFUL CONTACTS

Auckland
Auckland Explorer tel 0800 4 EXPLORER www.explorerbus.co.nz
Britomart Transport Centre tel 09-374 3873 www.britomart.co.nz
MAXX tel 09-366 6400 www.maxx.co.nz

Christchurch
Metro tel 03-366 8855 www.metroinfo.org.nz
Trams tel 03-366 7830 www.tram.co.nz
Tram dining tour tel 03-366 7511 www.tram.co.nz

Wellington
Metlink tel 04-801 7000 www.metlink.org.nz

Getting Around in Christchurch

Christchurch is a walkers' city but it does have a tramline and a good bus network with a new terminal, the Bus Exchange, on the corner of Lichfield and Colombo streets.

BUS

● Nearly all Christchurch buses serve the central Bus Exchange. An exception is the Orbiter, which provides a useful link between suburban hubs and shopping malls.

● Bus fares use a three-zone system, with all the central city in zone 1 (NZ$2.50). Buy your ticket from the driver, or get a Metrocard smart card from the Bus Exchange.

● The hybrid electric free yellow City Shuttle takes in a north–south route from the Casino through Cathedral Square and down Colombo Street and back, and operates every 10–15 minutes, Mon–Fri 7.30am–10.30pm, Sat 8am–10.30pm and Sun 10–8.

● The Best Attractions Express Shuttle links the Christchurch

Travel on the vintage tram

Gondola, Christchurch Tramway, International Antarctic Centre and Willowbank Wildlife Reserve and departs regularly from Cathedral Square, directly opposite the tram stop. An all-day pass (with bonus second day free) allows you to visit each venue as often as you wish (adult NZ$15, child NZ$10).

TRAM

Between 1905 and 1954 Christchurch had a thriving tram system. Since 1995 the restored trams have followed a 2.5km (1.5-mile) loop around the heart of the city, passing various sights of interest on the way (commentary provided).

● Trams operate Apr–end Oct daily 9–6 and Nov–end Mar daily 9–9. A restaurant car offers a daily dining tour at 7.30pm.

● The trams stop at or near many of the main attractions, including the Botanic Gardens and Cathedral Square.

● For more information tel 03-366 6943, **www**.tram.co.nz.

Getting Around in Wellington

Wellington's transportation system is efficient and extensive, with buses, trolley buses, trains, ferries and a vintage cable car. Information on all services is available from Ridewell, tel 04-801 7000.

BUS

● GOWellington buses operate daily 7am–11pm. City and suburban coverage is good and there is a 10-trip ticket system available. Services depart from the main city bus stop at the Railway Station and Courtenay Place.

● The yellow City Circular bus runs every 15 minutes daily 10–4.45 (adult NZ$3, child NZ$1; free with a NZ$6 Daytripper or NZ$9 Starpass ticket), taking in major sights, including Te Papa, Cuba Mall, the cable car on Lambton Quay and the Parliament Buildings. A free shuttle service runs to the Interislander ferry terminal from the rail station.

● If you intend to visit the Kapiti Coast or Hutt Valley it's worth considering the Capital

Explorer Pass, which allows a day of unlimited travel on regional buses and trains (NZ$15).

● Cityline runs regular daily services to the Hutt Valley. The Stagecoach Flyer offers express services from Lower Hutt to Wellington and Wellington Airport. The Wellington–Airport fare is NZ$5.50 adult, NZ$3 child.

● The Daytripper ticket (adult NZ$6) is valid on all GOWellington buses, including the City Circular. The STARPass (adult NZ$10) is valid on GOWellington buses and also on Cityline Hutt Valley and Stagecoach Flyer buses.

CABLE CAR

The cable car terminus is on Lambton Quay, and the car runs every ten minutes (Mon–Fri 7am–10pm, Sat 8.30am–10pm, Sun 9am–10pm) to the Botanic Garden at Kelburn, via Victoria University. One-way journey NZ$2.50 (child NZ$1), both ways NZ$4.50 (child NZ$2, family NZ$12).

FERRY

● The Dominion Post ferry sails from Queens Wharf to Matiu (Somes) Island and Days Bay, and to Petone and Seatoun on weekends.

● For information tel 04-499 1282, **www**.eastbywest.co.nz.

TRAIN

● Tranz Metro operates suburban trains to Johnsonville, Melling, Paraparaumu and Upper Hutt, as well as trains to Masterton and Palmerston North.

Driving

Although it is possible to negotiate the country by train or bus, for sheer convenience driving is the best choice. Many of the country's attractions are off the beaten track and a long walk from the nearest bus stop. You will also free yourself of organised schedules.

Beyond the cities, parking and traffic congestion are rarely problematic. In some remote areas of the country, especially in the South Island, the roads are single track and unpaved, so a little more driving skill is required. Keep the speeds and gears low on these roads. There may well be sheep or cattle along the verges in rural areas, so take extra care. There are very few wild mammals in New Zealand, but you might well encounter the cat-sized, brush-tailed possum, of which there are 70 million or so (▷ 21).

Insurance is generally offered by the car rental companies. If you are planning to visit for several months, many car rental companies offer temporary purchase or long-term rental (▷ 41).

Rules and regulations
- Traffic in New Zealand drives on the left.
- Speed limits are generally 100kph (62mph) on the open road (although they may be lower in some places) and 50kph (31mph) in built-up areas. Be aware that police patrol cars and speed cameras are omnipresent.
- Police operate random breath and blood tests. The alcohol limit for drivers is 80mg (0.003oz) in 100ml (0.2 pints) of blood; for drivers under 21 no alcohol at all is allowed.
- When you are turning, always give way to the right—the oncoming car has right of way. Always check your way is clear in all directions before turning.
- If you are turning left, give way to vehicles coming towards you that are turning right.
- If you are turning right, you

Above, busy Lambton Quay, Wellington

NORTH ISLAND DRIVING DISTANCES (IN KM)

	Auckland	Cape Reinga	Gisborne	Hamilton	Napier	New Plymouth	Palmerston North	Rotorua	Tauranga	Wellington
Auckland		440	507	127	422	366	530	235	208	656
Cape Reinga	440		943	566	861	805	967	672	645	1100
Dargaville	185	285	685	312	605	554	713	420	390	845
Gisborne	507	943		394	215	600	390	292	300	540
Hamilton	127	566	394		295	242	402	109	108	533
Hicks Bay	508	945	180	398	396	600	574	289	302	730
Kaitaia	325	114	827	450	748	692	853	560	535	982
Masterton	638	1077	448	511	233	343	109	444	530	100
Napier	422	861	215	295		412	178	227	312	320
New Plymouth	366	805	600	242	412		234	315	308	355
Paihia	241	220	745	368	664	610	773	476	447	900
Palmerston North	530	967	390	402	178	234		340	420	145
Rotorua	235	672	292	109	227	315	340		86	460
Taupo	280	720	335	153	143	296	259	84	165	378
Taumarunui	295	726	450	162	264	183	240	172	230	360
Tauranga	208	645	300	108	312	308	420	86		545
Thames	115	554	413	106	360	348	470	200	114	586
Waiouru	423	819	446	267	261	288	145	195	279	264
Wanganui	454	893	466	328	252	160	74	305	439	195
Wellington	656	1100	540	533	320	355	145	460	545	
Whangarei	170	270	680	295	597	540	700	405	381	818

Fuel stops often supply coffee, snacks and basic supplies, too

should give way to vehicles on your right that are turning right.
● Seatbelts must be worn in front seats at all times, and in rear seats where fitted.
● Turn on your headlights from dusk until dawn, or at any other time when you can't see vehicles clearly at a distance of 100m (110 yards) away.
● Dip your headlights when other vehicles are coming towards you, when following other vehicles, when police are directing traffic and when you stop.

Documents

You need a valid driver's licence from your own country or an international driving permit. This must be produced if you rent a vehicle (▷ 41).

Fuel

● Petrol (gas) comes in 91, 95 or 98 octane (all unleaded). LPG (liquified petroleum gas) and diesel are also available. CNG (compressed natural gas) is available only in the North Island.
● Challenge is New Zealand's own brand of fuel, with a network of service stations throughout the country. For a list of locations go to **www.challenge.net.nz**.

Car breakdown

Most rental companies include a free breakdown service within the deal.
● Members of the the AA in the UK, AAA in the US or driving organisations affiliated to the AIT receive six months' free reciprocal membership of the New Zealand Automobile Association (AA), including breakdown assistance (tel 0800-500 222).

At the scene of an accident

● If you are involved in an accident in which someone is hurt, you must inform a police officer as soon as possible, and no later than 24 hours afterwards.
● If no one is hurt, you must give the owner or driver of any damaged vehicle or property your name and address (and the name and address of your vehicle's owner) as soon as possible and no later than 48 hours after the accident.
● If this isn't possible, report the incident to the police as soon as you can and no later than 60 hours afterwards.
● If your vehicle is insured, tell your insurance company as soon as possible.
● If you injure an animal, tell its owner; if this isn't possible, tell the police or the SPCA (Royal New Zealand Society for the

SOUTH ISLAND DRIVING DISTANCES (IN KM)

	Blenheim	Christchurch	Dunedin	Greymouth	Invercargill	Kaikoura	Mount Cook	Nelson	Queenstown	Timaru
Alexandra	775	455	190	661	202	641	242	870	93	307
Arthur's Pass	440	150	451	100	668	308	408	385	645	250
Blenheim		318	675	324	900	132	645	116	798	475
Christchurch	318		362	255	579	186	331	425	487	163
Collingwood	251	509	871	384	1088	383	840	135	961	672
Dunedin	675	362		565	217	548	331	790	283	199
Franz Josef Glacier	502	410	563	179	575	518	498	469	404	493
Gore	825	513	151	705	66	699	378	941	169	350
Greymouth	324	255	565		760	339	510	290	583	352
Haast	645	554	421	321	433	660	356	611	262	418
Hokitika	370	270	570	41	700	380	520	337	530	360
Invercargill	900	579	217	760		765	444	1007	187	416
Kaikoura	132	186	548	339	765		517	248	673	349
Milford Sound	1085	773	411	860	278	959	550	1145	291	610
Mount Cook	645	331	331	510	444	517		756	271	211
Nelson	116	425	790	290	1007	248	756		910	590
Oamaru	560	247	115	445	332	433	216	675	319	84
Queenstown	798	487	283	583	187	673	271	910		335
Te Anau	964	652	290	739	158	838	434	1025	170	489
St Arnaud	100	352	710	222	932	232	682	119	839	514
Timaru	475	163	199	352	416	349	211	590	335	

TRAVELLING TIMES AND DISTANCES FROM AUCKLAND

	DISTANCE	CAR	BUS	TRAIN	AIR
WELLINGTON	647km	9hrs 15mins	10hrs 30mins	12hrs	1hr
CHRISTCHURCH	1,000km	2 days	2 days	2 days	1 1/2hrs
DUNEDIN	1,358km	2–4 days	3 days	Not available	2 1/2hrs
QUEENSTOWN	1,484km	2–4 days	3 days	Not available	2hrs 35mins
BAY OF ISLANDS	241km	4hrs 15mins	4hrs 30mins	Not available	50mins
ROTORUA	235km	3hrs 30mins	4hrs	Not available	45mins

Prevention of Cruelty to Animals, tel 09-827 6094) no later than 48 hours after the accident.

Parking
● Parking in the cities can be very expensive. Do not risk parking in restricted areas or exceeding your time allotment on meters.
● Note that you must park with the flow of traffic, never against it.
● At night, a car parked on the road must show two tail

Right, pay-and-display parking machines are in most cities. Below, prepare to give way on narrow rural bridges—very few have traffic lights

lights and one front light on the side of the car nearest the middle of the road, unless it's under a street light and visible to other vehicles at a distance of 50m (55 yards) in a 50kph area or 100m (110 yards) in an area with a higher limit.

Buying a car
Although by no means essential, buying a car is a cost-effective option for long stays. Second-hand cars are inexpensive and readily available.

Buying procedure and legalities
● A current international or accepted driver's licence is essential.
● All cars need a safety certificate to be legally on the

road and to obtain registration. Most garages and specialist 'drive in, drive out' Vehicle Testing Stations do a Warrant of Fitness (WOF) test for about NZ$35. If passed, this is valid for six months. If you buy a car with a WOF make sure it is not more than 28 days old.

● Registration can be gained (for a fee) with legal ownership and a valid WOF certificate for six months (about NZ$100) or twelve months (NZ$200).

● The buyer and seller must fill in an MR13A form, which can be bought and submitted at any Post Shop (NZ$10).

● Insurance is not compulsory but a minimum of third party coverage is highly recommended.

● The New Zealand AA offers good insurance rates, emergency breakdown help, free maps and information (tel 09-377 4660, www.nzaa.co.nz).

● To have the car's credentials checked before you purchase, contact AA Auto Report on the New Zealand AA's website (NZ$25) or tel 0800-500 333 and quote the chassis and licence plate number of the vehicle.

● The New Zealand AA provides vehicle inspections, as do other companies found in the *Yellow Pages* (www.yellowpages.co.nz).

Where to buy a car

● There are several auto magazines available at newsagents. The major daily newspapers (such as the *New Zealand Herald*, on Wednesday and Saturday) and auctions are also recommended sources of information.

● Car fairs are held at:
Ellerslie Racecourse, Greenlane (Sun 9–noon), tel 09-529 2233, www.carfair.co.nz;
Manukau Car Market, Manukau City Centre Car Park (Sun 9–1), tel 09-358 5000;
Sell It Yourself, 1106 Great South Road, Otahuhu (daily 8–6.30), tel 09-270 3666;
60 Wairau Road, Glenfield (daily 7–7), tel 09-443 3800.

● Car auctions are held at:
Turners Car Auctions, corner of Penrose and Leonard roads, Penrose (Thursday, Saturday), tel 09-525 1920,
www.turnersauctions.co.nz;
Hammer Auctions, corner of Neilson and Alfred streets, Onehunga (Monday, Thursday, Saturday), tel 09-579 2344,
www.hammerauctions.co.nz.

● Sale and guaranteed buy-backs are offered by:
Budget Car Sales, 12 Mount Eden Road, Mount Eden, tel 09-379 4120;
Downtown Rentals, 31 Neilson Street, Onehunga, Auckland, tel 09-625 6469;
Rex Swinburne, 825 Dominion Road, Mount Roskill, tel 09-620 6587.

SELECTED ROAD SIGNS

Speed limit on major roads, in kph

Hazard (penguins crossing) ahead

Slow down—sharp bends ahead

Main route sign, with distance to the destination given in km

Unmade road ahead

HOW TO NAVIGATE A ROUNDABOUT (TRAFFIC CIRCLE)

Slow down on the approach to a roundabout and give way to all vehicles that will cross your path from your right. Most multi-laned roundabouts are marked with lanes and arrows, to guide you into the correct lane—but note that not all are marked the same way. If you need to cross lanes near an exit, give way to any vehicles in the lane that you want to enter.

If you're continuing straight ahead (across the roundabout) don't signal on the approach, but signal left before your exit.

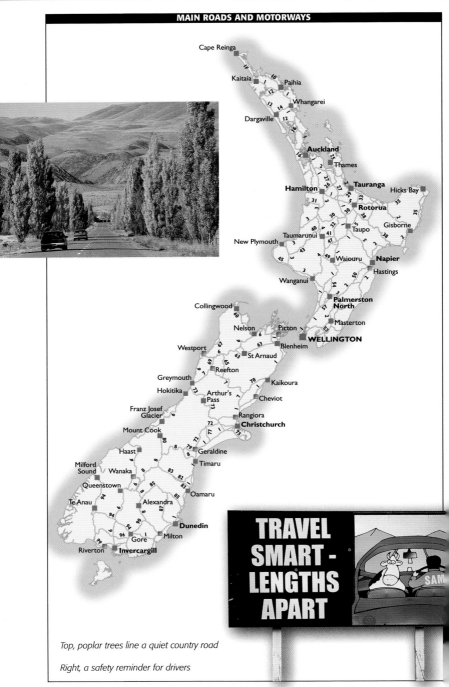

Cape Reinga

Kaitaia
Paihia
Whangarei
Dargaville

Auckland
Thames
Hamilton
Tauranga
Hicks Bay
Rotorua
Gisborne
Taumarunui
Taupo
New Plymouth
Waiouru
Napier
Hastings
Wanganui
Palmerston North
Masterton
WELLINGTON

Collingwood
Nelson
Picton
Westport
Blenheim
St Arnaud
Reefton
Greymouth
Kaikoura
Hokitika
Arthur's Pass
Cheviot
Franz Josef Glacier
Rangiora
Christchurch
Mount Cook
Geraldine
Haast
Timaru
Milford Sound
Wanaka
Queenstown
Oamaru
Te Anau
Alexandra
Dunedin
Gore
Milton
Riverton
Invercargill

TRAVEL SMART - LENGTHS APART

SAM

Top, poplar trees line a quiet country road

Right, a safety reminder for drivers

Buses and Taxis

National bus travel in New Zealand is generally well organised, with high standards of comfort, efficient networks and reliable daily schedules. Several shuttle companies serve the South Island. There are also many local operators and independent companies providing shuttles to accommodation establishments, attractions and activities.

ON THE MOVE

- The two main long-distance bus brands, Intercity (**www.intercitycoach.co.nz**) and Newmans (**www.newmanscoach.co.nz**), are operated by the same organisation.
- For information and reservations about bus travel call the following regional offices: Auckland tel 09-623 1503 Wellington tel 04-385 0520 Christchurch tel 03-365 1113 Dunedin tel 03-471 7143.
- In Northland, Northliner Express (tel 09-307 5873, **www.northliner.co.nz**) runs in cooperation with Intercity.
- Other companies in North Island include White Star (tel 06-758 3338, **www.yellow.co.nz/site/whitestar/**), which serves the route between New Plymouth and Wellington, taking in Wanganui and Palmerston North; and the Pavlovich Express (tel 0800-759 999, **www.pavlovichexpress.co.nz**), operating between Auckland, Rotorua, Tauranga and Taupo via Hamilton. Coromandel Explorer Tours (tel 07-866 3506, **www.coromandeltours.co.nz**) operates around Coromandel.
- The principal backpacker bus companies (▷ 50) are: Kiwi Experience, tel 09-366 9830, **www.kiwiexperience.com**; Magic Travellers, tel 09-358 5600, **www.magicbus.co.nz**; Stray, tel 09-309 8772, **www.straytravel.co.nz**; and Flying Kiwi, tel 0800-693 296, **www.flyingkiwi.com**.
- Bottom Bus (tel 03-434 7370, **www.bottombus.co.nz**) runs

Bus stops are clearly signed

around the Southern Scenic Route between Dunedin and Milford Sound, via Queenstown.

Concession fares

All bus companies offer a variety of concession fares.
- Infants younger than three travel free and children younger than twelve travel at 33 per cent discount on Intercity and Newmans.
- Passengers over the age of 60 travel at 20 per cent discount, backpackers (YHA, VIP, BBH, Nomads cardholders) and students at 15 per cent.
- Saver fares of 25 per cent discount and supersaver fares of 50 per cent discount are available, but these must be reserved in advance.
- Intercity and Newmans also operate a Club Free-Way Card. This accrues points that can later be redeemed for discounts or free tickets.

Bus passes

Intercity/Newmans Countrywide bus passes can be bought for a choice of four 'hop on–hop off' routes throughout the North and

South islands, ranging from an Auckland-to-Christchurch trip from NZ$565 to an Auckland-and-back deal from NZ$729, both driving the length of the South Island.

Intercity/Newmans North Island bus passes

- The Pacific Coast Highway goes from Auckland to Thames (via the Coromandel Peninsula), through Tauranga and Rotorua, and then rejoins the coast at Whakatane before continuing to Gisborne and Napier to Wellington; adult NZ$204, child NZ$140.
- The North Island Value Pass is a flexi-plan ticket between Auckland and Wellington, taking in either Coromandel or Waitomo; adult NZ$155, child NZ$105.

Intercity/Newmans South Island bus passes

- The West Coast Passport operates between Nelson and Queenstown (optional start in Picton or Greymouth); adult NZ$175, child NZ$117.
- The Milford Bound Adventurer is available on services from Christchurch via Mount Cook to Queenstown and then onto Milford Sound; adult NZ$235, child NZ$157.
- The Southern Discovery departs from either Christchurch or Greymouth, taking in Mount Cook, Queenstown and Milford Sound; adult NZ$355, child NZ$238. This trip is best combined with the famous TranzAlpine rail journey between Greymouth and Christchurch (▷ 199).
- The West Coast Passport covers the whole of the West Coast, from Picton through Nelson and Greymouth to

Queenstown; adult NZ$175, child NZ$117. Shorter options are available from Nelson (adult NZ$145, child NZ$97) and from Greymouth (adult NZ$125, child NZ$84).

BACKPACKERS AND NO-FRILLS TRAVEL

● An increasingly popular way to get round the country is to use services provided primarily for backpackers by companies like Stray (tel 09-309 8772, **www.**straytravel.com) and Kiwi Experience (tel 09-366 9830, **www.**kiwiexperience.com). This travel option is a cross between a bus service and backpacker-oriented coach tour.

● Different passes are offered: Stray's prices start with a NZ$35 Auckland day tour, or a tour round the bottom of the South Island from Dunedin for $330, and go up to a 22-day nationwide tour for NZ$1,200; Kiwi Experience passes range from NZ$89 for a one- or two-day Auckland–Paihia (Bay of Islands) trip or NZ$165 for Queenstown–Milford Sound, to NZ$1,850 for a 38-day comprehensive tour round the whole country.

● No-frills buses have also hit New Zealand roads, with fares on Nakedbus starting from just NZ$1.70, including booking fee (tel 0900-NAKED—calls cost at least $1.80 per minute— **www.**nakedbus.co.nz). This company doesn't have the comprehensive network of the more established operators, but its services are expanding in both main islands. Bookings must be made on the internet.

TAXIS

● You can take taxi cabs from ranks or hail one in the street.

● If there are three or more of you, taking a taxi can be less expensive than taking the bus, and no tip is expected.

● Long-distance fares should be negotiated in advance of the journey.

● Combined Taxis New Zealand runs a central service putting callers in touch with registered and approved taxi firms in different towns and cities. Call 0800-505555 and when prompted add:

    11 for Auckland
    13 for Christchurch
    14 for Dunedin
    36 for Greymouth
    15 for Hamilton
    31 for Nelson
    34 for Queenstown
    16 for Rotorua
    18 for Tauranga
    12 for Wellington or
    21 for Whangarei.

Other destination numbers are listed in the phone prompts.

● Information on special needs, meet-and-greet packages and taxi tours is available from the New Zealand Taxi Federation (tel 04-499 0611, **www.**taxinet. org.nz).

Taxis in New Zealand generally offer good value and are a comfortable option for shorter trips

Bicycling

● For information on bicycle rental ▷ 41.

● In towns, some bicycle lanes are coloured to mark them out from the road—for instance, some Christchurch and Hamilton lanes are red; Auckland's bicycle lanes are green.

● Helmets are compulsory for all bicyclists.

● All bicyclists must have a rear reflector (preferably red) on the back of the bicycle; yellow pedal reflectors or reflective leg-straps, and good brakes on the front and back wheels.

● You must have lights (white in front, red behind) to cycle after dark.

● Bicyclists must follow the same rules as drivers, including giving way at intersections (▷ 44).

● Bicyclists can only ride beside another cyclist or a moped—not alongside a car or truck.

● Bicyclists passing another vehicle must ride in single file.

● For more information: Land Transport New Zealand, tel 0800 699 000, **www.**landtransport. govt.nz; Cycling Advocates' Network (CAN), tel 04-472 2552, **www.**can.org.nz.

Trains

The rail network throughout the country is disappointing and in a seemingly incessant state of flux. New Zealand has struggled for years to maintain even a core network between its main hubs of population and provincial towns.

● Apart from commuter services in Auckland and Wellington, in the North Island Tranz Scenic (tel 0800 TRAINS, **www.**tranzscenic.co.nz) operates the Overlander between Auckland and Wellington daily in summer, Friday–Sunday in winter.
● In the South Island are Tranz Scenic's daily TranzCoastal services between Christchurch and Picton, connecting with the Interislander ferry to Wellington, and the daily TranzAlpine between Christchurch and Greymouth.

● The trains themselves are quite comfortable. Service is usually good and most trains have a viewing car at the rear, great for taking in the scenery.
● The tourist Taieri Gorge Limited (tel 03-477 4449, **www.**taieri.co.nz) runs daily between Dunedin and Pukerangi or Middlemarch, and weekly to Palmerston.

Fares

Tranz Scenic fares range widely from Standard to Super Saver; check your entitlements and any available deals.

● All trains are single class.
● Reservations and timetables are available from Wellington and Christchurch rail stations, i-SITES and travel agents throughout New Zealand.
● Several specialist travel packages are on offer, including Great Train Escapes and Day Escapes, comprising a range of one- to six-day excursions, most of which include accommodation. Prices range from NZ$79 for a day excursion to NZ$545 for six days. Children travel for around 40 per cent of the adult fare.

The TranzAlpine Railway travels through the scenic countryside of the South Island

Domestic Flights and Ferries

In addition to the principal international airports of Auckland, Wellington and Christchurch, New Zealand has many well-served provincial town airports. Air New Zealand Link is by far the dominant carrier. Qantas also flies from Auckland to Wellington and Christchurch. Services are highly professional and efficient, so you will rarely have problems with delays.

ON THE MOVE

DOMESTIC FLIGHTS

Apart from the major domestic operators, there are many smaller companies with scheduled services. These include: Great Barrier Airlines (Great Barrier, Coromandel and Northland), Sounds Air (offering an alternative to the ferry between the North and South islands) and Stewart Island Flights (between Invercargill and Stewart Island). Air2there (tel 04-904 5130, 0800 777 000, www.air2there.co.nz), based at Paraparaumu just north of Wellington, offers services to Nelson, Blenheim and Wellington, bypassing the capital for people on the Kapiti Coast. Mountain Air (tel 09-256 7025, www.mountainair.co.nz,) operates flights between Auckland, Whangarei and Great Barrier Island. Flying anywhere in New Zealand is, on a clear day, a scenic delight.

Domestic discount fares

If you can, reserve domestic flights well in advance via the internet or through a travel agent. Most discounted fares can be bought only in New Zealand.

There are many available deals that can make considerable savings, depending on season and availability. Air New Zealand offers the South Pacific Airpass, which works on a zone and coupon system and must be ticketed prior to arrival. For more information ask your travel agent or see www.airnewzealand.co.nz.

DOMESTIC FERRIES

Other than a few small vehicle ferries and the short trip to Stewart Island from Bluff in Southland, the main focus of ferry travel is the inter-island route across Cook Strait. The two ports are Wellington, at the southern tip of the North Island,

Above, a Sounds Air plane
Below left, Wellington Airport

and Picton, in the Marlborough Sounds, northern South Island.

Linking South and North

The scenic 85km (53-mile) journey across the Cook Strait takes up to three-and-a-half hours, depending on which vessel you take.

● In rough weather the crossing can be something of an ordeal. Sailings are stopped if considered too dangerous, but this does not happen often.

● Reserve tickets well in advance, especially in December and January. Most major visitor information centres and travel agents can organise reservations and tickets.

● On board the Interislander's *Arahua, Kaitaki* and *Aratere* ferries there are bars, food courts, cafés, movies, visitor information points, children's play areas and nurseries, and private work desks. The slightly higher-priced Club Class ticket gives access to a private lounge and complimentary tea, coffee, magazines and newspapers.

● A free shuttle bus to the terminal (2km/1 mile) runs from

DOMESTIC AIRLINES
Air New Zealand tel 0800-737 000 www.airnewzealand.co.nz
Great Barrier Airlines tel 0800-900 600 www.greatbarrier.co.nz
Qantas tel 0800-900 600 www.qantas.co.nz
Sounds Air tel 0800-505 005 www.soundsair.co.nz
Stewart Island Flights tel 03-218 9129 www.stewartislandflights.co.nz

Wellington Rail Station 35 minutes before each scheduled ferry departure.

● Fares for passengers range from the standard NZ$65 (child NZ$33) to the saver NZ$45 (child NZ$31). Cars cost NZ$99–NZ$160. The vehicle fare does not include the driver. Motorcycles cost NZ$36–NZ$55, bicycles NZ$10. Best of New Zealand Pass and Travelpass New Zealand are accepted, and children under the age of four travel free.

● Various day/limited-excursion, family and group fares and standard discounted fares are available but must be reserved in advance and are subject to availability. At peak periods (particularly December/January) discounts are rarely available.

● The latest operator making the crossing is the independent Bluebridge, with the ex-Mediterranean vessels *Monte Stello* and *Santa Regina*. Facilities are more basic, but adequate; the service is efficient and the staff friendly. The standard fare is NZ$49 for a passenger (child NZ$25), and NZ$120 for a vehicle.

Getting to Stewart Island

● Stewart Island Experience sails October to May 9.30, 11.30 and 5, and May to September 9.30 and 4.30, from the port of Bluff. The crossing by fast catamaran takes about an hour and costs NZ$51 (child NZ$25.50) one way.

● Secure parking is available in Bluff for NZ$5 per day.

FERRY CONTACTS

Bluebridge tel 0800-844 844 www.bluebridge.co.nz

Campbelltown Passenger Services tel 03-212 7404

Interisland Line tel 0800-802 802 www.interislander.co.nz

Stewart Island Experience tel 0800-000 511 www.stewartislandexperience.co.nz

● Campbelltown Passenger Services offer a regular daily shuttle to and from Invercargill to coincide with the Stewart Island ferries (NZ$12 one way). Reservations are advised.

Northland

● A car ferry operates across the Hokianga from Rawene (tel 09-405 2602, **www.**fndc.govt.nz), providing a useful link up the west coast of Northland. Fullers Bay of Islands (tel 09-402 7421, **http://**fboi.co.nz) operates car ferries linking the Russell area to Opua and passenger-only ferries to Paihia.

Hauraki Gulf

● Passenger ferries operated by Fullers (tel 09-367 9111,

Above, small ferries provide a shuttle service across Auckland's Waitemata harbour
Below, an Interislander ferry passing Pencarrow lighthouse entering Wellington harbour

www.fullers.co.nz) and Kawau Kat (**www.**360discovery.co.nz) criss-cross the Waitemata Harbour and the Hauraki Gulf, serving the North Shore and out to Great Barrier Island.

● Sealink (tel 09-300 5900, 0800 732 546, **www.**sealink. co.nz) operates frequent vehicle ferries to Waiheke Island from Half Moon Bay near Pakuranga, and from central Auckland, and daily (except Saturdays) from central Auckland to Great Barrier Island.

VISITORS WITH A DISABILITY

ON THE MOVE

For visitors with disabilities, New Zealand can be frustrating. While the majority of public facilities are accessible to wheelchairs, older lodgings and some public transportation systems (especially rural buses) are not as well organised. However, the good news is that the situation is improving slowly, and it is now a legal requirement for new buildings to include facilities for people with disabilities.

● Air New Zealand's International Boeing 747, 767 and 737-300 and Airbus A320 planes have onboard skychairs, which are designed to fit within narrow aisles. These are not available on domestic flights, but airports will provide skychairs for wheelchair-users for arrivals and departures.
● Facilities for people with disabilities at Auckland and Christchurch airports include automatic doors, elevators, wheelchair access, accessible toilets and showers, and ATMs with Braille keys. There are also parking spaces for card-holders in front of the terminals and in the airport parking areas.
● A useful sign to look for is the International Symbol of Access. It is awarded by local authorities to inspected properties that meet the needs of the mobility impaired.
● The Youth Hostels Association (YHA) runs 27 hostels in New Zealand, of which 11 are suitable for people with restricted mobility: Auckland International, Christchurch City Central, Franz Josef, Greymouth, Kaikoura, Lake Tekapo, Nelson, Queenstown, Te Anau, Tauranga and Wellington City.

● Visitors with disabilities often receive discounts on travel and some admission charges.
● Parking concessions are available and temporary cards can be issued on receipt of a mobility card or medical certificate.
● *Accessible New Zealand*, by Alexia Pickering, is a guide for visitors with restricted mobility. It covers a range of topics, including attractions, accommodation, shopping and parking, toilets, restaurants, transport and activities.

SPECIALIST TOUR COMPANIES

Accessible Kiwi Tours Ltd
PO Box 550, Opotiki,
Bay of Plenty
Tel 07-315 6988
Fax 07-315 5144
www.tours-nz.com,
Email info@accessible-tours.co.nz
Themed tours for individuals and groups, plus information for independent travel.

Galaxy Motors
PO Box 22114, Otahuhu,
Tel 0800 GALAXY
www.galaxyautos.co.nz
Email: f.hall@xtra.co.nz
Specially equipped cars and vans; tour guides and companions are also available.

Physical Freedom and Manawatu Jet Tours
PO Box 53, Ashhurst,
Tel/fax 06-329 4060
Email man-jet-tours@inspire.net.nz
Range of activities, including jet-boat river rides, drift-rafting, four-wheel driving, clay-bird shooting. Bus accommodates five wheelchairs. Personalised tours available.

USEFUL CONTACTS

Disability Persons Assembly (DPA)
Tel 04-801 9100
Fax 04-801 9565
www.dpa.org.nz
Email gen@dpa.org.nz
Umbrella organisation for people with disabilities, covering the whole country from its offices in Wellington.

Enable New Zealand
69 Malden Street, PO Box 4547, Palmerston North
Tel 0800 ENABLE
www.enable.co.nz
This organisation aims to help people with disabilities, as well as their families, employers and health professionals.

New Zealand Federation of Disability Information Centres
PO Box 24-042, Royal Oak, Auckland
Tel 0800 NZFDIC
www.nzfdic.org.nz
Provides information for people with disabilities via local (independent) information centres.

Weka
Tel 0800 171 981
www.weka.net.nz
New Zealand's disability information website, for people with disabilities, as well as their families and caregivers, health professionals and disability information providers.

This chapter is divided into six regions, which are identified on the map on the inside front cover. Places of interest are listed alphabetically within each region. Major sights are listed at the start of each region. To locate all the sights, turn to the atlas on pages 311–325.

The Sights

AUCKLAND, NORTHLAND AND COROMANDEL

The northern stretch of New Zealand is warm, humid and sparsely populated, with impressive coastal landscapes and the sunny Coromandel Peninsula. Auckland is the country's biggest city—ferries give access to prettier areas such as Devonport and Waiheke Island.

MAJOR SIGHTS

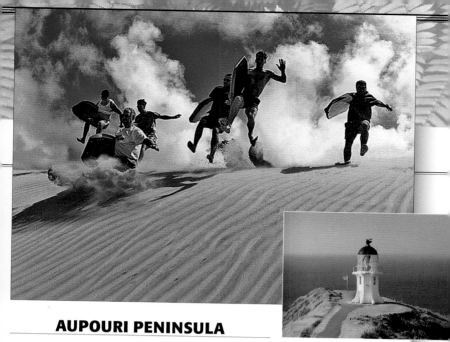

AUPOURI PENINSULA

A stretch of windswept beaches and remote villages in the far north.

New Zealand's most northerly finger of land is bounded by Ninety Mile Beach to the west, and Great Exhibition Bay and Rangaunu Bay and Harbour to the east. At its tip are Cape Reinga and the North Cape—the northernmost point of the North Island. The whole peninsula was once covered in kauri forest; now it consists mainly of extensive dune systems and swamps, interspersed with commercial forestry such as Aupouri Forest.

BEYOND KAITAIA

First stop after Kaitaia (▷ 68) is the Ancient Kauri Kingdom in Awanui, 8km (5 miles) north (daily 9–5), which sells kauri furniture and crafts and displays an imposing, 50-tonne (55-ton) log sculpture. About 17km (10 miles) farther north at Gumdiggers Park (daily 9–5), a reconstructed gumdiggers' village illustrates workers' lives, digging for fossilised kauri gum, around 1900. The route north passes Ninety Mile Beach, an uninterrupted sweep of empty white sand backed by impressive dunes. Join a tour—soft sands and quicksands make driving along it inadvisable, and forbidden by car rental companies.

In the small fishing village of Houhora there are guided tours of the Subritzky/Wagener Homestead, a 19th-century Polish settler's residence little changed since 1900 (11.30, 1.30 and 3.30).

THE FARTHEST POINTS

From Te Kao the road leads north to the vast Te Paki Station and Recreation Reserve, covering 23,000ha (56,830 acres) in all and giving access to the two capes, about 21km (13 miles) away. Local Maori own almost a quarter of the land here, and regard areas around North Cape as sacred. The tip of North Cape is a scientific reserve and has limited public access.

Most visitors head for Cape Reinga and its lighthouse. Views from the hill above extend as far as the Three Kings Islands, 57km (35 miles) offshore. They were named by Abel Tasman, who first spotted them at Epiphany in 1643. The Northland coastline has claimed more than 140 ships since 1808, most foundering around the Cape. The lighthouse contains the lens of an older structure which stood on Motuopao Island, to the south.

Top, enjoying the sand dunes at Te Paki
Above, the lighthouse at Cape Reinga dates from 1941

RATINGS

Historic interest	●●
Photo stops	●●●●
Walkability	●●●●

BASICS

✚ 314 G1

🛈 Information Far North, Jaycee Park, South Road, Kaitaia, tel 09-408 0879; daily 8.30–5

🚍 Daily tours from Kaitaia, Paihia and Mangonui

www.fndc.govt.nz/infocentre
Information on travel, climate, events, car rental and places to stay.

TIPS

● Pukenui is the last major settlement on the way to the Cape, so it pays to buy fuel and provisions at the café and general store.
● The drive to the Cape from Kaitaia takes about an hour and a half. The road is sealed to Te Paki Station; beyond this point it is metalled and speeds should be kept low.

Auckland

New Zealand's largest city and the arrival point for most visitors.
A cosmopolitan city on a narrow strip of land between two attractive harbours.

RATINGS	
Historic interest	● ●
Photo stops	● ● ● ● ●
Shopping	● ● ●
Walkability	● ● ●

*Above, looking across the
Waitemata Harbour to
Devonport and the volcanic
cone of Rangitoto
Above right, the Sky Tower is
illuminated in changing colours
at night
Right, the French-style Art Gallery*

SEEING AUCKLAND

Auckland sits between two natural harbours: the Waitemata, to the east, and the Manukau, to the southwest. At its heart is the CBD (Central Business District) and the main thoroughfare of Queen Street. To either side, the jungle of high-rises occasionally gives way to older buildings such as the Auckland Art Gallery and the green sanctuaries of Albert Park and the Domain, with its crowning glory, the Auckland Museum. Immediately north, the sails and ferries of Waitemata Harbour herald the end of the concrete sprawl, and the 1912 Ferry Building is a sharp contrast to the modern tower blocks behind it.

Viaduct Basin, along the waterfront, was formerly the America's Cup Village and is the home of the New Zealand National Maritime Museum. The Harbour Bridge (1959) leads to the huge expanse of the North Shore, an area of modern suburbs and relatively calm beaches stretching along to the Whangaparaoa Peninsula and the edge of the city, 40km (25 miles) away. The small suburb of Devonport, across the Waitemata Harbour, has a more intimate, affluent atmosphere, with a marina, a lively beach culture and smart villas. Two volcanic cones at Devonport—Mount Victoria and North Head—give excellent city views.

Dominating the southern horizon are Mount Eden and One Tree Hill. South of these landmarks, the low-income suburbs of South Auckland spread to the southern edge of the built-up area at the Bombay Hills, and encompass the Botanic Gardens. In the inner western suburbs, the zoo and the Museum of Transport and Technology (MOTAT) border the lakeside park of Western Springs. Auckland's westward expansion is restricted by the Waitakere Ranges, a hilly recreational area which takes in Auckland Centennial Park.

HIGHLIGHTS

AUCKLAND ART GALLERY (TOI-O-TAMAKI)

➕ 61 C2 ✉ Corner of Wellesley and Kitchener streets ☎ 09-307 7700 ⏱ Daily 10–5. Free guided tours 2pm 🎟 Adult Collection displays free; special exhibitions NZ$7 day pass, child (under 12) free 🍴 🏛
www.aucklandartgallery.govt.nz

The Auckland Art Gallery occupies two buildings in the middle of the city: one in Kitchener Street and the other on the corner of Wellesley and Lorne streets. Together they form the country's largest and most comprehensive collection of national and international art.

The original gallery in Kitchener Street is more than 100 years old and, although it has undergone major reconstruction over the years, it retains its handsome French Renaissance style, with steeply pitched roofs. Works from the permanent collections include international masters, focusing on the 17th century, but the most interesting are those by Charles Goldie (1870–1947) and Gottfried Lindauer (1839–1926), two early European settlers who specialised in oil landscapes and portraits of Maori elders.

The New Gallery, opened in 1995, is across the road. It houses temporary exhibitions and contemporary artists' installations, with a permanent exhibit by modern artist Colin McCahon (1919–1987).

➕ 313 J4
ℹ SKYCITY, corner of Victoria and Federal streets, tel 09-367 6008/0800 AUCKLAND; daily 8–8
🚌 Britomart Transport Centre

www.aucklandnz.com
Comprehensive visitor information including history, places to stay, events and section on other regions.

● Get your bearings from the observation decks of the Sky Tower.
● The best time to visit Mount Eden is at dawn, especially on a misty winter morning, before the crowds arrive.

AUCKLAND, NORTHLAND AND COROMANDEL AUCKLAND **59**

AUCKLAND

Devonport →

Waitemata Harbour

0   500 m
0   500 yds

Birkenhead

Stanley Bay

Brigham

Wynyard Wharf

Princes Wharf
Passenger Terminal

Queens Wharf

Captain Cook Wharf

Marsden Wharf

Powerhouse Lane

Bledisloe Terminal

Bledisloe Wharf

Fergusson Wharf

Jellicoe Wharf

Freyberg Wharf

America's Cup Village

Hobson Wharf

Ferry Berth

MECHANICS BAY

Viaduct Harbour

National Maritime Museum

QUAY

CUSTOMS

EAST

Sturdee

Commerce

Tinley

Plumer

Tooley

French

Sunderland

FANSHAWE

HOBSON

Swanson

QUEEN

Fort

Shortland

Police Station

Eden

Crescent

ANZAC

BEACH

QUAY

Kelly Tarlton's
Antarctic Encounter
and Underwater World

Auckland Mail Service Centre

St Patricks

Wyndham

Federal

Chancery

AVENUE

A WEST

VICTORIA

ALBERT

A WEST

WEST

Kitchener

Victoria East

Bowen Ave

Waterloo Quadrant

Roxeyne

The

Strand

AUCKLAND

The Strand

Television Centre

Sky Tower

Elliott

Lorne

High

Albert Park

Auckland Art Gallery

Auckland University

Princes

Alfred

St Andrews

PARNELL RISE

Augustus

York Ter

Earle

St Georges Bay

WELLESLEY

St Matthews

HOBSON

NELSON

Aotea Centre

Methodist Mission

QUEEN

WELLESLEY EAST

Auckland University

SYMONDS

Grafton

Garfield

Windsor

PARNELL

Police Station

Town Hall

WAKEFIELD

DRIVE

Auckland University of Technology

Cheshire

Scarborough Terrace

St Georges Bay

Auckland Hebrew Congegation

VINCENT

MAYORAL

Greys Ave

Myers Park

Airedale

AUCKLAND CITY

Auckland Domain

Lower Domain

PARNELL

Birdwood Cres

ape

Pitt

QUEEN

Liverpool

Liver city

SYMONDS

GRAFTON BRIDGE

PARK

Auckland Hospital

Drive

North

The Crescent

Domain Drive

Cathedral of the Holy Trinity

Kinder House

School of Medicine

Wintergardens

Auckland Museum
Tamaki Paenga Hira

Maunsell

GRAFTON

St Benedicts

KHYBER

Carlton

Claremont

Gore

Huntly Ave

CARLTON GORE

George

Morgan

Clayton

PARNELL

Sarawia

Ewelme Cottage

Ayr

wich

Exmouth

Nikau

Shaddock

MOUNT EDEN

Burleigh

NUGENT

PASS

BOSTON

BOSTON ROAD

KHYBER

PASS

Newmarket Park

NEWMARKET

Lauder

Mount Eden Prison

Auckland Grammar School

Mountain

Maunganawhau

Melrose

CROWHURST

Kent

Teed

Kingdon

Marl

Grove

Mamie

Middleton

CE

MT EDEN

Enfield

NORMANBY

Mountain

AUCKLAND

HAMILTON

(SOUTHERN

GILLIES AVE

Eden

Morrow

Mortimer Pass

BROADWAY

NEWMARKET

Nutfield

REMUERA

denvale

EDWIN

Clive

Gilgit

Almorah

Auckland Surgical Clinic

scent

Esplanade

Mercy Hospital

Withiel Thomas Park

St Marks Hospital

MacMurray

view

EDEN

Glenfell Place

Omana Hospital

Withiel

ALPERS AVE

GILLIES AVENUE

MANUKAU

GREAT SOUTH

MOTORWAY)

ue

en

Mount Eden Domain

Omana Ave

Albury Ave

Cornwall Park,
One Tree Hill

Auckland Regional
Botanic Gardens

SH1

Lovelock Avenue

Mount Eden

B   **C**   **D**

AUCKLAND MUSEUM TAMAKI PAENGA HIRA
🖽 61 D3 ✉ Domain Drive ☎ 09-304 0443 🕐 Summer daily 9–5.30; winter daily 9–4.30 💲 Adult NZ$5 donation, child (under 18) free. Maori Concert NZ$15, child NZ$7.50 🎁 Excellent gift shop with jewellery, knitwear, ceramics and books
www.aucklandmuseum.com

Rising above New Zealand's oldest and biggest park, the Domain, the museum is a neoclassical building of 1929 housing the outstanding collections of the Auckland Museum. Among its displays are the Pacific and Maori Taonga (treasures), which combine to form the largest such collection in existence. Other attractions include a children's discovery centre with computers, games and interactive displays; social and settlement history sections; natural history galleries; and Scars on the Heart, the story of New Zealanders at war,

Below, Auckland's famous Harbour Bridge spans Waitemata Harbour
Below middle, Viaduct Basin
Below right, floral display in the Botanic Gardens

Right, jumping from the Sky Tower; far right, Mount Eden

MORE TO SEE

PARNELL
🖽 61 D3

Parnell is a fashionably restored suburb 2km (1 mile) east of downtown, full of craft shops, galleries and restaurants. At the top of Parnell Rise is the modern Auckland Cathedral of the Holy Trinity (Mon–Sat 10–4, Sun 11–4); just behind it, the older St. Mary's (1888) is one of the world's largest wooden churches. Parnell Rose Gardens (daylight hours) bloom from November to March. Nearby St. Stephen's Chapel (1857) is a fine example of the Gothic style that evolved under Bishop Selwyn (1809–78).

NEWMARKET
🖽 61 D2

A modern commercial suburb best known for its shopping, quality restaurants, cafés and entertainment. The grand Highwic House at 40 Gillies Avenue (Wed–Sun 10.30–12, 1–4.30, enter from Mortimer Pass) was the 1860s home of 'colonial gentleman of property' Alfred Buckland (1825–1903). Lion Breweries give tours of their facilities (Mon, Wed–Sat 9.30, 12.15, 3), with samplings included.

from the New Zealand Wars of the 19th century to the campaigns in Gallipoli and Crete in the two world wars (▷ 32).

The highlight of the collection is Maori Gallery, He Taonga Maori, housing a variety of craftwork ranging from woven baskets to lethal hand weapons carved from bone and greenstone. Its focal points are the 25m (82ft) *Te Toki a Tapiri* (Tapiri's Battleaxe), last of the Maori war canoes (*waka*), carved from a single tree trunk in 1836; and Hotunui, a beautifully carved meeting house of 1878. A Maori concert is staged daily at 11am, noon and 1.30 (additional performance Jan–Mar 2.30) by Manaia, the museum's cultural performance group.

The museum was built in tribute to the fallen of World War I; it houses a War Memorial Hall, and veterans gather on the forecourt at dawn every year on 25 April—Anzac (Remembrance) Day. Spread around the museum are the Domain's 80ha (198 acres) of fields, gardens and woods, protected as a reserve by Governor Hobson in 1840. Look for the Wintergarden, and the regular orchestral and operatic outdoor events in summer.

AUCKLAND ZOO
🖽 60 A4 ✉ Motions Road, Western Springs ☎ 09-360 3800 🕐 Sep–end May daily 9.30–5.30; Jun–end Aug daily 9.30–5 💲 Adult NZ$18, child (4–14) NZ$8 ☕ 🎁
www.aucklandzoo.co.nz

New Zealand's premier wild animal collection is set in parkland near Western Springs, 4km (2.5 miles) west of the city's hub. The zoo has an active programme of conservation and captive breeding of native species including kiwi and tuatara, both of which are on display. Elephants are also on view, and are sometimes taken for walks around the zoo. Imaginative themed exhibits include a huge walk-through aviary, and a rainforest where primates swing freely through the trees. Recent additions include Pridelands—a spacious home for the giraffes, lions and zebras; the adjoining Hippo River; and a state-of-the-art Sealion and Penguin Shores.

CORNWALL PARK
🖽 61 C5 ✉ Greenlane Road, Manukau Road, Campbell Road ☎ 09-630 8485 🕐 Daily 7–dusk 💲 Free
www.cornwallpark.co.nz

Just south of Mount Eden and 5km (3 miles) south of the Sky Tower, Cornwall Park offers a great escape from city life. Its main claim to fame is One Tree Hill, an extinct volcanic cone with well-preserved

MOUNT EDEN
✠ 61 B5
At 196m (643ft), the closest volcano to downtown Auckland (15 minutes' drive, or bus 274/275 from Customs Street East) provides a terrific view. At its southern base Eden Garden (daily 9–4.30) contains flowering shrubs and native New Zealand plants. Mount Eden village has a fine delicatessen, interesting shops and a number of good cafés and restaurants.

KINDER HOUSE
✠ 61 D4 ✉ 2 Ayr Street, Parnell
☎ 09-379 0202 ⏰ Tue–Sun 11–3
🎟 Adult NZ$2, child 50c
This two-floor building was built in 1856 as the home of pioneer churchman and artist John Kinder (1819–1903). It now displays some of his art works.

EWELME COTTAGE
✠ 61 D4 ✉ 14 Ayr Street, Parnell
☎ 09-379 0202 ⏰ Fri–Sun 10.30–12, 1–4.30 🎟 Adult NZ$3, child free
Not far from Kinder House is Ewelme Cottage, built in 1863 as the Auckland home of the family of Archdeacon Vicesimus Lush (1817–82). It was altered in 1882 but has since remained largely unchanged, and contains colonial furniture and household effects.

AUCKLAND REGIONAL BOTANIC GARDENS
✠ 61 D5 ✉ 102 Hill Road, Manurewa
☎ 09-267 1457 ⏰ Summer daily 8–8; winter daily 8–6; visitor office hours vary 🎟 Free
www.aucklandbotanicgardens.co.nz
A 64ha (158-acre), 10,000-plant collection is laid out 20 minutes south of downtown Auckland. Planting began in 1974 and consists mostly of New Zealand natives. There is also an ornamental lake, a nature trail and a fragrant display of New Zealand-bred roses.

remains of Maori fortified settlements around the summit (the lone pine tree which gives the hill its name was cut down in 2000). Kiwi Tamaki, chief of the Wai O Hua tribe, lived here in the 18th century with thousands of his family and followers, and you can still see the ditches and ramparts that marked their dwellings. Scottish settler and Auckland mayor Sir John Logan Campbell bought the hill and surrounding land, and Huia Lodge, now the visitor office, was his gate-keeper's house. Directly across the road is restored Acacia Cottage (Dec–end Mar 7–dusk, Apr–end Nov 7–4), in which Campbell lived; the oldest house in Auckland, from 1841, it was relocated here from the city in the 1920s.

DEVONPORT
✠ 61 C1 ⛴ Every half hour from Ferry Building, Quay Street; 10-minute crossing
A bronze sculpture on King Edward Parade marks the spot where the first Polynesians landed in their canoe, *Tainui,* in the 14th century. Devonport was later a European settlement and still has many splendid 19th-century buildings, including the restored Esplanade Hotel. Ferries dock at Devonport Wharf, at the end of the main street, Victoria Road, which is lined with cafés and shops selling books, crafts, souvenirs and antiques. A footpath from its far end leads up Mount Victoria, an extinct volcanic cone with traces of a Maori *pa* around the summit. The views of the Hauraki Gulf and offshore islands are magnificent. At the tip of the peninsula, North Head Historic Reserve is another volcanic cone, pocked with 19th-century gun emplacements and tunnels, evidence of a Russian invasion scare. Spring Street leads from the waterfront to the Royal New Zealand Navy Museum (daily 10–4.30).

KELLY TARLTON'S ANTARCTIC ENCOUNTER AND UNDERWATER WORLD
✠ 61 D2 ✉ 23 Tamaki Drive, 6km (4 miles) from downtown ☎ 09-528 0603/ 0800 805050 ⏰ Daily 9–6 (last entry 5) 🎟 Adult NZ$28, child (4–14) NZ$14, under 4 free 🅿 ♿
www.kellytarltons.co.nz
This hugely popular attraction, the brainchild of diver Kelly Tarlton, was set up in subterranean storage tanks behind Orakei Wharf. Visits are

divided into two main parts. The Antarctic Encounter displays relate the story of early Antarctic exploration. Before entering a replica of Captain Scott's 1911 South Pole expedition hut, you are primed by a weather update from the modern base, citing barely imaginable sub-zero temperatures and wind speeds. From here a snow cat carries you through Penguin Encounter, where king and gentoo penguins breed in carefully maintained natural conditions.

Through Stingray Bay is the original Underwater World, where Tarlton pioneered the concept of viewing sea life through fibreglass tunnels. Stingrays and sharks glide directly above your head, and smaller tanks contain a host of species including beautiful

Below, explore beneath the waves at Kelly Tarlton's Below right, One Tree Hill provides great views over the city

ONE TREE HILL

✚ 61 D5

A single totara tree once stood on One Tree Hill and gave the area its original name: Te-Totara-a-Ahua (the totara that stands alone). Settlers cut this tree down in 1852, and to make amends a new totara and several Monterey pines were planted in its place. Most failed to flourish and by 1960 only one pine was left, providing Auckland's greatest landmark before the advent of the Sky Tower. In 1994 this tree was damaged by a pro-Maori activist, and after a further attack in 1999 it was decided that the pine must be removed for safety's sake. On the day of its felling hundreds of people gathered to say goodbye, and a Maori *karakia* (prayer service) was said at dawn.

seahorses, moray eels and the poisonous scorpion fish. Open rock pools and a separate education facility provide a learning experience for children.

MUSEUM OF TRANSPORT, TECHNOLOGY AND SOCIAL HISTORY (MOTAT)

✚ 60 A4 ✉ Great North Road, Western Springs, 4km (2.5 miles) west of downtown ☎ 09-815 5800/0800 668 2869 ◉ Daily 10–5 🦶 Adult NZ$14, child (5–16) NZ$7, under 5s free, family NZ$30 📠 🏛
www.motat.org.nz

MOTAT is near Auckland Zoo, on a site that once pumped water from Western Springs Lake to the city's houses. The original pumphouse and beam engine are part of a complex ranged over two sites and housing an eclectic 30,000-item collection that includes vintage cars, fire engines and motorcycles, telephone boxes and printing presses. MOTAT 2, on Motions Road, occupies the Sir Keith Park Memorial Site (named after New Zealand's most famous wartime aviator) and concentrates on aviation, rail and the military. Prize exhibits include the only Solent Mark IV flying boat in the world, and a World War II Avro Lancaster bomber. The two sites are connected by a vintage tram (NZ$2 round trip), which also stops at the zoo.

NEW ZEALAND NATIONAL MARITIME MUSEUM

✚ 61 B1 ✉ Corner of Quay and Hobson streets ☎ 0800-725897/09-373 0800 ◉ Oct–end Apr daily 9–6; May–end Sep daily 9–5 🦶 Adult NZ$16, child (5–17) NZ$7, family NZ$36. Cruises NZ$15, child NZ$7, family NZ$35 (*Ted Ashby*)
www.nzmaritime.org

Ranged around the waterfront on Hobson Wharf, the New Zealand National Maritime Museum is as diverse and interesting as you might expect in the City of Sails. The layout is chronological, beginning with a video presentation of early Polynesian arrivals and replicas of their vessels, before moving on to European maritime history. The living quarters of an early immigrant ship are replicated, complete with moving floor and sound effects.

Next come the galleries of New Zealand's yachting history, tracing the nation's participation and triumphs in the Louis Vuitton Cup, the Whitbread Round the World Yacht Race and the America's Cup.

Harbour cruises include a trip aboard the 17m (56ft), traditionally built scow *Ted Ashby*, and excursions aboard the *Pride of Auckland*.

SKY TOWER

🕂 61 B2 ✉ Corner of Victoria and Federal streets ☎ 09-363 6000 🕐 Daily 8.30–11 (observation deck) 👜 Adult NZ$22, child (5–14) NZ$8, under 5s free, family NZ$44; extra NZ$3 for Sky Deck 🍴 Orbit revolves to give 360-degree views of the city; the Observatory gives diners access to the main deck www.skycity.co.nz

In 1997 Auckland's skyline gained a dramatic addition in the concrete needle-shape of the Sky Tower, the southern hemisphere's tallest

Below, the Sky Tower, likened to a hypodermic needle, dominates the city skyline
Bottom, glass floor panels in the Sky Tower's observation platform give vertiginous views

building, at 328m (1,076ft) high, and part of the SKYCITY casino, hotel and shopping complex. It takes a mere 40 seconds for the elevator to reach the main observation deck, and there are even more stunning views from the Sky Deck.

If admiring the view isn't quite exciting enough you can opt for Vertigo Climb—a two-hour guided tour up the interior of the tower's mast, culminating in an internal climb from the upper observation deck to the first crow's nest. For an even bigger adrenalin boost there's Sky Jump, the world's highest land-based bungy jump, leaping from 192m (630ft).

BACKGROUND

The first Maori to settle in this area were thought to be hunters of the now extinct moa bird, who arrived before AD1000. From the 12th to the 14th century Maori tribes migrated here, and in the early 18th century Kiwi Tamaki's tribe rose to power, establishing *pa* (fortified Maori settlements) on almost every volcano in the district. A series of brutal conflicts with rival tribes, along with an epidemic of smallpox brought here by the early Europeans, subsequently decimated the area's Maori population.

In 1820 missionaries Samuel Marsden and John Gare Butler were the first white Europeans to pay an 'official' visit. Low-key European settlement followed, and 20 years later Lieutenant-Governor Captain William Hobson bought a triangular section of the isthmus from the Ngati Whatua for £55 and a few blankets. He called this area Auckland in tribute to George Eden, First Earl of Auckland, then Governor General of India.

As a result of the New Zealand Wars (▷ 30) and the discovery of gold in Otago and the nearby Coromandel Peninsula, Auckland entered a period of decline and, in 1865, lost its status as capital to Wellington. By the end of the 19th century its fortunes had revived, thanks to its fertile soils, good climate and a booming kauri industry. Growth continued during the 20th century and a combination of geography, climate, industry, agriculture, and sporting and business opportunities have encouraged its development as a vibrant, cosmopolitan city.

Coromandel Peninsula

Spectacular coastal scenery, rugged mountain bush and a relaxed way of life.

Cathedral Cove, where a natural arch links two beaches

Riding the waves at Whangamata

Visitors on the Driving Creek Railway

BASICS

✚ 315 K4

🛈 206 Pollen Street, Thames, tel 07-868 7284; Mon–Fri 8.30–5, Sat, Sun, pub hols 9–4

✈ Coromandel–Auckland flights Fri, Sun

⛴ Coromandel–Auckland ferries Tue, Thu, Fri, Sat

www.thamesinfo.co.nz

Gathering mussels on the seashore

SEEING THE COROMANDEL PENINSULA

The Coromandel Peninsula's varied landscapes and laidback style make it the main attraction on the Pacific Coast Highway. The west coast, bounded by the Firth of Thames, is the least developed side, with a ragged coastline of islands and pebble beaches lined with pohutukawa trees. In contrast, the east coast is a stretch of beautiful bays, resort development and some of New Zealand's most popular beaches. Between the two coasts, a spine of bush-covered mountains makes up the Coromandel Forest Park, with historic logging and mining remains.

HIGHLIGHTS

COLVILLE AND THE CAPE ROAD

✚ 315 K4

North of Coromandel town the Colville Road enters the most remote and scenic area of the peninsula. From the beach at Waitete Bay it climbs a hill and drops to the tiny village of Colville, with just a general store-cum-café and a fuel station. Beyond Colville the interior is dominated by 893m (2,930ft) Moehau. The road eventually climbs around the northern tip of the cape and descends to Port Jackson, where there are superb views of Great Barrier Island. Fletcher Bay marks the beginning of the three-hour Coromandel Walkway to Stony Bay, and thence the east coast road and all points south.

COROMANDEL

✚ 315 K4 🛈 355 Kapanga Road, tel 07-866 8598

www.coromandeltown.co.nz

The township of Coromandel is 56km (35 miles) north of Thames (▷ 73), on the peninsula's west coast. It was built to serve the kauri timber trade, but boomed when gold was discovered at nearby Driving Creek. During the peak gold-rush years of the 1860s and 1870s its population reached 12,000. Today its inhabitants number around 1,000, and it has a carefully nurtured village atmosphere.

Most of Coromandel's cafés and shops are on Kapanga Road, which runs at right angles to the port. Two sites give an insight into gold-hunting days. The Coromandel School of Mines and Historical Museum on Rings Road (summer daily 10–4; winter Sat, Sun

1.30–4) is in the original School of Mines (1897) and includes New Zealand's first prison; the Coromandel Gold Stamper Battery on Buffalo Road (summer daily 10–5) lets you pan for gold in its stream.

A short drive north of town is the Driving Creek Railway and Potteries (daily). You can ride up to the ridge-top Eyefull Tower terminus, through tunnels and across viaducts and past potter and railway restorer Barry Brickell's sculptures.

NEW CHUMS BEACH
✚ 315 K4

This is one of the best beaches in the Coromandel, accessible only on foot. To reach it, take the SH25 east from Coromandel town over the

OPOUTERE
✚ 316 L5

Quiet and magical Opoutere, on the east coast, is one of the Coromandel's best-kept secrets. White-sand Ocean Beach is guarded by Wharekawa Harbour and a narrow tract of forest. At the tip of the sand spit is the Wharekawa Wildlife Refuge, where oystercatchers and rare New Zealand dotterels breed.

Above, panning for gold
Left, Coromandel Harbour

ranges before descending steeply to Te Rerenga and Whangapoua Harbour, then continue 4km (2.5 miles) north to Whangapoua village and take a 30-minute walk north from the road there to negotiate the headland. Even in bad weather, this stunning beach is definitely worth the walk.

WHITIANGA
✚ 315 K4 **ℹ** 66 Albert Street, tel 07-866 5555
www.whitianga.co.nz

Whitianga is on glorious Mercury Bay, within walking distance of several fine beaches. There are plenty of leisure activities, but Whitianga is most famous as a sea- and big-game-fishing base.

The Mercury Bay Museum (Dec–Easter daily 10–4), which traces the area's social history, faces the main wharf, where a passenger ferry shuttles across the narrows to Ferry Landing. This was the township's original site, and the stone wharf (built in 1837) is said to be the oldest in the country.

The main waterfront beach is named after a timber ship, HMS *Buffalo*, wrecked here in 1840. Two smaller resorts lie within reach of Whitianga: Cooks Beach, on its southern edge (where Captain James Cook planted the British flag on 5 November 1769 and claimed the country for George III), and Hahei (▷ 220), 35km (22 miles) farther by road and accessible by ferry. Both have wonderful beaches. A track north of Hahei on Grange Road leads in half an hour to Cathedral Cove, a fabulous beach guarding the Te Whanganui-A-Hei Marine Reserve (▷ 228). Strictly speaking, there are two beaches here, connected by a natural rock arch negotiable at low tide.

BACKGROUND

First to set foot here was the Maori explorer Kupe, 1,000 years ago. Captain Cook paid a brief visit in 1769, and from 1795 ships landed regularly to load timber for the British navy. Nearly three quarters of the kauri forests were felled, leaving just 5,000ha (12,355 acres). Coromandel is named after the timber ship HMS *Coromandel*, which called here in 1820. Charles Ring discovered gold in 1852; at the peak of the boom, around 1880, the peninsula's population topped 12,000.

WAIHI
✚ 316 K5 **ℹ** Seddon Street, tel 07-863 6715
www.waihi.org.nz

Waihi once had 1,200 gold mines, producing half the country's gold. The Martha Mine (free guided tours most weekdays), which sits like a huge bomb crater right in the middle of town, was one of the first, and reopened after a brief redundancy in the mid-1900s. Today, from a lookout behind the information office, you can watch earthmoving trucks winding in and out of the massive, terraced hole.

WHANGAMATA
✚ 316 L5 **ℹ** 616 Port Road, tel 07-865 8340

The Coromandel's main surfing venue is well served with places to stay and eat, and with water-based activities. There are several good short coastal walks, and south of town the Wentworth and Parakiwai valleys offer longer trails, taking in waterfalls and remnants of the gold-mining industry. The beach at Whangamata is more than 4km (2.5 miles) long.

A natural rock hole by Piercey Island, in the Bay of Islands

The scenic Kai Iwi lakes are a focus for summer activities

Decorative pillars in the unusual public toilets at Kawakawa

BAY OF ISLANDS

🚩 314 J2 ℹ️ Marsden Road, Paihia, tel 09-402 7345 🚌 Maritime Building, Paihia ⛴ Ferry between Russell and Paihia; car ferry to Opua, 9km (5.5 miles) south of Paihia ✈️ Bay of Islands airport, between Paihia and Kerikeri www.northland.org.nz

A group of 150 islands huddled in their large bay on the east Northland coast has become a major draw for holidaymakers, who come for watersports and superb coastal scenery. This area is also of huge historic significance, as the site of the signing of the 1840 Treaty of Waitangi—the document that set in train New Zealand's bicultural society (▷ 27). You can explore the islands—now designated a Historic and Maritime Park—by kayak, yacht or sailing ship; you can also go fishing for marlin or shark, dive among shoals of blue maomao, swim with dolphins, bask on the beaches or jump out of a plane.

Most facilities are based in Paihia (▷ 72). From here a ferry crosses the bay to the small village of Russell (▷ 72). State Highway 11 runs to the bay, though a more interesting route

is via the Old Russell Road, which leaves SH1 for the coast at Whakapara, about 26km (16 miles) north of Whangarei (▷ 75). You reach the coast at Helena Bay, which, along with Whananaki and Mimiwhangata to the south and the Whangaruru Peninsula to the north, offers remote and beautiful coastal scenery. From Whangaruru the road passes the neck of the beautiful Cape Brett Peninsula before turning inland and slowly negotiating its way to Russell.

COROMANDEL PENINSULA

See pages 66–67.

HAURAKI GULF ISLANDS

See pages 70–71.

KAI IWI LAKES

🚩 314 H3 ℹ️ Normanby Street, Dargaville, tel 09-439 8360 www.kauricoast.co.nz

Located about 30km (19 miles) south of the Waipoua Kauri Forest (▷ 75), and only 10km (6 miles) from the coast, three freshwater lakes—Kaiiwi, Taharoa and Waikere—form part of the Taharoa recreation reserve. On

their crystal clear waters you can enjoy sailing, windsurfing, water-skiing, jet-skiing and fishing, and you can explore the area along an extensive walking track. Note that, lacking cover and so close to the western coast, the lakes can be exposed to the elements.

KAITAIA

🚩 314 H2 ℹ️ Jaycee Park, South Road, tel 09-408 0879 🏢 Kaitaia Travel Bureau, 170 Commerce Street ✈️ Airport 6km (4 miles) north

Kaitaia is the last significant out-post of the Far North, and a good start point for exploring Ninety Mile Beach (▷ 57). It frequently registers the hottest temperatures in the country. Its population is mainly Maori but includes a Croatian minority, whose fore-bears arrived during the kauri gum boom years of the late 19th century. The Far North Regional Museum (Mon–Fri 10–5, Sat, Sun 1–4) has a number of Maori treasures, including the Kaitaia Carving, one of the earliest Maori carvings in existence, and a 1,500kg (1.5-ton) anchor left by French navigator Jean-François de Surville in 1769. Other collec-tions include moa remains and remnants from the Greenpeace ship *Rainbow Warrior* (▷ 34). The Okahu Estate Winery, on the corner of Okahu Road and the Ahipara/Kaitaia highway, 3.5km (2 miles) from Kaitaia (daily 10–5, closed winter weekends), is New Zealand's northernmost winery and offers free tastings.

KARIKARI PENINSULA

🚩 314 H1

This peaceful, beautiful T-shaped spur juts out on the northeastern coast, before it extends into the long, straight run of the Aupouri Peninsula (▷ 57). Its remote beaches separate Doubtless Bay from the mangrove swamps of

A sparkling inlet of white sands in the Bay of Islands

The stone-built warehouse at Kerikeri was built up a barely navigable creek and is known as 'Kemp's folly'

The kauri timber industry is explained at Matakohe

Rangaunu Harbour and the broad, empty sweep of Karikari Bay to the north. Whales are frequently stranded here. In 1995 more than 100 pilot whales were refloated by locals and officials, only to beach themselves again the following day. Tokerau Bay is the main settlement on the peninsula.

KAWAKAWA

➕ 314 H2

Bizarre as it might seem, the main attraction in this town 17km (10.5 miles) south of Paihia is the public toilet. The Hundertwasser public toilets are the imaginative creation of Austrian artist Friedensreich Hundertwasser (1928–2000). The interior uses tiles of all sizes and shades and stained glass to produce a cheerfully chaotic effect, and the whole building is topped with a grass roof.

South of Kawakawa, local Maori guides give tours of the Kawiti Caves (daily 8.30–4.30), a series of subterranean passages originally occupied by a Maori woman fleeing from her tribe.

KERIKERI

➕ 314 H2 ✈ Airport between Paihia and Kerikeri
www.kerikeri.co.nz

North of Paihia, rolling hills give way to corridors of windbreaks hiding trees of citrus, grape and kiwifruit, for which the area is famous. *Keri* means 'dig', and it was here that the first plough cut into New Zealand soil in 1820. Kerikeri is rich in Maori and early European history; the Kerikeri Historic Basin, 2km (1 mile) northeast of the present town, was the nucleus of New Zealand's first European colonisation.

Where the road meets the Kerikeri River stands the Stone Store (Nov–end Apr daily 10–5;

May–end Oct daily 10–4), the country's first stone building, completed in 1836 and used by the first Anglican bishop, George Selwyn, as a library in the early 1840s. It later housed ammunition during conflicts with Ngapuhi chief Hone Heke, before assuming its intended purpose as a general mission store. A museum occupies the top floor.

Almost immediately next door is the two-floor Mission Station or Kemp House (Nov–end Apr daily 10–5; May–end Oct daily 10–4), the oldest surviving wooden building in New Zealand. The Reverend John Gare Butler had it built in 1821 on land offered by the great local Maori warlord Hongi Hika, who accepted 48 felling axes in return. In 1832 it became the home of lay missionary and blacksmith James Kemp, whose family lived in the house until 1974, when it was given to the nation. The house now contains Kemp family relics.

Overlooking both buildings is the ancient Kororipo *pa*, which was chief Hongi Hika's territory until the 1820s, when he had a European-style house built near by. A stroll across the river leads to Rewa's Village (Dec–end Mar daily 9–5; Apr–end Nov daily 10–4), a re-created pre-European Maori fishing settlement, or *kainga*, named after Hongi Hika's successor. Its reed-and-thatch huts have beds of bracken and fern; traditional cooking areas occupy separate shelters.

In addition to its fruit, Kerikeri is also famous for its arts and crafts. Among many venues are Origin Art and Craft Co-op on SH1 (daily 9.30–5), which displays and sells pottery, stained glass and other crafts; and the Kauri Workshop, on the approach to town on Kerikeri Road (daily 9–5), where kauri and other native wood products are made.

The Aroha Island Ecological

Centre, on Rangitane Road 12km (7 miles) northeast of town (Tue–Sun 9.30–5.30; also overnight visits), and the nearby Rangitane Scenic Reserve are important remnant habitats of the brown kiwi. The island is kept predator-free and offers a small but valuable sanctuary for a few birds. As the kiwi is nocturnal, daytime visitors can only see interpretive material, but if you stay overnight you may see and hear the birds on a guided tour.

MATAKOHE KAURI MUSEUM

➕ 314 J3 ✉ Church Road, Matakohe
☎ 09-431 7417 🕐 Nov–end Apr daily 8.30–5.30; May–end Oct daily 9–5
💲 Adult NZ$15, child (5–15) NZ$3, family NZ$30 🚌 SH12 at Brynderwyn; all Twin Coast Discovery Highway routes stop here 🚍
www.kauri-museum.com

Highly imaginative displays in this museum in the village of Matakohe, 45km (28 miles) south of Dargaville, give a detailed account of the natural history of the kauri tree and its exploitation. The Volunteer Hall contains a 22.5m (74ft) kauri slab, a local specimen which was felled by lightning. On the wall at its base are the circumference outlines of larger recorded trees, the largest having a diameter of 8.5m (28ft). Around the hall are exquisite examples of kauri furniture, and models of kauri scows that used to ply the Kaipara Harbour. Other sections include a working Steam Sawmill, monstrous moving equipment and saws, and a superb kauri gum display, with carvings, busts and ornaments fashioned from the tree's resin or sap, some of it hundreds of thousands of years old. Restored kauri buildings in the museum grounds include the 1867 Pioneer Church and 1909 Post Office.

THE SIGHTS

Hauraki Gulf Islands

**Dozens of islands within easy reach of Auckland.
Volcanic terrain, beach barbecues, diving
sites and wildlife sanctuaries.**

*Above, Matiatia Bay, Waiheke
Top, a takahe*

*Dining al fresco at the Mudbrick
Restaurant, Waiheke (▷ 254)*

*Pohutukawa trees on the shore
of Tiritiri Matangi Island*

BASICS

✚ 315 K4
🛈 Department of Conservation office,
Ferry Building, Quay Street, Auckland,
tel 09-379 6476; Mon–Fri 9–5, Sat 10–3
🚢 Fleet of ferries run by Fullers, Quay
Street, Auckland, tel 09-367 9111,
www.fullers.co.nz: see individual islands
for sailings
✈ Airfields at Waiheke (3km/2 miles
east of Ostend) and Great Barrier
(Claris, Okiwi)

www.aucklandcity.govt.nz
Information for all the main islands,
including history and contact numbers.

Vineyard on Waiheke Island

SEEING THE HAURAKI GULF ISLANDS

The scattering of islands between the Coromandel Peninsula
to the east and the mainland to the south and west provide an
easy escape from the city for day trips or overnight stays. Most
of the Hauraki Gulf lies within Hauraki Gulf Maritime Park,
which takes in 47 islands and one mainland reserve (North
Head in Devonport). Some are wildlife sanctuaries. The most
densely populated island is Waiheke, a 35-minute ferry ride
from Auckland.

HIGHLIGHTS

GREAT BARRIER ISLAND
✚ 315 K3 🛈 Tel 09-367 6009, www.greatbarrier.co.nz 🚢 Sailings
Apr–end Oct Sun–Tue, Thu, Fri; more frequent in summer; always check ahead,
tel 09-300 5900 ✈ Daily flights from Auckland
Rugged Great Barrier (or 'the Barrier') is the largest island in the gulf,
with a population of around 1,000. This is the habitat for some rare and
endangered species, including brown teal and New Zealand's largest
skink (lizard), the cheveron. Over half of the island is conservation land.
   Great Barrier earned its name from Captain Cook because it
appeared to bar the entrance to the gulf. It was one of the first islands
to be colonised by Europeans, who mined for gold and copper and
plundered its extensive kauri forests. There are old kauri dams, the
remains of whaling stations and tramping tracks to explore.

KAWAU ISLAND
✚ 315 J4 🛈 1 Baxter Street, Warkworth, tel 09 425 9081 🚢 From Sandspit at
10.30am, 2, 3.30
www.warkworth-information.co.nz
Kawau, 8km (5 miles) off the Mahurangi Peninsula, was once the
headquarters of Maori pirates. Europeans took possession in 1837,
and the island was mined first for manganese, then for copper.
Operations ceased in 1869, but remnants of copper mines can be
found near the wharf. In 1862 Sir George Grey, Governor of New
Zealand, bought the island for £3,500 and began a 26-year stay in
Bon Accord Harbour, where he created the Mansion House (daily
10–3.30). Grey amassed a small collection of exotic animals and

plants here, unaware of the environmental damage he was unleashing on native flora and fauna. To this day, Australian wallabies and kookaburras inhabit the bush.

RANGITOTO ISLAND

🕂 315 J4 🛈 Rangitoto Island Heritage Conservation Trust, tel 09-634 1398
🚢 From Ferry Building daily at 9.15, 12.15, 3.15
Rangitoto's comparatively young volcanic cone (about 600 years old) dominates views of the Hauraki Gulf from almost every vantage

point in Auckland. Of the island's many walks, most culminate at the summit (two hours). The island's vegetation is of international importance, with 200 species of native tree and flowering plants, 40 kinds of fern, and orchids and lichens. Underfoot are mounds of loose laval scoria.

TIRITIRI MATANGI ISLAND

🕂 315 J4 🚢 Ferries from Pier 3, Ferry Building Wed–Sun at 9am; or the same ferry from Z Pier, Gulf Harbour on the Whangaparaoa Peninsula, 45 mins later
Visitors can wander freely on a network of walkways on this open bird sanctuary 4km (2.5 miles) off the Whangaparaoa Peninsula. The 220ha (544-acre) island has become a haven for rare and endangered species including the takahe, little spotted kiwi, kokako, whitehead, saddleback, North Island robin, kakariki and stitchbird.

WAIHEKE ISLAND

🕂 315 K4 🛈 Korora Road, Oneroa, tel 09-372 1234 🚢 Auckland Ferry Building, daily
The busiest island has a thriving arts and crafts community. Its main village is Oneroa, at the western end of the island. Behind the visitor information office, in the Artworks Complex, Whittakers Musical Museum (daily 10–4) displays instruments dating back 500 years. Live performances are staged at 1pm (except on Tuesday).
  Waiheke enjoys average temperatures 5°C (9°F) warmer than the mainland, and has many vineyards and wineries. The island is fringed with beaches, and inland there are walkways through native bush and farmland. One of the most popular is the track to Stony Batter, where an underground complex is linked by a series of tunnels built in World War II as defence against a possible Japanese invasion.

BACKGROUND

Traces of Maori *pa* sites can still be seen on many hillsides. After the arrival of Europeans in the 19th century some of the islands were sold for gold, arms and ammunition.

RATINGS				
Historic interest	●	●		
Photo stops	●	●	●	●	●
Shopping	●			
Walkability	●	●	●	

TIPS

● Take your own picnic to Rangitoto and Tiritiri Matangi as the shops there do not sell food.
● There is no mains electricity—or streetlight—on Great Barrier Island, so bring a torch: lights out at 10pm.
● Water, sun block and a hat are essential, as the black scoria (volcanic rock) can emanate a lot of heat.

Top, Governor George Grey's gracious Mansion House on Kawau Island

Above, the familiar shape of Rangitoto Island, viewed from Auckland

Pleasure cruisers moored in the bay at Paihia

Divers make the most of the clear waters around the protected Poor Knights Islands, off the Tutukaka Coast

MATAURI BAY

✚ 314 H2
www.matauribay.co.nz

The views above Matauri Bay, studded with the Cavalli Islands, are sublime. Captain Cook named the islands after buying travally (a species of fish) from local Maori. The Samuel Marsden memorial church in Matauri Bay commemorates the missionary who first preached the gospel in the Bay of Islands, on Christmas Day 1814.

This prime venue for deep-sea fishing and diving is probably more famous as the site of the remains of the *Rainbow Warrior*. This flagship of the environmental movement Greenpeace was bombed by French secret service agents in Auckland in 1985 to prevent her leading a protest flotilla to the French nuclear test grounds on the Pacific atoll of Mururoa. Matauri Bay's local Maori tribe, the Ngati Kura, offered the ship a final resting place, and her sunken hull now lies 3km (2 miles) offshore. A memorial on the hill overlooking the islands near the beach pays tribute to the ship, her crew (one of whom was killed) and the campaign for establishing a nuclear-free region.

The Maori *waka* (war canoe) *Mataatua II*, nearby, was built in 1990 to commemorate the Pacific migration from Polynesia in about AD1100.

MURIWAI BEACH

✚ 315 J4
www.muriwai.com

Muriwai, 45km (28 miles) west of Auckland, is the west coast's most visited beach. During summer weekends, locals and visitors flock to its black sands to soak up the sun, enjoy the surf, fish, or look over the gannet colony. Gannets have taken up residence

on the flat rock outcrops at its southern end to breed, forming a small seabird city. In spring you can witness at close range the fluffy white chicks being fed by their angry-looking parents. Muriwai boasts the only major North Island colony, after Cape Kidnappers (▷ 77).

Muriwai itself is well equipped for visitors and has a fine golf course. If Muriwai beach is too busy, you can try another surf spot, Maori Bay, just south of Muriwai and reached via Waitea Road.

PAIHIA

✚ 314 H2 ℹ Maritime Building, Marsden Road, tel 09-402 7345
🚢 Maritime Building
www.paihia.co.nz

Paihia is the most convenient base for cruises or other activities in the Bay of Islands Historic and Maritime Park (▷ 68), and for visiting Russell (see below), Kerikeri (▷ 69) and Waitangi (▷ 74). It has a wide range of motels, hotels and other places to stay, as well as plenty of restaurants, cafés and shops. At the Maritime Building on the quayside there are several booking and information offices, including the visitor office. Behind it, Paihia wharf is busy with charter vessels, dolphin-watch boats and the Russell ferries. Next to the wharf, Aquatic World aquarium (daily 9.30–6; extended hours in summer) provides an insight into marine life in the Bay of Islands.

RUSSELL

✚ 314 J2 ℹ www.russell.gen.nz
🚢 Paihia Wharf every 20–30 mins Oct–Mar 7.30–10.30; Apr–Sep 7.30–8.30

About 2km (1 mile) across the water from Paihia is the settlement of Russell, which has a village feel and a rich history.

Soon after the signing of the Treaty of Waitangi (▷ 27), Captain William Hobson purchased a block of land at nearby Okiato—renamed Russell after Lord John Russell, then British Colonial Secretary—with the aim of establishing the country's capital there. Nine months later, in March 1841, the capital was transferred to Auckland, and in 1844 the notoriously rowdy whaling port of Kororareka was given the name Russell.

The economic decline that followed the shift of the capital to Auckland provoked resentment among local Maori, who sacked the town in 1845. It was rebuilt the following year, and by the turn of the century had become a quiet summer resort. In 1930 a road was laid between Whangarei and Russell, allowing access by car for the first time.

The Russell Museum (Jan daily 10–5; rest of year 10–4) has a collection of early settler relics and a lot of information about Captain Cook, including a 1:5 scale model of his ship *Endeavour*.

A short distance south along the shore from the museum is Pompallier (Dec–Apr daily 10–5; May–Nov tours at 10.15, 11.15, 1.15, 2.15, 3.15), a French-style dwelling set up in 1842 by early Roman Catholic missionaries as a printing works. It later served as a tannery and a private home, and became a museum in 1990.

The 1836 Anglican Christ Church on the corner of Church and Robertson streets was one of the few buildings to survive the 1845 sacking and ensuing Maori war (bar a few visible musket ball holes), and is the oldest church in New Zealand.

A steep climb up Flagstaff Hill (Maiki) gives grand views. The flagstaff itself was raised after the signing of the Treaty of Waitangi.

A cannon in Russell dates from the 1847 Maori conflict

The view over historic Thames and the Hauraki Plains from the War Memorial Lookout

It was cut down several times by local Maori chief Hone Heke Pokai (▷ 28) and replaced in the 1850s as a gesture of conciliation.

A farther 1km (0.6 mile) north, the earth terraces of the ancient *pa* on the Tapeka Point Reserve make an interesting walk. Long Beach, 1km (0.5 mile) behind Russell, is a pleasant venue on a hot summer's day.

THAMES

✚ 316 K5 🛈 206 Pollen Street, tel 07-868 7284 🚌 From Auckland, Tauranga **www.thamesinfo.co.nz**

The historic town of Thames is at the western base of the Coromandel Peninsula (▷ 66–67), at the mouth of the Waihou River and on the fringe of the Hauraki Plains. Behind the town rise the hills of the Coromandel Forest Park.

The best place to start exploring is the War Memorial Monument Lookout on Waiotahi Creek Road, at the northern end of the town, where the panorama takes in the Hauraki Plains and Firth of Thames. Also

at the northern end of town, on attractively preserved Pollen Street, is the Thames Gold Mine and Stamper Battery (daily 10–4). Regular tours take in the impressive ore-crushing stamper and horizontal tunnels, with a commentary about the process and history of gold mining along the way. On the same theme, the Thames School of Mines and Mineralogical Museum (Wed–Sun 11–4) has a collection of rocks and minerals from around the world.

Other places of interest include the Matatoki Cheese Farm (daily 10–4), and the Piako Ostrich Farm (tours daily 11 and 2; closed Tue, Wed, Oct–end Jun). There are also several notable gardens in the area, including Lyndell and Stony Creek Gardens.

Every Saturday the town's popular market is held in Grahamstown, at the north end of Pollen Street.

TUTUKAKA COAST

✚ 315 J2 🛈 Otaika Road, Whangarei, tel 09-438 1079 🚌 Coastal shuttle from Walton Street supermarket, Tutukaka **www.whangareinz.org.nz**

The Tutukaka coastline's ruggedly scenic bays are best known for their safe access to some of the best deep-sea fishing and diving in the world. Tutukaka itself has a large, sheltered marina, and the village of Ngunguru, 5km (3 miles) away, has most of the visitor and resident amenities.

Accessed from Tutukaka, the Poor Knights Islands are a popular diving venue, which lie 25km (15.5 miles) offshore— the remnants of a large volcano which erupted more than 10 million years ago. They provide a predator-free refuge for land animals such as the tuatara (a reptile that has changed little in 60 million years), native lizards, giant weta (the largest insect in the world— around the size of a mouse), flax snails, giant centipedes and a wide variety of rare seabirds. They are also home to several species of plants, including the Poor Knights lily, found only here and on the Hen and Chickens Islands off Whangarei Heads (▷ 75). Landing on the Poor Knights Islands is forbidden without a permit.

Tranquil Russell was once a rowdy whaling port tipped to become the country's first capital

Left, the modest exterior of the Whare Runanga conceals
a richly carved interior of native woods, above

WAITANGI

**Site where the treaty was signed that would shape
European-Maori relationships to the present day.
The place where New Zealand's modern history began.**

BASICS

✠ 314 H2
✉ Waitangi Treaty Grounds, 1 Tau
Henare Drive, Waitangi
☎ 09-402 7437
🕐 Daily 9–6
💳 Adult NZ$12, child (under 14) free;
tours extra (see below); *kapa haka*:
NZ$12, child (under 5) free
🚢 Services from Auckland
⛵ Self-guided Discovery (NZ$12, child
free); Embrace Waitangi (NZ$22, child
NZ$5), 9.15, 10.30, noon, 1.30, 2.30
🍴 Waikokopu café/restaurant:
breakfast, snacks, lamb, beef,
seafood (9–5)
🎴 Traditional local arts and crafts

www.waitangi.net.nz
Basic background and visitor
information, plus details of all tours,
events and shows.

TIP

● The 75-minute Maori Sound
and Light Show is staged on
Monday, Wednesday, Thursday
and Saturday at the Whare
Runanga.

The haunting sound of piped Maori song draws you into the visitor
complex of the Waitangi National Reserve, where an audiovisual
display outlines the events that led to the signing of the Treaty of
Waitangi in 1840 (▷ 27), and highlights the significance of the
document to this day. A daily 30-minute Maori *kapa haka*
performance takes place in the visitor centre's theatre (10.30, 11.30,
1.30, 2.30).

The main focus of the reserve is the beautifully restored wooden
Treaty House, built between 1833 and 1834 and once the home of
British resident James Busby, who played a crucial role in the lead-up
to the signing. The house is full of detailed and informative displays
that help clarify the confusing series of events surrounding the
creation of the treaty.

AROUND TREATY HOUSE

Near Treaty House is perhaps the most visited Maori meeting house
in the country—Whare Runanga. The word 'house' is misleading;
Maori meeting houses are essentially works of art, and this is a
magnificent example, erected in 1940 and incorporating carved
panels contributed by major tribes.

In front of the Treaty House and Whare Runanga a spacious lawn
overlooks the bay to Russell. A flagstaff marks the actual spot where
the treaty was signed. From the lawn it is a short walk down to the
shore where the war canoe (*waka*) *Ngatokimatawhaorua* is housed.
This impressive craft, 35m (115ft) long, is named after the canoe in
which Kupe, the great Maori ancestor and navigator, discovered
Aotearoa (New Zealand). It was commissioned, along with the
Whare Runanga, as a centennial project to commemorate the signing
of the treaty. The *Ngatokimatawhaorua* continues to be launched
every year as part of the Waitangi Day ceremonies hosted on and
around the reserve.

The Huia Creek Walkway, which begins near Treaty House, is an
easy two-hour walk through the reserve to the Haruru Falls, taking in
a good example of mangrove habitat on the way.

Waipu Caves are famous for their glow-worms

A massive kauri log shows the value of such timber in the 19th and early 20th centuries, Parry Kauri Park

WAIPOUA KAURI FOREST

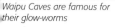 314 H2 🔒 Off SH12 towards southern end of the park,
tel 09-439 3011
www.doc.govt.nz

On the west coast within the 15,000ha (37,065-acre) Waipoua Forest is Waipoua sanctuary, of which 2,639ha (6,521 acres) contain mature kauri trees. Walking tracks at the northern end of the forest, immediately next to the highway, give access to the two largest known kauri specimens: Tane Mahuta, or Lord of the Forest, and Te Matua Ngahere, Father of the Forest. Tane Mahuta is an awesome sight, 51.5m (169ft) high, with a girth of 13.8m (45ft). It is estimated to be more than 1,500 years old.

From a parking area 2km (1 mile) south, a 20-minute walk leads to Te Matua Ngahere; a shorter path reaches the Four Sisters, a stand of trees growing together.

WAIPU

315 J3 🔒 36a The Centre,
tel 09-432 0746 🚌 Whangarei–Auckland routes (reserve in advance)
www.waipu.co.nz

A party of 120 Scottish settlers founded Waipu in 1853, and its ethnic origins are reflected in names such as Braemar Lane, Argyll Street and Caledonian Park. The war memorial in the square is made of Aberdeen granite and was shipped from Scotland in 1914 to commemorate the 60th anniversary of the town's founding. The community's heritage is explored in the Waipu House of Memories (daily 9.30–4), which has cases full of early settlers' personal effects.

Every New Year's Day since 1871 the Waipu Highland Games have been celebrated, with highland dancers, pipe bands and kilted, caber-tossing men (Waipu Caledonian Society, www.highlandgames.co.nz).

At the Waipu Caves, 13km (8 miles) west via Shoemaker Road, you can see glow-worms through a 200m (656ft) passage, part of an extensive limestone cave system. You'll need to take a torch and have sturdy footwear.

WARKWORTH

315 J3 🔒 1 Baxter Street,
tel 09-425 9081 🏢 Outside visitor office, Baxter Street
www.warkworth-information.co.nz

This former kauri-milling town is now a farming and tourism service base on the banks of the Mahurangi River. The Warkworth and District Museum (daily 9–4), in the shadow of two 600- to 800-year-old kauri trees within the Parry Kauri Park, uses reconstructed rooms to illustrate the life of early pioneers.

About 4km (2.5 miles) north of Warkworth is Sheepworld (daily 9–5, show 11–2), where you can feed the lambs and get involved in some shearing. A farther 3km (2 miles) north, at the Dome State Forest, walks range from 40 minutes to 3 hours, the best climbing to the Dome Summit, from where you can spot the Auckland Sky Tower (▷ 65) on a clear day.

WHANGAREI

314 J3 🔒 Tarewa Park, Otaika Road,
tel 09-438 1079 🚌 Rose Street and outside visitor office ✈ Onerahi, 9km (5.5 miles) southeast; shuttle bus
www.whangareinz.org.nz

Whangarei is the Northland district's biggest city. Mount Parahaki, on Memorial Drive (off Riverside Drive), once the site of one of the largest Maori *pa* (fortified site), is a good place for an overall view of the city and the bay. You can also walk up via the Mair Park, which has remains of an old gold mine and of further Maori fortifications.

Town Basin is a lively waterfront development with museums, art galleries and craft shops. Its most unusual attraction is Claphams Clock Museum (daily 9–5), a collection of timepieces gathered from around the world.

In the suburb of Maunu, 6km (4 miles) west of town, the Whangarei Museum, Clarke Homestead and Kiwi House (daily 10–4) is a colonial farming complex with a modern gallery housing Maori treasures, including a musket that belonged to the great warrior Hone Heke.

A Scot, William Carruth, was the first to buy land from the Maori in 1839 and settle at the mouth of the Hatea River. The quest for kauri gum and the building of a shipyard in the 1860s brought prosperity, and in the 1930s road and rail links with Auckland were completed.

WHATIPU

315 J4

Solitude and wilderness are the attractions of Whatipu, 45km (28 miles) southwest of downtown Auckland, at the southernmost tip of the Waitakere ranges. Its huge expanse of sand forms part of the narrow mouth of Manukau Harbour.

At the terminus of the winding, unpaved road a small cluster of buildings called Whatipu Lodge is the last sign of habitation and last chance of accommodation before the beach stretches 6km (4 miles) north to Karekare. Hidden inland among the dune grasses and cabbage trees are extensive wetlands that are home to paradise shelduck, pied stilts and black swans.

CENTRAL NORTH ISLAND

You can't escape the volcanic nature of this landscape, from the volcanoes around active Mount Ruapehu to the geothermal activity that surrounds Rotorua, the tourist capital of Maori culture. Art deco Napier, rebuilt after a devastating earthquake in 1931, is a highlight.

THE SIGHTS

MAJOR SIGHTS

Cape Kidnappers was the scene of a struggle in 1769 when local Maori tried to 'liberate' the servant of Cook's Tahitian interpreter

An Italian Renaissance setting in Hamilton Gardens

CAPE KIDNAPPERS

➕ 319 M8 ℹ️ 100 Marine Parade, Napier, tel 06-834 1911 🚌 Cape Shuttle between Napier and Clifton or Te Awanga; subject to season and tides

This remote and jagged white peninsula marks the southern boundary of Hawke's Bay. Its name recalls the 'rescue' in 1769 of a young Tahitian servant on Captain Cook's ship by local Maori, who mistakenly believed he was being held captive.

In summer up to 15,000 gannets gather here to breed, forming New Zealand's biggest mainland colony (visits Oct–late Apr). An 8km (5-mile) walk leads to the colony from Clifton Motorcamp, but since tides restrict the access times it's best to join one of the many available tours.

EAST CAPE

➕ 317 P6 ℹ️ District Council Building, Te Puia, tel 06-864 6853. See also Gisborne, below; Opotiki, page 81 🚌 Opotiki and Gisborne; services between Hick's Bay and Whakatane or Gisborne Mon–Sat ✈️ Gisborne airport 2km (1 mile) west of town

Most of the wild East Cape—the heel of New Zealand's upturned boot—is sparsely populated and mountainous, and much of the Raukumara mountain range, which dominates the interior, remains impenetrable by road. Early European settlers here were few, and the population remains predominantly Maori.

The 343km (213-mile) Pacific Coast Highway (SH35) follows the coast from Opotiki around the mouth of the Motu River and passes near Potala, the northern edge of the East Cape. It continues to Hicks Bay, which has a wild surf beach and is a popular viewing point for the planet's earliest sunrise. Look out here for the Tuwhakairiora Marae (1870),

one of the grandest meeting houses in the area. A beautiful stretch of road passes beaches and rivers on its way to East Cape lighthouse and the North Island's most easterly point.

On the more populous, east side of the cape, a turn-off before the Mata River crossing leads to 1,752m (5,748ft) Mount Hikurangi, the North Island's highest non-volcanic mountain. The mountain is sacred in Maori myth, as the first point of land to appear when Maui fished the North Island from the sea—a statue depicting Maui's canoe faces the rising sun today.

The road continues to Tolaga Bay—a coastal town with a wharf that is 660m (720 yards) long—to Gisborne. At the tiny junction settlement of Nuhaka, south of Gisborne, a scenic coastal road leaves SH2 towards the barren, windswept Mahia Peninsula, which marks the boundary between the Pacific and Hawke's Bay.

GISBORNE

➕ 317 N7 ℹ️ 209 Grey Street, tel 06-868 6139 🚌 Grey Street www.gisbornenz.com

This small city is set in an area of fertile land, with fruit growing and vineyards its main staples— it labels itself the Chardonnay capital of the country. Gisborne was the first place that Captain Cook set foot in on his return to New Zealand in 1769, before retreating from hostile Maori. Cook's Landing Site (marked by a statue of the explorer) and National Historic Reserve are next to the main port and the base of Titirangi (Kaiti Hill). To the west is Te Poho-O-Rawiri Marae (1930), one of the largest carved meeting houses in the country.

A statue on the southern bank of the Turanganui River commemorates Captain Cook's

cabin boy, Young Nick, who was first to sight land in 1769 and gave his name to the promontory Young Nicks Head, which forms the southern edge of Poverty Bay.

The Tairawhiti Museum on Stout Street (Mon–Fri 10–4, Sat, Sun 1.30–4) has regional displays. In the adjacent Te Moana Maritime Museum is the restored wheelhouse of *The Star of Canada*, which foundered at the base of Kaiti Beach in 1912.

HAMILTON

➕ 316 K5 ℹ️ Transport Centre, corner of Bryce and Anglesea streets, tel 07-839 3580 🚌 Transport Centre 🚆 Fraser Sreet, Frankton ✈️ Airport 15km (9 miles) south of city www.hamiltoncity.co.nz www.waikatonz.co.nz

New Zealand's fourth largest city grew out of an 1864 military settlement on the Waikato River. Garden Place lies on Victoria Street, at the heart of the downtown area, which was modernised in the 1990s.

The Waikato Museum (daily 10–4.30) overlooks the river on the corner of Victoria and Grantham streets and contains an impressive collection of Maori treasures, including the exquisitely decorated war canoe *Te Winika*, presented to the museum in 1973 by Te Arikinui Dame Te Atairangikaahu, the late Maori Queen.

South of the city are the 58ha (143-acre) Hamilton Gardens (daily 7.30–sunset), a conglomerate of Japanese, Chinese and English flower gardens. Hamilton Zoo (daily 9–5, extended hours Jan), 8km (5 miles) away on SH23, mixes native New Zealand species with others important to international conservation breeding projects, and has a vast walk-through, free-flight aviary.

Art deco architecture is a feature of the rebuilt town of Hastings

A relic of the Lord of the Rings film-making, strictly for fans

Sunset bathes the hills around Te Mata in scarlet

HASTINGS

🗺 319 L8 🚉 Westerman's Building, corner of Russell and Heretaunga streets, tel 06-873 0080 🚌 Weekday services from Napier
www.hastings.co.nz

Hastings is a lively agricultural town 20km (12 miles) south of Napier (▷ 82–83), lined with hanging baskets during the summer flower festival. Like Napier, Hastings was devastated by the earthquake of 1931. In rebuilding the town the architects echoed Napier's art deco and Spanish Mission styles, the best examples of which are the Westerman's Building on Russell Street and the Municipal Theatre on Hastings Street. The art deco clock tower in the middle of town was built in 1935 to house the bells from the Post Office tower, which collapsed in the quake.

HAVELOCK NORTH

🗺 319 M8

Vineyards and orchards surround this prosperous village, which sits in the shadow of the 399m (1,309ft) Te Mata Peak. There are tremendous views from the top of the peak.

Arataki Honey Ltd, on Arataki Road (daily 9–5), is one of the largest beekeeping enterprises in the southern hemisphere, with a staggering 17,000 hives and 40,000 very busy bees.

HAWERA

🗺 318 J8 🚉 55 High Street, tel 06-278 8599 🚌 Daily from Wellington and New Plymouth

Hawera is the largest of the south Taranaki townships, near the coast at the junction of SH45 and SH3. Its most obvious landmark is the water tower, built in 1914 at the request of insurance underwriters who were dismayed at the town's propensity to catch

fire, which it did in 1884, 1895 and 1912. The Historic Hawera heritage trail leaflet, available at the visitor office, details other major buildings.

Realistic life-size wax exhibits and scale models to depict Taranaki's past are made on-site and shown at the privately owned Tawhiti Museum, on Ohangai Road (Boxing Day–end Jan daily 10–4; Feb–end May, Sep–end Dec Fri–Sun 10–4; Jun–end Aug Sun 10–4). A narrow gauge railway runs on the first Sunday of each month, bringing to life the history of logging in the area.

Equally unusual is the Elvis Presley Memorial Record Room, at 51 Argyle Street (call for appointment, tel 06-278 7624), where avid collector and fan Kevin Wasley has amassed memorabilia and around 2,000 of the King's records.

KAWHIA

🗺 316 J6 🚉 Kawhia Regional Museum and Gallery, tel 07-871 0161
www.kawhia.co.nz

Outside the summer, when the population almost trebles, Kawhia (pronounced Kafia) is a sleepy village southwest of Hamilton on the shores of Kawhia Harbour. Most of its points of interest are on the shoreline, extending around to the port entrance and Ocean Beach. This is the most popular beach, best reached through the Tainui Kawhia Forest Track, southwest of central Kawhia.

At the Te Puia Hot Springs on Ocean Beach you can dig your own spa bath, but it's difficult to know exactly where unless you join a local tour.

When the Tainui people first landed here some 750 years ago they tied their canoe to a pohutukawa tree and named it Tangi-te-Korowhiti. The tree

(unmarked) is one of a small grove at the northern end of Kaora Street, and the canoe's burial site is marked with two stones, Hani and Puna, behind the Maketu *marae*, about 500m (545 yards) south of the landing site (ask for viewing permission at the *marae*).

MATAMATA

🗺 316 K6 🚉 45 Broadway, tel 07-888 7260 🚌 Broadway

Large ranches and farmsteads sprawl over this fertile agricultural landscape, which was never a visitor hotspot—until the *Lord of the Rings* movie trilogy came along. A plot of private farmland near Matamata was transformed into the village of Hobbiton (daily tours from visitor office 9.30, 10.45, 12, 1.15, 2.30, 3.45). Director Peter Jackson was obliged to clear away all traces of his sets, including this one, so other than a hobbit hole with a plywood frontage the only real attraction is the view across the Kaimai Ranges.

East of the town on Tower Road, Firth Tower is the main focus of the local history museum (Thu–Mon 10–4).

The Firth Tower, built in 1882 by Yorkshireman Josiah Firth

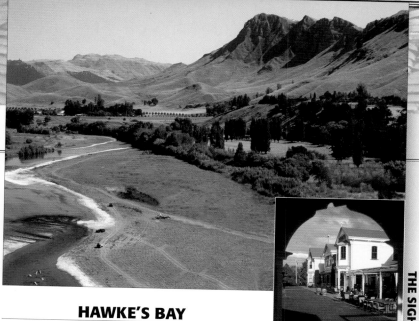

HAWKE'S BAY

Pretty coastal settlements, wine trails, art deco architecture and Pacific beaches.

Bleached cliffs embrace this scenic bay on the east coast between Havelock North and the Mahia Peninsula. Its fertile soils prompted early European settlers to plant vines, using the wine primarily for religious services; the Catholic Society founded its Mission in Taradale in 1851 and since then the wine industry has boomed, with its capital at Napier (▷ 82–83). Hawke's Bay's diverse 'sub regions'—such as Bay View and the Esk Valley—produce a wide range of wines, and there are more than 25 vineyards in all, most offering sales and tastings. Some have additional attractions—notable architecture, for instance, or fine restaurants and cafés. Chardonnay and Cabernet Sauvignon are two of the region's top wines (for wine tours contact Napier's visitor information office).

ALONG SH2

South of the wine region, SH2 winds its lonely way through the little-visited but stunning region of the Wairarapa (▷ 106), before arriving in Wellington (▷ 101–105). On SH2 there are a number of small towns including Waipawa, Waipukurau, Dannevirke and Norsewood (the last two having strong Scandinavian links). Activities available in the area include ballooning and hiking (▷ 172–179). The wild Kaweka and Ruahine Ranges are good for tramping, but you should plan carefully and go well prepared. The Department of Conservation at 59 Marine Parade, Napier (Mon–Fri 9–4.15) has all the necessary information.

A CURIOSITY

There is one other place worth visiting (if only for the novelty value) on a minor route into the back country. The point of this diversion is to see an unremarkable hill called Taumatawhakatangihangakoauauota-mateaturipukakapikimaungahoronukupokaiwhenuakitanatahu, and a sign declares this 85-letter place name the longest in the world. Roughly translated, it means 'the place where Taumata (known as Land Eater), the man with the big knees, who slid, climbed and wallowed mountains, played his flute to his loved one'. To reach the hill from Waipukurau, take the coast road towards Porangahau. After about 40km (25 miles) turn right and follow the AA Historic Place sign.

Top, a stream in the Hawke's Bay area
Above, Mission Estate Winery, one of the oldest in the region

RATINGS

Historic interest	●
Photo stops	●●●●
Walkability	●●●

BASICS

➕ 319 L8

ℹ Central Hawkes Bay Visitor Information Office, Railway Esplanade, Waipukurau, tel 06-858 6488; Mon–Fri 9–5, Sat 9–1

🚌 Services link all main towns and suburbs

www.hawkesbay.com
Well laid-out site with links to local information offices and main attractions.

TIPS

● The Hawke's Bay Wine Trail is outlined in the free leaflet of the same name, and gives details of each vineyard's facilities.
● Tours with exclusive access to the 252m (827ft) summit of Taumata's hill are available through Airlie Mount Farm Walks, tel 06-858 7601.

A walkway spans the steaming silica terraces at Orakei Korako Thermal Reserve

The nocturnal kiwi can be observed at Otorohanga

THE SIGHTS

MOUNT EGMONT NATIONAL PARK

✚ 318 H8 🅸 16km (10 miles) from North Egmont Village, end of Egmont Road, tel 06-756 0990 🚍 Shuttle services from New Plymouth www.taranakinz.org.nz

At the heart of Mount Egmont National Park is a 2,518m (8,261ft), beautifully symmetrical dormant volcano with two names: Taranaki, the original Maori name, and Egmont, the name given by Captain Cook in 1770. It was formed by numerous eruptions over 12,000 years—most recently about 350 years ago. Experts believe another may be due any time. The mountain vegetation is called 'goblin forest' due to its diminutive appearance at higher altitudes.

There are 140km (87 miles) of walks in the park, with a duration ranging from 30 minutes to four days. Many people have lost their lives here: in winter the slopes are covered in snow and ice, so climbing boots, crampons and an ice axe are essential. Even in summer crampons are advised on the summit. Visitor offices here and in New Plymouth can advise on routes, hut stays and weather.

Surfers head for the beach at Mount Maunganui

MOUNT MAUNGANUI

✚ 316 L5 🅸 Salisbury Avenue, tel 07-575 5099 🚍 Services from Tauranga

Dominated by its namesake mountain and graced by golden beaches, the town of Mount Maunganui, 6km (4 miles) north of Tauranga, is inundated with sunbathers every summer. The Hot Salt Water Pools, on Adams Avenue (Mon–Sat 6am–10pm, Sun 8am–10pm), are a popular attraction.

A network of pathways criss-crosses the mountain's wooded slopes, once an important Maori refuge and defensive site. The summit climb, best started south of the motor camp, takes about 45 minutes one-way. From the narrow neck of the Mount, Ocean Beach begins a stretch of sand that sweeps east around the Bay of Plenty. Just offshore are two small islands: Moturiki, noted for fishing, and Motuotau, important for its wildlife.

NAPIER

See pages 82–83.

NEW PLYMOUTH

✚ 318 H7 🅸 Puke Ariki Museum and Library, tel 06-759 6080 🚍 Corner of Queen and King streets ✈ 10km (6 miles) north of town www.newplymouthnz.com

Prosperous New Plymouth, the main population hub of the Taranaki region, is a good base for exploring Mount Egmont National Park. It has an excellent modern art gallery, the Govett-Brewster Gallery, at the corner of Queen and King streets (daily 10.30–5). Puke Ariki, on Ariki Street (Mon–Fri 9–4.30, Sat, Sun 1–5), has a collection of Maori items, and includes Richmond Cottage (daily 11–3.30), on Ariki Street, a colonial cottage of 1853.

Other notable sites include the oldest stone church in the country, St. Mary's, on Vivian Street, built in 1846, and the Pou Tutaki (Fitzroy Pole), on the corner of Devon Street East and Smart Road, erected by Maori in 1844 to commemorate Governor Fitzroy's clamp-down on settler acquisitions. The 45m (148ft) Wind Wand, created for the 2000 millennium celebrations on the waterfront by local artist Len Lye, sways gently in the breeze, and lights up at night.

New Plymouth is famous for its parks and gardens, the oldest and finest of which are Pukekura and Brooklands, best reached at Fillis Street, south of the heart of town. Pukekura, opened in 1876, is a well-maintained tract of lakes and gardens, and nearby Brooklands has an outdoor amphitheatre, ponds and gardens, and a historic colonial hospital museum/gallery.

Boats sail from West Quay to the volcanic Sugar Loaf Island's Marine Park, near the port and power station, home to fur seals and seabirds. The shore is part of a 7km (4-mile) Coastal Walkway, culminating in a strenuous climb up Paritutu Rock, which involves pulling yourself up by a cable.

NGARUAWAHIA

✚ 316 K5 🚍 Pharos Corner

The Maori capital of New Zealand, set at the confluence of the Waipa and the mighty Waikato, 19km (12 miles) north of Hamilton, is home to the Maori King, Tuheitia Paki, and of one of the country's most significant marae, Turangawaewae. The marae, on River Road, is open just once a year, in March

Raglan is a popular holiday resort for families

Fishing boats moored in the natural harbour at Tauranga

Gates mark the entrance to the Turangawaewae marae

during the annual regatta, when *waka* (war canoes) are raced on the river. The Mahinarangi House, built in 1929, is beautifully carved both inside and out. Next door is the King's official residence.

OPOTIKI

🚩 317 M6 🚹 Corner of St. John and Elliot Streets, tel 07-315 8484 🥖 Hot Bread Shop, 43 St. John Street **www**.opotiki.co.nz

Opotiki, 60km (37 miles) east of Whakatane on the Bay of Plenty, near the mouths of the Waioeka and Otara rivers, is a small town with fine beaches. It was once the base of the Hauhau—a revivalist sect of Maori rebels who were fierce enemies of the early Pakeha.

The Hukutaia Domain, signed about 6km (4 miles) from town, is 1ha (2.5 acres) of bush with many native trees, including a sacred 2,000-year-old puriri tree called Taketakerau, with a girth of about 22m (72ft) and standing over 23m (75ft) high. Its hollow was used by the local *iwi* to store the bones of their dead. The Church of Hinoa (St. Stephen's Anglican Church, 1864), at the north end of Church Street, was built for the Church Missionary Society and the Lutheran missionary Karl Volkner, who was suspected of being a government spy and beheaded by Hauhau emissaries in 1865.

ORAKEI KORAKO THERMAL RESERVE

🚩 316 L6 ✉ 494 Orakei Korako Road, 40km (25 miles) north of Taupo ☎ 07-378 3131 🕐 Daily from 8am; last boat leaves 4.30pm Nov–end Mar, 4pm Apr–end Oct 💵 Adult NZ$26, child (16 and under) NZ$8 🚌 Shuttle from Taupo **www**.orakeikorako.co.nz

One of the best thermal parks in the country occupies a tranquil

lakeside spot behind the Ohakuri Dam. Jet-boats carry visitors across the Waikato River to the colourful algae-covered silica terraces, boiling pools, geysers and bubbling mud. There's also the subterranean Ruatapu Cave to explore, with the warm Waiwhakaata pool (pool of mirrors) at its 40m (131ft) base, where it's said your wishes will come true if you dip your hand in the water. Look for silver ferns—the national emblem of New Zealand—in the surrounding bush and scrub.

OTOROHANGA

🚩 316 K6 🚹 57 Maniapoto Street, tel 07-873 8951 🚉 Corner of Maniapoto and Tuhoro streets 🚌 Services from Wellington, Hamilton and Auckland **www**.otorohanga.co.nz

This small town is the main point of access to the Waitomo caves (▷ 90–91) and the site of the Otorohanga Kiwi House and Native Bird Park, on Alex Telfer Drive (daily 9–5). It was established in 1971, and is one of the oldest native bird and reptile parks in the country. More than 50 species are housed here, including three of the four known species of kiwi.

RAGLAN

🚩 316 J6 🚹 4 Wallis Street, tel 07-825 0556 🚌 Services from Hamilton **www**.raglan.org.nz

Raglan, on the coast west of Hamilton, is the Waikato's main seaside resort and is internationally renowned for its surfing. The most convenient and safest beach for swimming is Te Kopua, reached from the end of Bow Street. Ocean Beach has good views across the bar (port entrance); access is off Wainui Reserve Road. Manu Beach is next, and then Whale Bay—which can only be reached over rocks.

Remote Ruapuke Beach has wild coastal scenery and is reached along the old coast road and Ruapuke Beach Road. Safe and child-friendly beaches near town include Coxs Bay (from the walkway along Government Road) and Puriri Park (Aro Aro Bay) at the end of Wallis Street.

The 756m (2,480ft) summit of Mount Karioi can be climbed from Te Toto Gorge, 12km (7 miles) southwest, in around six hours.

ROTORUA

See pages 84–87.

TAURANGA

🚩 316 L5 🚹 95 Willow Street, tel 07-578 8103 🚉 Corner of Wharf and Willow streets 🚢 Spirit Harbour Ferry, Coronation Wharf to Mount Maunganui daily 7–5.30 (winter hours vary) ✈ 4km (2.5 miles) east **www**.bayofplentynz.com

Busy Tauranga, on the Bay of Plenty, has enjoyed enormous growth in recent years, and cruise liners as well as merchant ships now negotiate the narrow entrance to its superb natural port. Its proximity to Rotorua (▷ 84–87) and Mount Maunganui (▷ 80) are a significant part of the town's appeal.

The main historical attraction is the Elms Mission House on Mission Street (Wed, Sat, Sun 2–4), site of the original mission, established here in 1834. Nearby, in Robbins Park on Cliff Road, on the eastern side of the peninsula, are the remnants of the Monmouth Redoubt (daily 9–6), built by government forces during the New Zealand Wars of the 1860s. At the base of the hill, on The Strand, is *Te Awanui Waka*, a Maori war canoe carved in 1973.

A series of superb beaches stretches from Mount Maunganui east to Papamoa.

Napier

The wine capital of the North Island.
Famous for its world-class art deco architecture.

Busy Marine Parade, and the art deco Sound Shell

Right, a gecko hesitates at the National Aquarium

An underwater tunnel gives a fish's-eye view at the Aquarium

SEEING NAPIER

Napier is a bright, dynamic coastal community with a relaxed atmosphere. At first glance it seems to enjoy a perfect relationship with nature; its fertile surroundings and the warm climate have made it the capital of the wine-producing region (▷ 79) of Hawke's Bay. Nature has not always been kind to Napier, however, and on 3 February 1931 an earthquake almost razed the town. The inhabitants set about its rebuilding with a collection of art deco buildings now considered among the finest in the world. Much of the city is negotiable on foot and, given its architectural appeal, is best appreciated from the street. Many of Napier's chief attractions line the long waterfront promenade, Marine Parade.

HIGHLIGHTS

ART DECO ARCHITECTURE

Napier's two central streets, Emerson and Tennyson, have many impressive art deco buildings. The ASB Bank, on Emerson Street, incorporates Maori designs and a fine doorway, while on Tennyson Street the highlights are (from east to west) the *Daily Telegraph* Building, the restored Municipal Theatre and the Desco Centre (art deco heritage society and shop).

Farther afield is perhaps the most attractive building of all, the 1932 Rothmans Pall Mall Building, at the corner of Bridge and Osian streets, in the port area of Ahuriri. The façade and entrance are worth the diversion—especially at night, when they are imaginatively lit. During the day it is possible to have a look at the interior, which shows exquisite attention to detail. A more modern example of art deco is the pharmacy at the southern end of Emerson Street.

MARINE PARADE

Marine Parade creates an impressive perspective, its long promenade lined with Norfolk pines and old wooden houses (the few that survived the earthquake). At its northern end are elegant gardens, including the Centennial Gardens, at the base of Bluff Hill. Farther south the renovated Ocean Spa (Mon–Sat 6am–10pm, Sun 8am–10pm) has hot pools, private spas, health and beauty therapies

RATINGS				
Historic interest	●	●	●	
Photo stops	●	●	●	●
Walkability	●	●	●	

BASICS

✚ 319 M8

ℹ 100 Marine Parade, tel 06-834 1911; Mon, Tue, Thu, Fri 8.30–5, Wed, Sat, Sun 9–5

🚌 Travel Centre, Munroe Street

🚌 Munroe Street

✈ Airport north of town; shuttles

www.isitehawkesbaynz.com
Busy site, with visitor information.

The Tom Parker Fountain

and a café. More gardens are laid out immediately to the south of the spa complex, dominated by a floral clock, the Tom Parker Fountain (which becomes an aquatic light show after dark) and a statue called *Pania of the Reef*, depicting a Maori maiden.

Heading south you reach the art deco Colonnade and Sound Shell. Once a dancing and skating hall, the Colonnade now houses a bell and memorial dedicated to the crew of HMS *Veronica*, which was in port at the time of the earthquake. Members of the crew were among the first to come to the city's aid and pull victims from the rubble. Every New Year the bell is rung to commemorate their brave efforts. Opposite the Sound Shell, which is occasionally used for open-air concerts, are the Art Deco Tower

TIPS

● The view from Bluff Hill, at the northern tip of town, is worth the climb.
● A good view down Marine Parade and across the city can also be enjoyed from Lighthouse Road, above the Centennial Gardens (reached via Lucy Road, off Coote Road).

(A&B building), which is also lit at night, and the Masonic Hotel.

Past the modern visitor office and Mini Golf Park are the Sunken Gardens, complete with water-lily ponds and a lazy waterwheel. Beyond them, seal and dolphin displays are combined with a project aimed at wild penguin and gannet rehabilitation at Marineland (daily 10–4.30). In daily sessions you can feed and swim with the dolphins. Continuing south you encounter the intriguing Millennium Sculpture, a work using reflective steel discs, by local artist David Trubridge.

HAWKE'S BAY MUSEUM

✉ 9 Herschell Street ☎ 06-835 7781 🕐 Oct–end Apr daily 10–6; May–end Sep daily 9–5 💲 Adult NZ$7.50, child (under 16) free
www.hawkesbaymuseum.co.nz
A wide range of exhibits set in modern surroundings relates to the history and art of the Hawke's Bay region. Nga Tukemata (The Awakening) presents the art and *taonga* (treasures) of the local Maori and rare evidence that dinosaurs once existed in New Zealand—remains unearthed in the Maungahouanga Valley of northern Hawke's Bay. Special attention is given to the earthquake of 1931, when 100 fires raged over 30 hours after the initial shock, and 258 people lost their lives.

BACKGROUND

When Captain Cook first mapped Hawke's Bay in 1769, Maori were already well established here. In the 1830s seasonal whalers arrived from Australia, and the first significant group of European settlers arrived 20 years later. In 1854 the town was named after British general Charles Napier.

During the New Zealand Wars of the 1860s the residents, with the help of local Maori, defended themselves against aggressive northern tribes. With the development of agriculture, the settlement flourished. The earthquake of 1931 destroyed everything, but the land surrounding Bluff Hill had risen several feet and huge tracts of land, previously underwater or covered in swamp, were now available for use. Earthquake-resistant concrete buildings with art deco designs reflecting the optimism of the jazz era gave the town a new face within a decade, thanks largely to architect Louis Hay (1881–1948).

Left, stylish architectural detailing on a bank
Above, the modern entrance to the National Aquarium
Below, ornamental fountain at the Mission

MORE TO SEE

NATIONAL AQUARIUM OF NEW ZEALAND

✉ Marine Parade ☎ 06-834 1404
🕐 Daily 9–5 (Wed until 4.30) 💲 Adult NZ$14, child (up to 14) NZ$7.50
www.nationalaquarium.co.nz
The newest of Napier's waterfront attractions hosts an eclectic mix of native and non-native water and land creatures, including seahorses and kiwis. Divers enter the tanks to feed the fish at 10am and 2pm; they also act as guides, conducting tours behind the scenes (extra charge applies).

Rotorua
●

Boiling lakes, spouting geysers and steaming streets in the volcanic heart of the North Island. A lively place for Maori culture. Hair-raising outdoor pursuits for the adventurous.

Demonstrating the traditions of Maori cooking

A natural steam-cloud engulfs the Rotorua Museum

The crater rim of Tarawera shows geological upheaval

RATINGS	
Outdoor pursuits	● ● ● ○
Photo stops	● ● ● ● ●
Walkability	● ● ○

BASICS
✚ 316 L6
🛈 1167 Fenton Street, tel 07-348 5179; daily 8–6
🚻 i-SITE, Fenton Street
✖ Eastern shores of Lake Rotorua, about 10km (6 miles) from town; shuttle service

www.rotoruanz.com
Impressive site with interactive maps and community and visitor information.

TIP
● The visitor office has an in-house travel section administering local and national bus, air and rail ticketing.

SEEING ROTORUA

Rotorua—alias Sulphur City—is the thermal and volcanic resort capital of New Zealand, and is often smelt before it's seen. In addition to exploring the geysers, pools and vents of bubbling mud in its immediate vicinity, you can enjoy a Maori *hangi* (feast), throw yourself down a waterfall in a raft, jump out of a plane or shop until you drop—preferably into one of the city's many restorative hot thermal pools. Rotorua sprawls on the southern shores of the lake of the same name, its half-timbered, mock-Tudor buildings recalling its development as a European-style health spa at the start of the 20th century.

HIGHLIGHTS

HELL'S GATE AND WAI ORA SPA

✚ 316 L6 ✉ 15km (9 miles) from Rotorua on SH30 ☎ 07-345 3151 🕐 Daily 8.30–8.30 💷 Adult NZ$20, child (under 16) NZ$8. Spa only NZ$12, child NZ$8 www.hellsgate.co.nz

The aptly named Hell's Gate thermal reserve is one of the most active, with two levels separated by a tract of bush and connected by a warm thermal stream, complete with steaming waterfall. The pools of bubbly mud and water on the lower levels hiss menacingly. The upper level has steaming lakes and tiny steaming vents, scattered with mini mud volcanoes and cauldrons of boiling water. Best of all is the Devil's Cauldron, a pit where a lively, globular mud pool makes wonderfully disgusting noises. Services include massage, sulphur spas, therapeutic mud facials, scrubs and private mud baths.

LAKE ROTORUA

✚ 316 L6

This flooded volcanic crater is the largest of the 17 lakes in the Rotorua thermal region, covering an area of 89sq km (34 square miles) and sitting 279m (915ft) above sea level. Boat trips from the city take in the nature reserve of Mokoia Island. Recreational activities include boating, water-skiing and trout-fishing. On the northern shores are the Hamurana Gardens, at 733 Hamurana Road, where a spring erupts with beautiful clarity and a volume of more than 3,780,000 litres (831,600 gallons) an hour.

OHINEMUTU

Narrow streets lined with steaming drains lead to the former Maori settlement and thermal area of Ohinemutu, on the city's lakefront. The focal point is the Tamatekapua Marae, a beautifully carved meeting house, renovated in 1939 but containing 19th-century carvings. Facing it is St. Faith's Church (daily 8–5), built in 1910. The interior pillars, beams, rafters and pews are carved with Maori designs, and on a window overlooking the lake a Maori Christ is sandblasted, as if walking on the lake, dressed in a *korowai* (chief's cloak). Members of the Arawa tribe are buried in the graveyard, among them the only European to be admitted to full chieftainship: Captain Gilbert Mair (1843–1923), who twice saved the Arawa from inter-tribal attacks.

Above, the fizzing Champagne Pool at Wai-O-Tapu

Inset, fierce carved figures with paua shell eyes guard the Tamatekapua Marae

AGRODOME

✚ 316 L6 ✉ 10km (6 miles) north of Rotorua on SH5 ☎ 07-357 1050
🕐 Daily 8.30–5; shows 9.30, 11, 2.30
🎟 Show NZ$22, child (5–15) NZ$11
www.agrodome.co.nz

The Agrodome Complex has a wide array of attractions, from bungy jumping to farm activities. The principal attraction is the Sheep Show, at which you are introduced to 19 different breeds of sheep.

*Above, the Artist's Palette
Right, meeting the sheep at
the Agrodome*

BLUE AND GREEN LAKES

✚ 316 L6 ✉ Southeast of city, off SH30

Mount Tarawera Road leads to Blue Lake (Tikitapu), used for boating and swimming, and Green Lake (Rotokakahi), which is sacred and off limits. Beyond them the road enters the Te Wairoa Valley, home of the Buried Village, where the Pink-and-White Terraces, the village and its hotel were laid waste by the 1886 eruption.

BLUE BATHS

✉ Government Gardens ☎ 07-350 2119 🕐 Mon–Fri 10–5 🎟 Adult NZ$9, child (5–14) NZ$6
www.bluebaths.co.nz

Built in the Spanish Mission style during the Great Depression of 1933, the pools flourished as a major social and recreational venue, and were one of the first public baths to have mixed bathing. Restored and reopened in 1999, today they offer hot pools and a museum.

MOUNT TARAWERA

✚ 316 L6

Tarawera is 1,111m (3,645ft) high, with a 6km (4-mile) converging gash of craters. It is a conglomerate of three mountains: Wahanga to the north,

POLYNESIAN SPA

✉ Hinemoa Street ☎ 07-348 1328 🕐 Daily 8am–11pm 🎟 Adult NZ$12, child NZ$8
www.polynesianspa.co.nz

Rain or shine, this luxury spa complex is a delight. Among the treats are hot springs and pools, private spa pools, a family spa—and massage treatments are also available. Outside, in timber-style tubs, therapeutic adult hot springs overlook the lake and range in temperature from 33°C (91.4°F) to 43°C (109.4°F). The best times to go are at lunch and dinner, when the tour buses are elsewhere.

ROTORUA MUSEUM OF ART AND HISTORY

✉ Government Gardens ☎ 07-349 4350 🕐 Oct–end Mar daily 9–8; Apr–end Sep daily 9–5. Guided tours daily 11, 2 🎟 Adult NZ$11, child NZ$5
www.rotoruamuseum.co.nz

People used to come from all over the world to the 1908 red-and-white half-timbered Bath House, which now houses this museum, to take advantage of the thermal water's therapeutic and curative powers. In one wing you can see some of the original baths, changing rooms and equipment used by the early visitors. A superb collection of Te Arawa *taonga* (treasures) contrasts with modern Maori artworks. An excellent audiovisual display, Rotorua Stories, introduces the area's history and legends—complete with shuddering pews during the dramatic account of the 1886 eruption.

WAI-O-TAPU

✚ 316 L6 ✉ 29km (18 miles) south of Rotorua off SH5 ☎ 07-366 6333
🕐 Daily 8.30–5 🎟 Adult NZ$25, child (5–15) NZ$8.50 📷
www.geyserland.co.nz

Wai-O-Tapu is the best thermal park in the region, with an almost surreal range of volcanic features, from mud pools and silica terraces to the beautiful Champagne Pool. If you can, time your arrival with the daily 10.15am eruption of the Lady Knox Geyser, which is signposted on the Wai-O-Tapu Loop Road (off SH5). A self-guided walk around the park takes about two hours, passing the Artist's Palette—a steaming silica field in pastel yellow, green and blue, and the Champagne Pool—an orange-rimmed pool which heats the water to a surface temperature of around 74°C (165°F).

Ruawahia in the middle and Tarawera to the south. Helicopter flights and 4X4 tours give access to the interior. Independent access is discouraged.

SKYLINE SKYRIDES
✉ Fairy Springs Road ☎ 07-347 0027
🕐 Daily 9–late 🎫 Gondola only, adult NZ$22, child (14 and under) NZ$10, gondola and 5 luge rides, NZ$26
www.skylineskyrides.co.nz
Visitors travel up the mountain in gondolas and return on the

infamous luge, which involves riding down a concrete course on a plastic tray with wheels and primitive brakes. A family course provides a gentler version.

TARAWERA FALLS
✚ 316 L6 ✉ 70km (43 miles) from Rotorua on SH30
In the heart of the Tarawera Forest, the Tarawera River flows from the eastern shores of Lake Tarawera and northern slopes of Mount Tarawera. A walkway leads to the point where the river disappears underground before emerging from a sheer cliff face.

*Above, the sacred Green Lake
Below, Tarawera Falls*

WAIMANGU
✚ 316 L6 ✉ 26km (16 miles) south of Rotorua, off SH5 ☎ 07-366 6137
🕐 Daily 8.30–5 🎫 Adult from NZ$28, child (6–16) NZ$7.50
www.waimangu.com

The volcanic features of the Waimangu volcanic valley were created as a result of the 1886 eruption of Tarawera (▷ 31). Lake Rotomahana is a water-filled crater which, before the eruption, was the site of the famous Pink-and-White Terraces. Both silica terraces were obliterated by the eruption, replaced by the Waimangu Cauldron—the world's largest boiling lake; the Inferno Crater Lake, which rises and falls up to 10m (33ft); steaming cliffs; and boiling springs and steaming fumaroles.

TE PUIA, WHAKAREWAREWA
✉ 3km (2 miles) south of downtown along Fenton Street ☎ Maori Arts and Crafts Institute 07-348 9047 🕐 Oct–end Feb daily 8–6; Mar–end Sep daily 8–5; Maori guided tours hourly 9–5; cultural performances 12.15, 3.15 🎫 Tours NZ$28, child (5–15) NZ$14; evening performance NZ$85, child NZ$50
www.nzmaori.co.nz

This is the most famous of the region's thermal reserves, and includes within its grounds the Rotowhio Marae, the Mai Ora Village (a replica of the former Te Arawa Maori settlement) and the modern Te Puia arts and crafts institute. There are two geysers here: Pohutu, or Big Splash, which goes off 10 to 25 times a day (more recently for days on end), achieving a height of over 30m (98ft), and Prince of Wales Feathers, which is less spectacular. Tracks negotiate other small mud pools and volcanic features and lead back to the Rotowhio Marae, which has a banquet and weaving house, and hosts daily cultural performances. A longer performance in the evening includes a *hangi* (feast).

BACKGROUND
The shores of Lake Rotorua and Whakarewarewa were first settled by Maori from the Arawa canoe in the 14th century. By the 1840s the first missions had been established. When inter-tribal war broke out the Te Arawa sided with the government. After the end of the New Zealand Wars, European settlement began. The population rapidly expanded, drawn by the aesthetic and therapeutic qualities of the thermal waters, and tourism flourished.

Tongariro National Park

**Dramatic and sometimes dangerous volcanic peaks
in New Zealand's oldest national park.
Excellent skiing and walking, as well as stunning scenery.**

*The snow-clad peaks of
Mount Ruapehu*

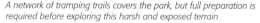

*A network of tramping trails covers the park, but full preparation is
required before exploring this harsh and exposed terrain*

RATINGS				
Outdoor pursuits	●	●	●	●
Photo stops	●	●	●	
Walkability	●	●	●	●	●

BASICS

➕ 316 K8

ℹ Department of Conservation office,
Whakapapa Village, SH48, tel 07-892
3729; daily 8–5; www.doc.govt.nz

🚌 All surrounding townships. Local
shuttles to Whakapapa Village and walk
drop-off/pick-up points

🚆 Services from Auckland and
Wellington to Ohakune and National
Park

✖ At intersection of SH47 and SH48

www.mtruapehu.com
Information on the whole
region, including ski areas,
transportation and
weather reports.

SEEING TONGARIRO NATIONAL PARK

In 1887 Horonuku Te Heuheu Tukino, the visionary chief of Ngati
Tuwharetoa, gave the sacred volcanoes of Ruapehu, Ngauruhoe
and Tongariro to the nation to preserve them, creating the heart
of Tongariro National Park—the fourth oldest in the world. Since
then the park has expanded to cover an area of 75,250ha
(185,940 acres), taking in forest, tussock country and volcanic
desert. Dominating everything are the majestic volcanic peaks of
Tongariro, Ngauruhoe and Ruapehu—all active volcanoes, and
quite different in size and appearance. Whakapapa and Turoa
offer some of the best skiing in the country (Jul–Oct).

HIGHLIGHTS

MOUNT NGAURUHOE

➕ 316 K7

The youngest of the three volcanoes lies 3km (2 miles) south of
Tongariro and reaches 2,287m (7,503ft). Its classic symmetrical cone
shape is due to its relative youth and the fact that it has only one
vent. In recent years, Ngauruhoe has been the most continuously
active, frequently venting steam and gas, and occasionally ash and
lava. Its last significant eruption occurred in 1954.

NORTHERN CIRCUIT

ℹ SH48, Whakapapa, tel 06-892 3729; Visitor Centre, SH48, Whakapapa,
tel 06-892 3729

The Tongariro Northern Circuit walking trail winds its way over Mount
Tongariro and around Mount Ngauruhoe, passing unusual landforms
and volcanic features, including lakes, craters and glacial valleys.
The walk takes three to four days to complete. The track starts
from Whakapapa Village and finishes at the Mangatepopo Road, just
off SH47.

MOUNT RUAPEHU

➕ 316 K8 ℹ 54 Clyde Street, Ohakune, tel 06-385 8427
www.mtruapehu.com

About 16km (10 miles) south of Ngauruhoe is the truncated cone of
Ruapehu, with its perpetually snow-covered summit peaks and azure

crater lakes. This is the North Island's highest mountain, at 2,797m (9,176ft), and in the last century it has seen the most violent activity of the three volcanoes, last errupting in 1995/6. Thousands of visitors come to ski or climb on its slopes, or enjoy its walking tracks—the longest of these, the Round-the-Mountain Track, takes five to six days. Ruapehu has three ski fields: Whakapapa, serviced by Whakapapa and Iwikau villages; Turoa, serviced by Okahune; and Tukino, the smallest of the three, on the eastern slopes.

TONGARIRO CROSSING

🏠 SH48, Whakapapa Village, tel 07-8923729
www.tongarirocrossing.co.nz
When the weather is clear, the views and volcanic features on this one-day hike are unforgettable. The 16km (10-mile) trail involves

steep climbs and the occasional scramble, and can take up to 10 hours. In winter it can be impassable and even in summer it may be dangerous. The walk can be tackled from either north or south.

BACKGROUND

According to local Maori legend, the volcanoes were formed around the 14th century when Ngatoroirangi, navigator and priest of the Arawa canoe, came to New Zealand.

On Christmas Eve of 1953 the wall of Mount Ruapehu's crater collapsed and a mighty lahar (a wash of volcanic rock debris and water) rushed down the Whangaehu River, destroying the rail bridge at Tangiwai. The night train to Auckland arrived moments later, and 151 lives were lost in the disaster. The mountain erupted in September 1995, and again a year later.

Left, Ngauruho, from Chateau Tongariro hotel
Above, snowboarding at Whakapapa ski field;
Above right, the Emerald Lakes

■ MORE TO SEE
OHAKUNE

🏠 318 K8 🏠 Clyde Street, tel 06-385 8427 ☐ Holiday Shoppe
www.ohakune.info
The pretty little ski resort of Ohakune sits near the southern edge of the park. Turoa ski field is 17km (10.5 miles) up the Ohakune Mountain Road. The Department of Conservation field centre, at the base of the road (Mon–Fri 9–12.30, 1–3), shows a video of the 1995/6 Ruapehu eruption.

WHAKAPAPA VILLAGE

🏠 316 K8 🏠 SH48, tel 07-892 3729 ☐ Shuttles to village and ski field
www.mtruapehu.com
Whakapapa is the headquarters and information base for the national park, and gives access to the Whakapapa Skifield and several good shorter walks. Its main landmark is the magnificent Chateau Tongariro Hotel, built in 1929. The Department of Conservation field centre (daily 8–5) has excellent displays and a seismograph monitoring the moods of Ruapehu.

(Map: Tongariro National Park, showing Oio, Hukapapa, Taurewa, Raurimu, National Park, Waikune, Erua, Pokaka, Horopito, Ohakune, Rangataua, Tongariro, Papakai, Lake Rotoaira, Rangipo, 1967 Mount Tongariro, 2294 Mount Ngauruhoe, Whakapapa Village, Iwikau Village, Tukino, Tongariro, 2797 Mount Ruapehu, Rangipo Desert, Lake Moawhango, 0 5 km, 0 3 miles)

Waitomo

Bizarre limestone formations in a landscape of caves, gorges, holes and arches. An astonishing network of more than 360 recorded caves, the longest over 14km (9 miles).

Black-water rafting tours of the caves are for the adventurous

A galaxy of glow-worms on the roof of the Waitomo cave

The natural stone arch—once a cave—at Mangapohue

SEEING WAITOMO

Visitors come in droves to the district of Waitomo and its underground world of limestone caves. Above ground, the typical farmland and the resort village itself give no clue to what lies below. Many of the region's features can be enjoyed along the three-hour Waitomo Walkway, which begins opposite the Glow-worm Caves and follows the Waitomo Stream to the Ruakuri Scenic Reserve. A short circular track in the reserve takes in caves and natural limestone bridges, hidden among lush native bush.

HIGHLIGHTS

ARANUI CAVE
✉ 3km (2 miles) west of Glow-worm Caves, in Ruakuri Scenic Reserve 🕐 Hourly tours 10–3 💳 Adult NZ$30, child (5–14) NZ$14; under 5s free. Combined Glow-worm and Aranui ticket NZ$50, child NZ$23
Just 2km (1 mile) away, Aranui is a less frenetic, more sedate experience than the Glow-worm Caves at Waitomo. It was discovered by chance by Maori hunter Ruruku Aranui, in 1910, while he was hunting pigs. Effective lighting brings out the hues and variety of the formations.

GLOW-WORM CAVES
✉ Waitomo Caves Road, off SH3 ☎ 07-878 8227 🕐 Tours half-hourly 9–5 💳 Adult NZ$30, child (5–14) NZ$14; under 5s free. Combined Glow-worm and Aranui ticket NZ$50, child NZ$23; Glow-worm and museum ticket NZ$33, child NZ$14 🚌 Shuttle from Waitomo and Otorohanga
www.waitomocaves.co.nz
This cave network is Waitomo's biggest attraction, and the most commercial, drawing almost 250,000 visitors annually. The network was first extensively explored in 1887 by a local Maori, Tane Tinorau, and an English surveyor, Fred Mace, and the caves were opened to visitors in 1889. Despite the crowds, the highlight of the 45-minute tour—the silent trip to the glow-worm colony by boat—is still magical. The glow-worm *Arachnocampa luminosa* emits light to attract its prey and is unique to New Zealand. It is the larval stage of a two-winged insect.

MANGAPOHUE NATURAL BRIDGE SCENIC RESERVE

✉ Marokopa Road 🎫 Free

A short streamside walk on the route between Waitomo and Te Anga leads to an impressive natural limestone arch with unusual stalagmites. This was once part of a large cave, and it is hard to imagine that the now rather inconspicuous little stream created it all. About 5km (3 miles) farther on are the Piripiri Caves, reached by a short but stiff climb up a boardwalk. These caves are in stark contrast to the well-lit, visitor-friendly offerings in Waitomo: They are dark and forbidding, and the path into them is steep and quite dangerous. If you are alone do not venture far, and take a torch (flashlight).

MUSEUM OF CAVES

ℹ️ In the visitor office, Main Street, Waitomo, tel 07-878 7640 🕐 Dec–end Mar daily 8–8; Apr–end Nov daily 8–5 🎫 Adult NZ$5, child (pre-school) free www.waitomo-museum.co.nz

A thorough introduction to the area is presented at this museum, considered the best of its kind in the world. Displays cover cave formation, the history surrounding the local caves and the natural history, including the spectacular glow-worms. There's a small collection of everyday implements and treasures once belonging to the Tainui Maori, who lived in this valley for 500 years. These include *toki* (adzes), *waka kereru* (bird traps) and an exquisite oyster-shell necklace discovered in a local cave. There are also fascinating exhibits relating to early tourism in the area.

BACKGROUND

The limestone around Waitomo was once a seabed, formed about 30 million years ago. Over the ages its layers have been raised by the action of the earth's plates, bending and buckling and creating a maze of cracks and joints. As rainwater drains into these cracks it mixes with small amounts of carbon dioxide in the air and soil, forming a weak acid. This slowly dissolves the limestone, widening its faults. Over time small streams flow through converging cracks and create underground caves. The caves themselves have a finite lifespan—as is evident at the Lost World, near Waitomo, where part of a cave system has collapsed in on itself.

THE SHEARING SHED

✉ Waitomo Caves Road, Waitomo ☎ 07-878 8371 🕐 Shows daily at 12.45 📅 🎫 Free

Large, fluffy Angora rabbits are cuddled to within an inch of their lives at this unusual venue, and then shorn for their highly prized, fine hair. Angora products—yarn, duvets, underlay and sweaters—are on sale, and there are guided tours to tell you about it all.

WOODLYN PARK

✉ 1177 Waitomo Valley Road, Otorohanga ☎ 07-878 6666 🕐 Shows daily, 1.30; reserve tickets 🎫 Adult NZ$18, child (school age) NZ$9, under 5s NZ$5, family NZ$52 www.woodlynpark.co.nz

This is the main above-ground attraction in Waitomo, if not the whole region—a show hosted by ex-shearer Barry Woods, giving an informative, interactive and very funny interpretation of old and modern-day Kiwi country life. The production is an eccentric affair involving a clever pig, a not-so-clever pig, an axe, an ingenious home-made computer, dogs, sheep, a 'Kiwi bear' and underwear.

THE SIGHTS

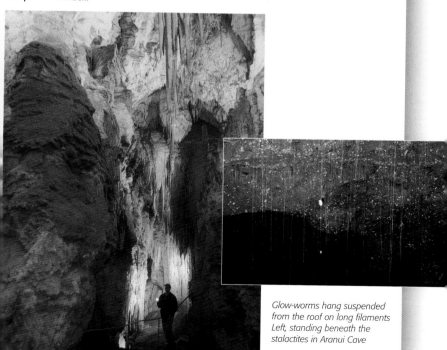

Glow-worms hang suspended from the roof on long filaments Left, standing beneath the stalactites in Aranui Cave

Sailing on Lake Taupo, a stretch of water famed for its fishing

A fern uncurls in the sunshine, Te Urewera National Park

The Wairaka Statue guards the entrance to Whakatane harbour

THE SIGHTS

TAUPO

➕ 316 L7 ℹ️ Tongariro Street (SH1), tel 07-376 0040 🚌 Gascoigne Street ✈️ 10km (6 miles) south of town www.laketauponz.co.nz

Massive volcanic eruptions formed the Taupo region's landscape over 250,000 years. The latest occurred in AD186, spewing out ash and debris at up to 900kph (560mph). Its effects were visible from China and Rome, and it was one factor in the creation of the vast and now placid 619sq km (239 square-mile) expanse of Lake Taupo.

The busy resort town of Taupo sits on the northern lakeshore and offers a multitude of activities—principally trout-fishing in the lake, but also bungy jumping, tandem skydiving, mountain biking, golf, sailing and walking. Longer lake cruises take in a remarkable set of Maori carvings, showing a huge tattooed face and covering an entire rockface. These relatively recent creations, can only be seen from the water, at Mine Bay.

The Taupo Museum and Art Gallery at Story Place (daily 10.30—4.30) focuses on the early days of the region. West of the museum, the Waikato River begins its 425km (264-mile) journey to the Tasman Sea, winding north behind the town towards Wairakei Park. Mid-river just before the park is Cherry Island (daily 9—5), a small wildlife attraction.

TE PUKE

➕ 316 L6 ℹ️ 130 Jellicoe Street, tel 07-573 9172 www.tepuke.co.nz

Te Puke, 31km (19 miles) southeast of Tauranga, claims to have launched New Zealand's kiwifruit industry. Take a Kiwikart tour at Kiwi360 (daily 9—5), 5km (3 miles) east of the town on SH2.

Next door, at the Vintage Auto Barn (daily 9—5), there are more than 90 classic and vintage vehicles.

TE UREWERA NATIONAL PARK

➕ 317 M7 ℹ️ SH38, Aniwaniwa, Lake Waikaremoana, tel 06-837 3900

Te Urewera is a daunting and mysterious place of almost threatening beauty. The national park, northwest of Wairoa, encompasses the largest block of native bush in the North, home to rare kiwis, kakas and kokakos. The focus is Lake Waikaremoana—the Sea of Rippling Waters, created 2,000 years ago, when the Waikaretaheke River was dammed by a huge landslide.

TONGARIRO NATIONAL PARK

See pages 88—89.

TURANGI

➕ 316 K7 ℹ️ Ngawaka Place, off SH1, tel 07-386 8999 www.taupodc.govt.nz

This small village on the scenic Tongariro River is famous for trout-fishing, and makes a good base for exploring the Tongariro National Park to the south (▷ 88—89). At the Tongariro National Trout Centre, 3km (2 miles) south of the village on SH1 (daily 9—5), you can see a trout hatchery in operation, with adult fish in a large pool and an underwater viewing area.

WAIRAKEI PARK

➕ 316 L7

In the heart of the Wairakei Park, north of Taupo, is one of the country's most spectacular waterfalls. Huka Falls, reached via Huka Falls Road, start as the sedately flowing Waikato River before being forced through a

cleft of solid rock 15m (49ft) wide and 100m (328ft) long. From here they emerge to fall 7m (23ft) into a foaming cauldron. Depending on the flow (regulated at Lake Taupo for electricity generation), the falls vary from 9m to 10m (29ft to 33ft) in height.

Wairakei Terraces, north of Taupo (daily 9—5), are the region's latest thermal attraction. About 1km (0.5 miles) farther on is the Wairakei Thermal Valley.

WAITOMO

See pages 90—91.

WHAKATANE

➕ 317 M6 ℹ️ Corner of Quay and Kakahoroa Drive, tel 07-308 6058 🚌 Intercity services and East Cape shuttle ✈️ Northwest of town www.whakatane.com

The principal town in the eastern Bay of Plenty sits at the mouth of the Whakatane River and has a rich Maori history dating back to 1150, when the Polynesian explorer Toi te Hauatahi landed here. This historic town is a departure point to the active volcano of Whakkaari/White Island, which on a clear day can be seen steaming 50km (31 miles) offshore. Other major activities include swimming with dolphins and fishing. The island closest to shore is Moutohora (or Whale) Island, a wildlife refuge.

Pohaturoa is a large rock outcrop at the corner of The Strand and Commerce Street, used for 600 years as a Maori meeting place. The summit was a sacred place for the bones of early chiefs, and newborns were dedicated to the gods in a stream at its foot. More local history is related in the Whakatane Museum and Gallery on Boon Street (Tue–Fri 10–4.30, Sat, Sun 11–3).

SOUTHERN NORTH ISLAND

The citizens of Wellington take their breaks
on the white-sand beaches of the Kapiti Coast, or
perhaps amid the vineyards of the remote Wairarapa
region. The capital itself boasts the outstanding
Te Papa national museum and dozens
of excellent cafés.

MAJOR SIGHTS

Martinborough's Wine Centre lies at the heart of the town, within walking distance of around 20 small vineyards

A polished act at the Steam Inc Engine Shed, Paekakariki

CAPE PALLISER

⊞ 318 K11

The road to the North Island's most southerly point passes the eroded rocky spires and turrets of the Putangirua Pinnacles, and the fishing village of Ngawihi, where tractors and bulldozers wait on the beach to launch the boats. The road ends at the Cape Palliser lighthouse, where a climb up the 250 steps is rewarded with outstanding views towards the South Island. A colony of New Zealand fur seals live on the bluff year-round—keep your distance, especially during the breeding season (Nov–Jan).

Be aware, the drive to Cape Palliser and back takes a day.

CASTLEPOINT

⊞ 319 L10 ⓘ 316 Queen Street, Masterton, tel 06-370 0900
www.wairarapanz.com

Castlepoint is the highlight of the Wairarapa's wild coastline. At the eastern end of the main beach the weather-beaten Castlepoint Lighthouse perches on a stark, rocky headland, that sweeps south to enclose a large lagoon. Just below it is a cave that can be explored at low tide, but take care: a small memorial stone commemorates those who have drowned while exploring the offshore reef.

KAPITI ISLAND

⊞ 318 J10 ⓘ DoC, Government Buildings, Lambton Quay, Wellington, tel 04-472 7356 ⓦ Access by arrangement with DoC, tel 04-472 5821 ⓦ Landing permits from DoC NZ$9, child (17 and under) NZ$4.50 ⛴ Boats depart from Paraparaumu Beach, 9–9.30, return 3–4 ⓡ From Wellington to Paraparaumu

Kapiti Island lies 5km (3 miles) offshore from Paraparaumu, and with its adjunct marine reserve is

administered by the Department of Conservation. The 10km- (6-mile) long, 2km- (1-mile) wide island has been cleared of possums, rats and other predators, and after numerous plant and animal reintroductions is now a haven to native New Zealand species. You can follow tracks through native bush, while inquisitive robins, saddlebacks and stitchbirds flit about your head, and weka and takahe poke about for insects disturbed by your feet. Other occupants include kiwi, little blue penguins and the endangered kokako, which has one of the loveliest bird songs ever to grace the air.

The island has a rich history as the 19th-century stronghold of the Maori warrior Te Ruaparaha, and in the 20th century as a whaling hub. The resorts that line the stretch of mainland between Otaki and Paekakariki, known as the Kapiti Coast, are popular weekend destinations for the people of Wellington.

MARTINBOROUGH

⊞ 318 K10 ⓘ 316 Queen Street, Masterton, tel 06-370 0909 ⛴ Services from Featherston

This attractive, busy little town at the hub of the Wairarapa region (▷ 106) was founded in the 1880s by British settler John Martin, who laid out the village square and its radiating streets in the form of the Union Jack flag. Today there are no fewer than 20 vineyards within walking distance of the square, most of which offer tastings, and a wine centre in the heart of the village (daily 10–5) can advise on tours and hours. The Colonial Museum on the square (Sat, Sun, 2–4) occupies the former library, built in 1894.

A limestone gorge, the Patuna Chasm, with stalactites, fossils and waterfalls, can be visited on

Patuna Farm, Ruakokopatuna Road (Oct–Easter, guided tours only). The nearby Ruakokopatuna glow-worm caves can be accessed with permission from Blue Creek Farm (tel 06-306 9797); take a torch and sturdy footwear.

OTAKI

⊞ 318 K10 ⓘ Centennial Park, SH1, tel 04-364 7620 ⓡ Services from Wellington
www.naturecoast.co.nz

Otaki is a small town steeped in Maori history. It has several marae, including the finely carved 1910 Te Pou O Tainui Marae on Te Rauparaha Street, as well as the Maori Rangiatea Church, rebuilt after it was destroyed by arsonists in 1995. Otaki is the main eastern base for exploring the Tararua Forest Park: Otaki Gorge Road, 2km (1 mile) south of town, leads to Otaki Forks, where several tracks wind into the mountains.

PAEKAKARIKI

⊞ 318 J10 ⓡ Services from Wellington

Train enthusiasts flock to this tiny seaside village on the Kapiti Coast to appreciate the restored vintage trains—some still running at the Steam Inc Engine Shed (Sat 11–3), by the rail station. More vintage transport is shown at the Wellington Tramway Museum (Sat, Sun, 11–5), 5km (3 miles) north of here in Queen Elizabeth Park, where four trams are currently in operation.

PARAPARAUMU

⊞ 318 J10 ⓘ Coastlands shopping centre, off SH1, tel 04-298 8195 ⓡ Services from Wellington
www.naturecoast.co.nz

Paraparaumu is the principal township on the Kapiti Coast and has two main beaches: Raumati

Kaka (bush parrots) are popular feature Pukaha Mount Bruce

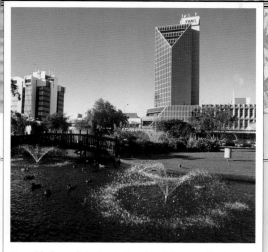

Tower blocks mark the heart of modern Palmerston North

PALMERSTON NORTH

A university town, gateway to the south and west, and a place of pilgrimage for rugby fans.

➕ 319 K9
ℹ️ The Square, tel 06-350 1922; daily 9–5
🚌 Corner of Pitt and Main streets
🚆 Services from Auckland and Wellington
✈️ 4km (2.5 miles) northwest of city

www.manawatunz.co.nz
Clearly laid-out guide to events and places to stay in the whole region.

RATINGS	
Cultural interest	●●●○
Historic interest	●●○○
Walkability	●●●○

TIP
● Because it is so flat, you can easily get lost. Don't stray too far from the central square and visible tall buildings without a street map from the tourist office.

This agricultural and university community is set on the Manawatu River, and makes a good base for exploring the southern sector of the North Island. It also gives access through the impressive Manawatu Gorge to the Wairarapa (▷ 106) and Hawke's Bay (▷ 79). The heart of the city is the vast green, tree-lined Square.

Other than Massey University (second in size only to Auckland's university, and named after former prime minister William Massey), the town is perhaps most famous for the New Zealand Rugby Museum at 87 Cuba Street (Mon–Sat 10–12, 1.30–4, Sun 1.30–4). It has a huge collection of memorabilia, and an archive resource of videos with accounts of every All Black game since 1870. The excellent Te Manawa Science Centre, Museum and Art Gallery, at 396 Main Street (daily 10–5), integrates social, cultural and artistic heritage with hands-on science displays. In the museum are Maori *taonga* (treasures) and several significant artworks by contemporary figures such as Colin McCahon and Ralph Hotere. There is also a popular hands-on science section.

AROUND PALMERSTON NORTH

In the Manawatu flatlands north of Palmerston sits Feilding. It is a pretty place on the banks of the Oroua River, relatively prosperous and particularly well known for its gardens. These have played a key role in the town's success in the nation's Most Beautiful Small Town Awards, which it has won a remarkable 12 times. Feilding has a scattering of small museums (traction engines being a local speciality), craft outlets and gardens, and it is a tranquil place to explore on foot, or by horse and cart. It's also fun to watch local farmers bidding at the stock sales on Friday.

Beach, to the south, and Paraparaumu Beach, to the north. The latter is also the base for trips to Kapiti Island (▷ 94).

North of town, off SH1, Southward Car Museum (Nov–Easter daily 10–5; Easter–end Oct daily 10–4.30) has an outstanding collection of 250 vehicles dating from 1895, including cars, traction engines, motorbikes, bicycles and a model railway. Highlights include a Rolls Royce that once belonged to film star Marlene Dietrich.

PUKAHA MOUNT BRUCE WILDLIFE CENTRE

➕ 319 K10 ✉️ 30km (18 miles) north of Masterton on SH2 ☎️ 06-375 8004 🕐 Daily 9–4.30 💷 Adult NZ$8, child (17 and under) free 🅿️
www.mtbruce.org.nz

Pukaha Mount Bruce is the flagship of the Department of Conservation's endangered species breeding policy, where you can see rare species such as takahe, stitchbird and kokako. Wild indigenous eels live in the stream running through the reserve and gather beneath the bridge at feeding time (1.30pm) in a swirling mass. Cheeky kaka (bush parrots), bred here and now living wild in the area, will happily nibble your ear before cracking open a peanut. They are fed by staff at 3pm.

Vintage style: a Buick at Southward Car Museum

THE SIGHTS

Te Papa Tongarewa-
Museum of New Zealand

One of the largest new museums in the world, covering more than 36,000sq m (387,500sq ft). A museum with an ambitious mission—to explore New Zealand's bicultural heritage and natural history and environment. NZ$317 million has been spent achieving this end since its opening in 1998.

RATINGS	
Cultural interest	● ● ● ● ○
Good for kids	● ● ● ○ ○
Historic interest	● ● ● ● ○
Shopping	● ● ● ● ○

SEEING TE PAPA

Te Papa sprawls on the waterfront and uses its setting to great effect, incorporating gardens, waterways, outdoor exhibits and performance areas on the bayside. A vast lobby on ground level gives a wonderful view out over the harbour. From this space, 20m (66ft) high, there is access to the exhibition areas. Te Papa holds a staggering variety of items, including the largest Maori collection held by any museum in the country—almost 16,000 *aonga*, from woodcarvings, personal ornaments and musical instruments to sections of meeting houses, canoes and store-houses, weapons, woven raincapes and feather and dogskin cloaks, and a contemporary *marae*. European history is repre-ented by 23,500 items, including costume, fine furniture and a major archive of 19th-century photographs (all Level 4).

Among other sections are the world's biggest collection of marine mammal skeletons; the national fish collection; 230,000 dried plant specimens; 65,000 specimens of birds, most from New Zealand (all Level 2); artworks from the late 19th century to the present day by artists including Charles Frederick Goldie, Rita Angus and Colin McCahon (Levels 5–6), and much, much more.

HIGHLIGHTS

MANA WHENUA (LEVEL 4)

This fabulous display of Maori art treasures and artefacts is a great introduction to Maori culture, with personal genealogical histories brought to life on audiovisual screens, and stories and legends told in the carved meeting house. Learn about the myth of the sacred *pounamu* (greenstone), and admire the feathered cloaks and other ornaments.

TIME WARP (LEVEL 2)

The Time Warp section is about information through entertainment. Blastback and Future Rush are two high-tech simulated rides—the former taking you back in time to show the creation of New Zealand from both Maori and geological perspectives (15 minutes), and the latter whisking you to Wellington of 2055, where you'll visit a

BASICS

➕ 103 C4
✉ Cable Street, Wellington
☎ 04-381 7000
🕐 Fri–Wed 10–6, Thu 10–9
💲 Free; charge for visiting exhibitions; Time Warp rides from NZ$8, child (4–14) from NZ$6, family from NZ$19
🚌 City Circular
🎫 Daily introductory tour Nov–end Mar 10.15, 11.15, 12, 1, 2, 3; NZ$9, child NZ$5
🏬 Level 1: excellent collection of museum merchandise, books, gifts, crafts, jewellery; Level 2 for kids' toys
🚻 Wheelchair access on all levels; unisex on levels 1 and 4
🍴 Licensed café (level 1) and espresso bar (level 4)
📖 Te Papa Explorer, NZ$2 (on sale at information desk, Level 2)

www.tepapa.govt.nz
Excellent comprehensive site with information on amenities, exhibitions and research collections.

Signs of a Nation (Level 4) explores the Treaty of Waitangi super-modern house and fly around in a futuristic car (18 minutes). In the Present Zone you can make a virtual bungy jump or shear a virtual sheep.

GOLDEN DAYS (LEVEL 4)

Golden Days re-creates a cluttered junkshop, where the drama of New Zealand's landmark historical events is played out in a 12-minute movie. The absorbing Made in New Zealand, on the same level, showcases the creativity and ingenuity behind 300 years of Kiwi visual arts and culture.

Below, the building stands on the waterfront
Below right, Future Rush, part of the Time Warp

STORYPLACE (LEVEL 2)

Children aged from 18 months to 5 years old can settle down here, an interactive space where carers are at hand to play and tell stories (tickets cost NZ$2 for a 45-minute session). Discovery Centres on Levels 2 and 4 also give children the chance to make their own animated films, read, have a go at weaving or study the world's largest flower.

Don't miss the underground Quake Braker exhibition, which shows how the museum building is designed to reduce the effects of earthquakes.

Left, the Boulevard Gallery on Level 5
Above, learning in a Discovery Centre

Below, a lively display including a Holden car, made in New Zealand

Wellington

**A national capital with a small-town atmosphere.
Well-preserved historical buildings and a
vibrant arts and café culture.**

*Richard 'King Dick' Seddon
watches over the Beehive*

*Catching the cable car down
from the Botanic Garden*

*Admiring the view from the
top of Mount Victoria*

SEEING WELLINGTON

Wellington is New Zealand's capital, and the port for ferries from
the South Island. The city is sandwiched between green hills and
the waterfront, and anyone arriving by road or rail is delivered
right into its high-rise heart. Lambton Quay, the main business
and shopping street, leads to Molesworth Street, Thorndon
and the Parliamentary district. The harbour, with its bordering
main roads of Waterloo Quay, Customhouse Quay, Jervois Quay,
Cable Street and Oriental Parade, sweeps south and east,
encompassing the modern, revitalised waterfront. Here the main
landmark is the Te Papa museum (▷ 96–99), the city's top
visitor attraction, which explores New Zealand's bicultural
heritage. Cuba Street leads towards funky Cuba Mall, and
Courtenay Place, lined with restaurants and cafés. Behind the
Central Business District (CBD) are the Botanic Garden and
the hillside suburb of Kelburn. Dominating the view southeast is
Mount Victoria, an ideal place to get your bearings.

HIGHLIGHTS

BOTANIC GARDEN AND CABLE CAR

✛ 102 A3 ✉ Glenmore Street, Thorndon; cable car 280 Lambton Quay
☎ 04-499 1400; cable car 04-472 2199 🕐 Daily dawn–dusk; cable car Mon–Fri
7am–10pm, Sat, Sun 9am–10pm, every 10 mins 🎫 Free; cable car NZ$2.50, child
(school age) NZ$1, under 5s free 🚌 3, all buses along Lambton Quay 🍽 Skyline
Café has great views over the city
www.wbg.co.nz

Wellington's Botanic Garden is magnificent but excruciatingly hilly. The
best way to get there is on the red cable car, an attraction in itself,
which takes about five minutes to climb 121m (440ft). There are
four stations on the way up, and from the summit station there's a
splendid view across the city. Gracing the precarious slopes are 26ha
(64 acres) of specialist gardens, flowerbeds, foreign trees and native
bush. A crowning glory is the Carter Observatory (▷ 186), with static
displays, planetarium shows and audiovisuals. The other highlight is the
Lady Norwood Rose Gardens, a circular display of more than 300
varieties at the northern end of the garden, at the base of the hill,
seen at their best between November and April.

BASICS

✛ 318 J11
🛈 101 Wakefield Street (Civic Square),
tel 04-802 4860; Mon–Wed, Fri 8.30–5,
Thu 9–5, Sat, Sun 9.30–4.30
🚆 Bunny Street
🚌 Bunny Street
⛴ Daily services to Picton, South Island
✈ Rongotai, 6km (4 miles) southeast;
Stagecoach Flyer bus and shuttles to
downtown

www.wellingtonnz.com
Basic visitor information and online
booking service, but limited in detail.

TIP

● Tourism Wellington
promotes a 'four quarters'
map system to help negotiate
the city's streets. The quarters,
mentioned on many maps
and in brochures, run clockwise from Mount Victoria:
Courtenay, Cuba, Willis
and Lambton.

*Native timbers including totara,
matai and kauri were used in the
construction of Old St. Paul's*

THE SIGHTS

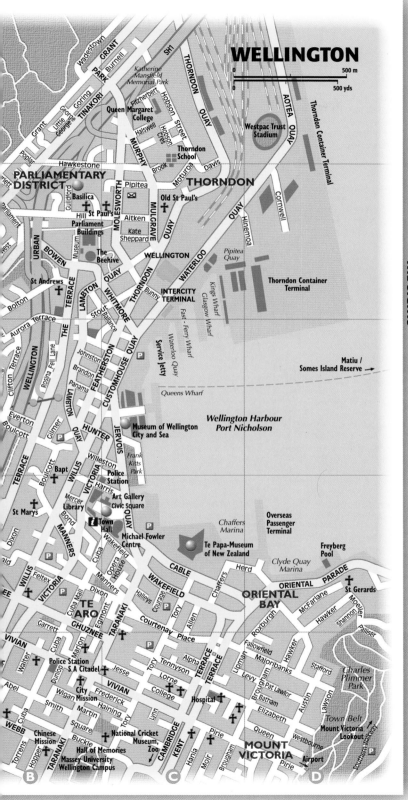

WELLINGTON

0   500 m
0   500 yds

WELLINGTON

Westpac Trust Stadium

Thorndon Container Terminal

THORNDON

Katherine Mansfield Memorial Park

Queen Margaret College

Thorndon School

Old St Paul's

PARLIAMENTARY DISTRICT

Basilica

St Paul's

Parliament Buildings

The Beehive

St Andrews

Kate Sheppard

WELLINGTON

Pipitea

Pipitea Quay

Thorndon Container Terminal

INTERCITY TERMINAL

Fast - Ferry Wharf

Kings Wharf

Glasgow Wharf

Service Jetty

Waterloo Quay

Queens Wharf

Matiu / Somes Island Reserve →

Museum of Wellington City and Sea

Frank Kitts Park

Wellington Harbour Port Nicholson

Police Station

Art Gallery

Civic Square

Mercer Library

St Marys

Town Hall

Michael Fowler Centre

Opera House

Chaffers Marina

Overseas Passenger Terminal

Freyberg Pool

Te Papa-Museum of New Zealand

Clyde Quay Marina

TE ARO

CABLE

WAKEFIELD

ORIENTAL PARADE

St Gerards

ORIENTAL BAY

Courtenay Place

Police Station S A Citadel

City Mission

VIVIAN

Hospital

National Cricket Museum, Zoo

Chinese Mission

Hall of Memories

Massey University Wellington Campus

MOUNT VICTORIA

Charles Plimmer Park

Town Belt

Mount Victoria Lookout

Airport

B   C   D

CIVIC SQUARE AND THE WATERFRONT

✛ 103 C4 🚌 City Circular

A beautiful silver fern orb is suspended above the middle of this public space, which is often used for outdoor events. This is the setting for the excellent City Gallery (daily 10–5), which hosts regular shows of contemporary art in various media and has regular film screenings and performances. Also on the square is Capital E (daily 10–5), where children's events and exhibitions are staged; there's a large toyshop attached.

From Civic Square it's a short walk to the waterfront across the City-to-Sea Bridge, by artist Para Matchitt, which sprouts sculptures celebrating the arrival of the Maori in New Zealand. The waterfront itself is a major focus for the city's museums and recreational activities, and sunny weekends here are abuzz with visitors and locals.

Below, the restored birthplace of writer Katherine Mansfield
Middle, dining out on lively Cuba Street
Right, a view over the city and the harbour from the Botanic Garden

MORE TO SEE

COLONIAL COTTAGE MUSEUM

✛ 102 A5 ✉ 68 Nairn Street, Brooklyn ☎ 04-384 9122 🕐 Jan–Easter daily 10–4; Easter–end Dec Sat, Sun 12–4 🎟 Adult NZ$5, schoolchild free 🚌 7, 8, 9
www.colonialcottagemuseum.co.nz
A restored and furnished Victorian interior housed in one of the city's oldest buildings (1858), which belonged to the family of carpenter and timber merchant William Wallis for 119 years. Early settler life and Wellington's growth are charted.

KARORI WILDLIFE SANCTUARY

✛ 102 A3 ✉ Waiapu Road, Karori ☎ 04-920 9200 🕐 Dec–end Mar daily 10–5 🎟 Adult NZ$10, child (under 14) NZ$4, family NZ$24 🚌 3, 17, 18, 21, 22, 23 www.sanctuary.org.nz
In 1994, 250ha (618 acres) in a valley of regenerating bush and hills of Karori was set aside and protected with a predator-proof fence. The benefits are already apparent, as native species are reintroduced and birdsong returns to the bush. The area around the perimeter fence is popular for walking and mountain biking.

MOUNT VICTORIA LOOKOUT

✛ 103 D5 🚌 20

From a distance, the wooded slopes of 196m (643ft) Mount Victoria hardly seem in character with the movie trilogy the *Lord of the Rings*, but they provided a location for several scenes depicting the Shire in the first film, *Fellowship of the Ring*. Although it is not easy to miss from downtown, reaching the lookout is something of an expedition. The best route is by car, to Thane Road via Majoribanks Street, at the bottom of Courtenay Place. If you lose your way in the web of residential hillside streets, keep heading uphill. On foot, the summit is part of the Southern Walkway. At the top you can watch planes make the tricky landing into Wellington Airport, enjoy the city view and investigate the Byrd Memorial, a tribute to US-born aviator and Antarctic explorer Richard Byrd (1888–1957).

MUSEUM OF WELLINGTON CITY AND SEA

✛ 103 C3 ✉ Queens Wharf ☎ 04-472 8904 🕐 Daily 10–5 🎟 Free 🚌 City Circular
www.museumofwellington.co.nz
Housed in the former Bond Store, this superb museum competes very successfully with its much bigger neighbour, Te Papa. Its interior, multilevel design combines a modern and rustic feel; its emphasis is on local history, with a particular maritime slant. Of special note is the *Wahine* Disaster Gallery, using original film footage set to a dramatic score to recall the loss of 51 lives on the *Wahine* passenger ferry, which came to grief at the port entrance in 1968.

NEW ZEALAND CRICKET MUSEUM

✛ 103 C5 ✉ The Old Grandstand, Basin Reserve ☎ 04-385 6602 🕐 Nov–end Apr daily 10.30–3.30; May–end Oct Sat, Sun 10.30–3.30 🎟 Adult NZ$5, child (13–16) NZ$2; 12 and under free if with an adult 🚌 1, 3, 4, 22, 23, 43, 44 www.nzcricket.co.nz
Enthusiasts will love this small but well arranged museum in the old 1924 grandstand of the Basin Reserve cricket ground. It displays national and international memorabilia, dating back to 1743, with emphasis on encounters with arch-enemy Australia. The ground occupies the site of a planned dock, made impractical after the earthquake of 1855. The curious Grecian temple structure inside the eastern boundary fence is a memorial to William Wakefield, leader of the New Zealand Company Wellington settlement from 1840 until 1848.

PARLIAMENTARY DISTRICT

✚ 103 B2 ☎ 04-471 9999 🚌 City Circular, 14

A stroll around this district, focused on Molesworth Street, takes in several of Wellington's most interesting buildings. One is the aptly named Beehive, a city landmark which houses government offices. Designed by British architect Sir Basil Spence and built in 1980, it is hated and loved in equal measure. Tours of Parliament, including the 1922 Parliament House, start here (Mon–Fri 10–4, Sat 10–3, Sun 12–3), and you can watch the House of Representatives in session (times vary). Old Government Buildings on Lambton Quay, built in 1876 to house Crown Ministers, was designed to look like stone, but is actually the world's second largest wooden building (after Japan's Todaji Temple). It was restored in 1994, complete with fibreglass replica chimneys. On Mulgrave Street, Archives New Zealand (Mon–Fri 9–5, Sat 9–1) contains historical documents including the original Treaty of Waitangi (▷ 27). The neo-Gothic Old St. Paul's Cathedral, built in 1866, has impressive interior timberwork and stained-glass windows, and is well worth a look.

The Prime Minister's official residence, Premier House, is a much-enlarged 1843 building on Tinakori Road. Farther north on the same road at No. 25 is the Katherine Mansfield Birthplace (Tue–Sun 10–4), where New Zealand's best-known writer, born in 1888, lived until the age of five (▷ 33). The simple house features in her short stories *Prelude* and *A Birthday*, and has been faithfully restored.

TE PAPA TONGAREWA-MUSEUM OF NEW ZEALAND

See pages 96–99.

BACKGROUND

According to Maori legend Kupe, the great Polynesian explorer, landed here in about AD950. The first European ships to arrive were the *Rosanna* and the *Lambton*, on a preliminary exploration for the first New Zealand Company in 1826, and the first settlers came in 1839 and 1840. The original community was in the area that is now Thorndon. A major earthquake in 1855 created new, flat land suitable for building, and Wellington began to prosper. It became the capital in 1865 and takes its name from Arthur Wellesley, the 1st Duke of Wellington (1769–1852).

The modern Byrd Memorial on top of Mount Victoria

MATIU/SOMES ISLAND RESERVE

✚ 103 D3 ✉ Wellington Harbour
☎ 04-499 1282 🕐 Daily 8.30–5
🚢 Ferry, adult NZ$18.50, child (3–15) NZ$10, under 3s free
www.eastbywest.co.nz

Once a quarantine station, this island now supports a number of protected native birds. Ferries travel here from Queen's Wharf three times a day on the way to Days Bay, near the coastal resort of Eastbourne.

WELLINGTON ZOO

✚ 103 C5 ✉ Daniell Street, Newtown
☎ 04-381 6750 🕐 Daily 9.30–5
🎟 Adult NZ$15, child (3–16) NZ$6
🚌 10, 23 💳 🏛
www.wellingtonzoo.com

Conservation projects are central to this zoo, whose residents include kiwi, tuatara and a wide variety of non-native species including Sumatran tigers, Malayan sun bears and a troupe of chimps—the second largest in the southern hemisphere.

Castlepoint Lighthouse (▷ 94) stands proud on the rugged eastern seaboard of the Wairarapa region

Modern art displayed at the Sarjeant Gallery, Wanganui

THE SIGHTS

WAIRARAPA

➕ 319 K10 ℹ 316 Queen Street, Masterton, tel 06-370 0900 🚌 Services from Wellington to Masterton
www.wairarapanz.com

Wild coastal scenery, relaxed rural towns like Martinborough (▷ 94), vineyards and the North Island's southernmost point (Cape Palliser, ▷ 94) all make this little-visited region worth getting to know.

From Masterton, the chief town, SH2 leads south to Carterton. Here, at the Paua World factory (▷ 180) on Kent Street, you can watch jewels being crafted from exquisite paua (abalone) shells, which are subject to strict quotas and harvesting rules. One of the best views in the Wairarapa can be enjoyed from Mount Dick, 14km (9 miles) along Dalefield Road, at the southern end of the town.

At the Waiohine Gorge, 22km (14 miles) south of Carterton, walks lead high above the river and negotiate the heart-stopping, 40m-high (130ft) swing bridge. Greytown, farther along SH2, is best known for its antiques and craft shops housed in a row of beautifully restored wooden-fronted buildings on Main Street. The Cobblestones Museum on Main Street (daily 9–4.30) is a collection of buildings and memorabilia from early settler days.

Featherston is the Wairarapa's southern point of access, set in the shadow of the Rimutaka Range. In the 1870s this was the base during construction of the Wairarapa–Wellington rail link. Its main attraction now is the Fell Engine Museum on Fitzherbert Street (Mon–Fri 9.30–4, Sat, Sun 10–4), housing the beautifully restored engine that used to climb the 265m (870ft) rise of the Rimutaka Incline. The incline is now part of the Rimutaka Rail Trail, starting at the end of Cross Creek Road, 10km (6 miles) south of Featherston, and leading in a day to Summit and back or to Kaitoke.

WANGANUI

➕ 318 J9 ℹ 101 Guyton Street, tel 06-349 0508 🚌 Ridgeway Street, Ingestre Street ✖
www.wanganuinz.com

Wanganui lies at the mouth of the Whanganui River, once a vital north–south supply route. Formerly a bustling port, Wanganui is now the southern gateway to Whanganui National Park. The area of Queen's Park, east of the central thoroughfare of Victoria Avenue, with its restored Victorian and Edwardian houses, is the city's cultural heart. It's also home to the modern Whanganui Regional Museum (daily 10–4), which contains a fine collection of Maori canoes and illustrates ingenious Maori methods of catching fish and birds. Crowning Queens Park hill is the domed Sarjeant Gallery (daily 10.30–4.30), with more than 4,000 permanent artworks.

Sailings of the restored *Waimarie* paddlesteamer, which worked the river for 50 years before sinking in 1952, leave from Wanganui Riverboat Centre on Taupo Quay (Nov–Apr daily 2pm; May–Oct Sat, Sun 1pm).

Within Cooks Gardens, on St. Hill Street, are the 1899 colonial-style Opera House; a stadium and wooden velodrome; and the Ward Observatory (Fri 8–9.30), built in 1901.

Across the city bridge from Taupo Quay a tunnel takes you 200m (656ft) into the hillside to ride the Durie Hill Elevator (1919) to the top (Mon–Fri 7.30–6, Sat 9–6, Sun 10–5), where you can climb the Durie Hill War Memorial Tower, built of shellrock.

WELLINGTON

See pages 100–105.

WHANGANUI NATIONAL PARK

➕ 318 K8 ℹ 74 Ingestre Street, Wanganui, tel 06-348 8475; Cherry Grove, Taumarunui, tel 07-8958201; Owairua Road, Pipiriki, tel 06-385 5022
www.doc.govt.nz

From its source high on the volcanic slopes of Tongariro National Park, the Whanganui River travels 290km (180 miles) to the sea, carving through some of the North Island's least accessible country. At its most remote parts it cuts deep into the soft sand and mudstone and is joined by tracts of forest, which form the heart of the Whanganui National Park. The entire area is difficult to reach, but there are walking tracks and jet-boat and kayak trips along the river itself. Be aware that slips and flooding are real dangers; consult the Department of Conservation before an excursion.

The windy and scenic Whanganui River Road branches off SH4 15km (9 miles) north of Wanganui and follows the river to Pipiriki before turning inland to Raetihi, where it rejoins SH4. The 106km (66-mile) round trip, passes a number of mission settlements that were created in the 1840s by the Reverend Richard Taylor.

Paua shell

NELSON AND MARLBOROUGH

The northern tip of the South Island is known for its gentle, sunny climate, attracting wine-growers to the Marlborough region and artisans to Nelson and its environs. The coastal Abel Tasman is one of the best-loved national parks in the country.

MAJOR SIGHTS

← AWAROA LODGE 17 MINS

Abel Tasman National Park

The smallest and busiest national park in New Zealand. Some 23,000ha (56,830 acres) of the best coastal scenery, beaches and walks in the country.

Sparkling sand and sea at Awaroa Inlet

Rich hues glimpsed in a crystal-clear tidal rockpool

Water taxis help visitors access sections of the Coast Track

SEEING ABEL TASMAN NATIONAL PARK

More than 170,000 visitors a year come to appreciate the Abel Tasman's rolling hills of native bush; its granite, limestone and marble outcrops; its clear, azure waters; and its 91km (56 miles) of coastline indented with more than 50 sandy beaches. Birds such as tui and bellbirds inhabit lush pockets of forest, and pukeko feed in the wetlands—outside the park's boundaries, these are protected as the Tonga Island Marine Reserve.

Walkers come to enjoy the world-famous Coast Track, sea kayakers to make the most of an internationally renowned venue. On an average summer's day the park attracts up to 4,000 people, and you must reserve well in advance for all places to stay and most activities.

HIGHLIGHTS

AWAROA BAY
🛨 320 G10
A 6km (4-mile), three- to six-hour walk makes the most of this glorious inlet tucked into a fold of land south of Totaranui. Its starting point is reached from Takaka along the Totaranui Road, via Pohara, Wainui Inlet and the Pigeon Saddle, with tremendous views on the way. From the Totaranui Road, a right turn takes you on to the Awaroa Road and the Awaroa parking zone.

To enjoy the walk you need to time your arrival with an outgoing tide, as it begins on the beach (this stage is best done barefoot). It ends at Awaroa Lodge, where you can buy beer, coffee or tea, before retracing your steps to the Awaroa parking zone, keeping a careful eye on the tide.

COAST TRACK
This world-famous two- to five-day, 51km (32-mile) walk requires medium fitness; the track itself is well maintained. The only obstacles and difficult sections are the two estuary crossings at Awaroa Inlet and Torrent Bay—the most scenic beaches on the route—which must be negotiated at low tide. There are several ways to tackle the track in whole or in part.

RATINGS	
Outdoor pursuits	●●●●●
Photo stops	●●●
Walkability	●●●●●

BASICS

🛨 320 G10

ℹ️ Wallace Street, Motueka, tel 03-528 6543; daily 8–7

ℹ️ Department of Conservation field centre, corner of King Edward and High streets, Motueka, tel 03-528 1810; Mon–Fri 8–4.30

🚌 Services from Nelson to Kaiteriteri and Marahau via Motueka (southern entrance), and to Totaranui (northern sector)

🚤 Water taxis from Motueka, Kaiteriteri and Marahau; can also be hailed within park

✈️ Awaroa Bay (from Nelson or Motueka): Abel Tasman Air (tel 03-528 8290)

www.doc.govt.nz
A guide to DoC parks and services, with useful links to other sites and DoC contact details.

Left, primitive-style wooden sculpture at Awaroa Lodge
Opposite, marker post on the Abel Tasman Coast Track

- Visitor information and DoC offices in Motueka can help with reserving places to stay, passes, transportation, activities and tide times.
- General information, hut reservations, maps and leaflets are also available at the DoC office.
- Unmanned DoC information stations and intentions sheets are available at Marahau and Totaranui (seasonal).

MORE TO SEE

KAITERITERI

✚ 320 G10 🚌 Services from Nelson Scenic launches, water taxis and kayak trips set off from this very pretty village on the dead-end road to the southern boundary of the park. There are two exceptionally good beaches here. At the eastern end of the main beach is the Kaka Pa Point Lookout. Idyllic Breakers Beach, below, looks eastward.

MARAHAU

✚ 320 G10 🚌 Services from Nelson Marahau is 6km (4 miles) east of Kaiteriteri, on the same southern approach road to the park. It offers a wide range of places to stay and activities, water taxis and a café. Controversy is raging about a NZ$15 million resort development given resource consent on the environmentally sensitive wetlands at the entrance to the park—a project that confirms the worst fears of conservationists about threats to the unspoiled beauty of the Abel Tasman.

Right, trampers
Below, boardwalk on the trail

The most popular routes are from the south (Marahau) to the north (Wainui), or from Totaranui in the north (by water taxi from Marahau) to Marahau in the south. There are plenty of campsites and huts along the way and a few independent lodges. The walk involves a lot of bush walking, where views of the sea and beaches are obscured for long periods of time.

INLAND TRACK

The Inland Track is a quieter but more energetic walk than the Coast Track, and leads away from the coast and its hordes of visitors. It provides a link between Marahau and Wainui via the Pigeon Saddle on the Takaka–Totaranui Road, and takes three to five days to cover 37km (23 miles). The main appeals here, other than the fact that the walk is far less popular than the coastal track, are the undisturbed regenerating bush and the occasional sublime views. You may also hear kiwis at night.

TORRENT BAY TO MARAHAU WALK

This 14km (8.5-mile) route takes from three to six hours to complete. From Marahau you can take an early morning water taxi to Torrent Bay (NZ$15; first taxi leaves 8.30), making sure that your arrival at Torrent Bay coincides with low tide. From here the route joins the Coast Track heading south, for which you need to take off your boots and follow the markers across the estuary, and continues via the lovely sands of Anchorage Bay Beach, intimate Watering Cove, and Stillwell and Appletree bays.

BACKGROUND

Maori communities have lived along this coast for at least five centuries, and in 1642 the Ngati Tumatakokiri people saw off the first European visitors—part of Dutch explorer Abel Tasman's crew. From 1855 European settlement got underway, which meant the clearing of forests and quarrying of granite. Fears that logging would strip the coast of its vegetation led to a campaign for the protection of this stretch of shoreline, and in 1942—largely as a consequence of the tireless efforts of conservationist and resident Perrine Moncrieff—the national park was opened. Many place-names within the park are associated with explorations by the French explorer Jules Sébastien César Dumont d'Urville.

Blenheim is at the forefront of South Island wine production

Inside the Te Anaroa cave system, near Collingwood

A gannetry occupies the tip of Farewell Spit

BLENHEIM

🚩 321 H11 🚃 Rail Station, SH1, Sinclair Street, tel 03-577 8080 🚌 Services to Christchurch, Picton and Nelson 🚍 Grove Road; services from Christchurch and Picton ✖ On Middle Renwick Road, 7km (4 miles) west; shuttles **www.**destinationmarlborough.com

The Marlborough region's largest town is a resort known for its wineries—over 50 of them, most clustered off SH6 near the village of Renwick, 10km (6 miles) west of town on the fertile soils of the Wairau Plains. Famous names include Montana, Cloudy Bay and Nautilus Estate, and tours and tastings are widely available (▷ 189). Blenheim's dry climate has its disadvantages: in recent years the whole region has suffered from a severe lack of rain.

The Marlborough Provincial Museum at Brayshaw Park, New Renwick Road, 3km (2 miles) south of town (daily 10–4), is a mainly open-air reconstruction of an early settlers' village. It is at the end of the narrow-gauge Blenheim Riverside Railway (tel 03-578 9442).

COLLINGWOOD

🚩 320 G10

This tiny village on Golden Bay was once known as Gibbstown and—unlikely as it now seems—was once a booming gold-mining town promoted as a suitable capital for the nation. That dream turned to dust when the gold reserves ran out and a fire almost destroyed the village. Rebuilt and renamed Collingwood in tribute to Admiral Lord Nelson's second-in-command, the community was struck by fire again in 1904 and yet again in 1967, when the town hall, hotel and two shops

were reduced to ashes. Despite its calamitous history, Collingwood retains a few historic buildings, including the courthouse, which is now a café.

South of the village, in the attractive Aorere River Valley, are the privately owned Te Anaroa and Rebecca Caves, on Caves Road, near Rockville (reservations essential, tel 03-525 6044). The Te Anaroa Caves are 350m (1,148ft) long and include stalactites and fossilised shells, and the Rebecca Caves are known for their glow-worms.

If you have time, an exploration of the pretty Aorere River valley (Heaphy Track Road) is recommended, taking in the river gorge at Salisbury Bridge and the Bainham Store, an original store that has changed little in decades and is still open for business.

FAREWELL SPIT AND GOLDEN BAY

🚩 320 G9 🎫 Freemans Access, Puponga, tel 03-524 8454

Countless tons of sand have been ejected into the northerly ocean currents from river-mouths scattered all the way up the west coast, forming this dynamic though desert-like landscape at the northwest tip of the South Island, with sparse vegetation struggling to take root in the dry and shifting sand. Both Cape Farewell and Farewell Spit were

noted by Abel Tasman in 1642, and named by Cook when he left New Zealand in 1770. The lighthouse at the very tip of the spit was first erected in 1870, and relocated after the sea almost washed it away.

The majority of the spit is a nature reserve, and the mud flats that it creates along its landward edge are one of New Zealand's most important habitats for wading birds. More than 100 species have been recorded around the spit, but it is the sheer numbers of each species that are most notable. Migrating flocks of godwits and knots can run well into the thousands. Black swans are also found here.

The spit is remarkable for its powerful sense of isolation, but from afar and from sea level its extensive dune system appears no more than a coastal mirage. For an impression of its scale, the best viewpoint is around the Pillar Point Light Beacon, accessed from Wharariki Road and Puponga. A marked walk leads from the beacon along the cliffs to Cape Farewell, where you may see or hear (or smell!) fur seals. From here you can descend to Wharariki Beach, one of the most beautiful in the country (you can also reach it from Puponga along Wharariki Road), where golden sands are punctuated with caves, dunes and rock arches.

THE SIGHTS

The grey sands of Farewell Spit

The famous Mussel Boys restaurant makes the most of Havelock's local produce—green-lipped mussels

A peaceful mooring at Motueka

THE SIGHTS

HAVELOCK

🔲 321 H10 🚹 65A Main Road, tel 03-574 2114 🚌 Main Road 🚢 Services from Blenheim and Nelson
www.rutherfordtravel.co.nz

Travelling west from Blenheim (▷ 111), the SH6 passes through the small village of Renwick before winding through the rolling hills of the Inner Marlborough Sounds to Nelson. About 41km (25 miles) along, at the head of the Pelorus Sound, is the enchanting little fishing settlement of Havelock. The village has a fine café, a famous restaurant (Mussel Boys, ▷ 262), art and craft galleries, a pub and a small but interesting museum on Main Road (daily 9–5). It's also an ideal base for exploring the glorious Pelorus and other outer sounds. Takorika Hill, behind the town, has extensive views.

Havelock was once a thriving gold-mining town and was the boyhood home of one of New Zealand's most famous sons, atomic physicist Ernest Rutherford (1871–1937)—the man who split the atom. His former home is now the youth hostel, and a memorial stands on the main street. These days Havelock's gold is the green-lipped mussel, without doubt the finest-tasting thing in a shell, and a major export industry within the Sounds.

A network of old bridleways makes up the 27km (17-mile) Nydia Track, which begins near Havelock at Kaiuma Bay. The two-day walk takes in an old timber-milling site and magnificent forest on the way to Duncan Bay.

About 18km (11 miles) west of Havelock is the Pelorus Bridge Scenic Reserve, where the Rai and Pelorus rivers flow through bush-clad hills. You can walk in

Fruit is grown around Motueka

the area, and there's a great café by the bridge.

KAHURANGI NATIONAL PARK

🔲 320 G10 🚹 DoC field centres, Millers Acre, 79 Trafalgar Street, Nelson, tel 03-546 9339; corner of King Edward and High streets, Motueka, tel 03-528 1810; Commercial Street, Takaka, tel 03-525 8026 🚌 Services from Nelson, Takaka and Karamea
www.doc.govt.nz

Kahurangi, opened as a national park in 1996, is a wide and remote landscape in the north-west of rugged alpine ranges and river valleys. The most notable of these is the Heaphy, which meets, in part, the park's most famous walking route, the 82km (51-mile) Heaphy Track—named for Major Charles Heaphy, the first to traverse the coastal section, in 1846. It takes four to six days to cover the whole route, which reaches its highest point of 915m (3,002ft) at Flannigan's Corner, near Mount Perry. The eastern Heaphy Track trailhead is reached via Collingwood (▷ 111), and Bainham (Aorere River Valley), at the end of the Heaphy Track Road. The route is signposted from Collingwood. The western trailhead starts about 15km (9 miles) north of Karamea. Book hut accommodation ahead in summer.

Some of the country's oldest rock landforms—spectacular

limestone caves, plateaux, arches and outcrops—are contained within the park, and it provides a home for more than half New Zealand's native plant species (over 80 per cent of all alpine species) and more than 18 native bird species, including the New Zealand falcon and the great spotted kiwi, as well as the huge New Zealand land snail.

MOTUEKA

🔲 320 G10 🚹 Wallace Street, tel 03-528 6543 ✈ Airport on College Street, 2km (1 mile) west
www.abeltasmangreenrush.co.nz

Motueka sits among sun-bathed hop farms and orchards, a short distance from several beautiful beaches. Many visitors pass through en route to the Abel Tasman National Park and Golden Bay, making this a bustling resort in summer and a sleepy service town in winter. The best beaches near Motueka (and before the national park) are in Kaiteriteri (▷ 110). For a short walk try the Motueka Quay, reached via the waterfront west of downtown. Motueka has a small museum (Dec–Apr daily 9–4; May–Nov Mon–Fri 10–4).

The route between Motueka and Richmond (SH60), known as Nelson's Coastal Way, is the place to go for arts and crafts and wineries, plus the Touch the Sea Aquarium (daily 9–5) and the Cool Store art gallery next door.

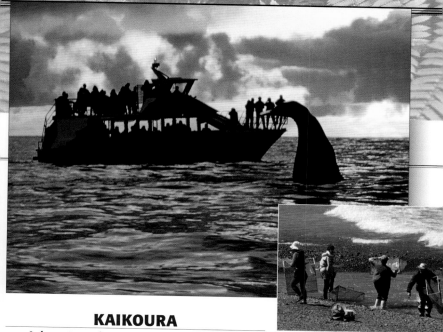

KAIKOURA

A chance to get close to whales and dolphins, seals and albatrosses on a sparkling azure bay.

The small town of Kaikoura sits on the spectacular northeast coast, in the shadow of the snow-capped Kaikoura mountains. South, a sea trough extends unusually close to the coastline, creating an upsurge of nutritious plankton soup and attracting an extraordinary variety of ocean inhabitants.

Modern Kaikoura was established as a whaling station in the early 19th century. Station manager George Fyffe built Kaikoura's oldest remaining house (Fyffe House) near the Old Wharf in 1860, and gave his name to the mountain immediately behind the township. The whaling industry was replaced by fishing, particularly for crayfish. Today Kaikoura's wildlife is hunted only by the camera, and the resident and migratory whales are the big draw.

WATER-BASED ACTIVITIES

The sea around Kaikoura abounds with dolphins, from the common and bottlenose to the smaller, rare Hector's dolphin. You are most likely to encounter or swim with dusky dolphins; pods running into the hundreds, if not the thousands, are common. Kaikoura is home to its own pod of sperm whales. Whale-watching trips depart from the Whaleway Station off Beach Road, offering a chance to spot dolphins, seals and other wildlife. Other whale species that appear regularly include humpbacks, rights and orcas, and if you are very lucky you may see an enormous blue whale. For details of tours, ▷ 190.

LAND-BASED SIGHTS

Clifftop and shoreline walkways link the northern and southern settlements of Kaikoura, and cross the head of the Kaikoura Peninsula. A good spot to get an overall impression of the town, the peninsula and its mountain backdrop is the lookout just off Scarborough Terrace (off SH1 between the northern and southern settlements). See also the walk, ▷ 234.

There are three historical venues of note: the Kaikoura District Museum, at 14 Ludstone Road (Mon–Fri 12.30–4.30, Sat, Sun 2–4), offering an insight into early Maori and whaling activities; Fyffe House, on Avoca Street near the Old Wharf (Nov–end Apr daily 10–5; May–end Oct Thu–Tue 10–4); and the Maori Leap Cave, 2km (1 mile) south of Kaikoura, a sea-formed limestone cave, discovered only in the 21st century (daily tours).

Top, watching as a sperm whale dives off the Kaikoura coast Above, fishing from the shingle beach

RATINGS

Historic interest	●●
Outdoor pursuits	●●●
Walkability	●●●●

BASICS

✚ 321 H12

🛈 West End, Kaikoura, tel 03-319 5641; Jan, Feb daily 8–6; Mar–end Dec daily 9–5

🚌 Services from Christchurch, Blenheim, Picton and Hanmer Springs. Shuttles to all main sights

🚉 Clarence Street; services from Christchurch, Blenheim and Picton

www.kaikoura.co.nz
Comprehensive guide to the area's wildlife, environment, activities, art and history, places to stay and eat, and other visitor information.

TIPS

● In midsummer it's advisable to reserve all activities ahead, and essential if you want to go whale-watching or dolphin-swimming.
● Kaikoura is subject to changeable weather. Trips may be cancelled at short notice, so request inclusion on alternative trips.

Nelson

A vibrant modern town steeped in history, and surrounded by beaches and national parks.
Claims the title of Sunshine Capital of New Zealand.

Dining al fresco at Olivia's, on the waterfront

Right, the Boatshed Restaurant overhangs the water

Far right, South Street's houses are among the oldest in the country

BASICS

✚ 321 G10
🛈 Corner of Trafalgar and Halifax streets, tel 03-548 2304; daily 9–5
🚌 Outside visitor information office; services from Christchurch, Blenheim, Picton, Golden Bay, Abel Tasman, Takaka and West Coast
✈ Airport 6km (4 miles) southwest of town off SH6

www.nelsonnz.com
Well-designed site with wide-ranging information on the Nelson region, including a search database on food and wine and places to stay.

SEEING NELSON

Nelson is known as the sunniest place in the country—and this could apply to its atmosphere, its people and its surroundings, in addition to its Mediterranean climate. The city's colonial heart is around Trafalgar Street, and the Saturday market is a highlight (▷ 191). Within 100km (60 miles) of town are superb beaches and coastal scenery, as well as three diverse national parks: Abel Tasman (▷ 108–110), Nelson Lakes (▷ 117) and Kahurangi (▷ 112). Little wonder that Nelson is considered one of the top places to visit—and to live—in the country.

HIGHLIGHTS

BEACHES

No visit to Nelson would be complete without a trip to the beach. The most popular stretch of sand is at the Tahunanui Beach Reserve, just southwest of downtown. It may not have the same scenic beauty (or solitude) of more remote beaches in the region, but it is a convenient place to relax. About 20km (12 miles) farther round Tasman Bay towards Motueka, off SH60, are the seemingly never-ending sands and forest swathe of Rabbit Island.

BROADGREEN HISTORIC HOUSE

✉ 276 Nayland Road, Stoke, 6km (4 miles) southwest of downtown ☎ 03-547 0403 🕐 Daily 10.30–4.30 💰 Adult NZ$3, child (school age) NZ$0.50, pre-school free 🚌 From Travel Centre, 27 Bridge Street
An 11-room cob house of 1855, made of clay, sand and straw, has been furnished in its original style and opened to the public. It was built for Englishman Edmund Buxton, following the model of a Devon farmhouse, and sits amid lawns and rose gardens.

NELSON MUSEUM PUPURI TAONGA O TE TAI AO

✉ Corner of Hardy and Trafalgar streets ☎ 03-548 9588 🕐 Mon–Fri 10–5, Sat, Sun 10–4.30
www.museumnp.org.nz
The new regional museum covers the natural and human history of the top of the South Island. Displays include photos of everyday life from an outstanding collection made in the 1860s, as well as

Maori *taonga* (treasures), works of art and a range of domestic and technical objects.

SUTER TE ARATOI O WHAKATU

✉ 208 Bridge Street ☎ 03-548 4699 ⏱ Daily 10.30–4.30 💰 Adult NZ$3, schoolchild NZ$0.50 🍴 🏧 🚌 From Travel Centre, 27 Bridge Street; Double-Decker Express

www.thesuter.org.nz

The Suter, next to Queen's Gardens, is foremost among several major galleries in this city known for its thriving arts and crafts. Four exhibition spaces showcase permanent and temporary historical and contemporary collections. There is also a theatre on the site.

WORLD OF WEARABLE ART AND CLASSIC CARS (WOW)

✉ Quarantine Road, Annesbrook ☎ 03-547 4573 ⏱ Jan–Easter daily 10–6; Easter–end Dec daily 10–5 💰 Adult NZ$18, child (5–14) NZ$7, under 5s free, family from NZ$26 🚗 🏧 🚌 From Travel Centre, 27 Bridge Street; Double-Decker Express

www.wowcars.co.nz

In 1987 Nelson sculptor Suzie Moncrieff created and directed a unique stage show called Wearable Art. Contributors were asked to create a piece of themed artwork in any medium in a form that could be worn in motion. The show became an annual event and has now shifted to Wellington (▷ 187), but the best entries can be seen in this gallery. A fully scripted moving parade of extreme costumes is displayed, reflecting an astonishing array of creative thought and eccentric wit—not to be missed. A second gallery in the same complex houses vintage cars.

BACKGROUND

Maori tribes migrated to this area from the North Island in the 16th century. In the 1840s New Zealand Company agent Colonel William Wakefield negotiated a land purchase at Nelson. Subsequent disagreements about ownership of further land led to the Wairau Affray and the death of his brother, Captain Arthur Wakefield, and 27 others. In 1844 the NZ Company collapsed, leaving many destitute. Recovery began in 1857, when gold was discovered, and by the end of the 19th century Nelson's rich agricultural potential was finally being realised.

Above, strolling on the town's Tahunanui Beach
Below, New Zealand's central point is celebrated

TIPS
● Nelson's vineyards are overshadowed by the reputation and scale of those in Marlborough, but the wine they produce can be of excellent quality. For more information see www.nelsonwines.co.nz.
● A half-hour's climb to the viewpoint above the Botanical Gardens, off Milton Road or Maitai Road, gives a great view of the town from a site claimed as New Zealand's geographical mid-point.

Above, a coastline indented with appealing little bays characterises Queen Charlotte Sound; left, a fishing boat in the Sounds

BASICS

✚ 318 J10

🛈 Foreshore, near the ferry terminal, Picton, tel 03-520 3113; daily 8.30–5

🚌 Services to Picton from Christchurch, Nelson and Blenheim

🚆 Daily service Christchurch–Picton: arr 12.13pm, dep 1pm

⛴ Ferries to Picton from Wellington

✈ Koromiko airport, 10km (6 miles) south of town

www.destinationmarlborough.com
Straightforward site with web directories for the region, plus Picton and New Zealand generally.

TIPS

● Marlborough Sounds can be explored on foot or by boat. Several water-based operators will drop off or pick up from a number of points along the Queen Charlotte walking track.
● Sea access is possible at Ship Cove, Resolution Bay, Endeavour Inlet, Camp Bay (Punga Cove), Bay of Many Coves, Torea Bay (the Portage), Lochmara Bay, Mistletoe Bay (Te Mahia) and Anakiwa.

MARLBOROUGH SOUNDS

A mosaic of tiny islets, coves and waterways, to be enjoyed along coastal paths or from the water.

The Marlborough Sounds are the South Island's giant entrance foyer. This vast, convoluted system of drowned river valleys, wooded peninsulas and remote green islets has sublime coastal scenery and offers every opportunity for kayaking, wildlife-watching or just relaxation. From its base at Picton (▷ 117) it is only a short journey to Blenheim (▷ 111), the region's capital. On the map, the Sounds take up a relatively small area, but the myriad drowned river valleys create an astonishing 1,500km (932 miles) of coastline, known for seabirds and dolphins. The two main inlets are Queen Charlotte and Pelorus sounds.

EXPLORING THE SOUNDS

There are two popular walking tracks in the sounds: the Nydia Track (Havelock ▷ 112) and the Queen Charlotte Track, a 71km (44-mile), coastal route which leads in three to five days from Ship Cove to Anakiwa. The track is suitable for most people of average fitness, and is open in part to mountain bicycles. It winds its way around sheltered coves, over skyline ridges and through native forest, fringing an extensive network of sunken river valleys.

Boat access in the Sounds is well organised and readily available. Other options include guided and self-guided walks, as well as kayaking trips and a ride on the Magic Mail Run (tel 03-573 6175, www.mailboat.co.nz). There is road access for drivers at Camp Bay (Punga Cove), Torea Bay (The Portage) and Mistletoe Bay (Te Mahia).

EARLY VISITORS

There is evidence of Maori settlement here from as early as the 14th century. Captain Cook visited the Sounds on each of his voyages between 1770 and 1777. He was particularly fond of Ship Cove, near the mouth of Queen Charlotte Sound, which he visited five times: a monument there commemorates the occasions. Less celebrated visits by other early explorers include those of Abel Tasman (before Cook), and French navigator Jules Dumont d'Urville in 1827. In the same year, London whaler John Guard established Marlborough's first European settlement, and the country's first land-based whaling station, at Te Awaiti Bay in Tory Channel, on Arapawa Island.

River at the southern end of Lake Rotoiti, Nelson Lakes

MURCHISON

⊞ 320 F11 ⓘ 47 Waller Street, tel 03-523 9350 🚌 Services from Nelson and the West Coast
www.nelsonnz.com

Murchison sits at the head of the Buller Gorge, where the Matakitaki and Buller rivers meet, and gives access to the west coast from the north. Although once an important gold-mining town—and nearly wiped out by a violent earthquake in 1929—it is now a quiet place, primarily of interest for activities such as fishing, white-water rafting, kayaking, caving and mountaineering.

The Murchison Museum, on Fairfax Street (daily 10–4), has exhibits on gold-mining and the town's past.

NELSON

See pages 114–115.

NELSON LAKES NATIONAL PARK

⊞ 320 G11 ⓘ St. Arnaud, tel 03-521 1806 🚌 Services from Nelson to St. Arnaud

This somewhat underrated national park protects 102,000ha (252,042 acres) of the northernmost Southern Alps range. Dominating the park are two long, scenic and trout-filled lakes, Rotoroa and Rotoiti, which lie cradled in beech-covered alpine ranges, surrounded by beautiful tussock valleys and wildflower-strewn meadows.

The ranges and river valleys offer superb walking, notably the 80km (50-mile), four- to seven-day Travers-Sabine Circuit and the excellent two- to three-day Robert Ridge/Lake Angelus Track. The principal base for the park is the pretty little hamlet of t. Arnaud, at the northern end f Lake Rotoiti—ask at the visitor nformation office here about horter walks in the vicinity.

Inside the restored teak hull of the Edwin Fox

PICTON

The gateway to South Island and Marlborough Sounds, in summer a buzz of sailing activity, in winter a sleepy port.

⊞ 321 H11
ⓘ Foreshore, near ferry terminal, tel 03-520 3113; daily 8.30–5
🚌 Services from Christchurch, Nelson and Blenheim
🚆 Service from Christchurch
⛴ Ferries from Wellington
✈ 10km (6 miles) south of town

www.picton.co.nz
Directory information for Picton and Marlborough Sounds.

RATINGS			
Historic interest	●	●	●
Outdoor pursuits	●	●	● ●
Walkability	●	●	● ●

TIP
● For a comprehensive guide to the walks around Picton, get hold of the excellent broadsheet *Picton by Foot*, available free from the visitor information office.

After you have arrived on the modern ferry, with its comfy seats and state-of-the-art radar screens, you will thank your lucky stars for progress when you encounter the old hulk of the 1853 East India trading ship *Edwin Fox*, between the ferry terminal and the heart of town (daily 9–5). Ranked the ninth oldest ship in the world, she carried troops in the Crimean War before being commissioned to bring immigrants to Australia and New Zealand.

MUSEUMS

Next door is the Seashore World (daily 9–6), whose inhabitants include an octopus called Larry, seahorses and rays. Farther towards the town on London Quay is the Picton Community Museum (daily 10–4), which contains a cluttered but interesting range of items focusing mainly on the 1800s whaling operations in the sounds, as well as Maori *taonga* (treasures) and early pioneer settler pieces.

ACROSS THE WATER

A short walk across the footbridge and the inlet leads to the eastern side of the waterfront and Shelley Beach. Here, the Echo Café and Bar (daily 10–late) is based around a scow, built in 1905 and gradually restored after her retirement in 1965. She was the last commercial trader under sail in New Zealand, and served in World War II. During her eventful life, *Echo* was stranded 15 times and damaged 16 times, had two new engines, propellers and shafts, suffered fires in 1911 and 1920, not to mention having seven collisions involving 75 different vessels and being sunk twice. She now has a quieter time as a restaurant.

THE SIGHTS

Tours explore the natural wonders of Rawhiti Cave in Golden Bay, east of Takaka

The Labyrinth Rocks were scoured out by river water

RAWHITI CAVE

➕ 320 G10 ✉ Clifton Road, Golden Bay

This ancient cave 7km (4 miles) east of Takaka has one of the largest cave entrances in the world, laden with thousands of multi-hued tufa stalactites. It can be accessed independently, but the best way to see it is on a three-hour guided walk with Kahurangi Walks (tel 03-525 7177, www.kahurangiwalks. co.nz) through the wonderful gorge of the Dry River. The ground is slippery, so you'll need to wear sturdy shoes.

TAKAKA

➕ 320 G10 🚶 Willow Street, tel 03-525 9136 🚌 Willow Street; services from Abel Tasman and Kahurangi ✈ Airfield 6km (4 miles) west of town on SH60 www.nelsonnz.com

Takaka was founded in 1854 and is the principal business and shopping area for Golden Bay (▷ 111). Particularly busy during summer, it has a life of its own all year as a cosmopolitan art and crafts hub. It is also the main base for visits to the northern sector of the Abel Tasman National Park (▷ 108–110), the vast Kahurangi National Park, and the remote 35km (22-mile) Farewell Spit (▷ 111). The small seaside village of Pohara, about 10km (6 miles) northeast of Takaka on the road to the northern boundary of the Abel Tasman National Park, boasts the best local beach and provides safe swimming.

In the town itself the Golden Bay Museum and Gallery (daily 10–4, closed Sun in winter) displays local treasures and a special feature on explorer Abel Tasman's unfortunate first encounter with the local Maori (when four of his crew were killed). The gallery next door showcases the

cream of local arts and crafts talent. There are many other independent studios and galleries in the area, listed in the free *Arts of Golden Bay* leaflet, available at the visitor information office.

The odd and shapely karst features of the Labyrinth Rocks (daily 1–5) form an intriguing sight 3km (2 miles) outside the town on Labyrinth Lane. More interesting land formations can be seen at the Grove Scenic Reserve at Clifton. Here a short 10-minute walk brings you to a spot where massive rata trees grow out of curiously shaped limestone outcrops. There are fine views and a fabulous summer flowering of begonias at nearby Begonia House on Richmond Road (Nov–end May daily 10–5; Jun–end Oct Mon–Fri 10–3).

The Abel Tasman Memorial on the headland just beyond Tarakohe, on Totaranui Road, was erected in 1942 to commemorate the tercentenary of the Dutch explorer's arrival. Drive on towards Totaranui and at the base of Wainui Bay is an easy 40-minute walk to the pretty Wainui Falls. The same road can

also take you to the northern beaches and walking access points of the Abel Tasman National Park.

TE WAIKOROPUPU SPRINGS

➕ 320 G10 ✉ North of Takaka, Golden Bay 🕐 Daily 🎫 Free

The biggest attraction in the Takaka area is the beautiful, crystal-clear Te Waikoropupu, or Pupu Springs. Turquoise waters bubble out of the ground to create the clearest freshwater lake outside Antarctica, with an extraordinary 62m (203ft) of horizontal visibility. It provides a habitat for a wide range of aquatic plants and fish, including brown trout. The main spring has a basin 40m (131ft) across, and there are several smaller springs, identifiable by the white sand thrown up towards the surface by the action of the water. The spring is a sacred Maori site, and bathing in its chilly waters is not permitted.

The source of the water is the Takaka River and its tributaries, which flow over karstified marble to the south, entering swallow holes and flowing through a massive underground cave system until it reaches this outlet.

To get to this peaceful place follow SH60 north of Takaka, turning left just after the bridge over the Takaka River. Follow Pupu Valley and Pupu Springs Road to the parking zone. There are well-maintained paths and boardwalks through forest and swamp, and the reserve can be explored thoroughly in about 45 minutes (access is free). Nearby the Pupu Walkway, which starts at the end of Pupu Valley Road, retraces an old gold-mining water race.

The clear waters of Pupu Springs give exceptional visibility

Vineyards stretch as far you can see; right, Montana Brancott Winery

WAIRAU VALLEY

World-class wineries in New Zealand's largest wine-growing region.

More than 50 wineries operate in the sunbaked Marlborough region, concentrated in the fertile Wairau Valley and producing highly acclaimed Chardonnay, Riesling, Cabernet Sauvignon, Merlot, Pinot noir, sparkling *méthode champenoise* and some of the best Sauvignon blanc in the world. Montana sowed the first seeds of success in the early 1970s and is now the largest winery in the country, joined by a host of other international names and providing a major national export industry.

Like Hawke's Bay in the North Island, the wineries have been quick to take advantage of the influx of summer visitors. Most offer tours, tastings (free or inexpensive) and good restaurants. The vineyards may lack the architectural splendour or variety of Hawke's Bay (▷ 79), but the wine itself is outstanding.

TOURING THE AREA

Several excellent tours offer full- or half-day overviews of the whole Wairau Valley area, taking in the pick of the crop and the widest variety of wine types. There is always an informative commentary on offer—and often a lunch stop, too. If you have particular tastes, many tour operators will create a personal itinerary; and if you wish to explore by yourself there are plenty of maps and leaflets available at the visitor information office. Most of the wineries are located off SH6, west of Blenheim, and the best time of year to visit them is in April, when the vines are ripe for the picking.

Montana Brancott Winery, at Riverlands on Main South Road (SH1) just south of Blenheim (▷ 111), started it all and is well worth visiting (daily 9–5). It is the central venue for the famous Wine Marlborough festival, held in February (▷ 194), where you can sample more than 150 wines.

In addition to wineries there are distilleries, breweries and orchards in the Wairau Valley, producing everything from liqueurs and fruit wines to olive oil. Prenzel Distillery on Sheffield Street, Riverlands Estate is the country's first commercial fruit distillery, with a whole range of products including fruit liqueurs, schnapps and brandies. The Mud House on Rapaura Road (daily 10–5) has an olive shop, crafts, a coffee house and a restaurant.

RATINGS
Good for food	●●●
Specialist shopping	●●●●
Value for money	●●

BASICS

✚ 321 H11

ℹ Sinclair Street, Blenheim, tel 03-577 8080; summer daily 8.30–6.30; winter Mon–Fri 9–5.30, Sat, Sun 9–4

🚌 Services to Blenheim from Christchurch, Nelson and Picton

🚉 Services to Blenheim from Christchurch and Picton

✈ Airport on Middle Renwick Road, 7km (4 miles) west of Blenheim

www.winemarlborough.net.nz

TIPS

● The visitor information office produces a *Wines and Wineries of Marlborough* wine trail map and a broadsheet called *The Marlborough Wine Region*.

● Detailed information about New Zealand wines can be found in the magazine *Cuisine Wine Country*, available in most bookshops and magazine outlets.

CANTERBURY AND THE WEST COAST

From the expansive farms of the Canterbury Plains the region rears up into the jagged peaks of the Southern Alps. Glaciers are the attraction on the west coast, and the star of these great mountains is Mount Cook/Aoraki. Christchurch—the Garden City—is the South Island's largest settlement.

MAJOR SIGHTS

Heading towards the Southern Alps and Arthur's Pass on the TranzAlpine scenic rail route from Christchurch

Lake Brunner, the West Coast's biggest area of fresh water

ARTHUR'S PASS

323 F13 • SH73, tel 03-318 9211 • Services from Christchurch and Greymouth • TranzAlpine service from Christchurch and Greymouth • www.doc.govt.nz

At the northern edge of Craigieburn Forest Park, road and rail penetrate the vast, open-braided Waimakariri River valley before entering Arthur's Pass National Park. From there it is a short drive to the tiny alpine outpost of Arthur's Pass, 924m (3,031ft) above sea level.

Arthur Dudley Dobson, a pioneer surveyor, first explored the route to the west coast via the east Waimakariri and west Otira river valleys in 1864. A road based on his observations was built within a year; a rail link for the coal and timber trade took another 60 years to complete. To the north, the impressive Otira Viaduct gives a sense of the scale of the engineering challenges.

ARTHUR'S PASS NATIONAL PARK

323 F13 • See Arthur's Pass, above

This area of 114,500ha (282,930 acres) extends from Harpers Pass in the northern Southern Alps, to the mountains around the head of the Waimakariri and Otira rivers. Designated a national park in 1929, it embraces mountain ranges, gorges and braided river valleys. One of the highest mountains is 2,270m (7,447ft) Mount Rolleston, southwest of Arthur's Pass. In the eastern part of the park the forests are almost entirely made up of mountain beech, while to the west, on the other side of the Great Divide, the vegetation is more complex, with a variety of podocarp species, beech, kamahi and kaiwakawaka. Many indigenous alpine plant species thrive above the treeline. The most notable native bird is the green mountain parrot, the kea, which may well fly down to greet you and relieve you of your sandwiches (and your vehicle of anything flexible, from window seals to wipers).

The park has a network of tracks. Braided rivers and their tributaries are notorious for flash floods, so take extra care.

BANKS PENINSULA

See page 122.

CHRISTCHURCH

See pages 124–129.

GERALDINE

323 E15 • Corner of Cox and Talbot streets, tel 03-693 1006

Set among the Four Peaks and Peel Forest Mountain ranges, this pleasant country town has a lively arts and crafts community and two museums. The Vintage Car Club and Machinery Museum on Talbot Street (daily 10–4) houses cars and tractors dating back to 1900, and some notable aircraft. A small town museum is on Cox Street (Mon–Sat 10–12, 1.30–3.30, Sun 1.30–3.30) in the 1885 former Town Board office. The town's most unusual attraction is found in the back room of a sweater shop. The shop, called the Giant Jersey, claims to have the biggest sweater in the world: a faithful copy of the Bayeux Tapestry made from a glittering mosaic of more than two million tiny pieces of spring steel, the on-going work of enthusiast Michael Linton. There are good walks in the Talbot Forest Scenic Reserve.

GREYMOUTH

320 E12 • Corner of Mackay and Herbert streets, tel 03-768 5101 • Mackay Street • TranzAlpine service from Christchurch • www.greydistrict.co.nz

Greymouth is the west coast terminus of the spectacularly scenic TranzAlpine rail journey from Christchurch across the Great Divide and the northern ranges of the Southern Alps. The town was founded during the gold rush, and continued to prosper thanks to the coal and timber industries and its status as the west coast's principal port. The region's mining and nautical past is explored at the History House Museum on Gresson Street (Mon–Fri 10–4).

The Grey River was a famous source of greenstone (pounamu), or New Zealand jade, which the Maori sought out. The Jade Boulder Gallery on Guinness Street (Oct–end Apr daily 8.30am–9pm; May–end Sep daily 8.30–5) has a range of crafted greenstone jewels and sculptures, a Jade Discovery Walk, master sculptors at work and a huge, river-polished jade boulder. Also worth a look is the Left Bank Art Gallery on Tainui Street (Nov–end Apr Mon–Fri 10–5, Sat, Sun 10–3; May–end Oct Tue–Sat 10–4), showing the work of west coast artisans in a variety of media.

Shantytown, off SH6 (Rutherglen Road) 11km (7 miles) south of Greymouth (daily 8.30–5), is a re-created 1880s gold-mining settlement complete with shops, bank, saloon, jail, a working sawmill and a steam train which runs daily (9.45–4). You can also try your hand at gold-panning or even tie the knot in the original church.

Lake Brunner (Moana), 37km (23 miles) east of Greymouth, is the west coast's largest lake and one of the prettiest, offering fishing and other water-based activities. Watch for the beautiful white herons (kotuku), which visit outside the summer breeding season.

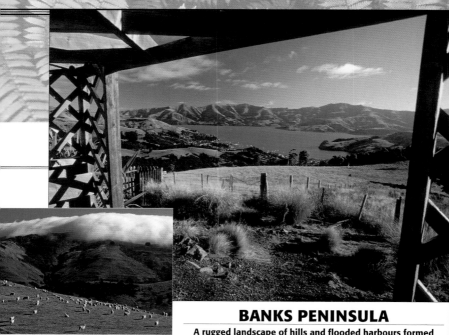

Top, view from the Akaroa Heritage Path
Above, sheep graze the hill pastures of the peninsula

RATINGS

Historic interest	●●●
Outdoor pursuits	●●●●
Photo stops	●●●●

BASICS

⊞ 323 G14

🛈 80 rue Lavaud, Akaroa, tel 03-304 8600; 20 Oxford Street, Lyttelton, tel 03-328 9093; daily 9–5

🚌 Lyttelton: 28 from the Bus Exchange, Christchurch; Akaroa: daily shuttles from Christchurch

www.akaroa.com
Informative and accessible site with local places to stay and eat, events and peninsula map.

TIP

● Staff at the Akaroa information office have local knowledge and can direct you to the peninsula's more remote places.

BANKS PENINSULA

A rugged landscape of hills and flooded harbours formed by two violent volcanic eruptions.

Like the bulb on a jigsaw piece, Banks Peninsula juts out into the Pacific Ocean from Christchurch (▷ 124–129). Its largest harbours are Lyttelton to the north and Akaroa to the south. Akaroa is its main settlement. It has refreshing hill and coastal scenery, historic sites and activities that include cruising and looking for the world's smallest and rarest dolphin, the Hector's dolphin. Captain Cook was the first European to discover the peninsula, but he charted it as an island, naming it after his ship's naturalist, Sir Joseph Banks.

LYTTELTON

Lyttelton, on the opposite side of the volcanic crater of Lyttelton Harbour, is only 12km (7 miles) from Christchurch via the Lyttelton Tunnel. Explorers Robert Falcon Scott and Ernest Shackleton used the port as a base during their Antarctic expeditions, and relics from these heroic times can be seen in the Lyttelton Museum on Gladstone Quay (Tue, Thu, Sat, Sun 2–4). The Lyttelton Timeball Station, high on the hillside off Sumner Road (Wed–Sun 10–5), is the only survivor of three timing contraptions built in New Zealand to aid mariners' calculations of longitude.

Rapapa Island was originally a Maori *pa* and subsequently the base of Fort Jervois, built in 1886 to repel a feared Russian invasion. There are daily sailings (Dec–end Mar 10.20, 12.20; Oct–end Nov, Apr 12.20) to Quail Island, a former leper colony and now a refuge for native birds.

AKAROA

Sprinkled with attractive old colonial wooden houses and picket fences, the pretty village of Akaroa has distinctly French roots. In 1835 Jean Langlois established a whaling station at French Bay and, seeing its potential for settlement, made a down-payment on the land with the local Ngai Tahu Maori. French settlers arrived, knowing nothing of the Treaty of Waitangi (which had placed New Zealand under British sovereignty only 13 days before), and were obliged to sell their claims and integrate. The community's rich history is traced at the Akaroa Museum, on the corner of rue Lavaud and rue Balguerie (Nov–end Apr daily 10.30–4.30; May–end Oct daily 10.30–4). **Don't miss** Barry's Bay Cheese factory tours (Oct–end Apr daily).

The thermal reserve at Hanmer Springs offers the indulgence of naturally heated mineral pools in a landscaped setting

Carving greenstone, or pounamu, at Hokitika

HAAST

🔢 322 C14 ℹ️ SH6 beyond Haast River Bridge, tel 03-750 0809 🚌 North and southbound services

The Haast region of South Westland contains some of New Zealand's purest ecosystems, taking in mountains, coastal plains and wetlands, dense tracts of forest, swamps, hidden lakes and beaches. From the north, a lush corridor of coastal forest and the 750m (2,460ft) Haast River Bridge brings you to the splintered settlement of Haast, named after German geologist Julius von Haast, who explored the coast in 1863. Several tiny conglomerations make up the community: Haast Junction, Haast Beach, and the remote village of Jacksons Bay. Haast township is inland on SH6.

South of Haast, the unsealed Cascade Road follows the Jackson River valley (a tributary of the Awawata) to tranquil Lake Ellery, then rises to a high point in the valley, where views take in the Cascade Valley and the dramatic glacial sweep of hills to the coast. Inland, the Olivine Range and Red Hills (coloured by magnesium and iron) mark the boundary of Mount Aspiring National Park (▷ 146).
Don't miss at Jackson Bay, the iron-framed grave of Claude Morton Ollivier, who died of pneumonia just weeks after arriving in 1875. The oldest known European grave on the West Coast, it commemorates the first, disastrous attempts at European settlement.

HAAST PASS

🔢 322 C15

From Haast township SH6 turns inland and follows the bank of the Haast River before being enveloped by mountains and surmounting the 563m (1,847ft)

Haast Pass, an ancient Maori greenstone trail plagued by floods and landslips. The first of three waterfalls, Roaring Billy, can be viewed on a short loop walk, and about 25km (15.5 miles) farther on, Thunder Creek Falls drop 28m (92ft) into the Haast River. Beyond are the boulders and precipitous rock walls of the Gates of Haast gorge, which foiled road-building attempts until 1960. Above it, Fantail Falls tumble over a series of rocky steps. From here it is a short distance to the Haast Pass and the boundary of Westland and Otago.

Maori greenstone carving, Hokitika

HANMER SPRINGS

🔢 320 G12 ℹ️ Amuri Avenue, tel 03-315 7128 🚌 Services from Kaikoura and Christchurch

Hanmer's biggest attraction is its Thermal Reserve on Amuri Avenue (daily 10–9). The natural hot springs were first discovered by Europeans in 1859 and became a commercial venture in 1907. Steaming streams connect a series of pools, and the mineral-rich waters range in temperature from a lukewarm 32°C (89.6°F) to a balmy 42°C (107.6°F). The alpine resort is a popular base for mountain bicycling and walking, and in winter for skiing.

HOKITIKA

🔢 322 E13 ℹ️ Carnegie Building, corner of Hamilton and Tancred streets, tel 03-755 6166 🚌 Tancred Street 🚗 1km (0.6 miles) east www.hokitika.org

More gold passed through Hokitika in the 1860s than through any other town on the West Coast. From 1865 to 1867, 37,000 prospectors poured in. Today this is the West Coast's craft capital, attracting crowds to watch glass-blowers and greenstone-carvers and to browse in its galleries, concentrated on Tancred Street. To the south the mountain ranges climb steadily towards the peaks of the Westland Tai Poutini National Park and Mount Cook/Aoraki. Hokitika Gorge, 25km (15.5 miles) east of Hokitika, is crossed via a swinging footbridge—an exciting experience when the river becomes a raging torrent.

KARAMEA

🔢 320 F10 ℹ️ Bridge Street, tel 03-782 6652 🚌 Services from Westport and Heaphy Track 🚗 Karamea airstrip

This former frontier settlement, perched on its namesake rivermouth and overshadowed by the peaks of the Kahurangi National Park, is the northernmost town on the West Coast and a base for walkers tackling the Heaphy Track (▷ 112). The limestone caves and arches of the Oparara Basin, 26km (16 miles) north and east of Karamea, are some of the South Island's most remarkable karst scenery. A thick veil of rainforest covers the bizarre formations, creating the eerie mood of a lost world. Bones found in the caves include those of the now extinct New Zealand eagle, with a 3m (10ft) wingspan. Residents include the gradungula spider, the country's biggest, with a leg span of 10cm (4in).

Christchurch

New Zealand's Garden City, where river punts, cricket pitches and parkland serve as reminders of its English roots.

Above, a kea at Willowbank

Stained glass in Christchurch's Anglican cathedral

The snow-capped Southern Alps form the classic city backdrop

RATINGS	
Historic interest	●●●○
Photo stops	●●○○
Walkability	●●●○
Shopping	●●●●

BASICS

✚ 323 G14

ℹ Old Chief Post Office, Cathedral Square, tel 03-379 9629; Mon–Fri 8.30–5, Sat, Sun 8.30–4

🚌 Corner of Lichfield and Colombo streets

🚉 Troup Drive, Addington, 3km (2 miles) from downtown. Services to Kaikoura, Blenheim, Picton and TranzAlpine scenic journey to West Coast (▷ 199)

✈ 12km (7.5 miles) northwest of city

www.christchurchnz.net
News, events, visitor information, weather reports, a video intro-duction to Christchurch, photo gallery and maps.

Opposite, roses flourish in the Botanic Gardens, Hagley Park

Right, a seagull rests on the statue of John Robert Godley (1814–61), founder of Christchurch, outside the cathedral

SEEING CHRISTCHURCH

Christchurch, the largest city in the South Island, has a winning combination of cosmopolitan vivacity, quiet charm and a proud cultural and architectural heritage. Its heart is around Cathedral Square, to the west of the immense, tree-lined Hagley Park, and its borders are known as the Four Avenues: Rolleston Avenue, on the eastern fringe of Hagley Park; Moorhouse Avenue to the south; Fitzgerald Avenue to the east; and Bealey Avenue to the north. One of the most attractive features of the city is the River Avon, which winds its way gently through Hagley Park and down-town from west to east. The city is essentially flat, and has a grid system of streets extending in all directions from Cathedral Square, with most good shopping on the north–south Colombo Street. The central area is easily negotiable on foot.

HIGHLIGHTS

ARTS CENTRE

✚ 127 D3

The lively Arts Centre on Worcester Boulevard occupies the original site of the University of Canterbury. The Gothic-revival buildings now house arts and crafts workshops, galleries, sales outlets, theatres, cinemas, cafés, restau-rants and bars. There is a weekend craft market and local entertainment, including buskers. Historical features include the 'den' of physicist Ernest Rutherford (1871–1937), the Great Hall, with its stained-glass windows, and the Townsend Observatory.

AVON RIVER

✚ 126 C3

This pretty river meanders from the northwest tip of the Four Avenues through Hagley Park, the Botanic Gardens and downtown, before continuing through the city's eastern suburbs to the sea. You can feed the ducks, and go punting from the eastern bank, just beyond Cathedral Square and beside the Worcester Street Bridge (summer daily 9–6; winter daily 10–4). Across the bridge and on the right,

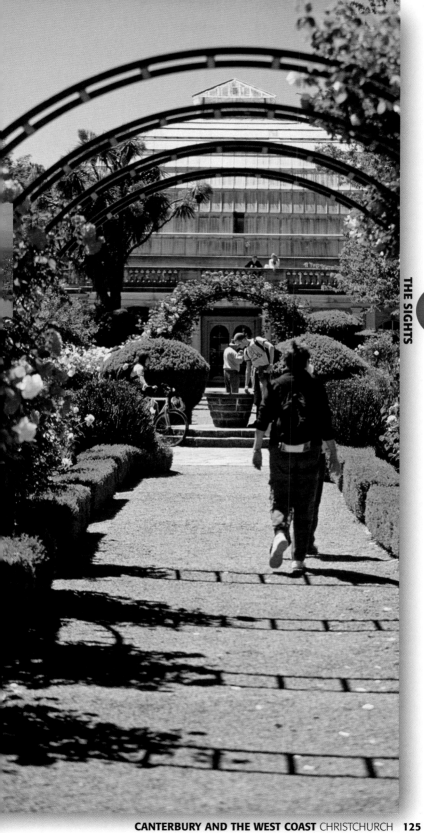

CHRISTCHURCH

0 ___ 400 m
0 ___ 400 yds

Rhodes
Hewitts
Clissold
MILL
CARLTON

BE

PARK
TER

Millbrook
Reserve

Little Hagley
Park

Mona
Vale

Christchurch Airport,
International
Antarctic Centre,
Hägglund Ride,
Orana Wildlife Park,
Willowbank Wildlife Reserve

Christchurch Girls'
High School

HARPER AVENUE

Hagley Golf Course

Matai East

KILMARNOCK

Clubhouse

Hagley Park

Victoria
Lake

Albert
Lake

Ayr

Riccarton Bush,
Riccarton House

RICCARTON

Croquet
Field

Tennis
Courts

Bartlett

Bowls
Field

Christ's
College

McDougall
Art Gallery

Tennis
Courts

Botanic
Gardens

Canterb
Muse

Freyberg

RICCARTON

AVENUE

Avon

Christchurch
Hospital

Christs College
Sports Ground

P

Mayfair
Airforce World,
Railway Station

BLENHEIM

Christchurch
Hospital

Canterbury
Brewery

Hagley
Community
College

Netball
Courts

HAGLEY

AVENUE

Selwyn

Waller

Stewart

Balfo

Horatio

MOORHOUSE AVENUE

A   B   C

DEANS AVENUE
DEANS AVENUE

THE SIGHTS

TIP

- If you're driving it's a good idea to park free south of Moorhouse Avenue (the old rail station and Hoyts 8 Cinema), then catch the free shuttle to the heart of the city.

farther up Worcester Street, is the Christchurch Art Gallery Te Puna O Waiwhetu (Thu–Tue 10–5, Wed 10–9), designed to evoke the river—but dubbed by locals 'a warehouse in a tutu'. More than 3,000sq m (32,292sq ft) of exhibition space are devoted to New Zealand artists such as Charles Goldie and Ralph Hotere, as well as contemporary artworks and national and international shows.

CATHEDRAL SQUARE

➕ 127 E3 🚌 12, 20, 33

Dominated by its Gothic-revival Anglican cathedral, Christchurch's main square underwent a facelift in the late 1990s, resulting in a profoundly controversial display of sharp angles and steel-and-concrete façades. The cathedral itself (tours Mon–Fri 11, 2, Sat 11, Sun 11.30) has an unusual interior design combining Maori and

Striking modern architecture in the heart of the city

Punting on the Avon reveals the city's English origins

The grand Edwardian mansion of Riccarton House

MORE TO SEE

MONA VALE

➕ 126 A1 ✉ 63 Fendalton Road
☎ 03-348 9660 🕐 Summer daily 9.30–4; winter daily 10–3. Gardens: daily dawn–dusk 🎟 Free 🅿
🚌 Airport bus, 9

In 1905 a beautiful Elizabethan-style homestead was built in 5ha (12 acres) of grounds by Annie Townend, who named it Mona Vale after her mother's birthplace in Australia. The homestead is now a restaurant and café, and the surrounding gardens include a lily pond, rhododendrons, azaleas and exotic trees, all set on the River Avon and accessible by punt.

NGA HAU E WHA NATIONAL MARAE

➕ 127 F2 ✉ 250 Pages Road
☎ 03-388 7685 🕐 Mon–Fri 9–4.30; evening performance and *hangi* 6.45
🎟 Free, or by donation; performance from adult NZ$65 🚌 5, 51

The Marae of the Four Winds is the country's largest *marae*, with a beautifully constructed meeting house complete with green-stone-inlaid steps, which should be rubbed for good luck. Guided tours introduce you to Maori culture, and you can stay to experience the evening perform-ance and *hangi* (feast).

European styles, and its spire can be climbed in part, offering a panoramic view of the city.

Two notable characters inhabit the square, one permanently and the other between November and March. The former is the statue of founding father John Robert Godley; the latter is the Wizard, a local eccentric who wears a pointed hat and has been entertaining the masses with his views on life, the universe and everything for decades. The Four Ships Court, a memorial to the first four immigrant ships, stands outside the 1879 Old Chief Post Office (now the i-SITE visitor information office). The tall cone sculpture was commissioned for the millennium celebrations. Guided walks of the city leave from the southeast corner of the Square (Oct–end Apr 10am, 1pm; May–end Sep 1pm).

HAGLEY PARK

➕ 126 B2 🚌 A, 5, 7, 14, 27, 33

This enormous swath of parkland, covering more than 200ha (495 acres), is divided in two by Riccarton Avenue, and comprises tree-lined walkways, sports fields and, in its central reaches, the well-maintained and varied Botanic Gardens (7–dusk; Conservatory Complex 10.15–4). At the entrance to the Botanic Gardens, on Rolleston Avenue, is the Canterbury Museum (daily 9–5), founded in 1867 and housed in an 1870 neo-Gothic building. The museum's highlights are the impressive Maori collection and the Hall of Antarctic Discovery. Just north of the museum is Christ's College (guided tours Oct–end Apr, tel 03-366 8705), New Zealand's most famous public school, built in 1850. At the southern end of Rolleston Avenue you can hire a punt at the Antigua Boat Sheds, a former boatbuilders' premises dating from 1882.

INTERNATIONAL ANTARCTIC CENTRE AND HÄGGLUND RIDE

➕ 126 A1 ✉ Airport (signposted), Orchard Road ☎ 03-358 9896 🕐 Oct–end Mar daily 9–7; Apr–end Sep daily 9–5.30 🎟 From NZ$30, child (3–15) NZ$20; combination ticket NZ$48, child NZ$36 🚌 A, 10 from Bus Exchange

Since the turn of the 20th century and the days of polar explorers Scott and Shackleton, Christchurch has been an important point of access to the Antarctic (Scott is also commemorated with a statue by

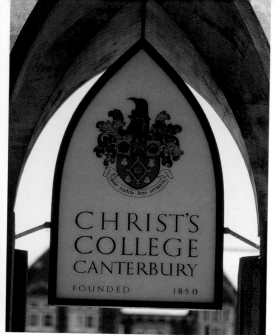

ORANA WILDLIFE PARK
⊞ 126 A1 ✉ 743 McLeans Island Road, near airport ☎ 03-359 7109 ⊙ Daily 10–5 💰 Adult from NZ$19, child (5–14) NZ$7, under 5s free, family NZ$45 🚌 Sunshine Shuttle from Cathedral Square, 10 and 1 www.oranawildlifepark.co.nz
New Zealand's largest captive wildlife reserve is set in 80ha (198 acres) of parkland and has a mix of native and international wildlife, with an emphasis on African animals. Giraffes and rhinos are among the inhabitants, along with the ever-popular inquisitive meerkats, and there is a nocturnal kiwi house.

WILLOWBANK WILDLIFE RESERVE
⊞ 126 A1 ✉ 60 Hussey Road, off Gardiners Road ☎ 03-359 6226 ⊙ Daily 10–10 💰 Adult NZ$20, child (5–15) NZ$10, under 5s free, family NZ$44 🚌 Best Attractions from Cathedral Square
www.willowbank.co.nz
Native wildlife and farm animals are the focus here, with daily guided tours and night and day kiwi-viewing. The reserve has a very successful kiwi-breeding programme. You can also see the cheeky kea (mountain parrots) being fed.

his widow Kathleen on Worcester Boulevard). The Antarctic Centre is a working campus occupied by Antarctica New Zealand (managers of New Zealand's scientific activities in the Antarctic), the Antarctic Heritage Trust and other official groups. The visitor centre gives an excellent introduction to the great white continent, with displays including the Snow and Ice Experience—a chill-inducing room kept at -15°C (-5°F) and decked with manufactured snow and ice. The Hägglund is a tracked vehicle originally used by the US and New Zealand Antarctic programmes at Scott and McMurdo bases. A 15-minute ride takes you to see some of the centre's main facilities before giving you a taste of the vehicle's all-terrain abilities on an adventure course.

RICCARTON BUSH AND RICCARTON HOUSE (PUTARINGAMOTU)
⊞ 126 A2 ✉ 3km (2 miles) west of downtown; entrance to reserve 16 Kahu Road ☎ 03-341 1018 ⊙ Deans cottage daily; homestead Mon–Fri 1–4; tours Sun–Fri 💰 Adult NZ$10, child NZ$5, family NZ$25 🚻 🚌 24
www.riccartonhouse.co.nz
The Riccarton Estate, set in 12ha (30 acres) of parkland, was the home of Scottish pioneers and brothers William and John Deans, the first European settlers on the Canterbury Plains. You can see the faithfully restored original 1843 Deans cottage, in which they first lived, and the grand Victorian-Edwardian homestead built by the next generation between 1856 and 1874. Riccarton Bush reserve, Canterbury's sole remnant of kahikatea floodplain forest, has survived for 3,000 years.

BACKGROUND
Given Christchurch's strong and obvious English links, it is ironic that the first European settlers on the Canterbury Plains were Scottish. Brothers William and John Deans settled here in 1843, calling it Riccarton. Five years later the government bought this and surrounding land for more concerted settlement.
  In 1849 Robert Godley founded the Canterbury Association (mainly worthies from his old university college of Christ Church, Oxford) to establish a new Anglican settlement. In 1850 the first four ships brought 782 colonists to the whaling base of Lyttelton. Despite the collapse of the Association in 1855, the colony flourished and much of its founding English influence prevails.

Above, Christ's College school was built around an open quadrangle

Below, looking for sport in Mona Vale

Lake Kaniere is home to a variety of waterfowl including crested and little grebes, scaup and teal; see also Drive 12 (▷ 236–237)

Glacier-fed Lake Tekapo, milky turquoise from fine rock dust

THE SIGHTS

LAKE KANIERE

✚ 323 E13 ℹ Carnegie Building, corner of Hamilton and Tancred streets, Hokitika, tel 03-755 6166

Swimming, water sports, picnicking and walking are all popular at this summer haven about 14km (9 miles) inland from Hokitika. The surroundings of the lake, which is the heart of the Lake Kaniere Scenic Reserve, can be explored on foot or by car, boat or bicycle. The two best short walks are the Kahikatea Walk at Sunny Bight (10 minutes) and the Canoe Cove Walk (15 minutes)—both include good beaches. If you are feeling more energetic, the Lake Kaniere Walkway (four hours), which also starts at Sunny Bight, follows the western shore of the lake to Slip Bay at its southern edge. The road on the eastern edge gives access to the hardest walk (seven hours): the ascent of Mount Tuhua.

LAKE OHAU

✚ 322 D15 ℹ Northern entrance to Market Place, Twizel, tel 03-435 3124 🚌 Twizel: services from Christchurch and Queenstown ⊠ Omarama **www.twizel.com**

Lake Ohau provides a pleasant diversion off SH8 between Omarama and Twizel. In winter it becomes a ski resort, known for its views and quiet atmosphere. Most activity focuses on Lake Ohau Alpine Village, above the southern shores just west of Lake Middleton, a small sub-lake separated from Ohau by a strip of land. In summer the lake and its surroundings are popular for walking, fishing and mountain bicycling. Six forests lie around its shores, with a number of tracks, access points and campsites.

LAKE TEKAPO

✚ 322 E14 ℹ Kiwi Treasures, Main Street, tel 03-680 6686 🚌 Services from Christchurch and Queenstown

Between Lake Tekapo and Twizel (▷ 133) is the heart of the Mackenzie Country, where lake and mountain ranges give way to the tussock grasslands of the Tekapo River basin. The SH8 delivers you to the southern shores of Lake Tekapo and the settlement of the same name, where the most famous landmark is a solitary stone church overlooking the lake. The Church of the Good Shepherd was built in 1935 in memory of the Mackenzie Country pioneers, who cleared this land of matagouri and speargrass for Merino sheep. Close by is a statue of a sheepdog—a moving tribute to the high-country shepherd's best friend.

If you have time and a robust vehicle it's worth exploring the unpaved roads on either side of Lake Tekapo. The road to the west passes lakes Alexandrina and McGregor before winding its way north to terminate at the Godley Peak Station. On the eastern side the road travels along the lake's edge past the Mount Hay and Richmond

stations before continuing up into the wilds of Macaulay and Godley river basins.

There are plans to open a Mackenzie Heritage Centre in Tekapo.

LEWIS PASS

✚ 320 G12

From Hanmer Springs, SH7 crosses the northern ranges of the Great Divide (Southern Alps) to the West Coast via the Lewis Pass, Maruia Springs, Springs Junction and Reefton. At the top of the Hope River Valley the road skirts the borders of the Lake Sumner Forest Park and begins to follow the Lewis River to its headwaters and the saddle known as the Lewis Pass, 864m (2,834ft) high.

In pre-European times the Ngai Tahu Maori of Canterbury used this route to access the west coast in search of greenstone. Having negotiated the pass on their return, they are said to have killed their slaves and feasted on their bodily parts. A valley known as Cannibal Gorge immortalises this rather grim tale.

The pass itself was named in 1860 in tribute to pioneer surveyor Henry Lewis. The Lewis Pass offers excellent walks, ranging from one hour to several days, and its lichen-covered beech forests are superb. The five-day St. James Walkway begins near the Lewis Pass summit parking area and is best negotiated in summer or autumn.

Just beyond The Lewis Pass, heading west, is the oasis of Maruia Springs, an attractive Japanese-themed thermal resort.

The bronze statue at Tekapo was sculpted by a farmer's wife in tribute to the dogs that faithfully guarded the remote boundaries of the sheep runs

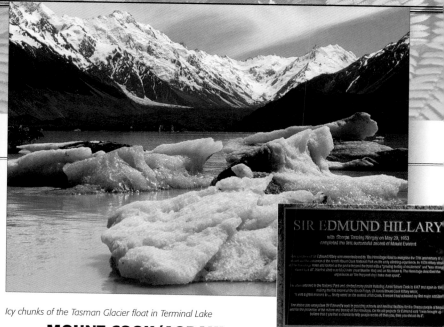

Icy chunks of the Tasman Glacier float in Terminal Lake

MOUNT COOK/AORAKI NATIONAL PARK

A breathtaking array of mountain peaks crowned by Mount Cook/Aoraki. Training ground of mountaineer Sir Edmund Hillary, who conquered Everest in 1953.

This spectacular 70,696ha (174,690-acre) park backs onto the Westland Tai Poutini National Park (▷ 134–135). The 3,754m (12,316ft) peak of Mount Cook/Aoraki—New Zealand's highest mountain—sits at its heart, towering over lower peaks such as Tasman, at 3,498m (11,476ft), and Mount Sefton, 3,157m (10,361ft), and surrounded by another 19 peaks reaching more than 3,000m (9,840ft). Tipping down from this great chancel are the vast and impressive Hooker and Tasman glaciers. The area is considered sacred by Maori, who see Aoraki as a powerful symbol of being, an ancestor from whom the Ngai Tahu people, the tangata whenua, are descended, and a link between the supernatural and natural world.

MOUNT COOK VILLAGE AND BEYOND
The village is the hub for all activities in the region, including scenic flights and heli-skiing. The only distinctive building is the Hermitage Hotel—the third version to have been built. The original, erected in 1884 farther down the valley, was destroyed by floods in 1913; a second, on the present site, was gutted by fire 44 years later.

In addition to the gargantuan vista of Mount Cook/Aoraki and Mount Sefton, the associate glacier valleys are worthy of investigation. Directly north of the Hermitage is the Hooker Valley. To the east, dwarfing the Wakefield Range, is the vast Tasman Valley, with its own massive glacier—the longest in New Zealand. Both act as watersheds that feed Lake Pukaki, and were once full of ice, hence the incredible expanse of boulder fields that precede the lake waters. Fine glacial moraine (rock flour) gives the glacial lakes their exotic azure shade.

Walks within the park take in every variation, from a strenuous climb to the Muller Hut, 1,768m (5,800ft) up on the ridge of Mount Oliver (the first peak in the region climbed by Edmund Hillary), to the 10-minute Bowen Bush Walk, which starts from behind the Alpine Guides Centre in Mount Cook Village and takes you through classic totara forest. Other tracks lead to the Hooker Valley, Muller Glacier and the Tasman Valley.

RATINGS
Outdoor pursuits	● ● ● ● ●
Photo stops	● ● ● ● ●
Walkability	● ● ●

BASICS
322 D/E14

Bowen Drive, Mount Cook Village, tel 03-435 1818; Oct–end Apr daily 8.30–6; May–end Sep daily 8.30–5

Services to Mount Cook Village from Christchurch and Queenstown

3km (2 miles) south of Mount Cook Village, sightseeing flights

www.mtcooknz.com
Wide-ranging site with information on history, activities and amenities in the region.

TIP
● Always seek up-to-date information on track and weather conditions before embarking on walks in the park, and beware of rock falls.

Above and left, tributes to mountaineer and national hero Sir Edmund Hillary, who trained in this area

Layers of limestone at Punakaiki, on the northern West Coast, stacked like pancakes 30 million years ago, now exposed by the sea

The Court House, one of many old timber buildings in Reefton

THE SIGHTS

MOUNT SUNDAY

 322 E14

Mount Sunday dominates the Rangitata valley, in stark contrast to the mountainous skyline of the Southern Alps, and was used as the set for Edoras and King Theoden's grand hall in *The Two Towers*, the second of the *Lord of the Rings* movies. From Mount Somers the road leads west through the Ashburton Gorge towards lakes Camp and Clearwater, before opening into a wide tussock valley. A route west towards the end of the valley and the edge of the Mount Harper Range (Harpers Knob) gives a sudden and dramatic view down into the Rangitata valley and, in the far distance, Mount Sunday's prominent outcrop, 611m (2,004ft) high. Direct access to the hill is forbidden.

PAPAROA NATIONAL PARK

320 F12 SH6, Punakaiki, tel 03-731 1895 Services from Greymouth and Nelson www.doc.govt.nz

Paparoa National Park covers 30,000ha (74,130 acres) on the West Coast, with a predominantly karst (limestone) topography. Its most famous features are the pancake rocks and blowholes of Dolomite Point at the small settlement of Punakaiki. Erosion has produced fluted vertical columns here known as karren, and a 20-minute track loops around lookout points and blowholes. At high tide the spectacle can be amazing, with the ground physically shaking to the thunderous pounding of the waves, and sea spray hissing from the cracks.

Tiromoana, 13km (8 miles) north of Punakaiki, is the northern trailhead for the Inland Pack Track, a 27km (17-mile), two- to three-day route that takes

in the Fox River gorge. This is a system of caves including one 100m (328ft) long, and the 100m-by-30m (328ft by 98ft) Ballroom Overhang, which sits like half an umbrella embedded in the riverbed.

Closer to Punakaiki is the Bullock Creek valley, which leads to Cave Creek—a deeply incised limestone gorge. In 1995 a viewing platform set high above the cavern collapsed, killing 15 students, and as a result there was a complete review of similar structures countrywide.

The area is also home to rare wildlife, such as the Westland black petrel, which nests only on Paparoa's mountains.

PUKEKURA

322 E13 18km (11 miles) south of Ross 03-755 4144 www.pukekura.co.nz

The population of this tiny west-coast settlement is two: Peter Salter and Justine Giddy. The township was originally a stage-coach stop; a saw mill opened in the 1950s and shut down in the 1980s, and in 1993 Salter and Giddy established the Bushman's Centre here. In later years they bought the pub, houses and heli-pad, which lie within the scenic forest reserve. At the heart is an interactive museum, where you can learn about bushcraft and stroke a pig. Other activities based here include horse-trekking, gold-panning and Canadian canoe safaris (▷ 202).

REEFTON

320 F12 Broadway, tel 03-732 8391 www.reefton.co.nz

In 1888 this former gold town at the head of the Lewis Pass (▷ 130) became the first town in the southern hemisphere to receive a public electricity supply

and street lighting. Today Reefton has fine fishing in the local rivers and a wealth of walking and mountain bicycling opportunities, mainly within the 180,000ha (444,780-acre) Victoria Conservation Park, the largest forest park in the country.

On the Strand is the Single Fairlie R28 locomotive, the sole survivor of its type. An easy 40-minute walk crosses the river to the former powerhouse that once proudly lit up the town. Blacks Point Museum, just beside SH7 in Blacks Point (summer, Wed–Fri, Sun 9–noon, 1–4, Sat 1–4), has displays about the region's goldfields.

TIMARU

323 E15 Landing Service Building, 2 George Street, tel 03-688 6163 Services from Christchurch and Dunedin

Timaru, halfway between Christchurch and Dunedin, is New Zealand's second biggest fishing port and makes an enjoyable and interesting stop. The South Canterbury Museum, on Perth Street (Tue–Fri 10.30–4.30, Sat, Sun 1.30–4.30), contains exhibits on local maritime history and Maori rock art, of which hundreds of examples can be seen in the area. It also traces the exploits of aviator Richard Pearse (1877–1953), said to have made the first manned flight in 1903, nine months before the Wright brothers of America (▷ 33). A full replica of his impressive flying machine is on display.

The Aigantighe Art Gallery on 49 Wai-iti Road (Tue–Fri 10–4, Sat, Sun 12–4, gardens dawn–dusk), founded in 1956 in a 1908 building surrounded by a sculpture garden, is one of the best art galleries in the country, with works dating back to the seventh century.

Modern Scandinavian chalet-style accommodation at the holiday centre of Twizel

A fur seal basks on the rocks at Cape Foulwind

At Caroline Bay, to the north of the town centre, there's a beach formed in 1877 by land reclamation and harbour development, which provides the focus for the popular Summer Carnival.

TWIZEL

🚌 322 D15 ℹ️ Northern entrance to Market Place, tel 03-435 3124
🚌 Outside information office; services from Christchurch and Queenstown
www.twizel.com

Right in the heart of the Mackenzie Basin stands the rather featureless holiday centre of Twizel, a former hydroelectric-scheme construction town built in the 1970s. Pioneer surveyor John Thompson bestowed the name in tribute to the Twizel Bridge, which crosses the River Tweed on the border between England and Scotland. Twizel's most famous residents are the endangered kaki, or black stilts, which, along with the town's proximity to the Mount Cook National Park, are its biggest draw. Once common in the heartlands and braided-river beds throughout New Zealand, kaki are now one of the rarest wading birds in the world, currently numbering fewer than 100 in the wild. Guided visits to a viewing hide on Lake Ruataniwha, 3km (2 miles) south of Twizel, allow you to view the stalwart survivors and a captive population of 66, bred in enclosed aviaries (late Oct to mid-Apr, daily; winter by prior arrangement only).

WAITAKI VALLEY

🚌 325 E16

From Oamaru, SH83 turns through this pretty valley on its way to Omarama, Mackenzie Country and Mount Cook/Aoraki. Its lakes and the Waitaki River are

regulated by an extensive system of hydroelectric dams, and activities include fishing and water sports on lakes Benmore and Aviemore, gliding from Omarama airfield and winter skiing at Lake Ohau (▷ 130). The Clay Cliffs, between Omarama and Twizel, echo the bizarre eroded rock and gravel formations of the Pinnacles in the Wairarapa, North Island (▷ 106).

Travelling from east to west the first settlement of any significance is Duntroon. With the discovery of gold in 1868, the town enjoyed a very brief boom before the diggings proved a failure, earning them the label 'poor man's field'. After a return to relative obscurity, there was more excitement with the discovery of a quartz reef between the Maerewhenua and Otekaike rivers in 1870, but, like the gold, its extraction was short-lived. Duntroon is now a small farming settlement with a number of amenities, activities and scenic attractions. The Elephant Rocks, reached from Livingstone Road, near the Maerewhenua River Bridge, are unusual limestone outcrops, and there are Maori rock drawings at Takiroa, on the other side of the Maerewhenua valley, dating back more than 1,000 years.

West of Duntroon are Lake Aviemore, whose dam has a

1km- (0.6-mile) long fish-spawning race used by up to 3,000 adult trout at a time; and Lake Benmore, with the biggest dam in New Zealand.

WESTLAND TAI POUTINI NATIONAL PARK

See pages 134–135.

WESTPORT

🚌 320 F11 ℹ️ 1 Brougham Street, tel 03-789 6658 🚌 Services from Greymouth and Nelson ✖️
www.westport.org.nz

The West Coast's oldest town has a long main street fed by a flat expanse of orderly blocks and wide roads, and is most often used as an overnight base before heading north to Karamea and the Heaphy Track or south towards Greymouth. The excellent Coaltown Museum on Queen Street South (daily 9–4.30) has a range of displays with an emphasis on coal mining, but also including gold, pioneer and maritime exhibitions. Of note are the simulated walk-through mine and the massive brake drum from the Denniston Incline, with a coal wagon pitched at the incline's 47-degree angle.

Cape Foulwind, 11km (7 miles) south of Westport, is a buttress of land where a fur seal colony thrives on beautiful Tauranga Bay.

Westport's busy main street

Westland Tai Poutini National Park

Forested mountains, deep gorges, coastal wetlands and two magnificent glaciers.

Above, the snout of Fox Glacier Top, heli-hiking on the ice

Sunset reflected in the perfectly still waters of Lake Matheson

Helicopters land visitors on the glaciers

RATINGS	
Outdoor pursuits	●●●●●
Photo stops	●●●●●
Walkability	●●●●

BASICS

✛ 322 D13–14

🅸 DoC Franz Josef Glacier, southern end of Franz Josef, tel 03-752 0796; summer daily 8.30–12, 1–6, winter 8.30–noon, 1–4.45

🅸 DoC Fox Glacier, SH6, northern end of Fox, tel 03-751 0807; Mon–Fri 9–noon, 1–4.30

🚌 Services to Franz Josef and Fox from Queenstown and Greymouth

www.doc.govt.nz
Official Department of Conservation website, covering natural features and visitor information.

SEEING WESTLAND TAI POUTINI NATIONAL PARK

Westland Tai Poutini National Park is separated from Mount Cook/Aoraki National Park (▷ 131) by the jagged summits and peaks of the Southern Alps. To the west of the Alpine Fault the forests and ravines of the Southern Alps are crowned with permanent snow-fields. Among the glaciers they feed are the two most famous: Franz Josef (Ka Roimata o Hine Hukatere) and Fox (Te Moeka o Tuawe), which flow from a height of 3,000m (9,840ft) at over 1m (3ft) a day, down into forest. Each has its own access village, offering a variety of walking opportunities and scenic flights.

HIGHLIGHTS

BRUCE BAY AND LAKE PARINGA

✛ 322 D14 🚌 Atomic Shuttle and Intercity services to Copeland Valley entrance
From Fox Glacier township SH6 winds its scenic way to the most remote region of the west coast—South Westland. Until 1965 the road from Fox was rough and petered out at Paringa, and even now much of South Westland remains unspoiled. South of the heavily forested Copeland Valley, Bruce Bay is a quiet coastal spot where a false gold claim was made by three miners during the rush of 1865. More than 2,000 hopeful prospectors made the long and difficult journey south, and on realising they had been duped went on the rampage, destroying the settlement's makeshift stores and shanties.

SH6 continues south, crossing the Paringa River before arriving at Lake Paringa. The river is the farthest point south that explorer Thomas Brunner reached in his epic 18-month journey from Nelson and the Buller Gorge in 1848—a feat marked by a riverside plaque.

FRANZ JOSEF GLACIER

✛ 322 D14 ✉ 5km (3 miles) south of Franz Josef village along Glacier Access Road
New Zealand's steepest and fastest-moving glacier is a dazzling landscape of ice crevasses, pinnacles, caves and ravines descending almost to sea level through dense rainforest. The juxtaposition of ice and greenery is unforgettable, and provides an ecosystem found nowhere else in the world. The glacier access road runs alongside the cold, grey Waiho River, which appears dramatically from beneath its

face. From the parking area you can walk along the wide, rocky riverbed to within 500m (1,640ft) of the glacier, but to walk on the glacier itself you must join a guided trip (▷ 200). Perhaps the best view of the glacier is from the 280m (920ft) viewpoint on Sentinel Rock, a stubborn remnant of previous glacial erosion, which is easily reached from the main parking area.

FOX GLACIER
✚ 322 D14 ✉ 5km (3 miles) southeast of Fox Glacier village
Many visitors head for Franz Josef and neglect Fox Glacier, but it is no less impressive. Fox Glacier valley and the chilly Fox River, which surges from the glacier terminus, create a significantly different mood, with precipitous, ice-carved cliffs looming over the village parking area. Like nearby Franz, Fox can be explored at its terminus independently, or climbed with a guide.

KNIGHTS POINT AND SHIP CREEK
✚ 322 C14 ✉ South of Lake Moeraki
On the coastline south of the National Park, Knights Point gives spectacular views of sea stacks and virtually inaccessible beaches, and beyond the viewpoint you may see fur seals dozing on the beach. At the base of the hill, about 3km (2 miles) south, a small parking area gives access to Murphys Beach, where, when the tide is out, you can explore the sweep of sand and the rugged coast.

Farther south is the more popular beach at Ship Creek, where several excellent short walks explore the beach, the coastal forest and a small lake between the dunes. In summer it is not unusual to see Fiordland crested penguins coming ashore to their breeding areas hidden in the coastal fringe. Ship Creek was named in memory of a shipwreck on the Australian coast at Cape Otway in Victoria. The *Schomberg* ran aground on her maiden voyage in 1854, and several years later pieces of the vessel washed up here, more than 1,500km (930 miles) away.

BACKGROUND
Franz Josef Glacier was sighted and documented by both Abel Tasman in 1642 and Captain Cook in 1770, but the first thorough exploration was carried out in 1865 by geologist Julius von Haast, who named it for the Austrian emperor. Until 1985 the glacier was receding steadily, but it now seems to be slowing down. Many are worried that global warming will see the glaciers recede at an unnatural rate due to a lack of snow at the summits.

MORE TO SEE

LAKE MOERAKI AND MUNROE BEACH
✚ 322 C14 ✉ 18km (11 miles) south of Lake Paringa
The waters of Lake Moeraki are popular for swimming, kayaking and birdwatching, and its outlet river leads to a wonderful west coast beach. The parking area and trailhead to Munroe Beach are 200m (220 yards) north of Moeraki River bridge. A path takes you through forest to the sands and pounding surf, where, in the breeding season (Jul–Dec) or during their late summer moult, rare Fiordland crested penguins fight their way through the waves to waddle into the bush.

Opposite, waiting for transport
Below, hiking with a guide on Franz Josef Glacier

THE SIGHTS

OTAGO AND THE FAR SOUTH

Queenstown is New Zealand's adventure capital, with world-renowned bungy jumping and jet-boating. The Victorian and Edwardian architecture of Dunedin provides a sedate contrast, with access to the wildlife of the Otago Peninsula. Fiordland, in the far southwest, is the wettest, wildest corner of the country.

MAJOR SIGHTS

Arrowtown's former postmaster's house, now a top-notch B&B

The reservoir of Lake Dunstan generates hydroelectricity

Giant fruit by the town sign indicate Cromwell's claim to fame

ARROWTOWN

⊞ 324 C16 ⓘ Lakes District Museum, 49 Buckingham Street, tel 03-442 1824 🚌 Services from Queenstown www.arrowtown.org.nz

This is the best known of New Zealand's former gold-mining settlements, beautifully set beneath the foothills of the Crown mountain range, with pretty tree-lined streets and historic miners' cottages. The Lakes District Museum, on Buckingham Street (daily 8.30–5), depicts the area's chaotic and feverish gold-mining boom (1861–65), and even rents out gold pans for you to try your luck. At the far end of leafy Buckingham Street, reconstructed mud-walled huts illustrate the hardship suffered by Chinese miners.

BLUFF

⊞ 324 C18 🚌 Services from Invercargill

The small port of Bluff heralds the end of the road in the South Island, and is dominated by its aluminium smelter—a jointly run New Zealand-Japanese project. Most visitors come here on their way to or from Stewart Island/Rakiura (▷ 150), or to photograph the windblasted signpost at the terminus of SH1, which tells them they are several thousand miles from anywhere. En route to the signpost is the quirky Paua Shell House on Marine Parade (daily 9–5), which has become something of a New Zealand legend. Its former owners, Myrtle (who died in 2000) and Fred (who died in 2002) Flutey lined the interior walls with paua shells and amassed a huge collection of other shells.

CATLINS COAST

⊞ 325 C18 ⓘ 4 Clyde Street, Balclutha, tel 03-418 0388 🚌 Services to Balclutha and Gore from Queenstown, Dunedin and Invercargill www.southland.org.nz

The almost impenetrable coastal forests of the Catlins Coast were thought by the Maori to be the home of a race of hairy giants known as Maeroero. Timber-millers began their relentless destruction of the forest from the 1860s, but a few tracts of podocarp and silver woods have survived and this southeast tip, bordered by the Clutha and Mataura rivers, is still a wonderfully remote area with glorious scenery and rich flora and fauna.

Slope Point, the South Island's southernmost point, can be reached from a roadside parking area and has impressive views of the dramatic headlands. Beautiful Porpoise Bay is a superb place to try and spot Hector's dolphins. At Curio Bay, about 500m (545 yards) west, the petrified stumps and logs of a fossilised forest more than 160 million years old scatter the rock platform.

Both Surat Bay, across the Owaka River 2km (1 mile) south of Owaka, the Catlins' largest town, and Cannibals Bay, north of Owaka, are good places to see Hookers sealions. About 3km (2 miles) east of Owaka is Tunnel Hill Scenic Reserve: the tunnel was dug in 1895 as part of the Catlins River branch railway line, which ran

between Balclutha and Tahakopa and closed in 1971.

Just beyond the hill is the turn-off to Nugget Point, best visited at sunrise, when the spectacular rock pillars and outcrops take on an orange glow. The islets and rocky, inaccessible coastline are home to seals, yellow-eyed and blue penguins, sooty shearwaters and gannets.

CLYDE

⊞ 325 C16 🚌 Services from Queenstown and Dunedin

The pretty and historic village of Clyde, backed by Clyde Dam and Lake Dunstan (a reservoir), has several notable buildings dating from the 19th century. On Fraser Street, the Clyde Historical Museum and Briar Herb Factory (Dec–end Apr Tue–Sun 2–4), which began processing local thyme in the 1930s, now displays the original machinery and exhibits on early settler life. The Clyde Stationary Engine Museum, at the former railway station on Fraser Street (Sun 2–4), shows stationary steam engines.

CROMWELL

⊞ 325 C16 ⓘ 47 The Mall, tel 03-445 0212 🚌 Services from Queenstown, Christchurch and Invercargill www.cromwell.org.nz

A sculpture of giant pieces of fruit gives a clue to Cromwell's status as 'the fruit bowl of the south'. Its main point of interest is the Old Cromwell Town Precinct, at the end of Melmore Place, where many restored or reconstructed houses are open for viewing (daily 10–4.30). Former gold-mining sites in the area include the Goldfields Mining Centre, 6km (4 miles) west along SH6 (daily 9–5). It lets you explore historic gold workings, a Chinese settlers' village, gold stamper batteries and a sluice gun.

**BLUFF
NEW ZEALAND**
LATITUDE   LONGITUDE
46°36 min 54 sec   168°21 min 26 sec
SOUTH   EAST

EQUATOR
LONDON 18958 km
15008 km NEW YORK
1401 km CAPE REINGA
HOBART 1680 km
SYDNEY 2000 km
RUAPUKE ISLAND
WELLINGTON 784 km

THE SIGHTS

Dunedin

The South Island's second-largest city, with strong Scottish roots.

Flower stall in The Octagon, Dunedin's central square

A photostop on the scenic Taieri Gorge Railway

Dunedin's university was the first in the country

RATINGS

Historic interest	● ● ●
Outdoor pursuits	● ● ●
Walkability	● ● ● ●

BASICS

✚ 325 E17

ℹ️ 48 The Octagon, below Municipal Chambers Building, tel 03-474 3300; Mon–Fri 8–6, Sat, Sun 8.45–6

🚌 Services from Christchurch, Invercargill, Queenstown and Te Anau

✈️ 27km (17 miles) south of city

www.dunedinnz.com
Well-illustrated site with thorough information on events, transport, dining, shopping and sightseeing.

www.cityofdunedin.com
News, weather and visitor information.

TIPS

● Centennial Lookout and Lookout Point have grand views of the bay and city—reach them via Signal Hill Road, beyond Lovelock Avenue.

● Baldwin Street, off North Road, is said to be the world's steepest street, with a gradient of nearly 1 in 3—a 19-degree angle.

SEEING DUNEDIN

The influence of Scottish architecture is everywhere in this lively and attractive city: grand buildings of stone, built to last and to defy inclement weather. Its streets share the names of Edinburgh's most famous thoroughfares, and presiding over the scene is a statue of one of Scotland's greatest sons, the poet Robert Burns—his nephew Thomas (1796–1871) was one of the city's founding fathers. Princes Street and George Street combine to form the main downtown route, with the open square of the Octagon, surrounded by grand public buildings, at its heart. Dunedin's beautiful backyard, the Otago Peninsula, is where the only mainland breeding colony of albatrosses thrives, along with rare yellow-eyed penguins and Hooker's sealions (▷ 244–245).

HIGHLIGHTS

ARCHITECTURE

During term time, Dunedin's population is boosted by 18,000 students at New Zealand's oldest seat of learning, founded in 1869. The 1906 railway station at the end of Lower Stuart Street is probably the most famous and photographed building in the country, with stained-glass windows, Royal Doulton tiles, mosaics and brass fittings. The New Zealand Sports Hall of Fame, on the first floor (daily 10–4), celebrates the legacy of more than a century of New Zealand champions. Otago University's grand administration building and clock tower on Leith Street (modelled on Glasgow University) is another fine building.

BOTANIC GARDEN

✉️ Opoho Road ☎ 03-477 4000 🕐 Daily dawn–dusk 🎟️ Free
There are many New Zealand firsts in Dunedin, including the Botanic Garden, first laid out in 1914. The 28ha (69-acre) site is split into upper and lower gardens that straddle Signal Hill and specialise in rhododendrons, plants from Asia, the Americas and Australia, native species and winter and wetland gardens. Access to the Lower Garden is via Cumberland Street; the Upper Garden via Lovelock Lane.

OLVESTON HOUSE

✉ 42 Royal Terrace ☎ 03-477 3320 🕐 Daily guided tours 9.30, 10.45, 12, 1.30, 2.45, 4 💵 Adult NZ$14.50, child (school age) NZ$5 🚌 Moana Pool

This Edwardian time capsule was built in 1906 and bequeathed to the city in 1966 by the last surviving member of the wealthy and much-travelled Theomin family. The Jacobean-style 35-room mansion had been left unaltered since the death of its first owner, David Theomin, in 1933, and its library, oak gallery and billiard room give a vivid glimpse of prosperous family life in the early 20th century. Contents include ceramics, carpets, arms, antiques, silverware and art acquired by the family during their travels in Asia and Europe.

CHURCHES

Dunedin's churches are worth more than a passing glance, particularly the Gothic First Church of Otago (1873), on Moray Place, and St. Paul's Cathedral (1915), in The Octagon, which contains the only stone-vaulted ceiling in the country.

THE SIGHTS

OTAGO MUSEUM

✉ 419 Great King Street ☎ 03-474 7474 🕐 Daily 10–5 💵 Free; donation of NZ$5 suggested. Tours (daily 11.30) from NZ$10 ♿
www.otagomuseum.govt.nz

Established in 1868, this museum is one of the oldest in the country, housing a staggering 1.7 million items. Its primary themes are culture, nature and science. The Southern Land–Southern People exhibit, the museum's centrepiece, is designed to reflect the beauty and diversity of southern New Zealand, and there is a hands-on Discovery World for children (fee payable).

OTAGO SETTLERS MUSEUM

✉ 31 Queens Gardens ☎ 03-477 5052 🕐 Daily 10–5 💵 Adult NZ$4, child (school age) free ♿
www.otago.settlers.museum/

The emphasis here is firmly on people and transport. Among the permanent exhibits are a couple of monstrous steam engines, and the temporary exhibitions cover unexpected topics such as Scotland's second national drink—tea. There is also an extensive archive.

BACKGROUND

The largest Maori *pa* in this area was on the Otago Peninsula. Following on the trail of the whalers and sealers, Dunedin's permanent settlement was begun in 1842 by Scot George Rennie, who planned a Presbyterian colony in a New Edinburgh of the South. With the discovery of gold the population exploded, growing by 500 per cent between 1861 and 1865. Dunedin was the largest city in New Zealand by the late 1860s—and its grandest buildings date from this period.

DUNEDIN PUBLIC ART GALLERY

✉ 30 The Octagon ☎ 03-474 4000 🕐 Daily 10–5 💵 Free
www.dunedin.art.museum

Traditional and contemporary art are shown in the country's oldest gallery, including an interesting collection of New Zealand works from 1860 to the present day.

TAIERI GORGE RAILWAY

✉ Departs from train station, Anzac Avenue ☎ 03-477 4449 🕐 Oct–end Apr daily 2.30, also Fri, Sun 9.30; rest of year daily 12.30 💵 Adult from NZ$67

The four-hour Taieri Gorge Railway journey encompasses the history and superb scenery of Otago's hinterland. Completed in 1891, the line negotiates the Taieri Gorge, with 12 viaducts, and leads to the Otago Central Rail Trail.

Opposite, Robert Burns' statue in The Octagon
Above, the extraordinary Tunnel Beach, southwest of St. Clair

Fiordland National Park

●

A vast wilderness area of snow-capped mountains, lakes, forests and fiords.

A helicopter flight offers access into remote Doubtful Sound

Visitors sightseeing from the water in Milford Sound

Mountainous terrain makes this one of the least explored parks

SEEING FIORDLAND NATIONAL PARK

Fiordland National Park, in the remote southwest corner of the South Island, covers 1.25 million ha (3,088,750 acres) and is the largest of New Zealand's 14 national parks. Even when this wettest part of the country is under heavy rain (over 7,500mm/ 300 inches are recorded each year), Fiordland has a moody magnificence, with its high mountains, forested hills and deep inlets. Although the vast majority of the park remains inaccessible, there are more than 5,000km (3,100 miles) of walking tracks. The most accessible of the park's 14 fiords and one of the country's biggest visitor attractions is Milford Sound. For cruises see page 208. See also Lake Manapouri (▷ 144) and Te Anau (▷ 147).

HIGHLIGHTS

DOUBTFUL SOUND

⊞ 324 A16 ⛴ Excursions by boat then bus from Pearl Harbour, Manapouri
www.realjourneys.co.nz

Fiordland's mountain topography is generally lower the farther south you go, and its fiords become longer and more indented with coves, arms and islands. Captain Cook named this Doubtful Harbour in 1770, and did not explore beyond the entrance. It was not until 23 years later that Italian explorer Don Alessandro Malaspina, leading a Spanish expedition, sent a small crew into the fiord.

Doubtful Sound, though not as steep as Milford Sound, offers a sense of space and wilderness, and is the deepest of the fiords at 421m (1,381ft). It has three distinct arms and several superb waterfalls, including the 619m (2,031ft) Browne Falls. At the entrance to Hall Arm is an impressive 900m (2,953ft) cliff. Tours take in the dripping beech forests and a hydroelectric plant, and the sound has its own pod of about 60 bottlenose dolphins.

DUSKY TRACK

🚌 Shuttle services from Te Anau to Manapouri and Tuatapere ⛴ Boat access to southern trailhead from Tuatapere and Manapouri ✈ Floatplane and helicopter services to Supper Cove and Lake Hauroko from Te Anau and Tuatapere
Remote Dusky Sound, at the very heart of Fiordland, is a true wilderness that has changed little since Captain Cook first set foot there.

RATINGS	
Outdoor pursuits	●●●●
Photo stops	●●●●●
Walkability	●●●●●

BASICS
⊞ 324 A17
ℹ Lakefront Drive, Te Anau, tel 03-249 8900; daily 8.30–5.30; DoC, Lakefront Drive, tel 03-249 7924
🚌 Services from Queenstown and Te Anau to Milford Sound
✈ Te Anau airfield between Te Anau and Manapouri; airfield in Milford

www.doc.govt.nz
Basic information on a link from the government's website.

TIPS
● About 30 tour buses regularly make the 12-hour journey to Milford Sound from Queenstown; most run daily in summer from 11am.
● Remember to take insect repellent: the sandflies at Milford are legendary.

Opposite, the regular point of Mitre Peak is Fiordland's most famous landmark

The Dusky Track offers the widest range of experiences of any track in Fiordland, from glacial valleys and densely forested mountains to the possibility of complete immersion in icy water. Both its location and grade of difficulty make it a challenge that should be attempted only by serious walkers and only in summer.

HUMP RIDGE TRACK

Services to trailhead from Tuatapere
Opened in late 2000 and privately owned, the Hump Ridge Track is a 60km (37-mile), three-day, moderate-grade circuit track at the south-eastern end of Fiordland National Park, reached from the western end of Bluecliffs Beach. Its main attractions are a mix of coastal and podocarp and beech forest landscapes. It also takes in four viaducts, including the 125m (410ft) Percy Burn Viaduct, reputedly the largest wooden viaduct in the world. Wildlife to look for includes keas,

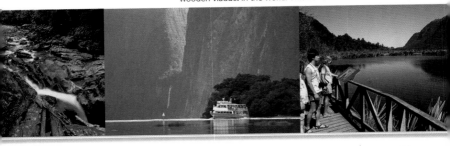

Water tumbles through the Chasm at Milford

Cruise boats make the most of day trips through the fiords

Admiring the view and the reflections at Mirror Lake

bellbirds, fur seals and Hector's dolphins. Boardwalk is laid through the areas most subject to flooding, but always check on track conditions before departure.

KEPLER TRACK

Services to trailhead (Lake Te Anau outlet control gates) from Te Anau   Boat services from Brod Bay
This 60km (37-mile), three- to four-day tramp combines lake, mountain and river valley scenery. After skirting the edge of Lake Te Anau the track climbs to the Luxmore Hut, with one of the best views in Fiordland. From here it negotiates the open tops of the Luxmore Range before descending through silver beech and podocarp forest to the Iris Burn Valley, and back to civilisation via Shallow Bay on Lake Manapouri. At night the forest often echoes with the cries of kiwis.

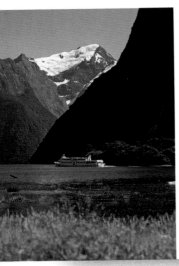

Cruise boats make the remote sounds accessible to visitors

MILFORD SOUND

324 B15   Boat Terminal, tel 03-249 8110
The approach to majestic Milford Sound is an exciting experience, with the mountains closing in on either side of Milford Road as you enter the Homer Tunnel, an amazing 1,200m (3,937ft) feat of engineering. You emerge in the spectacular Cleddau Canyon, where in heavy rain the water gushes from the steep outcrops in all directions, and where the Cleddau River has, over the millennia, sculpted round shapes and basins in the rock. Presently, Mitre Peak, at 1,683m (5,552ft), and Mount Tutoko, Fiordland's highest peak at 2,723m (8,934ft), are in view. Facing Mitre Peak is The Lion (1,302m/ 4,272ft), and behind it is Mount Pembroke (2,045m/6,709ft).

The fiord itself is 15km (9 miles) long and about 290m (951ft) at its deepest, and its mouth is only about 120m (394ft) wide. Cruises along the sound take about two hours. In heavy rains the whole sound can seem like one great waterfall, but by far the most impressive at any time are the powerful 160m (525ft) Lady Bowen Falls, a 10-minute walk from the cruiseboat terminal.

The Milford Deep Underwater Observatory (visits as part of cruise packages or by arrangement, tel 0800-326969) opened in 1995 in the sheltered waters of Harrison Cove, about a third of the way out of the sound on its eastern edge. From its interpretive centre you descend 8m (26ft) into a circular viewing chamber, where you can see at close quarters the very rare black coral (which is actually white)—a species that can live for more than 300 years.

MILFORD TRACK

✉ Independent reservations: 03-249 8514. Guided walks: 03-441 1138/0800 659255 🚌 Services to Te Anau Downs from Te Anau 🚤 Boat services from Te Anau and Te Anau Downs to Glade House (south); from Te Anau and Milford Sound to Sandfly Point (north) ✈ Floatplane services from Te Anau www.doc.govt.nz

Often spoken of as the world's greatest walk, this four-day, 53km (33-mile) walk must be booked (Apr–end Oct). Numbers are limited to no more than 100 people entering the track each day either as an independent or a guided walker, and everyone goes in the same direction from south to north to maintain the integrity of the environment. Highlights include the awesome vista from the top of the McKinnon Pass at 1,073m (3,520ft), the Sutherland Falls (New Zealand's highest at 580m/1,903ft), and walking through lush rainforest and beside Milford Sound at the end of the track. It rains a lot here—over 6m (235 inches) a year, and winter conditions can be treacherous. Always consult the Department of Conservation (tel 03-249 7924) before setting off. Reservation well in advance is essential.

BACKGROUND

Fiordland was gouged out by glaciers in the last Ice Age. Flora and fauna that once lived on the ancient supercontinent of Gondwana still thrive in this remote terrain. In 1986 its role in evolutionary history, along with its outstanding natural features, earned the park the status of a World Heritage Area. In 1990 Fiordland and three other national parks—Mount Aspiring, Westland and Mount Cook/Aoraki—were linked to form the UNESCO World Heritage Area of Te Wahipounamu—South West New Zealand, its Maori name meaning place of greenstone.

The Fiordland National Park is noted for its rainfall—all the better for spectacular waterfalls

Negotiating a swing bridge over a gorge on the Routeburn Track

Curious natural spheres of rock, formed around 60 million years ago, litter Hampden Beach at Moeraki

GLENORCHY

🕂 324 B16 🚹 DoC Visitor Centre, corner of Mill and Oban streets, tel 03-442 9937 🚌 From Queenstown

The tiny former frontier village of Glenorchy lies 48km (30 miles) northwest of Queenstown via the superb Lake Wakatipu scenic drive, and is surrounded by the rugged peaks of the Fiordland and Mount Aspiring national parks, the glacier-fed Rees and Dart rivers and ancient beech forests. A little settlement aptly named Paradise, 20km (12 miles) farther north in the Dart River valley, became a principal filming venue for the *Lord of the Rings* movies as Isengard. Activities available in Glenorchy include jet-boating and horse-trekking, and the village is the main access point for the Routeburn, Greenstone/Caples and Rees-Dart walking tracks (▷ 246).

GORE

🕂 325 C18 🚹 Corner of Hokonui Drive and Norfolk Street, tel 03-203 9288 🚌 Services from Dunedin, Invercargill and Queenstown

Gore, on the banks of the Mataura River, is the Southland region's second-largest town and is most famous for its unusual mix of trout-fishing, country music and its once illegal whiskey-distilling. Attractions include the Hokonui Moonshine Museum and the Gore Historical Museum (Oct–May daily 9–5; Jun–Sep Mon–Fri 9–5, Sat, Sun 1–4), both in the Hokonui Heritage Centre and revealing Gore's days of prohibition and boot-legging. The Reservation (daily 10–5.30), at the top of Coutts Road, has a small menagerie including chinchillas and miniature horses.

INVERCARGILL

🕂 324 C18 🚹 Gala Street, tel 03-214 6243 🚊 Leven Street station ✈ 2km (1 mile) south of city; shuttles www.visit.southlandnz.com

Though not much to look at and sandblasted by the worst extremes of the southern weather, Invercargill is the capital of the richest agricultural region in the South Island. Founded by Scots from Dunedin in 1856 on reclaimed swamp, it is the country's southernmost city, serving a wide farming district.

Its main highlight is the Southland Museum and Art Gallery (Mon–Fri 9–5, Sat, Sun 10–5), housed in a large white pyramid on Victoria Avenue, which includes the excellent tuatara display and breeding project. This reptilian species, older than the land on which you stand, can be seen face-to-face in the Tuatarium; its oldest resident, Henry, is more than 120 years old. Beyond the museum is Queen's Park—80ha (198 acres) of trees, flowerbeds and duck ponds. For a fine view over the city head for the 1889 redbrick Water Tower (Sun 1.30–4.30) on the corner of Gala Street and Queen Drive.

The 30km (19-mile) expanse of Oreti Beach lies 10km (6 miles) west of the city past the airport, and nearby Sandy Point, reached from Sandy Point Road,

Advertising the big attraction in Gore

offers a range of short walks and other recreational activities.

LAKE HAWEA

🕂 325 C15 🚹 100 Ardmore Street, Wanaka, tel 03-443 1233 ✈ 11km (7 miles) east of Wanaka www.lakewanaka.co.nz

North of Wanaka on SH6 towards the west coast is Lake Hawea and the small resort settlement of Hawea. Lake Hawea—like nearby Lake Wanaka (▷ 147)—occupies an ancient glacial valley, and only a narrow strip of moraine known as the Neck separates the two. Lake Hawea is noted for its fishing and delightful scenery, with mountain reflections that disappear towards its remote upper reaches, 35km (22 miles) north of Hawea. The lake level was raised by 18m (59ft) in 1958 as part of the Clutha River hydropower system. Hawea itself nestles on the southern shore on the former site of an important and strategic Maori *pa*.

LAKE MANAPOURI

🕂 324 B17 🚹 Real Journeys, Pearl Harbour, tel 03-249 7416 🚌 Services from Te Anau and Invercargill

Thirty-five islands disguise the boundaries of Lake Manapouri, which is a forbidding 420m (1,378ft) deep. To appreciate its size and complexity you have to get out on the water, which is on the route to Doubtful Sound. Hidden away on the west arm, right in the heart of Fiordland National Park (▷ 140–143), is the country's largest hydroelectric power station, the source of much controversy and around

Tulips in bloom in Invercargill's Queen's Park

10 per cent of the country's electricity. A 2,040m (6,693ft), 1:10 tunnel carved into the hillside allows access to the underground machine hall, where seven turbines and generators are fed by the water penstocks from 170m (558ft) above. The most impressive part is the 9.2m (30ft) diameter tailrace tunnel that expels used water at the head of Doubtful Sound, 10km (6 miles) away.

MOERAKI BOULDERS

✚ 325 E16 ⓘ Corner of Itchen and Thames streets, Oamaru, tel 03-434 1656 🚌 Tours from Oamaru, Dunedin and Invercargill

According to Maori legend, these strange and much-photographed spherical boulders littering the beach at Moeraki, between Oamaru and Dunedin, are *te kai hinaki*, or food baskets and sweet potatoes, washed ashore after a shipwreck. The scientific explanation is that they are septarian concretions—massive rocks left behind from the eroded coastal cliffs. Their formation is described at the Moeraki Boulderpark Visitor Centre, in a building shaped like the boulders themselves, and in an interpretive panel at the parking area, where the path to the boulders starts. Other, smaller boulders can be seen at Katiki Beach and Shag Point, beyond the village of Moeraki.

The small fishing village of Moeraki, 3km (2 miles) from the boulders, can be reached along the beach by foot or via SH1; it offers fishing, swimming, wildlife cruises (to see the rare Hector's dolphin) and pleasant coastal walks, as well as a historic lighthouse.

MOUNT ASPIRING NATIONAL PARK

See page 146.

Yellow-eyed penguins come ashore to their burrows at night

OAMARU

A limestone town of grand architecture, and a haven for rare penguins.

✚ 325 E16
ⓘ Corner of Itchen and Thames streets, tel 03-434 1656; Dec–Easter Mon–Fri 9–6, Sat, Sun 10–5; Easter–end Nov Mon–Fri 9–5, Sat, Sun 10–4
🚌 All major east coast services; summer service (Mon, Wed, Fri) from Mount Cook

www.tourismwaitaki.co.nz
Well-designed website that covers the whole Waitaki district.

RATINGS			
Historic interest	●	●	● ●
Outdoor pursuits	●	●	● ●
Specialist shopping	●	●	

TIPS
● For local crafts and produce visit Harbour and Tyne Market, 2 Tyne Street (Saturday, Sunday in summer; Sunday in winter).
● The Janet Frame Heritage Trail (▷ 17) starts from the Oamaru i-SITE.

Oamaru is an intriguing town on the east coast shores of Friendly Bay. Thanks to the prosperity of the 1860s to 1890s and the discovery of limestone that could easily be carved and moulded, the early architects of Oamaru created a settlement rich in imposing, classic buildings, earning it the reputation of New Zealand's best-built town. Styles range from Venetian to Victorian, and antiques shops, craft outlets, secondhand book stores and cafés add to the appeal. The Oamaru steam train (Sun), operated by the Oamaru Steam and Rail Restoration Society, is worth a look, too. The shiny engine hisses into action beside the visitor office by the harbour. The North Otago Museum on Thames Street (Mon–Fri 10.30–4.30) has interesting displays about Oamaru stone.

SEEING THE PENGUINS

No visit to Oamaru would be complete without seeing its penguin colonies. The town has two species in residence: the little blue (the smallest in the world) and the larger, yellow-eyed penguin. There are two colonies and observation points—one at Bushy Beach, where you can watch the yellow-eyed penguins from a hide for free; and the official harbourside Oamaru Blue Penguin Colony (tel 03-443 1195), which charges a fee for access. If you know nothing about penguins the best option is to join a tour, or to visit the official colony, before venturing out alone. The only time to view the penguins is from dusk (specific times are posted at the colony reception)—at other times they are at sea. There is a large covered stand from which you are given a brief talk before the penguins come ashore and waddle to their burrows.

Diamond Lake is a highlight of the national park

RATINGS

Outdoor pursuits	●●●●●
Photo stops	●●●●○
Walkability	●●●●○

BASICS

✚ 322 C15

🛈 100 Ardmore Street, Wanaka, tel 03-443 1233; summer daily 8.30–6.30; winter 9.30–4.30

🛈 DoC office, Upper Ardmore Street, Wanaka, tel 03-443 7660; daily 8–4.45

🚌 Services to Wanaka from Christchurch, Dunedin and Queenstown; Mount Aspiring Express trailhead connections to Raspberry Creek, Mount Roy and Diamond Lake

✈ Wanaka region airfield 11km (7 miles) east of Wanaka

www.doc.govt.nz
Basic information on a link from the government website.

TIPS

● The park's alpine areas are suitable only for experienced trampers and mountaineers.
● Jet-boat trips are available on the park's larger rivers, such as the Dart and the Wilkin (▷ 207).

MOUNT ASPIRING NATIONAL PARK

New Zealand's third-largest national park, with towering peaks, more than 100 glaciers and unique wildlife.

Like most of New Zealand's majestic national parks, Mount Aspiring has an impressive list of vital statistics. Designated in 1964, the park has been extended to cover 355,000ha (877,205 acres), stretching for about 140km (87 miles) from the Haast Pass to the Humbolt Range at the head of Lake Wakatipu. At its widest point it is 40km (25 miles), and it contains five peaks over 2,600m (8,530ft), including Aspiring itself—at 3,027m (9,931ft) the highest outside the Mount Cook Range.

AWESOME TERRAIN

Glaciers include the Bonar, the Therma and the Volta, and among the wildlife are the New Zealand falcon, the kea and the giant weta. The names associated with the area speak volumes about its terrain: Mount Awful, Mount Dreadful, Mount Chaos, The Valley of Darkness, Solitude Creek and Siberia River are just a few. Wanaka is the main base for trips into the park, and the small settlement of Makarora, about 67km (42 miles) away (almost on the border of the Otago and West Coast regions), acts as the portal to its northern trails and activities.

WALKING IN THE PARK

Mount Aspiring National Park offers endless opportunities for walking and tramping. The 33km (20-mile) Routeburn Track crosses Mount Aspiring and Fiordland national parks between the head of Lake Wakatipu and SH94, the Te Anau–Milford Road.

The walk to Rob Roy Glacier takes one day from the Raspberry Creek parking area in the West Matukituki Valley, along the river and up into the Rob Roy Valley. From here the track follows the chaotic Rob Roy River through beautiful rainforest, revealing occasional views of the glacier above. After about an hour and a half it reaches the treeline and enters a hidden valley rimmed with solid rock walls of waterfall and ice.

Farther up this road, past Glendhu and before the entrance to the Treble Cone ski field, is the Rocky Mountain and Diamond Lake Walk, with grand views of Mount Aspiring and the Matukituki River Valley, Lake Wanaka, and rocks that form unusual mounds and folds across the landscape. It is a stiff climb, but the path is marked and it is definitely worth the three-hour round trip.

Items preserved in the Skippers Park Museum, Skippers Canyon

Above, a meadow full of Californian poppies, Mount Iron, Wanaka
Below, royal albatrosses breed on the Otago Peninsula

OTAGO PENINSULA

🔲 325 E17 ℹ️ 48 The Octagon, Dunedin, tel 03-474 3300 🚌 Tour buses from Dunedin

The beautiful Otago Peninsula extends 33km (20 miles) northeast from Dunedin into the Pacific Ocean. Its star attraction is the breeding colony of royal albatrosses on Taiaroa Head, at the very tip—the world's only mainland breeding albatross colony. The first egg was laid here in 1920; the colony now numbers almost 100 and can be seen from the Royal Albatross Centre observatory (Oct–end Mar daily 9–dusk; Apr–end Sep Wed–Mon 10–4, Tue 10.30–4). Rare Stewart Island shags also breed on the headland. Watch one of the rarest penguin species in the world from the Yellow-eyed Penguin Conservation Reserve or Penguin Place at Harington Point (Oct–end Apr daily from 10.15; May–end Sep daily 3.15–4.45). You also can visit the Department of Conservation hide at Sandfly Bay at dawn or dusk.

Larnach Castle (daily 9–5), a Scottish-style Baronial mansion perched on the highest point of the peninsula off Castlewood Road, is the former residence of William Larnach (1833–98), a politician and financier known for his personal excesses.

QUEENSTOWN

See pages 148–149.

RIVERTON

🔲 324 B18 ℹ️ 127 Palmerston Street, tel 03-234 9991 🚌 Services from Invercargill

Riverton—or Aparima, to use its former Maori name—is the oldest permanent European settlement in Southland and one of the oldest in the country, established in the 1830s. The Riverton Museum, at 172 Palmerston Street (Nov–Easter daily 10.30–4; Easter–Oct daily 1.30–4), houses displays and photos of the early Maori, whaling and gold-mining days, with more than 500 portraits of the early pioneers. The Riverton Rocks and Howell's Point, at the southern edge of Taramea Bay, provide safe swimming, fishing and fine views across to Stewart Island (▷ 150).

SKIPPERS CANYON

🔲 324 C16 ℹ️ Corner of Shotover and Camp streets, Queenstown, tel 03-442 4100

Drivers of rented cars are warned at the entrance to the Skippers Canyon road that their insurance does not cover this route. No wonder, given its rough, pot-holed surface and vertiginous 120m (394ft) drops to the Shotover River below—but it's well worth joining a tour from Queenstown to be driven along this spectacular valley.

The road was funded by taxes raised on gold found in the river, and the remains of the gold-mining town of Skippers can be seen at the head of the canyon. The area's majestic mountains and valleys, terraced by the gold-mining process, were used as backdrops in the *Lord of the Rings* movies.

STEWART ISLAND/RAKIURA

See page 150.

TE ANAU

🔲 324 B17 ℹ️ Lakefront Drive, tel 03-249 8900 🚌 Services from Christchurch, Invercargill, Dunedin and Queenstown ⊠ Between Te Anau and Manapouri

Every summer the township of Te Anau, on the shores of New Zealand's second-largest lake at the edge of Fiordland National Park (▷ 140–143), is inundated by crowds of trampers eager to visit its magnificent surroundings. Lake Te Anau is 61km (38 miles) long and 10km (6 miles) at its widest point. Along its western edge, between the Middle and South Fiords, are the 200m (656ft) Te Anau Caves, whose rock formations, whirlpools, waterfalls and glow-worms can be accessed only on boat trips from Te Anau wharf, which last around 2 hours (several times daily).

WANAKA

🔲 325 C15 ℹ️ 100 Ardmore Street, tel 03-443 1233 🚌 Services from Christchurch, Dunedin and Queenstown ✈ 11km (7 miles) east of town www.lakewanaka.co.nz

The quiet service town of Wanaka borders the very pretty Roy's Bay, which opens out beyond Ruby Island into the southern and indented bays of Lake Wanaka. The lake occupies an ancient glacier bed more than 45km (28 miles) long. The town becomes a popular ski venue in winter.

One of the most immediate ways to get acquainted with the Wanaka area is to make the 45-minute ascent up Mount Iron (240m/787ft), along a well-marked track starting shortly before the township on the main road.

On SH6, by Wanaka airfield, is the Wanaka Transport and Toy Museum (daily 8.30–5), with more than 15,000 items on display. The NZ Fighter Pilots Museum (daily 9–4) gives a fascinating insight into general aviation history, with a good collection of World War II fighters and trainers.

THE SIGHTS

Queenstown

More than 150 activities in a year-round, 24-hour-a-day adventure capital set among mountains and lakes.

Aerial view of Lake Wakatipu and Queenstown

Boutiques and restaurants flourish around Steamer Wharf

The Mall is busy even in winter, when the town is a ski destination

RATINGS	
Good for food	● ● ●
Outdoor pursuits	● ● ● ● ●
Walkability	● ● ● ●

BASICS

➕ 324 C16
ℹ Corner of Shotover and Camp streets, tel 03-442 4100; daily 7–7
ℹ DoC, 37 Shotover Street, tel 03-442 7935
🚌 Services from Christchurch, Invercargill, Dunedin, Wanaka, Greymouth, Mount Cook, Te Anau and Franz Josef
✈ 8km (5 miles) east in Frankton

www.queenstown-nz.co.nz
Excellent site with links to activities, wineries and places to stay.

*Top, Shotover jet-boat ride
Below, bungy jumping*

SEEING QUEENSTOWN

Queenstown is the biggest tourist draw in New Zealand, as one of the top adventure venues in the world. More than a million visitors a year partake in a staggering range of activities, from sedate steamboat cruises to heart-stopping bungy jumps. In winter the walking boots are simply replaced by skis. The town is compact and easily negotiable on foot. The main street for information and activity bookings is Shotover Street; the Mall is the principal shopping and restaurant area.

HIGHLIGHTS

A.J. HACKETT BUNGY AND SHOTOVER JET

✉ The Station, corner of Shotover and Camp streets ☎ Bungy 0800-286 495, jet-boat 0800-SHOTOVER 🕐 Summer daily 7am–9pm; winter daily 8am–10pm 🎟 Bungy from NZ$125; jet-boat adult NZ$95, child NZ$55
www.AJHackett.com; www.shotoverjet.com
The Station is the main pick-up point for these two longest-established activity operators. A. J. Hackett started professional bungy jumps at Kawarau Bridge, 43m (141ft) over the river east of Queenstown, in 1988. Since then he has created the 102m (335ft) Pipeline Bungy over the Shotover River and the 134m (440ft) Nevis Highwire, among others.
Shotover Jet are the only operators to ply the lower reaches of the Shotover River. A 70kph (43mph) jet down the river includes thrilling 360-degree turns.

QUEENSTOWN GARDENS

✉ Marine Parade 🎟 Free
Founded in 1867 on a small promontory pointing out into Lake Wakatipu, the gardens offer some respite from the crowds. There are oaks, sequoias and 1,500 roses planted in 26 named rosebeds. At the entrance is the restored 1865 Williams Cottage.

REMARKABLES LOOKOUT

✉ Ski field road off SH6, 2km (1 mile) south of Frankton

Although it takes a rugged drive and a scramble to get there, the view of Lake Wakatipu and Queenstown from the Remarkables Lookout is worth every rut and step. Check that the weather is clear, wear warm clothes and sturdy walking boots and make sure that your car will survive the 1,500m (4,920ft) climb up the unsealed road to the ski fields; in winter you may need chains. If the ski field is open you can take a shuttle from Queenstown, and in winter you can use the Shadow Basin Chair Lift from the parking area. In summer, follow the path up the slopes behind the main building to Mid-Station, and from there continue roughly in line with the chairlift to its terminus. The lookout is about 200m (656ft) behind and farther up from this point.

SKYLINE GONDOLA

🔢 Brecon Street ☎ 03-441 0101 🕐 Daily 9–dusk 🎟 Adult from NZ$20, child (5–14) NZ$9, under 5s free, family NZ$47 🎒 🍴 🛒
www.skyline.co.nz

A cable car soars up to Bobs Peak, over 450m (1,476ft) above town, where there's a world-class view and a host of activities, including the Ledge Bungy, the Luge, the Sky-Swing, paragliding and helicopter sightseeing. There are also Maori cultural shows (daily from 5.30).

SS EARNSLAW

🔢 Steamer Wharf ☎ 0800-656 501 🕐 Oct–end Apr daily every 2 hours, 10–8; winter 12, 2, 4 🎟 Adult from NZ$40, child NZ$15

It won't take you long to spot the delightful twin-screw steamer Earnslaw plying the waters of Lake Wakatipu from Queenstown Bay. The steamer is named after the highest peak in the region, Mount Earnslaw (2,819m/9,249ft), and was launched at Kingston in 1912. Options include dinner cruises and trips to Walter Peak Station for an insight into farming life.

BACKGROUND

The first European to visit the area was Scotsman Donald Hay, who explored Lake Wakatipu in 1859. Gold was found in the Shotover River Valley in 1862, and within a year some 2,000 hopefuls were camped here. The Shotover is the richest gold-bearing river of its size in the world, but after a decade the gold was exhausted. By the mid-20th century tourism was already taking hold.

Top, thrill-seeking on the Sky-Swing
Above, Queenstown is a good place to catch a Maori cultural performance

TIP
● Despite the wide range of places to stay it is essential to reserve a room two or three days in advance in mid-summer and during the ski season, particularly in mid-July.

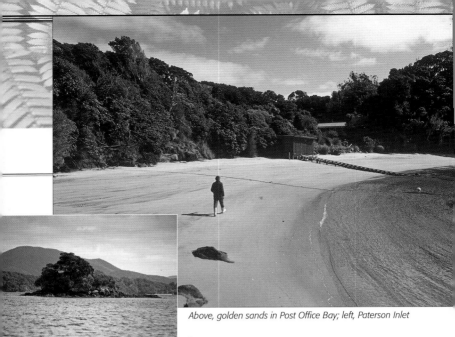

Above, golden sands in Post Office Bay; left, Paterson Inlet

STEWART ISLAND/RAKIURA (RAKIURA NATIONAL PARK)

One of the country's most unspoiled and ecologically important areas—and New Zealand's newest national park.

RATINGS

Outdoor pursuits	●●●●
Photo stops	●●●●
Walkability	●●●●●

BASICS

✚ 324 A15
🛈 DoC Visitor Information and Field Centre, Main Road, Oban, tel 03-219 0009; Mon–Fri 8–5, Sat, Sun 9–4
🚍 Shuttle services from Invercargill to coincide with ferries
⛴ Foveaux Express ferries from Bluff Sep–end Apr 9.30–5; May–end Aug 9.30–4.30; Stewart Island Adventures ferries from Bluff 10am daily
✈ Flights from Invercargill to Halfmoon Bay, Masons, Doughboy, West Ruggedy and Little Hellfire

www.stewartisland.co.nz
Straightforward site packed with information on walks, activities, shops, eateries and wildlife, including a list of resident birds.

www.doc.govt.nz
Basic information on a link from the government website.

TIP

● Only 15kg (33lb) of personal baggage can be flown to Stewart Island/Rakiura, but additional baggage can be taken on subsequent flights.

Lying 20km (12 miles) southwest of Bluff, across the Foveaux Strait, is Stewart Island/Rakiura, land of the glowing skies. In 2002, 85 per cent of the island was designated a national park. The island is home to 21 threatened plants, some of which are indigenous or occur only on the island. Thanks to the absence of trout, there are 15 native fish species, and birds include mollymawks (a kind of albatross), petrels and shearwaters (muttonbirds), many of which breed on the offshore islets in vast numbers. Even on the main island (and fighting to survive the ravages of introduced vermin), breeding birds include two of the rarest and most unusual in the world: an odd and enchanting flightless parrot called a kakapo (of which only about 60 remain), and—perhaps most famous of all—*Apteryx australis lawryi*, better known as the Stewart Island brown kiwi, the largest and the only diurnal kiwi in New Zealand. Other inhabitants include the rare yellow-eyed penguins and Hookers sealions.

OBAN AND AROUND

Oban, on Halfmoon Bay, is the island's principal settlement. A short, steady climb to Observation Rock, up Ayr Street at its southern end, gives great views of Paterson Inlet and the impenetrable forests that deck its southern shores. Oban's Rakiura Museum (Mon–Sat 10–12, Sun 12–2) traces a history of Maori occupation, whaling, saw-milling, gold-mining and fishing. The beach on the waterfront (Elgin Terrace) is a fine place to sit and watch the world go by, play industrial-size chess, or contemplate the many water-based trips available.

WALKS

Stewart Island/Rakiura has 245km (152 miles) of walking tracks, ranging from short walks around Oban to the Northwest Circuit, a mammoth 125km (78-mile), 10- to 12-day tramp around the island's northern coast with a side trip to climb Mount Anglem (980m/3,215ft), the island's highest peak. All tramping on Stewart Island/Rakiura presents challenges, as the island is so undeveloped and wet underfoot. Information is available from the Department of Conservation.

This chapter gives information on things to do in New Zealand other than sightseeing. It is divided into six regions, which are identified on the map on the inside front cover. Within each region, towns are listed alphabetically.

What to Do

SHOPPING

Wits used to quip that they had visited New Zealand, but it was closed. Not any more. Liberalised trading hours mean you can shop every day in the cities and major towns. Although in the tourist resorts you might be forgiven for thinking there is little to buy except fluffy sheep or kiwis dressed in rugby jerseys, shopping in New Zealand can be a rewarding experience, and the quality of locally made goods is generally high. In the cities, you'll find everything from chic boutiques and old-fashioned department stores to lively markets, factory outlets, craft co-operatives and supermarkets. In many places, undercover suburban shopping malls are replacing traditional central-city shops.

made into jewellery. Pendants, associated with status and fertility, are carved from bone and greenstone and often depict sacred animals or spirits. If you buy such an object, it is customary to offer it as a gift. Paua (abalone) is harvested naturally under strict controls and the shells are a by-product. You can buy the shells polished and varnished, or as iridescent jewellery.

ARTS AND CRAFTS
New Zealand culture has a strong basis in craft. Wherever you go, you'll probably find a gallery, craft co-operative or community market selling paintings, pottery, wood or stone carving, hand-knits, weaving or the produce of country kitchens. Places such as the Christchurch Arts Centre (▷ 124) enable you to meet the artist and buy direct. Much of the art reflects the

vibrant blues and greens of the environment. Native woods, such as kauri and rimu, are fashioned into bowls, ornaments and furniture.

MAORI ART
The Maori carvings on canoes and meeting houses depict ancestors and tell traditional stories. Greenstone (New Zealand jade, or *pounamu*)—traditionally used for weapons and symbolic gifts—is now

SHEEP PRODUCTS
In a country with an estimated ten sheep to every person, sheepskin and woollen goods are ubiquitous. Choose from jumpers, hats, coats, gloves, full sheepskins and slippers. The knits are usually home-spun, hand-knitted and high quality. Wool is also made into rugged Swanndri bush jackets and luxuriously soft merino underwear. Lanolin is used in popular skin-care products.

WHAT TO DO

CHAIN STORES

NAME	Menswear	Womenswear	For children	Shoes	Cosmetics and toiletries	Sports equipment and clothes	Accessories	Household items	Books, music and DVDs	Perfume	CONTACT
Canterbury of New Zealand	✔	✔	✔			✔	✔				04-238 4719
The CD and DVD Store									✔		0508-289 223
Country Road	✔	✔	✔								0800-105 655
Esprit	✔	✔	✔	✔			✔				09-271 2472
Farmers	✔	✔	✔	✔	✔			✔		✔	09-272 6996
Glassons	✔										03-366 0784
Hallensteins	✔										09-306 2500
Kimberleys		✔									0800 401 701
Kumfs				✔							09-633 2000
Line 7	✔	✔									09-308 7700
Living and Giving								✔			0800-548 464
Michael Hill Jeweller							✔				09-430 4810
Overland Footwear				✔							0800-OVERLA
PostiePlus	✔	✔									03-339 5700
Smiths City						✔		✔			03-983 3000
The Warehouse	✔	✔	✔	✔	✔	✔	✔	✔	✔	✔	09-489 7000
Whitcoulls									✔		0800-377 831

CLOTHING

You will see the All Black rugby jerseys, made by Adidas, wherever you go, and the original Canterbury Clothing Company (CCC) jerseys worn by other international sides are excellent quality cotton. The company also makes leisurewear, and has stores up and down the country and a factory shop in Christchurch. Christchurch is a good place for all types of outdoor adventure clothing and high-tech sports gear.

New Zealand fashion designers are making a name for themselves and their designs are often available here at a much better price than overseas. Look out for labels such as Zambesi, Karen Walker and Kate Sylvester. Some designers have their own boutiques, but larger cities also have fashion quarters that are worth exploring—try Newmarket in Auckland, Cuba Street in Wellington and High Street in Christchurch.

WINE AND FOOD

New Zealand is best known for Marlborough Sauvignon blanc, but the country also produces other excellent and distinctive wines, including Pinot noir, Chardonnay, Riesling, red blends and sparkling wines. You can buy wine in supermarkets, but you'll get a better range at specialist stores such as the Glengarry chain in Auckland and Wellington and Vino Fino in Christchurch. Many wines are made in such small quantities that they may be available only at restaurants or from the winery itself.

Most New Zealanders shop for food at the supermarket, but the quality is often better and the produce fresher at specialist stores such as the Auckland Seafood Market and Moore Wilson Fresh in Wellington. In the country, buy from roadside stalls and farms selling local produce. Native flower honeys, such as rata and manuka, make attractive gifts. Kiwifruit (zespri) and other fruits are made into chocolates and preserves.

OPENING HOURS

● Most shops open Monday to Saturday 9 to 5 or 5.30pm and have one late shopping night (usually Friday). In larger places and tourist areas, many open on Sunday.
● Large mall multi-complexes open daily.
● Larger supermarket chains open daily 8am to 9pm at least, some 24 hours, and the small convenience stores known as 'dairies' often open until 10 or 11pm.

PAYMENT

Most city shops accept credit cards and take EFTPOS transactions. You may have to pay cash in rural areas and at markets.

TAX REFUNDS

Goods posted direct to overseas destinations are free of the 12.5 per cent GST tax. Many stores offer mailing and shipping services.

WHAT TO DO

In addition to countless individual boutiques and specialist shops, New Zealand has some chain stores, including well-known American names. The chart below gives details of some of them, stating the number of branches each chain has in the country and the telephone number of the main store or head office.

NUMBER OF SHOPS	DESCRIPTION	WEBSITE
14	Rugby shirts, rugby boots and activewear for men, women and children	www.canterburyofnz.com
25	CDs, DVDs, music accessories	www.thecdanddvdstore.co.nz
6	Classic, elegant clothing for men, women and children	www.countryroad.com.au
8	Smart and sporty casual clothing for men, women and children	www.esprit.com
55	Department store selling clothing, accessories, cosmetics and household items.	www.farmers.co.nz
30	Casual fashion for women	www.glassons.co.nz
52	Reasonably priced clothing for men	www.hallensteins.co.nz
14	Fashion knitwear for women	www.kimberleysfashions.com
17	Shoes and boots for women	www.kumfs.com
15	Nautically inspired casual clothing, accessories, America's Cup gear	www.line7.co.nz
9	Household items and gifts	www.livingandgiving.co.nz
50	Mid-priced jewellery	www.michaelhill.co.nz
28	Fashion shoes and boots for women and men	www.overlandfootwear.co.nz
70	Inexpensive clothing for women and men	www.postieplus.co.nz
17	Department store	www.smithscity.co.nz
88	Discount department store	www.thewarehouse.co.nz
81	Books, magazines, cards, videos, DVDs, stationery, artists' materials	www.whitcoulls.co.nz

ENTERTAINMENT

New Zealand has a strong musical culture, both from its Maori roots and from its Pacific Island and European immigrants. Maori history is told through song and story, with games and dances originally devised to train and support warriors. The culture of Kapa Haka is taught in schools and contested in competitions. You can experience a version of it in concert parties in Rotorua and most large cities. Auckland's Pacific Island cultures are expressed in the Pasifika festival (▷ 171). Choral singing is particularly strong in Christchurch, while Dunedin celebrates its Scottish roots in Burns' Night festivities.

Many New Zealand cities have attractive Victorian theatres and modern venues hosting concerts and shows. Drama, orchestral concerts, ballet, dance, comedy, rock and jazz are all well represented, including tours by international performers. In rural New Zealand, people are used to making their own entertainment through amateur theatrical societies, choirs and local DJs.

Pipe bands are a tradition introduced by Scottish settlers

DRAMA
The Auckland Theatre Company lacks a home venue and performs in various places. Wellington has a lively drama scene, with professional companies performing at Downstage, Circa and the alternative Bats, as well as touring shows. Christchurch's Court Theatre and Dunedin's Fortune Theatre are both professional companies presenting repertory seasons.

BALLET AND CONTEMPORARY DANCE
The Royal New Zealand Ballet Company (www.nzballet.org.nz) is based at the Westpac St.

James Theatre in Wellington. It presents classical and modern works, and tours the country. Contemporary dance tends to be presented by troupes created for specific events. A wide range of dance styles is incorporated in festivals such as Wellington's Dance Your Socks Off (www.feelinggreat.co.nz) in September, Auckland's Tempo (www.tempo.co.nz) and Christchurch's The Body (www.thebody.co.nz), both in September or October.

OPERA
The NBR New Zealand Opera (www.nzopera.com) combines companies in Auckland and Wellington. They present several seasons of classic opera a year, to a high standard.

CLASSICAL MUSIC
The New Zealand Symphony Orchestra (www.nzso.co.nz) is based in Wellington at the Michael Fowler Centre. It presents classical and modern works and tours widely. The main cities also support excellent semi-professional orchestras—the Auckland Philharmonia (www.akl-phil.co.nz),

Wellington Symphonia, Christchurch Symphony (www.christchurchsymphony. co.nz) and Dunedin Symphonia, which give regular performances. Christchurch also has a fine choir, the Christchurch City Choir (www.christchurchcitychoir. co.nz), which gives several performances a year. Chamber music concerts by local and visiting groups are arranged by Chamber Music New Zealand (www.chambermusic.co.nz), with nationwide tours.

MAORI PERFORMANCES
Maori groups in the main cities

Traditional posturing for a haka, *with extended tongue*

organise performances for tourists. Check with the visitor information office for details.

CINEMA
Cinemas range from country halls to multi-venue city complexes where the popcorn is pushed as hard as the movie. Most big cities also have art-house cinemas, and most cinemas show first-release films. Many city complexes have daytime showings for parents and children, with prices to match, and specials early in the week. Typical ticket prices range from NZ$8 to NZ$14, with children around NZ$7.

BOOKING TICKETS AND INFORMATION

Ticketek are the main national administrators for information and ticketing; their website (www.ticketek.co.nz) lists up-and-coming shows and events. Other good sources of information are local newspapers—the *New Zealand Herald* in Auckland, the *Dominion Post* in Wellington, *The Press* in Christchurch and the *Otago Daily Times* in Dunedin.

New Zealand has several excellent orchestras

NIGHTLIFE

By world standards, New Zealand nightlife may be nothing remarkable, but there's still plenty to keep you entertained, especially in the cities. Auckland has a humming club life focusing on Karangahape Road, Wellington's Courtenay Place buzzes with night-time activity, Christchurch has the cafés along the restaurant Strip and Dunedin has hangouts popular with students. Queenstown is the place most dedicated to fun, with bars and clubs regularly open until 5am. There are casinos in Auckland, Christchurch, Hamilton, Queenstown and Dunedin, which are open most of the night. By law you need to be 20 to enter a casino, and dress codes are applied.

PUBS AND BARS

Traditionally, pubs in New Zealand were the preserve of hard-drinking men. Such places still exist, typically in rural areas, but in most places you can now enjoy a good beer and conversation in mixed company by a fire in winter or outside in the summer. Some boutique breweries also have their own bars. Irish pubs have become common, and although some are gimmicky, others try to be authentic and have a good selection of beers to match. Many restaurants and cafés have bars with outdoor seating, which are especially popular in summer.

Pubs and bars are generally open from 11am to 10.30pm. They serve a standard range of food, and many have an extended licence to midnight or 3am on weekends. Many also host gigs, some of which don't start until nearly midnight. You need to be 18 and have proof of age.

GAY AND LESBIAN SCENE

Gay sex was only decriminalised in New Zealand in 1986. Although some homophobia still exists, the larger cities are generally gay- and lesbian-friendly.

Gaytravel New Zealand (www.gaytravel.net.nz) and Go Gay New Zealand (www.gaynewzealand.co.nz) give information on gay and lesbian holidays, accommodation, venues, bars and activities, including events such as the Hero Parade (www.gaynz.com) in Auckland and Gay Ski Week (www.gayskiweeknz.com) in Queenstown.

SPORTS AND ACTIVITIES

New Zealanders are avid followers of spectator sports. Sport takes up a sizeable chunk of daily news coverage on television, radio and in newspapers, and armchair enthusiasts can spend all Saturday afternoon tuned into coverage of their chosen sports. As for activities—New Zealanders love the great outdoors. The vast range of outdoor pursuits available is a big attraction to visitors. The major cities are at or near the sea, and the countryside is never far away. Many Kiwis spend their leisure time at the family *bach* (holiday home) by the sea or in the mountains, tramping (hiking) in the bush (native rainforest), fishing from the family boat or gathering shellfish.

SPECTATOR SPORTS

Rugby is the national game, followed obsessively by young and old alike, who don team jerseys and travel to watch

The Coast to Coast is the ultimate endurance race

their heroes in action. Soccer, by contrast, has never really taken off. In summer, cricket is the major sport, and horse racing, motor sport and netball are all popular, New Zealand having won international events in these disciplines. The country also gets behind the national sailing team during the America's Cup, particularly when the event was held in Auckland. New Zealand also prides itself on mounting some of the world's toughest multi-sport events.

CRICKET

Cricket is popular at both local and national levels. During the

summer, city parks and rural domains (parks) are filled with white-clad players and the thwack of bat on ball. New Zealand Cricket (www.nzcricket.co.nz) operates the New Zealand cricket team, known as the Black Caps, organising test tours and one-day internationals with other nations. It also organises domestic cricket matches, including the State Championship first-class competition and the State Shield one-day competition. On sunny summer days, crowds of New Zealanders equipped with rugs, food and drinks settle on grassy embankments to watch the game, or tune in to the radio to keep score wherever they are on holiday.

ENDURANCE EVENTS

Held in February, the Coast to Coast (www.coasttocoast.co.nz, ▷ 15) across the Southern Alps is one of the most gruelling and well-known multi-sport events in the world.

In March, the Ironman New Zealand Triathlon (www.ironman.co.nz) draws crowds in Taupo to cheer on the more than 1,450 competitors from 39 countries who swim 3.8km (2.4 miles) in the lake, cycle 180km (112 miles) and run 42km (26 miles) through the town.

Travel in the vicinity is likely

to be slow on competition days, as roads may be partly closed.

GOLF

With 400 golf courses—more per person than anywhere else in the world—New Zealand has a full calendar of events at both amateur and professional levels. New Zealand Golf (www.nzga.co.nz) organises a number of competitions, including the New Zealand Open, held at a different links each year in February. Also held in February, the NZPGA championship (www.pgachampionship.co.nz), held at Clearwater Golf Club in Christchurch, attracts some of the world's top golfers and an estimated 25,000 spectators.

HORSE RACING

Horse racing, in both thoroughbred (the gallops) and harness (the trots) forms, is so popular that even the smallest towns are likely to have a racecourse, and races are held throughout the year. The main events are a great excuse to dress up and drink up: Cup Week in Christchurch in November, which includes the New Zealand Trotting Cup at Addington Raceway and the New Zealand Cup at Riccarton Park; Derby Day at Ellerslie—Auckland Racing Club on 26 December; and the Auckland Cup in March. Details of events are available through Harness Racing New Zealand (www.hrnz.co.nz) and New Zealand Racing (www.nzracing.co.nz). Bookmaking is banned; wagers are totalisator-based and the minimum bet is NZ$1.

MOTOR SPORTS

Motor sports in all their forms have a keen following, with New Zealand having produced world champions in Formula

One Grand Prix and motorcycle racing. Although most spectators watch the races on television, you can catch the sound and smell of live action at raceways such as Manfeild (Manawatu) and Ruapuna (Christchurch), the Rally of New Zealand based in Manukau in April or the Asia Pacific World Rally Championships in Whangarei in May. For details of events, see **www.**nzmotorsport.co.nz and **www.**motorcyclesport. co.nz (V8 Supercars, 2L touring cars and karting).

NETBALL
After rugby, the winter sport with the second-highest player numbers is netball (a game

New Zealand excels at the sport of netball

similar to basketball). It is the number one sport for women and is played extensively in schools. The Southern Sting, based in Invercargill, has been a frequent national champion and the national team, the Silver Ferns, has won the world championship several times. Go to **www.**netballnz.co.nz for details of matches.

RUGBY
Rugby Union is the most popular spectator sport in New Zealand, and the fortunes of New Zealand's national rugby team, the All Blacks– the world's best, according to international ranking–are

followed with much enthusiasm. When they win, it's a national celebration; when they lose, a time of national soul-searching.

Rugby has three levels of competition. The international Tri-Nations is played between New Zealand, South Africa and Australia. Super 14 Rugby, played in late summer and autumn, has teams from regions in the three countries. The domestic teams—the Highlanders based in Dunedin, Crusaders based in Christchurch, Hurricanes based in Wellington, Chiefs in Hamilton and Blues in Auckland—all command passionate regional followings.

At the next level down is the Air New Zealand Cup, which is played in winter and is divided into two pools. The most coveted provincial trophy is the Ranfurly Shield. In addition, there are occasional test matches between Australia and New Zealand. All the main cities have large stadia that host national matches and international tests. It's worth attending a live game, if you can, to catch the atmosphere; otherwise, find a pub with a big screen, where passions among the crowd run equally high. The New Zealand Rugby Union's website (**www.**allblacks.com) gives details of matches.

Rugby League (**www.**rugby-league.co.nz) has a single professional team, the New Zealand Warriors, who are based in Auckland and play in the Australian National Rugby League.

New Zealand is also part of the IRB Sevens World Series (**www.**sevens.co.nz), the New Zealand leg of which is usually held in Wellington.

SAILING
New Zealand sailors have won more than 60 world titles, and sailing is the country's most successful Olympic sport.

Youngsters start early, and you will see them sailing their P-class yachts in regattas all over the country. The Royal New Zealand Yacht Squadron (**www.**rnzys.co.nz) in Auckland is home to Team New Zealand, the only non-US syndicate to have successfully defended the America's Cup. The Club organises events such as the New Zealand Match Racing Championships, held in November. Yachting New Zealand (**www.**yachtingnz. org.nz), the national body for competitive and recreational sailing, has details of events.

SKIING
Competitors in the New Zealand Speed Ski

Christchurch's Jade Stadium is a venue for rugby matches

Championships (**www.**speed ski.co.nz), held at Turoa in October, hurtle down the mountain at speeds of up to 173kph (107mph). Other events include the Australia New Zealand Cup final at Whakapapa in September, the ANZ FIS (International Ski Federation) series held at Mount Hutt in August, and the New Zealand nationals held at Turoa in September. The Ski Racing New Zealand website (**www.**skiracing.org.nz) lists upcoming events.

SURF LIFE-SAVING
Throughout the summer, the main New Zealand beaches

are patrolled by surf life-savers. Surf Life Saving New Zealand (**www.**slsnz.org.nz) trains children in water safety and also holds contests including swimming, running, paddling a surf ski, board or canoe, rowing a surfboat or racing an inflatable rescue boat. The national championships are held every two years, and a tri-nations series between Australia, South Africa and New Zealand is hosted in alternate years.

TENNIS

One of New Zealand's richest sporting events for women, the ASB Classic international women's tennis tournament is part of the WTA Tour and

The thrill sport of bungy jumping was invented in New Zealand

attracts players among the top 25 in the world. It is played in the first week of January each year at the ASB Bank Tennis Centre in Auckland and is followed by the Heineken Open for men. Tickets start from NZ$32. The website of Auckland Tennis (**www.**aucklandtennis.co.nz) carries details.

The ITF International Women's tournament, held at the Renouf Tennis Centre in Wellington, is the largest international tournament in New Zealand for juniors. The Wellington Tennis website (**www.**wellingtontennis.org.nz) has details.

ACTIVITIES

For visitors, New Zealand has become synonymous with outdoor activities, along with adventure sports such as jet-boating, bungy jumping, kayaking, white-water rafting, sky-diving and ever more daring variations on the theme. Queenstown calls itself the Adventure Capital of New Zealand, but most of these activities are available in other tourist spots as well. Ensure that your insurance covers you to participate in such extreme sports.

BUNGY JUMPING

Diving off a very high bridge with a rubber band attached to your ankles is the best known of New Zealand's thrill-seeking activities (▷ 15).

CAVING

Virtually every part of New Zealand has caves, formed in limestone, marble or volcanic rocks. The most important caving areas are at Waitomo, northwest Nelson and north Westland. The region around Waitomo contains most of the North Island's best-known caves. The New Zealand Speleological Society (**www.**caves.org.nz) and many guided tours operate from there.

In Nelson, the marble mountains at Takaka Hill, Mount Arthur and Mount Owen contain New Zealand's deepest and longest caves: the Bulmer Cavern (39km/ 24 miles), Ellis Basin system (28km/17 miles) and Nettlebed Cave (24km/ 15 miles). Harwoods Hole, one of the world's largest sinkholes, is just off the main Motueka–Takaka road.

On the west coast, Karamea has the 13km (8-mile) Honeycomb Hill Cave, with 70 entrances and New Zealand's largest limestone arches. The Nile River caves also have glow-worm and stalactite displays.

Guided caving trips are listed on **www.**newzealand.com.

FISHING

As well as being one of the best trout-fishing areas in the world, New Zealand provides superb sea- and big-game fishing. The prime trout-fishing spots in the North Island are the lakes around Taupo and Rotorua; in the South Island, around Gore in Southland. Both experienced and novice anglers are well catered for, with numerous boat charters and guides. The warm Pacific waters around the North Island attract dozens of salt-water species from snapper to marlin. Areas particularly well geared up for game- and

Fishing for trout in the glacial waters of Lake Pukaki

sea-fishing include the Bay of Islands, Tutukaka (Northland), Whitianga (Coromandel) and Tauranga/Whakatane (Bay of Plenty). Options range from the three-hour novice trip to the highly organised three-day 'Hemingway' trips to catch that prize marlin. Check the **www.**fishing.net.nz website for information.

FLIGHTSEEING

Almost every provincial airport, airstrip or local flying club in New Zealand offers flights in a small, fixed-wing aircraft or a helicopter. There are several operators on the West Coast and the Southern Lakes district. If you take only one flight, make it the helicopter flight around the glaciers and summit of Mount Cook/Aoraki. For a more sedate ride consider a hot-air balloon trip, available in a number of locations (see the local visitor information office). Alternatively, you can don goggles and scarf and get strapped into a biplane. The flightseeing section of **www.**newzealand.com lists many of the operators.

FLY-BY-WIRE

This is claimed to be the world's fastest adventure ride, reaching speeds of 171kph (106mph). Brave souls are strapped to what resembles a metal hospital stretcher with a microlight engine on the back and suspended from a wire. Rides are available only in Queenstown.

GOLF

New Zealand has hundreds of golf courses, from those that require a cute wedge shot to avoid sheep to others with well-manicured greens fit for an open championship. They are frequently set in stunning surroundings, overlooking snowy mountains, lakes, seascapes or forests. World-class courses in New Zealand include Formosa in Auckland, Wairakei in Taupo and Millbrook in Arrowtown. The main season is March to October, both because the winters are relatively mild and because in summer many New Zealanders concentrate on water sports. Most courses have clubs for hire. Green fees start at around NZ$15, and attitudes to golfing etiquette tend to be relaxed. The New Zealand Golf website is **www.**nzga.co.nz.

HIKING

See Tramping, page 161.

HORSE TREKKING

The New Zealand landscape is ideal for horse trekking, and it can be enjoyed around almost every provincial town. Both the experienced and the novice are well catered for in treks lasting from an hour to several days. The approach tends to be informal, and specialised riding gear is not usually necessary. Helmets are provided. For additional information countrywide contact the International League for the Protection of Horses (ILHNZ), **www.**horsetalk.co.nz, or the national tour organisation via **www.**ridenz.com.

JET-BOATING

This usually involves whizzing down a river at high speed in remarkably shallow water, and turning 180 degrees. Although it looks scary, it is actually great fun. A New Zealand invention, the jet-boat was developed by a Canterbury farmer, Bill Hamilton, to navigate the shallow local rivers. Jet-boating is now one of New Zealand's best-known adventure activities. Some of the most exhilarating trips are available near Queenstown, the Buller Gorge, and the Waiau, Whanganui and Waikato rivers, but jet-boating is available on most New Zealand rivers. Not all are adrenalin-pumping trips; some (especially in the North Island) are more scenic affairs. The website **www.**newzealand.com lists many of the operators.

KAYAKING

New Zealand is a renowned playground for kayaking and canoeing, whether on river, lake, sea or fiord. It is also popular as an eco-sensitive way of interacting with wildlife, such as seals, dolphins and birds. Guided trips are particu-larly popular in the Abel Tasman National Park, but they are also available throughout New Zealand, and kayak operators can be found in just about every major town. Multi-day trips are available in all the main tourist spots, ranging from family-oriented paddles on calm rivers to the adrenalin rush of white water and rapids. The website **www.**newzealand.com lists many of the operators.

MOUNTAIN BIKING

New Zealand is a paradise for mountain bikers, with a choice of on- and off-road trails in spectacular locations. Cycling is also a great way to see the country, and many operators offer tours in which your gear is carried from one destination to the next. Some even drive you uphill so you only have to ride the downhill sections. Bicycle hire is available in most towns, and

Jet-boating can now be enjoyed all over the country

you can choose from gentle family expeditions to the multi-day Otago Central Rail Trail or heli-biking from mountain peaks. The New Zealand Mountain Bike website **www.**mountainbike.co.nz is a comprehensive resource.

MOUNTAINEERING

New Zealand's major peaks, although not especially high, are spectacular, challenging and potentially dangerous. The majority are in the South Island. The Mount Cook Range, Mount Aspiring (Wanaka) and the peaks of the Nelson Lakes National Park are the most accessible. Guides are available and definitely recommended.

Mount Taranaki/Egmont in the North Island is the country's most-climbed mountain. Other grand peaks in the North Island include Mount Ruapehu and the little-climbed (but superb) Hikurangi in Eastland. If you are a novice, seek advice and above all go well prepared: Check the weather forecast and tell someone of your intentions. Many lives have been lost through lack of common sense and over-confidence. Numerous guided trips are available, especially around Taranaki and Mount Cook/Aoraki (Franz Josef and Fox Glaciers).

There's little margin for error on Lake Taupo's golf course

For specialist enquiries contact the NZ Alpine Club, based in Christchurch, **www.**alpineclub.org.nz. The NZ Mountain Guides Association, **www.**nzmga. org.nz, is also good for further information and contacts.

PARAFLYING AND PARAPENTING

Paraflying (also called para-sailing) involves sitting on a seat under a parachute being pulled by a boat. Suitable for all ages, it requires no skill and is available at coastal and lake resorts.

Parapenting (or paragliding) is great fun but is difficult to

master. As with skydiving, the novice is taken in tandem with an expert. There is a limited number of tourist venues: Te Mata Peak in Hawke's Bay is the North Island's top site, while Wanaka is the capital for the South Island.

RAFTING

This is another premier New Zealand activity. The principal locations are the rivers of central and east North Island and throughout the South Island. Rivers and the rapids are graded from I to VI. Although the 45-minute trips are great fun and packed with adrenalin-pumping moments, the real rafting experience only comes with a multi-day expedition. Trips are generally well organised and safe; most will even do the campfire cooking for you. The New Zealand Rafting Association's website is **www.**nz-rafting.co.nz.

RIVER SLEDDING

River sledding involves rafting down a river on a body-board with little except a wet suit, flippers and a crash helmet. The prime location for this is the Waingongoro River in Hawera.

ROCK CLIMBING

Many locations offer great rock climbing—but remember, you need tuition and a guide. Many places also have climbing walls for practice. Visitor information offices can give you contacts.

SAILING

For the experienced sailor New Zealand—and in particular the Hauraki Gulf, off Auckland, and the Bay of Islands—provides one of the best sailing play-grounds in the world, and novices are well catered for. Try at least a few hours out on the water and, if you can, go on a multi-day trip. Bare boating gives you a choice of any vessel that matches your

expertise. Skippered yacht charter/rental companies are based in Auckland and the Bay of Islands. Picot's (**www.**charterguide.co.nz) has a comprehensive list of yacht charter operators.

SCUBA DIVING

New Zealand has some world-class dive sites, including the Poor Knights Islands off Tutukaka (**www.**diving.co.nz) in Northland, famed for their geology, marine life and water clarity. In many locations local operators will take you for a full- or half-day basic first dive experience. The main diving locations in the North Island are the Hauraki Gulf (Auckland), Whitianga (Coromandel)

Rock climbing requires expertise as well as fitness

and New Plymouth (Taranaki). In the South Island they are the Marlborough Sounds, Fiordland and Stewart Island/Rakiura. There are also many accessible wrecks on the coast. The prime months are February to June. The website **www.**newzealand.com lists many operators.

SKIING AND SNOWBOARDING

New Zealand is the principal skiing and snowboarding venue in the southern hemisphere. Most of the major commercial ski fields are in the South Island. They include Coronet Peak and the Remarkables near Queenstown (▷ 148), Treble Cone and Cardrona near Wanaka, Mount Hutt, Mount Potts and Porter Heights west of Christchurch, and the Craigieburn ranges, Arthur's Pass, Hanmer Springs and Nelson regions. The choice is vast. For an authentic Kiwi experience, try skiing the club fields, where the facilities are basic and the skiing is challenging, but the welcome is friendly and the cost is comparatively modest. The Canterbury Snowsports Association (**www**.skisouth. org.nz) has 13 affiliated clubs, from Tukino in the North Island to Fox Peak in the South. In the North Island the commercial fields are on the slopes of Ruapehu (Whakapapa and Turoa) in the Tongariro National Park.

There are a number of packages that include lift pass, equipment hire and one or more lessons. For contacts, see **www**.nzski.com, **www**.snow.co.nz, and **www**.brownbear.co.nz.

SKYDIVING
Tandem skydiving is available in many locations throughout both islands. Jumps range in height from 2,744m (9,000ft) to 4,573m (15,000ft). The latter will give you about 40 seconds free-fall. Prices increase the higher you go, although commercial operators will generally not take first-timers beyond 4,570m (15,000ft).

SURFING
The North Island's west coast locations of Raglan and Piha are perhaps the most famous for surfing, but other great surf spots include Whangamata (Coromandel), the Eastland beaches, and the beaches on Surf Highway 45 around Mount Taranaki/Egmont. To get a taste of surfing, try boogie-boarding or bodysurf-

ing. Boogie-boards, about half the size of a surfboard and made of compressed foam, are readily available and inexpensive to buy or rent. The website **www**.surf.co.nz gives an overview of surfing across New Zealand.

SWIMMING
Rotorua and Taupo are the natural hot-pool capitals but there are many other hot springs throughout the country, including Waiwera north of Auckland, Te Aroha in the Waikato, and Hanmer Springs in Canterbury. You can swim in all the lakes in the Rotorua region, except the Green Lake, which is sacred to Maori.

Coastal swimming can be very dangerous, with notorious riptides, so take care and swim only between the flags on beaches patrolled by surf lifeguards. If in difficulties raise your arm and keep it aloft; lifeguards will come to your rescue.

TRAMPING (HIKING)
Not only is tramping one of the principal pastimes for many New Zealanders, it is also the reason many visitors come to the country. There is a vast network of routes and literally thousands of kilometres of track the length and breadth of the country, from the famous and well-trodden Milford Track to the sporadic trail and markers of the lesser-known Dusky Track (▷ 246).

Under the administration and advocacy of the Department of Conservation (DoC), all advertised tracks are clearly marked, well maintained and have designated campsites and huts offering clean water, basic accommodation, cooking facilities and toilets. Detailed tramping information is available, including route descriptions, with the tracks classified by type and fitness required, and

up-to-date weather forecasts. Guided trips are also offered for those who would like to be accompanied by an expert.

A word of warning: Many of the tracks are very busy, so accommodation must be reserved weeks in advance. Always make sure you are well prepared, properly equipped and at the required level of fitness. Unless you are experienced, tramping alone on the more remote tracks is not advisable.

For detailed information about all the major tramping tracks and Great Walks contact the local DoC Field Centre, **www**.doc.govt.nz. For accommodation reservations and information, visit the office

Walking on the Coromandel Peninsula—it's not all trekking

or send an email to: greatwalksbooking@doc. govt.nz.

WALKING
The opportunities are endless and most visitor information offices or regional DoC offices compile lists of the most notable walks in each region.

For New Zealand walk suggestions, ▷ 214–245 or try **www**.doc.govt.nz; another useful site is **www**.sparc.org.nz.

WHALE- AND DOLPHIN-WATCHING
The Bay of Islands and Whakatane are the dolphin-watching and swimming

capitals of the North Island, while Kaikoura in the South Island is world-famous for both dolphins and whales. The tiny, endangered Hector's dolphin can also be viewed from Curio Bay in the Catlins, Southland, and around Banks Peninsula in Canterbury. Encounter success rates are generally very high in New Zealand, to the extent that many operators offer a refund or another trip if the whales and dolphins do not turn up.

WINDSURFING
New Zealand is very well suited to the experienced windsurfer, with endless locations. The Estuary in Christchurch is particularly popular with novices, as you can travel considerable distances without getting deeper than chest height in water. Windsurfing schools and board hire are available at most of the principal beach resorts. Contact **www.**windsurfingnz.co.nz.

ZORBING
Invented in Rotorua, zorbing (**www.**zorb.co.nz) involves climbing into a clear plastic bubble and rolling down a hill (▷ 177). The hair-raising ride lasts about 10 seconds.

HEALTH AND BEAUTY

WHAT TO DO

New Zealand is located on the active volcanic geothermal belt known as the Pacific Rim of Fire, and is dotted with hot spring mineral water sites, the most famous of which are around Rotorua. Local Maori had long known of the geothermal region's therapeutic powers, and in 1840 gave the new town an area of thermal springs 'for the benefit of the people of the world'. The Government lavished money on making Rotorua 'the spa city of the South Pacific', with a sanitarium, bath houses and landscaped gardens to draw people to 'take the cure'. The famous Blue Baths were one of the first public swimming pools in the world to allow mixed bathing for recreation. Thermal springs in other parts of New Zealand have been developed on a less grand scale.

mud baths, steam rooms, wet and dry massage and beauty therapies are available at the major thermal resorts, including Waiwera, Polynesian Spa and Hell's Gate Wai Ora at Rotorua, Taupo Hot Springs Spa at Lake Taupo, and Hanmer Springs. Spa packages are often available, involving a choice of pampering experiences for both men and women, such as aromatic massage, body wraps, facials, manicures and pedicures. Expect to pay from NZ$40 for a half-hour treatment. Similar massage and beauty therapies are available at day spas attached to luxury hotels and lodges, and in the major cities. Beauty salons tend to offer a more limited range of services, such as facials, make-up and manicures.

PUBLIC POOLS
Most of New Zealand's major hot springs have been developed commercially for recreation, with hot pools of varying temperatures, swimming pools, toddlers' pools, hydroslides, picnic areas and cafés. Towels and swimsuits are often available for hire. The main complexes are at Waiwera, Rotorua, Taupo, Te Aroha and Hanmer Springs.

Swimming complexes in the major towns and cities have a variety of pools and recreational facilities. The most modern also offer fitness classes and are equipped with saunas, steam rooms and a gym. Pool entrance starts at NZ$6 adult, NZ$4 child.

SPA TREATMENTS
Spa treatments involving a combination of thermal pools,

GYMS
City-dwelling New Zealanders are keen users of gyms and fitness facilities, which usually provide a range of workout options, including men's, women's and mixed gyms, aerobics classes, weight training, yoga and personal trainers. Some have crèche facilities and a café.

Casual rates are usually available, starting at around NZ$15. Health and fitness venues should be listed in the Yellow Pages of the telephone directory.

FOR CHILDREN

New Zealand is a generally child-friendly destination. Families can happily spend the day at a beach patrolled by lifeguards, take well-marked bush walks, or visit parks and playgrounds for free. During the summer holidays, from mid-December to the end of January, many local councils organise free concerts and family activities. Shopping malls in the big cities have children's play areas, and most public gardens have well-equipped playgrounds for young children. There are swimming pool complexes with hydroslides in most large towns, cinemas have special rates for children, and many attractions such as zoos and theme parks have reasonable family combo prices.

ACTIVITIES AND ATTRACTIONS

In New Zealand, children can do things which may be more expensive in other countries, such as horse-riding, skiing, farm experiences and water sports. Tame versions of jet-boating and rafting are available for families in many places, and although age restrictions apply to activities such as bungy jumping and paragliding, they may be open to children as young as 10.

Many cities and holiday areas have themed attractions that are popular with children.

In Wellington, the national museum, Te Papa, has a range of activities, including Story-Place, a haven for small children.

Visitor information offices are a good source of information about facilities and activities. There are also useful websites:

● Kidz Go! (www.kidzgo.co.nz) website and free magazine focuses on Christchurch and Queenstown, Wanaka and Fiordland, with sections on accommodation, activities, free things to do, age limits for adventure activities, and child-minding services.
● Kidspot (www.kidspot.com) is an online magazine.
● KidsNewzealand.com (www.KidsNewzealand.com) is a shopping and information site for families with children.

FESTIVALS AND EVENTS

From wild foods in Hokitika to art deco in Napier, Kiwis enjoy any excuse for a festival. Whether the official reason is fruit trees in blossom in Hastings, autumn foliage in Arrowtown, or the pohutukawas in the Coromandel, communities celebrate with everything from parades and concerts to art exhibitions, races, shop window competitions, flea markets and balls. In summer many councils sponsor free or low-cost entertainment, with buskers in the street, lunchtime concerts, family picnics and children's activities. Highlights are the free evening concerts in local parks, which draw huge crowds to join in Christmas carols or listen to opera, classical music or popular singers. For many, the most significant national event is Waitangi Day (6 February), when the founding treaty of the nation is celebrated at Waitangi and in *marae* all over the country.

WINE AND FOOD

Almost every city holds a wine and food festival. One of the oldest and best known is Wine Marlborough (February). Held under marquees in a vineyard, it has tastings from local wineries, food stalls, entertainment and seminars on wine-related subjects. At Toast Martinborough (November), the approach is different: You go from vineyard to vineyard, where tastings are matched with food prepared by local chefs, and the music ranges from jazz to string quartets. The focus is on local bounty of a different sort in Kaikoura's Seafest (October) and the Bluff Oyster and Southland Seafood Festival (April).

ARTS

The largest cities hold biennial arts festivals, those in Auckland and Christchurch alternating with the month-long International Festival of the Arts, held in February and March in even years in Wellington. Literary, dance and jazz festivals are held annually in the main cities.

AGRICULTURAL SHOWS

Agricultural and pastoral shows are important events in each region of New Zealand—even in the cities, when the country comes to town. Competitions for prize cattle, sheep-shearing and wood-chopping are held alongside food stalls and funfairs. The most popular are Auckland's Royal Easter Show and Showtime Canterbury, held in Christchurch in November.
● Tourism New Zealand's website has more details (www.newzealand.com).

AUCKLAND, NORTHLAND AND COROMANDEL

Auckland is not called 'the City of Sails' for nothing. One in every four Aucklanders is reckoned to have a boat, and a glance at the map gives one reason: The city sprawls around such a narrow strip of land that everywhere the view is of water, beaches, harbours and islands. The same is true in the Coromandel Peninsula and Bay of Islands. Water-based activities are a popular leisure pursuit in the whole northern region—sailing, surfing, windsurfing, water-skiing, kayaking, canoeing, fishing, snorkelling, diving and collecting seafood. The Bay of Islands has an international reputation for game-fishing.

A sophisticated, fashion-conscious city, Auckland has plenty of smart bars and restaurants, a casino complex that dominates the skyline, and a humming club scene based on Karangahape Road. The main focus of performance is the Edge complex in Aotea Square. The city has the excellent Auckland Philharmonia orchestra, and the Auckland Theatre Company produces drama of a high standard. The 'Time Out' section in Saturday's *New Zealand Herald* is a good place to see what's on.

The city's downtown shopping area, Queen Street, is an odd mix of smart and tawdry. While you'll find some of New Zealand's leading fashion designers—such as Kate Sylvester, Trelise Cooper, Zambesi and Karen Walker—in the central city, many also have stores in the chic suburb of Newmarket, where locals prefer to shop. Suburban shopping malls such as St. Lukes are popular for day-to-day shopping, and a wander around the Otara market on a Saturday morning reminds you that Auckland is the largest Pacific Island city.

KEY TO SYMBOLS	
	Shopping
	Entertainment
	Nightlife
	Sports
	Activities
	Health and Beauty
	For Children

AUCKLAND

AOTEA SQUARE MARKET
Aotea Square, Queen Street, Auckland
Tel 09-307 5493
In the heart of downtown Auckland, this market sets up under sun umbrellas in Aotea Square on Fridays and Saturdays. The stalls are a mix of arts and crafts, Pacific culture, funky fashion and ethnic food, with the added fun of street entertainers.
🕐 Fri–Sat 10–6

⊕ ELEPHANT HOUSE
237 Parnell Road, Parnell, Auckland
Tel 09-309 8740
www.nzcrafts.co.nz
A co-operative owned and operated by local craftspeople, Elephant House sells direct to the public. It carries only items handmade in New Zealand and the range is huge: wood, mobiles, leather, greenstone, clothing, honey and kiwifruit products, ceramics, Maori carving, paua and other jewellery, glass, souvenirs and gifts.
🕐 Mon–Fri 9.30–5.30, Sat, Sun 10–5
🚌 On the Link bus route

⊕ KATE SYLVESTER
47 High Street, Auckland
Tel 09-307 3282
www.katesylvester.com
One of New Zealand's leading fashion designers, Kate Sylvester has a minimalist approach to tailoring and a

quirky sense of humour. Also at 1 Teed Street, Newmarket.
🕐 Mon–Thu 9.30–6, Fri 9.30–7.30, Sat 10–5, Sun 11–4

🌐 OTARA MARKET
Newbury Street, Otara, Auckland
Tel 09-274 0830
On Saturday mornings the Otara shopping centre car park is crammed with stalls serving Auckland's Pacific Island communities, with fruit and vegetables, ethnic ingredients, clothing, Island music, crafts and prepared foods.
🕐 Sat 6–noon 🚌 Bus 487,497
🚗 20km (12 miles) south of Auckland CBD. Take the East Tamaki off-ramp (exit 444) from the Southern Motorway (SH1)

🌐 SMITH AND CAUGHEY'S
253–261 Queen Street, Auckland
Tel 09-377 4770
www.smithandcaughey.co.nz
This elegant, 1880s department store sells classy accessories, clothing, cosmetics, household items, perfume, shoes, stationery and food. Also at 225 Broadway, Newmarket.
🕐 Mon–Thu 9.30–6.30, Fri 9.30–7, Sat 10–5, Sun 10.30–5

🌐 TWO DOUBLE SEVEN
277 Broadway, Newmarket, Auckland
Tel 09-978 9400
www.twodoubleseven.co.nz
Shopping complex with smart international and local fashion boutiques such as Oroton, Polo Ralph Lauren, Esprit, Country Road, Scarpa, Barkers, Max and Keith Matheson. Also food, accessories, CDs, leisure and household items.
🕐 Mon–Wed, Thu, Fri 9–6, Sat 9–6, Sun 10–5 🚌 On the Link bus route
🚗 From downtown Auckland, exit SH1 at Gillies Avenue (exit 431), turn left then first right into Mortimer Pass

🌐 VICTORIA PARK MARKET
210 Victoria Street, West Auckland
Tel 09-309 6911
www.victoria-park-market.co.nz
Recognisable by its tall brick chimney, this shopping mall is housed in the former work-

shops and stables of the furnace that burnt the city's rubbish in the early 1900s. Shops around a cobbled court-yard sell crafts, clothing and souvenirs. Also a food court.
🕐 Daily 9–6 🚌 On the Link bus route
☕ Several cafés

🌐 WESTFIELD DOWNTOWN SHOPPING
11–19 Customs Street West, Auckland
Tel 09-978 5265
Centrally located between Queen Street and the water-front, this brings together more than 60 speciality and service stores under one roof, including fashion, books, handcrafts and souvenirs,

Auckland's Victoria Park Market is a mall with an unusual setting

America's Cup clothing and accessories, sheepskins, jewellery and an international food court.
🕐 Mon–Fri 8–6, Sat 10–6, Sun 10–4

🌐 ZAMBESI
Corner of Vulcan Lane and O'Connell Street, Auckland
Tel 09-303 1701
www.zambesi.co.nz
Zambesi is one of New Zealand's leading fashion labels, that of designer Elisabeth Findlay. Also found at 2 Teed Street, Newmarket (tel 09–523 1000), the shops carry other designer fashion, including Nom D., Martin Margiela, Dirk Bikkemberg

shoes, Comme Des Garçons and Bisonte. Zambesi Man carries leading international and local men's fashion (10 O'Connell Street).
🕐 Mon–Thu 9–6, Fri 9–8, Sat 9–5, Sun 11–4

🎭 AUCKLAND THEATRE COMPANY
Level 2, 108 Quay Street, Auckland
Tel 09-309 0390
www.atc.co.nz
Performs at various venues. Shows are listed on the website.

🎭 THE EDGE
Aotea Square, Queen Street, Auckland
Tel 09-309 2677
www.the-edge.co.nz
Several venues make up The Edge: the multipurpose Aotea Centre, built in 1990 and adjoining Aotea Square; the Auckland Town Hall, built in 1911 and favoured as a concert hall; and the opulent Civic Theatre, built in 1929 as a cinema, and now popular for music theatre.

🎭 MAIDMENT THEATRE
8 Alfred Street, Auckland
Tel 09-308 2383
www.maidment.auckland.ac.nz
Twin theatre complex on the University of Auckland city campus. Events are listed on the website.

🎭 SKYCITY METRO
291–297 Queen Street, Auckland
Tel 09-369 2411
This futuristic building bordering Aotea Square has a six-level atrium and houses an entertainment complex including a 13-screen cinema, Time Out games, Borders bookstore and a food hall.
🕐 Cinema: Mon–Thu, Sun 10–9.30, Fri, Sat 10am–11.30pm 🎟 Adult NZ$9–NZ$14, child (3–15) NZ$7–NZ$8.50

WHAT TO DO

⊙ SKYCITY THEATRE
Corner of Federal and Victoria streets, Auckland
Tel 09-363 6010
www.skycity.co.nz
Part of the SKYCITY complex. Hosts live shows and concerts.

⊙ CLASSIC COMEDY AND BAR
321 Queen Street, Auckland
Tel 09-373 4321
www.comedy.co.nz
Professional comedians and new faces entertain from Wednesday to Saturday. The venue also hosts cabaret, films and music. Events are listed on the website.
⊙ Daily 7–late ⦿ NZ$10–NZ$20
⦿ Two bars

⊙ DOGS BOLLIX IRISH BAR
2 Newton Road, Auckland
Tel 09-376 4600
www.dogsbollix.co.nz
As well as having all the usual mock-Irish paraphernalia, this bar pulls in the crowds with gigs featuring New Zealand bands, jam sessions and Irish music nights.
⊙ Mon–Wed 3–late, Thu–Sun noon–late ⦿ NZ$5 cover charge for some performances

⊙ THE LOADED HOG
204 Quay Street, Viaduct Basin
Tel 09-366 6491
www.theloadedhog.co.nz
A combination of its prime location on the Viaduct Basin, beer brewed on site and good food ensure this is always a popular place. Part of a chain, it serves its own tap lager, draught, wheat beer and dark ale. Paintings of famous New Zealanders adorn the walls.
⊙ Daily 11am–late

⊙ SKYCITY CASINO
Corner of Federal and Victoria streets, Auckland
Tel 09-363 6010
www.skycity.co.nz
Part of the SKYCITY complex, the casino has table games and 1,200 gaming machines.
⊙ Daily 24 hours

⊙ STAIRCASE NIGHTCLUB AND BAR
340 Karangahape Road, Auckland
Tel 09-374 4278
A gay-friendly nightclub and venue on Auckland's nightlife strip, the Staircase has resident DJs, a bar, pool tables and a dance auditorium. It also hosts concerts and events.
⊙ Tue–Sat 4–late

⊙ SURRENDER DOROTHY
175 Ponsonby Road, Ponsonby, Auckland
Tel 09-376 4460
A small gay, lesbian and transsexual bar, Surrender Dorothy has a friendly neighbourhood atmosphere with couches

Labelling at the vineyards makes sense for visitors

inside, tables outside, and a ceiling decorated with high-heeled shoes.
⊙ Tue–Sat 5pm–12.30am

⊙ ELLERSLIE RACECOURSE
80–100 Ascot Avenue, Greenlane East, Auckland
Tel 09–524 4069
www.ellerslie.co.nz
Ellerslie is the home of the Auckland Racing Club, which hosts 26 horse-racing events a year. Details of dates are listed on the website. A highlight is the Auckland Cup, held in March. It is also the venue for other major events.
🚗 Take Greenlane off-ramp (exit 433) from SH1

⊙ FULLERS
Fullers Cruise Centre, Ferry Building, 99 Quay Street, Auckland
Tel 09-367 9111
www.fullers.co.nz
Fullers operates ferry services to destinations such as Devonport, Rangitoto and Waiheke Island, and cruises including a 90-minute Harbour Cruise. The day trip to Tiritiri Matangi (▷ 71) is particularly recommended.
⊙ Harbour cruise daily 10.30, 1.30
⦿ Harbour cruise adult NZ$30, child NZ$15, family NZ$76

⊙ MOUNT SMART STADIUM
Beasley Avenue, Penrose, Auckland
Tel 09–571 1603
www.mountsmartstadium.co.nz
The main venue for rugby league matches and other sports events, the stadium also hosts celebrity concerts.
🚗 Take Mount Wellington off-ramp (exit 438) from SH1

⊙ AUCKLAND BRIDGE CLIMB
Westhaven Reserve, Westhaven Marina, Auckland
Tel 09-361 2000
www.ajhackett.co.nz
Specially designed walkways provide a safe and not-too-demanding experience with great views over the harbour and city. The experience lasts 1.5 hours and can be combined with bungy jumping. No children under 7, and children 7 to 15 must have written parental consent. Night trips are available on Saturday in summer on request.
⊙ Daily 9, 11.30, 2.30 ⦿ NZ$65

⊙ DOLPHIN AND WHALE SAFARI
PO Box 105-337, Auckland
Tel 09-357 6032
www.dolphinsafari.com
Trips lasting 4 to 5 hours with a marine research team in the Hauraki Gulf Marine Park viewing dolphins, whales and a variety of seabirds. You can also swim with the dolphins (conditions apply).

◷ Daily 9.30am (weather permitting) from Pier 3 on the waterfront
🎫 Adult NZ$140, child (5–15) NZ$100, family NZ$380

✪ FORMOSA COUNTRY CLUB

110 Jack Lachland Drive, Beachlands, South Auckland
Tel 09–536 5895
www.formosa.co.nz
Best known for its 160ha (395-acre), 18-hole golf course designed by Bob Charles with views over the Hauraki Gulf. Also villa accommodation, fine dining, sports stadium including heated pool.
◷ From 7am 🎫 Green fees with cart from NZ$77

✪ HOWICK HISTORICAL VILLAGE

Bells Road, Lloyd Elsmore Park, Pakuranga, Auckland
Tel 09–576 9506
www.fencible.org.nz
Life in Auckland's colonial past is re-created in this museum of living history, where characters in 19th-century costume inhabit authentic buildings, including a store, church, forge and settlers' houses.
◷ Daily 10–4 🎫 Adult NZ$13, child NZ$7 (under 5 free), family NZ$35

✪ LIONZONE

Lion Breweries, 380 Khyber Pass Road, Auckland
Tel 09–358 8366
www.lionzone.co.nz
Interactive tour of New Zealand's largest brewery, home of Steinlager and Lion Red, with tastings.
◷ Wed–Mon 9.30, 12.15, 3 🎫 Adult NZ$15, child (5–15) NZ$7.50, family NZ$40 🚌 On the Link bus route

✪ SAILNZ

Tel 09–359 5987
www.sailnz.co.nz
Experience life on America's Cup racer *NZL40* or *NZL41*. You can become the crew and take the helm, pump the grinders or sit back and enjoy the action.
◷ Daily, usually 2pm 🎫 Adult from NZ$135, child NZ$110

✪ SKY JUMP

SKYCITY, corner of Victoria and Federal streets, Auckland
Tel 0800-SKYJUMP
www.skyjump.co.nz
A harness jump from just above the restaurant of the Sky Tower (▷ 65); maximum weight 120kg (265lbs). No children under 10; written parental consent is required for children aged 10 to 13.
◷ Daily 10–5.15 🎫 NZ$195

✪ AUCKLAND ZOO (▷ 62)

✪ KELLY TARLTON'S ANTARCTIC ENCOUNTER AND UNDERWATER WORLD (▷ 63–64)

Auckland's Harbour Bridge is a landmark with fabulous views

✪ RAINBOW'S END

Corner of Great South and Wiri Station roads, Manukau City, Auckland
Tel 09–262 2030
www.rainbowsend.co.nz
This theme park has a mix of entertainment, with wild rides like the corkscrew roller coaster and tame rides for the little ones, as well as dodgems, go-karts, bumper boats, mini golf, a pirate ship and interactive games. Refreshments and free parking are available.
◷ Daily 10–5 🎫 Adult NZ$40, child (4–13) NZ$33, (2–3) NZ$31, under 2 free. Family discounts 🚌 Bus 471 or 472 from 55 Customs Street East
🚗 Take Manukau off ramp (exit 448) from SH1

CLEVEDON

⊕ CLEVEDON COAST OYSTERS

914 Clevedon–Kawakawa Bay Road, Clevedon
Tel 09–292 8017
www.clevedonoysters.co.nz
Buy live oysters direct from the farm and watch them being processed. You can also buy live and smoked mussels and wines from the owner's Pakihi Island vineyard.
◷ Mon–Fri 7–4.30, Sat 9–2

⊕ CLEVEDON GALLERY

9 North Road, Clevedon
Tel 09–292 8660
www.countryknits.co.nz
In this gallery you'll find local arts and crafts, especially knitwear, sheepskins and mohair rugs made from wool, mohair and possum/merino blend yarns. The local information centre is also here.
◷ Daily 10–5

✪ VIN ALTO

424 Creightons Road, Clevedon
Tel 09–292 8845
www.vinalto.com
A high hillside vineyard inland from Clevedon specialising in Italian grape varieties and traditional Italian wine-making methods, including Retico, made from grapes dried in the Amarone style. Cellar-door tastings, wine museum, shop and wine-tasting lunches of antipasto, tasting of four wines, dessert and liqueur (NZ$50).
◷ Sep–end Jul Sat, Sun 11–4.30

COROMANDEL TOWN

⊕ THE COROMANDEL SMOKING COMPANY

70 Tiki Road, Coromandel Town
Tel 07–866 8793
www.corosmoke.co.nz
Coromandel seafood is smoked daily over native manuka sawdust at this smokehouse and deli. Specialities include mussels, oysters, kingfish, trevally, tarakihi and kahawai. They'll also smoke the fish you catch.
◷ Daily 9–5.30

WHAT TO DO

COROMANDEL ARGO ADVENTURE TOURS
PO Box 132, Coromandel
Tel 07-866 7667
The Coromandel's mussel farms are a popular recreational fishing ground. Mussel Barge Snapper Safaris take you there on a traditional flat-bottomed wooden scow. Rods are available for hire. If you prefer to stay on land, the same operator takes tours of old gold-mine workings on eight-wheel-drive all-terrain vehicles.
Daily From NZ$35

HAHEI

CATHEDRAL COVE KAYAKS
88 Hahei Beach Road, Hahei
Tel 07-866 3877
www.seakayaktours.co.nz
Explore the dramatic volcanic coastline of the Coromandel Peninsula by kayak in half- or full-day tours, with all equipment provided. The scenery is spectacular and cappuccino is served on the beach to revive you.
Daily Oct–end May, otherwise on demand From NZ$75

KAITAIA

HARRISONS CAPE RUNNER
123 North Road, Kaitaia
Tel 09-408 1033
www.ahipara.co.nz/caperunner
These bus tours to Cape Reinga via Ninety Mile Beach include a break for some exciting sand-dune tobogganing, and a picnic lunch is included in the cost. Harrisons also offer a more personalised 4x4 Reef Runner tour, which includes sand tobogganing.
Daily 9am Adult NZ$45, child NZ$25

KAWAKAWA

BAY OF ISLANDS ADVENTURE COMPANY
Tirohanga Road, Kawakawa
Tel 09-404 1142
www.bushnbike.co.nz
Guided tours of a 62ha (153-acre) cattle farm on either horseback or quad bikes

explore farmland, native bush and the Tirohanga River. No experience is necessary, and the horse treks are suitable for beginners or advanced riders. Families can opt for a 4x4 safari, and the children can meet the farm animals.
Daily Adult from NZ$55, child NZ$25 3km (2 miles) north of Kawakawa

KERIKERI

MAHOE FARMHOUSE CHEESE
SH10, Oromahoe, Kerikeri
Tel 09-405 9681
Bob and Anna Rosevear make Dutch-style cheese out of milk from the cows that line the

Macadamia chocolate by Makana Confections

driveway to the factory on their dairy farm. You can buy the cheeses from the rustic shop.
Mon–Sat 8.30–5, Sun 10–5
12km (7 miles) south of Kerikeri on SH1

MAKANA CONFECTIONS
Kerikeri Road, Kerikeri
Tel 09-407 6800
www.makana.co.nz
A viewing window allows you to watch chocolates being made by hand, often using local ingredients such as macadamia nuts. The shop is elegant, the quality of the chocolates excellent, and you can taste before you buy.
Daily 9–5.30

MATAKANA

MORRIS AND JAMES
Tongue Farm Road, Matakana
Tel 09-422 7116
www.morrisandjames.co.nz
Clay dug from the banks of the Matakana River is the inspiration for Morris and James pottery. The showroom, filled with their vibrant ware, has become a popular attraction on the Matakana wine trail. The restaurant is an added draw, serving food on their ceramic ware with local wines.
Mon–Fri 8–4.30, Sat, Sun 10–5
Mon, Tue 9–3, Wed–Sun 9–3, 6–9

MATAURI BAY

KAURI CLIFFS GOLF COURSE
Kauri Cliffs, Matauri Bay Road, Matauri Bay
Tel 09-407 0010
www.kauricliffs.com
Aimed at the luxury market, this spectacularly sited golf course overlooks the ocean and is designed to use the natural features of the site. You can stay in beautifully appointed, secluded cottages and dine at the lodge, which also has tennis courts, a swimming pool and fitness centre.
From NZ$300 a round Turn off SH10 at Matauri Bay Road

MERCER

MERCER CHEESE
Old Great South Road, Mercer
Tel 09-232 6778
You can drive past Mercer without blinking, but it's worth slowing down to stop at the cheese shop. The shelves inside are stacked with fine Dutch-style cheeses, made at the nearby farm, which can be cut to order.
Daily 10–5

MIRANDA

☼ MIRANDA SHOREBIRD CENTRE

283 East Coast Road, Miranda
Tel 09-232 2781
www.miranda-shorebird.org.nz
More than 60 species of shorebirds congregate here, including the rare wrybill and the New Zealand dotterel, which flock on the tidal flats at the Firth of Thames. Some species fly 12,000km (7,455 miles) from Arctic breeding grounds to over-winter from October to March. The centre has displays, information, birdwatching and accommodation.
🕐 Daily 9–5 💰 Donation 🏛
🚌 20km (12 miles) off SH2

☺ MIRANDA HOT SPRINGS

East Coast Road, Miranda
Tel 07-867 3055
www.mirandahotspring.co.nz
Don't miss a visit to what is reputedly the largest naturally heated mineral pool in the southern hemisphere. The hot springs complex also has a toddlers' pool, private spa, barbecue area and a holiday park next door.
🕐 Daily 8am–9.30pm 💰 Adult NZ$14, child (5–13) NZ$7, (1–4) NZ$4.50 🏛
🚌 12km (7 miles) off SH2

MURIWAI

⛳ MURIWAI GOLF CLUB

Coast Road, Muriwai
Tel 09-411 8454
www.muriwaigolfclub.co.nz
This links course is located in a bird sanctuary, on naturally rolling fairways with views of the sea and forests. Book well in advance. ▷ 72
🕐 Daily 7am–4pm 💰 From NZ$35
🚌 Take Muriwai Road off SH16

PAIHIA

🏵 THE CABBAGE TREE

Williams Road and the Maritime Building, Paihia
Tel 09-402 7318
www.thecabbagetree.co.nz
With three outlets in Paihia, the Cabbage Tree has a comprehensive range of New

Zealand-made products, including men's and women's fashion clothing, All Black merchandise, possum-fur products, knitwear, bone and jade carving, wood, jewellery and paintings.
🕐 Mon–Sat 9–6, Sun 9.30–6

☼ FULLERS BAY OF ISLANDS

Maritime Building, Waterfront, Paihia
Tel 09-402 7421
www.fullers-bay-of-islands.co.nz
Fullers runs ferry services between Paihia and Russell, Opua and Okiato, and catamaran tours around the islands, including the famous Hole in the Rock at Cape Brett, making them the major sight-

Galloping on the sands at Pakiri Beach

seeing operator in the region. Choose from lunch cruises, swimming with the dolphins, an island stopover, or land tours to Cape Reinga, Russell and Kerikeri.
🕐 Daily 💰 Adult from NZ$45, child from NZ$25

☼ THE ROCK

Corner of Marsden and Williams roads, Paihia
Tel 09-402 7796
www.rocktheboat.co.nz
Dubbed "the backpackers' cruise ship", this 24-hour trip combines sightseeing with activities such as snorkelling and mussel diving, fishing for your dinner, night kayaking,

dolphin- and penguin-watching, and island walks. You sleep in dormitories or double cabins on a purpose-built craft. Meals are included.
🚢 From NZ$148

☼ SALT AIR

PO Box 293, Paihia
Tel 09-402 8338
www.saltair.co.nz
If you want to see a lot in a short time, Salt Air's half-day trip to Cape Reinga combines scenic flights with a 4X4 driving tour. You can also choose from a number of scenic flights around the Bay of Islands by Cessna aircraft or helicopter.
🕐 Daily from 8am 💰 From NZ$115

PAKIRI BEACH

☼ PAKIRI BEACH HORSE RIDES

Rahuikiri Road, Pakiri Beach
Tel 09-422 6275
www.horseride-nz.co.nz
Horseback-riding on the beach is the speciality here. Choose from a one-hour ride to a seven-day trek, taking in the beach, pine forest and native bush. There are horses to suit all ages and skill levels, with tuition available. Overnight accommodation is in cabins with farmhouse cooking.
🕐 Daily 💰 From NZ$40 🚌 SH1 to Warkworth, turn right, follow signs to Leigh and Goat Island Marine Reserve. Continue over the hill to Pakiri. At the village turn 2nd right into Rahuikiri Rd

RUSSELL

☼ CAPE BRETT WALKWAYS

PO Box 149, Russell, Bay of Islands
Tel 09-403 8823
www.capebrettwalks.co.nz
This gives access to walking tracks on the Cape Brett peninsula on both DoC and Maori Trust land, with spectacular seascapes and forested ridges. Walks take from two hours to two days over easy to moderate terrain, and are suitable for people of all ages as long as you are fit.
💰 From NZ$30 independent, NZ$250 guided

TUTUKAKA

✪ DIVE TUTUKAKA
Poor Knights Dive Centre, Marina Road, Tutukaka
Tel 09-434 3867
www.diving.co.nz
Diving around the Poor Knights Islands is the main attraction here, with underwater caves, tunnels and archways, and shipwrecks to explore. You can also go snorkelling, kayaking or whale- and dolphin-watching.
🖐 From NZ$119

WAIHEKE ISLAND

🍷 GREENHILLS WINES AND SPIRITS
153 Ocean View Road, Oneroa, Waiheke Island
Tel 09-372 6139
This impressive wine store in Oneroa specialises in Waiheke wines. For NZ$15 you can taste four local wines and sample Waiheke olive oil.
🖐 NZ$15

✪ ANANDA TOURS
20 Seaview Road, Ostend, Waiheke Island
Tel 09-372 7530
www.ananda.co.nz
Visit Waiheke artists in their studios, tour the island's vineyards, do coastal walks (moderate fitness required), or take an eco-tour in Whakanewha Regional Park. Other options include garden tours and overnight stays.
🕐 Daily 🖐 From NZ$85

✪ STONYRIDGE VINEYARDS
80 Onetangi Road, Waiheke Island
Tel 09-372 8822
www.stonyridge.co.nz
Stephen White aims to make the highest quality Cabernet blend in the world. His flagship Larose is one of New Zealand's most sought-after wines, with a price tag to match. Vineyard tours and tastings are held at 11.30am on weekends. Olives are also grown on the estate, and the café serves Mediterranean food.
🕐 Sat, Sun 11.30–5, daily in high summer 🖐 Tours NZ$10 💻

WAIMAUKU

🐝 BEESONLINE HONEY CENTRE AND CAFÉ
791 State Highway 16, Waimauku
Tel 09-411 7953
www.beesOnline.co.nz
A working honey centre with a bee theatre, a range of honey products, tastings, a retail outlet and a café serving indigenous and organic food.
🕐 Mon–Fri 9–4, Sat, Sun 9–5 🖐 💻

🏛 CORBAN ESTATE ARTS CENTRE
426 Great North Road, Henderson
Tel 09-838 4488/4455
www.ceac.org.nz
Former winery buildings on the original Corban's Wine Estate

Birdwatching from Whangamata with Kiwi Dundee Adventures

have been turned into studios for artists and artisans. The Pacific Island community holds regular markets and events.
🕐 Daily 10–4.30 🖐 Free 🚗 Near the intersection of Lincoln Road and Mount Lebanon Lane

✪ BUSH AND BEACH
Tel 09–837 4130
www.bushandbeach.co.nz
Coach tours tailored to age and fitness explore the black-sand beaches and lush native bush within 30km (18 miles) of Auckland. Half-day, full-day and overnight tours are available.
🕐 Daily 🖐 From NZ$110

WAITANGI

🎭 CULTURE NORTH SOUND AND LIGHT SHOW
Waitangi
Tel 09-402 5990
www.culturenorth.co.nz
This informative, entertaining show gives a Maori perspective on events right through from the story of Kupe, the first Maori chief to discover New Zealand, to the signing of New Zealand's founding document and the present day.
🕐 Oct–end Apr, Mon, Wed, Thu, Sat 7.30pm–9.30pm 🖐 NZ$50

✪ COASTAL KAYAKERS
Te Karuwha Parade, Ti Bay, Waitangi
Tel 09-402 8105
www.coastalkayakers.co.nz
Choose to explore the outer islands, lagoons, natural rock caves and beaches, or challenge the Haruru Falls on these guided kayaking and canoeing trips, which last from half a day to several days. All equipment and refreshments provided.
🕐 Daily 🖐 From NZ$55

WAIWERA

✪ ♡ WAIWERA INFINITY SPA
21 Main Road, Waiwera
Tel 09-427 8800
www.waiwera.co.nz
This complex of 26 indoor and outdoor naturally heated thermal pools is popular with families. There are waterslides for the children, facial and body treatments for adults, spa packages and a fitness centre.
🕐 Sun–Thu 9am–10pm, Fri, Sat 9am–10.30pm 🖐 Adult NZ$22, child NZ$11, family NZ$53 🖐 💻

WHANGAMATA

✪ KIWI DUNDEE ADVENTURES
PO Box 198, Whangamata
Tel 07-865 8809
www.kiwidundee.co.nz
Personalised walks and nature tours, from relatively easy day walks to challenging hikes, taking in native bush, beaches and former gold mines.
🖐 From NZ$190

JANUARY

ASB CLASSIC AND HEINEKEN OPEN

ASB Tennis Centre, 1 Tennis Lane, Parnell, Auckland
Tel 09-373 3623
www.asbbankclassic.co.nz
www.heinekenopen.co.nz
These annual international tennis tournaments are held consecutively over two weeks.

FEBRUARY

DEVONPORT FOOD AND WINE FESTIVAL

Winsor Reserve, Devonport
Tel 09-378 9031
www.devonportwinefestival.co.nz
This beachside food, wine and music festival in the picturesque village of Devonport has two stages, with non-stop entertainment and 30 stalls of New Zealand's wine and food.

NZ$25 via www.ticketmaster.co.nz and door sales From the Auckland ferry terminal

WAIHEKE ISLAND WINE FESTIVAL

Isola Estate, Onetangi Road, Waiheke Island
Tel 09-372 7676
www.waihekewinefestival.co.nz
Wines from the island's vineyards are showcased in a one-day festival, which also includes food and live music at several vineyards. Tickets are limited, so book early.

Tickets NZ$65 (NZ$89 including return ferry trip). Bookings at Ticketek, tel 09-307 5000, www.ticketek.co.nz From the Auckland ferry terminal

FEBRUARY–MARCH

AUCKLAND FESTIVAL

PO Box 3787, Shortland Street, Auckland
Tel 09-309 0101
www.ak05.co.nz
This biennial arts festival is held over three weeks in venues all over the city. Book through Ticketek, tel 09-307 5000.

MARCH

PASIFIKA

Western Springs Lakeside and Stadium, Great North Road, Auckland
Tel 09-379 2020
www.aucklandcity.govt.nz
This annual one-day festival is New Zealand's largest Pacific Island celebration, with contemporary arts and music, traditional food, craft and cultural performances. Parking is limited, but public transport goes to the venue.

Free Bus 045 from Downtown

EASTER

ROYAL EASTER SHOW

ASB Showgrounds, 217 Greenlane West, Epsom, Auckland
Tel 09-623 7728
www.royaleastershow.co.nz
As well as the traditional agricultural competitions such as shearing, dog trials and equestrian events, the show puts on family entertainment with carnival rides, children's stage shows and Farmworld 'petting pens'. At the same venue are artworks from the Royal Easter Show Art Awards.

Adult NZ$15, child (2–12) NZ$5, family NZ$30 Buses 302–312, 327–359 from Midtown Exit Southern Motorway at Greenlane (exit 433)

WAIHEKE ISLAND OF JAZZ

PO Box 170, Oneroa, Waiheke Island
Tel 09-372 5301
www.waihekejazz.co.nz
Concerts featuring local and international performers are held over five days at pubs, cafés and vineyards around Waiheke Island, linked by a shuttle bus. Book your accommodation well ahead.

From the Auckland ferry terminal

SEPTEMBER

AIR NEW ZEALAND FASHION WEEK 2004

PO Box 147240, Auckland
Tel 09-377 8033
www.nzfashionweek.com
This is aimed at fashion buyers and media, but the public can get close with shows such as ANZFW 4 U public access day (tickets through Ticketek, tel 09-307 5000), and big-screen coverage at Viaduct bars.

NOVEMBER

ELLERSLIE INTERNATIONAL FLOWER SHOW

Auckland Regional Botanic Gardens, Manukau City
Tel 09-579 6260
www.ellerslieflowershow.co.nz
The largest flower show in the southern hemisphere, Ellerslie showcases New Zealand horticulture, landscape design and garden art, with food, wine and entertainment.

Adult NZ$35, child (5–14) NZ$5 Manukau Station and shuttle bus Exit the Southern Motorway (SH1) at Manukau (exit 433) and follow signs

NOVEMBER–DECEMBER

POHUTUKAWA FESTIVAL

PO Box 592, Thames, Coromandel Peninsula
Tel 07867 9077
www.pohutukawafest.com
Timed to coincide with the flowering of the 'New Zealand Christmas tree', this 17-day festival is an umbrella for many different events in the area, including swimming and diving competitions, an adventure run, outdoor expo, food and wine festival and jazz brunch.

Bookings at Ticketek, tel 09-307 5000, www.ticketek.co.nz

WHAT TO DO

CENTRAL NORTH ISLAND

Maori culture and geothermal wonders are what bring most visitors to the central North Island, but Rotorua and Taupo also vie with each other in catering for thrill seekers, whether it's bungy jumping, water sports, off-road adventures, throwing yourself out of aeroplanes or hurtling downhill at high speed. Children are offered tamer versions of many activities, and those who get their thrills in more sedate ways find the fishing and golf world class. After so much exertion, you'll want to soak in the hot pools or be pampered in a spa, of which there are plenty. After that, you may well be too tired to do much other than have a good meal—which is as well, since the nightlife is limited. The most interesting shopping tends to be souvenirs of Maori culture, such as greenstone, carved bone and woven flax.

The North Island's only commercial ski fields are on Mount Ruapehu, one of several volcanoes in the region, not all of them extinct—which adds an extra frisson to the experience. The landscape of the Central Plateau is also well worth exploring in summer, either on short treks from Whakapapa or on the famous Tongariro Crossing. To the west, the lone, almost perfect cone of another volcano, Taranaki/Mount Egmont, is also a magnet for hikers, and surfers love the nearby beaches on Surf Highway 45. Catch a concert if you can at one of New Zealand's prettiest venues, the TSB Bowl of Brooklands at New Plymouth. On the eastern coast, Gisborne and Hawke's Bay are traditional fruit-growing areas, which also produce some of New Zealand's best wine. Hawke's Bay leads the country in wine and food tourism, with many producers open to the public. Napier also makes the most of its art deco heritage with guided tours and a not-too-serious festival.

KEY TO SYMBOLS	
⊕	**Shopping**
🎭	**Entertainment**
▽	**Nightlife**
🏀	**Sports**
✪	**Activities**
♡	**Health and Beauty**
✕	**For Children**

CAMBRIDGE

✪ CAMBRIDGE THOROUGHBRED LODGE
SH1, Karapiro, Cambridge
Tel 07-827 8118
www.cambridgethoroughbredlodge.co.nz
An hour-long New Zealand

Horse Magic Show on a 40ha (100-acre) farm showcases various horse breeds, which perform with audience participation. Afternoon tea and a horse ride are included.
⏰ Daily 10–3, shows at 10.30 or 11.30. Check for times and dates. Bookings are essential ✋ Adult NZ$12, child NZ$5
🚌 6km (4 miles) south of Cambridge

GISBORNE

⊕ BULMER HARVEST CIDER
Customhouse Street, Gisborne
Tel 06-868 8300
You can taste and buy a range of ciders made on site by

New Zealand's largest cider producer. They also make honey mead and a liqueur.
⏰ Mon–Fri 10–4

▽ SMASH PALACE
24 Banks Street, Gisborne
Tel 06-867 7769
A bar, barbecue and museum of eccentricities in the heart of Gisborne's industrial area, Smash Palace hosts DJs and live bands, particularly in summer. It also has a reputation for its flaming pizza.
⏰ Mon–Thu 3pm–late, Fri, Sat 12pm–3am, Sun 3pm–late

CHALET SURF LODGE
2 Moana Road,
Wainui
Tel 06-868 9612
www.chaletsurf.co.nz
Surfing is the theme of this
lodge, 8km (5 miles) north of
Gisborne, which combines
with a local surf retailer, The
Boardroom, to provide an
experience of the region's surf
beaches. Surf coaching,
accommodation and board
rental are also available.
From NZ$22

MILLTON VINEYARDS
119 Papatu Road, Manutuke,
Gisborne
Tel 06-862 8680
www.millton.co.nz
The Millton vineyards were
the first in New Zealand to
have full organic certification.
Vines here are grown
biodynamically, mixing
organics with the theories of
Rudolf Steiner. The flagship
Clos de Ste. Anne Pinot noir
and Chardonnay from
Naboth's Vineyard are
particularly highly regarded.
Dec daily 10–5; Oct, Nov, Jan–end
Apr Mon–Sat daily 10–5; otherwise by
appointment Off SH2

NEW ZEALAND
SAFARI ADVENTURES
Tangihau Station Enterprise,
Rere
Tel 06-867 0872
www.tangihau.com
Hunting is the focus of this
operation, spread over
6,667ha (16,474 acres) at
Tangihau Station, where you
can pursue big game such as
red stag and fallow buck, or
water fowl, turkeys and ducks
in season. Non-hunters can
experience station life with
farm tours, rock sliding,
swimming at the Rere Falls,
golf and wine trails.
NZ$75–NZ$800 44km
(27 miles) from Gisborne

ANIMAL KRACKERS
PET PARK
Oakland Truffière, Ferry Road,
Waerenga-a-hika, Gisborne
Tel 06-862 5597
www.oaklandtruffles.co.nz
Children can cuddle and feed
the rabbits, miniature horses,
deer, llama and kunekune pigs
at this little pet park. Their
parents may also be interested
in visiting the *truffière*, New
Zealand's first commercial
producers of prized Périgord
black truffles. A trained dog
sniffs out the delicacies from
May to the end of August.
Daily 1–4; *truffière* visits by appointment Adult NZ$5, child NZ$2
Turn off SH2 at the Bushmere Arms

*An Italianate building forms a
backdrop at Hamilton Gardens*

HAMILTON

DONOVANS CHOCOLATES
137 Maui Street, Hamilton
Tel 07-847 5771
www.donovanschocolates.co.nz
A family firm specialising in
European-style chocolates,
Donovans has a factory shop
selling 40 kinds of confec-
tionery, including truffles,
fudges and liqueur chocolates.
Mon–Sat 9.30–5, Sun 10–4
Serves espresso and snacks

THE GOUDA CHEESE SHOP
245 Cambridge Road, Hillcrest, Hamilton
Tel 07-856 6633
www.meyer-cheese.co.nz
Ben and Fieke Meyer make
Dutch-style cheeses using

the milk from their farm outside Hamilton. You can buy the
cheeses cut to order at this
retail outlet in the suburb of
Hillcrest, which also carries a
selection of Dutch foods.
Mon–Fri 9.30–5.30, Sat 9.30–1

FOUNDERS THEATRE
221 Tristram Street, Hamilton
Tel 07-838 6600
Hamilton's major performance
venue, this 1,250-seat auditorium is located in Boyes Park
and hosts international acts,
musicals and concerts, opera,
dance and cultural events.
More intimate concerts and
plays are staged at the
Clarence Street Theatre (59
Clarence Street), and alternative theatre and dance at The
Meteor (1 Victoria Street).

RIVERSIDE
ENTERTAINMENT CENTRE
346 Victoria Street, Hamilton
Tel 07-834 4900 (Sky City)
www.skycityhamilton.co.nz
This complex houses SKYCITY
Hamilton Casino, with 23
gaming tables and 339 gaming
machines. On level two, The
Bowlevard has 10-pin bowling,
laser games, a sports bar and
nightclub. Minimum age 20,
smart casual dress required.
Sky City: Sun–Wed 9am–3am,
Thu–Sat 9am–5am. The Bowlevard:
Mon 4pm–10pm, Tue, Wed
10am–11pm, Thu–Sat 10am–2am,
Sun 10am–11pm

HAMILTON GARDENS
Cobham Drive, State Highway 1,
Hamilton
Tel 07-856 6782
www.hamiltongardens.co.nz
Hamilton's most famous
attraction, this is a collection
of themed gardens with river
walks, lakes and exotic
pavilions. Guided tours are
available. The Gardens Pavilion
hosts a full schedule of shows
and other events.
Oct–end Apr daily 7.30am–8pm;
May–end Sep 7.30–6

WHAT TO DO

⊕ MV *WAIPA DELTA*

Memorial Park Jetty, Memorial Drive,
Hamilton
Tel 07-854 7813
www.waipadelta.co.nz
Replica 'paddleboat' cruises
explore the Waikato River, with
lunch, afternoon tea or a buffet
dinner. There is a bar on board.
🕐 Thu–Sun 12, 2.45, 6.30 💰 From
NZ$20 adult, child (under 15) half price

♡ WATERS DAY SPA

1226a Victoria Street,
Hamilton
Tel 07-838 2202
www.waters.net.nz
Spa treatments including
facials, massage, pedicures
and a range of body treatments are offered in premises
overlooking the Waikato
River. There is also an
infrared sauna.
🕐 Tue–Sat 9–5 💰 From NZ$45

✪ EXSCITE

1 Grantham Street,
Hamilton
Tel 07-838 6553
www.exscite.org.nz
With a name that stands for
Explorations in Science and
Technology, Exscite is an inter-
active science exhibit aimed at
children, attached to the
Waikato Museum (▷ 77).
🕐 Daily 10–4.30 💰 Adult NZ$6, child
NZ$5, under 3s free, family NZ$20

HASTINGS

⊕ HAWKE'S BAY FARMERS' MARKET

Hawke's Bay Showgrounds,
Kenilworth Road, Hastings
Tel 06-974 8931
Local growers and artisan food
producers sell their wares from
market stalls, and local people
come here to buy fresh food
direct from the grower. Stalls
include fruit and vegetables,
meat, poultry, small goods,
eggs, herbs, coffee, ice cream,
preserves, confectionery and
flowers.
🕐 Sun 8.30–12.30

⊕ RUSH MUNRO'S ICE CREAM GARDENS

704 Heretaunga Street West,
Hastings
Tel 06-878 9634
www.rushmunro.co.nz
Rush Munro's have been
making delicious handcrafted
natural ice creams to their
own traditional recipes since
1926. They use no colourings
or additives, and their fruit
ice creams contain real fruit.
The choice of flavours
offered is huge, ranging from
passionfruit to cappuccino or
hokey pokey.
🕐 Dec–end Feb Mon–Fri 11–8, Sat,
Sun 10–9; Mar–end Nov Mon–Fri 12–5,
Sat, Sun 11–5

*Fun in the sunshine at Splash
Planet water park*

✪ EARLY MORNING BALLOONS

71 Rosser Road, RD4, Hastings
Tel 07-879 4229
www.early-am-balloons.co.nz
Hot-air balloon flights over
Hawke's Bay last approxi-
mately an hour, but allow four
hours' total excursion time as
balloons are launched from
the best sites according to the
conditions. The flight fee
includes a picnic. Minimum
four people, maximum six, and
not recommended for children
under 10.
💰 Adult NZ$290, child (under 12)
NZ$240

✪ ON YER BIKE WINERY TOURS

129 Rosser Road, RD4,
Hastings
Tel 06-879 8735
www.onyerbikehb.co.nz
Visit the wineries of the
Ngatarawa area on these
self-guided bicycle tours.
Comfortable mountain bikes,
maps and a picnic lunch are
provided, as well as a mobile
phone for back-up (such as
arranging to have your wine
purchases collected). Routes
up to 28km (18 miles) long
cater to various levels of
fitness. Minimum age 18.
🕐 Oct–end Apr daily 10–5.30;
May–end Sep daily 11–4 💰 From
NZ$50

✪ SPLASH PLANET

Grove Road,
Hastings
Tel 06-873 8033
www.splashplanet.co.nz
There's something for the
whole family to enjoy at this
themed water park, with 15
rides and attractions including
the Sky Castle Screamer,
Master Blaster and Never-
Ending River ride. For the less
adventurous there are land-
based activities such as
mini-golf and a toddlers' pool.
🕐 Mid-Nov to Feb daily 10–6
💰 Adult NZ$25, child (15 and under)
NZ$19.50

HAVELOCK NORTH

⊕ VILLAGE GROWERS' MARKET

Black Barn Vineyards, Black Barn Road,
Havelock North
Tel 06-877 7985
www.blackbarn.com
This delightful small market
takes place on Saturday
mornings in the summer
months under a ring of trees in
the heart of the vineyard. Local
growers and producers sell
their seasonal wares, along
with artisan breads, coffee,
flowers, meat, pickles, olive oil
and lavender products.
🕐 Late Oct to end Apr Sat 9–12

WHAT TO DO

✪ AIRPLAY
...e Mata Peak,
...avelock North
...el 0274 512 886
www.airplay.co.nz
...pecialists in foot-launched
...aragliding, Airplay fly from a
...ariety of graded sites. Tandem
...aragliding flights range from
...5 minutes over the cliffs of
...e Mata Peak to cross-country
...lights lasting up to four hours.
...ourses are also available.
🚄 From NZ$140

✪ ARATAKI HONEY
...6 Arataki Road,
...avelock North
...el 06-877 7300
www.aratakihoneyhb.co.nz
... honey factory and shop
...ith a bee wall and tours on
...eekdays at 1.30pm (▷ 78).
🅾 Daily 9–5

HAWERA

✪ DAM DROPPING
...aitiaki Adventures, Surf Highway,
...awera
...el 021-461 110/0800 DAMDROP
www.damdrop.com
...his three-hour trip on water
...ledges on the Waingongoro
...iver includes an 8m (26ft)
...rop over a dam. It differs
...om white-water rafting as
...ou are in control of your
...ndividual sledge.
🅾 Oct–end Mar daily 9, 12, 3.30
🚄 From NZ$100

✪ HAWERA WATER TOWER
...5 High Street, Hawera
...el 06-278 8599
...limb to the top of the 54m
...77ft) tower, built in 1914 for
...re-fighting, for views over the
...whole of South Taranaki, and
... the mountain.
🅾 Mon–Fri 8.30–5, Sat, Sun 10–2
🚄 Adult NZ$2

NAPIER

✪ ART DECO SHOP
...eco Centre, 163 Tennyson Street,
...apier
...l 06-835 0022
www.artdeconapier.com
...he shop stocks a wide range
... art deco products, including

books, posters, clothing,
writing paper, needlepoint,
place mats, coasters and
table napkins.
🅾 Daily 9–5

🎭 NAPIER MUNICIPAL THEATRE
119 Tennyson Street,
Napier
Tel 06-835 1087
www.venues.co.nz
An art deco building that has
been sensitively extended to
create a modern performing
space, this theatre seats 970
and is regularly used for
concerts, drama, dance and
international acts. The website
gives performance details.

The gannet colony is the big
draw on Cape Kidnappers tours

✪ ART DECO TOURS
Art Deco Trust, 163 Tennyson Street,
Napier
Tel 06-835 0022
www.artdeconapier.com
Enjoy a guided or self-guided
art deco tour of the city, by car
or on foot. A 2.5-hour tour,
starting at 2pm at the Art Deco
shop (▷ this page), includes a
two-hour guided walk and
video screening with refreshments. Shorter morning walks
start at 10am from the visitor
information office, or you can
pick up an *Art Deco Walk*
booklet (NZ$4) for a self-
guided tour. Self-drive touring
maps (NZ$4) are also avail-
able, or you can tour in a

vintage Buick (NZ$99 for up to
three people).
🅾 Daily 🚗 From NZ$10, children free

✪ CHURCH ROAD WINERY
150 Church Road, Taradale,
Napier
Tel 06-844 2053
www.churchroad.co.nz
Founded in 1897, the Church
Road winery is one of the
oldest in New Zealand and is
known particularly for the
work of pioneering wine-
maker Tom McDonald, after
whom the winery's top red
wine and cellar are named.
The winery also houses New
Zealand's only wine museum.
🅾 Daily 9–5; tours daily at 10, 11, 2
and 3, NZ$10 📷

✪ GANNET BEACH ADVENTURES
PO Box 1463,
Hastings
Tel 06-875 0898
www.gannets.com
Tours leave from Clifton Beach
on trailers pulled by vintage
tractors, following the Cape
Kidnappers coastline to the
gannet colonies. Stopping for
90 minutes allows time to
swim or see the displays at the
shelter and get a close view of
the birds. Departure times
depend on the tides.
🅾 Oct–early May daily 🚗 Adult from
NZ$33, child NZ$19

⊘ OCEAN SPA
Marine Parade,
Napier
Tel 06-835 8553
Built on the site of the original
Hot Sea Water Baths, the
complex has pools of differing
depths and temperatures,
spas, sauna, steam room,
massage and beauty therapies.
The stylish Soak café is
licensed and has good food.
🅾 Mon–Sat 6am–10pm, Sun
8am–10pm 🚗 Admission adult NZ$6,
child (2–14) NZ$4, private spa NZ$8,
massage from NZ$35 📷

NEW PLYMOUTH

🌐 KINA

101 Devon Street West, New Plymouth
Tel 07-759 1201
www.kina.co.nz
Kina is located in the 1894 Exchange Chambers and specialises in New Zealand-made arts and crafts, including jewellery, pottery, glass, prints, turned wood, flax weaving and paua. Monthly local exhibitions are held in the adjacent art space.
🕒 Mon–Thu 9.30–5.30, Fri 9.30–7, Sat 9.30–4, Sun 11–4

🎭 TSB BOWL OF BROOKLANDS

Pukekura Park, New Plymouth
Tel 07-759 6080
www.bowl.co.nz
Attractively set in parkland, with a lake in front of the stage, this natural amphi-theatre seating up to 15,000 is a popular summer venue for Christmas in the Bowl, ballet, concerts, international acts and events such as the WOMAD world music festival.
🕒 Events listed on the www.newplymouthnz.com website

🎟 YARROW STADIUM

Maratahu Street, New Plymouth
Tel 07-759 6060
Major local and national sporting events are held in the 25,000-seater stadium, includ-ing rugby, cricket and soccer.
🕒 Events listed on the www.newplymouthnz.com website

❤ TARANAKI MINERAL POOLS

8 Bonithon Avenue, New Plymouth
Tel 06-759 1666
www.windwand.co.nz/mineralpools
Incorporating the original Tarawhata Mineral Baths, the Bonithon Spa Health company has reopened the artesian mineral well and transformed it into a modern healing facility. Communal and private pools are available. Advance booking essential.
🕒 Mon, Wed–Fri 9am–8pm, Tue 9–5, Sat, Sun 12–9 💲 From NZ$6

✪ FUN HO! NATIONAL TOY MUSEUM

25 Rata Street, Inglewood
(Inglewood is around 20km/12 miles southeast of New Plymouth)
Tel 07-756 7030
www.funho.com
For more than 50 years Fun Ho! miniature vehicles and other toys could be found in every New Zealand playground and sandpit. This collection contains more than 3,000 of them, made between the 1930s and 1980s, as well as other New Zealand-made toys. Replica toys are also made at the museum.
🕒 Daily 10–4 💲 Adult NZ$6, child NZ$3, family NZ$15

A guided river trip with Canoe Safaris of Ohakune

OHAKUNE

✪ TUROA SKIFIELD

Ohakune
Tel 07-385 8456
www.mtruapeu.com
On the Ohakune side of Mount Ruapehu, with reputedly the biggest vertical drop of all ski fields in Australasia, Turoa is popular with both skiers and snowboarders. It covers 500ha (1,200 acres) and has 11 lifts, equipment hire and cafés. Ski passes are also valid at Whakapapa on the other side of Mount Ruapehu.
🕒 Usually mid-Jun to end Oct 💲 From NZ$60, youth NZ$29

✪ CANOE SAFARIS

Tay Street, Ohakune
Tel 06-385 9237
www.canoesafaris.co.nz
Guided canoeing trips lasting from one to five days can be taken on the Whanganui and Rangitikei rivers. Rafting trips are also available on the Mohaka River. Most trips are suitable for families with children aged five upwards, with guides going ahead to set up campsites and lunches.
🕒 Oct–end Apr 💲 From NZ$95, child NZ$65

ORAKEI KORAKO THERMAL RESERVE

✪ NZ RIVERJET

Vaile Road, Reporoa
Tel 07-333 7111
www.riverjet.co.nz
Jet-boat trips take in lovely scenery on the Waikato River for one hour, or head to the hidden valley of Orakei Korako Thermal Reserve.
🕒 Daily 10.30 💲 From NZ$125, child NZ$50, family NZ$300 🚗 37km (23 miles) north of Taupo, off SH5

RAGLAN

✪ RAGLAN SURFING SCHOOL

5 Whaanga Road, Whale Bay, Raglan
Tel 07-825 7873
www.raglansurfingschool.co.nz
You can learn to ride Raglan's famed 'Endless Summer' breaks at the Raglan Surf School, which offers three-hour lessons and two- to five-day surf adventure packages, including equipment and accommodation.
🕒 Daily 10am 💲 From NZ$89

ROTORUA

🌐 JADE FACTORY

1288 Fenton Street, Rotorua
Tel 07-349 3968
www.jadefactory.com
Visit the workshop to watch jade carvers create pendants and sculptures in traditional and contemporary designs, many of which have symbolic associations—as the carvers will explain. The adjacent gift

entre sells their works as well as souvenirs, woollen products, clothing, jewellery and items made from native wood.
ⓘ Daily 9–6

🏛 TE PUIA MAORI ARTS AND CRAFTS INSTITUTE
Hemo Road, Whakarewarewa, Rotorua
Tel 07-348 9047
www.tepuia.com
Part of the Whakarewarewa complex (▷ 87), the institute preserves the arts of wood carving (*whakairo*) and weaving (*raranga*). You can walk around the carving school, visit a greenstone jeweller's studio and watch women weaving flax to make clothing, baskets and mats. Many products are for sale.
ⓘ Daily 8–5 🎟 General admission
adult NZ$28, child (5–15) NZ$14

🎭 TAMAKI MAORI VILLAGE
220 Hinemaru Street, Rotorua
Tel 07-349 2999
www.maoriculture.co.nz
Maori life in pre-European times is re-created at this village, which gives an insight into *marae* protocol with demonstrations of culture and crafts, a concert party and a *hangi* (food cooked in an earth oven, ▷ 251). You can also buy carvings, flax weaving, foods, Maori medicines and clothing.
ⓘ Oct–end Apr daily 5.30, 6.30, 7.30; May–end Sep 5.30, 7.30 🎟 Adult NZ$90, child (5–15) NZ$50

🍺 THE PIG AND WHISTLE
182 Tutanekai Street, Rotorua
Tel 07-347 3025
www.pigandwhistle.co.nz
Housed in a former police station (which gives rise to plenty of jokes), this lively bar sells micro-brewed beers with names like Swine Lager. Live bands play on Thursday, Friday and Saturday nights, and a guitarist on Wednesday and Sunday. There's also a big screen in the garden bar with Sky Sport.
ⓘ Daily 11.30am–late

🌀 MOKOIA ISLAND TOURS
Memorial Drive, Lakefront, Rotorua
Tel 07-348 6634
www.mokoiaisland.com
Paddleboat cruises on the lake are combined with breakfast, lunch, afternoon tea or dinner and dancing. A trip to Mokoia Island Nature Reserve includes a Maori cultural experience related to the history of Hinemoa and Tutanekai.
ⓘ Daily 10, 12, 2, 4 🎟 Adult from NZ$85, child NZ$49

🌀 MOUNT TARAWERA NZ LTD
171 Fairy Springs Road, Rotorua
Tel 07-349 3714/0274 963083
www.mt-tarawera.co.nz

Traditionally carved greenstone (pounamu), New Zealand jade

A choice of six tours is available from one of the few operators licensed to take visitors to the crater left by the eruption of 1886. You can travel by 4X4 or helicopter, walk the crater rim or scree slide, and combine Tarawera visits with other Rotorua attractions.
ⓘ Daily 8, 1 🎟 From NZ$121, child (under 12) NZ$71.50

🌀 MV *REREMOANA*
The Landing, Lake Tarawera
Tel 07-362 8595
A morning cruise on Lake Tarawera retraces the route of Maori canoes that visited the famed Pink and White Terraces before the 1886 Mount Tarawera eruption, with a stop to walk to Lake Rotomahana. Afternoon scenic cruises are also available. Advance booking essential.
ⓘ Daily 11, 1.30, 2.30 🎟 From NZ$27, child NZ$13.50

🌀 WET 'N' WILD
2 White Street, Rotorua
Tel 07-348 3191
www.wetnwildrafting.co.nz
Depending on the level of adrenalin rush desired, you can choose from white-water rafting at various grades on five rivers. Trips last anything from 45 minutes to a highly recommended multi-day trip down the remote Motu River.
🎟 From NZ$85

🌀 ZORB ROTORUA
Agrodome Adventure Park, Western Road, Ngongotaha, Rotorua
Tel 07-357 5100
www.zorb.co.nz
Zorbing is a local invention: rolling downhill in an inflated ball at up to 50kph (30mph). You can choose to go harnessed in a dry Zorb, or loose in a Hydro Zorb (known as the 'wash cycle'), or try the zigzag track. The Hydro Zorb can be done alone or with friends, which reduces the cost. There's also a children's Zorb for playing on flat ground.
ⓘ Nov to mid-Feb daily 9–8.30; mid-Feb to end Oct 9–5 🎟 NZ$45

🌀 BLUE BATHS (▷ 86)

🌀 HELL'S GATE AND WAI ORA SPA (▷ 84)

🌀 POLYNESIAN SPA (▷ 86)

🌀 AGRODOME (▷ 86)

WHAT TO DO

🟠 RAINBOW SPRINGS

Fairy Springs Road,
Rotorua
Tel 07 350 0440
www.rainbowsprings.co.nz
This nature park sets out to be family friendly, with bush walks, kiwi and other native birds, and trout that can be fed. An entertaining farm show also gives an insight into life on a New Zealand farm.
🕐 Daily 8–5 💷 Adult NZ$23.50, child (5–15) NZ$13.50, under 5s free, family NZ$69 💷 🍴

TAUPO

🟢 KURA GALLERY

47A Heu Heu Street,
Taupo
Tel 07-377 4068
www.kura.co.nz
This small gallery specialises in contemporary New Zealand ethnic art and craft, including jewellery, carving, wood turning, paintings and flax weaving.
🕐 Mon–Fri 10–6, Sat, Sun 10–4

🟢 THE MERCHANT OF TAUPO

14 Spa Road, Taupo
Tel 07-378 4626
www.themerchant.co.nz
The Merchant provides all the ingredients for a slap-up picnic: cheese, pâté, olives and cured meats, salmon, sauces, biscuits and chocolates, wines, beers and spirits. He also does glassware and gifts.
🕐 Daily 9–6

🟠 CHRIS JOLLY OUTDOORS

Taupo Boat Harbour,
Taupo
Tel 07-378 0623
www.chrisjolly.co.nz
A wide-ranging tour operation, Chris Jolly offers scenic cruises, lake fishing, fly fishing, hunting, water skiing, jet skiing, self-drive boats, guided walks and scenic flights. One option is to take a two-hour guided bush walk, be met by boat, and fish and cruise back to Taupo (NZ$1,040 for 2–4 people).
💷 From NZ$30, child NZ$16

🟠 ECO EXPLORER

PO Box 1725, Taupo
Tel 07-378 7902
www.ecoexplorer.co.nz
Aimed at people seeking gentle eco-adventure experiences rather than an adrenalin rush, these tours include a half-day guided kayak trip to the Maori carvings on Lake Taupo, a half-day kayak and launch cruise combo, guided forest walks.
💷 From NZ$95

🟠 WAIRAKEI INTERNATIONAL GOLF COURSE

State Highway 1, Taupo
Tel 07-374 8152
www.wairakeigolfcourse.co.nz

Kiwifruit provides the theme at Kiwi360's theme park

Designed as a green-fee course rather than a club, this internationally recognised golf course welcomes visitors and has a driving range, pro shop, bar and restaurant.
💷 From NZ$135 🚗 9km (6 miles) north of Taupo on SH1

♥🟠 TAUPO HOT SPRINGS SPA

Tel 07-377 6502, SH5, Taupo
www.taupohotsprings.com
Beauty treatments and family fun are combined at this thermal complex, which has hot pools, private spas and an interactive warm-water children's playground with hydroslide. Spa treatments include therapeutic massage, skin care, beauty treatments and features such as wet massage, acupressure jets and air massage seats.
🕐 Daily 7.30am–9.30pm 💷 From NZ$12, child (3–12) NZ$4; treatments from NZ$65

TAURANGA

🟠 BAYCOURT ENTERTAINMENT CENTRE

Durham Street, Tauranga
Tel 07-577 7198
www.baycourt.co.nz
Baycourt supports Tauranga's lively performing arts scene, with a modern 590-seat theatre hosting local and touring shows, and a 1926 Wurlitzer theatre organ.

🟠 BUTLER'S SWIMMING WITH DOLPHINS

Tel 0508 BUTLER
www.swimwithdolphins.co.nz
Gemini Galaxsea, an eco-friendly 20m (65ft) sailing boat, takes you on a leisurely trip to watch and swim with dolphins. It leaves from either Tauranga or Mount Maunganui. The boat has a swim bar for hanging onto when the dolphins swim faster than you can. Whales, seals and seabirds are also plentiful.
🕐 Daily 9am Tauranga Marina, 9.30 Salisbury Wharf, Mount Maunganui 💷 Adult NZ$110, child (under 13) NZ$85

TE AROHA

♥🟠 TE AROHA MINERAL POOLS

Te Aroha Hot Springs Domain, Te Aroha
Tel 07-884 4498
www.tearohapools.co.nz
Established in 1883 to take advantage of the health-giving properties of the mineral soda hot springs, the complex is in a landscaped domain (park) and retains many Edwardian buildings. You can choose from modern or Edwardian private bath houses or outdoor spas.
🕐 Spa daily 10–10; pool Mon–Fri 10–6, Sat, Sun 10–7 💷 From NZ$6, child NZ$4

TE PUKE

🌀 KIWI360
State Highway 2, Te Puke
Tel 07-573 6340
www.kiwi360.com
Kiwifruit orchard tours and
horticultural theme park (▷ 92).
🕐 Daily 9–5 💷 Tours adult NZ$23,
child (5–12) NZ$10, family NZ$60
🚍 36km (22 miles) south of Tauranga

WAIPUKURAU

🌀 AIRLIE MOUNT WALKS
PO Box 368, Waipukurau
Tel 06-858 7601
Itineraries lasting from half a
day to three days combine
walks on private farms with
visiting grand 1800s home-
steads not otherwise open to
the public. The walks take in
native bush, bird and marine
life, beaches and pa sites.
🕐 Daily 💷 From NZ$90

WAITOMO

🌀 THE LEGENDARY BLACK
WATER RAFTING COMPANY
PO Box 13, Waitomo Caves
Tel 07-878 6219
www.blackwaterrafting.co.nz
Best known for its underground
cave-tubing experience, Black
Labyrinth, this company also
offers Black Abyss abseiling
(rappelling). Reasonable fitness
is required. Minimum age 13.
🕐 Black Labyrinth daily 9, 10.30, 12,
1.30, 3; Black Abyss daily 9.30, 2.30
💷 Black Labyrinth NZ$90; Black Abyss
NZ$175

🌀 WAITOMO GLOW-WORM
CAVES (▷ 90)

WHITE ISLAND

🌀 PEEJAY WHITE ISLAND
TOURS
15 The Strand East, Whakatane
Tel 07-308 9588
www.whiteisland.co.nz
Enjoy an 80-minute launch trip
to White Island's active volcano,
and a guided walk (with hard
hat and gas mask) through the
remains of a sulphur factory to
the rim of the volcano.
🕐 Daily 9.15 (more trips Dec–end Feb)
💷 From NZ$150, child (1–13) NZ$110
(child rates not available Nov–end Mar)

FESTIVALS AND EVENTS

FEBRUARY
BREBNER PRINT ART DECO
WEEKEND
Deco Centre, 163 Tennyson Street,
Napier
Tel 06-835 11911
www.artdeconapier.com
This not-too-serious celebration of Napier's art deco
heritage has become so
popular it now runs into
several days, with walks and
tours, events on stage and
screen, a vintage car cruise,
street jazz and a seaside ball.

HARVEST HAWKE'S BAY
Hawke's Bay Wine Country
Tel 0800-442 946
www.harvesthawkesbay.co.nz
Around 30 Hawke's Bay
vineyards open their doors to
show off their wines in this
festival of tastings, tours,
concerts, art exhibitions
and workshops.
💷 Adult NZ$15

MARCH
WOMAD NEW ZEALAND
TSB Bowl of Brooklands,
New Plymouth
Tel 06-759 8412
www.womad.co.nz
This three-day biennial
celebration of world music,
arts and dance is held in odd
years, with concerts, workshops, storytellers, crafts and
Kidzone for children.

EASTER
MONTANA NATIONAL
JAZZ FESTIVAL
Baycourt, corner of Durham and
Wharf streets, Tauranga
Tel 07-577 7188
www.jazz.org.nz
Concerts at Baycourt span the
decades from New Orleans,
Chicago and Latin America,
with a New Zealand spin,
while downtown Tauranga
holds a Mardi Gras celebration
of wine, food and music.

JUNE
MATARIKI
Hawkes Bay Showgrounds
Tel 06-873 3526
www.matarikifestival.co.nz
This celebrates the Maori New
Year, the first new moon after
the rising of Pleiades star cluster in the eastern sky at dawn.
There are feasting and fun
activities here, and in other
parts of the country.

NEW ZEALAND NATIONAL
AGRICULTURAL FIELDAYS
Mystery Creek, Mystery Creek Road,
Hamilton
Tel 07-843 4499
www.fieldays.co.nz
The biggest agricultural trade
show in the southern hemisphere, Mystery Creek attracts
1,000 exhibitors and more
than 115,000 visitors. It is also
famous for its Rural Bachelor
of the Year contest.
💷 Adult NZ$15, child (5–14) NZ$6

SEPTEMBER
HASTINGS BLOSSOM
FESTIVAL
106 Russell Street South, Hastings
Tel 06-878 9447
www.blossomfestival.co.nz
The apple orchards are in full
bloom for this celebration
of spring in one of New
Zealand's leading fruit-
growing regions. The 10 days
of concerts and events include
a blossom parade.

NOVEMBER
TASTE GISBORNE
Showgrounds Events Centre
Tel 06-868 4123
www.gisbornenz.com
Taste Gisborne is a day-long
festival held in the events
centre at the showgrounds. It
involves many of the region's
top wineries, food and beverage producers, craftspeople
and chefs, with continuous
live entertainment.
💷 Adult NZ$30, child (under 12) free

WHAT TO DO

SOUTHERN NORTH ISLAND

New Zealand's most cosmopolitan and lively city, Wellington is the country's arts capital as well as the seat of government. The politics may be on the dull side, but the arts are definitely not, particularly during the biennial month-long International Festival of the Arts and concurrent Fringe Festival, when the city barely sleeps. Wellington is the home of the New Zealand Symphony Orchestra, the Royal New Zealand Ballet, some excellent professional theatre companies, Te Papa (the national museum), interesting art galleries, the child-focused Capital E, and a humming jazz and alternative arts scene, so even outside festival time, there is always something going on. See the *Dominion Post* newspaper for listings.

The city also has the advantage of being compact, making walking the easiest way to get around. It has resisted other New Zealand cities' drift towards suburban shopping malls, so the locals shop, eat and are entertained downtown. For nightlife, head for Courtenay Place; for quirky shops and alternative boutiques, stroll down Cuba Street; for smart shopping browse Lambton Quay. You'll find great coffee in cafés on almost every corner. Also downtown, or very close, is the Basin Reserve, one of New Zealand's oldest and certainly most characterful sports grounds.

Its location on the harbour makes Wellington popular for water sports, especially sailing. The inner-city beach is more suitable for sunbathing than swimming, but it does have good indoor baths. Lyall Bay is popular with surfers. For a family excursion, take the ferry to Days Bay, where there is a beach with kayaks and small boats for rent.

Over the Rimutaka hills to the northeast of Wellington, about an hour's drive away, is the highly regarded Martinborough wine region, one of the few places in New Zealand where the vineyards are so close together that you can walk between many of them—a particular advantage during the popular Martinborough Wine Festival.

KEY TO SYMBOLS

🏬	Shopping
🎭	Entertainment
🍸	Nightlife
🏃	Sports
✪	Activities
♥	Health and Beauty
☺	For Children

CARTERTON

🏬 PAUA WORLD
54 Kent Street, Carterton
Tel 06 379 6777
www.pauashell.co.nz
The iridescent bluey-green shell of the paua (abalone) is turned into all sorts of distinctive New Zealand souvenirs at this factory and outlet. Boggle at the paua hallway, watch a video about the life of this curious mollusc, and take the free factory tour for an insight into the processing of the shells. There's also a children's playground and a salt-water aquarium.
🕐 Daily 9–5 💵 Free

✪ BALLOONING NEW ZEALAND
54B Kent Street, Carterton
Tel 06-379 8223
Early-morning flights complete with a café 'champagne

breakfast' are a speciality. Flights last an hour.

⏲ Oct–end Apr daily 6am; May–end Sep daily 7am 💰 NZ$260 including breakfast

GREYTOWN

🏠 THE FRENCH BAKER MOÏSE CERSON

81 Main Street,
Greytown
Tel 06-304 8873
www.frenchbaker.co.nz

Croissants, palmiers, *religieuse*, *pissaladière*—artisan baker Moïse Cerson bakes wonderful authentic French breads, savouries and pâtisserie at his bakery and espresso bar.

⏲ Tue–Sun 8.30–4

✪ THE ADVENTURE CENTRE

76 Main Street,
Greytown
Tel 06-304 8565
www.ecoadventure.co.nz

Interactive ecology tours on the Waiohine Gorge involve rafting the gentle Grade II river, studying flora and birdlife as part of a conservation project. Night rafting is also available, finishing with a barbecue, roaring fire and mulled wine. Half-day rafting trips are suitable for all ages, with 'river bugging' for the more adventurous, caving and a full-day 'extreme' trip including bridge swing and 'rap jumping', which finishes with a winery tour.

💰 From NZ$70

MANAKAU

🏠 SOO'S BROWN ACRES

Main Road,
Manakau, Levin
Tel 06-362 6029

Home-grown vegetables, fruit and berries ripened on the property are sold at Soo's stall on the main road near Levin. Tree-ripened apples of many varieties are a speciality. They also sell confectionery and ice cream.

⏲ Daily 9–5.30

MANGATAINOKA

🏠 TUI BREWERY

State Highway 2, Mangatainoka
Tel 06-376 0615
www.tui.co.nz

Tui beer has been associated with the Tararua region since it was first brewed on this site in the 1880s. The building is known by some as the local equivalent of the Taj Mahal! Brewery tours are available (advance booking essential), and there is promotional clothing for those so inclined.

⏲ Tours Mon–Fri 10.30, 1, Sat, Sun 1, 2 💰 NZ$10, under 16s free 🍴 Mon–Fri 10–4 🚗 On SH2, 24km (15 miles) east of Palmerston North

Local delicacies are brought together in Martinborough

MARTINBOROUGH

🏠 MARTINBOROUGH WINE CENTRE

6 Kitchener Street,
Martinborough
Tel 06-306 9040
www.martinboroughwinecentre.co.nz

A good starting point for the Wairarapa wine trail, the centre has information about local wineries and an excellent selection of wines to taste and buy. They also stock wine books and local products such as olive oil.

⏲ Daily 10–5

🏠 MARTINBOROUGH BEER AND ALES

Corner of New York and Princess streets, Martinborough
Tel 06-306 8310

Martinborough may be best known for its wine, but it also produces some fine craft beers. Martinborough Beer and Ales makes wheat beer, lager, ale and stout, which you can taste while you watch the beer being made.

⏲ Late Oct to end Mar Wed–Sun 11–7; Apr–late Oct Fri, Sat 11–7

🏠 SUNDAY MARKET

6 Kitchener Street, Martinborough
Tel 06-306 9040
www.martinboroughwinecentre.co.nz

Wairarapa food producers and craftspeople sell their wares at the weekly Sunday market. It's held in a rustic workshop at the back of the Martinborough Wine Centre.

⏲ Sun 10–2

🏠 TASTE OF MARTINBOROUGH WINE AND CHEESE SHOP

8 Kitchener Street, Martinborough
Tel 06-306 8383
www.tasteofmartinborough.co.nz

Fine boutique cheeses can be cut to order at this shop, which also stocks local wines and gourmet items. The store has a café selling coffee, snacks, drinks and wine by the glass.

⏲ Daily 9–5 🍴

✪ ATA RANGI

Puruatanga Road, Martinborough
Tel 06-306 9570
www.atarangi.co.nz

Wines of international stature are made at Ata Rangi, known particularly for its Pinot noir, which is regarded as one of New Zealand's top wines. The Paton and Masters families who make the wines live on site, and you're likely to meet them if you visit their rustic cellar door.

⏲ Oct to mid-Apr Mon–Fri 1–3, Sat, Sun 12–4

⭐ MCLEODS QUAD ADVENTURES

White Rock Road, Martinborough
Tel 06-306 8846
www.mcleodsadventures.co.nz
If you've ever wanted to experience the thrill of exploring by quad bike, then this could be your chance. Tours across farmland take in river crossings and fabulous views. No experience required, but advance booking is essential.
✋ From NZ$100

⭐ OLIVO

Hinakura Road, RD4, Martinborough
Tel 06-306 9074
www.olivo.co.nz
Wander through the Wairarapa's first commercial olive grove, which is located in beautiful gardens. You can also taste and buy the oil and learn about its production.
🕐 Sat, Sun 🚗 3km (2 miles) from Martinborough Town Square

⭐ TORA COASTAL WALK

Wairewa Farm, RD2 Martinborough
Tel 06-307 8115
www.toracoastalwalk.co.nz
This three-day, circular, 40km (25-mile) walk crosses the southern Wairarapa hills and drops down to the coast. The hosts are farmers who give you a warm welcome—you dine at their homes. You stay in well-equipped farm cottages and can opt for provisions or take your own food. Your baggage can also be carried.
🕐 Oct–end Apr ✋ Adult NZ$330

♡ AU SPA BELGE

41 Strasbourge Street, Martinborough
Tel 06-306 8188
Yvette Françoise Bonfond brings European techniques to this women's day spa, offering facials, massage therapy, mud treatments, full body treatments, detoxification and hydrotherapy spa baths.
🕐 Wed–Sun 9.30–5 ✋ From NZ$50

MASTERTON

🧀 KINGSMEADE CHEESE

8b First Street, Masterton
Tel 06-378 7178
www.kingsmeadecheese.co.nz
Kingsmeade specialises in sheep cheeses made from milk from its own flock. You can buy the cheeses, as well as jams, chutneys, crafts and local products, at their retail outlet. To find out more about how the cheese begins life, join a farm tour to watch the sheep-milking take place.
🕐 Mon–Fri 9–5, Sat 10–1

⭐ PUKAHA MOUNT BRUCE WILDLIFE CENTRE (▷ 95)

Olive oil products are for sale at Olivo, in Martinborough

⭐ WAIRAPAPA GOURMET WINE ESCAPES

Tranzit Coachlines, Masterton
Tel 06-377 1227
www.tranzit.co.nz
Wine tours depart daily from Wellington (by train to Featherston), Masterton, Carterton, Greytown, Featherston and Martinborough, visiting four Martinborough wineries and the Martinborough Wine Centre, with lunch in a vineyard café.
🕐 Daily ✋ From NZ$76

PALMERSTON NORTH

🏢 EZIBUY

170–178 John F Kennedy Drive, Palmerston North
Tel 06-952 2112
www.ezibuy.co.nz
The retail outlet of a well-known Palmerston North mail-order company, Ezibuy has shopping areas for women, men and children, and stocks clothing, footwear, homeware and gift lines. There is also a four-screen video wall and a children's play area.
🕐 Mon–Wed, Fri 8.30–5.30, Thu 8.30am–8pm, Sat 9–5, Sun 10–5
💻

🎭 CENTREPOINT THEATRE

Corner of Pitt and Church streets, Palmerston North
Tel 06-354 5740
www.centrepoint.co.nz
One of the few theatres to have its own full-time professional theatre company, Centrepoint stages regular shows, from comedy to classic drama, with an emphasis on local New Zealand plays.
🕐 Tue 6.30, Wed–Sat 8, Sun 5
🎟 NZ$35

🎭 REGENT THEATRE

Broadway Avenue, Palmerston North
Tel 06-350 2100
www.regent.co.nz
Opened in 1930, the original picture palace of Palmerston North was restored in 1998. With a seating capacity of almost 1,400, it hosts events such as ballet, musicals, orchestra concerts and comedy.

⭐ GO 4 WHEELS

Horne Road, Ballance, Pahiatua
Tel 06-376 7043
Two-hour trips to the Tararua Wind Farm are the main attraction on these rides—from the hilltops you can see both sides of the North Island. Expect it to be windy! One-hour trips are also available (NZ$65). Advance booking is essential.
✋ NZ$95

PARAPARAUMU

🌐 LINDALE CENTRE

State Highway 1, Paraparaumu
Tel 04-297 0916
A complex of agricultural speciality shops, this is well worth stopping at for local Kapiti cheeses, honey, olive products, sheepskins, and a farm-kitchen restaurant.
🕐 Daily 9–5 🍴

✪ PARAPARAUMU BEACH GOLF CLUB

376 Kapiti Road, Paraparaumu
Tel 04-902 8200
www.paraparaumubeachgolfclub.co.nz
An international-standard golf links ranked 73rd in the world, graced by Tiger Woods at the NZ Open in 2001, and the venue for 12 New Zealand golf opens.
💲 NZ$90

PIPIRIKI

✪ BRIDGE TO NOWHERE TOURS

Pipiriki, RD6 Wanganui
Tel 06-348 7122
www.bridgetonowhere-lodge.co.nz
You can hunt deer, pigs, goats or possums from this remote lodge, but it is also accessible to daytrippers with a four-hour jet-boat ride along the Whanganui River and a guided walk to the Bridge to Nowhere. Overnight accommodation can be arranged. Also trips to the Matemateaonga Track, and Tieke Marae, for an experience of Maori river culture.
💲 From NZ$75

TAIHAPE

✪ MOKAI GRAVITY CANYON

Mokai Bridge, Taihape
Tel 06-388 9109
www.gravitycanyon.co.nz
This company offers the North Island's highest bungy (80m/262ft) and New Zealand's longest Flying Fox (aerial cableway), stretching 1km (0.6 miles), on which you can reach 160kph (107mph)—not for the faint-hearted! If you still have the nerve, a Giant Swing swoops into the Mokai Canyon.
💲 From NZ$99 📍 Off SH1, south of Taihape

UPPER HUTT

✪ EFIL DOOG GARDEN OF ART

1995 Akatarawa Road, RD 2, Upper Hutt
Tel 04-526 7924
www.efildoog-nz.com
Explore 4ha (10 acres) of beautiful gardens full of quirky sculpture. There's also a small art gallery, which specialises in early New Zealand paintings. Guided tours are available.
🕐 Oct–end Mar Wed–Sun 10–4.30
💲 Adult NZ$14, child (5–16) NZ$6

Lilac-hued irises by a pool at Efil Doog Garden of Art

✪ SILVER STREAM RAILWAY

Silverstream, Upper Hutt
Tel 04-563 7348
www.silverstreamrailway.org.nz
Take a Sunday afternoon ride on a vintage steam train, leaving from the site of the country's biggest collection of historic railway engines.
🕐 Trains operate Sun 11–4
💲 Adult NZ$10, child (5–15) NZ$5, family NZ$25

WAIKANAE

✪ KAPITI ISLAND (▷ 94)

WANGANUI

🎭 ROYAL WANGANUI OPERA HOUSE

Saint Hill Street, Wanganui
Tel 06-349 0511
www.royaloperahouse.co.nz
Small but very grand, the opera house was built in 1899. It seats 800 and is used for touring shows, opera and rock bands.

✪ WANGANUI RIVERCITY TOURS

PO Box 4224, Wanganui
Tel 06-344 2554
www.rivercitytours.co.nz
No experience is needed for these escorted canoe adventures over four days in Whanganui National Park. The service includes hotel pick-up, safe vehicle storage, fresh food supplies and informed guides. Sleeping bags and mats are available for hire.
🕐 Nov to mid-Apr 💲 Adult NZ$545, child (under 16) NZ$272

✪ WHANGANUI RIVER CRUISES

Whanganui Riverboat Centre
1A Taupo Quay, Wanganui
Tel 06-347 1863
www.riverboat.co.nz
New Zealand's last operating coal-fired passenger paddle steamer, PS *Waimarie*, was built in 1899 and restored in 2000, and now runs scheduled cruises on the Whanganui River.
🕐 Late Oct–end Apr daily 2pm; May–end Jul, Sep–late Oct Sat, Sun 1pm 💲 Adult NZ$30, child (5–15) NZ$12, family NZ$84

WELLINGTON

🌐 FRUTTI

166 Cuba Street, Wellington
Tel 04-384 6965
One of Cuba Street's many funky designer shops, Frutti has a lively mix of streetwear and party gear. Many items are made out of vintage fabrics, including one-off designs, bags and accessories.
🕐 Mon–Thu 10.30–6, Fri 10–9, Sat 10–6, Sun 11–5

WHAT TO DO

KIRKCALDIE AND STAINS
165–177 Lambton Quay, Wellington
Tel 04-472 5899
www.kirkcaldies.co.nz
Wellington's grand department store, founded in 1863, retains an elegant air, with a commissionaire still present. Originally a draper's store, it still specialises in fashion for men and women, but also carries cosmetics, stationery, lingerie, children's wear, household items, gifts and food.
🕙 Mon–Thu 9–5.30, Fri 9–6, Sat 10–5, Sun 11–4

MOORE WILSON FRESH
Corner of College and Tory streets, Wellington
Tel 04-384 9906
www.moorewilson.co.nz
A must for food lovers, Moore Wilson Fresh is the leading fresh produce store in New Zealand, selling artisan breads, fresh meat, fresh chicken, fresh fish, a huge cheese selection and deli range, coffee and flowers. (Also at Porirua Masterton.)
🕙 Mon–Fri 7.30–7, Sat 7.30–6, Sun 9–5.30

OLD BANK SHOPPING ARCADE
223–237 Lambton Quay, Wellington
Tel 04-922 0600
www.oldbank.co.nz
The arcade contains 27 shops, many of them exclusive to the Wellington region, including fashion, food and cosmetics. It occupies the former banking chamber of the heritage BNZ bank building, with the buried remains of the ship *Inconstant* on display in the basement.
🕙 Mon–Thu 9–6, Fri 9–7, Sat 10–4, Sun 11–3

SCOTTIES
4 Blair Street, Wellington
Tel 04-384 3805
www.fashionz.co.nz/scotties
Scotties sells high fashion womenswear by New Zealand designers such as Marilyn Sainty, Julia Fong and Beth

Ellery. You'll also find international labels, including Issey Miyake, Lanvin and Comme des Garçons.
🕙 Mon–Fri 9.30–6, Sat 10–5

SOMMERFIELDS
296 Lambton Quay, Wellington
Tel 04-499 4847
www.sommerfields.net
Specialising in New Zealand-made gifts and souvenirs, this store carries many items made exclusively for them. The range includes Maori carvings, greenstone, native timber products, hand-blown glass and paua shell.
🕙 Mon–Thu 9–5.30, Fri 9–6, Sat 10–5, Sun 11–3

You'll find a top-class range of souvenirs at Sommerfields

STARFISH
128 Willis Street, Wellington
Tel 04-385 3722
www.starfish.co.nz
Wellington designers Laurie Foon and Carleen Schollum create innovative clothing for men and women reflecting the New Zealand lifestyle and environment. The shop also stocks the luxury Laurie Foon range and other New Zealand designer labels, including Doris De Pont, Fix, Din and Sabatini. You can also buy national and international accessories. Samples, seconds and sale items are available

at Star X (213 Left Bank, Cuba Mall, tel 04-384 7827).
🕙 Mon–Thu 9.30–6, Fri 9.30–8, Sat 10–5, Sun 11–4

TAMARILLO
102–108 Wakefield Street, Wellington
Tel 04-473 6095
www.tamarillonz.com
A dealer gallery and craft shop, Tamarillo holds monthly exhibitions and carries contemporary New Zealand works of art by established and emerging artists, including glass, ceramics, wood, sculpture and jewellery. Worldwide shipping is available.
🕙 Mon–Fri 9.30–6, Sat 10–4, Sun 12–4

UNITY BOOKS
57 Willis Street, Wellington
Tel 0800-486 489
www.unitybooks.co.nz
An excellent bookshop committed to New Zealand publishing, Unity is strong on fiction, politics, history and cookery. It has useful review boards and a knowledgeable staff.
🕙 Mon–Thu 9–6, Fri 9–7, Sat 10–5, Sun 11–4

BATS THEATRE
1 Kent Terrace, Wellington
Tel 04-802 4176
www.bats.co.nz
Alternative and experimental theatre and dance are regularly performed in this casual and intimate theatre, which specialises in New Zealand works. It is also a venue for the annual Fringe Festival (▷ 187).

CIRCA THEATRE
1 Taranaki Street, Wellington
Tel 04-801 7992
www.circa.co.nz
Located next to Te Papa (▷ 96–99), Circa is a professional theatre which presents international drama and comedy as well as New Zealand works on two stages. The atmosphere is casual but

the standard of productions is high.

🕐 Usually Tue–Wed 6.30, Thu–Sat 8, Sun 4 💷 From NZ$35 🎭

🎭 DOWNSTAGE THEATRE
12 Cambridge Terrace, Wellington
Tel 04-801 6946
www.downstage.co.nz
Downstage, New Zealand's longest-running professional theatre, is an intimate venue which presents classic and contemporary drama, dance and comedy, as well as touring shows.

🕐 Mon–Thu 6.30, Fri, Sat 8 🎭

🎭 EMBASSY THEATRE
10 Kent Terrace, Wellington
Tel 04-384 7657
www.deluxe.co.nz
A restored cinema with a giant screen, this is a popular venue during film festivals and hosted the world première of *Lord of the Rings—Return of the King.* The first-floor café, Blondini's, is also a venue for live jazz. Details of films and jazz concerts are carried on the website.

🎟 From NZ$9

🎭 THE OPERA HOUSE
111 Manners Street, Wellington
Tel 04-802 4060
www.stjames.co.nz
The Opera House is the grand old lady of Wellington theatres—typical of lavish early 1900s architecture, and with a large stage. It is a popular venue for concerts, musicals and touring shows.

🎭 READING CINEMAS COURTENAY CENTRAL
100 Courtenay Place, Wellington
Tel 04-801 4601
www.readingcinemas.co.nz
A 10-screen complex located on level 3 of a shopping and entertainment complex, Reading Cinemas shows popular films and has good parking. Details of films are listed on the website.

🎟 From NZ$9.50, child NZ$8.50

🎭 WELLINGTON CONVENTION CENTRE
111 Wakefield Street, Wellington
Tel 04-801 4231
www.wellingtonconventioncentre.com
An umbrella for 19 venues around Wellington, this includes the modern Michael Fowler Centre (111 Wakefield Street), which stages opera and concerts and is home to the New Zealand Symphony Orchestra; the beautifully restored 1904 Wellington Town Hall next door, which is also a concert hall; and the modern TSB Bank Arena (Queens Wharf), used for sports and pop concerts, accommodating up to 5,000.

Wellington's best-known cinema, the Embassy Theatre

🎟 Tickets available through Ticketek, tel 04-384 3840, www.ticketek.co.nz

🎭 WESTPAC ST. JAMES THEATRE
Courtenay Place, Wellington
Tel 04-802 4060
www.stjames.co.nz
The St. James was built in 1912 as a vaudeville and picture theatre, and extended and refurbished in 1998. Today it has one of the best stages in New Zealand. The ornate interior has been retained and a spacious foyer with a café added. It hosts musicals, dance and touring shows and is home to the Royal New Zealand Ballet.

🍷 BAR BODEGA
101 Ghuznee Street, Wellington
Tel 04-384 8212
www.bodega.co.nz
Bar Bodega hosts local and occasional international music events, and is dedicated to real ale and good music.

🕐 Daily 4pm–3am

🍷 THE ESTABLISHMENT
Corner of Courtenay Place and Blair Street, Wellington
Tel 04-382 8654
www.theestablishment.co.nz
You can dance until late at this popular hangout on Courtenay Place, listen to jazz or watch the weekend's big match. The Establishment serves Southwest American food and tapas in its restaurant, and there's also a lounge bar.

🕐 Mon–Fri 11–late, Sat, Sun 10–late

🍷 HAPPY
Corner of Vivian and Tory streets, Wellington
Tel 04-384 1965
www.happy.net.nz
A relaxed basement venue, Happy has nightly gigs featuring alternative live music and jazz. It is one of the venues in the Wellington Jazz Festival.

🕐 Gigs 8pm and/or 10pm

🍷 SPICEHAMMER
71 Cuba Street, Wellington
Tel 04-389 2120
www.pound.co.nz
A gay nightclub, Spicehammer has resident and guest DJs and weekly drag shows.

🕐 Tue–Sat 5–late

⚽ BASIN RESERVE
Rugby Street, Wellington
Tel 04-384 3171
www.westpacstadium.co.nz
Arguably New Zealand's most famous sports ground, and the only one with heritage status, the Basin Reserve is maintained largely for regional and national cricket fixtures. It is also home to the New Zealand Cricket Museum (▷ 104). During the winter it is used for club rugby.

WHAT TO DO

⭐ WESTPAC STADIUM

Waterloo Quay, Wellington
Tel 04-473 3881
www.westpacstadium.co.nz
Seating 34,500, with seven
food and beverage outlets,
this is the main venue for
national and international
rugby fixtures, international
rugby sevens tournaments
and cricket. It also hosts big
popular events, such as Carols
by Candlelight and rock
concerts.

✪ FERGS ROCK 'N' KAYAK

Shed 6, Queens Wharf, Wellington
Tel 04-499 8898
www.fergskayaks.co.nz
Owned by Olympic champion
Ian Ferguson, Fergs guides
and coaches kayaking, climbing and in-line skating on the
waterfront. You can have a
paddle along the shore or a
full guided tour, and the indoor
rock wall caters to all levels of
climbing.
🕐 Mon–Fri 10–8, Sat, Sun 9–6
💲 From NZ$9

✪ HELIPRO

Queens Wharf, Wellington
Tel 04-472 1550
www.helipro.co.nz
Scenic helicopter flights
give views over the city and
harbour, or can take you
farther afield on a wine tour to
the Marlborough Sounds or
lunch at Wharekauhau.
💲 From NZ$45

✪ MUD CYCLES

338 Karori Road, Wellington
Tel 04-476 4961
www.mudcycles.co.nz
Close to Makara Peak
Mountain Bike Park, standard
mountain bikes and 24-speed
cycles are available for hire,
with the option of central city
drop-off and collection. Mud
Cycles also offer instruction
classes and tours, which range
from easy sightseeing to
advanced technical trails for
eager thrill seekers.
💲 From NZ$25

✪ SEAL COAST SAFARI

32 Salamanca Road, Wellington
Tel 0800-732 527
www.sealcoast.com
Tours of Wellington's wild
south coast take in the Red
Rocks and the wind turbine, as
well as the fur seal colony at
Tongue Point and Sinclair
Head. There is time to meet
the seals, learn about their life
cycle and have refreshments.
Tours leave from the visitor
information office.
🕐 Daily 10.30, 1.30 💲 NZ$74,
child (under 14) NZ$40

✪ WALK WELLINGTON

Tel 04-472 8280
www.wellingtonnz.com/Walk-Wellington/

*Seal Coast Safaris get you close
to these intriguing creatures*

Knowledgeable locals take
guided walks around the city,
which can be personalised to
suit your interests or focus on
arts, heritage, shopping or
nature. Book at least three
days ahead. Scheduled
Essential Wellington walks give
a general introduction to the
city. They leave from the visitor
information office and you
can book them there
(tel 04-802 4860).
🕐 Essential Wellington: Nov–end Mar
daily at 10am; Apr–end Oct call ahead
to find out times and days 💲 From
NZ$20, child (5–16) NZ$10, under
5s free

✪ WELLINGTON ROVER TOURS

PO Box 11167, Wellington
Tel 021-426211
www.wellingtonrover.co.nz
With these coach tours you
can visit *Lord of the Rings*
locations (including lunch at
Rivendell), take a 'hop on hop
off' day pass or search for
glow-worms on a sunset drive
around the south coast.
💲 From NZ$40, child NZ$25

⭐ CAPITAL E

Civic Square, Wellington
Tel 04-913 3720
www.capitale.org.nz
A creative technology and
performance facility for
children, located in Civic
Square, Capital E has professional theatrical shows,
including puppets, masks and
music. There are also events,
exhibitions, activities, and
workshops, which include a
TV studio.
🕐 Daily 10–5

⭐ CARTER OBSERVATORY AND PLANETARIUM

40 Salamanca Road, Wellington
Tel 04-472 8167
www.carterobservatory.org.
The observatory is located in
the Botanic Garden, close to
the top terminal of the Cable
Car (▷ 101), and includes
a planetarium, several
telescopes and a giftshop.
Choose from two shows at the
planetarium (one of which is
always the current night sky),
and enjoy solar viewing or
night sky telescope viewing.
🕐 Nov–end Feb Sun–Tue 10–5, open
late Wed–Sat; Mar–end Oct Mon–Thu
11–4, open late Fri, Sat 📅

⭐ KARORI WILDLIFE SANCTUARY (▷ 104)

⭐ WELLINGTON CABLE CAR (▷ 101)

⭐ WELLINGTON ZOO (▷ 105)

FESTIVALS AND EVENTS

JANUARY

WELLINGTON CUP WEEK
Trentham Racecourse, Upper Hutt
www.trentham.co.nz
The highlight of the Wellington race calendar also marks Wellington's Anniversary Weekend. And high fashion is all part of the race-day fun.

WINGS OVER WAIRARAPA
Hood Aerodrome, Masterton
Tel 027-477 417
www.wings.org.nz
Organised by the New Zealand Sport and Vintage Aviation Society, this biennial show (odd years) commemorates milestones in aviation, with displays of World War I and II warbirds and many other famous and interesting vintage aircraft.

FEBRUARY–MARCH

FRINGE FESTIVAL
Abel Smith Street, Wellington
Tel 04-382 8015
www.fringe.org.nz
The Fringe started as an offshoot of the International Festival to cater for people with smaller pockets and alternative tastes. It has now become an annual festival in its own right, with comedy, dance, new media, parties, spoken word, music and free performances.

MARTINBOROUGH FAIR
The Square, Martinborough
Tel 06-304 9933
www.martinboroughfair.org.nz
This country fair—the largest event of its type in New Zealand—is held on two days, one month apart, and includes arts, crafts and food from all over the country. It attracts around 480 stallholders and more than 40,000 visitors each year.
🎫 Free

NEW ZEALAND INTERNATIONAL ARTS FESTIVAL
PO Box 10113,
Wellington
Tel 04-473 0149
www.nzfestival.telecom.co.nz
The city barely sleeps during this month-long biennial festival (held in even years) as Wellington hums with top international acts that would not normally come to New Zealand—cabaret, jazz, circus, classical music and avant-garde theatre—along with fresh, commissioned local work.

MARCH

GOLDEN SHEARS
12 Dixon Street,
Masterton
Tel 06-378 8008
www.goldenshears.co.nz
Reckoned to be the world's premier shearing and wool-handling championship, this three-day event gives a unique insight into New Zealand's rural community as sheep are shorn at lightning speed.

SEPTEMBER

MONTANA WORLD OF WEARABLE ART
TSB Bank Arena,
Wellington
Tel 03-548 9299
www.worldofwearableart.com
Art is taken off the wall to adorn the body in wildly wonderful ways in this annual show, which started in Nelson and has spread to the extent that it has had to make a home in Wellington. The WOW exhibition remains in Nelson (▷ 115).

OCTOBER–NOVEMBER

WELLINGTON INTERNATIONAL JAZZ FESTIVAL
PO Box 11981, Manners Street,
Wellington
Tel 04-385 9602
www.jazzfestival.co.nz
From jazz standards to avant cabaret, free jazz to funky dance grooves, there is jazz for every taste in cafés, bars and venues all over the city during this annual two-week festival of international and local talent.
🎫 From NZ$10; tickets from Ticketek

NOVEMBER

SCARECROW'S BIG DAY OUT
Gladstone School, Gladstone
Tel 06-372 7601
www.gladstone.org.nz
Scarecrows are scattered throughout the Gladstone district in this lighthearted fair, which includes a 'Scarecrow Scamper' 10km (6-mile) walk and fun run.

TOAST MARTINBOROUGH
Kitchener Street, Martinborough
Tel 06-306 9183
www.toastmartinborough.co.nz
A highlight of the New Zealand wine calendar, this festival is so popular that the 10,500 tickets sell out fast. Festival-goers move from vineyard to vineyard, where local and Wellington chefs match food to the wine-maker's selection, and there is top live entertainment. You also get the chance to sample vintages that have been saved for the festival, but have other-wise sold out. There is a free shuttle bus.
🎫 NZ$60

NELSON AND MARLBOROUGH

Nelson is reckoned to be New Zealand's sunniest region; it is also one of the prettiest, with acres of golden-sand beaches, rolling hills and lush farmland, orchards and vineyards. Nelson also has one of the country's most popular walks, the Abel Tasman Coast Track. Every settlement is crowded with craft studios, and Nelson city has an astonishing number of restaurants. Eco-tourism on both land and sea is especially popular here.

The same is true of the Marlborough Sounds, an intricate network of bays and inlets, many of them reachable only by boat. A cruise on the Sounds is a must; better still, stay at one of the isolated resorts, where you can spend the day doing bush walks such as the Queen Charlotte Track, swim, cycle, kayak or sail, then pamper yourself with spa treatments, and eat and sleep in comfort. (Note: Outdoors you'll need to protect yourself against biting sandflies.)

Marlborough is also New Zealand's largest wine region, famous for its Sauvignon blanc but also producing a wide range of styles. A comprehensive wine trail map is available from visitor information offices, or you can choose from several tours. Don't expect great shopping, entertainment or nightlife, however.

Whale-watching made Kaikoura's name as a destination. Because of the marine geography, whales come close to the coast, and the environment attracts rare seabirds and other marine life. You can view them from a boat, a plane, a helicopter or a kayak, and swim with some of them. Landlubbers can get close to the seal colony by driving along the Kaikoura Peninsula. The road south from Kaikoura hugs the precipitous coast and is particularly scenic, as is the train journey from Picton to Christchurch, stopping at Kaikoura. The township itself comes alive during the annual Seafest.

KEY TO SYMBOLS	
🛍	Shopping
🎭	Entertainment
🍸	Nightlife
🏃	Sports
✪	Activities
♡	Health and Beauty
✹	For Children

ABEL TASMAN NATIONAL PARK

✪ ABEL TASMAN WILSON'S EXPERIENCES
265 High Street, Motueka
Tel 03-528 2027
www.abeltasman.co.nz
Depending on your budget and the time you have available, you can choose from half-day to five-day experiences of the Abel Tasman Coast Track (▷ 109–110), cruising, walking and/or kayaking, with or without a guide. There's also the opportunity to stay overnight in beachfront accommodation, with food provided.
🛏 Adult from NZ$53, child NZ$26

✪ KAITERITERI KAYAKS
Sandy Bay Road, Kaiteriteri
Tel 03-527 8383
www.seakayak.co.nz
As well as kayaking trips lasting from two hours to five days, this company offers the option

f swimming with the seals
t the Tonga Island Marine
Reserve. Swimming is
ombined with kayaking, water
axi trips or walking the Abel
asman Coast Track.
🏊 Adult from NZ$55, child NZ$40

BLENHEIM

🐝 MARLBOROUGH
FARMERS' MARKET
.&P Showgrounds, Maxwell Road,
lenheim
el 03-579 3599
www.mfm.co.nz
resh local produce is sold
direct to the community at this
ummer market, where more
han 30 producers supply
wild game, organic salmon
nd koura, preserves and
ickles, roasted coffee, potato
lates, fresh vegetables,
eirloom potatoes, half-
aked baguettes and other
natural products.
🕐 Nov–end Mar Sun 9–12

🐝 THE VILLAGE
93 Rapaura Road,
lenheim
el 03-579 3520
everal speciality stores are
ound under one roof here,
ncluding coffee, olive products, giftware, Mud House and
e Grys wines, Prenzel fruit
queurs and schnapps (▷ 119).
🕐 Daily 10–5

☘ CLOUDY BAY
acksons Road,
lenheim
el 03-520 9140
www.cloudybay.co.nz
New Zealand's most
nternationally acclaimed
auvignon blanc is made here,
nd so are some other less
well known but equally
nteresting wines, including
arrel-fermented Chardonnay,
Pinot noir, Pelorus *méthode
raditionelle* and Te Koko, an
ak-aged Sauvignon blanc
ermented with wild yeasts.
🕐 Daily 10–5

☘ DANIEL LE BRUN
Terrace Road, Renwick
(west of Blenheim)
Tel 03-572 8859
www.lebrun.co.nz
With its courtyard café and
cellars tunnelled into the
hillside, Daniel Le Brun is a
romantic spot for a bite to eat
or a winery tour. The company
makes a range of wines, and is
best known for its *méthode
traditionelle* sparkling wine—
it's well worth taking a winery
tour, which explains the
specialist techniques involved.
🕐 Daily 10–4.30 🖥

☘ HUNTERS WINES
(▷ 232–233)

*Searching for bargains at a
Marlborough farmers' market*

☘ MARLBOROUGH OLIVES
NEW ZEALAND
Fell Street, Grovetown,
Blenheim
Tel 03-577 8834
www.marlborough-olives.co.nz
New Zealand's first commercial
olive grove was established
here in 1986 by the late Gidon
Blumenfeld, and the oil they
press here is named after him.
The grove is part of a world-
wide trial based on the olive
collection at Córdoba, Spain,
and the research centre of
Israel. Phone before you visit.
🕐 Mon–Fri 8.30–4.30

☘ MARLBOROUGH RIVER
QUEEN
Riverside Park, Horton Street,
Blenheim
Tel 03-577 5510/0800-266 322
www.riverqueencruise.co.nz
Gentle Cruises along the
Opawa River in a replica pad-
dle steamer, Mississippi-style.
Lunch cruises take two
leisurely hours, afternoon ones
last an hour, and dinner
cruises three.
🕐 Thu–Sat 12, 3.15, 6.30, Sun 12, 3.15
🏊 From NZ$12.50

☘ MARLBOROUGH TRAVEL
PO Box 1000,
Blenheim
Tel 03-577 9997
www.marlboroughtravel.co.nz
Insights into many aspects of
Marlborough life are offered in
these land- and sea-based
tours. The signature Greenshell
Mussel Cruise visits a mussel
farm in the Sounds, and serves
mussels cooked on board
with a glass of locally made
Sauvignon blanc. A gourmet
tour focuses on wine and food
matching. Other tours visit
gardens, olive groves,
vineyards and craftspeople.
Tours can be personalised to
your interests.
🏊 From NZ$95

☘ MONTANA BRANCOTT
WINERY (▷ 119)

☘ PRENZEL DISTILLING
COMPANY (▷ 119)

☘ WINE TOURS BY BIKE
191 Bells Road, Blenheim
Tel 03-577 6954
www.winetoursbybike.co.nz
Cycling is a popular way to
see the vineyards in this flat
countryside. This service,
operated by Argrove Lodge,
allows you to join a guided
tour or hire a bicycle and have
it delivered to your door.
Trailer bicycles cater for
young children.
🏊 From NZ$40

COLLINGWOOD

✪ CAPE FAREWELL HORSE TREKS

McGowan Street, Puponga, Collingwood
Tel 03-524 8031
www.horsetreksnz.com
Horse treks in this beautiful countryside take in stunning views over farmland and beach, with river crossings, caves and the option of a gallop along the sands. Trips can last from 1.5 hours to four days.
🖐 From NZ$35

✪ FAREWELL SPIT TOURS

Tasman Street,
Collingwood
Tel 03-524 8257
www.farewellspit.com
This company has more than 50 years experience of taking people out onto Farewell Spit. The tours go to the lighthouse, the gannet colony, Cape Farewell, and to see the wading birds (▷ 111). Trips last from 3 to 6.5 hours.
🖐 Adult from NZ$80, child (under 16) NZ$45

KAIKOURA

☻ DONEGAL HOUSE

Schoolhouse Road, RD1,
Kaikoura
Tel 03-319 5083
www.donegalhouse.co.nz
Donegal House is a lively Irish pub, restaurant and B&B surrounded by beautiful gardens and run by Murray Boyd, whose ancestors arrived from Donegal, Ireland, in 1865. The bar is a popular place to meet the Kaikoura locals and there is often live music, as well as Guinness and Kilkenny on tap and a choice of 140 whiskeys.
🕐 Daily 7am–midnight 🚗 4km (2.5 miles) north of Kaikoura on SH1; turn left into Schoolhouse Road

✪ DOLPHIN ENCOUNTER AND ALBATROSS ENCOUNTER

96 Esplanade, Kaikoura
Tel 03-319 6777
www.dolphin.co.nz
www.oceanwings.co.nz
You can swim with dolphins or watch rare seabirds on launch trips by these sister companies. Wetsuits and snorkelling equipment are provided for swimmers, and there are hot showers on board.
🖐 Adult from NZ$60, child NZ$40
🕐 Oct–end May daily 5.30, 8.30, 12.30; Jun–end Sep 8.30, 12.30

✪ KAIKOURA HELICOPTERS

PO Box 5, Kaikoura
Tel 03-319 6609

A traditional Maori greeting (hongi), Maori Tours Kaikoura

www.worldofwhales.co.nz
In a helicopter you don't get as close to the wildlife as you can on a boat, but you do get a bird's-eye view of the whole whale on these World of Whales flights. Other scenic flights are also available.
🕐 Daily on demand (weather permitting) 🖐 From NZ$195, family NZ$680

✪ KAIKOURA KAYAK

Tel 021-462 889
www.seakayakkaikoura.co.nz
Kayaking is a good way to encounter seals and watch ocean-going birds such as albatrosses, while keeping the impact on the environment to

a minimum. You can freedom-hire or take a half-day guided tour, combined with optional diving and snorkelling. Kayak training is also available.
🕐 Oct–end Apr daily 8.30, 12.30, 4.30; May–end Sep daily 9, 1 🖐 Adult from NZ$70, child (under 12) NZ$50. Freedom hire from NZ$55

✪ MAORI TOURS KAIKOURA

10 Churchill Street, Kaikoura
Tel 03-319 5567
www.maoritours.co.nz
A good introduction to local culture and protocol, these tours visit local *pa* sites and a Maori home, and explore native bush to see how the Maori used plants. Tours leave from the Kaikoura Information Office.
🕐 Daily 9, 1.30 🖐 Adult NZ$85, child (under 15) NZ$45

✪ WHALEWATCH KAIKOURA

Whaleway Station, off Beach Road (SH1), Kaikoura
Tel 03-319 6767
www.whalewatch.co.nz
You need to book well in advance for these boat trips. As well as whales, you can expect to see dolphins, seals, albatrosses and other seabirds (there is an 80 per cent refund if no whales appear). An on-board computer animation explains the marine geography of the Kaikoura Canyon. Trips are weather-dependent. Children under 3 are not permitted.
🕐 Mar–end Oct daily 7.15, 10, 12.45; Nov–end Feb 7.15, 10, 12.45, 3.30
🖐 Adult NZ$130, child NZ$60

✪ WINGS OVER WHALES

Kaikoura Airfield, 6km (4 miles) south of Kaikoura
Tel 03-319 6580/0800-226629
www.whales.co.nz
Sightseeing flights give you a bird's-eye view of whales, dolphins and seals, as well as the spectacular Kaikoura scenery.
🕐 Daily 9–4 🖐 Adult from NZ$135, child (4–13) NZ$75

WHAT TO DO

MAPUA

🏛 COOL STORE GALLERY
7 Aranui Road, Mapua
Tel 03-540 3778
www.coolstoregallery.co.nz
The works of more than 70 artists and craftspeople from the Nelson and West Coast regions are displayed here.
🕐 Daily 10–5

🏛 THE NAKED BUN
66 Aranui Road, Mapua
Tel 03-540 3656
Grab a croissant or Danish pastry for breakfast, stock up for a picnic with speciality breads, quiches and pastries at this village bakery, or have a coffee and eat in the café.
🕐 Wed–Sun 7–5 🔲

✪ MAPUA ADVENTURES
8 Aranui Road, Mapua
Tel 03-540 3833
www.mapuaadventures.co.nz
Jet-boating, mountain biking, birdwatching and kayaking are among the diversions available, with options for individuals, families and children. Trips explore the Mapua estuary, coastline and forests.
🎫 From NZ$35

MOTUEKA

🏛 MOTUEKA SUNDAY MARKET
Decks Reserve Carpark, Motueka
Tel 03-540 2709
This eclectic market mixes food, New Zealand crafts, Asian and Peruvian clothing, collectables, second-hand items, plants, seasonal fruits and vegetables with live music and street drama.
🕐 Sun 8–1

✪ ABEL TASMAN AIR
PO Box 125, Motueka
Tel 03-528 8290
www.abeltasmanair.co.nz
If you are short of time and want to see a lot, this may be the way to go. Tours fly to Abel Tasman National Park for lunch at Awaroa Lodge, to the West Coast for part of the Heaphy

Track, or head to Kaikoura for whale-watching and a crayfish lunch. The company also operates scenic flights and connecting flights for trampers.
🎫 From NZ$65

✪ BUSH AND BEYOND
35 School Road, RD3 Motueka
Tel 03-528 9054
www.naturetreks.co.nz
Bush and Beyond is a conservation-based guiding business specialising in flora and birds. Treks last from one to eight days in Kahurangi National Park. Itineraries cater for all ages and fitness levels and can be personalised. You can stay in comfortable lodges,

Checking out the coffee roaster at Pomeroy's, Nelson

walk the Heaphy Track or go off-track wilderness backpacking.
🎫 From NZ$115, family NZ$350

MURCHISON

✪ RUSSELL FROST'S TICKLISH TROUT TOURS
PO Box 30, Murchison
Tel 03-523 9868
www.guidedflyfishingnz.com
Russell Frost specialises in 'New Zealand-style stalking' of wild brown trout in high country streams, braided rivers and glacial lakes. Trips can last from half a day to an overnight camp-out.
🎫 From NZ$450 for two people

✪ ULTIMATE DESCENTS
51 Fairfax Street, Murchison
Tel 03-523 9899
www.rivers.co.nz
Despite the name, this company arranges family-friendly rafting trips on the Buller River, as well as adrenalin-pumping whitewater kayaking and rafting, camp-outs, and one- to five-day heli-journeys. Minimum ages apply to all trips.
🕐 Adult from NZ$95, child NZ$75
🎫 🔲

NELSON

🏛 NELSON MARKET
Montgomery Square, Nelson
Tel 027-270 2600
www.nelsonmarket.com
On Saturday mornings a dreary car park in central Nelson is transformed into a marketplace, with a flea market mix of clothes and crafts and a fine selection of food. Look for local organic fruit and vegetables, speciality breads, local sheep's cheese, bratwurst made from local pork, and Blackbird Valley Forge's knives made from recycled materials.
🕐 Sat 8–1

🏛 POMEROY'S COFFEE AND TEA CO.
80 Hardy Street, Nelson
Tel 03-546 6944
www.pomeroys.co.nz
An old-fashioned boutique coffee roaster, Pomeroy's sells 25 blends of coffee and a huge variety of speciality teas. It also serves excellent coffee to drink on the spot, and stocks Nelson olive oils and deli items.
🕐 Mon–Fri 9–5, Sat 9.30–12.30

🎭 THEATRE ROYAL
Rutherford Street, Nelson
Tel 03-548 3840
New Zealand's oldest wooden theatre, built in 1878, the Royal is in need of restoration but it still hosts the Nelson Repertory and other local and visiting shows.

WHAT TO DO

🎵 PHAT CLUB
137 Bridge Street, Nelson
Tel 03-548 3311
www.phatclub.co.nz
A mix of dance music and live acts makes this a popular late-night dance club and venue. Whether your taste runs to techno, dub, rock, hip-hop, indie or punk reggae, you can find it here.
🕐 Thu–Sat 10pm–late

🎵 VICTORIAN ROSE
281 Trafalgar Street, Nelson
Tel 03-548 7631
www.victorianrose.co.nz
A firm supporter of local music, the Victorian Rose pub has regular Tuesday night gigs with the Nelson Jazz Club, Wednesday and Thursday nights devoted to freewheeling jazz, and weekends get feet dancing with jazz-rock blends of local and imported bands. There's a blackboard menu, Mac's beers and local wines.
🕐 Daily 11am–late

⭐ HAPPY VALLEY ADVENTURES
194 Cable Bay Road, Nelson
Tel 03-545 0304
www.happyvalleyadventures.co.nz
This 650ha (1,600-acre) farm offers eco-tours on 4X4 motor-cycles, taking in an extensive native forest valley with a 2000-year-old matai tree. Other attractions include bush-walks, Skywire rides reaching up to 100kph (60mph), and rides on an eight-wheel drive amphibious all-terrain vehicle.
💰 From NZ$70, child (under 16) NZ$1 per year of age

⭐ JJ'S QUALITY TOURS
31a Stansell Avenue, Nelson
Tel 03-546 5470/0800-568 568
www.jjs.co.nz
As well as wine tours of the region that made their name, JJ's now offer a tour of five Nelson breweries, and sight-seeing and craft tours. You may be able to mix and match, according to your interests.
💰 From NZ$50

⭐ NELSON GOLF CLUB
38 Bolt Road, Nelson
Tel 03-548 5029
www.nelsongolf.co.nz
This championship-standard, 18-hole course is near the air-port on the shores of Tasman Bay—a short drive from the city. It has fine views over the sea and mountains, a fully stocked pro-shop and clubs, trundlers and carts for hire.
🕐 Daily 7–7 💰 NZ$40

⭐ VERTICAL LIMITS
34 Vanguard Street, Nelson
Tel 03-545 7511
www.verticallimits.co.nz
Even if you have no previous experience you can join a

Strapped in for the Skywire ride at Happy Valley Adventures

rock-climbing expedition, or learn the principles indoors on a climbing wall.
🕐 Mon–Thu 12–9, Fri–Sun 10–6 💰 From NZ$40

⭐ FOUNDERS HISTORIC PARK
87 Atawhai Drive, Nelson
Tel 03-548 2649
www.founderspark.co.nz
This collection of buildings from the late 1800s houses several businesses, including a bone carver and a café. There are also displays of vintage transport, and train rides daily between 26 December and 10 January. Children can enjoy the

playground and 3-D maze, and their parents can sample the excellent organic brews produced on-site by Founders craft brewery.
🕐 Daily 10–4.30 💰 Adult NZ$5, child NZ$2, family NZ$13

❌ NATURELAND
Tahunanui Beach, Tahunanui (southwest of downtown Nelson)
Tel 03-548 6166
www.naturelandzoo.co.nz
This little family-oriented zoo has exotic, domestic and native wildlife, a walk-through aviary and an aquarium. Families can feed the animals and enjoy a picnic by the playground.
🕐 Daily 9–4 💰 Adult NZ$5, child (2–14) NZ$2

❌ NELSON FUN PARK
Tahunanui Beach, Tahunanui (southwest of downtown Nelson)
Tel 03-548 6267
A hydroslide, bumper boats and mini-golf are the attractions at this beachside family fun park. The hydroslide is closed from May to the end of September.
🕐 Sat, Sun 11.30–5, plus school holidays 💰 Adult from NZ$4, child NZ$2.50

PICTON
⭐ THE COUGAR LINE
The Waterfront, Picton
Tel 03-573 7925
www.cougarlinecruises.co.nz
Scheduled trips around the Marlborough Sounds visit various bays to drop off and take on passengers. Short cruises are also available, taking in up to 80km (50 miles) of coastline in three hours, with a commentary on the way. A popular option is the day trip to Ship Cove, with the opportunity to walk for five hours on the Queen Charlotte Track to Furneaux Lodge.
💰 From NZ$50

☼ DOLPHIN WATCH ECOTOURS
The Waterfront, Picton
Tel 03-573 8040
www.dolphinwatchmarlborough.co.nz
As well as the popular swimming with dolphins, this company takes trips to Motuara Island bird sanctuary, to walk a section of the Queen Charlotte Track, and do some birdwatching for king shags (found only in the Sounds), New Zealand robins, little blue penguins and saddlebacks.
🎫 From NZ$80

☼ MARLBOROUGH SOUNDS ADVENTURE COMPANY
London Quay, Picton
Tel 0800-283283
www.marlboroughsounds.com
Adventures of all kinds are on offer in trips that combine kayaking, mountain biking and walking on the Queen Charlotte Track. One of the most popular is the Ultimate Sounds Adventure, a guided one-day hiking, one-day sea kayaking, one-day mountain biking adventure. There is an overnight stay at Portage Resort Hotel, either backpacker-style or in twin-share ensuite accommodation.
🎫 From NZ$50

☼ SOUNDS CONNECTION
10 London Quay, Picton
Tel 03-573 8843
www.soundsconnection.co.nz
Choose from launch and coach tours, or fishing or wine tasting on scheduled and private half- to full-day tours.
🎫 From NZ$55

RICHMOND

⊕ CRAFT HABITAT
Champion Road, Richmond
Tel 03-544 1488
www.crafthabitat.co.nz
Watch the makers at work at Nelson's arts and crafts village, buy their work or commission them to make something for you. There is also a specialist food shop.
🕐 Daily 9–5 ☕ Courtyard café

⊕ THE GRAPE ESCAPE
Corner of McShane Road and Coastal Highway, Richmond
Tel 03-544 4341
www.grapeescape.co.nz
Organic vineyard Richmond Plains and Te Mania Estate share an outlet for their wines in this rustic complex, which also sells arts and crafts, the Prenzel range of liqueurs and schnapps (▷ 119), and chocolate.
🕐 Daily 10.30–4.30 ☕

⊕ HÖGLUND ART GLASS
Landsdowne Road, Richmond
Tel 03-544 6500
www.hoglund.co.nz

Watching the glass-blowing at Höglund Art Glass

Ola Höglund and Marie Simberg-Höglund have an international reputation as hot-glass blowers and their gallery is a candy store of brilliant hues and design. Their International Glass Centre includes a glass-blowing studio, exhibition hall, engraving studio, and cold-work studio for cutting, sandblasting and polishing. Guided tours show you the artists at work.
🕐 Daily 9–5; tours 10.30, 1.30, 3
🎫 Tours: adult NZ$15, child (under 14) free

STOKE

☼ MAC'S BREWERY
660 Main Road, Stoke
Tel 03-547 0526
www.macs.co.nz
Nelson's local brewery, Mac's makes naturally brewed lagers, ales and innovative limited-release beers. You can tour, sample the beers and browse in the shop.
🕐 Daily 10–5.30; tours daily 11, 2

TAKAKA

☼ ANATOKI SALMON
McCallums Road, Takaka
Tel 03-525 7251
www.anatokisalmon.co.nz
Catch your own salmon here and tour the salmon farm on the banks of the Anatoki River. Fishing rods and tackle are supplied, and you can hire a barbecue to cook your fish.
🕐 Daily 9–5

☼ BENCARRI NATURE PARK
McCallums Road, Takaka
Tel 03-525 8261
Feeding the Anatoki eels has been a popular holiday pastime here since 1914, and Bencarri has plenty of other friendly farm animals to feed, touch and interact with. Horse-riding and mini-golf are among the other attractions, and the gallery sells knitwear and alpaca/llama yarns.
🕐 Sep–end Apr daily 10–6 ☕

WAIRAU VALLEY

☼ LEIGHVANDER
RD1 Wairau Valley
Tel 03-572 2851
www.leighvandercottage.co.nz
A collection of 140 varieties of lavender grows in this lovely garden, which surrounds a restored 1859 cob cottage. Handmade soaps and body products made from lavender are among the products sold in the studio, which also offers gifts, including ribboned lace, candle wicking and furniture.
🕐 Nov–end Mar by appointment

FESTIVALS AND EVENTS

WHAT TO DO

JANUARY

NELSON JAZZFEST
Nelson Jazz Club, PO Box 7188, Nelson
Tel 03-546 9269
www.nelsonjazz.co.nz
A wide variety of jazz bands from the Nelson region and around the country perform in this week-long festival, with events on the streets and at various venues around the town. There's a grand finale on New Year's Day at Fairfield Park.
🎫 Tickets from Everyman Records, 249 Hardy Street, Nelson

NELSON SUMMER KITE FESTIVAL
Neale Park, Nelson
Tel 03-548 8707
http://nkc.nayland.school.nz
This two-day festival, hosted by Nelson Kite Club, fills the Nelson sky with kites in every conceivable shape and form. Don't be surprised to see a flying cat or a giant lizard.

JANUARY–FEBRUARY

MARLBOROUGH 4 FUN SUMMER CONCERTS
Various locations
Tel 03-577 8935
www.marlborough4fun.co.nz
Free outdoor concerts are held during the summer holiday season.

FEBRUARY

BLUES BREWS AND BBQS
A&P Park, Maxwell Road, Blenheim
www.bluesbrews.co.nz
Held on the first Saturday in February, this festival combines tastings of local ales, alcoholic lemonades, ciders and beers, with a variety of barbecue food, live bands and children's entertainment.
🕐 Noon–7.30 🎫 NZ$35 from Ticket Direct, tel 0800-224 224

WINE MARLBOROUGH FESTIVAL
Brancott Vineyard, Brancott Road, Blenheim
Tel 03-577 9299
www.wine-marlborough-festival.co.nz
This showcase for Marlborough wines, held in a vineyard on the second Saturday and Sunday in February, provides an opportunity to sample over 150 wines from more than 40 wineries. The event also includes wine workshops, wine and food matches, entertainment and music.
🕐 10–6 🎫 NZ$35 from Ticket Direct, tel 0800-224 224 🚌 Shuttle buses from Blenheim

EASTER

CLASSIC FIGHTERS MARLBOROUGH
Tel 03-578 8227
Omaka Aerodrome, Blenheim
www.classicfighters.co.nz
Aircraft are displayed as part of a theatrical spectacle, where battle scenes from both world wars are re-enacted on the ground as well as in the air.
🕐 From 7.30am 🎫 Gate sales: adult from NZ$15, child (6–12) NZ$5

JULY

NELSON SCHOOL OF MUSIC WINTER FESTIVAL
Nelson School of Music, 48 Nile Street, Nelson
Tel 03-548 9477
www.nsom.ac.nz
This annual two-week festival of music, comedy, dance and drama features local, national and international artists.

OCTOBER

KAIKOURA SEAFEST
Takahanga Domain, Kaikoura
Tel 03-319 5641
www.kaikoura.co.nz/seafest
Held on the first Saturday of October, Seafest is an annual celebration of the abundance of the ocean and all it represents for the Kaikoura region. It combines continuous live entertainment with cooking demonstrations and food, wines and beverages from the Kaikoura, Marlborough and North Canterbury regions. Beforehand, you can dance at the Big Top Bash.
🕐 10–5 🎫 Adult NZ$20, child (5–17) NZ$5

NELSON ARTS FESTIVAL
Nelson City Council, 110 Trafalgar Street, Nelson
Tel 03-546 0212
www.nelsonfestivals.co.nz
Entertainment of all kinds is provided in this annual two-week festival, which includes a mask carnival, sculpture symposium, street fun and other cultural events.

NOVEMBER

HUNTER'S GARDEN MARLBOROUGH
PO Box 1180, Blenheim
Tel 03-577 5500
www.garden-marlborough.co.nz
Green-fingered enthusiasts from all over New Zealand gather in Blenheim for this annual six-day celebration of gardening, which includes garden tours, seminars, workshops and a market day with 200 stalls in Seymour Square.

DECEMBER

KAHURANGI ENDURANCE TRIATHLON AND MOUNTAIN CLASSIC RUN
Golden Bay
www.nelsontriclub.co.nz
One-day multi-sport events in New Zealand started here in 1984, and this is still one of the best, combined with a classic off-road run. An endurance test strictly for the super fit, combining cycling, kayaking and running.

CANTERBURY AND THE WEST COAST

The 'English' city of Christchurch may lack the sophistication of Auckland or the liveliness of Wellington, but it makes up for it in ease of access to a wide range of facilities and activities. You can visit beautiful gardens or an interactive Antarctic exhibit, find trendy fashions in the High Street or see craftspeople at work in the Arts Centre, attend a concert by the Christchurch Symphony or play golf on one of many courses, take a gondola up the Port Hills or find some of the country's best windsurfing on the Estuary. *The Press* newspaper carries entertainment listings.

Christchurch's main shopping area is a pleasant network of pedestrian malls intersecting Colombo Street and fringing Cathedral Square, in which you can find speciality shops, international fashion and lifestyle chains, food courts, cafés and bookshops. The heart of New Zealand's high-tech sports and leisurewear industry, Christchurch is the home of labels such as Fairydown and Macpac. Locals tend to shop at look-alike suburban malls such as Eastgate, Westfield Riccarton and The Palms.

Shops are few and far between on the West Coast, where 'wild' sums up the scenery, the weather and the folks. You can sample the atmosphere of the place at the Mahinapua pub, south of Hokitika, and get it in spades at the annual Hokitika Wildfood Festival. Farther south, the Fox and Franz Josef glaciers are amazingly easily accessible.

An hour's drive north of Christchurch, Waipara is the region's main wine-growing area, with a number of vineyards open to the public, some with restaurants. In the same area, Hanmer Springs is noted for its thermal pools.

Less than two hours driving west from Christchurch gives you a great choice of skiing, from commercial fields such as Mount Hutt to the club fields of the Craigieburn Range, which offer a particularly New Zealand experience with primitive facilities, friendly people and ungroomed slopes.

KEY TO SYMBOLS

- 🛍 Shopping
- 🎭 Entertainment
- 🍸 Nightlife
- 🏅 Sports
- ⭐ Activities
- 💗 Health and Beauty
- ✪ For Children

AKAROA

🛍 AKAROA BLUE PEARLS
Main Wharf, Akaroa
Tel 03-304 7877
www.akaroabluepearls.com
Iridescent blue mabe (hemi-spherical) pearls are cultured in paua in Akaroa Harbour and Tory Channel. The Eyris Blue Pearl Centre tells the story of their creation and sells them.
🕐 Oct–end Mar daily 10.30–5.30; Apr–end Sep 11–4.30

🛍 BARRYS BAY CHEESE
Main Road, Barrys Bay, Akaroa Harbour
Tel 03-304 5809-
At Barrys Bay, Don and Jeanette Walker are carrying on a cheese-making tradition going back more than 150 years. They are the only people in New Zealand still making traditional cloth-bound rinded cheddar, and also make a range of European cheeses. You can watch the cheese

being made on alternate days during the season, and taste it in the shop, which also sells local wine and deli items.

🌐 Aug–end May Mon–Fri 8.30–5, Sat, Sun 9.30–5; Jun, Jul Mon–Fri 9–5, Sat 9.30–1, Sun 9.30–4.30

🌐 NATURALLY JADE

57 rue Lavaud, Akaroa
Tel 03-304 7781
www.naturallyjade.co.nz

You can watch the craftsman at work here, carving items from greenstone (*pounamu*, or New Zealand jade). The gallery has a superb collection of greenstone works, from large sculptures to jewellery—many show designs with symbolic associations, which he will explain. The shop also stocks gold, silver, paua and bone jewellery by other artists.

🌐 Mon–Fri 9–5, Sat, Sun 10–5

✪ AKAROA HARBOUR CRUISES

Main Wharf, Akaroa
Tel 03-304 7641
www.blackcat.co.nz

Two-hour scenic wildlife cruises at 11am and 1.30pm are on offer here. Although the highlight is the likely sighting of Hector's dolphins, you may also see little blue penguins, spotted shags and fur seals. You can also swim with dolphins and take a guided kayak trip.

🌐 Nov–end Apr 11, 1.30; May–end Oct 1.30 💲 Adult from NZ$52, child (5–15) NZ$20

✪ AKAROA SEAL COLONY SAFARI

PO Box 4, Akaroa
Tel 03-304 7255
www.sealtours.co.nz

The four-wheel-drive safari takes a crater-rim road and goes through sheep and cattle paddocks to the seal colony on the eastern bays of Banks Peninsula. You can observe the colony from a distance, or walk around the rocky coastline to see it at close quarters.

🌐 Daily 9.30am, 1pm 💲 Adult NZ$70, child NZ$50, family NZ$190

✪ BANKS PENINSULA TRACK

PO Box 54, Akaroa
Tel 03-304 7612
www.bankstrack.co.nz

Leaving from Akaroa, the track takes in 35km (22 miles) of spectacular coastline, native bush, waterfalls and beaches. It can be done in two or four days, staying in farm cottages with hot showers and well-equipped kitchens. You can take your own food and some supplies are available on route. Pack cartage is available (at extra cost) for parts of the track.

🌐 Oct–end Apr 💲 2 days NZ$125, 4 days NZ$225

A stunning greenstone carving at Naturally Jade, Akaroa

✪ LINTON ARTIST'S GARDEN VISITS

68 rue Balguerie, Akaroa
Tel 03-304 7501
www.linton.co.nz

Surprises are everywhere in Josie Martin's enchantingly eccentric artist's garden, dotted with sculptures and mosaics, including an extraordinary sculptural wall mosaic. The house is a showcase for her paintings, and the venue for art workshops and concerts. You can also stay on a bed-and-breakfast basis.

🌐 Oct to mid-Jun daily 2–4 💲 House NZ$10; garden NZ$12

✪ POHATU PENGUINS

Pohatu Flea Bay, Akaroa
Tel 03-304 8552
www.pohatu.co.nz

Pohatu is home to the largest white-flippered penguin colony on the South Island. The best time to come is during the breeding season, from September to January. Guided evening walks are available through the colony; as the road is only accessible to four-wheel-drive vehicles or mountain bikes, the recommended option is to join the tour at Akaroa. Scenic day tours and kayak rental are also available.

💲 Adult from NZ$55, child (under 12) NZ$40

♥ LUMIÈRE

8 rue Balguerie, Akaroa
Tel 03-304 7404
www.lumieremassage.co.nz

Therapeutic massage, exfoliation, body wraps, outdoor hot tubs and reflexology are among the services offered at this 'private outdoor wilderness'.

🌐 Daily 10–5 💲 From NZ$25

CHRISTCHURCH

🌐 ARTS CENTRE

Worcester Boulevard, Christchurch
Tel 03-366 0989
www.artscentre.org.nz

Take a guided retail therapy tour or browse around the 40 art and craft outlets, many of which are working studios (▷ 124). Try to catch the weekend market, when up to 70 stalls put up their awnings and the smell of cooking from many countries fills the air.

🌐 Daily 9.30–5

🌐 BALLANTYNES

City Mall, Christchurch
Tel 03-379 7400
www.ballantynes.co.nz

A Christchurch institution, this traditional, family-run department store stocks everything from perfume to household items, bed linen to toys, and furniture to fashions

WHAT TO DO

for men, women and children. Branches at Christchurch Airport and Timaru.
🕒 Mon–Thu 9–6, Fri 9–8, Sat 9–5, Sun 10–5

🏬 BIVOUAC OUTDOOR
Corner of Lichfield and Colombo streets, Christchurch
Tel 03-366 3197
www.bivouac.co.nz
Bivouac specialises in mountaineering and alpine sports equipment, including clothing, tents and packs, sleeping bags, ski gear and climbing equipment.
🕒 Mon, Wed, Thu 9–5.30, Tue 9.30–5.30, Fri 9–8, Sat, Sun 10–4

🏬 MAPWORLD
Corner of Manchester and Gloucester streets, Christchurch
Tel 03-374 5399
www.mapworld.co.nz
Mapworld has a wide range of digital and topographical city, town, provincial and national maps; also atlases and accessories such as binoculars.
🕒 Mon–Thu 8–6, Fri 8–8, Sat, Sun 9–5

🏬 MERIVALE MALL
189 Papanui Road, Christchurch
Tel 03-355 9692
www.merivalemall.co.nz
Serving a smart residential suburb, Merivale Mall has more than 40 speciality shops, many of them devoted to New Zealand and international fashion labels. It also houses several stylish restaurants and wine bars and a particularly good supermarket.
🕒 Mon–Wed, Fri 9–6, Thu 9–8, Sat 10–5, Sun 10–4

🏬 RICCARTON ROTARY MARKET
Riccarton Park Racecourse, Racecourse Road, Christchurch
Tel 03-339 0011
A community project operated by the local Rotary Clubs, this popular weekly market has more than 300 stalls selling crafts, food, clothing, jewellery, bric-à-brac and produce.
🕒 Sun 9–2

🏬 SWANNDRI CONCEPT STORE
132 Gloucester Street, Christchurch
Tel 03-379 8674
www.swanniestore.com
Best known for its famous bush shirts of checked wool—much loved by hunters, farmers and trampers needing rugged protection from the elements—Swanndri also produces a range of more fashion-conscious lightweight merino garments for men, women and children.
🕒 Mon–Fri 9–5.30, Sat 10–5

🏬 UNTOUCHED WORLD
155 Roydvale Avenue, Christchurch
Tel 03-357 9399

Stylish outdoor gear from the Untouched World collection

www.untouchedworld.co.nz
Located not far from the airport, Untouched World is a stylish modern store specialising in high-quality New Zealand lifestyle products, including its own-label merino-opossum blend knitwear, leisure and fashion clothing, skincare, art and food. A courtesy bus is available.
🕒 Daily 9–5 🍴 Restaurant and wine bar

🎭 ARTS CENTRE
Worcester Boulevard, Christchurch
Tel 03-366 0989
www.artscentre.org.nz
Several performance venues are clustered on the Arts

Centre site (▷ 124), including the Court Theatre (tel 03-963 0870, www.courttheatre.org.nz), one of New Zealand's leading professional theatre companies, which presents local and international drama, musicals and comedy. Occasional performances are also given at the University Theatre (tel 03-374 5483) and the Southern Ballet and Dance Theatre (tel 03-379 7219). The Academy Cinema and Cloisters Cinemas (tel 03-366 0167) screen art-house films. Plays and concerts, including Friday lunchtime concerts, are performed in the Great Hall.

🎭 CHRISTCHURCH TOWN HALL
95 Kilmore Street, Christchurch
Tel 03-366 8899
www.convention.co.nz
The 2,000-seat auditorium, noted for its acoustics, is a regular venue for concerts by the Christchurch Symphony Orchestra and Christchurch City Choir, as well as touring orchestras and performers. The smaller proscenium-arch James Hay Theatre hosts chamber music, opera and theatrical productions.

🎭 ISAAC THEATRE ROYAL
145 Gloucester Street, Christchurch
Tel 03-366 6326
www.isaactheatreroyal.co.nz
The grand old lady of Christchurch theatres, the Theatre Royal opened in 1908. It retains its ornate interior, and refurbishments backstage in 2005 brought it up to international standards. It hosts ballet, drama and musicals.

🎲 CHRISTCHURCH CASINO
30 Victoria Street, Christchurch
Tel 03-365 9999
www.chchcasino.co.nz
The casino has 350 gaming machines as well as blackjack, baccarat, Caribbean stud poker, American roulette, keno and *tai sai*. The dress code is smart casual and the

minimum age is 20. There are several restaurants and bars.
🕙 Daily 24 hours

🍸 CRUZ
90 Lichfield Street, Christchurch
Tel 03-379 2910
www.cruz.co.nz
A gay bar and nightclub upstairs in the Ministry night-club, Cruz provides a relaxed lounge environment with a free pool table early week-nights, before becoming a nightclub at 11pm.
🕙 Wed–Sun 7–late

🍸 DUX DE LUX
41 Hereford Street, Christchurch
Tel 03-366 6919
www.thedux.co.nz
A restaurant and pub in the Arts Centre, the Dux hosts regular gigs by local and visiting performers. The venue is tiny and noisy, but the large outdoor courtyard acts as a popular meeting place. The attached restaurant serves vegetarian dishes and seafood, but the pub is most highly regarded for its boutique brewery. The beers are available only on tap, and are given quirky local names such as Nor'Wester (after Canterbury's famous wind). Ginger Tom ginger ale is recommended.
🕙 Daily 11am–late

🍸 ILLUSIONS
Corner of Chancery Lane and Gloucester Street, Christchurch
Tel 03-379 0572
A popular dance hangout, Illusions plays 1960s and '80s disco classics to a young crowd, with live performers on Friday and Saturday nights.
🕙 Wed–Sat 10–late

🍸 SAMMY'S JAZZ REVIEW
14 Bedford Row, Christchurch
Tel 03-377 8618
www.sammys.co.nz
Sammy's has live jazz seven nights a week, and supports local musicians with regular weekly gigs, as well as hosting

visiting groups. There's also a good à la carte menu, so you can dine while you listen.
🕙 Mon–Sat 5–late, Sun 10.30–1.30, 5–late

🍸 THE TWISTED HOP
6 Poplar Street, Lichfield Lanes, Christchurch
Tel 03-962 3688
http://thetwistedhop.co.nz
The Twisted Hop brews its own English-style cask-conditioned Golding, Challenger and Twisted Ankle ales year-round, and India Pale Ale in summer. There's a quiz night every other Sunday, and live jazz on Wednesday and Thursday.
🕙 Daily noon–late

Celebrating a win at Christchurch's Addington Raceway

🏇 ADDINGTON RACEWAY
Jack Hinton Drive, Christchurch
Tel 03-338 9094
www.addington.co.nz
The New Zealand Metropolitan Trotting Club offers harness racing all year round, including the popular Christchurch Casino and New Zealand Trotting Cup. Advance booking is required.

🏊 CENTENNIAL LEISURE CENTRE
Armagh Street, Christchurch
Tel 03-941 6853
www.centennial.org.nz
Less than 10 minutes' walk from Cathedral Square in the heart of the city, Centennial

has both a leisure pool and a lap pool, sauna, steam and spa facilities, and a fitness centre.
🕙 Mon–Thu 6am–9pm, Fri 6am–7pm, Sat, Sun 7–7 🎫 Fitness centre NZ$8, pool NZ$5, child (under 16) NZ$2.50

🏉 JADE STADIUM
Wilsons Road, Christchurch
Tel 03-379 1765
www.jadestadium.co.nz
Major rugby fixtures and test cricket attract huge crowds here. Check events on the website and book tickets through Ticketek (tel 03-377 8899).

🏇 RICCARTON PARK RACECOURSE
Racecourse Road, Christchurch
Tel 03-342 0000
www.riccartonpark.co.nz
The Canterbury Jockey Club holds 20 race days through the year, including the New Zealand Cup, New Zealand Grand National and Easter Racing Carnival.

🏔 ADVENTURE CANTERBURY
PO Box 1259, Christchurch
Tel 03-358 5991
www.adventurecanterbury.com
Whether it's golf or skiing, Akaroa or Mount Cook/Aoraki, rafting or horse-trekking, farm visits, a wine trail or fishing, this company has a tour on offer.
🎫 From NZ$45

🚴 CHRISTCHURCH BIKE TOURS
4A Ramahana Road, Huntsbury, Christchurch
Tel 03 366 0337
www.chchbiketours.co.nz
Billed as the country's only guided city bike tours, the two hour route takes you through Hagley Park to Riccarton Bush and Mona Vale, taking advantage of the city's flatness and its good cycle facilities. Bikes are provided.
🕙 Nov–end Mar daily 2pm 🎫 NZ$25

❂ CHRISTCHURCH PERSONAL GUIDING SERVICE

1/28 Packe Street, Christchurch
Tel 03-365 8480
Daily two-hour walks leave
from a kiosk in Cathedral
Square, with trained guides
providing informative
commentary about historic
and modern buildings.
🕐 Oct–end Apr daily 10am, 1pm;
May–end Sep 1pm 💵 NZ$10

❂ EXPLORE NEW ZEALAND BY BICYCLE

Tel 03-339 4020
www.cyclehire-tours.co.nz
You can go bicycling almost
anywhere in the South Island
with this company, from
short-term hire of family bikes
for an excursion in Hagley
Park to taking the gondola up
the Port Hills and mountain
biking down, or touring
farther afield.
💵 From NZ$25

❂ HAGLEY GOLF CLUB

Hagley Park, Christchurch
Tel 03-379 8279
www.hagley.nzgolf.net
Located in Hagley Park, in the
heart of Christchurch, the golf
course caters for players of all
abilities. The regular Friday
morning 12-hole tee-off is a
feature, and non-members
are welcome.
🕐 Daily, open to green-fee players
after 10.30am 💵 NZ$20 for 18 holes

❂ NIMBUS PARAGLIDING

PO Box 17712, Sumner, Christchurch
Tel 03-389 1999
www.nimbusparagliding.co.nz
The Port Hills above
Christchurch make a good
take-off spot for paragliders.
You can do a tandem paraglide
without training, or Nimbus
will instruct you until you
are able to do a solo flight.
Flying at Taylors Mistake,
Scarborough Cliffs or Castle
Rock, you get great views
over the Canterbury Plains.
💵 From NZ$140

❂ TASTE CANTERBURY

3 Scarborough Road, Christchurch
Tel 03-326 6753
www.goodthings.co.nz
Tailor-made food and wine
tours take you to meet the
makers, see them at work,
and taste their wares. Half-day
and full-day tours explore
Christchurch city and plains,
Akaroa and Banks Peninsula,
West Melton, Ellesmere
and Waipara.
💵 From NZ$100

❂ TRANZALPINE HIGH COUNTRY EXPLORER TOUR

6 Fraser Place, Rangiora
(north of Christchurch)
Tel 03-377 1391

*Panoramic windows make a ride
on the TranzAlpine a treat*

www.high-country.co.nz
Enjoy a variety of Canterbury
attractions on this tour, with
a coach trip across the
Canterbury Plains, morning
tea, a jet-boat trip, a four-
wheel-drive safari, lunch and
then a scenic rail trip back to
Christchurch from Arthur's Pass
on the TranzAlpine train.
💵 Adult NZ$330, child (4–14) half price

❂ TRANZALPINE RAILWAY

Christchurch Railway Station, Troup
Drive, Addington
Tel 0800 872467
www.tranzscenic.co.nz
This 4.5-hour rail trip from
Christchurch to Greymouth
takes in spectacular mountain,

farm and rainforest scenery,
including areas not seen
from the road, such as the
Waimakariri Gorge. An open-air
viewing deck adds to the
experience, and there is a
buffet car. You can do the
return trip in a day.
🕐 Daily 8.15am 💵 Adult day return
NZ$182, child NZ$101

❂ UP UP AND AWAY

PO Box 36308, Merivale, Christchurch
Tel 03-381 4600
www.ballooning.co.nz
Early-morning balloon flights
over the Canterbury plains give
spectacular views of the
Southern Alps. You can help
with preparations for take-off
and, after landing in a farmer's
field, celebrate with a glass
of bubbly.
💵 Adult NZ$260, child (5–11) NZ$199

❂ QEII PARK

Travis Road, New Brighton
Tel 03-941 6849
www.qeiipark.co.nz
Built for the 1974 Common-
wealth Games, QEII is a multi-
sport and leisure complex. The
aquatic facility includes a 40m
(131ft) wave pool, lazy river
and children's play zone with
interactive water toy features.
Spa, sauna and café facilities
are available poolside. QEII
also has a modern fitness
centre and aerobic studio,
squash courts, Olympic
weight-lifting gym, athletic
stadium and cricket wicket.
🕐 Mon–Fri 6am–9pm, Sat, Sun
7am–8pm 💵 Adult from NZ$5,
child NZ$2.50

❂ SCIENCE ALIVE!

392 Moorhouse Avenue, Christchurch
Tel 03-365 5199
www.sciencealive.co.nz
The whole family can be entertained while learning about
science through hands-on
experiences and shows in this
interactive exhibit. There is also
a well-stocked science shop.
🕐 Mon–Thu 10–5, Fri–Sun 10–6
💵 NZ$12 ♿

WHAT TO DO

FOX GLACIER

⊕ ALPINE GUIDES

Main Road, Fox Glacier
Tel 03-751 0825
www.foxguides.co.nz
Trips leave throughout the day
to suit various fitness levels,
from a gentle walk to the
glacier terminal or a half-day
hike on the lower reaches
of the glacier to heli-hikes,
ice climbing or multi-day
mountaineering. Ice-climbing
instruction days are a speciality.
Some equipment is provided,
including crampons.
📷 Adult from NZ$79, child NZ$46

FRANZ JOSEF

⊕ AIR SAFARIS

Main Road, Franz Josef
Tel 03-752 0716
www.airsafaris.co.nz
A 30-minute scenic flight gives
overviews of the Franz Josef
and Fox glaciers, rainforest
and Westland Tai Poutini
National Park. The popular
50-minute Grand Traverse
also takes in the Southern
Alps, Aoraki/Mount Cook and
the Tasman and Murchison
glaciers.
📷 Adult from NZ$260, child NZ$180

⊕ FRANZ JOSEF GLACIER GUIDES

Main Road, Franz Josef
Tel 03-752 0763
www.franzjosefglacier.com
A choice of trips is available,
ranging from an easy 2km
(1.2-mile) walk to the glacier
terminal or a half-day hike on
pre-cut steps, to a full-day
climb on spectacular icefalls
and overnight trips staying in
alpine huts. Popular heli-hikes
combine a scenic flight with a
two-hour guided trip around
the ice pinnacles of the middle
glacier. Some equipment is
provided, including strap-on
crampons. Minimum ages
and numbers apply.
📷 Adult from NZ$90, child (6–16)
NZ$45

GERALDINE

⊕ BARKER'S BERRY BARN

Te Moana Road, Geraldine
Tel 03-693 8969
www.barkers.co.nz
Barker's fruit processors make
juices, jams, toppings, spiced
fruit sauces and condiments
from local and Central Otago
fruit. You can taste before you
buy at this retail outlet, which
also sells gift baskets, fruit
smoothies and sundaes.
🕐 Daily 9–5.30

⊕ TALBOT FOREST CHEESE

16 Talbot Street, Geraldine
Tel 03-693 1111
A remarkable range of cheeses
is produced at this little factory

A rich variety of preserves is sold at Barker's Berry Barn

in the heart of Geraldine's
shopping complex. You can
watch the cheeses being made
and sample them at the
attached retail outlet, which
also sells a variety of food-
related gift items.
🕐 Daily 9–5.30

GREYMOUTH

⊕ LEFT BANK ART GALLERY (▷ 121)

⊕ ECO-RAFTING

108 Mawhera Quay, Greymouth
Tel 03-768 4005
www.ecorafting.co.nz
Relaxing river excursions,
fly-fishing trips and extreme
white-water adventures are

offered in half-day to multi-day
trips on the Arnold, Grey
and Buller rivers.
📷 From NZ$100

⊕ MONTEITH'S BREWING COMPANY

Corner of Turumaha and Herbert
streets, Greymouth
Tel 03-768 4149
www.monteiths.co.nz
The Monteiths name has been
associated with brewing on
the West Coast since the
1850s, and this is the only
brewery in New Zealand
where the beer is made in
open fermenters by coal-fired
boilers. Tours fill you in on the
history, show the brewing
process, explain the different
beer styles and include a
formal tasting. Advance
booking is essential.
🕐 Tours Mon–Fri 10, 11.30, 2, Sat, Sun
11.30, 2 📷 NZ$10

⊛ SHANTYTOWN (▷ 121)

HANMER SPRINGS

⊕ HANMER FOREST CONSERVATION PARK

Hanmer Springs
Tel 03-315 7128
www.doc.govt.nz
Some of New Zealand's oldest
exotic forest can be accessed
in self-guided walks, ranging
from easy trails taking less
than an hour to hill climbs
taking between one and five
hours. Trail maps from the
visitor information office.

⊕ HANMER SPRINGS ADVENTURE CENTRE

20 Conical Hill Road, Hanmer Springs
Tel 03-315 7233
www.hanmeradventure.co.nz
You can rent mountain bikes of
all kinds from this store, as well
as in-line skates, motorised
scooters, skis and snowboards,
and fishing rods—with local fishing information and licences.
Transport to the Hanmer
Springs Ski Area is also available. The shop sells outdoor
clothing, swimwear, camping,
fishing, mountain biking and ski

gear. Quad-bike trips are available (minimum age 12), plus rental of mountain bikes (one hour NZ$14, full day NZ$28), scooters, motorbikes, ATVs, fishing tackle and ski equipment.
🕐 Daily 8.30–5.30 ✋ Mountain bike hire from NZ$14

✪ THRILLSEEKERS CANYON ADVENTURE CENTRE
Waiau Ferry Bridge, Main Road, Hanmer Springs
Tel 03-315 7046
www.thrillseeker.co.nz
Bungy jumping off the 135-year-old Waiau Ferry Bridge, jet-boat rides and rafting are organised on this spectacular stretch of the Waiau River gorge near the Hanmer turn-off from SH7. You can recover from your exertions at the on-site café.
✋ Adult from NZ$85, child NZ$50
🚌 9km (6 miles) south of Hanmer 🅿️

◐✪✪ HANMER SPRINGS THERMAL RESERVE (▷ 123)

HAWARDEN

✪ ALPINE HORSE SAFARIS
Waitohi Downs, Hawarden
Tel 03-314 4293
www.alpinehorse.co.nz
Lawrie and Jenny O'Carroll are best known for their high-country trail rides lasting up to 11 days. They also offer two-hour and half-day treks, and the opportunity to take part in farm life by joining a sheep or cattle round-up.
✋ From NZ$50

HOKITIKA

✪ JUST JADE EXPERIENCE
197 Revell Street, Hokitika
Tel 03-755 7612
www.jadeexperience.co.nz
Gordon Wells combines jade carving with a backpacker's stop in Hokitika. Spend a day learning how to carve and polish greenstone, then create a piece of your own.
✋ From NZ$20

✪ SCENIC WATERWAYS PADDLE BOAT CRUISES
Main South Road, Hokitika
Tel 03-755 7239
www.paddleboatcruises.com
Takutai Belle, a stern-drive paddleboat, takes trips through rainforest up the Mahinapua Creek to Lake Mahinapua, on the old Gold Trail Waterway route. Tours can be arranged to suit—ask for a refreshment stop at the Mahinapua pub, an authentic West Coast tavern.
🕐 Daily 2pm ✋ Adult NZ$25, child NZ$15

✪ NATIONAL KIWI CENTRE
Sewell Street, Hokitika
Tel 03-755 5251

Riding out on an Alpine Horse Safari from Hawarden

This is a kiwi house and indoor marine aquarium on the outskirts of Hokitika, which displays sea life unique to the West Coast. Watch sharks being fed by divers, as well as giant eels, crayfish, seahorses and octopuses. You can also catch a salmon in the lake and have it cooked in the restaurant.
🕐 Daily 9–5 ✋ Adult NZ$12, child NZ$6, family NZ$30

LAKE TEKAPO

✪ EARTH AND SKY
PO Box 112, Lake Tekapo
Tel 03-670 6960
www.earthandsky.co.nz
Day and evening tours to Mount John Observatory.

🕐 Daily 11–3. Also 10pm in summer and 8pm in winter ✋ Adult from NZ$42, child NZ$5

✪ LAKE TEKAPO ADVENTURES AND CRUISES
PO Box 129, Lake Tekapo
Tel 03-680 6629
www.laketekapo.co.nz
An attractive combination tour includes a cruise around Motuariki Island on Lake Tekapo with optional fishing plus a 4X4 trip up Mount John, giving spectacular views over the Mackenzie Basin and Southern Alps. Another option is a day's fly fishing with lessons and lunch.
✋ Combination NZ$120 with fishing, NZ$70 without; fly fishing NZ$600, for up to 3 people

✪ MOUNT COOK ALPINE SALMON
Tekapo-Pukaki Canal Road, Lake Tekapo
Tel 03-435 0085
www.mtcooksalmon.com
At 677m (2,221ft) above sea level, with a stunning view of the mountain after which it is named, Mount Cook Alpine Salmon is reckoned to be the highest salmon farm in the world. The farm makes use of the hydro canal, growing 70,000 salmon in cages. You can take a self-guided tour and feed the fish, catch your own fish (rod supplied), or buy one at the shop and barbecue it on the spot.
🕐 Daily, daylight hours ✋ Tour: 2 adults NZ$5, child free 🚌 From SH8, take Hayman Road at Lake Pukaki, or the Heritage Trail at Irishman Creek

LITTLE RIVER

✪ LITTLE RIVER GALLERY
Main Road, Little River, Banks Peninsula
Tel 03-325 1944
www.littlerivergallery.com
A popular stop halfway between Christchurch and Akaroa, this gallery shows the work of local artists in sculpture, painting and jewellery. The adjacent café and general store sells excellent country food.
🕐 Daily 9.30–5.30

LYTTELTON

✪ SEA CRUISES
B Jetty, Lyttelton
Tel 03-328 7720
www.sea-cruises.co.nz
Combine city sightseeing with dolphin-watching on the Scenic Lyttelton Tour, which includes pick-up, a scenic coach tour and dolphin cruise. Other cruises go to Ripapa and Quail islands.
🕐 Daily 🎫 Adult NZ$50, child (5–15) NZ$17.50, family NZ$117.50

METHVEN

✪ BLACK DIAMOND SAFARIS
PO Box 60, Methven
Tel 0274-508 283
www.blackdiamondsafaris.co.nz
These skiing enthusiasts take people to Canterbury's club fields for a special New Zealand skiing or boarding experience on ungroomed slopes, with rope tows and no tow queues. Tours include one-day and multi-day trips, safety equipment included.
🎫 From NZ$150

✪ MOUNT HUTT SKI AREA
Mount Hutt, Methven
Tel 03-302 8811
www.nzski.com
Canterbury's largest commercial ski area, Mount Hutt has nine lifts and a vertical drop of 675m (2,214ft), with snow-making equipment, and slopes suitable for everyone from beginners to advanced skiers. It has a ski shop, gear for rent, and a restaurant with a deck.
🕐 Jun–end Oct 🎫 Adult from NZ$79, child NZ$42

MOUNT COOK

✪ ALPINE GUIDES
Bowen Drive, Mount Cook
Tel 03-435 1834
www.alpineguides.co.nz
The only resident guiding company in the national park, they can take you on anything from half- and full-day walks to mountaineering trips and heli-skiing on the Tasman Glacier.
🎫 From NZ$130, child NZ$60

✪ HELICOPTER LINE
Tel 03-435 1801
www.helicopter.co.nz
Three flights are offered in the park: a 20-minute trip landing on the Ben Ohau Range, a 30-minute trip to the Richardson Glacier, and a 45-minute Mountains High adventure which takes you over the Tasman Glacier, makes a snow landing and flies across the Main Divide and the Franz Josef and Fox glaciers.
🎫 From NZ$195

OKARITO

✪ OKARITO NATURE TOURS
PO Box 89, Franz Josef
Tel 03-753 4014

Safety gear is part of the scene when rafting on the Buller River

www.okarito.co.nz
Kayaking is a good way to explore Okarito Lagoon, New Zealand's largest unmodified wetland (3,240ha/8,000 acres). It's the main feeding ground for kotuku (white herons), and visited by more than 70 other bird species.
🎫 From NZ$35

PUKEKURA

✪ PUKEKURA BUSHMAN'S CENTRE LODGE
Pukekura, Lake Ianthe, South Westland
Tel 03-755 4144
www.pukekura.co.nz
While staying in this tiny settlement, you can browse in the museum, try gold panning, or fish in a Canadian canoe, then revive yourself with a plate of possum pie at the Puke Pub and soak in the hot pools before retiring to the Lodge.
🕐 When it suits

STAVELEY

✪ TUSSOCK AND BEECH ECOTOURS
Staveley, RD1, Ashburton
Tel 03-303 0880
www.nature.net.nz
The 'In the Hobbits' Footsteps' tour includes a visit to Mount Sunday, site of Edoras in *The Lord of the Rings: The Two Towers*. The trip includes lodging in a heritage-registered cottage, meals, a tour through the spectacular glaciated landscape, a beech forest walk along a mountain stream, and lunch beside a lake. You can also join nature tours.
🎫 From NZ$275

WAIPARA

✪ ATHENA OLIVE GROVES AND MILL HOUSE
164 Mackenzies Road, Waipara
Tel 03-314 6774
www.athenaolives.co.nz
Producers of Canterbury's first olive oil, Athena presses its olives on a traditional Tuscan press within hours of picking them, producing extra virgin olive oil of high quality. You can watch the process in season or see a video, and taste the olive products in the shop.
🕐 Daily 9–4

WESTPORT

✪ BULLER ADVENTURES
Buller Gorge Road, Westport
Tel 03-789 7286
www.adventuretours.co.nz
You can choose from several adventures in and around the spectacular Buller Gorge, with rafting graded from family to white-water and heli-rafting, as well as jet-boating, horse-trekking and eight-wheel-drive Argo tours.
🎫 From NZ$75, child NZ$55

WHAT TO DO

FESTIVALS AND EVENTS

JANUARY–FEBRUARY

WORLD BUSKERS FESTIVAL
PO Box 845, Christchurch
Tel 03-377 2365
www.worldbuskersfestival.com
Street performers from around the world converge on Christchurch for 10 days in the summer. They come in many forms—acrobats, comedians, contortionists, escapologists, fire-eaters, jugglers, 'living statues', magicians, mime artists, sword swallowers and street artists. Performances are generally free.

FEBRUARY

CANTERBURY WINE AND FOOD FESTIVAL
North Hagley Park, Christchurch
Tel 03-343 5953
Around 40 local wine producers, food producers and restaurants set up stalls under the trees in Hagley Park, and families gather on the grass to listen to live music.

MARCH

HOKITIKA WILDFOODS FESTIVAL
Cass Square,
Hokitika
Tel 03-756 9048
www.wildfoods.co.nz
Hokitika has become famous for its annual Wildfoods Festival, on the second weekend of March, which attracts 18,000 visitors eager to sample 'bushtucker' such as huhu grubs, worms, grasshoppers, eels, mussels, snails, and the famous West Coast whitebait, washed down with local beer. There's a dance in the evening. Reserve accommodation well in advance.
🕐 11–5 🎟 Adult NZ$30, child (5–18) NZ$5

WAIPARA WINE AND FOOD CELEBRATION
Glenmark Church, Waipara
Tel 03-314 6962
Started as a European-style church and community celebration of grape-gathering and wine-making, the Waipara festival remains an appealingly small community event, which includes organ concerts in the church, and food and wine stalls and music outdoors.
🎟 NZ$25

JULY–AUGUST

CHRISTCHURCH ARTS FESTIVAL
PO Box 705, Christchurch
Tel 03-365 2223
www.artsfestival.co.nz
This two-week biennial winter festival is held in odd years, with live performances including opera, classical music, jazz, cabaret, drama and dance.

OCTOBER

HERITAGE WEEK
Tel 03-941 8688
www.heritageweek.co.nz
Plenty of heritage-related activities in the Christchurch area, including events, tours, quizzes and fairs.

REEFTON WILD WEST HUNT
Visitor Centre, 67 Broadway, Reefton
Tel 03-732 8391
The quality and variety of local wild foods are celebrated in this weekend hunt for the heaviest deer, pig and trout. There's a special section for children, too.

NOVEMBER

CANTERBURY A&P SHOW
Canterbury Agricultural Park, Christchurch
Tel 03-343 3033
www.theshow.co.nz
The country comes to town in New Zealand's largest agricultural and pastoral show, attended by more than 100,000 people each year. In addition to livestock competitions, showjumping, dressage, dog trials and wood-chopping, there are 350 trade exhibitors and a Canterbury food pavilion. Look for local 'A&P' shows all over the country, too.

TIMARU FESTIVAL OF ROSES
Caroline Bay, Timaru
Tel 03-688 5531
www.festivalofroses.co.nz
The largest annual community event in the central South Island, this three-day festival attracts around 15,000 gardening enthusiasts and others with seminars, workshops, displays, competitions, shows, demonstrations, tours and 150 stalls and exhibits from across New Zealand. There are also children's activities.

DECEMBER

WAIMATE STRAWBERRY FARE
Seddon Square, Waimate
Tel 03-689 7771
Waimate celebrates its berryfruit-growing tradition on the first or second Saturday in December—timed to coincide with the peak of the strawberry season. The festival is a mix of stalls, strawberry-picking competitions, free all-day family entertainment—and of course, lots of strawberries and ice cream.

DECEMBER–MARCH

SUMMERTIMES
Christchurch City Council Leisure
Tel 03-941 8999
www.summertimes.org.nz
Organised annually by the City Council, this festival of free outdoor entertainment includes musical, sporting, children's and community events, including the Classical Sparks orchestral concert with fireworks. The festival takes place for two months some time between December and March.

OTAGO AND THE FAR SOUTH

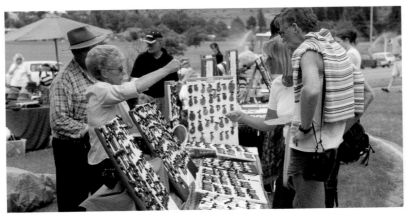

Queenstown dominates this region, with its spectacular location and a reputation as New Zealand's adventure capital. You can do almost anything here, with companies vying to offer the most extreme experience—from flying like a rocket to bungy jumping from a parachute. It's a very tourist-oriented town, with service and prices to match, but compensatingly long shop-opening hours (daily 9–9) and a nightlife that goes on until 5am. Queenstown is also the site of two contrasting ski slopes: the lower, more sophisticated Coronet Peak, and the higher Remarkables. Wanaka is less frenetic and more popular with locals, who enjoy sailing and fishing on the lake and skiing at Treble Cone, one of New Zealand's top ski slopes.

The Central Otago wine region has pockets of vineyards producing remarkable wines in good years. A wine trail map is available from visitor information offices.

By contrast with Queenstown, Invercargill, Dunedin and Oamaru are redolent of their past, with grand Victorian buildings and a quieter pace of life. Expect to visit fine gardens, view penguins or albatrosses at close quarters, and meet locals speaking with a distinctive burr. Dunedin celebrates its Scottish heritage with Burns' Night celebrations. The site of New Zealand's first university, it is still very much a university city, and a large student population makes for a humming café and pub scene. It also has lively performing arts and music, with a professional theatre and local orchestra.

In the interior, the region's gold-mining past has left its mark on the land and its people: one good way to experience this is by taking the Otago Central Rail Trail by bicycle, on horseback or on foot, stopping at the conveniently located old pubs on the way. Central Otago also has more than 100 rivers, streams, lakes and dams, where you can fish for brown and rainbow trout.

Southland is the heart of one of New Zealand's most prosperous dairy regions, and is also famous for its fishing and wild game. For a wilderness experience, take a slow journey through the Catlins or cross Foveaux Strait to Stewart Island/Rakiura, which is still largely undeveloped.

KEY TO SYMBOLS	
🖰	Shopping
🎵	Entertainment
🍸	Nightlife
🏃	Sports
✪	Activities
♥	Health and Beauty
✹	For Children

ALEXANDRA

✪ BLACK RIDGE VINEYARD AND WINERY

Conroys Road, Alexandra
Tel 03-449 2059
www.blackridge.co.nz
A wild, rocky ravine makes a dramatic and unusual location for this vineyard, where bulldozers had to reshape the schist to allow pockets of vines to be planted. The resulting wines are distinctive, in particular a highly regarded, flinty Gewürztraminer. You can purchase cheese and cured meats to go with wine tastings. Cheeseboard and nibbles are available alfresco from 27 December to mid-January,

and there is often live music on weekends.
🕐 Daily 10–5

ARROWTOWN

🏢 THE GOLD SHOP
29 Buckingham Street, Arrowtown
Tel 03-442 1319
www.thegoldshop.co.nz
The Gold Shop reflects Arrowtown's gold-mining heritage in jewellery fashioned from gold bought from local miners. Gold flakes are shown off in lockets, and nuggets fashioned into pendants and bracelets.
🕐 Daily 8.30–5.30

🏢 OUT THERE CLOTHING
18 Buckingham Street, Arrowtown
Tel 03-442 1500
www.otclothing.co.nz
Two local sisters design this relaxed, easy-to-wear but trendy clothing for men and women who want to be 'out there' doing things (also at 27 Beach Street, Queenstown).
🕐 Daily 10–5

✪ AMISFIELD
Lake Hayes Winery, 10 Lake Hayes Road, Arrowtown
Tel 03-442 0556
www.amisfield.co.nz
Just outside Arrowtown, Amisfield is the closest winery to Queenstown. It has vine-yards at picturesque Lake Hayes, and extensive plantings on the shores of Lake Dunstan. Specialists in Pinot noir and *méthode traditionelle,* it also produces Pinot gris, Sauvignon blanc, Riesling and an excellent rosé. The attractive stone winery has a spacious cellar door facility, which hosts art exhibitions, and an under-ground barrel hall.
🕐 Daily 10–8

✪ ◐ MILLBROOK
Malaghans Road, Arrowtown
Tel 03-441 7000
www.millbrook.co.nz
The resort is based around one of New Zealand's most

beautiful and well-appointed golf courses, designed by Sir Bob Charles. Casual players can pay green fees and rent clubs, and packages are available (from NZ$200) that include green fees, golf clubs and shoes, golf cart, balls, tees, and a taxi to and from your accommodation. You can also stay on site. Millbrook has extensive facilities, including tennis courts, a swimming pool, a gymnasium, spa pools and sauna. It also has an associated day spa (tel 03-441 7017) offering massage, hydrotherapy, facials and body treatments.
🏌 Green fees from NZ$75

Trackers Ecotours take you to the heart of the Catlins

THE CATLINS

✪ CATLINS WILDLIFE TRACKERS ECOTOURS
Papatowai, RD2, Owaka
Tel 03-415 8613
www.catlins-ecotours.co.nz
These very informative two- and four-day tours give an in-depth look at the area's flora and fauna, geology, history and conservation. Small groups are taken to remote places to walk and appreciate rare wildlife, such as Hooker's sealions and yellow-eyed penguins. Accommodation is provided, and connections from Balclutha can be made.
🚌 From NZ$345

CROMWELL

✪ THE BIG PICTURE
Corner of Sandflat Road and SH6, Cromwell
Tel 0800 wineadventure
www.wineadventures.co.nz
The Big Picture offers 'the essential wine adventure', combining an interactive wine and film experience with an adjoining restaurant where you can sample Central Otago wines as you dine. There's an 'aroma room' featuring up to 60 aromas associated with wine, and an auditorium where you are taken on a virtual flight over the region while wine-makers from various vineyards lead you through a tutored tasting.
🕐 Dec–end Feb 9am–11pm; Mar–end Nov 9–6 🎟 NZ$15

DUNEDIN

🏢 MERIDIAN SHOPPING MALL
267–287 George Street, Dunedin
Tel 03-474 7500
Meridian Mall is a multi-level shopping precinct housing 40 speciality stores, including Arthur Barnett's department store, K-Mart, fashion chains, food outlets, books, sporting goods and computer games.
🕐 Mon–Thu 9–6, Fri 9–9, Sat 9–5, Sun 10–5

🏢 OTAGO FARMERS' MARKET
Dunedin Railway Station, Anzac Square, Dunedin
Tel 03-477 6701
www.otagofarmersmarket.org.nz
Up to 4,000 people visit this Saturday market on a fine day, to buy fruit and vegetables, venison, free-range eggs, free-range pork, fresh fish, organic lamb and beef direct from the growers. Artisan producers also bring speciality breads, pies, pastries and chocolates. In season you can also find wild mushrooms, quinces, artichokes, hazelnuts and chestnuts.
🕐 Sat 8–1.30

PLUME
310 George Street, Dunedin
Tel 03-477 9358
One of the country's leading fashion designers, Margi Robertson exports her Nom D. label worldwide but remains in Dunedin, where she started in 1986. She reinvents stylistic conventions on how a garment is cut, assembled and worn, using New Zealand wool.
⏱ Mon–Thu 9–5.30, Fri 9–7.30, Sat 10–4

THE SCOTTISH SHOP
17 George Street, Dunedin
Tel 03-477 9965
www.scottishshop.co.nz
Trading on Dunedin's Scottish heritage, this shop sells products made in Scotland alongside New Zealand-made items in a Scottish style. From tartan kilts, ties and stockings to oatcakes and shortbread—if it's Scottish, they'll have it.
⏱ Mon–Fri 9–5.30, Sat 10–3

DUNEDIN TOWN HALL
1 Harrop Street, Dunedin
Tel 03-474 3614
www.cityofdunedin.com
Excellent acoustics make Dunedin Town Hall a popular venue for chamber music, symphony and choral concerts.

FORTUNE THEATRE
Corner of Moray Place and Stuart Street, Dunedin
Tel 03-477 8323
www.fortunetheatre.co.nz
Dunedin's professional theatre operates from a converted 1870 church, staging regular productions of local and international drama in two venues: the Mainstage and Studio. Bookings can be made at the theatre or via the website.
⏱ Tue 6, Wed–Sat 8, Sun 4

REGENT THEATRE
17 The Octagon, Dunedin
Tel 03-477 6481
www.regenttheatre.co.nz
The beautifully restored Regent Theatre combines the spacious elegance of a 1920s movie palace with state-of-the-art projection and sound. It hosts live theatre, cinema, musicals and special events, including the annual film festival.
⏱ Booking office Mon–Fri 9–5, Sat 10.30–1

ARC CAFÉ
135 High Street, Dunedin
Tel 03-474 1135
www.arc.org.nz
The Arc is a combination of arts venue, recording studio and vegan/vegetarian café, and is popular with local artists, musicians and students. It's run by a non-profit trust, and holds regular live gigs.
⏱ Mon–Sat noon–late

Preparing to sample the ales at Speight's Brewery

CARISBROOK SPORTING COMPLEX
Burns Street, Dunedin
Tel 03-466 4010
www.orfu.co.nz
Carisbrook, home of the Otago Rugby Football Union and the venue for international rugby and cricket matches, is known locally as 'the house of pain'—because visiting teams find it so hard to succeed here.

EDGAR SPORTS CENTRE
Portsmouth Drive, Dunedin
Tel 03-456 1200
www.edgarcentre.co.nz
Non-members are welcome and you can rent equipment at this sports centre, which includes 21 tennis courts.
⏱ Mon–Thu 9am–10pm, Fri 9–8, Sat, Sun 9–6

DUNEDIN CASINO
Southern Cross Hotel, 118 High Street, Dunedin
Tel 0800-477 4545
www.dunedincasino.co.nz
This boutique casino in the boutique Southern Cross Hotel aims for a sophisticated atmosphere, with a dress code of smart attire. Play blackjack, roulette, baccarat, *tai sai*, poker, or gaming machines. There is also a restaurant. Minimum age 20.
⏱ Daily 10am–3am

NEW ZEALAND SPORTS HALL OF FAME
Dunedin Railway Station, Anzac Square, Dunedin
Tel 03-477 7775
www.nzhalloffame.co.nz
New Zealand's great sporting moments are relived in this exhibit, in the splendidly grandiose heritage Railway Station. A shop sells sporting paraphernalia.
⏱ Daily 10–4

SPEIGHT'S BREWERY
200 Rattray Street, Dunedin
Tel 03-477 7697
www.speights.co.nz
Still on the site it has occupied since 1876, Speight's Brewery has become synonymous with the 'Southern Man' image of rural Otago and Southland. The Heritage Centre takes tours through the gravity-fed working brewery and museum, ending with a tasting session. You can also bottle, label and cap your own beer to take away in a wooden gift pack. The Ale House Bar and Restaurant (tel 03-471 9050) is a popular meeting place and open until late.
⏱ Alehouse: Mon–Thu, Sat 11.30am–1am, Sun 11.30am–midnight; Heritage Centre tours: Mon–Thu 10, 12, 2, 7; Fri, Sun 10, 12, 2, 4 Tours: adult NZ$17, child (5–15) NZ$6

❂ CADBURY WORLD
280 Cumberland Street, Dunedin
Tel 03-467 7967
www.cadbury.co.nz
Cadbury World combines a
visitor centre with heritage
and interactive displays, a
theatre presentation and a
guided tour of the factory
showing how various products
are made. Reduced tours are
available when the factory is
not operating. A shop sells
chocolates, clothing, hats,
bags, toys, novelty items
and souvenirs.
🕐 Jan–end Apr daily 9am–7pm;
May–end Dec daily 9–3.30 💲 Mon–Sat
adult NZ$16, child (under 15) NZ$10,
family NZ$42; Sun, public holidays adult
NZ$10, child NZ$5 ♿

GLENORCHY

❂ DART RIVER SAFARIS
Mull Street, Glenorchy
Tel 03-442 9992
www.dartriver.co.nz
The safaris focus on the Dart
River, involving a bus ride from
Queenstown to Glenorchy,
4X4 drive through Paradise
(taking in *Lord of the Rings*
film locations on the way),
walks through beech forest
and a jet-boat trip back to
Glenorchy. Horseback riding
and kayaking options are also
available.
💲 Adult from NZ$209, child
NZ$104.50

GIBBSTON

❂ GIBBSTON VALLEY WINES AND GIBBSTON VALLEY CHEESERY
State Highway 6, Gibbston, RD1
Queenstown
Tel 03-442 6910 (winery); 03-441 1388
(cheesery)
www.gvwines.co.nz
www.gvcheese.co.nz
Gibbston Valley is a popular
spot with visitors, not just
because of the fine wines—
notably its flagship Pinot noir
and Chardonnay—but also for
the educational tours it offers
of the vineyard, winery and
barrel cave; the food,
featuring local produce in

its restaurant; and the adjacent
cheesery, where you can learn
how the handcrafted cow, goat
and sheep cheeses are made.
🕐 Daily 10–5; tours: 10–4 on
the hour 💲 NZ$9.50

INVERCARGILL

🍫 THE SERIOUSLY GOOD CHOCOLATE COMPANY
20 Windsor Street, Invercargill
Tel 03-217 5107
www.seriouslygoodchocolate.com
Jane Stanton specialises in
handmade chocolates with
special fillings, such as
branded wines, and is best
known for her truffles made
with local produce, such as
Bluff oyster cinnamon truffles

*Splash Palace offers swimming
and leisure facilities*

and tuatara chocolate eggs.
Buy them direct from her
shop or in stores in Invercargill
and nationwide.
🕐 Mon–Wed, Thu 9–6.30, Fri–Sun
9–5.30

🎭 CIVIC THEATRE
Tay Street, Invercargill
Tel 03-211 1777
A fine Renaissance-style
Victorian theatre, the
1,000-seat Civic was built in
1906 as a cinema and to host
opera, musicals, comedies
and ballets. It is now home
of the Invercargill Repertory
Society, and is used by professional touring companies.

🎭 EMBASSY THEATRE
112 Dee Street,
Invercargill
Tel 03-214 0050
www.bdlhire.co.nz
Originally a cinema, the
Embassy was revamped and
reopened in 1999 as a
performance and production
venue with high-tech facilities.
It is operated by an audio,
lighting and DJ company
and hosts functions and
rock concerts.

🎭 READING CINEMA
29 Dee Street,
Invercargill
Tel 03-211 1555
This five-screen cinema
complex shows first-release
movies. The phone line gives
information on the movies
currently showing.
💲 From NZ$7

⚽ STADIUM SOUTHLAND
Surrey Park, Isabella Street,
Invercargill
Tel 03-217 1200
www.stadiumsouth.co.nz
This modern stadium has four
squash courts and doubles as
a concert venue. Home to one
of the country's top netball
teams, Southern Sting, it also
has international-standard
indoor courts.
🕐 Mon–Fri 8.30am–10pm, Sat,
Sun 9–5

❂ SPLASH PALACE
Southland Aquatic Centre, Elles Road,
Invercargill
Tel 03-217 7506
www.splashpalace.co.nz
A modern indoor complex,
Splash Palace has a main
pool, diving pool, whirlpool
and steam room and leisure
pool. It is used for national
swimming championships
and other sports.
🕐 Mon–Fri 6am–9pm, Sat 6am–8pm,
Sun 8am–8pm 💲 Adult NZ$4.40, child
NZ$2.20 ♿

KINGSTON

⭐ KINGSTON FLYER
Kingston Railway Station, Kingston
Tel 03-248 8848
www.kingstonflyer.co.nz
The Kingston Flyer was originally a passenger service that operated between Kingston and the main railway line at Gore, from 1878 through to the mid-1950s. It provided a passage to Queenstown and the surrounding areas by meeting the lake steamers at Kingston Wharf. Today it puffs along a 14km (9-mile) track while passengers listen to 1920s music.
🎫 Oct–end Apr daily 10, 1.30 👤 Adult NZ$40, child NZ$20, family NZ$99
🚌 47km (29 miles) south of Queenstown

MANAPOURI AND DOUBTFUL SOUND

⭐ REAL JOURNEYS
Pearl Harbour, Manapouri
Tel 03-249 7416
www.realjourneys.co.nz
High tech and wild nature are combined in these trips to the Manapouri Power Station and Doubtful Sound. The Wilderness Day Cruise crosses Lake Manapouri by launch, takes a bus over the Wilmot Pass, and then a launch cruise on Doubtful Sound. You visit the hydro station on the way back. An overnight option lets you stay in Doubtful Sound on the *Fiordland Navigator*, designed along the lines of a trading scow. A shorter option visits only the power station.
🎫 Daily 9.30 (Te Anau 8.30) 👤 Adult from NZ$230, child NZ$55

MILFORD SOUND

⭐ MILFORD SOUND RED BOAT CRUISES
Milford Wharf Visitor Centre, Milford Sound
Tel 0800-264536
www.redboats.co.nz
Cruises explore the Sound to the Tasman Sea, taking in the majestic scenery, waterfalls, seal colonies and an optional underwater observatory (additional charge, ▷ 142).
🎫 Daily 👤 Adult from NZ$55, child NZ$15

⭐ ROSCO'S MILFORD SOUND SEA KAYAKS
Deep Water Basin, Milford Sound
Tel 03-249 8500
www.kayakmilford.co.nz
Choose from a variety of day, twilight or full-moon trips, as well as fly/kayak combinations, or paddle and walk part of the Milford Track.
👤 From NZ$98

OAMARU

⭐ BLUE PENGUIN COLONY (▷ 145)

Relive the glory days of steam travel on the Kingston Flyer

⭐ WHITESTONE CHEESE
3 Torridge Street, Oamaru
Tel 03-434 8098
www.whitestonecheese.co.nz
Whitestone cheeses are named after local landmarks, because handmade cheeses reflect the local geography, pastures and climate. All the cheeses are on display and can be tasted and bought in the adjoining licensed café, which has a cheese-influenced blackboard menu and Central Otago wines. You can see the Make Room from an exterior platform.
🎫 Daily 9–5

OTAGO PENINSULA

⭐ ELM WILDLIFE TOURS
Elm Backpackers Lodge, 19 Irvine Road, The Cove, Dunedin
Tel 03-454 4121
www.elmwildlifetours.co.nz
These informative guided nature tours of the Otago Peninsula include Hooker's sea lions, fur seals, albatrosses and yellow-eyed penguins. The five- to six-hour trip takes in the Albatross Centre, a New Zealand fur seal colony and their own yellow-eyed penguin-breeding beach at the remote Cape Saunders. Other options include kayaking, a cruise around the heads, and the Catlins. You can stay at the backpackers' lodge or be picked up from elsewhere.
👤 From NZ$75

⭐ E-TOURS
67 Stuart Street, Dunedin
Tel 03-476 1960
www.inmark.co.nz/e-tours
Packages for doing the Otago Central Rail Trail at your own pace, including accommodation, transport, maps and gear.
👤 From NZ$75

QUEENSTOWN

🛍 O'CONNELLS SHOPPING CENTRE
Corner of Camp and Beach streets, Queenstown
Tel 03-442 7760
This shopping mall has 25 stores selling everything from food to fashion.
🎫 Daily 9–9

🛍 OUTSIDE SPORTS
Shotover Street, Queenstown
Tel 03-491 0074
www.outsidesports.co.nz
Every kind of outdoor sport is catered for here, with clothing, footwear and equipment. They specialise in trekking, camping, rock climbing, mountain and road bikes, and performance multisport clothing. Their sister shop, Outdoor Adventure, is farther down the Mall.
🎫 Summer daily 8.30am–9pm; winter daily 7.30am–9.30pm

WINEDELI

40 Shotover Street, Queenstown
Tel 03-442 4482
www.winedeli.com
As the name suggests, this shop specialises in Otago and other New Zealand wines, deli items, cheese and preserves.
Daily 10–10

EMBASSY CINEMA

11 The Mall, Queenstown
Tel 03-442 9994
www.readingcinemas.co.nz
Three screens show first-release movies and host the International Film Festival. Details of screenings are carried on the movie line, tel 03-442 9990.
Adult from NZ$9.50, child NZ$8.50

HAKA PA MAORI VILLAGE

Waterfall Park, 345 Lake Hayes Road, Queenstown
Tel 03-442 1534
www.hakapa.com
The cultural experience starts with a traditional welcome and viewing of the Maori village, followed by a performance of traditional action songs and dances, *haka* (warrior dance) and *poi* (performed by the women). Dinner is a four-course feast, or *hangi*, based around meat and vegetables steamed in an earth oven. Pick-ups and drop-offs in Queenstown can be arranged.
Pa daily 9–5; dinner 7–10
Cultural experience: adult NZ$89, child (5–15) NZ$40

QUEENSTOWN EVENTS CENTRE

Joe O'Connell Drive, Frankton
Tel 03-442 3664
www.qtevents.co.nz
The Events Centre hosts local and touring shows and indoor sporting fixtures. There is also a climbing wall. Outdoor concerts are held in the adjoining Oval.

SKYCITY QUEENSTOWN CASINO

16–24 Beach Street, Queenstown
Tel 03-441 0400
www.skycityqueenstown.co.nz
Located above the Hard Rock Café, the casino offers live entertainment, table games, more than 70 gaming machines and a restaurant and bar. You need to be age 20 or over, and a dress code applies.
Daily noon–4am

SURREAL

7 Rees Street, Queenstown
Tel 03-441 8492
One of Queenstown's popular nightspots, this nightclub is

Spoilt for choice amid the wines at Queenstown's WineDeli shop

gay-friendly and has great DJs and sounds. It starts getting busy around 10.30pm. When the party swings, it's open until 5am.
Daily 11am–late

A.J. HACKETT BUNGY AND SHOTOVER JET (▷ 148)

APPELLATION CENTRAL WINE TOURS

Queenstown
Tel 03-442 0246
www.appellationcentral.co.nz
Philip Green has a Diploma of Wine and has been a wine collector for 15 years. He organises small group tours (up to nine people) which

depart daily, and customises tours for wine enthusiasts. Afternoon tours visit four wineries in the Gibbston and Bannockburn and Cromwell, and include lunch. Full-day tours include a wine cave tour, cheese tasting, lunch and a wine experience at The Big Picture.
Daily 9.30, noon   From NZ$135

CORONET PEAK/ REMARKABLES SKI AREAS

Queenstown Snow Centre, corner of Camp and Shotover streets, Queenstown
Tel 03-442 4640
www.nzski.com
The original commercial ski-field—and still one of the best when it gets a good covering of snow—Coronet Peak (1,649m/5,410ft) has excellent facilities and the added advantage of being an easy drive (18km/11 miles of sealed road) from Queenstown. Not surprisingly, it gets very busy. Its sister field across the valley, the Remarkables, is reached by a longer and more tortuous road (28km/17 miles of gravel road) but often has more snow as it goes higher (1,935m/6,348ft).
Late Jun to mid-Oct   Lift passes from NZ$72

EXTREME GREEN RAFTING

39 Camp Street, Queenstown
Tel 03-442 8517
www.nzraft.com
White-water rafting on the spectacular and action-packed Shotover and Kawarau rivers can be combined with jet-boating, helicopter flights, skydiving or bungy jumping, and the combinations can be done on different days.
From NZ$149

😊 FLY-BY-WIRE

Corner of Shotover and Rees streets, Queenstown
Tel 03-442 2116
www.flybywire.co.nz
The closest you'll get to flying a rocket, Fly-by-Wire is an adventure flight in a high-speed plane suspended from an overhead tether, which allows you to pilot it anywhere within the spectacular canyon. You will experience exhilarating speeds, a huge adrenalin rush, total weightlessness and, finally, serenity as the plane glides gently to the end—all in six minutes. Minimum age 15.
✋ NZ$139

😊 FLYFISHING NEW ZEALAND

Queenstown Bay, Queenstown
Tel 03-442 5363
www.wakatipu.co.nz
Queenstown and the surrounding area offers great opportunities for fly fishing, lake trolling, drift-boat fishing and heli-fishing. The high-country stream fishing season opens on 1 October and runs to 30 May. Lake Wakatipu and the Kawarau River are open all year round.
✋ From NZ$85, plus NZ$18 fishing licence

😊 GLENORCHY AIR

Queenstown Airport, Queenstown
Tel 03-442 2207
www.glenorchy.net.nz
www.trilogytrail.com
Capitalising on its experience of flying the *Lord of the Rings* cast and crew, this company does Trilogy trips to the locations used to represent Lothlorien, Amon Hen, Nen Hithoel, Amon Lhaw, Parth Galen, Ford of Bruinen, The Pillars of the King on the River Anduin, and the site of Gandalf's ride to Isengard. There is also a road trip to local filming sites (NZ$125 adult, NZ$62.50 child).
✋ From NZ$325, child NZ$162.50

😊 MILFORD SOUND SCENIC FLIGHTS

Tel 03-442 3065
www.milfordflights.co.nz
The quickest and easiest way to see Milford Sound, this flight is also spectacular. You can choose from a combination of tours, including a launch trip on the Sound and the option of going one way by coach or helicopter.
✈ Adult from NZ$295, child NZ$175

😊 TSS *EARNSLAW* (▷ 149)

🔵 BODY SANCTUM

50 Stanley Street, Queenstown
Tel 03-442 8006

The Fly-by-Wire is a unique adrenalin-pumping experience

www.bodysanctum.co.nz
A soothing place to recover from the rigours of the day's activities, Body Sanctum is in a new building, with fine views from the treatment rooms. There is an outdoor spa, steam room and sauna, and treatments include skier's, snowboarder's or tramper's foot revival, aromatic body wraps, massage, reflexology, facials and water therapies.
🕐 Daily 9–9 ✋ From NZ$20

STEWART ISLAND/ RAKIURA

😊 RUGGEDY RANGE WILDERNESS EXPERIENCE

170 Horseshoe Bay Road, Stewart Island
Tel 03-219 1066
www.ruggedyrange.com
Former Department of Conservation guide Furhana Ahmad organises a comprehensive itinerary of day and overnight guided walks, sea kayaking, kiwi-spotting and birdwatching trips on Stewart and Ulva islands. Packages are available and she assists with travel and accommodation bookings. Outdoor clothing and equipment is available for rent or sale. Some trips are suitable for children.
✋ Adult from NZ$85, child NZ$60

TE ANAU

😊 FIORDLAND BIKE AND HIKE

Sinclair Road, Te Anau
Tel 03-249 7098
www.bikefiordland.co.nz
Offering an appealing way of making the journey from Te Anau to Milford Sound, these trips combine mountain biking on the downhill sections of the Milford Road with nature walks and a cruise on the sound, and the option of hiking part of the Routeburn Track. All equipment is provided, including wet weather gear. Suitable for children 14 and over.
🕐 Oct–end Apr daily 7.30am ✋ From NZ$99

😊 KIWI REEL-RIFLE

175 Aparima Drive, Te Anau
Tel 03-249 9071
www.kiwireelrifle.com
Hunting, fishing and kayaking trips can be arranged to suit your level of experience and the time available. Overnight fishing trips run from October to the end of April, but one-day fishing and kayaking excursions are available all year. Hunting for small game or red deer and chamois can be combined with flying,

210 OTAGO AND THE FAR SOUTH Q–W

walking and/or kayaking. Fishing instruction is available.
 From NZ$140

😊 SINBAD CRUISES

15 Fergus Square, Te Anau
Tel 03-249 7106
www.sinbadcruises.co.nz
Help sail the 11m (36ft) gaff ketch *Little Ship Manuska*, or just sit back and enjoy the scenery. Trip options include day, afternoon, evening and overnight cruises, or you can combine cruising with a helicopter trip and/or walking at Mount Luxmore.
From NZ$20

WANAKA

🎬 PARADISO CINEMA AND CAFÉ

3 Ardmore Street, Wanaka
Tel 03-443 1505
www.paradiso.net.nz
A one-of-a-kind cinema, Paradiso shows first-release and art-house movies, but is best known for its quirky style. Seating includes a motley collection of old sofas and three seats in an old Morris Minor. A café and bar serves meals before, during or after the movie, and home-made ice cream and hot cookies at intermission.
Mon–Wed 5pm, Thu, Fri 2.30pm, Sat, Sun 11am NZ$12

😊 ALPINE AND HELI MOUNTAIN BIKING

Tel 03-443 8943
www.mountainbiking.co.nz
These folk put the mountain back into biking, with a choice of seven trips to some of the country's highest and most scenic track trailheads, including Mount Pisa, Mount Alpha and the Treble Cone. You can go by four-wheel drive or helicopter. The biggest range of options is available in summer, but some winter rides are also available. You can also do multi-day rides, staying overnight in old gold-miners' cabins.
From NZ$150

😊 LAKELAND ADVENTURES

The Log Cabin, Waterfront, Wanaka
Tel 03-443 7495
www.lakelandadventures.co.nz
From their lakeside log cabin, Lakeland Adventures organise jet-boat trips on the Clutha River, guided fishing trips on Lake Wanaka, and cruises to the islands. They also rent aqua bikes, kayaks, mountain bikes, fishing rods and boats.
Adult from NZ$50, child NZ$25

😊 RIPPON VINEYARD

246 Mount Aspiring Road, Wanaka
Tel 03-443 8084
www.rippon.co.nz
One of the most stunningly located vineyards in New

The bizarre Leaning Tower at Puzzling World

Zealand, Rippon was planted in 1981. Known for its Pinot noir, it also makes other wines, including a *méthode traditionelle*, Riesling, Gamay rosé and a Merlot Syrah blend. Picnic lunches are served in summer, and a rock festival is held on Waitangi weekend in even years.
Dec–end Apr daily 11–5; Jul–end Nov daily 1.30–4.30

😊 TREBLE CONE SKI AREA

Wanaka
Tel 03-443 7443
www.treblecone.co.nz
Treble Cone is one of the top ski and snowboarding areas in New Zealand, with more

skiable terrain than anywhere else, plus great views of Lake Wanaka and Mount Aspiring. Equipment rental and tuition are available, and there is a childcare facility. The area is open in high summer for walking and mountain biking.
Late Jun to early Oct for skiing; 30 Dec to mid-Jan for summer activities
Lift passes from NZ$89, child NZ$37, family NZ$217
20km (12 miles) northwest of Wanaka via Matukituki Valley Road

😊 WANAKA PARAGLIDING

PO Box 118, Wanaka
Tel 03-443 9193
www.wanakaparagliding.co.nz
Paragliders like the conditions in Wanaka so much they come here for the New Zealand championships. You can tandem paraglide from Treble Cone all year round, for magnificent views over Wanaka and the mountains. Short summer Eco Flights are also available from Mount Iron (but you walk up first).
From NZ$170

💗 ASPECTS BEAUTY AND HEALTH

61 Browston Street, Wanaka
Tel 03-443 5051
www.aspectsofbeauty.co.nz
Men and women can get a full range of therapies and beauty treatments at this salon, including massage, body wraps, pedicures and facials.
Mon–Sat 9–8, Sun by appointment
From NZ$60

😊 PUZZLING WORLD

State Highway 84, Wanaka
Tel 03-443 7489
www.puzzlingworld.co.nz
You can't miss the crazily angled towers of Stuart Landsborough's Puzzling World, on the road into Wanaka. Within is a modern maze and a variety of eccentric or puzzling attractions, including illusion rooms.
Nov–end Apr 8.30–5.30; May–end Oct 8.30–5 Adult NZ$10, child (5–15) NZ$7

FESTIVALS AND EVENTS

WHAT TO DO

JANUARY–FEBRUARY

CENTRAL OTAGO WINE AND FOOD FESTIVAL

Queenstown Visitor Centre,
PO Box 253, Queenstown
Tel 03-442 4100

The Central Otago Wine and Food Festival is held annually in the lovely setting of Queenstown Gardens, on the shores of Lake Wakatipu. It's a small but high-quality event. Foods of the region, prepared by members of the local Chefs Association, are matched with wines from 18 local wineries, and there is a farmers' market for small producers.

🕙 11–5 💲 NZ$25

APRIL

BLUFF OYSTER AND SOUTHLAND SEAFOOD FESTIVAL

Bluff Events Centre, Gore Street, Bluff
Tel 03-211 1400
www.bluffoysterfest.co.nz

Bluff's famous oysters are celebrated at the annual Bluff Oyster and Southland Seafood Festival, where restaurants and community groups from Invercargill and Bluff have stalls featuring fresh local seafood, and chefs create dishes matching wines from a regional winery. A formal Southern Seas Ball is held the night before.

🕙 11–5 💲 Adult NZ$20, child NZ$10

APRIL–MAY

ARROWTOWN AUTUMN FESTIVAL

PO Box 148, Arrowtown
Tel 03-442 0809

Arrowtown celebrates its brilliant autumn hues in a 10-day community festival of arts and crafts, talks and tours, with tournaments, markets and a street parade.

JUNE

COUNTRY MUSIC FESTIVAL GORE

PO Box 382, Gore
Tel 03-208 1978
www.goldguitars.co.nz

Gore has established itself as the country music capital of New Zealand, hosting a 10-day country music festival each June, which culminates in the Gold Guitar Awards.

JUNE–JULY

LINDAUER QUEENSTOWN WINTER CARNIVAL

Destination Queenstown, PO Box 353, Queenstown
Tel 03-441 2453
www.winterfestival.co.nz

This annual 10-day celebration of the mountains takes place at three venues—Coronet Peak, Earnslaw Park and Queenstown Bay—and is a great excuse to party. As well as concerts, music and arts events, it includes the Classic Challenge of wild and wacky events. Some events are ticketed, others—such as the opening party, the parade and Mardi Gras—are free.

SEPTEMBER

GAY SKI WEEK

Queenstown
www.gayskiweeknz.com

A national gay and lesbian event, the ski week takes advantage of Queenstown's proximity to four major ski resorts. For those who are neither skiers nor boarders, the adventure capital of New Zealand still has plenty of off-piste activities.

SEPTEMBER–OCTOBER

ALEXANDRA BLOSSOM FESTIVAL

PO Box 370, Alexandra
Tel 03-440 2097
www.blossom.co.nz

The fruit-growing district of Alexandra has been celebrating spring with this festival since the 1950s. Now held over two weeks, it includes crowning the Blossom Queen, a shearing competition, vintage car rally, motocross, boat races, a charity ball and the Grand Festival Parade with floats, bands, classic cars, floral princesses and animals. There is also a fair with arts and crafts, entertainment, wine and food (adult NZ$15, child (5–15) NZ$5, family NZ$30).

OCTOBER

DUNEDIN RHODODENDRON FESTIVAL

PO Box 980, Dunedin
Tel 03-474 5162
www.rhododunedin.com

Dunedin's famous Botanic Garden's planting of 3,500 rhododendrons is regarded as one of the most significant in the world. The annual four-day celebration involves events for families and visitors as well as gardening enthusiasts, including garden tours, golf and a fête.

NOVEMBER

BANNOCKBURN GUTBUSTER MOUNTAIN BIKE RACE

www.cromwell.org.nz

The Gutbuster is a marathon pub-to-pub cycle race over a distance of 75km (47 miles) across the precipitous heights of the Nevis Pass. It starts from the Garston Hotel and finishes at the Bannockburn Hotel, with many participants raising money for charity.

🕙 Entry from NZ$20

OAMARU VICTORIAN HERITAGE CELEBRATIONS

Visitor Information Office, Oamaru
Tel 03-434 1406

Oamaru celebrates its Victorian heritage in five days of festivities, when local people dress in period costume and take part in a fair, street parade, Penny Farthing races, a ball and other activities.

Get out and about in New Zealand with these eight driving tours and eight walks. They explore the varied attractions of both the North and the South islands. The locations of the walks and tours are marked on the map on page 214. It is advisable to buy a detailed map of the area before you set out.

Out and About

OUT AND ABOUT

KEY TO THIS MAP

1 Drive
2 Walk
■ Capital City
■ City / Town

KEY TO ROUTE MAPS IN THIS CHAPTER

★ Start point
━ Route
▪▪ Alternative route
► Route direction
5 Walk start point on drive
6 Featured sight along route
● Place of interest in Sights section
● Other place of interest
☀ Viewpoint
621 ▲ Height in metres

Cape Reinga
Kaitaia
Paihia
Whangarei
Dargaville
Auckland
Thames
Hamilton
Tauranga
Hicks Bay
Rotorua
Gisborne
Taupo
Taumarunui
New Plymouth
Waiouru
Napier
Hastings
Wanganui
Palmerston North
Collingwood
Masterton
Nelson
Picton
WELLINGTON
Westport
Blenheim
St Arnaud
Reefton
Kaikoura
Greymouth
Hokitika
Arthur's Pass
Cheviot
Franz Josef Glacier
Rangiora
Christchurch
Mount Cook/ Aoraki
Haast
Geraldine
Timaru
Milford Sound
Wanaka
Queenstown
Oamaru
Te Anau
Alexandra
Dunedin
Gore
Milton
Riverton
Invercargill

1. Drive
West Coast Beaches and the Waitakere Ranges (▷ 215–217)

2. Walk
Devonport and North Head (▷ 218–219)

3. Drive
Coromandel Countryside and Coast (▷ 220–221)

4. Drive
Around Lake Rotorua (▷ 222–223)

5. Walk
The Rotorua Walkway (▷ 224–225)

6. Drive
A Circuit of Tongariro National Park (▷ 226–227)

7. Walk
Hahei and Cathedral Cove (▷ 228)

8. Walk
The Waitomo Walkway (▷ 229)

9. Walk
A Taste of the Abel Tasman (▷ 230–231)

10. Drive
Queen Charlotte Drive (▷ 232–233)

11. Walk
Cliffs of Kaikoura (▷ 234–235)

12. Drive
Lake Kaniere and Hokitika Gorge (▷ 236–237)

13. Drive
Over the Port Hills (▷ 238–239)

14. Walk
First Steps to Mount Cook/ Aoraki (▷ 240–241)

15. Walk
Diamond Lake and Wanaka Views (▷ 242–243)

16. Drive
Otago Peninsula's Secret Side (▷ 244–245)

WEST COAST BEACHES AND THE WAITAKERE RANGES

This circular tour explores Auckland's wild west-coast beaches and the Waitakere Ranges, with their memorable city views.

THE DRIVE
Distance: 95km (59 miles)
Allow: 6–8 hours
Start/end: Sky Tower, SKYCITY, Auckland

★ From SKYCITY take Hobson Street south to the motorway on-ramps. Take the Northwestern motorway, SH16 (signposted). After 3km (2 miles) take the Great North Road exit (exit 8) onto urban route 11, then 19 southwest to Titirangi Road (urban route 24).

❶ The suburban village of Titirangi is considered the gateway to the Waitakeres and has a number of laid-back cafés, interesting shops and a good art gallery, Lopdell House (daily 10–4.30), on the corner of Titirangi and South Titirangi roads. Titirangi is part of Waitakere City, known for its liberal attitudes, art, vineyards and orchards, and its spectacularly wild unspoiled bush and beaches. As a result, it has attracted many seeking an alternative lifestyle, and is home to artists and craftspeople. On the last Sunday of the month the village market is held in the Memorial Hall (10–2).

From the middle of Titirangi continue west to the roundabout (traffic circle) and turn onto Scenic Drive, signposted to Piha (urban route 24). Take care on this road as it has many blind corners and connecting residential driveways. Follow Scenic Drive for another 5km (3 miles) to the Arataki Information Centre, which is on the left.

❷ The information centre is an impressive modern building with a vast amount of information and interesting interpretive and audiovisual displays, which provide the perfect introduction to the region and its natural history. There is also a short nature trail from here with spectacular views south over the Nihotupu Reservoir and Manukau Harbour. An impressive Maori *pou* (guardian post) dominates the entrance to the centre. It lost its not insignificant 'manhood' a few years ago through vandalism, but thankfully for this great warrior another was duly carved, and the glint in his little paua-shell eye restored.

From the information centre continue north along Scenic Drive for 4km (2.5 miles), then turn left onto Piha Road to Piha (11km/7 miles).

❸ Piha has been luring dreamers and surfers for years, and is one of the west coast's most popular beaches and coastal enclaves. If you swim at Piha you can do so in relative safety, but always stay

Titirangi's arts centre, at the heart of a thriving community

between the flags and under the vigil of the lifesavers. When you are weary of sunbathing, swimming or trying to hold on to your surfboard in the fierce surf, there are two things you must do. The first is to climb Lion Rock, the guardian of the beach, via the steep track (allow 30 minutes to reach the top). The second, especially when the surf is high, is to take the Tasman Lookout Track at the south end of the beach to The Gap, where breakers crash into the narrow rock crevice.

There is also an interesting, if less dramatic, walk at the northern end of Piha Beach, which leads to the isolated and beautiful Whites Beach. If you have time, also try to see the Kitekite Falls—they're reached via the Kitekite Track, up Glenesk Road behind the main camping ground in the middle of the village.

From Piha drive back up the hill and look for Karekare Road to Karekare Beach (right). Descend to the parking area.

④ Karekare is another fine west coast beach and was used as a backdrop to the hugely successful New Zealand film *The Piano* (1993). There are a number of short walks and tracks around Karekare, some of which head inland or south to join the network of

tracks in the Waitakeres. The short walk up the Taraire Track to Karekare Falls is worthwhile, especially if you intend to swim in the pool beneath it. Another is the Colmans Track from the end of Watchmans Road (signposted on the right before the parking area), where the path creeps up the hill at the northern point of Karekare Beach and terminates with a magnificent view. Looking south you can see well past Karekare Beach to the huge expanse of Whatipu Beach beyond, as well as the tiny, inaccessible Mercer Bay, immediately below and north.

Return to Piha Road and the junction with Scenic Drive (urban route 24). Turn left towards the TV mast. After 1km (0.6 miles) look for signs to Rose Hellaby House (right).

⑤ The Scenic Drive (28km/17 miles long) winds along the eastern fringe of the Waitakeres, offering stunning views across Auckland, but one of the best viewpoints is the garden of Rose Hellaby House. Its owner, Rose, who loved these hills with a passion, donated the property to the city.

Continue north along Scenic Drive, taking care on blind corners. There are a number of other viewpoints across the city along the way. Descend back to the fringe of the city and the junction with Swanson Road. Turn right along Swanson Road (urban route 24) to the roundabout, and then continue straight across onto Universal Drive. At the end of Universal Drive turn left onto Lincoln Road to rejoin SH16 Northwestern Motorway (signposted) back into the city centre and SKYCITY (exit 4B).

Top, on Scenic Drive
Below, Piha Beach, with its high surf and black sands

Rose Hellaby loved this view of the Waitakere hills from her house

A café spills out onto the street in the village suburb of Titirangi

WHERE TO EAT

Hardware Café
✉ 404 Titirangi Road (in the heart of Titirangi)
☎ 09-817 5059
Light, healthy meals with a traditional Kiwi edge—and good coffee.
🕐 Mon–Tue 9–5, Wed–Sun 7–10

BASICS

Tourist Information
✉ Auckland Visitor Centre, Atrium, Sky City, corner of Victoria and Federal streets, Auckland
☎ 09-363 7184
www.aucklandnz.com
🕐 Daily 9–5

Arataki Information Centre
✉ 333 Scenic Drive, Titirangi
☎ 09-366 2000
www.arc.govt.nz
🕐 Sep–end Apr daily 9–5; May–end Aug Mon–Fri 10–4, Sat, Sun 9–5

Rose Hellaby House
✉ 515 Scenic Drive
☎ 09-366 2000
🕐 Gardens: daily 8–5. House: Sat, Sun 1–4 💲 Free

DEVONPORT AND NORTH HEAD

Escape the city bustle by ferry to experience the history and village feel of Devonport, and the views from North Head, one of Auckland's most iconic (extinct) volcanoes.

THE WALK

Distance: 5km (3 miles)
Allow: 3 hours
Start/end: Devonport Wharf, Devonport

Located at the southernmost tip of the North Shore and named after the naval base in Plymouth, England, the suburb of Devonport was one of the first areas to be settled in Auckland and is home to the Royal New Zealand Navy.

Long before the first Europeans dropped anchor there in the early 1800s, the Maori used the two small but distinct volcanic mountains as *pa* (fortified settlements). They would almost certainly have witnessed the dramatic eruption of Rangitoto (▷ 71), the most recent and least modified volcano of the Auckland volcanic field and an unmistakable natural feature that dominates the view from North Head.

★ From the Devonport Wharf and ferry terminal, facing towards the middle of Devonport, turn right and walk along the waterfront (King Edward Parade), then turn left into Cheltenham Road. Turn right off Cheltenham Road onto Takarunga Road and climb to the summit of North Head.

❶ North Head (Maungauika) is one of about 50 dormant volcanoes within Greater Auckland, and at 65m (213ft) offers some of the most memorable views of the city and Waitemata Harbour. From here it is easy to see why Auckland is dubbed the City of Sails and is renowned as one of the most desirable sailing venues in the world. During international yachting events, including the Whitbread Round the World in 1993 and America's Cup campaigns in 2000 and 2003, this was a prime viewpoint for locals cheering on the New Zealand crews. Today huge cargo ships

and cruise liners are also a common sight.

In the days when tall ships brought the first European settlers to New Zealand, a small gun was sited on North Head to signal the much-anticipated arrival of mail ships.

The activity on North Head has not always been so celebratory in its mood. In response to the fear of a Russian invasion in the 1880s and of a possible Japanese invasion in World War II, the mound was heavily fortified and a maze of tunnels, bunkers and gun emplacements were constructed. Convicts built tunnels with nothing more than a pick, a shovel and their bare hands. The remnants of these tunnels, along with gun emplacements and lookouts, can be explored today (torch/flashlight recommended).

Take time to explore and walk around North Head. Then, from the northern slope, descend the steps onto Cheltenham Beach, the first of the northern beaches and considered by many to be the best on the North Shore. Walk to the top end of the beach onto Vauxhall Road. Head south along Vauxhall Road back towards Mount Victoria, looking for signs on the right for the Mount Cambria Reserve.

❷ The Mount Cambria Reserve was once a volcanic mount in its own right, and named Takaroro by Maori. Quarried for scoria in the late 1800s, it is now an attractive landscaped garden and home to the Devonport Museum. A relatively low-key affair, the museum showcases the early days of the historic suburb with artefacts and photographs.

Walk through Mount Cambria Reserve onto Church Street, turning left past the old power station to the Mount Victoria

Walkway steps (signposted right). Climb round the mount on the spiral walkway to the summit.

❸ At 881m (2,890ft), Mount Victoria (Takarunga) commands superb views across the harbour, city and surrounding suburban streets. From here you can see the wooden villas and colonial architecture that characterises the suburb.

Steeped in history and intrigue, Mount Victoria still has remnants of the Maori Kawerau tribe fortifications. At its foot, on the northern edge, there is an old cemetery where some of the North Shore's first settlers are buried.

From the Mount Victoria summit parking area follow the summit road onto Flagstaff Lane, then Victoria Road, Devonport's main thoroughfare.

❹ Victoria Street is the commercial and social heart of Devonport. Here you will find a range of tourist-oriented shops selling everything from secondhand books or antiques to local art. Alternatively, relax and enjoy a cappuccino in one of several streetside cafés. If you have an interest in naval tradition and antiquity you may also want to visit the Devonport Navy Museum in the dockyard, which forms the principal base for the Royal New Zealand Navy (▷ 63). Opened in 1888, its Calliope dry dock was once the largest dry dock in the southern hemisphere. Although often seconded for peacekeeping missions overseas, some vessels from the nation's limited fleet may be in evidence.

Walk down Victoria Street past the visitor information centre and Esplanade Hotel back to the Devonport Wharf and ferry terminal.

OUT AND ABOUT

Masts top the volcanic peak of Mount Victoria, left

The ferry terminal at Devonport

WHERE TO EAT

There is plenty of choice in Devonport, from streetside cafés for coffee or light snacks to à la carte restaurants. For a good coffee, healthy light meals and great atmosphere try Manuka, 49 Victoria Road. For a buffet dinner or Sunday brunch (from NZ$16), try the Watermark on the waterfront (33 King Edward Parade). For fish and chips it's hard to resist the Cod Piece, 26 Victoria Road, or the more traditional Catch 22, 19 Victoria Road.

HOW TO GET THERE

Fullers ferry from the Ferry Building, Quay Street, Auckland. Every 30 minutes, from NZ$9 return. Crossing: 15 minutes.

TIP

● Take binoculars, and a torch if you plan to explore the tunnels on North Head.

BASICS

Tourist Information
www.tourismnorthshore.org.nz
✉ 3 Victoria Road, Devonport
☎ 09-4460677

Devonport Museum
www.devonportmuseum.org.nz
✉ Mount Cambria Reserve
☎ 09-445 2661
🕐 Sat, Sun 2–4 or by arrangement

Navy Museum
www.navymuseum.mil.nz
✉ Spring Street
☎ 09-445 5186
🕐 Daily 10–4.30

The view of central Auckland from Mount Victoria

COROMANDEL COUNTRYSIDE AND COAST

A circular tour exploring the rugged hills, townships and spectacular coastal scenery of the Coromandel Peninsula.

Distance: 135km (84 miles)
Allow: 8 hours (or two days)
Start/end: Coromandel Township

★ From the old gold-mining township of Coromandel (▷ 66) take SH25 south for 3km (2 miles), then turn left onto The 309 Road. This is unsealed in places, but manageable with care. The first stop on The 309 Road is the Waiau Waterworks.

❶ Waiau Waterworks is a garden full of fascinating, whimsical water sculptures and gadgets. You are greeted by a metal stick figure who operates a waterwheel hung, not with wooden boards, but with pots, pans and other kitchenware. Within the gardens are many unusual interactive water-powered inventions, including an old bicycle that you peddle furiously to squirt a hose of water across a lily pond.

Continue south on The 309 Road, keeping an eye open (left) for the aptly named Castle Rock (526m/1,725ft), a knobbly volcanic plug that can be seen from many points on the peninsula.

❷ The stiff climb to the top of Castle Rock takes up to two hours. To reach the summit track (signed) take the forest road left 2km (1mile) south of the Waiau Waterworks. The track is more like a stream for much of the year, but the view is well worth the effort.

Just over 7km (4 miles) south from the Coromandel end of The 309 are the Waiau Falls, with a drop of 6m (20ft). View them from a lookout by the road, or via an access track.

Less than a kilometre (0.6 miles) south of the falls is Kauri Grove.

❸ Kauri Grove is a small stand of ancient kauri trees that survived the rapacious logging at the end of the 19th century. Now fully protected, they offer a glimpse of what much of the upper North Island must once have looked like. The walk (signed) takes 20 minutes.

From Kauri Grove continue southeast on The 309 to the junction with SH25. Turn right and drive through the settlement of Coroglen. Eight kilometres (5 miles) beyond Coroglen turn left, signed to Hahei and Hot Water Beach. Turn right to the beach.

❹ At Hot Water Beach, about two hours each side of low tide you can dig a hole in the sand to access natural hot water (the local store hires out spades for NZ$5). The beach is very pleasant, but it is also very dangerous for swimming, with notorious rips. Once suitably boiled in your own hot spa, pop your head into the Moko Artspace at 24 Pye Place, just opposite the main car park.

About 10km (6 miles) north of Hot Water Beach is Hahei, signposted right.

❺ Hahei is an unspoiled coastal settlement surrounded by some of the best coastal scenery on the peninsula. Dramatic Cathedral Cove is the highlight (▷ 228).

From Hahei return to SH25 and head back north to Whitianga.

❻ The peninsula's most popular holiday spot, Whitianga (▷ 67) presents the perfect opportunity for a lunch stop, or an overnight stay (book ahead October–March). There's plenty of accommodation in the town, with Villa Toscana one of the top bed-and-breakfasts in the region (▷ 275).

North from Whitianga, SH25 straddles bush-clad hills before descending towards the coast again at Kuaotunu.

❼ The small beachside hamlet of Kuaotunu is a lovely spot, especially for swimming, but it also acts as the gateway to Otama and Opito bays via the scenic Black Jack Road (this is unsealed but manageable for standard vehicles). Both bays have lovely beaches and magnificent views across to the Mercury Islands. This is a great spot to escape the crowds.

Back on SH25 and a little farther west (signposted 1km off SH25) is the sterile real-estate settlement of Matarangi. Although it's usually bypassed by visitors, you may like to spend time enjoying its 5km (3-mile) sweep of beach, or perhaps book a tee time at its well groomed golf course (tel 07-866 5394). From Matarangi continue west on SH25 to Te Rerenga. On a clear day you will see Castle Rock straight ahead. At Te Rerenga turn right, following signs to Whangapoua.

❽ Whangapoua is little more than a conglomeration of *baches* (holiday homes) that come alive in summer. The village is the gateway to one of

Sunset bathes the bay at Coromandel township in gold

OUT AND ABOUT

the most idyllic beaches on the peninsula—New Chums Beach (▷ 67), which can be reached only by foot. From the northern end of Whangapoua, cross the small river (at low tide) and follow the edge of the beach, where you will find a track. Follow this to the headland, where it ducks left through the bush, soon revealing the beach. The slopes surrounding the headland are noted for their pohutukawa trees, which flower crimson in December, earning it the label New Zealand's Christmas tree.

From Whangapoua return to SH25 at Te Rerenga then turn right. From here SH25 winds its way over the ranges, offering fine views of the Hauraki Gulf before descending steeply to the west coast and Coromandel township. On a clear day, with binoculars, you should be able to see the needle-sharp Sky Tower in Auckland (▷ 65), just beyond the volcanic cone of Rangitoto.

Digging on Hot Water Beach

WHERE TO EAT

Café Nina
✉ 20 Victoria Street, Whitianga
☎ 07-866 5440
Café Nina offers an imaginative black-board menu and a fine cup of coffee.
🕐 Daily 8–4.30

Top, pohutukawa blossom
Above, boats at Whitianga

WHERE TO STAY

Villa Toscana
✉ Ohuka Park, Whitianga
☎ 07-866 2293
www.villatoscana.co.nz
A grand villa offering memorable views.

BASICS

Tourist Information
✉ Coromandel Visitor Centre, 355 Kapanga Road, Coromandel
☎ 07-866 8598
www.coromandeltown.co.nz

Waiau Waterworks
✉ The 309 Road, Coromandel
☎ 07-866 7191
🕐 Oct–end Mar daily 9–dusk; Apr–end Sep daily 9–5
🎟 Adult NZ$10, child NZ$5

AROUND LAKE ROTORUA

Drive around Lake Rotorua to sample just a few of the natural and manmade features that first spawned tourism in New Zealand and made the region the tourism capital of the North Island.

THE DRIVE

Distance: 85km (53 miles)
Allow: 8 hours
Start/end: Rotorua Visitor Information Centre

Rotorua is where tourism began in New Zealand. The Government's Department of Tourist and Health Resorts took over the spa in 1901, and in 1902 appointed the first official balneologist. For over a century the diverse volcanic and geothermal features of the region have lured visitors with the hope of both drama and cure: Drama in the form of gushing geysers, bubbling mud, or the former pink silica terraces (▷ 87), and cure in the form of therapeutic pools and curative treatments. From its inception in 1908, the town's world-famous Bath House was the main focus for many making the journey to the Bay of Plenty. The Bath House now forms part of the Rotorua Museum of Art and History (▷ 86).

★ From Fenton Street head south, following signs for the airport (east) and SH30. After 2km (1.5 miles) turn right onto Tarawera Road. On the right is the northern fringe of the Whakarewarewa Forest Park.

❶ Whakarewarewa Forest Park has a good network of tracks that are mostly used for mountain biking. The park is said to be one of the best venues in the country, and if you have never tried the sport this presents a perfect opportunity. A small visitor centre and gift shop on Long Mile Road provides all the details, including advice on bicycle hire and organised tours.

❷ At the eastern fringe of the park (8km/5 miles along Tawarewa Road) are Lake Rotokakihi (the Green Lake) and Lake Tikitapu (the Blue Lake; ▷ 86). The difference in

colour between the two lakes is a result of the effects of subterranean minerals.

From Lake Tikitapu the road veers east towards Lake Tarawera and the partly excavated Maori Buried Village. Here you can gain a fascinating insight into the eruption of Mount Tarawera in 1886. Tarawera Landing is just a little farther east, from where boat trips are available on MV *Reremoana* (▷ 177).

From Tarawera Landing return to SH30 and head east (right) around the lake, past the airport to the junction between SH30 (Whakatane) and SH33 (Tauranga). Remain on SH30 as it heads east away from the lake, following signs to Hell's Gate **❸** (3km/2 miles, ▷ 84).

After your thermal experience at Hell's Gate, return to the lake and turn right onto the Tauranga Road (SH33). Cross over the Ouau Channel (that connects Lake Rotorua with Lake Rotoiti) and continue north to Okere (2km/1 mile). At Okere turn left, following signs to the Okere Falls Scenic Reserve, just before the river bridge.

❹ The Okere Falls Scenic Reserve offers an excellent opportunity for a short bush walk and to watch the rafting and white-water action on the tempestuous Kaituna River. It is one of the best venues for the sport in the North Island, and the 7m (23ft) drop from the Tutea Falls is a dramatic highlight. There is a viewing platform just a short distance from the main track (signposted) where you can watch the rafters plummeting over the edge with trepidation, or glee. If you are tempted, trips can be arranged through the visitor centre in Rotorua (from NZ$85).

From Okere return south and turn right just before the lake and Ohau Channel. This road hugs the northern fringe of Lake

Rotorua and offers pleasant views back towards Rotorua. Take a brief stop at the crystal-clear Hamurana Springs. (Look for the golf course on the right and park your car in the golf course parking area.)

❺ Hamurana Springs are the largest in the North Island, and erupt at a volume of over one million gallons per hour, creating a beautifully clear river that flows the short distance into Lake Rotorua. The head of the springs can be reached via a 10-minute walk through a glade of giant redwood trees that fringe the river. Access is from the former Hamurana Gardens parking area (which doubles as the Hamurana Golf Course parking area) beside the main road. Cross the bridge at the car park and follow the path upstream.

From Hamurana Springs continue west through Ngongotaha to join SH5 towards Rotorua. Continue south for 3km (2 miles), stopping at the Skyline Skyrides (▷ 87) on the left. Rainbow Springs (▷ 178) is opposite.

From Skyline Skyrides continue south on SH5, bearing left on Lake Road into the city to return to the visitor information centre on Fenton Street. Alternatively, a perfect end to your tour would be a soak in the thermal pools at the Polynesian Spa (▷ 86) at the southern end of Government Gardens, off Fenton Street. The best bet is to go at lunchtime, when the tour buses are elsewhere.

WHERE TO EAT

Skyline Skyrides complex
✉ On the slopes of Mount Ngongotaha, SH5
☎ 07-347 0027
Enjoy traditional Kiwi fare with views across the city and lake.
🕐 Jan–end Mar daily 9–8.30; Apr–end Dec daily 9–6. Entry fee applies for gondola: adult NZ$18, child (5–14) NZ$8 (▷ 87)

OUT AND ABOUT

● Before leaving the rather grand and well-stocked visitor information centre, gather any detailed information you may require about the sights on this drive that take your fancy.

TIP

BASICS

Tourist Information
✉ Rotorua Visitor Centre, 1167 Fenton Street, Rotorua
☎ 07-348 5179
www.rotoruaNZ.com
🕘 Daily 8–5.30

Whakarewarewa Forest Park visitor information centre
✉ Long Mile Road, off Tarawera Road
☎ 07-346 2082
🕘 Mon–Fri 8.30–5, Sat–Sun 10–4

Mist hangs above Waimangu volcanic valley

The Green Lake, or Rotokakihi, is sacred to the Maori

Left, exploring Rotorua's volcanic highlights

THE ROTORUA WALKWAY

This easy circular walk through the heart of the city and around the lakefront offers a great introduction to Rotorua's intriguing natural and human history.

THE WALK

Distance: 2km (1 mile)
Allow: 2–3 hours
Start/end: Polynesian Spa car park, lake end of Hinemoa Street

As the North Island's most popular tourist destination, and host to almost 2 million visitors a year, there is no doubting Rotorua's commercialism, or its ability to entertain. But amid all the hype and adrenalin-pumping activities, one of the best ways to get a feel for the place (if not to escape the crowds) is to explore part of the 26km (16-mile) Rotorua Walkway. The short section described below concentrates on the heart of the city and the lakefront and offers a mix of local history, architecture and—of course—a sample of the region's celebrated and unpredictable geothermal features.

★ From the Polynesian Spa (▷ 86) car park head west through the heart of the city along Hinemoa Street to the junction with Ranolf Street. Turn right and enter Kuirau Park at the junction of Pukuatua and Ranolf streets. Head north through the park.

❶ With your nose assailed by the pungent smell of sulphur, you quickly realise that Kuirau Park is not your average town park. It is pock-marked with fenced-off craters and steaming hot pools, and you could be forgiven for thinking you were on another planet. Once a dangerous swamp, the 30ha (74-acre) Kuirau Park was endowed as a reserve by the local Maori, Ngati Whakaue, and first developed during the Depression of the 1930s.
Although all the pools in Kuirau Park are now out of bounds to the public, for many decades locals and visitors used the more temperate among them for bathing and relaxation. Maori legend has it that a local girl, Kuirau, who

used to bathe in the biggest lake (originally known as Taokahu), was seized by a despicable *taniwha* (spirit) who inhabited a lair beneath the waters. This was noticed by the gods, who decided to boil the lake in order to destroy the *taniwha*. From that time on the lake was known as Kuiarau, or Kuirau, in memory of the unlucky girl.

From the northern fringe of Kuirau Park head right up Pukeroa Hill on Lake Road.

❷ Pukeroa Hill (also known as Hospital Hill) was a *pa* site used by the local Maori, Ngati Whakaue, who adapted the small hilltop for their defences. There are still some burial sites (*urupa*) present on the hill. In 1961 the hill became the site for a military hospital, which later developed into the King George V Hospital.

From Lake Road turn left down Haukotuku Street, then right along Tunohopu Street to the historic Maori settlement of Ohinemutu, home to St. Faith's Church and the magnificent Tamatekapua Meeting House ❸ (▷ 85).
Continue round the lakefront, which then forms the fringe of Government Gardens. A short distance from the Rotorua Museum of Art and History is another Rotorua icon, the Blue Baths ❹ (▷ 86).
From the museum, return to the lakefront and head east

to the Motutara Point and Sulphur Bay.

❺ From beyond Motutara Point Lake, Rotorua (▷ 84) is laid out before you, with Mokoia Island dominating the horizon. Among the waterbirds you may see here are brown teal, along with black swans and a colony of pied shags.

From Motutara Point continue south on the marked walkway to Sulphur Point.

❻ The view of Sulphur Bay, the southernmost bay on Lake Rotorua, is dominated by a steaming, sulphurous crust that sits above an active geothermal field. Although a hostile and unproductive habitat for wildlife, it still provides sanctuary for both roosting and nesting birds, including the omnipresent and handsome red-billed gulls. It was officially designated as a wildlife refuge in 1967.
Local Maori also made use of the thermal features and the small islands of Sulphur Bay, particularly Moturere Island—which before lake levels rose had a thermal pool known for its therapeutic properties. The soft rock and warm waters also made it a perfect site to sharpen greenstone tools and weapons.

From Sulphur Point continue south to return to the Polynesian Spa car park.

OUT AND ABOUT

Bathing outdoors in the thermal luxury of Rotorua's Polynesian Spa

Hoping for titbits: black swans beside the walkway

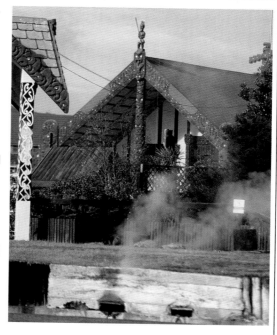

Above, the half-timbered former Bath House of 1908, now the city's museum, looms on the skyline

Right, natural steam vents at the Tamatekapua Marae

Left, relaxing in the sunshine on the lakeside

OUT AND ABOUT

A CIRCUIT OF TONGARIRO NATIONAL PARK

Throughout this tour you'll have the company of two large and unpredictable landmarks—Ruapehu and Ngauruhoe—the North Island's most celebrated volcanoes.

THE DRIVE

Distance: 328km (203 miles)
Allow: 8 hours
Start/end: Taupo

★ From Taupo (▷ 92) follow SH1 south along the eastern shore of Lake Taupo.

1 Given the sheer expanse of water and its apparent serenity, it is hard to imagine that Lake Taupo is a massive volcanic crater. It was formed after a massive eruption that occurred around AD230.

At the southeastern edge of the lake, near the mouth of the Tongariro River, is the small resort of Turangi **2** (▷ 92). The Tongariro is renowned for its excellent trout-fishing, and is also popular for white-water rafting and canoeing.

At the southern fringe of Turangi turn right onto SH41. Follow this for 3km (2 miles), and then turn left onto SH47.

SH47 climbs to a viewpoint looking back towards Lake Taupo before straddling a pass between Pihanga (1,325m/4,347ft) on the left and Kakaramea (1,301m/4,268ft) on the right. If you feel like a break, you might consider the relatively easy two-hour walk around Lake Rotopounamu, which is hidden in the bush on the western flank of Pihanga. The car park and track are signposted.

3 Just south of the Lake Rotopounamu car park, Lake Rotoaira comes in to view. Beyond this you will see the northern slopes of Mount Tongariro (1,967m/6,455ft) and the volcanic cone of Ngauruhoe (2,287m/7,501ft). Lake Rotoaira is another good place for trout-fishing, and is frequented by hundreds of black swans. If you look carefully, about two-thirds of the way up the slopes of Mount Tongariro (to the south), you may be able to see the Ketetahi Hut. This 'sanctuary in the clouds' has been a

welcome sight to many a tired soul undertaking the Tongariro Crossing (▷ 89), considered one of the best day hikes in New Zealand.

Continue south on SH47 and enjoy the spectacular views on the left over the Tongariro National Park (▷ 88–89). The dominant features are Mount Ngauruhoe, with its classic volcano shape, and Mount Ruapehu, also a volcano and at 2,797m (9,176ft) the highest mountain in the North Island.

At the foot of Mount Ruapehu you will see the historic Chateau Tongariro hotel (▷ 278), another icon of the national park.

Turn left onto SH48 following signs to the Chateau and Whakapapa Village (7km/4 miles).

4 Park in the middle of Whakapapa Village (▷ 89) to explore, then continue up the main road (Bruce Road) to reach the Whakapapa Ski Field (Top o' the Bruce). The dramatic rocky outcrops around the main skiing complex were used in the *Lord of the Rings* movies as Mount Doom in Mordor.

From Whakapapa, return via SH48 to SH47 and continue left (west) to the village of National Park (9km/6 miles).

5 A drab-looking place, National Park is an accommodation base for the ski fields.

Turn left again onto SH4 and continue south for 26km (16 miles) before turning left onto SH49 to Ohakune (▷ 89), the halfway point on the tour.

East of the heart of the village and signposted off SH49, the 17km (11-mile) drive up Mountain Road to the Turoa ski fields is well worth the journey in good weather, providing fine views to the west. If it is a

particularly clear day you may be able to see the snow-capped volcanic peak of Mount Taranaki/Mount Egmont (▷ 80).

According to Maori legend, there was a feud between the mountains of Tongariro and Taranaki after both fell in love with the beautiful Pihanga. A mighty battle ensued. Taranaki lost the fight and, wild with grief and anger, ripped himself from his roots and tore a path towards the coast, where he now stands alone. Perhaps through indifference or appeasement, Tongariro created the waters that filled Taranaki's path of destruction, and the Whanganui River was born.

From Ohakune follow SH49 east as it circles the southern fringe of Ruapehu. Twelve kilometres (7 miles) beyond Ohakune on the left are two lakes collectively known as Lake Rotokura (signposted). Access is on foot only.

6 The tranquil upper lake reflects the peak of Ruapehu, and can be reached with an easy 30-minute walk from the car park, just off SH49.

A little farther east on SH49 is the Whangaehu River, straddled by a new road bridge. Alongside it is the Tangiwai Memorial.

On Christmas Eve 1953, the walls of the crater lake of Ruapehu collapsed without warning and a mighty lahar rushed down the Whangaehu River, wiping out the rail bridge at Tangiwai. The night train to Auckland arrived moments later—151 lives were lost.

A further 7km (4 miles) brings you to Waiouru and a junction. Turn left, heading north on SH1.

7 Just north of Waiouru, SH1 cuts through a barren, flat expanse of grassland known as the Rangipo Desert, in the rain shadow of Ruapehu.

OUT AND ABOUT

Above, Lake Taupo is a famous fishing venue
Right, cruising the lake, with the snow-clad volcanic peaks behind

This stretch, dubbed the Desert Road, is often temporarily closed in winter due to snow.

Continue on SH1 back to Turangi. Three kilometres (2 miles) south of Turangi, pass the Tongariro National Trout Centre.

⑧ At this trout hatchery you can observe wild trout in the Waihukahuka stream through a viewing window. The visitor centre showcases the history of fishing in the region, and how to catch your own fish on Lake Taupo.

From Turangi return on SH1 to Taupo, where you can enjoy a dip at the Taupo Hot Springs.

Maori carvings in the cliffs above Lake Taupo

WHERE TO EAT/STAY
The Chateau Tongariro (▷ 278)

WHEN TO GO
Snow sometimes causes road closures.

BASICS
Tourist Information
✉ Taupo Visitor Centre, 30 Tongariro Street, Taupo
☎ 07-376 0027
www.LakeTaupoNZ.com
🕙 Daily 8.30–5

DoC Whakapapa Visitor Information Centre
✉ Whakapapa Village
☎ 07-892 3729
www.doc.govt.nz
🕙 Daily 8–6

Tongariro National Trout Centre
✉ Turangi
☎ 07-386 9254
🕙 Dec–Apr daily 10–4; rest of year 10–3
💲 Free, but donations appreciated

HAHEI AND CATHEDRAL COVE

The highlight of this walk is Cathedral Cove, where secluded beaches are connected by a natural arch and guarded by bizarre rocky stacks.

Distance: 6km (4 miles)
Allow: 3 hours
Start/end: Kotare Domain car park, Pa Road, Hahei

★ On entering Hahei village turn right onto Pa Road. Park in the Kotare Domain car park on the left, 200m (220 yards) from the end of Pa Road. Walk to the end of Pa Road, to Te Pare Point.

❶ The Te Pare Point Historic Reserve, which dominates the southern end of Hahei Beach, is the site of a *pa* occupied by the Ngati Hei people. This local tribe (and the settlement itself) is named after the Maori chief Hei, a *tohunga* (priest) who arrived at the time of the great Polynesian migration to New Zealand, around 1350. He settled his people here in Mercury Bay mainly because of its plentiful resources—but there is little doubt the stunning beauty of the area also influenced his decision. Hei's descendants, as *tangata whenua*, retain a strong ancestral and spiritual attachment to the site, and proudly continue their role as guardians, or *kaitiaki*, of the resources within it. Information panels at the Cathedral Cove Lookout (see below) give a brief history of the Ngati Hei and the influence of the first European settlers.

From Te Pare Point descend the steps to the beach—this is only possible at low tide. At high tide, walk back along Pa Road for 100m (110 yards) to the grass walkway on the right (marked) and cross the bridge. Steps onto the beach are signposted at the end of the road.
   Walk to the northern end of the beach and look for the steps and walkway up the hill to the Cathedral Cove Lookout (signposted). From the lookout take the Cathedral Cove track (signposted). The track ducks

Strolling through the natural rock arch of Cathedral Cove

through tracts of native bush and pine before descending to the first of the two beaches collectively known as Cathedral Cove.

❷ The scenic jewel in the region's crown, Cathedral Cove guards the Te Whanganui-A-Hei (Cathedral Cove) Marine Reserve. This reserve covers 9sq km (3.5sq miles) and became New Zealand's sixth marine reserve in 1992. Cathedral Cove is actually two coves and two beaches connected by a natural limestone arch, which is negotiable at low tide. There are sandstone pinnacles on both beaches, with the highest, Sail Rock, on the western beach. Although the beach can get very busy, it offers great sunbathing and swimming and unforgettable scenery. By far the best time to go is at dawn, when you can sometimes—if only for a short while—have the beach all to yourself.
   The snorkelling opportunities in Te Whanganui-A-Hei Marine Reserve are also outstanding, especially at Gemstone Bay and the western side of Mahurangi Island. In early 2004 a snorkel trail was installed at Gemstone Bay. Four marker buoys with information panels depicting which species inhabit each area are anchored from 50m (55 yards) to 165m (180 yards) offshore. For information contact the Department of Conservation in Thames, tel 07-867 9180.

Return to the lookout and take Grange Road back into Hahei

and the small shopping centre. From here, turn right onto the main road. Head south back to Pa Road and return to the Kotare Domain car park. If you wish you can take a short cut through the Domain itself, 100m (110 yards) south of the shopping centre on the left (signposted).

Luna Café
✉ 1 Grange Road (in the main shopping centre)
☎ 07-866 3016
Come here for a bite to eat during the day or a well-deserved cup of coffee.
🕒 Daily in summer from 9am until late, with reduced hours in winter

The Church
✉ 87 Beach Road, Hahei
☎ 07-866 3797
www.thechurchhahei.co.nz
This is the best-known and most characterful option in Hahei.
🕒 Wed–Sun

Hahei is 35km (22 miles) by road from Whitianga. Go Kiwi offers regular shuttle services from Ferry Landing, Whitianga (book at Whitianga information centre). In summer, the five-minute, passenger-only ferry crossing to Ferry Landing operates continuously 7.30am–6.30pm, 7.30pm–8.30pm, 9.30pm–10.30pm. In winter hours may be reduced.

Tourist Information
✉ Whitianga i-SITE, 66 Albert Street, Whitianga
☎ 07-866 5555
www.whitianga.co.nz

OUT AND ABOUT

THE WAITOMO WALKWAY

Often described as one of the finest short walks in the North Island, the Waitomo Walkway follows the meandering course of the Waitomo Stream, culminating in a 40-minute loop to take in the major limestone features within the Ruakuri Scenic Reserve.

THE WALK

Distance: 12km (7 miles)
Allow: 3 hours
Start/end: Waitomo Glow-worm Caves car park

The limestone around Waitomo was once the sea-bed, and formed about 30 million years ago from the layered remains of countless marine animals. Over millennia these layers have been raised by the action of the earth's plates, and in some places the limestone is more than 200m (656ft) thick.

Through its gradual uprising the limestone bends and buckles, creating a network of cracks and joints. As rainwater drains in to these cracks it mixes with small amounts of carbon dioxide in the air and soil, forming a weak acid. Over thousands of years this acid slowly dissolves the limestone and the cracks and joints widen. Yet more time sees small streams flow through converging cracks, to create the features we see within the Ruakuri Scenic Reserve. Eventually these streams disappear underground, where they can scour out dramatic underground caves such as Waitomo and Aranui.

Within these caves the acidic water continues to seep from the walls or drips from the roof, leaving a minute deposit of limestone crystal. Gradually these deposits form stalactites, stalagmites and other features. The size and rate of their formation depends on the rate of flow. In time, the caves collapse, forming gorges, holes or arches.

★ From the Waitomo Glow-worm Caves (▷ 90) car park follow the signposted walking track (Waitomo Walkway) southwest to the Ruakuri Scenic Reserve and Aranui Cave car park.

❶ According to local tradition, the Aranui Cave was inhabited by a pack of wild dogs—hence its name, '*rua*', which means cave and '*kuri*', the name for a Maori dog. There are burial caves in the cliffs along the track, making this a place of special significance for Maori. The entrance to Ruakuri Cave, marked by karaka trees with a burial cave above, is *waahi tapu* (sacred).

From the car park begin your circuit of the Scenic Reserve.

Top, blackwater rafting on inner tubes through the caves
Above, stalactites and stalagmites fused into columns

❷ The Ruakuri Scenic Reserve encompasses typical karst landscape, characterised by caves, natural arches, tunnels, gorges, depressions and sculpted rock outcrops, the presence and formation of which are explained and outlined on information boards along the way.

The first 50m (55 yards) of the walk are fringed with damp walls and small over-hangs that are inhabited by glow-worms (obviously best seen if you return after dark, but take a torch/flashlight).

One of the highlights of the walk is the Ruakuri natural bridge tunnel, which is home to a colony of native long-tailed bats. They are an endangered species and one of only two land mammals native to New Zealand (both of which are species of bats).

After completing the Ruakuri circuit return via the Waitomo Walkway to the Waitomo Glow-worm Caves car park.

WHERE TO EAT

Morepork Café
✉ Kiwipaka Hostel, School Road, Waitomo Caves Village
☎ 07 878 3395
A congenial pizza café with spacious deck.
🕐 Daily 8am–9pm

HOW TO GET THERE

The Waitomo turn-off is 16km (10 miles) south from Otorohanga on SH3, and Waitomo is 7km (4 miles) west of SH3 on SH37.

BASICS

Tourist Information
✉ Waitomo Museum of Caves Visitor Information Centre, 21 Waitomo Caves Road, Waitomo
☎ 0800-474839/07-878 7640
www.waitomo-museum.co.nz

TIP

● Take a tour to the Waitomo Glow-worm Caves (▷ 90) before or after your walk.

A TASTE OF THE ABEL TASMAN

This section of the Abel Tasman Coast Track, from Bark Bay to Anchorage, includes dense native bush, turquoise bays, golden beaches and idyllic swimming spots.

THE WALK

Distance: 12km (7 miles)
Allow: 7 hours; 4 hours of walking
Start/end: Marahau, 67km
(42 miles) northwest of Nelson

It takes up to five days to walk the entire Abel Tasman Coast Track (▷ 109–110), but water taxis make it easy to walk this delicious one-day taster. The walking track is in excellent condition, the climbs are gentle and there's plenty of time to relax and enjoy the beauty.

Abel Tasman is New Zealand's smallest and most popular national park. It was named after Dutch explorer Abel Janszoon Tasman (1603–c1659), who managed to upset the Maori without actually setting foot on land. His two ships moored off the northern coast of the South Island in 1642, watched warily by the Ngati Tumatakokiri tribe. A small boat, ferrying sailors between the ships, was rammed by one of eight Maori canoes. A skirmish erupted and four of Tasman's crew were killed. Tasman heatedly named the beach Murderers' Bay; it was later renamed Golden Bay.

★ Meet the water taxi at its Marahau base for the 9am departure to Bark Bay.

1 The hour-long trip takes you past Split Apple Rock, a huge ball of porous granite from Separation Point that, at some unknown time, broke clean in half. It is stained red by the iron oxide that gives the beaches their golden tone and the oysters an interesting tang.

As you step off the boat at Bark Bay, the track is at the south (left-hand) end of the beach. There are toilets here: it's 8km (5 miles) to the next ones, and the Department of Conservation does not encourage bushland emergencies.

2 Bark Bay was home to a family of European settlers—Timothy Huffam and his sons, who arrived in 1870. One of

their money-earning activities was to gather beech and rimu bark to sell in Nelson for the tanning process. They stayed until 1904. The DoC hut at the north end of Bark Bay beach is built on the site of their homestead, and the redwoods they planted are still there.

Follow the well-formed track as it gradually meanders away from the coast and through native bush, which includes tree ferns, kanuka and beech. After 1km (0.6 miles), a signposted track on the left points to South Head. The short track gives views over the sea and Pinnacle Island. Once back on the main track, take your time crossing the Falls River swingbridge—seals often cruise for fish here at high tide.

Descend into Torrent Bay **3** and walk down the two sandy 'streets' of holiday *baches*. At the south end of the beach a picturesque jetty gives a superb view of the bay and is a good spot for lunch. Toilets are another 500m (550 yards). Stay on the main track. (It is also possible to get to Anchorage across the bay at low tide; this route is 3km/2 miles shorter, but be sure of the tides.)

4 The bush in this section of the walk is lush compared to other areas. From Bark Bay to Onetahuti Beach, the next beach to the north, there is a lot of scrubby manuka and kanuka, while visitors to the park's northwestern entrance

at Wainui Bay pass a stretch of invasive, prickly gorse. It's all part of a massive experiment in land recovery. This land was leased to European settlers on the condition that it was cleared for productive use, and sawmills, granite quarries, boatyards and farms appeared. None were sustainable: Farmland was quickly drained of nutrients and stock failed to thrive. Through the 1930s Nelson conservationist Perrine Moncrieff led a vigorous campaign to have 15,000ha (37,000 acres) of the land made into a national park, and in 1942 the park formally opened.

The track follows a series of picturesque coves. Birdlife is prolific and seals often come up the rivers to play and forage. The seals that frequent these coves are New Zealand fur seals. Sealers decimated the population in the 19th century, but now they are fully protected, numbers are crawling back by around 2 per cent a year. The marine reserve around Tonga Island, north of Bark Bay, attracts them with a plentiful supply of squid and fish. Pups are born in early summer, and learn to swim at about four weeks old. As teenagers, they are playful and curious, and even climb aboard the odd sea kayak. As adults they can be fierce if disturbed.

In 2km (1 mile) look for a sign to Cleopatra's Pool, 1km (0.6 miles) inland from the main track. This detour follows a stream to a delightful freshwater swimming hole and picnic area **5**.

Return to the main track and continue south towards Anchorage. After 1.5km (1 mile) the path rises up; at the brow of the hill there's a signpost. Turn left down the hill and it's 500m (550 yards) to the broad curve of Anchorage Beach. Relax here until 4pm, when the water taxi will pick you up and take you back to Marahau.

A watchful cormorant

Tourist Information
✉ Wallace Street, Motueka
☎ 03-528 6543
www. AbelTasmanGreenRush.co.nz

Department of Conservation
✉ Corner of King Edward and High streets, Motueka
☎ 03-528 1810
www.doc.govt.nz

WHEN TO GO

Spring and autumn are more peaceful in the Abel Tasman, though the weather can be cool. December and January are very busy, while Christmas/New Year is plain crazy.

A combination of native bush and scenic coastline make the Abel Tasman Coast Track popular with trampers

Mind the gap—standing between the neat halves of Split Apple Rock provides a popular photo opportunity

Water taxis, booked ahead, enable you to walk sections of the track

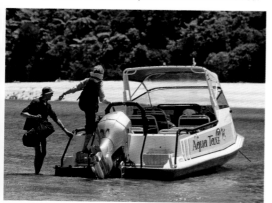

WHERE TO EAT

Have a picnic at Torrent Bay. Supplies can be ordered the day before from Hooked on Marahau at the Marahau Beach Camp (tel 03-527 8576, daily 8am–9pm, summer; 8–6, winter). Take ample drinking water with you, and a spare bag for rubbish.

TIP

● For a water taxi, book with Aqua Taxi at least one day ahead, tel 0800-278 282. The Beaches and Bays trip costs around NZ$48.

OUT AND ABOUT

QUEEN CHARLOTTE DRIVE

This route combines the Queen Charlotte scenic drive between Havelock and Picton with exploring the wine-making region of Marlborough.

THE DRIVE

Distance: 100km (62 miles)
Allow: 2.5 hours
Start/end: Picton Visitor Centre, near the ferry terminal

Beyond the towns of Blenheim and Picton, Marlborough is one of the country's least populated regions. Even the gorgeous coastline is under-whelmed by human inhabitants, and holiday homes far outnumber perma-nent residences. It could have been so different—in the 1860s Picton had high hopes of becoming New Zealand's capital city. Now it is most famous for being the South Island port for the interisland ferries (▷ 52–53), and more than a million travellers pass through every year.

★ From the visitor centre in Picton (▷ 117), drive south down Auckland Street to the intersec-tion with Broadway. Continue on the southeast fork, Wairau Road. The road goes around Nelson Square and continues out of Picton as SH1 towards Blenheim. This road wiggles comfortably south past the Para Wetlands ❶, a signposted area frequented by duck-shooters in season. Mount Richmond Forest Park rises up 4km (2.5 miles) to the west.

❷ The Wairau Plains—the flat area north of Blenheim—is superb farmland. The river valley soil is fertile, the sun-shine hours are long, and it's all sheltered by the Richmond Ranges. Grapes grow marvel-lously well, but so do apples, cherries and berries.

After 21km (13 miles) reach the small township of Spring Creek. At Spring Creek, turn right into Rapaura Road and within 1km (0.6 miles) you are deep in vineyard country. Rows and rows of vines make up the vista on both sides of the road, while mountains rise up to the north.
In 7km (4 miles) reach the acclaimed Hunter's Estate.

❸ Hunter's, with its pleasant winery, garden, restaurant and resident artist's studio, is well worth a stop. The estate has one of the highest international profiles of any in New Zealand. Its founder, Ernie Hunter, was a pioneer of Marlborough wine-making, putting grapes down in 1983 and winning major UK awards just three years later. The estate is now run by his wife, Jane Hunter, herself a viti-culturalist. In 2004 she won the inaugural Women in Wine award at the International Wine and Spirits Awards, held in London.

In another 4km (2.5 miles) reach the Mud House.

❹ The Mud House offers regional specialities such as olive oil, gifts and Prenzel liqueurs, as well as Mud House boutique wines.

Two kilometres (1 mile) after the Mud House, take SH6 to Havelock. The highway crosses the mighty Wairau River after 2km (1 mile), then follows the Kaituna River. After 25km (16 miles) there is a clearly sign-posted turn-off for Queen Charlotte Drive.
If you would like to buy fresh green-shell mussels, continue ahead for a detour into Havelock (▷ 112, try the Four Square supermarket or Mussel Boys Restaurant on the main street).
From Queen Charlotte Drive there's a view of Havelock's marina to the north, then the road starts winding upwards through Mahakipawa Scenic

Reserve. For 8km (5 miles) the road tracks the Mahakipawa Arm of Mahau Sound. The picnic area at the end of this stretch, developed by Linkwater locals, is the best place to stop and absorb the views. The next 6km (4 miles) are relatively straight with farmland on both sides, but it gives access onto Kenepuru Road, which leads to the Queen Charlotte Track.

❺ The Queen Charlotte Track is notable among New Zealand walking tracks for its accessibil-ity. The long sliver of land offers 55km (34 miles) of ridge and coastal walking and mountain biking. Apart from the beautiful bays and bush sections, the joy is the number of points connecting with boats or cars, so walkers can do as much or as little as they fancy. The other bonus is the amount of accommodation en route, from campsites to luxury rooms, so heavy packs aren't required.
The final 17km (11 miles) of Queen Charlotte Drive are the most rewarding. This tight stretch of road passes pretty marinas at Momorangi and Ngakuta bays, enclaves of secluded housing, cool tracts of native bush and views of the jagged inlets of Queen Charlotte Sound. Governor's Bay is a good place to stop, with safe parking and a look-out a couple of metres from the road, and a sandy swim-ming beach 1km (0.6 miles) down the hill.

Port Shakespeare's logging wharf is the first sign of Picton, 5km (3 miles) away. Before your final descent, there's a large roadside car park overlooking the ferry terminal and Picton township. In 1km (0.6 miles) reach a major roundabout (traffic circle), and turn east into Dublin Street. The next left (northward) turn is Auckland Street, which leads back to the visitor centre.

Roadside fern fronds

OUT AND ABOUT

Left, the winding route of the Queen Charlotte drive is well signed; above, Marlborough is famous for its vineyards

The forested flanks of Queen Charlotte Sound are indented with shallow bays and coves

CLIFFS OF KAIKOURA

This way-marked walk takes you from the seal colony to the cliff-tops, where you can look over colonies of birds to the same ocean vista as the early whalers.

THE WALK

Distance: 8.5km (5.5 miles)
Allow: 2 hours
Start/end: Peninsula car park
at the northeast end of the Kaikoura Peninsula

★ The Peninsula car park overlooks a large (and pungent) fur seal colony and tidal rock pools. Start at the eastern end, following a sign to the Cliff-Top Walk. A 200m (220-yard) climb is rewarded with a fantastic view of the Seaward Kaikoura Ranges, the shoreline and ocean. Take the southwest path over the stile and past the squat, yellow lighthouse. After 500m (550 yards), the fence line turns at a right-angle. Walk right to the corner.

1 In spring, you'll see the busy comings and goings of a red-billed seagull colony below this point—but don't lean on the fence, it may be electrified. Around 12,000 of these gulls nest on the peninsula, which is also popular with black-backed gulls, white-fronted terns and shags. The tidal platforms along the shoreline attract wading birds such as turnstones, oystercatchers and herons.

After another 200m (220 yards), a stile leads you onto the cliff-side of the fence, but the track is still clear and secure. In another kilometre (0.6 miles), you reach Whalers' Bay Lookout. There's a bench here, or in another 300m (330 yards) you can take a seat above the rocky white hump known as Sugar Loaf.

2 These points are where whalers sat in the 1840s, looking out to sea for spouting whales. Once they were spotted, a signal was sent to boats on the shore below and the oarsmen set to work. The preferred quarry was the southern right whale, which would rise to the surface when dead and usually yielded vast quantities of oil. The animal was hauled back to shore and

butchered on the beach. The oil was generally sent to England for lamp fuel and as a lubricant, while the pliable bone of the whale's jaw was used in corsets, stays and horsewhips. Demand dropped with the increased use of electricity. The last whale commercially killed in New Zealand was caught off Kaikoura in 1964.

Shortly, green signposts turn you inland towards South Bay, and soon you have a view of the wharves. White posts with orange triangles lead you down the hill, heading northwest. At the stile before Atia Point, turn north and follow the fence line straight down the hill. After a cliff-edge walk along a wider dirt track, pass through a double gate and walk beside pine trees, then along a stony beach until you enter South Bay Recreation Reserve.

3 The name Atia Point alludes to one of the Cook Islands. Such names are thought to be very old, as they hark back to the Maori homelands. Oral tradition testifies that Kaikoura's first Maori settlers, the Waitaha, arrived a thousand years ago with Chief Rakaihautu.

At the end of the grassy area, turn west onto Kaka Road to reach Moa Point, site of a whale-processing factory that closed in 1922. Now it shelters the boats of today's commercial whaling industry—Whalewatch Kaikoura (▷ 190).
Shortly turn inland up Tui Drive, then eastwards along South Bay

Parade for 1km (0.6 miles). Houses on the seaward side give way to reserve land; beyond this, white fences mark a stream bed and a green sign points inland to Kaikoura township (▷ 113). Follow this route across the grassy reserve towards a stile. Follow the white marker post to a steep climb heading north, with pine trees to the east. This brings you to a viewpoint overlooking South Bay. Continue north and cross two stiles onto Scarborough Street.

4 Across Scarborough Street is the site of Nga Niho *pa*. This terrace-edged village was fortified with defensive earthworks that still stand over 2m (7ft) tall. It was probably built in the 1820s, one of 15 *pa* known to have stood on the peninsula. Its position was ideal—easy to defend with a plentiful food source nearby.

Walk eastwards up Scarborough Street, turn north up Austin Terrace, then east onto Cromer Terrace at the corner. Where Cromer Terrace meets Ward Street there's a green signpost for Fyffe Quay. Cross the stile and follow the southern fence line until you see a track winding down the hill. In the northeast corner, a yellow triangle sign and stile lead onto a back road. Walk westwards and descend onto Jimmy Armer's Beach on Fyffe Quay. Continue east along the road for 1km (0.6 miles) to return to the car park.

Fur seal pups drying out on the rocky wave-cut platforms are a familiar sight along this route

The Kaikoura peninsula, with good bays on each side, proved a good defensive site in the past for Maori pa; inset, dolphins off the coast

Below, the Department of Conservation administers the Coastal Walkway

Right, Fyffe Quay, with the Kaikoura mountains behind

WHERE TO EAT

Pipi's Restaurant and Café
✉ 80 Beach Road, Kaikoura
☎ 03-319 7160
Here you'll find fresh Marlborough mussels cooked innovatively. Mussel fritters and spicy paella are popular. Relaxed atmosphere; counter meals and cakes during the day.
🕐 Daily 10.30–10

BASICS

Tourist Information
✉ West End, Kaikoura
☎ 03-319 5641
www.kaikoura.co.nz

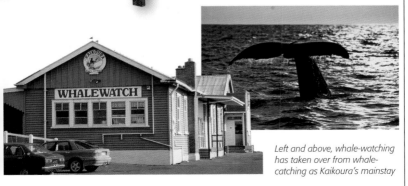

Left and above, whale-watching has taken over from whale-catching as Kaikoura's mainstay

LAKE KANIERE AND HOKITIKA GORGE

Easy walking detours enable you to explore the bush and a tumbling waterfall around the lake, then it's a short trek across farmland to the swingbridge across the Hokitika Gorge.

THE DRIVE

Distance: 95km (60 miles)
Allow: 3 hours
Start/end: Junction of Stafford Street and SH6, Hokitika, West Coast

★ Stafford Street is the more southerly of two roads heading inland from Hokitika (▷ 123). After 5km (3 miles) it forks; take the left arm signposted Lake Kaniere Road. In another 8km (5 miles) enter Lake Kaniere Scenic Reserve. The surroundings become markedly more lush and the Southern Alps dominate the horizon. In another 4km (2.5 miles) pass the Hokitika Angling Club. About 500m (550 yards) after this the road forks. In the middle is the start of a water-race known as The Landing, and your first view of Lake Kaniere.

❶ The Landing was built in 1875 to bring water to the Kaniere goldfield. By 1907 it had been reconstructed to feed the powerhouse 7km (4 miles) west on Lake Kaniere Road. This is now the smallest hydro-power station in Westland, supplying about 40 houses in Hokitika. The lake also provides Hokitika's drinking water.

Lake Kaniere was gouged out by glaciers some 12,000 years ago. It is 195m (640ft) deep and home to trout, eels and freshwater mussels, and attracts birds such as teal, scaup and crested and little grebes.

Turn south into Sunny Bight Road and drive for 1km (0.6 miles), passing a row of holiday *baches*. Park the car at Sunny Bight picnic area and take the Kahikatea Forest Walk.

❷ This 1km (0.6-mile) loop track begins on a boardwalk over wetland for 200m (220 yards) and continues on a wide, well-formed path. Kahikatea trees grow up to 60m (197ft) high, distinctively straight with branches that start high on the trunk. These characteristics make it ideal for milling, so thick stands of mature trees like this are few and far between. Kahikatea are great hosts to epiphytes—mosses, lichens and ferns.

Drive back up Sunny Bight Road and turn east into Dorothy Falls Road. In 1km (0.6 miles) there's a small parking area for Canoe Cove walk. Take your picnic and stroll through podocarp forest to a secluded beach. It's a great spot to enjoy the lake, the mountains and perhaps a quick dip.

Continue north on Dorothy Falls Road. In 1.5km (1 mile) you'll pass through Hans Bay, a quiet holiday village. The road then becomes unsealed and narrow in places. After 4.5km (2.5 miles) there's a car park for Dorothy Falls.

❸ You can see Dorothy Falls from the road, but for the full impact walk down and stand on the rocks near the bottom. The waterfalls are most dramatic from autumn to spring. If you didn't swim at Canoe Cove, now's your chance.

The gravel road continues for another 5km (3 miles), most of it on fair surface through farmland. After 3km (2 miles), pass the western end of Lake Kaniere

walkway, a 13km (8-mile) path through bush and lakeside that emerges near the Kahikatea loop. At the Mark Wallace Bridge over Styx River the road becomes sealed again. This marks the edge of the Kaniere Reserve and you continue through open farmland. Mount Lathrop, at 1,905m (6,250ft), is the highest of the ranges to the east.

Thirteen kilometres (8 miles) from Mark Wallace Bridge reach Kokatahi. At the eastern end is the Hokitika junction. Continue straight on towards Hokitika Gorge. After 1km (0.6 miles) the road turns southeast, so you have excellent views of the Southern Alps. The road takes five right-angle turns, all well signposted. Sixteen kilometres (10 miles) beyond Kokatahi, the road is unsealed again and you enter the Hokitika Gorge Scenic Reserve. The car park is in another 1.5km (1 mile).

❹ To see the gorge, walk from the car park down steep, rough steps. Once over the bridge, the track on your left (upriver) takes you down a difficult track to a view of the bridge. The original was built in the late 19th century, and marked the start of the Westland farmers' long journey across the Southern Alps into Canterbury, to the nearest sale yards. In 2004, the bridge became the focus of new controversy. An Australian company planned to surround it with an 'airwalk'— platforms enabling visitors to walk a loop around the tree tops, up to 21m (69ft) above ground. The 'pro' crowd said it would bring road improvements and economic spin-offs; the 'anti' group said the tranquillity and views would be disturbed.

Return to your car and retrace your path to Kokatahi. At the junction, turn north for the road back to Hokitika. It's 10km (6 miles) to the Stafford Street/Lake Kaniere Road junction, and another 5.5km (3 miles) to SH6.

OUT AND ABOUT

The Hokitika River is forced through a narrow gorge here—seen at its most dramatic after heavy rains

Kaihinu

Stafford

Goldsborough

Arahura

Hokitika

Humphreys

Takutai

Kaniere

Woodstock

Mananui

Lake Mahinapua

Ruatapu

Kokatahi

Lake Kaniere

1

2

Dorothy Falls

3

Styx

Kowhitirangi

Hokitika

4

Ross

0   5 km
0   3 miles

686
▲
Doctor Hill

Right, the swingbridge high above the Hokitika Gorge

Left, kahikatea trees were plundered for their long, straight timber

WHERE TO EAT

Have a picnic at Canoe Cove. Supplies can be bought from Café de Paris, 19 Tancred Street, Hokitika (tel 03-755 8933, daily 7.30am–11pm).

WHEN TO GO

On damp days with low cloud you won't see the mountains, but the lake and bushwalks are still magical.

BASICS

Tourist Information
✉ Carnegie Building, corner of Hamilton and Tancred streets, Hokitika
☎ 03-755 6166

LAKE KANIERE AND HOKITIKA GORGE 237

OVER THE PORT HILLS

This route climbs into the Port Hills and follows an impressive course along the historic Summit Road. The hilltop lookouts contrast the ragged inlets of Lyttelton Harbour with Christchurch's rambling flatness, while the dramatic Southern Alps rise up in the distance.

THE DRIVE

Distance: 40km (25 miles)
Allow: 2.5 hours
Start/end: Ferrymead Heritage Park, Christchurch

In 1849, Sumner, a beach town southeast of Christchurch, was expected to become a bustling business hub, buoyed by Evans Pass traffic between Lyttelton and Christchurch. It only happened on paper—the Lyttelton rail tunnel was built in 1867 and by the 1870s there was little more to Sumner than a hotel. Then, in 1888, a tramline opened between Sumner and the city. It started the trend for day-trippers.

★ From Ferrymead Heritage Park, drive east to the end of Ferrymead Park Drive and turn left (north) along Bridle Path Road. At the T-junction opposite the estuary, turn right onto Main Road. It's an easy drive past Mount Pleasant, Balmoral Hill, Redcliffs and Moncks Bay. After 4km (2.5 miles), Shag Rock marks the western end of Sumner Beach. Once you pass the Clifton turn-off (south) and the surf club (north), turn left (northeast) into the Esplanade.

❶ On the seaward side of the Esplanade, Cave Rock can be climbed for a lifeguard's lookout, or walk right through it at low tide. Opposite Cave Rock is the broad entrance to a cave where moa bones were found.

Drive 1km (0.6 miles) to the playground at the end of the Esplanade. Turn right (south) up Heberden Avenue and cross the speed bump at the Nayland Street intersection. After 1km (0.6 miles), turn left (south) onto Evans Pass Road and begin your climb into the Port Hills countryside. After 2km (1 mile), a viewing area looks over Sumner. Straight after this, turn west, following yellow signs for The Sign of the Kiwi and Summit Road.

❷ Summit Road is linked with the life of Harry G. Ell (1863–1934), maverick MP and conservationist. Ell envisaged a continuous network of paths along the Port Hills and across Banks Peninsula to Akaroa with 14 rest stations. By the time he died only four had been built—but even this was a feat. He had a knack of upsetting authorities from the Prime Minister down, and repeatedly brought his Summit Road trust to the brink of bankruptcy, only to be bailed out by friends.

The next 12km (7 miles) follow the winding Summit Road. At regular intervals on either side there are parking bays to enjoy the fabulous views over Christchurch, Lyttelton Harbour and Banks Peninsula. Good spots to stop are the Memorial to Pioneer Women, 1km (0.6 miles) after you pass under the Christchurch Gondola cables, and the Sugar Loaf Scenic Reserve car park, 7km (4 miles) after the memorial. By this point you will also have a good view of the 120m (394ft) television transmitter.

Summit Road is crisscrossed with walking tracks. For a break, stop at Tihiokahukura (Castle Rock), 1km (0.6 miles) after the memorial. It's a 500m (550-yard) track with unhindered views across the Canterbury Plains. In 2km (1 mile) you'll reach The Sign of the Kiwi restaurant.

❸ Compared to Ell's fanciful masterpiece, The Sign of the Takahe (finished 1939, ▷ 265), The Sign of the Kiwi is modest— a stone cottage with a warm, wooden interior and pleasant views towards Christchurch. It was opened in 1916 but, true to Ell's form, did not operate without controversy. When the Summit Road and Reserves Association publicly disowned Ell in 1920 (due to a NZ$5,000 debt), Ell moved into the Kiwi and refused to leave. His wife, Ada, came to the rescue by running the tearooms at a profit each year until 1926, when she suffered a nervous breakdown.

As you leave the Kiwi car park, turn south onto Dyers Pass Road, signposted Lyttelton. After 3km (2 miles) and some nerve-racking switchbacks, turn east to skirt Governor's Bay and follow the road to Lyttelton. Drive through the scenic hamlets of Rapaki and Cass Bay. As you leave Corsair Bay you will see the yachts of Lyttelton Harbour. At the T-junction of Simeon Quay, turn right (east). About 300m (330 yards) farther is the SH74 Lyttelton Tunnel roundabout.

❹ Governors Bay Road gives clear views of Quail Island. Now an attractive destination for walkers and daytrippers, it held a leper colony from 1907 to 1925, when the remaining sufferers were moved to Fiji. There are scant remnants of its huts, nurses' quarters and small hospital.

For a jaunt through Lyttelton, continue east towards the heart of town. After 500m (550 yards), turn left (north) into Oxford Street. Pass the visitor office, then turn left (west) into London Street. After 250m (275 yards), turn left (south) into Dublin Street and arrive back at the roundabout. Turn north through the tunnel on SH74. Exit SH74 immediately after the tunnel, following signs for the gondola and Ferrymead.

OUT AND ABOUT

Right, Banks Peninsula is named after botanist Joseph Banks (1744–1820)
Below, the precipitous Summit Road

CHRISTCHURCH

Ferrymead Heritage Park

Cave Rock
①
Sumner Head

Sumner

Godley Head

Dyers Pass Road

Summit Road

Sign of the Kiwi
③

Lyttelton

②

Lyttelton Harbour

Governor's Bay

④

Quail Island

Diamond Harbour

Port Levy

Charteris Bay

Teddington

G14

G14

0   3 km
0   2 miles

Right, cruise boat, Lyttelton
Left, the Christchurch Gondola in the Port Hills

OUT AND ABOUT

WHERE TO EAT

Sign of the Kiwi
✉ Corner of Dyers Pass and Summit roads
☎ 03-329 9966
Friendly arts and crafts-style bungalow with an all-day menu designed for walkers and sightseers. Three-course set-lunch menu NZ$20; morning and afternoon teas a speciality.
🕐 Jan–end Mar daily 10–6; Apr–end Dec daily 10–4

BASICS

Tourist Information
www.christchurchnz.net
✉ Old Chief Post Office, Cathedral Square (West), Christchurch
☎ 03-379 9629

Ferrymead Heritage Park
www.ferrymead.org.nz
✉ Ferrymead Park Drive, off Bridle Path Road, Christchurch
☎ 03-384 1970 🕐 Daily 10–4.30

WHEN TO GO

This is a popular Sunday drive route for all Christchurch, so go during the week if possible.

Below left and right, Lyttelton was the arrival port for early settlers, who had to haul everything over the steep hill (now cut through by two tunnels) to Christchurch

FIRST STEPS TO MOUNT COOK/AORAKI

The Hooker Valley Track is Mount Cook/Aoraki National Park's most popular route, offering perfect views of Mount Cook and the smaller giants around it. The linear track takes you past a glacier terminal lake via two dramatic swingbridges and ends at Hooker Lake.

THE WALK

Distance: 12km (8 miles) return; ascent 140m (460ft)
Allow: 4 hours
Start/end: Visitor information centre, Mount Cook Village

★ From the visitor centre in the village (▷ 131), 760m (2,493ft) above sea level, take the cobblestone path by the Hermitage Hotel, heading north. Cross the road to a green Department of Conservation sign for White Horse Hill Campground and Kea Point Track.

❶ The gravel track is fairly flat for this section (1.5km/1 mile) and winds through scrub and scree. The landscape was formed in 1913, when heavy rains caused the outwash stream of the Mueller Glacier to burst through the moraine wall, pushing a mass of boulders before it and destroying the original Hermitage. West is the Mueller range, 1,200m (3,936ft) above the track. North are the Footstool (2,764m/9,066ft), Mount Sefton (3,158m/10,358ft) and a glimpse of Mount Cook/Aoraki.

Forty per cent of the national park's area (70,000ha/172,970 acres) is covered by glacial ice. Five glaciers fill the upper reaches of the main valleys, including the Tasman Glacier, which at 29km (18 miles) is the longest in New Zealand. The mountains are being forced up by the Alpine Fault at the same pace their tops erode—about 1cm (0.3 inches) a year.

Turn east, following a sign for the campground and the Hooker Valley Track. Just south of the campground is the old Hermitage's fireplace. In the northeast corner of the campground is the track's official start. In 200m (220 yards) you come across a 3m (10ft)-high stone pyramid just north of the track, a memorial to lives claimed by Mount Cook/Aoraki. Shortly after, the track climbs to a stone wall lookout over Mueller Glacier lake, Mount Sefton and the Footstool. In another 600m (656 yards) it zigzags downhill to the first swingbridge across the Hooker River. The milky-blue of the water is due to fine particles of rock crushed by the Hooker Glacier.

❷ The Mount Cook lily—actually the world's largest buttercup—is symbolic of this region, but hundreds of other alpine plants thrive, too. After the white buttercups in spring come the mountain daisies of early summer and the gentians of early autumn. Many other plants put on more subtle displays, so it's worth taking a patient look on hands and knees. Ninety-three per cent of New Zealand's alpine species are endemic and many have no close relatives anywhere else in the world.

Once across the first swingbridge, the track skirts the eastern side of Mueller Glacier terminal lake. Uphill sections are made easier by stone steps. The trickiest part occurs at the bluff just before the second swingbridge, where the path is cut out of a rock face by the river. It may challenge the nerves, but a railing on the riverside means there is little real danger. Take special care in winter, when it may be icy.

❸ The dark green keas are the park's resident clowns. These protected alpine parrots are curious, sociable and intelligent. They are notorious for roughing up climbing gear and windscreen wipers, but often engage in harmless fun—sliding down hut roofs, skidding across snow fields, gliding in storm winds and tumbling on the Hermitage lawn. They are easily identified by a flash of red under the wing.

After the bridge, the track narrows but it's easier underfoot. Here you find the most magnificent views of Mount Cook/Aoraki, its south face framed by the rocky valley and underlined by the river. In summer there can be a profusion of Mount Cook lilies. After 1.2km (0.7 miles) you arrive at Stocking Stream ❹, which has a shelter and toilets.

Despite serious attempts from 1882, Mount Cook/Aoraki remained unconquered until 1894, when the imminent attempt of an English climber and his Swiss guide spurred three young Kiwis—Tom Fyfe, George Graham and Jack Clarke—to have a go. They made it to the top on Christmas day, much to the pride and relief of New Zealanders, although they had no flag and had to fly an old sugar bag instead.

The final kilometre (0.6 miles) begins with a flat section and some boardwalks. It then rises slightly and as you reach the top, you see Hooker Lake in front of you. It's often sunny and sheltered, a good place to lunch before you retrace your steps to the village.

Mount Cook lily, Hooker Valley

OUT AND ABOUT

WHERE TO EAT

Picnic at Hooker Lake. Supplies from The Hermitage Hotel, Mount Cook Village (tel 03-435 1809, ▷ 287). Hampers (from NZ$21) can be provided at two hours' notice.

WHEN TO GO

Peak seasons are October to April and July to September. There's a quiet window between April and June. This popular track is often busy, so start bright and early if you can.

Above, crossing a swingbridge in the Hooker Valley

Left, the Old Mountaineers' Café at Mount Cook Village reflects the mountain peaks

Below, lupins are among the wildflowers here

BASICS

Tourist Information
✉ 1 Larch Drive, Mount Cook Village
☎ 03-435 1186
www.doc.govt.nz

Stopping for a breather on the magnificent Hooker Valley Track

DIAMOND LAKE AND WANAKA VIEWS

A clear track takes you through bush and tussock farmland to the summit of Rocky Mountain (775m/2,542ft), where a 360-degree view reveals Lake Wanaka and surrounding mountain ranges in full splendour.

THE WALK

Distance: 7km (4 miles); ascent 400m (1,312ft)
Allow: 2.5 hours
Start/end: Diamond Lake Walking Track car park, near Wanaka, Central Otago

★ From the car park, cross the cattle grid and follow the gravel farm road up the hill. As you arrive at the top, there's a toilet eastwards (right) and a wooden sign marked 'track' on the left. Walk to this and you will see a sign for the start of the track proper, and a donation box— NZ\$2 per adult is asked for track maintenance. The next 300m (330 yards) follow the edge of Diamond Lake.

❶ Diamond Lake, surrounded by willows and raupo rushes, is an alpine tarn. It was formed some 10,000 years ago by the same receding glaciers that carved out Lake Wanaka. Minerals leaching out of the soil cause its dark appearance. It often freezes over in winter and was popular for ice-skating in the days before health and safety regulations took hold.

The track narrows and the ascent begins. The next kilometre (0.6 miles) takes you through bush, climbing on a series of flat rocks and wooden staircases before you emerge into open farmland. After 500m (550 yards), a hand-painted sign shows your place on the route, at the bottom of the figure-of-eight. For the first emergency exit, take the eastern branch. A signposted view of Lake Wanaka is 1km (0.6 miles) up this track. For Rocky Mountain, continue on the western branch.

❷ Like much farmland in Central Otago, this area is speckled with wiry brown bracken, which prohibits sheep from grazing and sticks in their wool, depreciating its quality. To combat this, sections of the hillside are burned between August and October. A specialist makes sure the fire is hot enough to burn bracken but not grasses or native flora.

After a glimpse of Lake Wanaka, the path turns west towards Mount Aspiring and returns to bush. In another 800m (875 yards), a stile leads you back into farmland. Soon you reach a large flat rock on which to sit and admire the lake. If you've had enough, the next emergency exit is only 300m (310 yards) farther, at the middle of the figure-of-eight.

For both routes, turn west towards the hills and follow two marker poles for 200m (220 yards). Shortly after a wooden bridge, you'll find another hand-painted sign. Continue uphill if you want the second emergency exit, or turn westwards to push for Rocky Mountain.

❸ You are approaching large schist rock-faces that are part of the area's attraction for climbers. The land on the opposite side of Wanaka Mount Aspiring Road is also popular. Its name—Hospital Flat—relates to its historic use as a recuperation spot for horses, rather than any association with climbing accidents.

The next 2km (1 mile) are a hard slog through tussocky farmland. The path zigzags steeply beneath large rocky overhangs, then turns east so you walk above them. After a tantalising glimpse of the lake, you burst over the brow of the hill to a wonderful view of Lake Wanaka, its islands and peninsulas, the Matukituki River and bridge ❹. At the western end of the valley is Mount Aspiring (▷ 146).

Much of this vista could have been lost but for a chance meeting in 1968. Plans were afoot to dam the outlet, at the east side of Lake Wanaka, for hydro-electricity; the community had been assured the water level would not rise significantly. Marion Borrie, a minister's wife, was walking up Mount Iron one day when she met a couple and stopped to commiserate over the plans. It turned out she was talking to the manager of the New Zealand Electricity Department, who quietly admitted the plan would raise the lake by 6m (20ft), drowning much of the land between Cromwell and Wanaka and parts of Wanaka township (▷ 147). Mrs Borrie raised the alarm, and after intense political furore the plans were shelved.

The descent starts north of the viewpoint—look for two red metal poles. The path becomes very steep and rocky; it can be slippy, so take care. The distinctive Piggyback Rock marks the end of this section. After 400m (440 yards) the path flattens to a dirt track. In another 100m (110 yards), there's an option to turn east and walk 500m (550 yards) for another view over the lake. Another 1,500m (1,640 yards) takes you back to the first painted signpost and you retrace your steps to Diamond Lake.

Lake Wanaka, surrounded by hills

OUT AND ABOUT

The beauty spot of Diamond Lake, in the hills above Wanaka

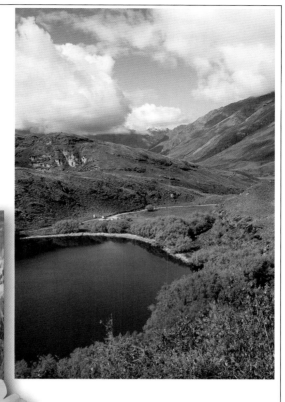

Left, a profusion of California poppies on the mountainside

WHERE TO EAT

The lake viewpoints are perfect for a picnic. Supplies can be bought from Kai Whaka Pai, at the corner of Helwick and Ardmore streets (tel 03-443 7795, daily 7am–late).

HOW TO GET THERE

From the information centre on the Wanaka lakefront, drive 18.5km (11 miles) west along Mount Aspiring Road. The car park is 6km (4 miles) after Glendhu Bay motor camp.

WHEN TO GO

Intense summer heat can make the walk more challeng- ing—an early morning start is recommended. The track may be closed in winter if conditions are not suitable— check with the DoC office (tel 03-443 7660).

BASICS

Tourist Information
✉ 100 Ardmore Street, Wanaka
☎ 03-443 1233

TIP

● For a half-day's effort, this walk offers exceptional rewards. Be prepared—the route is steep and a good level of fitness is required. However, its figure-of-eight structure provides two 'emergency exits' if it gets too tough, both affording excellent lake views.

Walkers near the start of the scenic Diamond Lake-Rocky Mountain track

OTAGO PENINSULA'S SECRET SIDE

Discover the inlets and beaches of the southeastern corner of the Otago Peninsula. The steeply rolling hills and sandy beaches belong to sheep, seals and wading birds. It's utterly remote, but just a short drive away from the friendly attractions of the northern side.

THE DRIVE

Distance: 32km (20 miles)
Allow: 2.5 hours
Start/end: The parking bay at the southern end of Portsmouth Drive, 3km (2 miles) from The Octagon, in the heart of Dunedin. It's marked by an information board and signposts to the peninsula.

Before you set off, look south to the opposite side of Portsmouth Drive, where Shore Street meets Portobello Road. There you will see a huge rock with 'Rongo' carved into it. This is a memorial to the Taranaki Maori prisoners of war held in Dunedin from 1869 to 1872 and from 1879 to 1881. They—and fellow European prisoners—built the seawall that runs all the way to Portobello. Rongo is the Maori god of peace.

★ From the car park turn east and cross Portobello Road's causeway. Continue straight on, following a blue sign for the peninsula. On your seaward side, pass Vauxhall yacht club. Take the first inland turn up Doon Street, which takes you behind a once grand private home. Stay on Doon Street as it turns abruptly left. At the end of Doon Street, turn right into Connell Street, then left into Larnach Road (a main road). This turns into McKerrow Street after 500m (550 yards). When you reach the T-junction, turn left onto Highcliff Road.

About 200m (220 yards) down Highcliff Road, Rotary Park

lookout gives a dramatic glimpse of Dunedin city and harbour. From here, the road narrows and enters countryside. After 1.5km (1 mile) pass a parking bay; just beyond is a well-marked track to the Soldier's Memorial, a 700m (765-yard) climb. Continue for another 5km (3 miles) and you come to Pukehiki, with its white, rectangular church tower and tiny public library on the north. The next intersection signposts Larnach Castle (▷ 147) to the north, but stay on Highcliff Road.

❶ Peninsula farms are distinctive for their use of drystone walls, rather than the typical No. 8 fencing wire (▷ 12). It shows skill and thrift on behalf of the early Scottish farmers—while neatly divvying up their paddocks, they cleaned up the volcanic stones that littered the ground. Look for the skewed macrocarpa trees, which tell tales about the southerly wind. Sandfly Bay did not get its name from the insects, but the gales.

After 2km (1 mile) pass the modern stone wall of Gatesheath bed-and-breakfast. At this corner, turn south down Sandymount Road. This marks the end of the tourist trail and after 600m (656 yards) the road is unsealed. To the north there are good views of Harbour Cone; to the south, the Pacific Ocean, beaches and rolling sheep country.

After 2km (1 mile) reach a triangular intersection. For a detour, continue up the steep road to Sandymount Recreational Reserve.

❷ From the reserve, well-marked tracks lead to the cliff known as Lovers Leap (2km/1 mile), and the high dunes of Sandfly Bay (5km/3 miles). Note that they are closed during the lambing season, from August to October.

To continue the tour, turn north onto Hoopers Inlet Road. After 1km (0.6 miles), the inlet is before you.

❸ The tidal mudflats of Hoopers Inlet (and Papanui Inlet to the northeast) offer good feeding for wading birds. Pied stilts, godwits, black and variable oystercatchers and spur-winged plovers are regular visitors, and spoonbills occasionally drop by.

Turn west and drive 2km (1 mile) around the inlet to a yellow sign-post for Portobello. Follow this sign left (northwards) along Allan's Beach Road for 1.5km (1 mile), which brings you over the hill and into Portobello. From here, the Royal Albatross Centre (▷ 147) is a farther 11km (7 miles) out from the city, while Westpac Aquarium is 1.5km (1 mile) down Hatchery Road. Turn left (west) onto Portobello Road and take the 'low road' 14km (9 miles) back to Portsmouth Drive. The Portobello Coffee Shop is on Highcliff Road, which is to the south, opposite the inlet.

❹ Thematically painted bus shelters punctuate the drive back to Dunedin. These concrete caves were brightened up in 1989 by Broad Bay artist John Noakes. There are 12 of them on the route, often with designs relating to local names—a flock of chooks (chickens) are near the Happy Hens shop, four-leaf clovers enliven Dublin Bay, while comic characters Wallace and Grommit appear for good measure.

The road is tightly snaking, with excellent views towards the city and north across the harbour towards Port Chalmers. It passes a number of well-signposted and worthwhile attractions such as the 1909 Fletcher House, Macandrew Bay beach and Glenfalloch Gardens. Take your time, especially as you go around Burns Point, 11km (7 miles) from Portobello. Despite the railings, cars end up in the harbour about once a year.

OUT AND ABOUT

Black oystercatchers are among the waders in Hooper's Inlet

The grand mansion of Larnach Castle makes for a worthy detour from the main route

DUNEDIN

Otago Peninsula

Potato Point
Heywood Point
E17
Waitati
Upper Waitati
Mihiwaka
Aramoana
Taiaroa Head
Royal Albatross Colony
Port Chalmers
Otago Harbour
Otakou
Harwood
Glenleith
Portobello
Papanui Inlet
4 Broad Bay
Larnach Castle
Hoopers Inlet
88
3
Pukehiki
1 Highcliff
2
Sandymount Recreational Reserve
Cape Saunders
Sandfly Bay
Harakehe Head
Maori Head

0 — 2 km
0 — 1 mile

E17

BASICS

Tourist Information
✉ 48 The Octagon, Dunedin
☎ 03-474 3300
www.cityofdunedin.com

Fletcher House
✉ 727 Portobello Road
☎ 03-478 0180
🕐 Daily 11–4, Boxing Day–Easter
🎟 Adult NZ$3, child free

Glenfalloch Woodland Gardens
✉ 430 Portobello Road
☎ 03-476 1775
🕐 Daily dawn–dusk
🎟 Adult NZ$3, child NZ$1

NZ Marine Studies Centre and Westpac Aquarium
☎ 03-479 5826
🕐 Daily noon–4.30; guided tours 10.30am
🎟 NZ$9; guided tour NZ$18

Drystone walls—field dividers skilfully built without mortar—are typical of this area

Above right, a royal albatross colony is the big attraction at the eastern tip of the peninsula

WHERE TO EAT

Portobello Coffee Shop
✉ 699 Highcliff Road, Portobello
☎ 03-478 1055
You'll get homestyle fare here, including traditional kiwi slices. Highlights are the craft gallery at the back featuring local knitting and pottery, and outdoor seating overlooking the bay.
🕐 Daily 9–5

LONG-DISTANCE WALKS

Tramping, trekking, hiking, walking—whatever you call it, New Zealanders like to do it, and manage a network that includes some of the finest walking tracks in the world. Most are equipped with simple hut accommodation or campsites, some require reservation ahead, and all offer a chance to get closer to native plants, wildlife and spectacular scenery. Some of the most popular are listed below, but there are many shorter options—just ask at any DoC or visitor information centre. More information on all these may be found on www.doc.govt.nz.

ABEL TASMAN COAST TRACK

Where: Marahau–Wainui
Distance: 51km (32 miles)
Time: 2–5 days
This easy-to-moderate walking track passes through a picturesque landscape of coastal forests and golden sandy beaches at the top of the South Island. While all the streams are bridged, some sections are tide-dependent. Water taxis give access to shorter sections (▷ 109–110).

DUSKY TRACK

Where: Lake Hauroko–West Arm, Lake Manapouri, via Supper Cove
Distance: 84km (52 miles)
Time: 8–11 days
One of the country's most remote walking trails, in the fiordlands of the southwest South Island, provides a challenge for dedicated trampers, with the promise of 21 three-wire bridge crossings, and access in summer only (▷ 141–142).

GREENSTONE AND CAPLES TRACKS

Where: End of Greenstone Road–Elfin Bay, western Lake Wakatipu
Time: 4–5 days
A round-trip through the open tussock valley of the Greenstone River and the wooded vale of the Caples River, which both flow into Lake Wakatipu, the South Island's second biggest lake. The valleys are linked by the McKellar Saddle, a high sub-alpine pass.

HEAPHY TRACK

Where: Aorere Valley, near Collingwood–near Karamea
Distance: 82km (51 miles)
Time: 4–6 days
A challenging trail in Kahurangi National Park, the Heaphy crosses various landscapes, from the junction of the Brown and Aorere rivers, over tussock grassland to the lush forests

and roaring sea of the South Island's West Coast (▷ 112).

KEPLER TRACK

Where: Circuit from Te Anau
Distance: 60km (37 miles)
Time: 3–4 days
A moderately difficult circuit in Fiordland takes in alpine meadows, beech forest and glacial valleys. You're recommended to tackle it in an anti-clockwise direction (▷ 142).

MILFORD TRACK

Where: Glade Wharf, Lake Te Anau–Sandfly Point, Milford Sound
Distance: 53.5km (33 miles)
Time: 4 days
Numbers are strictly controlled on this, New Zealand's most famous tramp, and advance booking is essential. It can be wet and muddy, but—weather permitting—the waterfalls, alpine flowers and viewpoints are spectacular (▷ 143).

QUEEN CHARLOTTE TRACK

Where: Ship Cove–Anakiwa
Distance: 71km (44 miles)
Time: 4 days
www.queencharlottetrack.co.nz
Easy access by water taxis means you can send luggage ahead by boat each day on this stunning walkway, which passes through ancient

forest and beside the coast, with fabulous Sounds views (▷ 116).

RAKIURA TRACK

Where: Stewart Island/Rakiura circuit from Halfmoon Bay
Distance: 36km (22 miles)
Time: 3 days
Stewart Island/Rakiura is a natural paradise, known for its plants and wildlife. This circular route around the coast and through forest is described as suitable for anyone with moderate fitness (▷ 150).

ROUTEBURN TRACK

Where: Routeburn Shelter, Mount Aspiring National Park–The Divide, Fiordland National Park
Distance: 33km (20 miles)
Time: 3–4 days
A high track through spectacular lake and mountain scenery, the ever-popular Routeburn links Mount Aspiring and Fiordland national parks via the Harris Saddle (▷ 140–143, 146).

ST. JAMES WALKWAY

Where: Lewis Pass
Distance: 66km (41 miles)
Time: 5 days
Through varied mountain, forest, open farmland and sub-alpine landscapes (▷ 130).

TONGARIRO NORTHERN CIRCUIT

Where: Circuit from Whakapapa village
Time: 3–4 days
The Tongariro Northern Circuit, in the central North Island, winds over the volcanic peak of Mount Tongariro and around Mount Ngauruhoe, with volcanic craters and glacial valleys to admire. In winter, you'll need alpine equipment and a guide (▷ 88).

Footpaths are well maintained across New Zealand, with detailed guide books readily available and touring options

This chapter lists places to eat and stay, broken down by region, then alphabetically by town.

Eating and Staying

EATING OUT IN NEW ZEALAND

You can eat almost any kind of food in New Zealand. The country's European heritage is largely British, with a tradition of roast meat, 'three veg' and hearty breakfasts, which can still be widely found. Good home baking still characterises many cafés. A typical family meal is likely to be a barbecue of sausages, chops or seafood that folk have caught or gathered themselves, usually washed down with beer or wine.

Eating out in New Zealand is getting more sophisticated, as Kiwis embrace the café society and bring back a taste for international cuisines from their overseas travels. Modern New Zealand chefs draw inspiration from Asia, the Mediterranean and the Pacific, developing a style of cooking that reflects New Zealand's position in the world. Often called Pacific Rim cuisine, it aims to enhance the tastes of fresh local produce. Indigenous ingredients, traditionally used by Maori, are increasingly being incorporated, with exciting results. With a climate ranging from subtropical to temperate, New Zealand can grow anything from oranges to avocados, saffron to swede, and sheep and cattle are fed year round on pasture. The quality of ingredients is superb.

Immigrants from many countries have opened restaurants, too, so it's easy to find Indian, Chinese, Malaysian, Thai, Japanese, Korean, Italian, Greek and Mexican food. Sometimes they modify their cooking to what they perceive as New Zealand tastes—so in a Chinese restaurant, for example, you may need to ask for the Chinese menu to get authentic dishes. Although New Zealand is still largely a nation of meat eaters, most restaurants offer vegetarian options.

WHAT TO EAT
New Zealand lamb is arguably the best in the world. Farm-raised venison, known as Cervena, is also a speciality (▷ 19). Farmed green-lip mussels, oysters and salmon are also of high quality, thanks to the pristine waters in which they are grown. Despite New Zealand's reputation as perhaps the best trout-fishing country in the world, buying and selling trout is illegal. However, if you

catch your own, many restaurants will be happy to cook it for you.

When you can get wild seafood, seize the chance. As an island nation, New Zealand's seafood resources are vast, but more than 80 per cent is exported, so chefs in New York, Tokyo or Sydney have a better chance of getting a regular supply than the locals. Look for snapper, monkfish, blue cod, hapuka, turbot, flounder (cooked on the bone is best) and swordfish. For an authentic experience, catch the fish yourself and barbecue it. Other seafood treats include crayfish (spiny lobster), Bluff oysters, paua (abalone), pipi, tuatua, cockles, scampi, koura (freshwater crayfish) and scallops.

Below ground, the kumara (sweet potato) is prized by Maori and used in many ways. Kiwifruit or 'zespri' are deservedly celebrated and most often appear sliced on top of New Zealand's most famous dessert, the pavlova—a concoction of meringue, whipped cream and fresh fruit. Other locally grown fruits worth trying are the feijoa and tamarillo.

WHERE TO EAT
Throughout New Zealand there are eateries to suit every taste and budget, from international fast-food joints to world-class restaurants. The main cities are rich in choice (reputedly, Wellington has more cafés and restaurants per capita than New York) with cafés, café-bars, brasseries, traditional and specialist restaurants flying the flags of many countries. Generally, there is little to distinguish between cafés and restaurants, although cafés tend to be more informal during the day and serve more substantial dishes at night. They also almost always serve coffee, breakfast or brunch, are often licensed (or at least

EATING

welcome BYO) and often provide outdoor seating. You can get good coffee almost everywhere.

Kiwis are a casual lot and few restaurants expect formal attire. The restaurants of many of the top hotels, motels and lodges are open to non-residents and can be a good option. If what you want is a hearty feed, you can generally find good pub grub in the cities and most major towns, particularly in popular Irish- and English-style pubs. Fish and chips is New Zealanders' most popular takeaway—with a menu so you can choose what fish you want.

OPENING HOURS

Hours vary and are often seasonal. Most cafés open for breakfast between 7 and 9am, often remaining open until 5pm. Some also stay open late into the evening or the early hours. This usually applies seven days a week, with special Sunday brunch hours. Most mid-range restaurants open daily for lunch (often 11–2) and dinner (from 6). The more exclusive establishments usually open for dinner from about 6, with some (especially in winter) opening selected weekday evenings only and on weekends.

BRING YOUR OWN (BYO)

BYO restaurants or cafés are licensed for the consumption of (but not the sale of) alcohol and allow you to bring your own wine or bottled beers, sometimes charging a corkage fee (typically NZ$2–NZ$10). Some restaurants are both licensed and BYO wine.

FOODSTORES

The main supermarket chains are Foodtown, Woolworths and New World, with Pak 'n Save and Countdown being marginally less expensive. Try to buy fresh vegetables and fruit from the roadside stalls or wholesale fruit markets, where the prices are lower and the quality fresher than the supermarkets.

BEER

Steinlager may be internationally famous, but the most interesting New Zealand beers are the boutique brews. Try Galbraith's in Auckland (Mount Eden Road), Dux de Lux in Christchurch and Emerson's in Dunedin. More widely produced beers worth trying are Speight's (the tipple of the Southern Man), Monteith's (especially lauded on the West Coast of the South Island) and Mac's, originally brewed in Nelson. All the main international brands and some specialist ones are available, and you can also get New Zealand-brewed Guinness. Beer and lager is usually sold by the 'handle' (pint) or the 'jug' (up to three pints). Half-pints come in a 12fl oz (350ml) glass. Rarely is a pint

a full imperial pint; it's usually just under. Drinks generally cost from NZ$6 to NZ$7 for a pint, about NZ$4 to NZ$5 for a jug of Lion Red and up to NZ$7 for a double shot. Drinks cost much less in rural pubs and RSAs (Returned Services Association clubs), where you can usually get yourself signed in. The minimum drinking age is 18. Liquor shops are everywhere and in most places you can buy alcohol seven days a week.

For further information on Kiwi beer visit the websites **www.**Realbeer.co.nz or **www.**brewing.co.nz.

WINE

New Zealand's diversity of climates and soil types has produced a distinctive array of wines. Wine is made the length and breadth of the country, but the Hawke's Bay and Nelson/Marlborough areas are the principal wine-producing regions. Sauvignon blanc from Marlborough is New Zealand's most internationally acclaimed wine, but there is growing recognition for its Chardonnay, Pinot noir, *méthode traditionelle* sparkling wine, Riesling, Cabernet Sauvignon and Merlot. Striking contemporary architecture and Pacific Rim cuisine combine to make vineyard restaurants exciting places to dine. Fruit wines, including kiwifruit, are also produced. Many vineyards offer tastings and cellar-door sales.

NON-ALCOHLIC DRINKS

All the major international soft-drink brands are available. New Zealand has its own soft drink, a brand called L&P, which stands for Lemon and Paeroa. The 'Lemon' speaks for itself and Paeroa relates to a town in the Waikato where the drink was founded and made famous by the use of the local mineral-rich spring water. Although it is not made there now, the traditional recipe is still used. Bright green spirulea drinks contain a mineral-rich seaweed.

Given New Zealand's colonial roots, tea is popular and widely available. Increasingly, the standard Bell teabag is being joined by green and herbal teas, often served in specialist shops. New Zealanders expect a high standard from their coffee, and support a number of local roasteries. Expect to ask for a flat white, latte, cappuccino, ristretto, long or short black, or any number of permutations.

TIPPING

Tipping is not normal in New Zealand, and most New Zealanders don't tip, but a service charge of 10 to 15 per cent may be included at some smarter restaurants.

SMOKING

New Zealand has banned smoking in the workplace—which includes restaurants, bars, pubs, clubs and casinos.

RESTAURANT CHAINS

RESTAURANTS, FAST FOOD AND CAFÉS	Price per meal (NZ$)	Alcohol	Child Menu	Takeout	Phone Number	Website
Cobb and Co	20–30	✔	✔		09-377 0595	www.cobb.co.nz
Domino's Pizza	12–15			✔	0800-304 050	www.dominospizza.co.nz
KFC	8–10		✔	✔	0800-KFC KFC	www.kfc.co.nz
McDonald's	3–8		✔	✔	09-306 5600	www.mcdonalds.co.nz
Pizza Hut	15–20			✔	0800-838383	www.pizzahut.co.nz
Valentines	20			✔	09-444 4819	www.valentines.co.nz

MENU READER

aubergine: eggplant
BBQ: barbecue
cervena: New Zealand venison
BYO: restaurants or cafés that allow you to bring your own wine or beer
capsicum: bell pepper
entrée: appetizer or hors d'oeuvre
feijoa: an aromatic fruit, also known as the pineapple guava
fritter: as in whitebait or crab fritters (also known as patties)—seafood or fish cakes
hokey pokey: aerated toffee, usually in vanilla ice cream
jug: as in jug of beer (about 4 pints)
hangi: traditional Maori feast cooked on hot stones underground (see opposite)
kai: Maori word for food (*kai moana*—seafood)
kumara: sweet potato. Originally from Peru, the kumara came to New Zealand via Samoa and was a staple food of Maori. Very popular because of its sweet taste and versatility, it may be steamed, boiled, baked or eaten raw
kina: sea eggs with a prickly shell and edible roe, usually eaten raw and an acquired taste
lollies: sweets or confectionery
manuka honey: honey with a distinctive taste from the flowers of the manuka (tea tree, known for its medicinal properties)
muttonbird: the young of the sooty petrel, with a strong, fishy taste
paua: abalone (a mollusc)
Pavlova: also known as 'Pav'. A traditional pudding made of cream and meringue. Though hotly debated and claimed on both sides of the Tasman Sea, it was thought to have originated in the 1930s to celebrate a visit to New Zealand by Russian ballerina Anna Pavlova
schooner: large glass of beer, usually 0.4L (0.75 pint)
stubby: a small bottle of beer
tamarillo: egg-shaped, deep-red or gold-skinned fruit with tart flesh and edible seeds

EATING

Outlets	Location	Description
16	Nationwide	Family dining, reasonably priced home-style fare
61	Nationwide	Dial-out pizzas
103	Nationwide	Chicken meals
104	Nationwide	Burgers and salads
106	Nationwide	Family dining
11	North Island	Buffet family meals

HANGI

Pronounced 'hungi', this is the traditional Maori and Pacific Island method of cooking. It's a great social occasion as much as anything else.

Traditionally, the men would light a large fire and place river stones in the embers. While the stones were heating, a pit was dug in the earth (in active thermal areas, such as around Rotorua, the stones and pit might be naturally heated).

The stones were then placed in the pit with sacking or plant material onto which the meat was laid. Nowadays this includes chicken, wild pig and lamb, but formerly it would have been moa, pigeon, seafood and vegetables, including kumara and watercress. Smaller items were wrapped in leaves or in foil and placed in a basket covered with earth. The steam slowly cooked the food, sealing in the wonderful tastes.

Although—due to modern health and safety requirements—it is not possible to sample an authentic *hangi*, the feasts produced for visitors are a good second-best.

EATING

AUCKLAND, NORTHLAND AND COROMANDEL

While most of New Zealand has a temperate climate, the 'winterless north' is generally regarded as subtropical. Oranges, kiwifruit and avocados grow in abundance, and are sold at roadside stalls around Kerikeri. The Bay of Islands is renowned for big-game fishing so you will find snapper, giant hapuka and marlin on many restaurant menus, as well as the locally farmed Orongo Bay oysters. Grapevines were introduced to New Zealand in Kerikeri and a number of boutique vineyards make up the Northland wine trail. Farther south, Puhoi is a cheese-making heartland. Boutique cheeses from Mahoe, Matatoki and Mercer are also a speciality of the region. The developing wine region of Matakana, with its attractive vineyard cafés, is well worth a detour off the main highway between Whangarei and Auckland. Some of the country's finest wines and olive oils are produced on Waiheke Island, and the Auckland wine regions of Henderson and Kumeu are both within easy reach of the city. Shellfish are farmed in Clevedon and around the Coromandel Peninsula—or you can gather them yourself from the beach.

AUCKLAND

KERMADEC
Viaduct Quay, Auckland
Tel 09-309 0412
www.kermadec.co.nz
This seafood complex in the Viaduct Basin is a clever combination of the owner's fishing business, a casual brasserie and bar with a balcony, and a classy restaurant. The restaurant carries the sea theme into

its décor, with tapa-cloth sails slung from the ceiling and water-walled *tatami* rooms. You can order traditional Japanese or modern New Zealand dishes such as seared snapper on corn risotto and chervil beurre blanc.
🅒 Brasserie daily 10–late; restaurant Mon–Fri 6–late
🅦 Brasserie L NZ$40, D NZ$50, W NZ$29; restaurant, D NZ$60, W NZ$29

LAVA
425 Tamaki Drive, St. Heliers, Auckland
Tel 09-575 9969
www.lavanz.co.nz
Opposite the beach, with great views over the harbour, Lava has become known for its modern New Zealand food, such as oven-baked veal roulade wrapped with prosciutto with bell peppers, polenta cake, ratatouille and rocket pesto. The décor is elegantly subdued: grey walls, brown leather chairs and white tablecloths, with artworks complementing the beachfront location.
🅒 Daily 9am–late
🅦 L NZ$25, D NZ$60, W NZ$40

OH CALCUTTA
151 Parnell Road, Parnell, Auckland
Tel 09-377 9090
www.ohcalcutta.co.nz
Oh Calcutta ranks highly in all departments, from food quality to ambience and service. The dishes are a mixture of northern and southern Indian. Whole snapper marinated, skewered and smoke-roasted in the tandoor is a speciality. A large, bustling place popular with expatriate Indians and families, it has indoor and outdoor seating.
🅒 Daily 5.30–11.30, also Wed–Fri 12–2
🅦 L NZ$25, D NZ$35, W NZ$25

ORBIT AND THE OBSERVATORY
Sky Tower, corner of Victoria and Federal streets, Auckland
Tel 09-363 6000
www.skycityauckland.co.nz
Up the Sky Tower, with views over the city, the Orbit à la carte restaurant revolves sedately while serving modern New Zealand brasserie food, such as *wakame*-seared tuna loin on a tabouleh salsa with

avocado aioli. Reservations are required. The Observatory, above the main level, serves buffets at a fixed price, with children charged according to age.

🅒 Daily 5.30–9.30; also Orbit Mon–Fri 11.30–2.30, Sat, Sun 10–3; Observatory Fri–Sun 12–2
🅦 Orbit L NZ$25, D NZ$57, W NZ$29.50; Observatory L NZ$37.50, D NZ$52.50, W NZ$29.50

SPECIAL IN AUCKLAND
PONSONBY FRESH FISH AND CHIP CO
127 Ponsonby Road, Ponsonby, Auckland
Tel 09-378 7885
Fish and chips are New Zealanders' takeaway food of choice, and this is one of Auckland's most popular places to get them. An institution in Ponsonby for many years, it may have reduced its portions over time, but the quality has stayed generally good. Try the local Pacific fish. If you don't want fish, the vegetarian burgers are also good. There is always a crowd but there's no place sit, so plan to place an order and return about 20 minutes later.
🅒 Daily 11–9.30
🅦 From NZ$6

WHITE

Hilton Hotel, Princes Wharf, 147 Quay Street, Auckland
Tel 09-978 2000
www.whiterestaurant.co.nz

For a combination of views across the water, classy atmosphere, food and service, White is hard to beat. Surrounded on three sides by the sea, it has the style of a cruise ship. The restaurant is split-level, with a long table at the entrance for single diners or couples who want to mix. It serves the best of local seafood and regional produce in a modern cooking style. The wine list is vast. It is within the Hilton Hotel, ▷ 273.

🕒 Mon–Fri 6.30am–10.30am, 12–3, 6pm–11pm, Sat, Sun 11–3
🍴 L NZ$39, D NZ$80, W NZ$70

SOUL BAR AND BISTRO

Viaduct Harbour, Auckland
Tel 09-356 7249
www.soulsearch.co.nz

With open-air decks over-looking the harbour, this stylish restaurant has award-winning chef Mark Wylie. The food blends influences from the Mediterranean, North Africa and the Middle East, as in quail stuffed with Moroccan sausage roasted in vine leaves. The seafood is excellent: you can choose to have the day's choices grilled, pan-fried, roasted or black-ened and served with accompaniments appropriate to the cooking style.

🕒 Mon–Fri 11am–late, Sat, Sun 10am–late
🍴 L NZ$55, D NZ$70, W NZ$38

COLVILLE

COLVILLE GENERAL STORE AND CAFF

Main Road, Colville, Coromandel Peninsula
Tel 07-866 6805

Take a photograph here, as places like this are disappearing fast. A classic Kiwi rural store, it is the last place to get provisions and fuel before continuing on a journey farther north. Like the store, the attached café is the day-time hub of social contact in these parts. It has the usual café fare, including cakes, pastries, pies and coffee,

but the real delight is listening to the local gossip.

🕒 Daily 9.30–4, also Fri–Sun 6–8pm
🍴 From NZ$6

COROMANDEL TOWN

PEPPER TREE RESTAURANT AND BAR

31 Kapanga Road, Coromandel Town
Tel 07-866 8211
www.coromandeltown.co.nz

In the heart of Coromandel Town, the Pepper Tree is a community meeting place, with a big-screen TV and weekly music club jam sessions. The buffets and à la carte menus focus on local seafood such as oysters, mussels, snapper, smoked fish and crayfish. You can also get hearty country fare like

steak, chips and eggs. Special children's dishes, such as spare ribs, are available. On summer evenings book in advance.

🕒 Daily 10–9
🍴 L NZ$25, D NZ$50, W NZ$25

KERIKERI

MARSDEN ESTATE

Wiroa Road, Kerikeri
Tel 09-407 9398
www.marsdenestate.co.nz

This winery and restaurant are named after Samuel Marsden, who planted New Zealand's first grapevines close by in 1819. The restaurant is charmingly located beside a lake among the vines. There is seating indoors, where wine-tasting takes place, or outdoors on the terrace. The menu includes dishes such as black pudding with blue cheese, pear and blueberry sauce, designed to complement the wines from the 4ha (10-acre) vineyard.

🕒 Aug–end May daily 10–5; Jun, Jul Sun–Thu 10–4, Fri, Sat 10–4, 6–late
🍴 L NZ$25, W NZ$19.50

ROCKET CAFÉ AND DELI

Kerikeri Road, Kerikeri
Tel 09-407 3100

Surrounded by gardens and orchards, this is a good place to stop for refreshments or lunch. It has excellent coffee, a small menu of hot dishes, and a tempting deli counter of cakes, muffins and quiches. You can sit inside or under a canopy among the fruit trees. Children have their own menu and playground.

🕒 Tue–Fri 8.30–3.30, Sat, Sun 9–4
🍴 L NZ$20, W NZ$26

MATAKANA

ASCENSION VINEYARD RESTAURANT

480 Matakana Road, Matakana
Tel 09-422 9601
www.ascensionvineyard.co.nz

An eye-catching building next to the Ascension winery, this popular restaurant on the Matakana wine trail serves a comprehensive menu of New Zealand cuisine with a Mediterranean twist. Ascension wines are served, and the gift shop in the wine-tasting room sells their own preserves, jellies, oils and relishes. The restaurant is open for dinner during summer and regularly hosts live music and gigs.

🕒 Mon–Fri 11–4, Sat, Sun 11–5

PAIHIA

ONLY SEAFOOD

40 Marsden Road, Paihia
Tel 09-402 6066

While in Paihia, the capital of game fishing in New Zealand, chances are you'll want to try the local speciality. At Only Seafood, located on the water-front above its companion restaurant Bistro 40, you get a fine view across the bay as well. Game fish is typically served seared in a light soy sauce. Other dishes include char-grilled hapuka, scallops and local Orongo Bay oysters. It's an informal place where you can feel comfortable coming straight from the beach. Eat indoors or out on the deck. The restaurant doesn't take reservations, but you can have a drink in the bar while you wait.

🕒 Daily from 5pm
🍴 Main and veg NZ$30

EATING

HOTEL DU VIN

Lyons Road, Mangatawhiri Valley, Pokeno
Tel 09-233 6314
www.hotelduvin.co.nz
Just off the main road to the Coromandel Peninsula, this restaurant is part of a luxury retreat amid the vines of Firstland Vineyard. The food is modern New Zealand, with a focus on seafood and game in dishes such as venison fillet with tomato, mozzarella, basil and macadamia-nut ravioli. On Sundays you can combine a fixed-price three-course lunch (NZ$45) with use of the hotel's leisure facilities. Reserve in advance.
🕐 Mon–Sat 12–2.30, 6–9.30, Sun 11.30–2.30, 6–9.30
🍴 L NZ$48, D NZ$65, W NZ$49

RAWENE

BOATSHED CAFÉ

Clendon Esplanade, Rawene
Tel 09-405 7728
A welcome refreshment stop before or after the ferry crossing, the Boatshed Café serves a surprisingly varied selection of light snacks and good coffee, with views across the Hokianga Harbour. Bright works by local artists are displayed and may be purchased.
🕐 Daily 8.30–4, closed mid-Sep to mid-Oct
🍴 L from NZ$10

RUSSELL

DUKE OF MARLBOROUGH

Duke of Marlborough Hotel, The Waterfront, Russell
Tel 09-403 7829
www.theduke.co.nz
It's hard to think of a more romantic place to dine than this old waterfront hotel, particularly if you can sit outdoors on the veranda and look out over the water while boats bob in the bay. Indoors, the grand dining room is more formal. You can order local fish and seafood, including Orongo Bay oysters, but the menu is also strong on char-grills and game.
🕐 Daily 7.30am–9pm
🍴 L NZ$25, D NZ$55, W NZ$30

KAMAKURA

The Strand, Russell
Tel 09-403 7771
www.kamakura.co.nz
A stylish restaurant on Russell's waterfront, Kamakura has a reputation for superb food and interesting wine. The menu is Pacific Rim, with an emphasis on fresh local produce including Orongo Bay oysters, and everything—including bread—is made on site. Advance booking is recommended.
🕐 Mon, Thu–Sat 12–2, 6–9, Sun 11–3
🍴 L NZ$45, D NZ$70, W NZ$45

WAIHEKE ISLAND

MUDBRICK RESTAURANT

Church Bay Road, Oneroa, Waiheke Island
Tel 09-372 9050
www.mudbrick.co.nz
Named after the earth bricks from which it is built, Mudbrick Restaurant is in a spectacular location, surrounded by vines, with expansive views over the Hauraki Gulf. The restaurant and winery blend in with the landscaped gardens, and are designed in a French provincial style. The food has a rural and Mediterranean theme, with Waiheke Pacific oysters, home-baked foccacia, and dishes such as saffron and spinach ravioli, set off by local wines. Advance booking is essential.
🕐 Daily 11–5, 6–late
🍴 L NZ$47, D NZ$70, W NZ$38

WAITANGI

WAIKOKOPU CAFÉ

Treaty Grounds, Waitangi
Tel 09-402 6275
www.waitangi.net.nz
A good place for coffee or lunch after exploring the Treaty Grounds (▷ 74), this attractive café has indoor and outdoor dining areas overlooking a bush walk and pond, the *waka* (Maori canoe) and the coastline. You can choose from snacks and cakes or a blackboard menu of substantial dishes such as corn and coriander fritters served with guacamole, sour cream and tomato salsa. There is also plenty of food on the menu that appeals to children.
🕐 Daily 9–5
🍴 L NZ$20, W NZ$22

WHANGAREI

A DECO

70 Kamo Road, Kensington, Whangarei
Tel 09-459 4957
Art deco décor, original combinations of tastes and good service make this place worth a detour off the main road between Auckland and the Bay of Islands. Chef Brenton Low's signature dish is a braised oxtail and wild mushroom tart with porcini polenta and Parmesan crumble, but the menu ranges widely, from chilled mushroom soup to pina colada crème brulée.
🕐 Tue, Sat 6–late, Wed–Fri 11–2.30, 6–late
🍴 L NZ$25, D NZ$50, W NZ$28

WHENUAKITE

COLENSO COUNTRY CAFÉ & SHOP

Main Road, Whenuakite, Coromandel Peninsula
Tel 07-866 3725
Surrounded by old-fashioned herb gardens, the Colenso Café is a pleasant place to stop for a snack or lunch on the road between Whitianga and Tairua. You can sit on a shady veranda or indoors, where local crafts are displayed for sale. The food is simple but good home baking. Although it's licensed for the sale of alcohol, the real treat here is freshly squeezed juice from the café's organic orchard. You can also buy orchard products from the roadside stall.
🕐 Sep–end Jul daily 10–5
🍴 L NZ$30, W NZ$25

WHITIANGA

THE FIRE PLACE

9 The Esplanade, Whitianga, Coromandel Peninsula
Tel 07-866 4828
www.thefireplace-restaurant.com
There is no escaping the motif of this rustic restaurant on the Whitianga waterfront—you are greeted by a giant fireplace and there are others inside. The food continues the theme, with pizza from the wood-fired oven, but there are many other dishes including pasta, salads and seafood. There's a good selection of coffees and teas, too, and wines are reasonably priced. Reservations are recommended.
🕐 Daily 5pm–9.30pm (also 11am–2pm in summer)
🍴 L NZ$30, D NZ$50, W NZ$25

EATING

CENTRAL NORTH ISLAND

The lush dairy country of Taranaki is the heart of the North Island's cheese industry, producing some excellent European-style cheeses like Raclette and St. Paulin, as well as New Zealand creations such as Shades of Blue, mainly under the Ferndale label. Fine boutique cheeses are also made in the Dutch style at Meyer Gouda near Hamilton. In Gisborne, look for the local Waimata cheeses. Paeroa has a national reputation thanks to L&P (lemon and Paeroa) mineral waters, originally from the town. Orchards surround Tauranga, producing citrus, tamarillos, feijoas and kiwifruit—nearby Te Puke calls itself the kiwifruit capital. Gisborne and Hawke's Bay are also traditional fruit- and vegetable-growing areas, producing citrus and stonefruit, berries, avocados, peas, beans, corn and many other crops. Both regions have a reputation for producing top-class wine—Gisborne is noted particularly for its Chardonnay and Hawke's Bay for its reds. More than 40 wineries are open to the public on the Hawke's Bay wine trail (▷ 79).

PRICES AND SYMBOLS

The prices given are for a two-course lunch (L) and a three-course dinner (D) for one person, without drinks. Many restaurants add a 15 per cent charge on public holidays. The wine price (W) is for the least expensive bottle. Restaurants are listed alphabetically by town. For a key to the symbols, ▷ 2.

CAMBRIDGE

SOUTER HOUSE

19 Victoria Street, Cambridge
Tel 07-827 3610
www.souterhouse.co.nz
Deep red carpeting, chandeliers and Royal Doulton china grace the dining room at Souter House, an 1870s Victorian mansion with a licensed restaurant and accommodation. The food is traditional European and beautifully presented. Starters include shrimp cocktail, scallops and bacon and deep-fried Camembert; main courses are strong on roasts and grills, including lamb, venison, ostrich and salmon; and desserts include dishes such as lemon meringue pie.
🕒 Tue–Sat from 6pm
🍴 D NZ$50, W NZ$25

GISBORNE

THE COLOSSEUM CAFÉ & WINE BAR

4 Riverpoint Road, Matawhero, Gisborne
Tel 06-867 4733
Matawhero is regarded as the cradle of Gewürztraminer in New Zealand, and its winemaker Denis Irwin is one of the wine industry's great characters, producing fine and sometimes unusual wines since 1970. You can taste his

wines and have brunch, lunch, evening meals and casual snacks at his vineyard café, the grandly named Colosseum, 10km (6 miles) south of Gisborne, off SH2. The antipasto platter (NZ$35) is a generous introduction to the menu.
🕒 Sep–end May daily 10.30–7
🍴 L NZ$25, D NZ$38, W NZ$20

THE WHARF CAFÉ

The Wharf, 60 The Esplanade, Gisborne
Tel 06-868 4876
www.wharfbar.co.nz
Set in a former wharf building, the café has big windows looking out over the marina. Inside the styling is simple, with sails stretched across the ceiling, and the outdoor tables are understandably popular. The food is mainly modern New Zealand, such as fresh crayfish with salad greens, roast gourmet potatoes, smoked salmon and roquette butter.
🕒 Daily 9am–late
🍴 L NZ$25, D NZ$60, W NZ$35

THE WORKS

The Wharf, 60 The Esplanade, Gisborne
Tel 06-863 1285
This harbourside winery and café houses the cellar door for the Gisborne Wine Company and several other local wineries. The brick building is a former freezing works, cleverly converted into a casual restaurant with indoor and outdoor dining, where you can have anything from coffee and a snack to lunch or dinner. The food has a regional focus; seafood and paua (abalone) are among the specialities.
🕒 Daily 10–10
🍴 L NZ$25, D NZ$45, W NZ$18

HAMILTON

IGUANA

Victoria Street, Hamilton
Tel 07-834 2280
www.iguana.net.nz
Spacious and popular, Iguana serves a mainly Pacific Rim menu, including steak, chicken

and lamb, and pizzas. Cook-your-own hot rocks are a speciality—a mini barbecue of heated granite with your choice of ingredients. Sit on the street or in a booth.
🕒 Mon–Wed 10am–late, Thu, Fri 10am–3am, Sat, Sun 9am–3am
🍴 L NZ$23, D NZ$55, W NZ$29

SPECIAL IN HAMILTON

CANVAS

Grantham Street, Hamilton
Tel 07-839 2535
www.canvas.net.nz
Modern art on the walls, lots of plants, muted lighting and jazz on the sound system give Canvas a sophisticated atmosphere, and the food and service are both highly regarded. The menu is modern New Zealand, with dishes such as twice-baked duck on kumara blinis with sweet soy, or salt and pepper squid with coriander (cilantro) and palm sugar dip.
🕒 Mon–Fri 11.30–2.30, 6–late, Sat 6–late
🍴 L NZ$25, D NZ$55, W NZ$31

TERRÔIR

Craggy Range Vineyards, 253
Waimarama Road, Havelock North
Tel 06-873 0143
www.craggyrange.com

This stunning modern stone-built winery restaurant looks out over vines to Te Mata Peak. There is seating indoors by a log fire or on the lakeside terrace. The restaurant has a French country theme, specializing in rôtisserie and wood-fired oven cooking, and showcasing Craggy Range wines. There is an outstanding international wine list. For a specifically New Zealand experience, try the paua sausage with potatoes and fern fronds.

🍷 Late Oct to mid-Apr Mon–Sat 11–3, 6–late, Sun 11–3; mid-Apr to late Oct Tue–Sat 11–3, 6–late, Sun 11–3
🍴 L NZ$44, D NZ$57, W NZ$35

HASTINGS

SILENI ESTATES RESTAURANT

Sileni Estates, 2016 Maraekakaho Road (SH 50), Bridge Pa, Hastings
Tel 06-879 4831,
www.sileni.co.nz

This striking modern winery complex is a landmark on the outskirts of Hastings. In addition to a stylish restaurant, it has a gourmet food store, cheese larder and wine-tasting room. You can dine indoors or out, overlooking the vineyard. The food is Mediterranean with global additions.

🍷 Dec to mid-Apr Sun–Wed 11–2, Thu–Sat 11–2, 6–late
🍴 L NZ$40, D NZ$60, W NZ$30

LAKE TARAWERA

THE LANDING CAFÉ

Spencer Road, The Landing, Lake Tarawera
Tel 07-362 8595
www.purerotorua.com

It would be hard to find a more idyllic spot than this café beside Lake Tarawera. Have a drink in the Old Trout Bar or take a veranda table overlooking the lake. The only trouble is, the sandflies love it too— so protect yourself. The menu includes open sandwiches, salads and pizza.

🍷 Daily 9.30–4.30, evenings by arrangement
🍴 L NZ$30, D NZ$45, W NZ$30

MOUNT MAUNGANUI

ASTROLABE

82 Maunganui Road, Mount Maunganui
Tel 07-574 8155
www.astrolabe.co.nz

A stylish restaurant and bar with modern minimalist décor, Astrolabe is laid out in separate but interrelated areas with a bar, café, courtyard and formal dining room, giving a range of options depending on your mood. It's popular for brunch/lunch, casual drinks or more serious meals, with standards like scrambled eggs and smoked salmon or Pacific Rim dishes such as coconut-fried prawns with saffron and vanilla risotto.

🍷 Daily 9am–10pm
🍴 L NZ$30, D NZ$45, W NZ$30

NAPIER

CAUTION AND SHED 2

West Quay, Ahuriri, Napier
Tel 06-835 2202
www.shed2.com

Cleverly converted from a 19th-century wool store, Shed 2 makes the most of its waterfront location, with large quayside decks overlooking the harbour. On cold days there's a welcome open fire. The international menu includes wood-fired pizzas—tandoori spiced chicken with onion, avocado and banana is popular—pasta, wok-cooked dishes and local seafood. The nextdoor Caution dining lounge provides a retreat from the big-screen TVs with a more formal menu, local wine list and brunch at weekends.

🍷 Mon–Fri 11.30am–late, Sat, Sun 9am–late
🍴 L NZ$25, D NZ$40, W NZ$33

CHAMBERS RESTAURANT

County Hotel, 12 Browning Street, Napier
Tel 06-835 7800
www.countyhotel.co.nz

Located on the Napier waterfront in the gracious Edwardian County Hotel (▷ 277), Chambers is one of the few silver-service restaurants in the city. It is noted for its elegant décor, attentive service and extensive wine lists. The menu is international, with dishes such as tiger prawns Thai style with saffron rice and sweet and sour sauce, and herb-crusted lamb rack on minted potatoes, caramelized

shallots, capsicums and a balsamic jus; and cranberry and frangipane tart.

🍷 Daily 6.30pm–late
🍴 D NZ$54, W NZ$28

MISSION ESTATE

198 Church Road, Taradale, Napier
Tel 06-845 9354
www.missionestate.co.nz

New Zealand's oldest winery, Mission Estate is located on a hillside overlooking Napier. The restaurant is in a restored seminary building, and offers a modern, seasonally focused, European-influenced menu—using Hawke's Bay produce when possible. Specialities are Aoraki salmon fillet panfried medium rare, in puff pastry with smoked salmon, spinach and summer greens and drizzled with salmon caviar butter sauce; and roast rack of venison encrusted with horopito spice, with roast potato, kumara and black pudding. There are only Mission Estate wines on the list, and the waiters are well briefed to advise on wine matches.

🍷 Daily 10am–late
🍴 L NZ$30, D NZ$50, W NZ$25

NEW PLYMOUTH

ANDRÉ L'ESCARGOT

37–43 Brougham Street, New Plymouth
Tel 06-758 4812
www.andres.co.nz

L'Escargot has been part of the New Plymouth restaurant scene since 1976. Its 1870s premises give the place a timeless quality, with dark wood furniture and crisp white linen. The menu is unashamedly French, with classics such as steak au poivre, goat's cheese soufflé and tarte tatin. A popular option is the platter of seasonal dishes for two (NZ$39.50 per person). The wine list includes French as well as New Zealand and Australian wines.

🍷 Mon–Sat from 5pm
🍴 D NZ$65, W NZ$40

SIMPLY READ

2 Dawson Street, New Plymouth
Tel 06-757 8667

A small, sunny café overlooking the sea, Simply Read has the added appeal of having a bookshop attached. The library-like atmosphere is peaceful, the coffee is good, and there's a choice of light,

EATING

healthy snacks, including plenty of vegetarian options.

🕐 Daily 9–5

🍴 L from NZ$8

OHAKUNE

FAT PIGEON GARDEN CAFÉ

Mountain Road, Ohakune
Tel 06-385 9423

This bright café is ideally located for skiers, at the bottom of the Mountain Road. There's a wood fire to snuggle up to in winter, and tables in the garden for warm weather. The coffee is good and the deli cabinet is full of snacks, such as filled panini. They also do a good line in pizzas, frittatas and pancakes. An à la carte menu is available in the evening.

🕐 Jul–end Oct daily 9am–10pm; Nov–end Jun Thu–Sun 9am–10pm

🍴 L NZ$20, D NZ$50, W NZ$22

RAGLAN

AQUA VELVET KITCHEN AND BALLROOM

17 Bow Street, Raglan
Tel 07-825 8588
www.aquavelvet.net.nz

Everything is prepared from scratch at this restaurant, including bread, cakes, pasta and desserts. The emphasis is on seasonal produce, much of which is organic. The coffee is organic and there's a choice of leaf teas. Brunches are particu-

larly good, with choices such as brioche French toast, and porridge with honeyed walnuts. The evening menu offers dishes like chicken on almond rice with saffron cauliflower. This is also a lively music venue.

🕐 Sun–Thu 8–3, Fri, Sat 8–3, 6–9

🍴 L NZ$14, D NZ$40, W NZ$28

ROTORUA

BISTRO 1284

1284 Eruera Street, Rotorua
Tel 07-346 1284
www.bistro1284.co.nz

An intimate restaurant in a 1930s wooden house, Bistro

SPECIAL IN ROTORUA

AORANGI PEAK

Top of Mountain Road, Rotorua
Tel 07-347 0036
www.aorangipeak.co.nz

Both the food and the view are worth experiencing at Aorangi Peak. Chefs with French and Japanese experience produce dishes such as sautéed spinach and smoked salmon in a sushi roll served with an aioli dressing, followed by chicken breast wrapped with prosciutto and flaky puff pastry, served with a melting prawn and escargot butter.

🕐 Daily 12–late

🍴 L NZ$30, D NZ$65, W NZ$33

1284 has frequently been voted Rotorua's best. The décor is stylishly minimalist, with cream walls and polished floors. The menu is also minimalist, but carefully considered, and the dishes are beautifully presented. A specialty is slow-roasted chicken with fried rice cake, shang-hi and mild red curry. Reservations essential.

🕐 Tue–Sat 6–9

🍴 D NZ$60, W NZ$34

FAT DOG

1161 Arawa Street, Rotorua
Tel 07-347 7586

One of Rotorua's most popular cafés, Fat Dog combines quirky décor with a casual atmosphere, a wide-ranging menu and good coffee. Choose from a blackboard menu of snacks or light meals, such as panini and steak sandwiches. In the evening there are additional main dishes such as venison

and sirloin steaks. Portions are generous. The café is always busy but the wait is worth it.

🕐 Sun–Wed 8am–9pm, Thu–Sat 8am–9.30pm

🍴 L NZ$15, D NZ$30, W NZ$25

TAUPO

THE BACH

2 Patuka Road, Lake Terrace, Taupo
Tel 07-378 7856
www.thebach.co.nz

The Bach offers a complete dining experience. A former fishing lodge with a view over Lake Taupo to Tongariro National Park, it combines innovative food with a remarkable wine list. The owner is a wine merchant, and the reserve list includes many rare labels. The cooking is modern New Zealand, with dishes such as crispy skinned quail tossed with spinach and shredded prosciutto served in a pastry tart case.

🕐 Nov to mid-Apr daily 6–late; mid-Apr to end Oct Tue–Sun 6–late; also Dec, Jan daily 12–2

🍴 L NZ$30, D NZ$55, W NZ$38

TAURANGA

HARBOURSIDE BRASSERIE AND BAR

The Strand, Tauranga
Tel 07-571 0520
www.harbourside-tga.co.nz

The former home of the local yacht club, the Harbourside has a prime waterfront location. Its vast menu is a mix of classical and modern Pacific Rim dishes with plenty of seafood.

Choices include sushi and sashimi, with Asian pickled vegetables, wasabi and ponzu; Asian-style mussels, infused with ginger, garlic, coriander (cilantro) and soy; and Whangamata scallops, pan seared with a potato blini, citrus salad and turmeric broth.

🕐 11.30am–late

🍴 L NZ$30, D NZ$60, W NZ$23

EATING

SOUTHERN NORTH ISLAND

The Wairarapa region has become noted internationally for its wines, particularly Pinot noir, and many of the vineyards around the town of Martinborough are open to visitors. The region also produces some excellent cheese, including the boutique Gladstone Chèvre (goat), Kingsmead (sheep), Rangiuru (Dutch-style) and Zany Zeus (Mediterranean). Kapiti, one of New Zealand's largest speciality cheesemakers, is based at Paraparaumu on the Kapiti Coast. Crabs from nearby Waikanae are highly prized.

PRICES AND SYMBOLS

The prices given are for a two-course lunch (L) and a three-course dinner (D) for one person, without drinks. Many restaurants add a 15 per cent charge on public holidays. The wine price (W) is for the least expensive bottle. Restaurants are listed alphabetically by town. For a key to the symbols, ▷ 2.

GREYTOWN

MAIN STREET DELI
88 Main Street,
Greytown
Tel 06-304 9022
A charming little café, snug inside and with a large outdoor eating area, the Main Street Deli serves breakfasts and lunches, along with excellent home-cooked slices, quiches and cakes. The coffee is good, too. The café is fully licensed and BYO.
🕐 Daily 8–6
🍽 L NZ$30, W NZ$15

SALUTÉ
83 Main Street,
Greytown
Tel 06-304 9825
www.salute.greytown.co.nz
Modern Mediterranean cuisine is the inspiration for this restaurant, which has an enthusiastic following. The menu is eclectic, with Spanish *chorizo*, Italian pizzas, Turkish *pide* (flat bread) and Moroccan *harira* (soup). Dinners can start with mezze and finish with baklava or lemon fritters rolled in cinnamon sugar with pomegranate molasses and lemon ice cream. If such things are unfamiliar, the staff are ready with explanations. There's an attractive outside seating area with trees and a fountain; indoors there's a fire in winter.
🕐 Tue–Sat 12–10.30, Sun 11–3
🍽 L NZ$25, D NZ$50, W NZ$27

THE WHITE SWAN
Main Street,
Greytown
Tel 06-304 8894
www.thewhiteswan.co.nz
Created from a former Railways building, the White Swan cleverly combines old and new. The hotel has a bar with pub food, and you can have a drink by the fire, in the library or on the veranda. The Lilac Dining Room also opens out onto the veranda and serves modern country food, such as chicken encrusted with basil pesto and pinenuts. Children's meals are also available.
🕐 Daily 10–4, 7.30–9.30
🍽 L NZ$17, D NZ$50, W NZ$27

MARTINBOROUGH

RIVERVIEW CAFÉ
Murdoch James, Dry River Road,
Martinborough
Tel 06-306 9165
www.murdochjames.co.nz
A beautiful location, good food and highly regarded wines combine to make a memorable lunch at this scenic vineyard 8km (5 miles) south of Martinborough. The grounds have been landscaped with a picnic area, walks, gardens and ponds. The 25ha (62-acre) vineyard produces Pinot noir, Syrah, Chardonnay, Sauvignon blanc, Cabernet Sauvignon, Cabernet Franc and Riesling, and the Mediterranean-themed lunches are designed to match them with dishes such as risotto or South Island smoked salmon. Reservations are essential.
🕐 Nov–end Feb daily 11.30–3.30;
Mar–end Oct Fri–Sun 11.30–3.30
🍽 L NZ$23, W NZ$25

THE VILLAGE CAFÉ
6 Kitchener Street,
Martinborough
Tel 06-306 8814
www.martinboroughwinecentre.co.nz
Centrally located next to the Martinborough Wine Centre, the café serves breakfast,

CAFÉ CECILLE
Queen Elizabeth Park,
Masterton
Tel 06-370 1166
www.cafececille.co.nz
Café Cecille is set in the pretty Queen Elizabeth Park near the heart of Masterton, and its menu uses local ingredients such as Gladstone ham, Kilrae olive oil and Parkvale mushrooms. It's a café by day, serving brunch and lunch, and a restaurant and wine bar in the evenings.
🕐 Tue 10–3, Wed–Fri 10–9, Sat 9–9, Sun 9–3
🍽 L NZ$20, D NZ$60, W NZ$35

brunch, lunch and snacks. The focus is on local products, such as manuka-smoked bacon, and they make their own sausages, bread, cakes and biscuits. A lunchtime menu of blackboard specials includes soups, pasta and meat dishes. You can also get local wines, locally brewed beer, organic coffee and speciality teas.
🕐 Daily 9–5
🍽 L NZ$20, W NZ$20

OTAKI

BROWN SUGAR CAFÉ
Corner of SH1 and Riverbank Road,
Otaki
Tel 04-364 6359
The Brown Sugar Café is a popular refreshment stop in a heritage building with an attractive garden on SH1, north of Wellington. The quality of the coffee may depend on the person making it, but the food tastes like home cooking, and the garden setting makes up for any deficiencies. There's a tasty breakfast menu.
🕐 Daily 9–5
🍽 From NZ$10

EATING

PAHIATUA

BLACK STUMP CAFÉ AND HARROWS RESTAURANT

106 Main Street,
Pahiatua
Tel 06-376 7123
www.blackstump.tripod.com

On the road between Palmerston North and Masterton, in the heart of a little-known scenic area, this is worth a stop for its rustic barn setting, with 'wool press' tables, native wood flooring and exposed-beam ceilings. You can warm yourself by the fire, play pool and eat bar snacks or stay for dinner in the 1900s-themed dining room. The food is unexpectedly modern and interesting, with choices such as bacon, potato and roast pear salad with blue-cheese dressing, or seared beef with caramelized red onions and Parmesan.

🕐 Tue–Sun 11.30–late
🍽 L NZ$22, D NZ$45, W NZ$22

PALMERSTON NORTH

BELLA'S CAFÉ

2 The Square,
Palmerston North
Tel 06-357 8616
www.bellas.co.nz

A popular café, Bella's mixes Italian with Thai and Pacific Rim dishes. For lunch, choose from tapas, home-made breads, salads or pasta. For dinner, Thai chicken curry is popular, but you can also get a range of grills and interesting vegetarian dishes. Desserts are good, too: Bella's Blitz of confectionery, fresh fruit and nuts, bound with chocolate cream and coulis, is made for sharing.

🕐 Tue–Sat 11.30–3, 6–10
🍽 L NZ$30, D NZ$50, W NZ$28

DÉJEUNER

159 Broadway Avenue,
Palmerston North
Tel 06-952 5581
www.dejeuner.co.nz

Déjeuner has a formal mood, knowledgeable service and a seasonally changing menu. The food is a fusion of European, Asian and Pacific cuisines. Twice-roasted lamb shanks are a speciality, but you can also get more adventurous dishes such as ostrich or tandoori beef salad. If you don't want to linger over your meal, the pre-theatre 'Eat and Out by 8' option on Thursday to Saturday nights is good value at NZ$45 for two courses.

🕐 Mon–Sat 6–late
🍽 D NZ$60, W NZ$29

WANGANUI

AMADEUS RIVERBANK CAFÉ

69 Taupo Quay, Wanganui
Tel 06-345 1538

In a prime position overlooking

the river, a short stroll from Victoria Avenue, the Amadeus is a good place for a relaxing, casual breakfast, light lunch or good coffee. 'The Works' (NZ$12) is their signature breakfast, guaranteed to fill you up with eggs, bacon and all the trimmings. There's an all-day menu, with blackboard specials and snacks such as samosas, bagels and nachos, along with cakes and tarts made on site.

🕐 Daily 8.30–4
🍽 L NZ$20, W NZ$17

WELLINGTON

THE BACKBENCHER

34 Molesworth Street, Wellington
Tel 04-472 3065

In the heart of the Parliamentary district, the Backbencher assures you of a good pub lunch and a fair assortment of tap ales, plus the entertainment of political satire on the walls in the form of cartoons and three-dimensional caricatures. Centre stage, of course, are the current and former New

Zealand prime ministers and noted parliamentarians, none of them very flattering portraits.

🕐 Daily 11–late
🍽 L NZ$15, D NZ$25

BOULCOTT STREET BISTRO AND WINE BAR

99 Boulcott Street, Wellington
Tel 04-499 4199
www.boulcottstreetbistro.co.nz

This is one of Wellington's top restaurants, occupying a charming Victorian house and headed by a celebrated chef, Chris Green. The menu mixes classics such as fillet béarnaise and crème brûlée with innovative dishes like shallot tarte tatin with lamb's brains and salsa verde, or five-spice pannacotta. The wine list showcases boutique wines, many available by the glass to

facilitate food matching. Bookings are accepted only for lunch.

🕐 Mon–Fri 12–2 (wine bar all day), 6–late, Sat 6–late
🍽 L NZ$40, D NZ$60, W NZ$30

CAFFE L'AFFARE

27 College Street, Wellington
Tel 04-385 9748
www.laffare.co.nz

Credited with introducing Wellingtonians to espresso, L'Affare is a thriving coffee business as well as a relaxed

café. Tucked down a side street off Tory Street, it is away from the main shopping area but worth searching out. It's a

CHOCOLATE FISH CAFÉ AND CONES

497a Karaka Bay Road, Seatoun, Wellington

Tel 04-388 2808

The Chocolate Fish—Wellington's most relaxed waterfront café—is hugely popular, especially since the cast and crew of The Lord of the Rings chose it as their preferred hangout. On sunny summer afternoons you'll have to queue, but it's worth trying to sit outside and soak up the atmosphere and the view over Scorching Bay. The ice cream is excellent, and there is a blackboard menu as well as counter snacks and cakes. The service is variable, but the place is child-friendly.

🕐 Daily 8.30am–5pm

🖐 From NZ$8

popular meeting place, with a children's play area, and serves filled paninis, counter snacks and all-day breakfast. Seafood chowder is a speciality, and as you might expect, the coffee is excellent.

🕐 Mon–Fri 7am-4.30, Sat 8am-4

🖐 L NZ$20, W NZ$35

THE DUBLINER

134 Courtenay Place, Wellington

Tel 04-384 2896

Located above the popular Molly Malone's pub, the Dubliner restaurant carries on the Irish theme in giving its dishes pseudo-Irish names, but the food is fairly standard hotel fare: soup of the day, salads and pasta, grills and apple crumble. Value for money and hearty portions are the main attractions, as well as its convenient location near Te Papa (▷ 96–99). Beware, however: lunch may become extended thanks to some fine ales and a good head on the Guinness.

🕐 Daily 12–late

🖐 L NZ$20, D NZ$35

KAI IN THE CITY

21 Majoribanks Street, Wellington

Tel 04-801 5006

www.kaicity.co.nz

This whare kai (restaurant) in the heart of the city is based on traditional Maori culture. The décor is of Maori design,

Maori names are given for all the foods (with an English glossary) and indigenous seasonings, such as piko piko ferns and miro berries, give a unique taste to the dishes. Kaimoana (seafood) is prominent. You are encouraged to ask the staff questions and there is entertainment on Saturday night. Reservations are essential.

🕐 Mon–Sat 5pm–late

🖐 D NZ$50, W NZ$26

LEUVEN

135 Featherston Street, Wellington

Tel 04-499 2939

www.leuven.co.nz

Leuven brings a touch of Belgium to central Wellington, with Belgian beers—Stella Artois, Leffe Blonde, Leffe Brune, Hoegaarden are all on tap—and Belgian food. The signature dish is a kilo of mussels served with frites and mayonnaise. You can sit outside and watch Wellington's world go by.

🕐 Mon–Fri 7am–late, Sat, Sun 10am–late

🖐 L NZ$25, D NZ$45, W NZ$32

LOGAN BROWN

192 Cuba Street, Wellington

Tel 04-801 5114

www.loganbrown.co.nz

Wellington's most elegant restaurant, Logan Brown is located in grand premises in a neo-Grecian 1920s banking chamber. Although it's large, booth seating gives diners some privacy and allows for conversation. The food is modern New Zealand, including dishes like duck with kumara (sweet potato) confit, or mango tarte tatin. A three-course bistro menu is available at lunch and pre-theatre. Reservations are essential.

🕐 Mon–Fri 12–2, 6–late, Sat, Sun 6–late

🖐 L NZ$38, D NZ$60, W NZ$39

MONSOON POON

12 Blair Street, Wellington

Tel 04-803 3555

Monsoon Poon brings the tastes of India, South China, Vietnam, Thailand, the Philippines, Malaysia and Indonesia together under one roof. This makes for a lively setting, as the chefs cook in full view of the dining room. The menu is designed so that

you can sample different cooking styles by sharing dishes. There are no reservations.

🕐 Mon–Thu 11–11, Fri 11am–midnight, Sat 5pm–midnight, Sun 5–11

🖐 L NZ$20, D NZ$40, W NZ$28

SHED 5

Queens Wharf, Wellington

Tel 04-499 9069

www.shed5.co.nz

Built in 1888 as a wool store, Shed 5 has been cleverly transformed into an elegant restaurant and bar. Indoors can get crowded and noisy, so take a table outdoors and watch

the boats come and go. The menu is modern New Zealand with a focus on seafood, with entrées such as crayfish risotto. Main courses include seafood, lamb, venison and poultry.

🕐 Daily 11am–late

🖐 L NZ$40, D NZ$60, W NZ$39

TULSI

135 Cuba Street, Wellington

Tel 04-802 4144

www.tulsirestaurant.co.nz

Deservedly popular in lively Cuba Mall, Tulsi serves contemporary Indian cuisine at affordable prices. Butter chicken is a speciality, voted best in Wellington on a local radio station. There are also Tulsi restaurants in Petone and Christchurch.

🕐 Daily 11.30am–late

🖐 L NZ$12.50, D NZ$35, W NZ$30

EATING

NELSON AND MARLBOROUGH

Marlborough is the largest wine-growing region in New Zealand, renowned internationally for its Sauvignon blanc—Cloudy Bay is probably the best known—but it also produces fine Chardonnay, Pinot noir and other varieties. Nearby Nelson also produces notable wines, outstanding among them Neudorf Chardonnay and Pinot noir. Many wineries welcome visitors and a number have vineyard restaurants attached. New Zealand's fledgling olive industry began in Marlborough, and small amounts of high-quality extra virgin oils are made by boutique producers across the region. You will find them on restaurant tables and at the farmers' market. Also look out for boutique sheep's milk cheeses produced by River Terrace Farm.

Nelson and Marlborough are known for fruit growing, especially berries and pip- and stone-fruit, which can be bought from roadside stalls in season. Surplus fruit is made into preserves. Nelson is also known for its hops, prized by the brewing industry. The Marlborough Sounds support mussel, oyster and salmon farms, and koura (native crayfish) are also farmed in the region. Nelson is the fishing capital of New Zealand, with the largest fishing port in Australasia—hoki is the main catch. Nelson scallops and Golden Bay crabs are highly regarded. Crayfish (lobster) is a speciality in Kaikoura, which is named after the Maori words for food and crayfish.

APPLEBY

SEIFRIEDS VINEYARD RESTAURANT

Corner of SH60 and Redwood Road, Appleby
Tel 03-544 1555
www.seifried.co.nz

The Seifried family pioneered wine-making in Nelson, starting in 1976, and remain one of the largest producers in the area. They are particularly noted for their Riesling, Chardonnay and dessert wines. The restaurant is surrounded by vineyards, with indoor and outdoor dining allowing families to sit by the playground. They serve seasonal local produce, including popular antipasto platters, and homemade breads and desserts.

🕒 Daily 10–5, and evenings in summer
🍴 L NZ$20, W NZ$15

BLENHEIM

BELLAFICO CAFFE AND WINE BAR

17 Maxwell Road, Blenheim
Tel 03-577 6072
www.bellafico.co.nz

A casual café by day and serious restaurant at night, Bellafico has excellent coffee, a German chef enthusiastic about local produce, and an outstanding list of local and international wines. Havelock mussels may come steamed either in a coconut cream and ginger broth, or battered in Marlborough Moa Noir beer.

SPECIAL IN BLENHEIM

HERZOG'S WINERY AND RESTAURANT

81 Jeffries Road, Blenheim
Tel 03-572 8770
www.herzog.co.nz

One of the top restaurants in the country, Herzog's has been created as a gourmet destination in the style of the celebrated restaurant Hans and Therese Herzog had in Switzerland. When they came to Marlborough to establish a vineyard they brought their chef and their superb collection of wines with them. The restaurant is furnished with Limoges china, Riedel crystal and French silverware. The food focuses on seasonal produce.

🕒 Mid-Oct to end Apr Tue–Sun 7–late; Dec–end Feb Tue–Sun 12–4,
🍴 L NZ$75, D NZ$98, W NZ$50

Wild venison cutlet is served on a home-made corn cake with a pomegranate jus.
🕒 Mon–Fri 10am–late, Sat 6pm–late
🍴 L NZ$25, D NZ$60, W NZ$29

TWELVE TREES RESTAURANT

Allan Scott Wines and Estates, Jacksons Road, Blenheim
Tel 03-572 7123
www.allanscott.com

This indoor-outdoor garden restaurant, named after the walnut trees that line the entrance to the winery, is constructed from rammed earth, with a walled courtyard and picnic area. The menu is simple and fresh, reflecting local seasonal specialities such as mussels and strawberries. There is usually a pasta dish and a salad, and the vineyard platter is always popular. Allan Scott is a pioneer of viticulture in Marlborough and noted for his wines, so it's a good place to try them, too.
🕒 Daily 9–4.30
🍴 L NZ$25, W NZ$20

COLLINGWOOD

COURTHOUSE CAFÉ

Corner of Gibbs Road and Elizabeth Street, Collingwood
Tel 03-5248 572

This is a great place to be found guilty of gluttony with intent to demolish three-fruit smoothies. The old colonial building, which was once the district courthouse, is a remnant of far busier times, when Collingwood was the focus of a gold boom. Alas m'lud, now the only case in session revolves around the levels of relaxation, the black-board menu (with some criminally good vegetarian

EATING

options) and the quality of the coffee bean.

⏰ Dec–end Jun daily 8am–late; Jul–end Nov 11–4
✋ L NZ$20, D NZ$40, W NZ$22

MUSSEL INN
Onekaka, Golden Bay
Tel 03-525 9241
www.musselinn.co.nz
Between Takaka and Collingwood on SH60, the Mussel Inn serves good pub grub, but the mussels, the beer and the atmosphere are what you come for. Local mussels are served simply steamed with bread. The beer is brewed on site, using home-grown hops. The range includes lager, stout, bitter and pale ale, the most unusual being Captain Cooker manuka beer. In the evening, it hosts regular gigs.
⏰ Sep–end Jul daily from 11
✋ L NZ$12, D NZ$35, W NZ$20

HAVELOCK
MUSSEL BOYS RESTAURANT
73 Main Road, Havelock
Tel 03-574 2824
www.musselboys.co.nz
Mussel Boys has done its best to put Havelock on the map as the green-lipped mussel capital of New Zealand. The distinctive restaurant, with out-size mussels on the roof, has spawned a franchise, and it would be hard to find fresher or tastier mussels. Choose from chowder, steamers or flats grilled with a choice of toppings (and there are meats and salads for diehard non-mussel eaters).
⏰ Mid-Apr to end Oct daily 11.30–7; Nov, Feb, Mar daily 11–9; Dec, Jan daily 10.30–9.30
✋ L NZ$20, D NZ$43, W NZ$28

KAIKOURA
FINZ OF SOUTH BAY RESTAURANT AND BAR
103 South Bay Parade, Kaikoura
Tel 03-319 6688
An intimate, family-run restaurant overlooking the sea, Finz is outstanding in Kaikoura. Many of the dishes are simple, relying on the superb taste of really fresh fish: crayfish grilled with butter and lemon zest, *sashimi* with Japanese accompaniments, or a succulent slab of citrus-dusted bluenose. Other dishes use contrasting accompaniments to highlight the seafood, such as scallops tossed with zucchini ribbons in pernod. The wine list showcases Marlborough vineyards. With only eight tables, Finz soon fills up, so book ahead.
⏰ Oct–end May daily 6pm–late; Jun–end Sep Wed–Sun 6pm–late
✋ D NZ$55, W NZ$30

HISLOPS CAFÉ
33 Beach Road, Kaikoura
Tel 03-319 6971
www.hislops-wholefoods.co.nz
A renovated villa with dining on the veranda and in the garden, Hislop's is a pleasant place to stop for refreshments or lunch. The café specialises in wholefoods, using organically grown ingredients where possible. Most vegetables come from the family farm, which has a long history of using organic methods. The beverage list also includes organic wines and beers. The cakes are a treat, notably the apricot and chocolate cream cheese slice.
⏰ Summer daily 10–9; winter Tue, Wed 10–4, Thu–Mon 10–9
✋ L NZ$25, D NZ$50, W NZ$26

KEKERENGU
THE STORE AT KEKERENGU
State Highway 1, Kekerengu
Tel 03-575 8600
Dramatically located on the coast halfway between Blenheim and Kaikoura, the Store is a must-stop for refreshments or lunch. The café has indoor seating around a double-sided fireplace, and tables on the deck outdoors with spectacular views over the thundering surf. The décor is modishly rustic with massive wharf piles supporting the hessian-draped roof. The food is all made on site, with light meals including pizza, filled focaccia and venison pies through to sophisticated dishes of crayfish and blue cod.
⏰ Oct to mid-Apr daily 7.30–7; mid-Apr to end Sep 8–6.30
✋ L NZ$23, D NZ$45, W NZ$33

MAPUA
FLAX RESTAURANT AND BAR
Mapua Wharf, Mapua
Tel 03-540 2028
Looking out over the Mapua estuary, Flax is one of the Nelson region's finest restaurants. A family affair, run by chef Tim Greenhough and *maître d'* Karen Hannan, it has an extensive wine list that also features Greenhough wines made by brother Andrew. The style of food is modern New Zealand, with interesting combinations such as lambs' brains with balsamic roast cherry tomatoes, ricotta pesto and bacon. The pork belly is also a popular choice. Service is friendly and informative.
⏰ Daily 10.30–3.30, 5–9
✋ L NZ$25, D NZ$45, W NZ$30

THE SMOKEHOUSE RESTAURANT
Shed 2, Mapua Wharf, Mapua
Tel 03-540 2280
www.smokehouse.co.nz
You can buy smoked fish to take away or eat in the restaurant overlooking the water at the Smokehouse. The menu is based on locally supplied fish, mussels and vegetables hot-smoked on site, using a traditional brick kiln, manuka wood shavings and no artificial additives. Some of the less-prized fish smoke best, so try the warehou, hake or trevally, as well as the snapper and salmon. Smoked mushrooms and smoked tomato soup are also good.
⏰ Daily 11–late
✋ L NZ$28, D NZ$50, W NZ$32

EATING

MARAHAU

PARK CAFÉ

Harveys Road, Marahau
Tel 03-527 8270
www.parkcafe.co.nz

Hikers finishing the Abel Tasman Coast Track can't believe their luck when they stumble on this café, with its blackboard menu, bar, good coffee and internet access. It's popular with daytrippers and hikers starting from Marahau, too. The café has indoor and outdoor tables and a children's playground. You can get anything from breakfast to evening meals or snacks and cakes, from burgers, soups and salads to steaks, pasta, fish and vegetarian dishes.

Oct–end May daily 8am–9pm
L NZ$20, D NZ$40, W NZ$28

MOTUEKA

HOT MAMAS CAFÉ

105 High Street, Motueka
Tel 03-528 7039

A bright and relaxed café with comfy sofas and lively murals, Hot Mamas has live music on Fridays and Saturdays. You can dine by the fire in winter, or out in the garden in summer. The blackboard menu has an Italian theme, with bruschetta, antipasto, pizza, pasta and Tuscan salads.

Daily 8.30am–late
L NZ$18, D NZ$32, W NZ$18

NELSON

THE BOAT SHED

350 Wakefield Quay, Nelson
Tel 03-546 9783
www.boatshedcafe.co.nz

You can't get much closer to the water than this converted

scallops, Golden Bay crabs and locally farmed salmon, oysters and green-lipped mussels. Non-seafood eaters are also well catered for.

Daily 9am–10.30pm
L NZ$30, D NZ$70, W NZ$36

THE OYSTER BAR

115 Hardy Street, Nelson
Tel 03-545 8955

The emphasis is on fresh seafood at this New York-inspired oyster bar. An intimate, narrow space with bar stools, it encourages you to chat with the chef as you watch him at work. As well as oysters every which way, there's a Californian sushi menu including smoked eel, blackened scallop, smoked salmon and vegetarian options.

Summer Tue–Sat 5.30pm–late; winter Thu–Sun 5.30pm–late
D NZ$40, W NZ$30

WATERFRONT CAFÉ AND BAR

341 Wakefield Quay, Nelson
Tel 03-546 6685
www.waterfrontcafenelson.co.nz

SPECIAL IN NELSON

LAMBRETTA'S CAFÉ-BAR

204 Hardy Street,
Nelson
Tel 03-545 8555
www.lambrettascafe.co.nz

Devoted to all things Italian, this café behind the grand Greco-Roman pillars of a former insurance office has the popular scooters bolted to the walls, along with a selection of Lambretta paraphernalia. The theme is carried on in the décor and the food, with pizza, pastas and antipasto to challenge

True to its name, Waterfront has views of the harbour and Tasman Bay from its upstairs restaurant, and a café and bar on the street frontage. Local seafood, venison and duck are on the menu, and the signature dish is a 650g Chateaubriand roast prime fillet steak for two, rolled in fresh herbs and spices, and served with a truffle potato purée, roast garlic bulbs, roast vegetables and a red wine jus.

Daily 11am–late
L NZ$25, D NZ$50, W NZ$30

RICHMOND

CAFÉ IN THE VINEYARD AT WAIMEA ESTATES

Appleby Highway, Hope, Richmond
Tel 03-544 4963
www.waimeaestates.co.nz

Just outside Richmond, Café in the Vineyard is the cellar door and café for Waimea Estates. You can sample and purchase the wines, including Sauvignon blanc, Riesling, Chardonnay and Merlot, and lunch in the extensive dining area, which flows out to the vines. Fresh, local ingredients are used in dishes like char-grilled ribeye.

Sep–end Mar daily 11–5; Apr–end Aug Wed–Sun 11–4
L NZ$24, W NZ$20

TAKAKA

WHOLEMEAL CAFÉ

Commercial Street, Takaka
Tel 03-525 9426
www.wholemealcafe.co.nz

In the old Takaka Theatre, the café has become an institution since it opened in 1977. The mood is bohemian, with modern art on the walls and visitors in bare feet and beads.

EATING

boatshed, with water lapping at the piles. The view over the harbour is stunning, particularly if you brave the breeze and take a table on the deck. Seafood is a speciality, particularly Nelson white fish and

the heartiest appetite. Children are welcome, with a special menu and play area.

Daily 9am–late
L NZ$20, D NZ$40, W NZ$22

It has good coffee, fresh juices and organic beers, and a daytime menu of free-range egg dishes, salads, sandwiches and cakes.

Daily 7.30am–9.30pm
L NZ$15, D NZ$35, W NZ$25

CANTERBURY AND THE WEST COAST

Canterbury is traditionally famous for its lamb, which is found on most restaurant menus, as is locally farmed deer, marketed as Cervena. Locally farmed ostrich can also be found. Salmon fishing is popular in the major rivers, and salmon is also farmed in Akaroa and in the high country lake district. Although vineyards are scattered through the region, the most successful wine-growing area is Waipara, known for its Riesling, Chardonnay and Pinot noir. A number of wineries are open to the public, some with restaurants attached. Several olive groves produce small quantities of extra virgin olive oil, which appears on menus along with locally produced hazelnut and walnut oils. Canterbury is also known for its pipfruit and berryfruit, and produces much of the country's asparagus. Boutique Dutch-style cheeses are made at Karikaas in Loburn; Barry's Bay Cheese on Banks Peninsula is most famous for its rinded cheddar; and boutique cheeses are made under the Talbot Forest label in Geraldine. Geraldine and Waimate are known for berry fruit, particularly blackcurrants and strawberries. Native honeys such as rata, kamahi and manuka are collected from the mountain beech forest. The West Coast is noted for its game and seafood, especially whitebait.

PRICES AND SYMBOLS

The prices given are for a two-course lunch (L) and a three-course dinner (D) for one person, without drinks. Many restaurants add a 15 per cent charge on public holidays. The wine price (W) is for the least expensive bottle. Restaurants are listed alphabetically by town. For a key to the symbols, ▷ 2.

AKAROA

HARBOUR 71

71 Beach Road, Akaroa
Tel 03-304 7656
Harbour 71 has great views over the water, and is set in one of Akaroa's character waterfront buildings, a former drapery, grocery and hardware business. It serves casual food during the day and has a more formal menu at night. Pizzas are the daytime speciality. The evening menu turns Pacific Rim, with dishes like coconut, lime and coriander-infused mussels.
🕒 Daily 10–late
🍴 L NZ$20, D NZ$65, W NZ$32

CHRISTCHURCH

ANNIE'S WINE BAR AND RESTAURANT

Arts Centre, Christchurch
Tel 03-365 0566
www.annieswinebar.co.nz
Annie's, in the heart of the Arts Centre, has outdoor dining in the cloisters or indoors where the brick walls are exposed and the furniture is recycled wood. The atmosphere is casual, with a menu of modern New Zealand food. The platter of breads and spreads is particularly popular. Annie's is

SPECIAL IN AKAROA

C'EST LA VIE

33 Rue Lavaud,
Akaroa
Tel 03-304 7314
With only eight tables at this intimate, highly regarded restaurant, you may be expected to share: once people get used to the idea, the owners say, it adds to the enjoyment, as you get to meet people from all over the world. The menu is French, changing seasonally with dishes such as duck à l'orange, venison with wild mushrooms and lamb provençal.
🕒 Mid-Sep to end Jun daily 6pm–late
🍴 D NZ$65, W NZ$30

well known for its wine list, served by knowledgeable staff. Reservation recommended.
🕒 Daily 11–late
🍴 L NZ$25, D NZ$60, W NZ$30

CAFFE ROMA

176 Oxford Terrace, Christchurch
Tel 03-379 3879
www.caffe-roma.co.nz
This European-styled coffee house with views over the river is a popular place for breakfast, brunch and lunch. As well as the usual egg dishes, breakfast specialities include home-

baked bagels and porridge cooked with apple juice, apples, honey, walnuts and sultanas, served with cream or milk. The lunch choices include pasta, risotto and salads.
🕒 Daily 7–4
🍴 L NZ$25, W NZ$34

COOK'N' WITH GAS

23 Worcester Boulevard,
Christchurch
Tel 03-377 9166
www.cooknwithgas.co.nz
A quirky restaurant in a converted villa opposite the Arts Centre, Cook'n' with Gas has walls covered in old photos, and a garden courtyard. The restaurant concentrates on New Zealand cuisine, serving, for example, baked *warehou* (fish) with a basil and karengo crust topped with garlic prawns, on a smoked tomato risotto, with a squid, lime and cucumber salad. They have a wide selection of local beers.
🕒 Mon–Sat 6pm–late
🍴 D NZ$55, W NZ$35

HAY'S

63 Victoria Street, Christchurch
Tel 03-379 7501
www.foodandwine.co.nz
Located opposite the Casino, this restaurant specialises in serving lamb grown on the Hay family's Banks Peninsula farm. The menu is modern New Zealand, with dishes such as lamb rack with Dijon mustard, parsley and tarragon crust, redcurrant and red wine jus and dauphinoise potatoes. The wine list focuses on top New Zealand wines.
🕒 Nov to mid-Apr daily from 5pm; mid-Apr to end Oct Tue–Sat from 5pm
🍴 D NZ$47, W NZ$31

EATING

MAINSTREET VEGETARIAN RESTAURANT
840 Colombo Street,
Christchurch
Tel 03-365 0421
Mainstreet is one of Christchurch's few vegetarian restaurants—a relaxed, informal place where you queue at the counter and point to what you want. The dishes are imaginative, substantial and well priced. Try the pumpkin and kumara (sweet potato) balls in spicy peanut and sesame seed sauce.
🕐 Tue–Thu 8am–9.30pm, Fri 8am–10pm, Sat 9am––10pm, Sun 9am–4pm
🍴 L NZ$12, D NZ$26, W NZ$20

OXFORD ON AVON
794 Colombo Street,
Christchurch
Tel 03-379 7148
www.oxfordonavon.co.nz

This popular carvery and buffet is the place to go when you're ravenously hungry. The restaurant operates on two floors, with a courtyard overlooking the Avon River. The Old English Breakfast (NZ$13.50) is available until 11am, when the queues start building for the set-price carvery lunch and all-you-can-eat buffet of European, Asian and Indian dishes. Children under 12 are charged NZ$1 for each year of their age.
🕐 Daily 6.30am–10.30pm
🍴 L NZ$16, D NZ$21, W NZ$19

PESCATORE
The George Hotel, 50 Park Terrace,
Christchurch
Tel 03-371 0257
www.thegeorge.com
The George Hotel's (▷ 285) classy restaurant triumphs in seafood. The style is Pacific Rim executed in exquisitely presented dishes, either à la carte or in dégustation menus showcasing

regional specialities matched with local wines. Typical dishes include crayfish bisque with cumin and fennel, or big eye tuna with red onion confit, kumara and ginger dauphinoise and spiced consommé. Fang au Chocolat is the signature dessert.
🕐 Oct–end Apr daily from 6pm; May–end Sep Thu–Sun from 6pm
🍴 D NZ$77, W NZ$45

THE SIGN OF THE TAKAHE
200 Hackthorne Road, Cashmere,
Christchurch
Tel 03-332 4052
www.signofthetakahe.co.nz
A 1908 neo-Gothic castle on the Port Hills overlooking Christchurch, the Sign of the Takahe provides à la carte dining and bar facilities, with a lunchtime buffet. The menu tends towards fusion, with dishes such as venison rack served with soft truffle polenta, broad beans, mushrooms and crispy parsnips topped with a spicy rice crust; oven-baked chicken breast with sweet pomegranate, eggplant two ways and a soft herb, Persian feta and lemon salad; and jasmine rice pudding.
🕐 Daily 10–4, 6–10
🍴 L NZ$25, D NZ$70, W NZ$30

DUNSANDEL
DUNSANDEL STORE
Main South Road,
Dunsandel
Tel 03-325 4037
On the main road south of Christchurch, the Dunsandel Store is an appealing combination of rustic café, deli, country store and shop selling local produce. You can buy anything from soap powder to local wines, there's a pretty courtyard planted with herbs, and the food is fresh and interesting. Typical dishes include old-fashioned pork pie, and rabbit and prune terrine. Apples feature strongly, as the owner makes juices and cider.
🕐 Daily 7am–8pm
🍴 L NZ$17, D NZ$27, W NZ$26

FOX GLACIER
CAFÉ NEVÉ
Main Road, Fox Glacier
Tel 03-751 0110
Café Nevé is small and friendly, with the feeling of being at home rather than in a restaurant. You can have breakfast,

THE OLD LIBRARY CAFÉ
7 Allandale Road, Fairlie
Tel 03-685 8999
The Old Library Café has made the small town of Fairlie a must-stop for visitors on the road to Mount Cook/ Aoraki and the Southern Lakes. The 1912 building has been converted into a sophisticated restaurant and friendly café, retaining the character of the building. There's an attractive outdoor dining area, and the menu caters both for people in a hurry and diners wanting to relax. Local Mackenzie Country lamb and beef are specialities.
🕐 Daily 10am–late
🍴 L NZ$27, D NZ$51, W NZ$20

lunch or an evening meal. Pizzas are served from 11am in various sizes, to eat in or take away, or choose from West Coast treats such as whitebait, venison, salmon and fresh

seafood. Espresso coffee is the speciality; hot chocolate and herbal teas are available too.
🕐 Daily 8am–late
🍴 L NZ$20, D NZ$40, W NZ$25

FRANZ JOSEF
BLUE ICE CAFÉ
Main Road (SH6),
Franz Josef
Tel 03-752 0707
Downstairs an à la carte restaurant serves local specialities such as whitebait patties and venison. Upstairs is a bar with a pool table, Sky TV, pizza, snacks and a well-stocked bar—the late-night party venue with regular DJs.
🕐 Oct–end Apr daily 2–10; May–end Sep daily 4–10
🍴 D NZ$45, W NZ$29

EATING

GREYMOUTH

THE SMELTING HOUSE CAFÉ

102 Mackay Street, Greymouth
Tel 03-768 0012

In a former bank building, this café is run by a dietitian, who cooks home-style food and serves good coffee. Enjoy a full

Farmer's Breakfast, and lunch dishes such as pasta.

🕐 Daily 8.30–4.30
🖐 L NZ$15, W NZ$26

HANMER SPRINGS

THE OLD POST OFFICE

2 Jacks Pass Road, Hanmer Springs
Tel 03-315 7461

The former post office retains much of its character in this country restaurant, with its flowery décor, lush drapes, deep-pastel walls and heavy linen. The menu is strong on beef, lamb and game, and portions are generous.

🕐 Daily 6–9pm
🖐 D NZ$60, W NZ$32

HOKITIKA

CAFÉ DE PARIS

19 Tancred Street, Hokitika
Tel 03-755 8933

Owners Joy (from New Zealand) and Pierre (from France) Esquilat have been in Hokitika for 20 years and bring a distinctive style to this West Coast café—French cuisine with a Kiwi accent. An airy café during the day, it serves coffee, pastries and blackboard lunches. In the evening enjoy classics like French onion soup

SPECIAL IN LAKE TEKAPO

KOHAN JAPANESE RESTAURANT

State Highway 8, Lake Tekapo
Tel 03-680 6688
www.laketekapo.cc/kohan

This restaurant has views over the lake and mountains and serves Japanese food of a high standard. The bento lunch boxes and combination menus are a good way of sampling several dishes, as they include appetizers, miso, rice, *sashimi*, pickles and a hot dish such as grilled fish.

🕐 Mon–Sat 11–2, 6–9, Sun 11–2
🖐 L NZ$18, D NZ$30, W NZ$25

and profiteroles, or more unusual dishes such as wild boar baked in pastry with mushrooms and red wine.

🕐 Daily from 7.30am
🖐 L NZ$15, D NZ$30

METHVEN

STEEL-WORX RESTAURANT AND BAR

36 Forest Drive, Methven
Tel 03-302 9900
www.steel-worx.co.nz

Steel is the principal material used in this 1910 building, which has been converted into a bar with a city feel, a restaurant and a beer garden. It's popular in the ski season, when the bar hosts party nights with DJs and dancing. The restaurant is warmed by a log-burning stove and serves après-ski dishes like venison on mushroom risotto.

🕐 May–end Nov daily 5pm–late
🖐 D NZ$46, W NZ$28

MOUNT COOK VILLAGE

OLD MOUNTAINEERS' CAFÉ AND BAR

Mount Cook Village
Tel 03-435 1890
www.mtcook.com

Opened in 2003, the Old Mountaineer is a welcome addition to the dining options in the village, with a casual atmosphere, great views, an open fire and a wide-ranging menu. You can have the usual breakfast items until 12.30, then lunch on paninis or fill up on a selection of steaks, curries and pizzas.

🕐 Nov–end Mar daily 9am–late;
Apr–end Oct 11am–late
🖐 L NZ$25, D NZ$43, W NZ$22

OMARAMA

CLAY CLIFFS ESTATE VINEYARD AND CAFÉ

Pinot Noir Court, Omarama
Tel 03-438 9654

This Tuscan-style vineyard café south of the village overlooks a pond and vine-covered hills. The 4ha (10-acre) vineyard is New Zealand's highest, at 440m (1,445ft) above sea level. The restaurant serves lunchtime snacks, as well as substantial meals such as rack of lamb.

🕐 Jul–end May daily 11am–late
🖐 L NZ$30, D NZ$60, W NZ$18

WAIPARA

PEGASUS BAY WINERY

Stockgrove Road, Waipara
Tel 03-314 6869
www.pegasusbay.com

A grand vineyard restaurant in landscaped gardens with outstanding wine and food, Pegasus Bay is a place for leisurely dining. The vineyard specialises in Riesling, Chardonnay, Pinot noir, late-harvest wines and reserve red blends. The menu is seasonal and created around the wine list, with suggested matches.

🕐 Daily 12–4
🖐 L NZ$45, W NZ$37

WESTPORT

THE BAY HOUSE CAFÉ RESTAURANT GALLERY

Tauranga Bay, Cape Foulwind
Tel 03-789 7133
www.thebayhouse.co.nz

The waves roll into the ruggedly beautiful Tauranga Bay by this café, where you can have excellent coffee, admire the art exhibitions and dine on distinctly Aotearoa fare. A typical dish is the Bay

House Platter, which changes to reflect West Coast produce such as green-lip mussels in manuka honey and soy.

🕐 Daily 9am–late
🖐 L NZ$30, D NZ$55, W NZ$30

EATING

OTAGO AND THE FAR SOUTH

Central Otago is famous for its stone fruit, especially apricots, nectarines and cherries, which can be bought from roadside stalls in season. The region is also successful with wine, and Gibbston Valley Winery is next to a cheese-making facility. Dairy farming is increasingly dominating local agriculture, with one of the world's largest cheese factories at Clandeboye, and highly regarded speciality cheeses made at Evansdale and Whitestone in Oamaru. The Oamaru region is also noted for its gourmet potatoes. Gore calls itself the capital of brown-trout fishing and although restaurants cannot put trout on their menus, they may be prepared to cook what you catch. Bluff is famous for its oysters and Stewart Island/Rakiura for its blue cod and crayfish. Paua (abalone) is also farmed on the island.

PRICES AND SYMBOLS

The prices given are for a two-course lunch (L) and a three-course dinner (D) for one person, without drinks. Many restaurants add a 15 per cent charge on public holidays. The wine price (W) is for the least expensive bottle. Restaurants are listed alphabetically by town. For a key to the symbols, ▷ 2.

CLYDE

OLIVER'S RESTAURANT

34 Sunderland Street, Clyde
Tel 03-449 2860
www.olivers.co.nz
Oliver's, part of a boutique historic lodge, was established in 1977 in an 1863 stone building, and features schist walls and two large stone fireplaces. Typical dishes on the menu are king salmon with wasabi-infused mash, wilted bok choi, rich honey mustard glaze and fresh coriander tomato confit; and glazed lamb shoulder rack served with warm lentil casserole and roast seasonal vegetables.
🕒 Tue–Sun 9–1, 6.30–8.30
🍴 L NZ$20, D NZ$50, W NZ$34

THE POST OFFICE CAFÉ AND BAR

2 Blyth Street,
Clyde
Tel 03-449 2488
Housed in Clyde's original post office (established in 1862), the restaurant retains much of the building's character, with stone walls and a dark wood interior. It's a pleasant place to have lunch, particularly on a sunny day when you can sit out in the garden. The food is simple but tasty, with a blackboard menu featuring anything from venison to blue cod. The pies are a speciality.
🕒 Daily 10am–late
🍴 L NZ$15, D NZ$30, W NZ$25

CROMWELL

LAZYDOG CAFÉ AND WINE BAR

Akarua Winery, Cairnmuir Road,
Bannockburn
Tel 03-445 3211
www.akarua.com
You can eat indoors or out at this attractive restaurant attached to Akarua Vineyard, 8km (5 miles) from Cromwell. Lamb and beef dishes are a strength, along with the produce of local orchards and Stewart Island salmon. Lamb backstrap with roasted tomato is a signature dish, served with kumara (sweet potato) and butternut squash, fettucine and a Pinot noir reduction.
🕒 Summer daily 11–3, 6–late; winter Wed–Sun 11–3, 6–late
🍴 L NZ$25, D NZ$50, W NZ$34

SPECIAL IN ARROWTOWN

SAFFRON

16 Buckingham Street, Arrowtown
Tel 03-442 0131
www.saffronrestaurant.co.nz
A quality restaurant in Arrowtown's heritage precinct, Saffron uses wild local ingredients whenever possible: Lindis Pass hare, West Coast boar, porcini and rosehips. The menu shows Mediterranean and Asian influences. Croutons come with creamy lambs' brains, and mussels are cooked with pernod. Central Otago wines head the wine list. The more casual Pesto restaurant next door is run by the same people, and serves a simple menu of pasta, pizza and salads. Their Blue Door Bar is a tiny, comfy cellar.
🕒 Daily 11–4, 6.30–late
🍴 L NZ$30, D NZ$90, W NZ$35

DUNEDIN

BELL PEPPER BLUES AND THE CHILE CLUB

474 Princes Street, Dunedin
Tel 03-474 0973
www.bellpepperblues.co.nz
The names of chef Michael Coughlin's restaurant and bar are tributes to his passion for the cooking of the south-western US, although he now takes inspiration from many cuisines. Cervena venison is a signature dish, which may be served as a grilled Denver leg cut with smoked venison sausage, kumara and leek hash cake. Both the service and presentation show meticulous attention to detail. The Chile Club offers a lunch menu.
🕒 Mon–Sat 6.30pm–late; also Wed–Fri 12–3
🍴 D NZ$60, W NZ$32

YELLOW TRAIN BISTRO

4 Dowling Street, Dunedin
Tel 03-477 1657
www.yellowtrain.co.nz
Yellow Train is in a historic building looking out onto the Queens Gardens, offering New Zealand food in a friendly atmosphere. Specialities are deep dish home-style pie, served with potato, and Lebanese vegetarian sambousik filo parcel.
🕒 Daily 5.30pm–late
🍴 D NZ$60, W NZ$32

INVERCARGILL

THE CABBAGE TREE

379 Dunns Road, Otatara, Invercargill
Tel 03-213 1443
www.thecabbagetree.com
On the way to the beach from Invercargill, The Cabbage Tree has been rebuilt from the old Beach Store using Central Otago schist and recycled timber, with lots of native planting outside. The menu includes giant sandwiches, all-day breakfast and high tea: a

speciality is the 'Chatter Platter'
of blue cheese, salami,
brie, pâté, smoked salmon,
squid rings, ham strips,
stuffed mushrooms, olives,
guacamole, basil pesto,
gherkins, sun-dried tomatoes,
marinated vegetables with
bread and crackers.
🕙 Tue–Sun 11am–late
✋ L NZ$25, D NZ$55, W NZ$35

HMS KING'S
80 Tay Street, Invercargill
Tel 03-218 3443
A traditional New Zealand fish
restaurant decked out like a
ship, King's is popular with

families and serves fresh,
locally caught seafood such as
Bluff oysters, crayfish and
whitebait. The cooking style is
simple, and many of the dishes
are fried. Seafood chowder is
a speciality and there is a
children's menu.
🕙 Mon–Fri 11.30–3, Sat–Sun 5–10
✋ L NZ$16, D NZ$40, W NZ$20

ZOOKEEPER'S CAFÉ
50 Tay Street, Invercargill
Tel 03-218 3373
A funky café and bar with
'wild' décor and a laid-back
atmosphere, Zookeeper's has

excellent coffee, and is a good
place for a casual lunch.
🕙 Daily 10am–late
✋ L NZ$20, D NZ$35, W NZ$30

MANDEVILLE
THE MOTH RESTAURANT AND BAR
Old Mandeville Airfield, SH94,
Mandeville
Tel 03-208 9662
www.themoth.co.nz
On the Gore to Milford highway, and next to an air
museum, The Moth is adorned
with aviation memorabilia.
The food is fresh and simply
presented, with home-made
bread, and the menu includes
roast chicken breast, lamb
rump seared in mint oil, spicy
BBQ pork loin and poached
blue cod. Leave space for
desserts such as dessert pizza
of the day (at the chef's whim)
and berry jelly pannacotta.
🕙 Nov–end Apr daily 10am–late;
May–end Oct Tue–Sun 10am–late
✋ L NZ$30, D NZ$50, W NZ$25

MOERAKI
FLEURS PLACE
The Old Jetty, Moeraki
Tel 03-439 4480
www.fleursplace.com
This quirky restaurant on the
waterfront is built from
demolition materials and
specialises in fresh fish straight
from Moeraki Bay fishing
boats. The blackboard menu
offers blue cod, dory, moki,
blue nose, gurnard, sole,
flounder, grouper, crayfish,
mussels and other delicacies
such as titi (muttonbird).
Reservations are essential.
🕙 Daily 9am–late
✋ L NZ$25, D NZ$47, W NZ$25

OAMARU
CRITERION HOTEL
Corner of Tyne and Harbour streets,
Oamaru
Tel 03-434 6247
www.criterion.net.nz
In the heart of the town's
Harbour and Tyne Historic
Precinct, this restored Victorian
pub has hand-pumped ales,
boutique beers and lots of
atmosphere. The food is
suitably traditional, with beef
hotpot, pies, roasts and
'bangers and mash' (sausage
and mashed potato). You can
also stay overnight in Victorian-
themed rooms. If you are
inspired to join your hosts
in Victorian dress, costumes
are available.
🕙 Mon–Wed 12–9.30, Thu 12–11, Fri,
Sat 12–12, Sun 12–8
✋ L NZ$15, D NZ$50, W NZ$18

QUEENSTOWN
THE BATHHOUSE CAFÉ AND RESTAURANT
15 Marine Parade, Queenstown
Tel 03-442 5625
www.bathhouse.co.nz
This was the original Victorian
bath house on the beach, and
it retains its period charm. You
can come for breakfast, lunch,
afternoon tea or dinner. The
menu is small. You can eat
simply with an omelette, miso
soup or waffles. For lunch
there are crispy duck
dumplings, roast lamb rump
and chocolate truffles. By
dinner time it's dishes like
roulade of local wild rabbit
with spinach, red rice risotto
and Canterbury goat's cheese.
🕙 Tue–Sun 10am–late
✋ L NZ$30, D NZ$80, W NZ$26

THE COW
Cow Lane, Queenstown
Tel 03-442 8588
The Cow—formerly a milking
shed—is cramped but full of
character. A Queenstown
institution, it specialises in
pizza and pasta, and serves
up simple, hearty fare at
reasonable prices. It's the
place to go after a hard day's
skiing when you need some
tasty fuel to replenish your
energy. You can expect to wait
for a table, and may be seated
at a large table with people
you don't know.
🕙 Daily 12–late
✋ L NZ$25, D NZ$35, W NZ$25

DUX DE LUX
14 Church Street, Queenstown
Tel 03-442 9688
In a heritage stone cottage in
central Queenstown, this
atmospheric pub and café was
formerly McNeills Cottage
Brewery. It still offers a range
of boutique beers, plus
vegetarian and seafood dishes.
🕙 Daily from 11am
✋ L NZ$20, D NZ$60, W NZ$27

GANTLEY'S
Arthur's Point Road, Queenstown
Tel 03-442 8999
www.gantleys.co.nz
Gantley's is 7km (4 miles) on
the road to Arrowtown, and
was a wayside inn during the
1860s gold rushes. The rough
stone walls of the building
contrast romantically with
deep red curtains, leather
sofas, white tablecloths and

candle-light. The restaurant is known for both its food and its wine, with an international list of about 300 vintages. The food is simple but can be exciting: pears are poached in Pinot gris and saffron and served with a chai jelly and lemongrass and ginger ice cream.

🕐 Daily 6.30–9pm
✋ D NZ$75, W NZ$38

RANFURLY

DANSEYS PASS INN
781 Kyeburn Diggings Road, Danseys Pass, Ranfurly
Tel 03-444 9048
www.danseyspass.co.nz
Built in 1862, during the height of the Otago gold rush, the inn is now quite isolated but retains much of its character. You can stay overnight, or stop for breakfast, lunch or dinner. Lunches tend to be from a blackboard menu; dinners are à la carte, with a wine list promoting Central Otago wines. Typical dishes include beef fillet with avocado béarnaise, salmon poached in vodka, and venison with morello cherries.

🕐 Daily 8am–9pm
✋ L NZ$22, D NZ$45, W NZ$32

ST. BATHANS

THE VULCAN HOTEL
1670 Loop Road, St. Bathans, Oturehua
Tel 03-447 3629
When gold fever was at its height, there were 14 hotels in St. Bathans. Now there is only one: the Vulcan, a mud-brick building dating from 1882. The walls are thick and the place is full of charm. As well as visitors, you're likely to meet some characterful locals propping up the bar. You can get bar snacks here and 'Devonshire' teas, and the hotel bistro serves a blend of traditional New Zealand with Polynesian, French, Italian and local ingredients. If you don't

mind basic accommodation, you can also stay the night.

🕐 Daily 8am–11pm
✋ L NZ$15, D NZ$35, W NZ$28

STEWART ISLAND

SOUTH SEA HOTEL
Half Moon Bay, Oban, Stewart Island
Tel 03-219 1059
www.stewart-island.co.nz
Right on the Oban waterfront, this is a typical country hotel and a popular meeting place for the locals. Don't expect sophistication, but you can get a good taste of the island from the restaurant, which serves

locally sourced oysters, mussels, salmon and scampi. The chowder is a speciality and the titi (mutton bird) is baked to order.

🕐 Daily 7am–9pm
✋ L NZ$20, D NZ$35, W NZ$18

TE ANAU

REDCLIFF CAFÉ AND BAR
12 Mokonui Street, Te Anau
Tel 03-249 7431
The Redcliff is a casual and intimate café with inside-outside dining and a convivial bar, set in a rustic cottage a block from the lake. It's also a popular venue for live entertainment. The menu focuses on fresh produce, with as much attention paid to the vegetables as the meat dishes. You can eat as simply as breads with spreads and pasta to hearty lamb and venison dishes, and finish with crème brûlée.

🕐 Daily 5–9.30pm
✋ D NZ$45, W NZ$25

WANAKA

MISSY'S KITCHEN
Level 1, 80 Ardmore Street, Wanaka
Tel 03-443 5099
www.missyskitchen.co.nz
Missy's has expansive views over the lake and mountains and a sophisticated city

SPECIAL IN WANAKA
CARDRONA HOTEL
Crown Range Road, Wanaka
Tel 03-443 8153
www.cardronahotel.co.nz
Today it's hard to imagine Cardrona as the thriving gold-rush town it was in 1870, with four hotels, European and Chinese stores, butcheries, a blacksmith and a baker. The Cardrona Hotel and the adjoining buildings are all that remain. The pub is full of atmosphere and you can stay in the modernised units. It's a great place to stop for an après-ski mulled wine, and in summer there's a garden with a children's playground. The restaurant serves an à la carte menu and regional and local wines.

🕐 Daily 11.30am–late
✋ L NZ$25, D NZ$45, W NZ$25

atmosphere. The food is modern Pacific Rim, with dishes such as Marlborough mussels fried with chilli jam, pickled carrot, coriander and mung bean salad; red braised pork belly, hot and sour Savoy cabbage salad, crispy shallots and garlic and steamed rice; round off the meal with Belgian chocolate soufflé with vanilla bean ice cream. The beverage list includes a good range of wines, beers, whisky and speciality teas, and the sommelier is knowledgeable.

🕐 Daily 4pm–late
✋ D NZ$46, W NZ$30

SARGOODS RESTAURANT
Edgewater Resort, Sargood Drive, Wanaka
Tel 03-443 8311
www.edgewater.co.nz
You can dine in the restaurant or outdoors with spectacular Wanaka views. The menu includes merino lamb, seared wild goat loin, three-tomato risotto and house-smoked Akaroa salmon pasta—but since chef Andrew Spiegel focuses on seasonal New Zealand ingredients, this can change.

🕐 Daily 7am–late
✋ L NZ$25, D NZ$60, W NZ$35

EATING

STAYING IN NEW ZEALAND

New Zealand offers a wide choice of accommodation, from backpackers' hostels to luxury lodges in stunning locations. Whichever part of the country you are in, you will rarely end up without a bed for the night, but book ahead in the high season (November to end February). To encounter real Kiwi hospitality, try to stay in a home or farmhouse. Visitor information offices can reserve all kinds of accommodation.

HOTELS

The hotels in New Zealand usually fall into one of four categories:

Large luxury hotels: There are a number of large, modern, luxury (four- or five-star) hotels in the main cities. Most are part of major international or trans-Tasman chains (▷ 272) and prices range from about NZ$250 to NZ$500 per night. All rooms are equipped with the latest technology, including laptop plug-in ports and satellite TV. Restaurants and leisure facilities such as swimming pools, spas and gyms are standard.

Standard chain hotels: Available in all the major cities and most of the larger provincial towns, they charge rates between about NZ$175 to NZ$300, but they have regular weekend or off-season deals. Again, most have in-house restaurants and additional facilities such as a heated pool.

Boutique hotels: Often used to enhance marketing, the 'boutique' label should still ensure that the hotel is small, luxurious and offers something a little different, be it in décor, location or service. The owners may live on site and extend a personal welcome. Very often the rooms or suites are themed. Although most boutique hotels are urban, you will find the boutique label applied to anything from a modern country home to a heritage building in a city suburb. Dinner is often available by arrangement. On average, double rooms cost from NZ$175 to NZ$400.

Traditional pubs and budget hotels: Many rural towns have retained their traditional old wooden hotels. Some of these may look grand from the outside, but invariably the interior doesn't match up. A basic, comfortable room can often be found, but there may be late-night noise from the bar. Prices are usually pitched somewhere between a standard backpackers' hostel and a basic motel unit (from NZ$20 to NZ$60).

LODGES

From heritage buildings furnished with antiques to purpose-built sporting retreats with fishing, hunting or golf, lodges are usually highly luxurious and often in outstanding rural locations. They may have up to 20 suites, often in self-contained units in secluded, park-like grounds, with opulent reception rooms in the main building. The price usually includes dinner, bed and breakfast, and extras such as pre-dinner drinks. Personal guiding, individuality and good food are assured. Prices range from NZ$200 to NZ$2,600 per night.
● www.lodgesofnz.co.nz.

BED-AND-BREAKFAST (B&B)

This covers a wide variety of hosted accommodation, from guesthouses to rooms in private homes, and can consist of anything from a basic double room with shared bathroom and cereal for breakfast to a luxurious room with private bathroom and full breakfast. Again prices vary, with the standard cost being around NZ$100 to NZ$150 for a double room. When looking at prices bear in mind a full breakfast costs at least NZ$12 in a café or restaurant. Many B&Bs also offer evening meals at extra cost, but advance notice is usually required.

HOMESTAYS AND FARMSTAYS

These give you the chance to stay in a family home and mix with your hosts. Breakfast is

STAYING

usually included, and an optional evening meal may be available on request. Farmstays offer the additional attraction of a taste of rural life. You are welcome to help around the farm, and children are particularly welcome. Rates for both homestays and farmstays are comparable with B&B prices.

● New Zealand Farm Holidays, based near Auckland, produce a free catalogue listing about 300 establishments, tel 09-412 9649, **www.**nzfarmholidays.co.nz.

● For farmstay options in Southland contact Western Southland Farm Hosting Group, tel 03-225 8608, **www.**farmhost.co.nz.

● Visitor information offices can help you find homestays or farmstays, and the Tourism New Zealand website (**www.**newzealand.com) also has a detailed listing of nationwide farmstays.

HOSTELS AND BACKPACKER ORGANISATIONS

As a popular destination for the independent traveller or backpacker, New Zealand is well served with hostels and budget accommodation.

The Youth Hostels Association NZ (part of the international YHA network) runs 64 hostels, from modern, purpose-built establishments in the cities to ex-churches. Many have double rooms, some with private bathroom. You can expect free linen, bedding and pillows, adequately equipped kitchens, laundry facilities, games room or TV room, secure storage facilities, phones and the internet. Prices vary from NZ$12 to NZ$20 for a dormitory bed, depending on season, and NZ$22 to NZ$30 per adult for doubles. Membership is available from **www.**yha.org.nz. The annual fee is NZ$40 (NZ$30 for renewals). YHA membership cards also entitle you to a number of discounts, including up to 30 per cent off air and bus travel. Other organisations include:

● VIP group, PO Box 60177, Titirangi, Auckland, tel 09-816 8903, **www.**vip.co.nz.

● Budget Backpacker Hostels Ltd (BBH), Foley Towers, 208 Kilmore Street, Christchurch, tel 03-379 3014, **www.**bbh.co.nz.

● Nomads, Travellers' Contact Point, 87 Queen Street, Auckland, tel 09-300 7197, **www.**travellersnz.com.

MOTORCAMPS AND CABINS

New Zealand is very well served with motorcamps (also known as holiday parks), where there are both powered sites for motor vehicles and tent pitches for campers. Camps are usually equipped with laundry facilities, hot showers and kitchens. Larger parks may also have a pool, games and sports facilities, a general store and café.

Motorcamps often also have a range of cabins, units or tourist apartments for rent. Cabins are the most basic, with little except a bed, sink and electric supply, but some also have a small kitchen. They cost between NZ$35 and NZ$60 for two. Units and apartments are similar to motels, being fully self-contained, some with multiple rooms. They vary in price but rarely exceed NZ$100 per night (for two people), with an additional charge of NZ$12 to NZ$15 per extra person.

● The Top Ten chain of motorcamps has a good reputation and a 'Club Card' scheme offering a 10 per cent discount, tel 03-377 9900, **www.**topparks.co.nz.

CAMPSITES

The Department of Conservation (DoC; **www.**doc.govt.nz) manages more than 200 vehicle-accessible campsites all over the country, many in prime locations. They are typically basic, provide clean running water, toilet facilities and barbecue areas, but rarely allow open fires. Sites in the national parks have well-equipped huts. The camping fee is NZ$2 to NZ$10 a night. Fees for huts are anything from NZ$5 to NZ$40 per night, depending on category and location. If you plan to use DoC campsites and huts, book well in advance.

SELF-CATERING

Holiday homes of all kinds, including tiny country cottages known as *baches*, are available for rent. *Bach* is pronounced 'batch', and is a shortened version of 'bachelor pad'. Most self-catering accommodation operates on a minimum weekend or week-long stay basis. Look in the travel or house-rental sections of national newspapers. Regional visitor offices may also be able to help. Motels are the choice of most New Zealanders. They range from the utilitarian to luxurious condos with a spa pool, but have at least a shower, kitchen facilities and a TV, and are usually clean and comfortable. Studio units cost about NZ$80 to NZ$100, one-bedroom units NZ$90 to NZ$120 and suites are available for an additional charge for each adult. Many of the larger motel complexes have a restaurant and a swimming pool, plus spas. Most motels offer breakfast, delivered to the door at extra charge.

RESERVATIONS AND PAYING

It is advisable to reserve at least three days in advance during the high season (November to March) and further ahead during New Zealand's summer holidays (from Christmas to the end of January). Payment is generally straightforward, with most establishments taking all major credit cards through EFTPOS (Electronic Funds Transfer at Point of Sale). Cash is also readily accepted, and recommended at B&Bs and homestays.

QUALMARK

Qualmark is New Zealand tourism's official symbol of quality, instigated to encourage high standards of hospitality and service. Lists of Qualmark-rated places to stay, graded from two to five stars, are available from visitor information offices and AA Travel Centres.

STAYING

Name of Hotel Chain	Description	Website	Telephone Numbers
Accor	The world's largest hotel group, encompassing the All Seasons, Ibis, Mercure, Novotel and Sofitel brand names. Full online search and booking service. 24 properties.	www.accorhotels.com.au	0800 444 422
Golden Chain	New Zealand-based, mid-range chain with hotels, motels and resorts nationwide. Offers two pre-booked or open-dated pass schemes or with a B&B 'mix and match'. 90 properties.	www.goldenchain.co.nz	0800-80 GOLDEN
Grand Hotels International	Asia-based chain with hotels in Auckland, Christchurch and Wellington. Full range of options including units, studios and apartments. 4 properties.	www.ghihotels.com	
Heritage	New Zealand-based group with luxury standard and apartment properties available in all major places. Online booking service. 9 properties.	www.heritagehotels.co.nz	0800 368 888
Intercontinental	Expensive international group including the Centra, Holiday Inn, Crowne Plaza and Park Royal brands. Properties in Auckland and Queenstown. 7 properties.	www.ichotelsgroup.com	0800 154 181
Langham	Expensive resort-style international hotel group with one hotel in Auckland. 1 property.	www.langhamhotels.com	09-379 5132
Mainstay	New Zealand-based, independently owned hotel chain. Wide variety of 3- to 4-star properties nationwide offering standard room types and self-contained apartments. 41 properties.	www.mainstay.co.nz	03-358 7900 0800 624 646
Millennium/ Copthorne/ Kingsgate	Chain with properties in all the main places around New Zealand. Regular special deals and weekend packages. 21 properties.	www.millenniumhotels.com	09-309 4420
Scenic Circle	New Zealand-based group with a diverse range of properties throughout the main places. Online booking service. 15 properties.	www.scenic-circle.co.nz	03-357 1919 0800 696 963

STAYING

AUCKLAND, NORTHLAND AND COROMANDEL

AUCKLAND

AACHEN HOUSE BOUTIQUE HOTEL
39 Market Road, Remuera, Auckland
Tel 09-520 2329
www.aachenhouse.co.nz
Aachen House is a five-star luxury B&B hotel in the chic suburb of Remuera. The grand 1904 house is superbly furnished with antiques and porcelain. Guest rooms look out on tranquil gardens and are decorated in period style, with king-size or twin beds.
🍷 NZ$345–NZ$590, inc pre-dinner drinks and gourmet breakfast
🛏 5 rooms, 3 suites
🚭 🅿 Off-street 🚌 Take Market Road exit (exit 432) signposted from SH1 Southern Motorway

CITY CENTRAL HOTEL
Corner of Wellesley and Albert streets, Auckland
Tel 09-307 3388
www.citycentralhotel.co.nz
A no-nonsense hotel, the City Central is well placed, clean and comfortable. There is a choice of rooms, some

sleeping up to five people, but all have TV, tea-making facilities and telephone, and some have air-conditioning. The standard rooms are very small. Continental and cooked breakfasts are extra.
🍷 NZ$99–NZ$160
🛏 104 rooms (25 non-smoking)
🚭 Except standard rooms
🅿 Parking available in Crowne Plaza

ESPLANADE HOTEL
1 Victoria Road, Devonport, Auckland
Tel 09-445 1291
www.esplanadehotel.co.nz
Ten minutes by ferry from the Central Business District (CBD), this boutique hotel is one of Auckland's oldest, built in 1903. It dominates Devonport's promenade and has fine harbour views. Rooms are spacious, with satellite TV and tea-making facilities. A

penthouse apartment has two bedrooms, two bathrooms, a lounge and fully equipped kitchen. The smart Esplanade restaurant and the more relaxed Mecca café both serve meals throughout the day.
🍷 NZ$210–NZ$560, inc breakfast
🛏 15 rooms, 2 suites, 1 apartment
🚭
🚌 On main bus route from Takapuna
⛴ Ferries half-hourly from Auckland

GREAT PONSONBY BED AND BREAKFAST
30 Ponsonby Terrace, Ponsonby, Auckland
Tel 09-376 5989
www.ponsonbybnb.co.nz
The Great Ponsonby is a stylish, century-old villa in a quiet cul-de-sac, a short stroll away from 'funky' Ponsonby Road. Brightly decorated rooms and self-contained studios are equipped with direct-dial phones and modems, coffee plungers, wine glasses, satellite TV, CD players, irons and de-mist mirrors—among other thoughtful touches. Bicycles, laundry facilities and beach towels are available on request. There's even a friendly dog and cat.
🍷 NZ$180–NZ$330, inc breakfast
🛏 5 rooms, 6 studios, 1 penthouse
🚭 🅿 Off-street
🚌 Near main bus route from CBD

HILTON HOTEL
Princes Wharf, 147 Quay Street, Auckland
Tel 09-978 2000
www.hilton.com
Completed in 2002, the Hilton sits in an enviable position, occupying a wharf in the harbour close to the heart of the city. The accommodation is first class, with custom woven carpets, contemporary furniture and spacious bathrooms.

Rooms have king-size or twin beds, private decks and internet access. Luxury suites have 180-degree views. There are also serviced apartments, a stylish restaurant, White (▷ 253), a cocktail bar, fitness facility and shops. Breakfast costs NZ$25–NZ$35.
🍷 NZ$461–NZ$1,142
🛏 160 rooms, 6 suites, 35 apartments
🚭 🏊 Outdoor 🛎 🅿 Valet

COROMANDEL TOWN

COROMANDEL HOLIDAY PARK
636 Rings Road, Coromandel
Tel 07-866 8830
www.coromandelholidaypark.co.nz
Coromandel Holiday Park is set in 1.4ha (3.5 acres) of parkland just five minutes' walk from Coromandel town. You can be a traditional camper in a tent or caravan, or stay in a fairly basic cabin or more upmarket motel room. Facilities include barbecues, a playground, trampolines and a games room, and fish-cleaning facilities for when you catch your own supper.
🍷 Tent sites from NZ$20, powered sites NZ$24, cabins NZ$50, motel units NZ$75
🛏 40 tent sites, 26 powered sites, 10 cabins, 6 motel units.
🏊 Outdoor
🚭

STAYING

KARAMANA HOMESTEAD

84 Whangapoua Road,
Coromandel Town
Tel 07-866 7138
www.karamanahomestead.com

One of the oldest homes on the Coromandel Peninsula, dating from 1872, Karamana has three guest rooms, named French, Victorian and Colonial and furnished accordingly.

There is also a two-bedroom cottage. Devonshire teas are a speciality. Breakfast includes fresh fruit and pancakes.

🖐 NZ$150–NZ$170
ℹ 3 rooms, 1 cottage
🚭 🅿 Off-street

POTTERY LANE COTTAGE

15 Pottery Lane, Coromandel Town
Tel 07-866 7171
www.geocities.com/potterylanecottage

These two cottages, plus a self-contained loft in the main house, are in a peaceful garden, a short stroll from the village. One cottage has two bedrooms (a twin and a double); the other is smaller and open-plan with a queen-size bed and a single bed. The wooden, single-storey buildings are simply furnished. Breakfast on request (NZ$5).

🖐 NZ$100–NZ$140
ℹ 2 cottages
🚭 🅿 Off-street

GREAT BARRIER ISLAND

OASIS LODGE

Tryphena, Great Barrier Island
Tel 09-429 0021
www.barrieroasis.co.nz

Set in a vineyard, this large homestead offers spacious, open-plan rooms with modern décor, TV and video, a bar and fridge, and outdoor decks overlooking the garden. There is also a self-contained chalet sleeping up to six. Diving, fishing, kayaking and horse-riding are available close by. A small restaurant serves international dishes.

THE CHURCH ACCOMMODATION

87 Beach Road, Hahei,
Coromandel Peninsula
Tel 07-866 3533
www.thechurchhahei.co.nz

Lovely gardens surround this former village church, which has been turned into a restaurant. Accommodation is in separate studio units or self-contained cottages, all with french doors leading onto verandas. Studios and cottages have a queen-size bed and window-seat bed, refrigerator and tea-making facilities. Self-contained cottages also have a separate living area, kitchen and TV; two have an open fire.

◎ Closed Aug
🖐 NZ$95–NZ$150, inc breakfast; additional adults NZ$20 extra
ℹ 4 studio units, 11 cottages
🚭 🅿 Off-street
🚗 37km (23 miles) southeast of Whitianga: turn off SH 25 at Whenuakite. No public transport

🖐 NZ$250, inc breakfast
ℹ 3 rooms, 1 chalet
🚭 🅿 Off-street
⛴ Ferry (4.5 hours) from Auckland or by air

KERIKERI

THE SUMMER HOUSE BED AND BREAKFAST

424 Kerikeri Road, Kerikeri
Tel 09-407 4294
www.thesummerhouse.co.nz

Subtropical gardens and a citrus orchard add to the appeal of this popular B&B, only two minutes' walk from Kerikeri. The two rooms have antique beds, while the self-contained suite is contemporary in style, with a South Pacific theme, including Maori weavings. Excellent breakfasts might include home-made bread and fruit from the orchard.

🖐 NZ$225–NZ$295, inc breakfast
ℹ 2 rooms, 1 suite
🅿 Off-street 🚭
🚗 2km (1 mile) off State Highway 10 on Kerikeri Rd. Airport pick-up available

MANGONUI

CARNEVAL

360 State Highway 10, Cable Bay,
Mangonui
Tel 09-406 1012
www.carneval.co.nz

This modern B&B, on a hill overlooking Doubtless Bay, provides a fine base to relax, or explore the Aupori Peninsula. The rooms, with king-size beds, refrigerators, ironing, tea-making facilities and private bathrooms, have either garden or ocean views. The Swiss-German owners have created a fine marriage of European and Kiwi hospitality and, as a former chef, Roly can ensure some memorable cooking. A sauna and log-burning fire add to the appeal.

🖐 NZ$140–NZ$170
ℹ 2 suites
🚭
🚗 Just after Mangonui on SH10

MATAURI BAY

HUNTAWAY LODGE

Wainui Road, Te Ngaere Bay, Matauri Bay
Tel 09-405 1611
www.huntawaylodge.com

You'll need your own transport or a helicopter to reach this exclusive lodge, in a superb setting overlooking the ocean and three secluded beaches. The three stylish guest rooms are named after them, and each has its own deck. Food is a speciality, with a three-course dinner available for NZ$90 per person. Activities include fishing, diving and golf.

🖐 NZ$375–NZ$425, inc breakfast
ℹ 3 rooms
🚭 🅿 Off-street
🚗 Take the Matauri Bay turnoff SH10 and follow the signs to Te Ngaere Bay. Veer left at the letter boxes

OHAEAWAI

LUDBROOK HOUSE

State Highway 1, Ohaeawai
Tel 09-405 9846
www.ludbrook.co.nz

The Ludbrook family have been farming their 420ha (1,037-acre) sheep and cattle property halfway between Paihia and the Kauri Coast since 1860. They welcome visitors for dinner, B&B at the

1920s homestead. Decorated in period style, Ludbrook House has four simple but comfortable guest rooms with private bathrooms. Chris Ludbrook makes preserves and cakes commercially, and many guests gravitate to the kitchen to chat as meals are prepared.

🖐 From NZ$760 per person, inc breakfast and dinner
ⓘ 4 rooms
🅿 Off-street
🚌 On SH1 near the junction with SH12

PAIHIA

ALLEGRA HOUSE

39 Bayview Road, Paihia
Tel 09-402 7932
www.allegra.co.nz

In the heart of Paihia, with fine views across the bay to Russell and beyond, this modern home offers two B&B rooms or a spacious apartment. Both rooms have TV, tea-making facilities and a fridge, and internet access is available. The owners are fluent in German and French. Minimum two-night stay required.

🖐 NZ$105–NZ$220
ⓘ 2 rooms, 1 apartment
🚭 🏊 🅿 Off-street
🚗 Turn left after the wharf and off Marsden Road onto Bayview Road. Follow Bayview to its terminus

COPTHORNE HOTEL AND RESORT BAY OF ISLANDS

Tau Henare Drive, Paihia
Tel 09-402 7411
www.copthornebayofislands.co.nz

Right on the waterfront, set in spacious grounds within the Waitangi National Reserve, this hotel has modern rooms with standard facilities. There is an in-house café restaurant serving Pacific Rim food. The hotel is well set up for children.

🖐 NZ$139–NZ$515
ⓘ 102 rooms (88 non-smoking), 7 suites
🅿 Off-street
🚗 2km (1 mile) past Paihia town centre. Follow signs on Marsden Road to the Waitangi Reserve; hotel is immediately right after the bridge

PUKENUI

PUKENUI LODGE

Corner of Main Highway North and Wharf Road, Pukenui
Tel 09-409 8837
www.pukenuilodge.co.nz

Close to Cape Reinga and Ninety Mile Beach, overlooking Houhora Harbour, Pukenui

PUKEMATU LODGE

Flagstaff Hill, Russell
Tel 09-403 8500
www.pukematulodge.co.nz

Perched high on the hill, this modern B&B has spectacular views to Waitangi and Paihia. The hosts go the extra mile to make sure your stay is memorable. The stylish suites are furnished in recycled native wood, with a sofa, fresh flowers, robes, fruit and organic bathroom products. Breakfast is served on the deck. Evening meals, including a Maori *hangi* barbecue, are available on request.

🖐 NZ$295, inc breakfast
ⓘ 2 suites
🚭 🅿 Off-street
🚌 10km (6 miles) from Opua vehicle ferry and 1km (0.5 miles) from the middle of Russell

Lodge has tidy, self-contained queen, family and studio motel units with their own kitchen and bathroom, satellite TV, in-house video, telephone and electric blankets. Breakfast is available (from NZ$8.50).

🖐 NZ$89–NZ$119
ⓘ 9 motel units, hostel
🏊 Outdoor 🅿 Off-street

RUSSELL

DUKE OF MARLBOROUGH

Waterfront, Russell
Tel 09-403 7829
www.theduke.co.nz

The 'Duke', right on the waterfront, holds New Zealand's oldest pub licence, granted in 1840. The bay views are stunning. Downstairs is a lounge with a log fire, the bar and an à la carte restaurant specialising in local seafood. The price includes Continental breakfast.

🖐 NZ$195–NZ$550, inc breakfast
ⓘ 25 rooms, 6 waterfront suites
🚭 🅿 Off-street
🚌 2km (1 mile) from Paihia by passenger ferry, or 20km (13 miles) by car and vehicle ferry via Opua

WAIHEKE ISLAND

ONETANGI BEACH APARTMENTS

27 The Strand, Onetangi
09-372 0003/0800-663 826
www.onetangi.co.nz

On the 2km-long (1-mile) Onetangi Beach, close to all facilities. The complex has

spa pools and a sauna, and kayaks are available. There are studios and beachfront and courtyard options.

🖐 NZ$100–NZ$350
ⓘ 8 units
🚭
🚢 Ferry from Auckland

POUHUTUKAWA RETREAT

40 Tiri Road, Oneroa
Tel 09-372 8219
www.pohutukawaretreat.com

The Pouhutukawa Retreat offers four modern self-contained chalets with sea and rural views, close to the ferry and walking distance from beaches, shops and restaurants.

🖐 From NZ$180
ⓘ 4 chalets
🚭
🚢 Ferry from Auckland

WHITIANGA

VILLA TOSCANA

Ohuka Park, Whitianga, Coromandel Peninsula
Tel 07-866 2293
www.villatoscana.co.nz

Villa Toscana is a grand villa high on a hill 4km (2.5 miles) north of Whitianga, surrounded by native bush. Lavishly furnished with Carrara marble and antique furniture, the suite has its own entrance,

two bedrooms, a granite kitchen, a large bathroom, an outdoor spa pool and a deck with views across the bay. Breakfast is provided. Gourmet Italian cuisine (dinner NZ$120) and an extensive wine cellar add to the appeal.

🖐 NZ$440–NZ$640
ⓘ 1 suite
🚭 🏊
🅿 Off-street
🚗 Take the main road past the airfield, turn left at the beach, left onto Centennial Drive, left onto Rimu Street and straight into Ohuka Park. The entrance is 1km (0.5 miles) on the right

STAYING

CENTRAL NORTH ISLAND

CAMBRIDGE

MAUNGATAUTARI LODGE
844 Maungatautari Road, Lake Karapiro, Cambridge
Tel 07-827 2220
www.malodge.com
Purpose built in 2002, this

luxury boutique hotel is on a 16ha (40-acre) stud farm. The spacious, sumptuously furnished suites in the main building and three villas next door all have super-king beds, double spa baths and private balconies or terraces with views of the gardens and Lake Karapiro. The four-course dinner features home-grown and organic produce. Mini-golf, horseback-riding, massage and beauty therapies are available.
✋ NZ$630–NZ$1,030, inc breakfast, pre-dinner drinks and dinner
🛏 5 suites, 3 villas
🚭 ♨ 🏊 Outdoor 🅿
🚗 9km (6 miles) south of Cambridge

DAWSON FALLS

DAWSON FALLS TOURIST LODGE
Manaia Road, Dawson Falls
Tel 06-765 5457
www.dawson-falls.co.nz
The Alpine-Swiss style lodge is set in native bush on the slopes of Mount Taranaki/ Egmont, in the heart of Egmont National Park. Rooms are furnished with hand-crafted furniture. A bar, with a log fire and a restaurant are added attractions.
✋ NZ$150
🛏 11
🚭 ♨ 🅿
🚗 Accessed from the north via Opunake (SH45) or Stratford (SH3), or from the south via Manaia (SH45)

GISBORNE

ONE ORANGE
98 Wairere Road, Wainui Beach, Gisborne
Tel 06-868 8062
www.oneorange.co.nz
This self-contained 'designer apartment' right next to the beach in Wainui encompasses a studio apartment and king-size bedroom that can be booked separately or in combination. Both are fresh, modern and minimalist in design, with leather furniture and a well-equipped kitchen. Food-and-wine-matching dinners and trout-fishing trips are a speciality. Two nights minimum.
✋ NZ$225, inc breakfast
🛏 1 room, 1 studio apartment
🚭 ♨ 🅿
🚗 On the right just past Wainui, 8km (5 miles) north of Gisborne

HAMILTON

NOVOTEL TAINUI HOTEL
7 Alma Street, Hamilton
Tel 07-838 1366
www.accorhotels.co.nz
Centrally located in the Central Business District (CBD), on the banks of the Waikato River, the four-star Tainui is Hamilton's premier hotel. Some rooms have river views, and all have internet access, a safe and ironing facilities. The restaurant has indoor and outdoor dining,

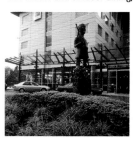

and the hotel offers a special package in conjunction with SKYCITY Hamilton Casino.
✋ NZ$135–NZ$334
🛏 177 rooms (130 non-smoking), including 4 suites
🚭 ♨ 🅿 Valet

HAVELOCK NORTH

MANGAPAPA PETIT HOTEL
466 Napier Road, Havelock North
Tel 06-878 3234
www.mangapapa.co.nz
Mangapapa Petit Hotel, a luxury hotel in a grand country home 3km (2 miles) from Havelock North, is surrounded by 9ha (22 acres) of orchards and manicured gardens. The rooms are opulently furnished in a blend of traditional and contemporary, with meticulous attention to detail. Guests can indulge in a four-course dinner matched with local wines, play tennis and rent bicycles.

✋ NZ$306–NZ$2,300, inc breakfast
🛏 12 rooms, 5 suites
🚭 ♨ 🏊 Outdoor 🅿 Off-road

OLEA COTTAGES
101 Ru Collin Road, Havelock North
Tel 06-879 7674
www.oleacottages.co.nz
These two functional, modern cottages occupy a peaceful rural setting in the heart of Hawke's Bay wine country. One cottage has two bedrooms and a pull-out couch; the other has one double bedroom. Both have well-equipped kitchens with dish-washer, satellite TVs and CD player. Complimentary breakfast supplies are provided the first two mornings, as are fresh flowers, local wine and fruit.
✋ NZ$220–NZ$230 inc breakfast (surcharge of NZ$30 for single-night stays)
🛏 2 cottages
🚭 🅿

KATIKATI

FANTAIL LODGE
117 Rea Road, Katikati
Tel 07-549 1581
www.fantaillodge.co.nz
This popular country lodge estate offers a fine base from which to explore the Bay of

STAYING

Plenty and the Coromandel Peninsula. Set in beautiful rural surroundings, it has luxury suite accommodation with lounge, bedroom, dressing room and bathroom, and self-contained two-bedroom villas. Additional attractions are the restaurant, in-house spa complex and informative eco-tours of the region.

🖐 NZ$356–NZ$394, inc breakfast
ⓘ 6 suites, 2 villas
🚭 🏊 Outdoor 🅿
🚌 35km (22 miles) north of Tauranga

NAPIER

COUNTY HOTEL
Browning Street, Napier
Tel 06-835 7800
www.countyhotel.co.nz

This Edwardian hotel in the middle of town was one of the few buildings to survive the 1931 earthquake. Restored in 1995, it has 18 spacious suites named after New Zealand birds, ranging from standard double to two bedrooms with private lounge, spa bath and balcony. All rooms have satellite TV and internet connection. The hotel also has a popular restaurant, Chambers (▷ 256) and bar. Parking is available across the road.

🖐 NZ$286–NZ$900
ⓘ 18 suites (all non-smoking)
🚭 🚭

MCHARDY HOUSE
11 Bracken Street, Napier
Tel 06-835 0605
www.mchardyhouse.com
High on a hill above Napier, McHardy House has been made into a luxury boutique hotel, with restored ornate stained glass, plasterwork ceilings and billiard room of the former grand residence, and each suite and deluxe room is furnished with a different theme, using fine fabrics and antiques. The

owner is a chef, and a speciality is his four-course menu using local produce.

🖐 NZ$615–NZ$695, inc breakfast, aperitifs and dinner
ⓘ 6 rooms
🚭 🏊 Outdoor 🅿 Off-street
🚌 From the city centre turn right off Tennyson into Carlyle Street, then right into Chaucer Road S. Continue up hill, turn left onto Napier Terrace, right onto Chaucer Road N., right into George Street and right again into Bracken Street

NEW PLYMOUTH

THE NICE HOTEL
71 Brougham Street, New Plymouth
Tel 06-758 6423,
www.nicehotel.co.nz
Art and history are the themes of this offbeat boutique hotel in the 1850s former Redcoats Hospital building. Each room is named after a local landmark, such as Len Lye's Wind Wand on the waterfront. In addition to stylish design and contemporary artworks, the rooms include luxuries such as double spa baths and comfy armchairs. The award-winning Table restaurant is spacious and airy, with good Pacific Rim cuisine. Complimentary airport transfers are available.

🖐 NZ$225–NZ$280
ⓘ 7 rooms, 1 suite
🚭 🅿 Off-street

OHAKUNE

POWDERHORN CHATEAU
Corner of Mangawhero Terrace and Thames Street, Ohakune
Tel 06-385 8888
www.powderhorn.co.nz
The Alpine-style Powderhorn Chateau is a popular base for skiing in winter. Each of the 30 suites has a queen-size bed, a double sofa bed, a lounge suite and satellite TV. The Mansion apartment can sleep up to eight. There is babysitting, a small casino and internet access. Two restaurants—the ski chalet-style Matterhorn and more informal Powderkeg—are lively après-ski venues. The *Lord of the Rings* cast stayed here during filming.

🖐 NZ$165–NZ$215
ⓘ 30 suites, 1 apartment
🚭 🏊 Indoor 📺
🚌 At the northern end of the village, at the start of Mountain Road

SOLSCAPE
611 Wainui Road,
Raglan
Tel 07-825 8268
www.solscape.co.nz
If you are looking for something completely different, this really is the place to stay in Raglan. The owners have renovated an array of railway guard's vans with native rimu floors and ceilings as bright lodgings, arranged as dormitories or self-contained units. Two self-contained cottages with open fires are also available. The property enjoys fabulous views across the Tasman Sea and there is also a menagerie of animals.

🖐 NZ$58–NZ$135
ⓘ 17 cabooses, 2 cottages
🚭
🚌 From Raglan follow the Wainui Road for 5.5km (3.5 miles)

ROTORUA

MILLENNIUM HOTEL ROTORUA
Corner of Eruera and Hinemaru streets, Rotorua
Tel 07-347 1234
www.millenniumhotels.co.nz
This popular chain hotel is located close to the Polynesian Spa. The modern rooms and suites have marble-floored bathrooms, direct-dial phones, ironing facilities, satellite TV and modem points. The nightly Maori cultural performance and *hangi* (feast) illustrates traditional myth and legend through song and dance. The restaurant has a wood-fired oven and is considered one of the city's best.

🖐 NZ$220–NZ$375
ⓘ 227 rooms (120 non-smoking)
🚭 🚭 📺 🏊 Indoor 🅿

REGAL PALMS MOTOR LODGE
350 Fenton Street, Rotorua
Tel 07-350 3232
www.regalpalmsml.co.nz
Of the dozens of motels in Rotorua, the Regal Palms is one of the newest and best. Its classy décor and attention to detail have helped earn it a five-star rating. It has one- and two-bedroom suites and three serviced apartments, all with kitchen facilities and a spa

STAYING

pool. Facilities also include a sauna, internet access, a bar, mini-golf, children's playground and barbecue area.

🖐 NZ$185–NZ$255
ℹ️ 41 suites, 3 apartments
🆂 🆂 📺 🏊 Outdoor 🅿️
🚌 On the main bus route
🚗 2km (1 mile) south of the CBD

SOLITAIRE LODGE
Lake Tarawera, Rotorua
Tel 07-362 8208
www.solitairelodge.co.nz
The staff know how to look after their guests at this celebrated hideaway on the shores of Lake Tarawera. There are nine spacious, luxurious suites, some with spa, private deck and lake views. Adding to the appeal is a fine art collection and the innovative New Zealand cuisine.

🖐 NZ$1,280–NZ$1,990, inc breakfast and dinner
ℹ️ 9 suites
🆂 🆂
❎ Helicopter access
🚗 20km (13 miles) south of the CBD

TAUPO

CABOOSE LODGE
100–102 Lake Terrace, Taupo
Tel 07-376 0116
www.taupocaboose.co.nz
In case something completely different takes your fancy, this hotel has an African rail safari theme. Built in a log-cabin style on the waterfront, it has standard double rooms with shower called Caboose Sleepers, larger Sleepers with full bathrooms, and three executive suites sleeping up to six. In-house facilities include spas, internet access, a lounge/bar with an open fire and a restaurant with ostrich on the menu. Fishing safaris are a speciality.

🖐 NZ$119–NZ$199
ℹ️ 22 compartments, 28 sleepers, 1 suite
🆂 🏊 Outdoor 🅿️
🚗 1km (0.5 mile) from Taupo CBD

STAYING

HUKA LODGE
Huka Falls Road, Taupo
Tel 07-378 5791
www.hukalodge.com
Huka Lodge remains New Zealand's most popular luxury lodge. Hidden in parkland beside the Waikato River, it regularly hosts royalty and rock stars seeking privacy. The complex has a classic lodge feel with wood predominating, a library, roaring fire and deep armchairs. The suites offer every comfort, and cuisine is first-class.

🖐 NZ$1,790–NZ$4,250, inc breakfast, cocktails, dinner, airport transfer
ℹ️ 20 suites
🆂 🆂
❎ Helicopter access
🚗 3km (2 miles) from Taupo CBD

WAIRAKEI RESORT
State Highway 1, Wairakei
Tel 07-374 8021/0800 RESORT
www.wairakei.co.nz
The resort, in the Wairakei Thermal Park, has a range of good facilities for sporty guests, with tennis, golf, squash and a gym, plus a spa, pool and sauna in which to relax afterwards. There is a wide variety of accommodation available, from standard rooms with a double and single bed to family villas, and air-conditioned executive suites with a separate lounge. All rooms have satellite TV, mini bar, hair dryer and tea-making facilities.

🖐 NZ$146–NZ$225
ℹ️ 157 rooms, 9 suites and 15 villas (most non-smoking)
🆂 🆂 📺 🏊 Outdoor
🚗 7km (4 miles) north of Taupo

TAURANGA

HARBOUR CITY MOTEL
50 Wharf Street, Tauranga
Tel 07-571 1435
www.taurangaharbourcity.co.nz

This classy motel is ideally located in the heart of Tauranga's shopping and café district. What strikes you most is its stylish design and the attention to detail. Modern furnishings and a minimalist décor make it seem like a chic boutique hotel. All rooms have spa baths. Harbour City also caters for children, with cots and high chairs provided free.

🖐 NZ$120–NZ$240
ℹ️ 16 studios, 4 one-bedroom units
🆂 🆂 🅿️
🚗 4km (3 miles) southwest of the airport

WHAKAPAPA

THE CHATEAU TONGARIRO
Whakapapa Village, State Highway 48, Mount Ruapehu
Tel 07-892 3809
www.chateau.co.nz
Perhaps the most famous hotel on the North Island, the Chateau Tongariro provides traditional luxury in a grand location—Tongariro National Park. Whether for relaxing or as a base for skiing or trekking the Tongariro Crossing, it offers elegance in keeping with its age (built in 1929), including a restaurant, bar, café, pool and golf course. It's worth paying extra for a guaranteed mountain view.

🖐 NZ$180–NZ$1,000
ℹ️ 95 rooms, 5 suites. Family units available in a separate building
🆂 🏊 Indoor 🅿️
🚗 45km (28 miles) south of Turangi on SH48

SKOTEL ALPINE RESORT
Whakapapa Village, State Highway 48, Mount Ruapehu
Tel 07-892 3719
www.skotel.com
A low mountain chalet, with extensive views over Tongaririo National Park, Skotel will appeal to budget-conscious visitors. With a restaurant and bar, lounge, games room, spa pools, drying room, ski shop and tramping gear rental, it provides a comfortable base for all activities in the park. Hostel accommodation and family chalets are also available.

🖐 NZ$130–NZ$160
ℹ️ 22 deluxe, 7 standard rooms
🆂 🅿️
🚗 46km (28 miles) south of Turangi

SOUTHERN NORTH ISLAND

CARTERTON

DORNEYWOOD HOMESTAY BED AND BREAKFAST
170 Park Road, RD2, Carterton
Tel 06-379 5099
Two private self-contained suites on a 7ha (17-acre) small farm, with a lake for kayaking. The farm is 3km (2 miles) from Carterton. One room is wheelchair accessible.
🖐 NZ$95, inc breakfast supplies
ⓘ 2 units
Ⓢ

FEATHERSTON

LONGWOOD
Longwood Road East, Featherston
Tel 06 308 8289
www.longwood.co.nz
Longwood, built in 1920 and reputedly New Zealand's largest private home, is surrounded by park-like grounds in the heart of the Wairarapa wine country. The lodge has magnificent reception rooms and four spacious bedrooms with canopied beds, antique furnishings, private bathrooms and fireplaces. The tariff includes breakfast, afternoon tea on arrival and a four-course dinner. There is also a choice of self-contained accommodation in the 1850s former gamekeeper's cottage, coach house and groom's quarters.
🖐 Cottages NZ$150–NZ$250, inc breakfast; lodge NZ$495 per person, inc breakfast and dinner
ⓘ 4 rooms, 3 cottages
Ⓢ Ⓟ

MANGAWEKA

MOUNT HUIA
906 Ruahine Road, RD 54 Kimbolton
Tel 06-382 5726
www.mthuia.co.nz
You can join in farm activities, walk through pastureland and native bush, or enjoy river sports at Mount Huia, a 351ha (867-acre) sheep and cattle

SPECIAL IN FEATHERSTON

WHAREKAUHAU COUNTRY ESTATE
Western Lake Road, Palliser Bay, Featherston
Tel 06-307 7581
www.wharekauhau.co.nz
Pronounced 'forry-coe-hoe', this is one of the country's

top luxury lodges. Part of its appeal is its location on a 2,000ha (5,000-acre) working sheep station overlooking the ocean, where you can relish getting away from it all. Lodging is in self-contained cottages dotted round the estate, with four-poster beds, open fireplaces and a naturalistic décor of cotton, clay, hemp and wool. TV, newspapers, internet and activities are available. Dinner in the lodge features French/ Italian cuisine matched with top local wines.
🖐 NZ$1,220–NZ$3,050 per person, inc breakfast, cocktails and dinner
ⓘ 12 cottage suites, 2 houses
Ⓢ Ⓢ Ⓨ ⌚ Ⓟ

farm in the Rangitikei hill country. Self-contained Hodd Cottage has three bedrooms, two bathrooms, a kitchen, and an open fire. Breakfast ingredients can be provided. Bed-and-breakfast accommodation in the 1920s farmhouse has private access, and a private bathroom and spa pool on the deck. Dinner is available (from NZ$20).
🖐 Farmstay NZ$180, inc breakfast; cottage NZ$50 per adult (breakfast provisions NZ$10)
ⓘ 1 room, 1 cottage
Ⓢ Ⓟ
🚌 9km (6 miles) from SH1

MARTINBOROUGH

AYLSTONE WINE COUNTRY RETREAT
Huangarua Road, Martinborough
Tel 06-306 9505
www.aylstone.co.nz
A spacious homestead, built in the early 1900s, Aylstone is surrounded by vineyards. The guest rooms are individually designed, in keeping with the house's colonial heritage, with a choice of super-king, queen or twin beds. All rooms have telephones, TV and internet facilities. Leisurely, seasonal breakfasts are a speciality, and there is a a restaurant in the summer. Bicycles are provided free of charge.
🖐 NZ$230, inc breakfast
ⓘ 6 rooms
Ⓢ Ⓟ

PEPPERS MARTINBOROUGH HOTEL
The Square, Martinborough
Tel 06-306 9350
www.peppers.co.nz
Dating from 1882, the hotel is a focal point of this Wairarapa village, in an area becoming internationally known for its wines. The 16 luxury rooms are individually designed and named after early European settlers. Attractive features include claw-foot baths and french doors opening onto either a private veranda or the garden. The bar has an open fire and serves pub food, while the Dining Room is noted for its wine list and more sophisticated fare.
🖐 NZ$275–NZ$355, inc breakfast
ⓘ 16 rooms
Ⓢ Ⓢ 2 rooms Ⓟ

PALMERSTON NORTH

AVENUE MOTEL
116 Fitzherbert Avenue, Palmerston North
Tel 06-356 3330/0888-116 333
www.avenuemotel.co.nz
This modern motel in a quiet location is just a few minutes' walk from the heart of the city. There are private spa pools and the standard, family and two-bedroom units are all on the ground floor. A studio unit is wheelchair-accessible.
🖐 NZ$88–$118
ⓘ 13 units Ⓢ
Ⓟ Off-street parking

STAYING

BENTLEYS MOTOR INN
Corner of Linton and Chaytor streets,
Palmerston North
Tel 06-358 7074/0800 BENTLEYS
www.bentleysmotorinn.co.nz
Refurbished in 2003, Bentleys
has 22 modern, ground-floor,
smoke-free units, including
studios, one- and two-
bedroom suites and a three-
bedroom apartment with full
kitchen and laundry. All suites
have spa pools or spa baths,
satellite TV, CD players,
business amenities and
cooking facilities. The inn is
quiet and within walking
distance of shops and cafés,
and there are on-site squash
courts, a sauna and a gym.
Breakfast is available.
🖐 NZ$135–NZ$280
🛈 22 rooms
🚫 🐾
🅿 Secure
🚭 Close to the main square, off
Fitzherbert Avenue

PARAPARAUMU
COPPERFIELD
SEASIDE MOTEL
7–13 Seaview Road,
Paraparaumu Beach
Tel 04-902 6414
www.seasidemotel.com
This modern Best Western
motel offers a convenient stop
on the Kapiti Coast. Close to
the beach and golf course, it
has studio units and one- and
two-bedroom apartments with
full kitchen facilities and
balconies. Many have sea
views and some have double
spa baths. Other facilities

include Sky and cable TV,
internet connection, hair dryers
and in-room ironing. A buffet
restaurant, vegetarian café,
wine bar and Italian restaurant
are on site.
🖐 NZ$95–NZ$135
🛈 15 units, studios and apartments
(9 non-smoking)
🚫 🅿
🚭 3km (2 miles) west of SH1

GREENMANTLE ESTATE
214 Main North Road,
Paraparaumu
Tel 04-298 5555
www.greenmantle.co.nz
Close to the site of the New
Zealand Open, this was where
champion golfer Tiger Woods
chose to stay in 2001. A
spacious, rambling 1940s
mansion set in gardens full of
native birds, it offers six beautifully appointed private rooms
and suites, with romantically
draped king beds, oak furniture and double showers.
Guests also have use of a gym,
heated pool and hot tub
hidden away in native bush.
A *table d'hote* dinner can be
booked in advance.
🖐 NZ$525–NZ$595, inc breakfast
🛈 6 rooms
🚫 🚭 🏊 Outdoor
🅿
🚭 3km (2 miles) north of
Paraparaumu

WANGANUI
BRAEMAR HOUSE
2 Plymouth Street, Wanganui
Tel 06-348 2301
www.braemarhouse.co.nz
Braemar House is an
Edwardian villa which retains
its period charm as a guest
house, in a quiet location close
to the Whanganui River.
Backpacker accommodation is
also available. The house has
attractive formal dining and
living rooms, a well-equipped
kitchen and simply but
appropriately furnished,
centrally heated single, double
and twin rooms, with shared
bathroom.
🖐 NZ$95
🛈 8 rooms
🚫 🅿 Off-street
🚭 1km (0.5 miles) from Wanganui
CBD

RUTLAND ARMS INN
Corner of Victoria Avenue and Ridgway
Street, Wanganui
Tel 06-347 7677
www.rutland-arms.co.nz
A heritage hotel centrally
located in downtown
Wanganui, the Rutland Arms
has individually designed
double, triple and twin suites
in the old English style.
Some have spa baths and all
have satellite TV, phone, fax,
hair dryers and ironing
facilities. The first floor is non-
smoking. A guest lounge is

available for relaxing, with
large screen TV and reading
material. A bar, restaurant,
courtyard café and shops
are attached.

🖐 NZ$145–NZ$175
🛈 8 suites
🏠 First-floor rooms
🅿 Off-street
🚭 5km (3 miles) from the airport

WELLINGTON
COPTHORNE HOTEL
ORIENTAL BAY
73 Roxburgh Street,
Wellington
Tel 04-385 0279/0800-404 010
www.millenniumhotels.co.nz
Visitors who revel in having a
five-star view without having
to pay for five-star accommodation are happy to walk
into the CBD from this hotel,
which clings to the hillside at
Oriental Bay. Located on the
waterfront, it has 113 rooms,
as well as an indoor swimming
pool, a restaurant and a bar.
Ask for a room with a harbour
view and a balcony. The
rooms are comfortable and
have direct dial telephone,
satellite TV, a hair dryer and
ironing facilities.
🖐 NZ$140–NZ$170
🛈 113 rooms, 3 suites
🚫 🏊 Indoor
🅿 Off-street
🚭 2km (1 mile) from the CBD

EIGHT PARLIAMENT
STREET
8 Parliament Street,
Wellington
Tel 04-499 0808
www.boutique-BB.co.nz
This stylish, artistic wooden
villa is typical of Wellington's
traditional colonial houses,
offering three rooms (one with
private bathroom, two with
shared bathrooms) with
bright decoration and modern
style. A courtyard offers outdoor relaxation and privacy
and there is a modern kitchen

STAYING

and living area. The house can be rented for NZ$270–NZ$370, which does not include breakfast.

🖐 NZ$120–NZ$185
ℹ️ 3 rooms
🚭 🅿️
🚌 2km (1 mile) from the CBD

HOTEL INTERCONTINENTAL

Grey Street,
Wellington
Tel 04-472 2722
www.wellington.intercontinental.com
A stone's throw from the waterfront, this striking, bronze-hued building is a city landmark, near the Lambton Quay shops, Parliament and the major sports stadium. The ambience is set as you are welcomed by the doorman, and the lobby gleams with marble. Rooms include luxury suites—queen, twin and standard—with the extras you

---

SPECIAL IN WELLINGTON
THE LIGHTHOUSE

326 The Esplanade, Island Bay,
Wellington
Tel 04-472 4177
www.thelighthouse.net.nz
If you have ever wanted to stay in a lighthouse, this is your chance. This replica offers impressive views across the harbour entrance and oozes character. All that is missing is the flashing light and pounding waves. There is a small kitchen and bathroom on one floor—the living and sleeping areas (two rooms, one main bedroom with spa) are above. Breakfast is included. For a different experience, the owners also offer bed-and-breakfast in a stone keep in Houghton Bay.

🖐 NZ$180–NZ$200
ℹ️ 2 rooms
🚭 🅿️
🚌 6km (4 miles) south of the CBD

---

would expect: direct-dial telephone, internet, ironing facilities, hair dryer and bathrobes. There is a fitness centre, and restaurants and bars include the Western-themed Arizona Bar and Grill.

🖐 NZ$245–NZ$1,824
ℹ️ 231 rooms, 7 suites (187 non-smoking)
🚭 🎥 🐕 🏊 Indoor
🅿️ Valet
🚌 In the CBD

MUSEUM HOTEL—HOTEL DE WHEELS

90 Cable Street
Wellington
Tel 04-802 8900, 0800 994 335
www.museumhotel.co.nz
The Museum Hotel is subtitled 'Hotel de Wheels' because the entire building was shifted 120m (395ft) on railway bogies from the other side of Cable Street to allow for the building of Te Papa. As a result it is very conveniently located for Te Papa, and also the rejuvenated waterfront and the Courtenay Place entertainment district. There are a lobby café and wine bar, a licensed restaurant and bar, and a fitness facility.

🖐 Mon–Fri NZ$149–NZ$269, Sat, Sun NZ$197–NZ$276
ℹ️ 65 rooms, 5 suites, 100 studio, one-and two-bedroom apartments
🐕 Some 🏊
🅿️ Limited on-site parking, valet parking

SHEPHERD'S ARMS HOTEL

285 Tinakori Road, Thorndon,
Wellington
Tel 04-472 1320
www.shepherds.co.nz
Located near Parliament, the Shepherd's Arms was established in 1870. Refurbished in 2001, it is still full of character. The 14 individually appointed rooms are decorated in keeping with their Victorian origins, some with four-poster king or queen beds. Most double rooms have hair dryers, coffee plungers and satellite TV, and all have private bathrooms. There is a popular bar and dining room with an open fire.

🖐 NZ$149–NZ$169
ℹ️ 14 rooms
🚭 🅿️
🚌 2km (1 mile) from the CBD

THE TERRACE VILLAS

202 The Terrace,
Wellington
Tel 04-920 2020
www.terracevillas.co.nz
A collection of historic houses on The Terrace, close to the Cable Car and the Lambton Quay shopping district, the Terrace Villas are divided into 50 self-contained serviced apartments, from studios to three-bedroom units. Although furnished in keeping with their age, all have modern facilities, cable TV, laundry and full kitchens. Breakfast is also available (NZ$9).

🖐 NZ$111–NZ$433
ℹ️ 50 apartments
🚭 🅿️ Off-street
🚌 In heart of the CBD

THE WELLESLEY HOTEL

2–8 Maginnity Street,
Wellington
Tel 04-474 1308,
www.thewellesley.co.nz
If you are fed up with flashy, modern, high-rise hotels, the 1920s neo-Georgian Wellesley is a splendidly restored heritage building offering furnished suites with character in the heart of the Lambton Quarter. Rooms have queen-size beds, spacious bathrooms with dual basins and claw-foot baths, air-conditioning, satellite TV, tea-making and ironing facilities, a hair dryer and bathrobes. Facilities include a gymnasium,

sauna, guest lounge and a popular English-style restaurant, which features an open fire and regular live music and entertainment (mainly jazz).

🖐 NZ$282–NZ$326
ℹ️ Luxury guest and executive suites and rooms
🚭 🐕 🎥
🚌 Near the Parliamentary district

STAYING

NELSON AND MARLBOROUGH

ABEL TASMAN NATIONAL PARK

AWAROA LODGE

Awaroa Bay, Abel Tasman National Park
Tel 03-528 8758
www.awaroalodge.co.nz

Inaccessible by road, Awaroa Lodge combines a wilderness experience with sophisticated accommodation and dining. The lodge is set in native bush, close to the beach and the Abel Tasman Track, and offers a choice of suites with a private deck, deluxe rooms and family rooms. All units are designed with natural materials, and have tea-making facilities and a fridge. Local seafood and organic garden produce are staples on the café menu.

🛏 NZ$235–400
ℹ 12 suites, 10 deluxe, 4 family
🚭
✈ Tasman Helicopters, Abel Tasman Air and Flightcorp fly to Awaroa airstrip from Nelson, Motueka and Wellington
🚗 No road access. On foot from the Abel Tasman Track or 1.5 hours by water taxi from Marahau

BLENHEIM

ANTRIA BOUTIQUE LODGE

276 Old Renwick Road, Blenheim
Tel 03-579 2191
www.antria.co.nz

Described as a modern European castle, Antria is certainly different—but don't

expect ramparts or moats. Mediterranean meets Antipodes in this cultural explosion, with massive neo-Gothic copper front doors, timber ceilings, Greek-inspired lime-washed walls, Italian ceramics and contemporary New Zealand artwork. Rooms are decorated with furnishings from around the world. It's built around a courtyard.

🛏 NZ$335, inc breakfast
ℹ 2 rooms
🚭 🏊 Outdoor 🅿 Covered
🚗 6km (4 miles) from Blenheim. Take Bells Road north off SH6 onto Old Renwick Road

HOTEL D'URVILLE

52 Queen Street, Blenheim
Tel 03-577 9945
www.durville.com

A boutique hotel full of character has been created in the old bank vaults of the grand Public Trust Building in downtown Blenheim. The individually themed suites have lofty ceilings, native wood floors scattered with rugs, and an eclectic mix of four-poster beds, exotic fabrics and antiques—from African textiles to a Javanese daybed. The central vault has been converted into a lounge. The hotel is also known for its lively bar and restaurant.

🛏 NZ$362
ℹ 11 suites
🚭 🚭 🅿 Limited off-street
✈ 7km (4 miles) from the airport

OLD SAINT MARY'S CONVENT

Rapaura Road, Blenheim
Tel 03-570 5700
www.convent.co.nz

This century-old two-storey convent has been transformed into an intimate retreat, surrounded by vineyards and olive groves. Seven spacious, airy rooms have expansive views, satellite TV and access to the balcony or garden. The original character of the building has been retained, with heating and air-conditioning hidden behind the native wood panelling and timbered floors. There is a billiard room, and a chapel in the garden.

🛏 NZ$550–NZ$650, inc breakfast
ℹ 5 rooms, 2 suites
🚭 🚭
🚗 15km (9 miles) from Blenheim

SPECIAL IN COLLINGWOOD

COLLINGWOOD HOMESTEAD

Elizabeth Street, Collingwood
Tel 03-524 8079
www.collingwoodhomestead.co.nz

A colonial-style home, Collingwood Homestead is beautifully decorated and maintained, with polished wooden floors and antiques mixed harmoniously with modern facilities to offer comfort and a homey setting. The lounge has a piano, open fire and veranda. The guest rooms are charmingly furnished, with private bathrooms. Breakfasts are gourmet and a four-course dinner is available (NZ$50, including pre-dinner drinks and wine).

🛏 NZ$265, inc breakfast
ℹ 4 rooms
🚭 🅿 Off-street
🚗 27km (16 miles) from Takaka

COLLINGWOOD

THE INNLET

Main Road, Pakawau
Tel 03-524 8040
www.goldenbayindex.co.nz

A good base for bush walks, kayaking, horseback-riding, cycling and trips to Farewell Spit, this backpackers' hostel has double and twin rooms (with shared bathroom), a rustic hut and a self-contained cottage in a lovely bush setting. The simply furnished cottage sleeps up to seven, with a downstairs double and loft bedrooms reached by ladder. Guests have access to a streamside barbecue and hot tub, and can gather shellfish at the sandy swimming beach 200m (219 yards) away.

🛏 NZ$60–NZ$146
ℹ 2 cottages, backpacker rooms
🚭 🅿
🚗 11km (7 miles) north of Collingwood

KAIKOURA

ANCHOR INN MOTEL

208 The Esplanade, Kaikoura
Tel 03-319 5426/0800-720 033
www.anchorinn.co.nz

One of the best motels in New Zealand, the five-star Anchor Inn is located right on the

STAYING

THE OLD CONVENT

Mount Fyffe Road, Kaikoura
Tel 03-319 6603/0800-365 603
www.theoldconvent.co.nz
In a quiet setting, this former convent, built for French nuns in 1911, has become an unusual B&B with loads of character. The cells and schoolrooms are now bedrooms with private bathrooms, and the former chapel is the guest lounge. An added attraction is the four-course French-style dinner (NZ$50 or NZ$75 with Kaikoura's famous crayfish). Guests also have access to bicycles, pétanque, croquet and tennis.

NZ$120–NZ$175
16 rooms
Outdoor Off-street
Signposted 5km (3 miles) north of Kaikoura

Kaikoura waterfront, with most rooms enjoying magnificent sea and mountain views. The complex includes executive, luxury and standard studios, as well as one- and two-bedroom apartments. All units are self-contained, with fully equipped kitchens, satellite TV, individual air-conditioning and double glazing. There is also a barbecue area. Breakfast is available.

NZ$125–NZ$245
15 units

FYFFE COUNTRY LODGE

State Highway 1, Kaikoura
Tel 03-319 6869
www.fyffecountrylodge.com
A striking building made of rammed earth and native timber, Fyffe Country Lodge is surrounded by English-style gardens. All rooms have tea

and coffee, a hair dryer, robes and TV. Seafood chowder is a

speciality of the in-house restaurant, which has an open fire, and the bar leads onto a pretty courtyard. Courtesy mountain bikes are available.

NZ$189–NZ$750, inc breakfast
6 studios, 1 suite

6km (4 miles) south of Kaikoura on SH1

MARAHAU

ABEL TASMAN MARAHAU LODGE

Marahau Beach, RD2 Motueka
Tel 03-527 8250
www.abeltasmanmarahaulodge.co.nz
Built close to the start of the Abel Tasman Coast Track, this attractive accommodation offers self-contained, two-room units and studio. Rooms are provided with fold-out desks, coffee plunger and local wine in the fridge. There is a communal kitchen for the six studio units that do not have kitchens, and the complex also includes a pool, sauna and spa. Room service breakfast and evening meals available.

NZ$130–NZ$185
8 suites, 4 self-contained units

16km (10 miles) north of Motueka

MARLBOROUGH SOUNDS

HOPEWELL

Kenepuru Sound
Tel 03-573 4341
www.hopewell.co.nz
You get an ideal blend of isolation, relaxation, value and comfort at this waterfront accommodation. Arriving by water taxi is recommended, as the road is tortuous. Five cottages provide shared rooms and doubles with bathrooms. A self-contained, two-bedroom cottage sleeps up to six. Linen is supplied, but not food. The well-equipped kitchen and lounge has a wood fire, TV, stereo and library. Other attractions include an outdoor spa, bush walks, kayaking, mountain biking, fishing, golf, water skiing and gathering shellfish.

NZ$64–NZ$84
8 double/twin rooms, 1 cottage

Soundsair flies from Wellington to the local airfield

85km (53 miles) from Picton, via Linkwater and Te Mahia. Water taxi from Picton or Havelock recommended

RAETIHI LODGE

Kenepuru Sound, RD2 Picton
Tel 03-573 4300
www.raetihi.co.nz
This modern, luxury lodge overlooking Double Bay is noted for its architecture, secluded location and stunning views. Superior sea view, garden and hillside rooms are individually themed to reflect aspects of the Sounds or exotic locations. The licensed restaurant offers cooked breakfasts (NZ$30), bar lunches and three-course dinners (NZ$70). The lodge has a helipad and is accessible, if required, by road, but is best approached by sea. Guests can enjoy walking and water-based activities, and aromatherapy massage.

NZ$125–NZ$250
13 rooms

85km (53 miles) from Picton, via Linkwater and Te Mahia. Water taxi from Picton or Havelock North recommended

MOTUEKA

MOTUEKA RIVER LODGE

Motueka Valley Highway, Ngatimoti, Motueka
Tel 03-526 8668
www.motuekalodge.co.nz
This luxury fishing lodge in the picturesque Motueka Valley is designed in French provincial style. It has an elegant, country-style interior with spectacular views in every direction. Anglers get guided trout-fishing in local rivers and streams, and even non-anglers will find plenty to enjoy. Guests tend to congregate in the farmhouse kitchen, where the chef uses local produce to offer a 'taste of Kiwi' with a touch of class. They can also sample Chardonnay from the lodge's own vineyard. Minimum two-night stay.

NZ$1,025–NZ$1,462, inc breakfast and dinner
5 rooms

30km (19 miles) southwest of Motueka

NELSON

THE HONEST LAWYER COUNTRY PUB

1 Point Road, Monaco, Nelson
Tel 03-547 8850/0800-921 192
www.honestlawyer.co.nz
Located near the airport on a peninsula in the Waimea estuary, the Honest Lawyer is

STAYING

a popular English-style pub, complete with exposed beams hung with memorabilia and a blazing open fire. It also has good food and accommodation, with king and twin rooms, a honeymoon suite, and a self-contained cottage. All rooms have internet connections, and a guest pantry has complimentary drinks and snacks.

🪙 NZ$170–NZ$230
ℹ️ 8 rooms, 1 suite, 1 cottage
🅿️ Off-street
🚗 6km (4 miles) from Nelson CBD. Turn right off Nayland Road into Songer Street which leads to Monaco

RUTHERFORD HOTEL
Trafalgar Square, Nelson
Tel 03-548 2299/0800-437 227
www.rutherfordhotel.co.nz

The principal hotel in the city, the Rutherford is centrally placed with a view of the cathedral gardens. It has spacious double rooms and two executive suites, all supplied with a hair dryer, bathrobes, an iron, tea-making facilities and a minibar. Executive rooms have a connection for laptops. The Japanese Miyazu restaurant is highly regarded.

🪙 NZ$159–NZ$199
ℹ️ 113 rooms
🅿️ Outdoor 🅿️

TE PUNA WAI LODGE
24 Richardson Street, Nelson
Tel 03-548 7621
www.tepunawai.co.nz

A restored early Victorian villa on the Port Hills, Te Puna Wai commands extensive views over Haulashore Island and the bay. One suite occupies the entire top floor and can sleep four, but the ground floor apartment is the most desirable, with french doors opening onto the veranda and garden, antique furniture, fresh flowers, a marble tiled bathroom with underfloor heating

and a designer kitchen stocked with local produce for breakfast. Another double with private bathroom can be booked with it.

🪙 NZ$145–NZ$325, inc breakfast
ℹ️ 3 rooms
🅿️ Limited off-street
🚗 Richardson Road is off the waterfront. Follow it uphill and through a sharp left-hand turn; Te Puna Wai is on the right

PICTON
BROADWAY MOTEL
113 High Street, Picton
Tel 03-573 6563/0800 101 919
www.broadwaymotel.co.nz

The four-star Broadway is on the edge of town and handy for the ferry terminal. Its top-range units have a private

balcony or courtyard, super-king and queen beds, and kitchens with microwaves. Some rooms also have spa baths. Continental or cooked breakfasts can be ordered.

🪙 NZ$105–NZ$185
ℹ️ 18 units
🅿️ Off-street
🚗 1km (0.5 miles) from the Interislander Ferry Terminal

ST. ARNAUD
ALPINE LODGE
Main Road, St. Arnaud
Tel 03-521 1869/0800-367 377
www.alpinelodge.co.nz

The Alpine Lodge offers a wide choice of accommodation, from self-contained two-bedroom apartments and spa bath suites to standard and superior double rooms, family units sleeping up to six, and a chalet for budget-conscious visitors which has double and shared rooms. Superior rooms have underfloor heating and double glazing. The Lodge has a house bar with an open fire, a café and a licensed restaurant specialising in fish and game dishes.

SPECIAL IN RAPAURA
CRANBROOK COTTAGE
Giffords Road, Rapaura RD3, Blenheim
Tel 03-572 8606
www.cranbrook.co.nz

Surrounded by vines and fruit trees, this 135-year-old cottage is private and romantic, with breakfast delivered to your door on a tray with fresh flowers. The cottage is self-contained, with queen and twin bedrooms decorated in white linen and nets, cooking facilities, lounge and dining area and private bathroom. Breakfast is likely to include home-grown produce and preserves. The hosts specialise in culinary tours.

🪙 NZ$180, inc breakfast
ℹ️ 1 cottage
🚗 Giffords Road is off Rapaura Road, reached from SH6 or SH1

🪙 NZ$135–NZ$160
ℹ️ 28 rooms (8 non-smoking), 4 studios and 4 apartments in the lodge

TAKAKA
SANS SOUCI INN
Richmond Road, Pohara, Takaka
Tel 03-525 8663
www.sanssouciinn.co.nz

Environmentally friendly accommodation is the theme of this inn, with rustic adobe-brick bungalows in a garden setting and an ecological sanitation system. Single, twin, double and family rooms are furnished with king-size futons and cane furniture. The popular licensed restaurant

serves home-style meals, with a set menu changing daily.

🪙 NZ$95
ℹ️ Single, twin, double and family bungalow rooms
🚗 8km (5 miles) northeast of Takaka

CANTERBURY AND THE WEST COAST

SPECIAL IN AKAROA
WILDERNESS HOUSE
42 rue Grehan, Akaroa
Tel 03-304 7517
www.wildernesshouse.co.nz
This charming 1878 villa, on a quiet street a short stroll from the village, is surrounded by old-fashioned gardens and has a small vineyard. Bedrooms, furnished with antiques, are thoughtfully appointed with wool duvets, fresh flowers and New Zealand-made toiletries. A lounge has TV and complimentary refreshments. Dinner is available by arrangement. No children under 14.
💶 NZ$240, inc breakfast
🛏 4 rooms
🚭 🅿 Off-street
🚌 Rue Grehan is on the left as you enter Akaroa

AMBERLEY
BREDON DOWNS HOMESTAY
233 Carters Road (SH1), Amberley
Tel 03-314 9356
www.bredondownshomestay.co.nz
Bredon Downs is an old farmhouse in English gardens with a pool and tennis court, and makes a good base for exploring the Waipara wine trail. You can choose between queen, twin or single rooms, all with private spa bathroom. The owners breed ostriches and are happy to show them to you. Dinner by arrangement.
💶 NZ$110–NZ$130, inc breakfast
🛏 3 rooms
🚭 🏊 Outdoor 🅿 Off-street
🚌 1km (0.5 miles) south of Amberley

ARTHUR'S PASS
THE TRANS ALPINE LODGE
Main Road, Arthur's Pass
Tel 03-318 9236
www.arthurspass.co.nz
Designed to look like a Swiss lodge, the Chalet combines alpine lodge accommodation with a European-influenced restaurant. Rooms are simply furnished, with en suite or shared bathrooms, and satellite TV. There is an outdoor spa pool. Cooked breakfasts, coffee and lunches are served in the bistro; at night there's fireside dining in the restaurant.
💶 NZ$120, inc breakfast
🛏 14 rooms (2 with shared bathroom)
🚭

CHRISTCHURCH
CROWNE PLAZA
Corner of Kilmore and Durham streets, Christchurch
Tel 03-365 7799/0800-154 181
www.crowneplaza.co.nz
A stylish building beside the Avon River, the Crowne Plaza is by the Town Hall, Convention Centre and Casino. It has a choice of standard rooms and suites, with views over Victoria Square or the city and Alps. The hotel has a sports bar, a café, a highly regarded restaurant and an authentic Japanese restaurant with traditional and *teppan-yaki* areas.
💶 NZ$176–NZ$475
🛏 298 rooms (177 non-smoking), 19 suites
🚭 🚲 📺 🏊 🅿

THE GEORGE HOTEL
50 Park Terrace, Christchurch
Tel 03-379 4560
www.thegeorge.com
Facing the Avon River and Hagley Park, the George combines an attractive location with attention to detail. It has 57 deluxe rooms and suites, some with balconies, spas and butler service, and a self-contained Residence wing. The emphasis is on understated elegance and good service. The Pescatore restaurant (▷ 265) specialises in seafood, and the brasserie has some of the best breakfasts in town.
💶 NZ$422
🛏 57 rooms and suites
🅿 Off-street
🚌 1.5km (1 mile) from Cathedral Square

STONEHURST ACCOMMODATION
241 Gloucester Street, Christchurch
Tel 03-379 4620
www.stonehurst.com

Stonehurst—best known as a top-end backpackers'—has expanded to include a modern motel annex with one- to three-

bedroom units and apartments. These are well appointed, with super-king beds and fully equipped kitchens; some also have spa baths, CD players and garages. The backpackers' also has single and double/twin rooms, some en suite. Facilities include a pool, pizza bar, internet access and travel shop.
💶 NZ$115–NZ$180
🛏 19 motel units, 9 apartments, 22 double/twin en suites
🚭 🏊 Outdoor 🅿 Off-street
🚌 1km (0.5 miles) from Cathedral Square

SUMNER BAY MOTEL AND APARTMENTS
26 Marriner Street, Sumner, Christchurch
Tel 03-326 5969, 0800 496 949
www.sumnermotel.co.nz
Every unit at the modern Sumner Motel has a private balcony or courtyard, and two have spa baths. The motel is only metres from Sumner Beach, with surfboards and bikes available for hire. Sumner has a village atmosphere, just 15 minutes' drive from the heart of Christchurch.
💶 NZ$145–NZ$195
🛏 12 units

FOX GLACIER
TE WEHEKA INN
Main Road, Fox Glacier
Tel 03-751 0730
www.weheka.co.nz
Te Weheka Inn is a modern, purpose-built, two-storey small hotel, four-star rated, with spacious modern bedrooms, a choice of en suite bath or shower, fluffy towels, hair dryer and ironing facilities. The lounge has a balcony, a small

STAYING

library and internet connection, and there is a laundry. Full or continental breakfast is included, and dinner is served during summer months.

🏨 NZ$236–NZ$348, inc breakfast
ⓘ 20 rooms
Ⓢ Ⓟ Covered
🚗 Opposite Visitor Information Office

FRANZ JOSEF

RAINFOREST RETREAT
Cron Street, Franz Josef
Tel 03-752 0220
www.rainforestretreat.co.nz
Log cabins nestle among the trees in this quiet bush setting. Some accommodation is on the forest floor, some up in the canopy. Standard tree houses have queen and single beds, en suites, satellite TV, electric blankets and heating. Tree

lodges upgrade to a full kitchen, air-conditioning and central heating. The complex also has motel and en suite accommodation, a spa, sauna, internet access, bar, café and restaurant.

🏨 NZ$129–NZ$199
ⓘ 6 tree lodges, 2 tree houses, 9 tree hut motel units
Ⓢ Ⓢ
🚗 One block from the shopping centre

SCENIC CIRCLE FRANZ JOSEF GLACIER HOTELS
Main Road (SH6), Franz Josef
Tel 03-752 0729
www.scenic-circle.co.nz
The hotel has two wings, 1km (0.5 miles) apart, in the village and on the outskirts. All

rooms have satellite TV, telephones, tea-making facilities and hair dryers. Rooms in the Douglas and Graham wings also have fridges and in-house video. Between them the

hotels have three restaurants, four bars, two spa pools and guest laundries.

🏨 NZ$298–NZ$360
ⓘ 177 rooms
Ⓢ Ⓢ
🚗 On SH6, 1km (0.5 miles) north of Visitor Information Office

GREYMOUTH

THE BREAKERS SEASIDE BED AND BREAKFAST
Nine Mile Creek, State Highway 6
Tel 03-762 7743
www.breakers.co.nz
Stunning ocean views and beach access add to the friendly welcome at this four-star seaside B&B lodge and homestay on the coast road between Greymouth and Westport. The rooms, inspired by the traditional Kiwi *bach* (holiday home), are close to the sea and have a large bedroom and lounge area, as well as en suite and a balcony. Dinner is available with 24 hours notice.

🏨 NZ$180–NZ$250, inc breakfast
ⓘ 4 rooms
Ⓢ
🚗 14km (8 miles) north of Greymouth

HAAST

MCGUIRES LODGE
State Highway 6, Haast Junction
Tel 03-750 0020/0800-624847
www.mcguireslodge.co.nz
Modern McGuires Lodge is on a 3.5ha (8.5-acre) deer farm. The 19-unit complex comprises standard, studio and family rooms. There is also a spa pool, barbecue and laundry. The restaurant serves local specialities such as crayfish from the house tank, venison, Hereford steak and blue cod. The bar is finished in recycled

native woods. Continental and cooked breakfasts are available.

🏨 NZ$95–NZ$190
ⓘ 19 rooms
Ⓢ Ⓟ
🚗 700m (760 yards) southeast of Haast River Bridge on SH6, by the DoC office at the Haast junction

HANMER SPRINGS

HERITAGE HOTEL AND RESORT
1 Conical Hill Road, Hanmer Springs
Tel 03-315 0060/0800-368 888
www.heritagehotels.co.nz
A local landmark, the former Hanmer Lodge was elegantly refurbished in 2000, retaining the Spanish design of its heyday in the 1930s, with Moorish arches, a bell tower and a Grand Dining Room to seat 120. Accommodation is a combination of rooms, garden suites and self-contained three-bedroom villas among mature trees. The restaurant serves Pacific Rim cuisine, such as local salmon on a *sushi nori* cake. In summer, take breakfast or dine more casually on the sunny patio.

🏨 NZ$150–NZ$361
ⓘ 36 rooms (31 non-smoking), 15 suites, 11 villas (non-smoking)
Ⓢ In restaurant Ⓢ 🏊 Outdoor
🚗 500m (545 yards) from the Visitor Information Office

HOKITIKA

BUSHLINE RETREAT BED AND BREAKFAST
Bluespur Road, RD2, Hokitika
Tel 03-755 8557/03-755 6603
www.bushline.co.nz
This bed-and-breakfast is ten minutes' drive from Hokitika, in a bush setting, with views of the sea. Three of the rooms have private facilities, and families are welcome.

🏨 NZ$95–NZ$180
ⓘ 5 rooms Ⓢ

SHINING STAR BEACHFRONT ACCOMMODATION
11 Richards Drive, Hokitika
Tel 03-755 8921/0800-744 646
www.accommodationwestcoast.co.nz
Sea views are a speciality at this beachfront motel with log cabin lodging, studios and family chalets. Double (queen) and triple (queen and single bed) chalets have a kitchen and bathroom; two-bedroom apartments sleep four to six. Executive spa chalets have

mezzanine floors, satellite TV, DVD and CD players. Breakfast (Continental) can be delivered.
🏨 NZ$55–NZ$145
🛏 20 rooms
🚭🅿
🚌 Turn onto Richards Drive off SH6 at the northern end of town; 1km (0.5 miles) from downtown

KARAMEA

KARAMEA HOLIDAY PARK

Maori Point Road, Karamea
03-782 6758
www.karamea.com
This campground, beside an estuary and surrounded by native bush, offers anything from tent sites to motel units. It's 3km (1.8 miles) south of Karamea, with transport to the Heaphy and Wangapeka tracks.
🏨 Tent sites NZ$20, power sites NZ$22, cabins NZ$25–NZ$35, motel NZ$60–NZ$65, all excluding breakfast
🛏 70 tent sites, 32 power sites, 20 cabins, 3 motel units

SPECIAL IN KARAMEA

LAST RESORT
71 Waverley Street, Karamea
Tel 03-782 6617
www.lastresort.co.nz
The Last Resort offers an opportunity to get back in tune with nature. This modern and imaginatively designed complex has lodge-style accommodation blocks interconnected by a walkway, with a large bar/café and restaurant. You can choose from two-bedroom cottages, studio en suites and shared accommodation. Room service and internet access are available.
🏨 NZ$65–NZ$140
🛏 Cottages, 13 studio en suites, 12 double lodge rooms (6 with en suite)
🚭
✈ Charter flights available from Karamea to Nelson and Takaka. Helicopter access
🚌 On SH67

LAKE MOERAKI

WILDERNESS LODGE LAKE MOERAKI

State Highway 6, Lake Moeraki
Tel 03-750 0881
www.wildernesslodge.co.nz
This eco-lodge in a remote West Coast location offers a high level of comfort in double lodge rooms and larger garden rooms. The restaurant overlooking the Moeraki rapids serves wilderness food, such as whitebait from the river, seafood from the coast and game from the forest. There are canoes for you to explore the lake and river, and guided nature walks. Minimum two-night stay in the busy season.
🏨 NZ$290–NZ$490, inc breakfast, dinner and some activities
🛏 22 rooms
🚭🅿
🚌 On SH6 at the Moeraki River outlet 30km (19 miles) north of Haast

LAKE TEKAPO

LAKE TEKAPO LUXURY LODGE

Aorangi Crescent, Lake Tekapo
Tel 03-680 6566/0800 LAKE TEKAPO
www.laketekapolodge.co.nz
Built in 1998, this spacious, earth-block lodge overlooks Lake Tekapo, a short stroll from the heart of the village. The four rooms have super-king or queen/single beds with en suites, one with spa bath. Most have lake and mountain views. Bathrobes and slippers are provided. The lounge has an open fire, and internet access and satellite TV are available.
🏨 NZ$200–NZ$395, inc breakfast
🛏 4 rooms
🚭🅿
🚌 1km (0.5 miles) from Tekapo village

MOUNT COOK VILLAGE

THE HERMITAGE

Mount Cook Village
Tel 03-435 1635
www.mount-cook.com
Spectacularly situated at the foot of the Alps, The Hermitage is one of New Zealand's most famous hotels, its isolation being part of the mystique. The complex includes rather tired traditional hotel rooms, a luxury wing, self-contained motels and chalets. There is a shop, sauna, tennis courts and a choice of bars and restaurants, including a buffet and the fine-dining Panorama Room in summer.

🌙 Chalets closed May–end Sep
🏨 Motel units NZ$235–NZ$275, inc breakfast; chalets NZ$240, inc breakfast; hotel rooms NZ$520–NZ$770, inc breakfast and dinner
🛏 221 rooms, 32 motels, 19 chalets
🚭🚬🅿
✈ 3km (2 miles) from Mount Cook airstrip
🚌 56km (35 miles) north of SH8

PUNAKAIKI

PUNAKAIKI ROCKS HOTEL AND VILLAS

State Highway 6, Punakaiki
Tel 03-731 1168/0800-786 2524
www.punakaiki-resort.co.nz
Only 400m (435 yards) from the Pancake Rocks and Blowholes, the resort has studio units with private decks facing the ocean or eco, solar-powered rooms set farther back from the highway, in bush. Rooms have cooking facilities, private outdoor seating and satellite TV. The villas are linked by suspended boardwalks, and a walk-through underpass gives easy beach access.
🏨 NZ$236–NZ$292
🛏 35 rooms
🚭🅿
🚌 400m (435 yards) south of Paparoa National Park Visitor Information Office

WAIPARA

CLAREMONT COUNTRY ESTATE

828 Ram Paddock Road, Waipara Gorge
Tel 03-314 7559
www.claremont-estate.com
Claremont blends five-star accommodation in a heritage building on a 980ha (2,400-acre) sheep station with stunning scenery. The suites and rooms have spacious bathrooms and are furnished with antiques, but also have central heating, satellite TV and internet access. There is a tennis court, and a spa and sauna. Families are accommodated in a separate self-contained cottage. Claremont is also a good base for exploring the Waipara wine region. Note that it is closed from July to September.
🏨 NZ$696–NZ$996, inc dinner and refreshments
🛏 5 suites, 1 cottage
🚭🅿
✈ Private airstrip
🚌 55km (34 miles) north of Christchurch. Turn off SH1 at Georges Road opposite Waipara Hills Winery and follow the road for 12km (7 miles)

STAYING

OTAGO AND THE FAR SOUTH

CLYDE

OLIVERS LODGE
34 Sunderland Street, Clyde
Tel 03-449 2860
www.olivers.co.nz
Equally lauded for the quality of its accommodation and its restaurant, Olivers offers a classic mix of old-world character and fine cuisine. Rooms are individually styled and range from the Stable and Homestead rooms to the individual Smokehouse room with its charming old shower and

sunken bath. The restaurant, which also exudes character with its cobblestone fireplace and red-brick floor, has been a focus for quality dining in the region for years.
🖐 NZ$140–NZ$300, inc breakfast
ⓘ 12 rooms
Ⓢ
🚌 1km (0.5 miles) off SH8

CROMWELL

GOLDEN GATE LODGE
Barry Avenue, Cromwell
Tel 03-445 1777
www.goldengate.co.nz
Smart and spacious, the lodge is designed to reflect the region's gold-mining heritage. Accommodation is in twin, double and king studios, suites (some with spa) and units, all with tea-making facilities. There are also a sauna and spa, licensed restaurant, café and wine bar. The Lodge is located at the entrance to the

town, opposite the shopping mall and by the golf course.

🖐 NZ$115
ⓘ 47 rooms
Ⓢ Ⓟ
🚌 500m (550 yards) from Cromwell Visitor Information Office

DUNEDIN

HULMES COURT
52 Tennyson Street, Dunedin
Tel 03-477 5319
www.hulmes.co.nz
Hulmes Court B&B is in a turreted 1860s Victorian mansion located two blocks from the Octagon. It is quiet, comfortable and friendly. Together with Hulmes Too, an Edwardian house next door, it has 14 bedrooms decorated in keeping with the period, with harbour and garden views, some with shared bath.
🖐 NZ$100–NZ$160, inc breakfast
ⓘ 14 rooms
Ⓢ Ⓟ Off-street
🚌 1km (0.5 miles) from Dunedin Visitor Information Office

MOTEL MORAY PLACE
97 Moray Place, Dunedin
Tel 03-477 2050
This modern, centrally located motel has quiet standard and executive units with comfortable beds and tiled bathrooms. Executive units come with spa baths. The units do not have full cooking facilities, but continental breakfast is available and each unit has a TV, a microwave, tea-making facilities, a toaster, a fridge and an iron.
🖐 NZ$97–NZ$150
ⓘ 40 unit
Ⓢ Ⓟ Off-street
🚌 200m (220 yards) from the Octagon and Dunedin Visitor Information Office

SOUTHERN CROSS
Corner of Princes and High streets, Dunedin
Tel 03-477 0752
www.scenic-circle.co.nz
Dunedin's premier hotel, located in the heart of the city, the Southern Cross dates back to 1883 when it was the original Grand Hotel. It has three in-house restaurants and two bars. The boutique casino is an added attraction for some guests. Rooms all have satellite TV, ironing facilities, hair dryers, tea-making facilities and internet access.
🖐 NZ$230–NZ$360
ⓘ 170 rooms, 8 suites
Ⓢ 🟦 Ⓟ Off-street
🚌 1km (0.5 miles) from the Octagon and Dunedin Visitor Information Office

SPECIAL IN DUNEDIN

CORSTORPHINE HOUSE PRIVATE HOTEL
23A Milburn Street, Corstorphine, Dunedin
Tel 03-487 6676/6672
www.corstorphine.co.nz
A listed 1863 heritage building, this five-star Edwardian-style private hotel sits in a 5ha (12-acre) estate and

commands fine views across the city. The house is beautifully appointed throughout, with stylish themed suites, from Scottish to art deco or a French boudoir. The estate produces flowers, vegetables, herbs, fruits, nuts and eggs for the house restaurant.
🖐 NZ$395–NZ$595, inc breakfast
ⓘ 7 rooms
Ⓢ Ⓟ
🚌 6km (4 miles) south of downtown

STAYING

INVERCARGILL

ASCOT PARK HOTEL

Corner of Tay Street and Racecourse Road, Invercargill

Tel 03-217 6195/0800-272 687

www.mainstay.co.nz

Ascot Park is in peaceful, park-like surroundings on the outskirts of Invercargill, and is the city's top hotel. Large and modern, it has a mix of deluxe,

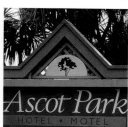

superior and standard rooms and motel units. It also has a restaurant, bar and tavern complex.

🍷 NZ$109–NZ$185

ℹ️ 72 rooms, 24 motel units

🚫 ♿ 🚗 🅿 Off-street

🚌 4km (2.5 miles) from the CBD

KAKA POINT

NUGGET VIEW, KAKA POINT AND CATLINS COAST MOTELS

11 Rata Street, Kaka Point

Tel 03-412 8602/0800-525 278

www.catlins.co.nz

As the name suggests, this complex has a variety of accommodation options, from economy to five-star luxury, all with ocean views. Open-plan studios have double beds; two-room apartments are suitable for families; superior spa units have a king bed and double spa bath. Kayaks and body boards are provided. The owners also operate fishing trips and eco-tours to The Nuggets.

🍷 NZ$75–NZ$280

ℹ️ 14 rooms

🚫 🅿

🚌 23km (14 miles) from Balclutha and SH1 via Highway 92. Turn off Highway 92 at Romahapa

MANAPOURI

BEECHWOOD LODGE

40 Cathedral Drive, Manapouri

Tel 03-249 6993

www.beechwoodlodge.com

A modern, deservedly popular boutique B&B that overlooks the lake and mountains, Beechwood accommodates

guests in two spacious en suites, which have their own private entrance and kitchen. The entire floor can also be booked as a suite. The real drawcard is the lounge, from which you can sit and muse upon the ever-changing moods of the lake. Not suitable for children.

🍷 NZ$300–NZ$400

ℹ️ 2 rooms

🚫 🅿 Off-street

🚌 20km (13 miles) south of Te Anau

MILFORD SOUND

MILFORD SOUND LODGE

Milford Road, Milford Sound

Tel 03-249 8071

www.milfordlodge.com

For the independent visitor, this backpackers' lodge is a great choice in Milford Sound. It can be very cosmopolitan and in midsummer, outside the local pub's opening hours, forms the hub of Milford's leisure activity. Single, double/twin and shared rooms are available, with shared bathrooms. The restaurant serves breakfast and pub meals. There's a kitchen, a large lounge and a store.

🍷 NZ$78

ℹ️ 8 double/twin units

🚫 🅿

🚌 On Milford Road, 1km (0.5 miles) east of Milford Sound airfield

OAMARU

KINGSGATE HOTEL BRYDONE

115 Thames Street, Oamaru

Tel 03-434 0011

www.millenniumhotels.co.nz

Oamaru's oldest and largest hotel, in the heart of town, the Brydone has an elegant Historic Wing, built in 1881 and furnished in period style, and a Pacific Wing, built in the 1970s. Despite the odd creaking floorboard, it's worth trying to book the former and soak up the atmosphere. The hotel has doubles or suites, some with spa baths, and there is a popular bar and restaurant.

🍷 NZ$140–NZ$248

ℹ️ 50 rooms

🚫 🅿

🚌 1km (0.5 miles) from Oamaru Visitor Information Office

QUEENSTOWN

EICHARDT'S PRIVATE HOTEL

Marine Parade, Queenstown

Tel 03-441 0450

www.eichardtshotel.co.nz

LARNACH LODGE

145 Camp Road, Otago Peninsula

Tel 03-476 1616

www.larnachcastle.co.nz

Larnach Lodge has beautifully appointed themed rooms, from the tartan Scottish Room to the Goldrush Room, with a king-size bed made

from an old cart found on the property. The views across the harbour and peninsula are superb. Breakfast is served in the former stables. Dinner is optional (NZ$50) in the castle. Less expensive rooms with shared bathrooms in the former coach house are also available. It's essential to book ahead.

🍷 NZ$270–NZ$240

ℹ️ 12 rooms

🚫

🚌 12km (8 miles) from Dunedin CBD via Highcliff and Camp roads

This centrally located, historic hotel was founded in 1866. Refurbished since the 1990s Queenstown floods, it now caters to the luxury boutique market. It has elegantly appointed suites with antiques and an open fire, and a guest parlour with overstuffed chairs and sofas against a backdrop of exquisite antiques.

🍷 NZ$1,375–NZ$1,595, inc breakfast

ℹ️ 5 suites

🚫

🚌 200m (220 yards) from Queenstown Visitor Information Office

HERITAGE QUEENSTOWN

91 Fernhill Road, Queenstown

Tel 03-442 4988/0800-368 888

www.heritagehotels.co.nz

The Heritage is on the western edge of town in a quiet position, with great views. Bedrooms include luxury suites, some self-contained with kitchen and laundry facilities, dishwasher and a full complement of crockery and glassware. There is an in-house restaurant with open fire.

🛏 NZ$140–NZ$618
🛏 197 rooms
🔲 🔲 🔲 🔲 🅿
🚌 2km (1 mile) west of Queenstown Visitor Information Office

MATAKAURI LODGE
Glenorchy Road, Queenstown
Tel 03-441 1008
www.matakauri.co.nz
This is a magnificent place, set in private bush with uninterrupted views across Lake Wakatipu. Accommodation is in modern villas and fully self-contained suites. The spacious lodge has a library and four fireplaces, and the spa pavilion in the grounds is perfect for après-ski. Dinner is served with top local wines.

SPECIAL IN QUEENSTOWN
QUEENSTOWN HOUSE
69 Hallenstein Street, Queenstown
Tel 03-442 9043
www.queenstownhouse.co.nz
Refurbished in 2002, this well-established modern upper-range B&B is in a central location overlooking the town. Accommodation

comprises elegant en suites and new villa suites with fireside sitting rooms. The pre-dinner hospitality hour is a speciality—you can sample NZ wine, cheeses and seasonal treats, while exchanging experiences and sharing restaurant recommendations. The full cooked or Continental breakfasts are excellent. Internet access.

🛏 NZ$225–NZ$895, inc breakfast
🛏 13 rooms
🔲 🅿 Off-street
🚌 500m (550 yards) from Queenstown Visitor Information Office

🛏 NZ$1,164–NZ$1,991, inc dinner
🛏 6 suites and villa suites
🔲 🔲 🔲
🚌 5km (3 miles) west of Queenstown

STEWART ISLAND/ RAKIURA
PORT OF CALL BOUTIQUE ACCOMMODATION
Jensen Bay, Stewart Island
Tel 03-219 1394
www.portofcall.co.nz
In an idyllic spot overlooking the entrance to Halfmoon Bay, surrounded by 8ha (20 acres) of native bush and abundant

bird life, this B&B has a charming double en suite, with great breakfasts and views from the deck. There are also the Bush and Tree cottages, both self-contained. The friendly hosts also have an eco-guiding operation.

🛏 NZ$285, inc breakfast, cottage NZ$160–NZ$250
🛏 1 guest room, 2 cottages
🔲
🚌 1km (0.5 miles) east of the village

SOUTH SEA HOTEL
Main Road, Oban
Tel 03-219 1059
www.stewart-island.co.nz
This is a great place to stay if you wish to mix with the locals and experience Stewart Island life. There are traditional hotel rooms (some with sea views) and self-contained motel units on a nearby property. There is a bar, and a restaurant where you can sample the local delicacy—muttonbird.

🛏 NZ$80–NZ$135
🛏 30 rooms, 9 motel units
🔲
🚌 100m (110 yards) from the ferry

TE ANAU
FIORDLAND LODGE
472 Te Anau–Milford Highway
Tel 03-249 7832
www.fiordlandlodge.co.nz
A purpose-built luxury lodge in the classic style, this has

stunning views across the lake and mountains. Facilities include smart guest rooms, two self-contained log cabins and a restaurant. The high

ceilings, full tree-trunk pillars and huge windows add to the appeal and sense of space.

🛏 Cabins NZ$300–NZ$420, inc breakfast; suites NZ$520–NZ$1,040, inc breakfast and dinner
🛏 10 rooms, 2 cabins
🔲
🚌 5km (3 miles) north of Te Anau

WANAKA
CARDRONA HOTEL
Crown Range Road (SH89), Cardrona
Tel 03-443 8153,
www.cardronahotel.co.nz
The Cardrona may be a little out of the way, but is well worth the journey. The hotel is over 140 years old and retains much of its character. Double rooms in the old stables look out over a beautiful garden and courtyard. There is a great rustic restaurant and bar. Advance booking essential.

🛏 NZ$185
🛏 16 rooms
🔲
🚌 On the Crown Range Road 26km (16 miles) south of Wanaka

THE MOORINGS
17 Lakeside Road, Wanaka
Tel 03-443 8479
www.themoorings.co.nz
This modern, classy boutique apartment and motel block overlooks the lake, and is only metres from the lakeshore and the heart of town. Stylish motel rooms have underfloor heating and balcony views, and the spacious apartments have log burners and individual carports. Satellite TV and ski-drying room are available.

🛏 NZ$160–NZ$345
🛏 14 motel units, 8 apartments
🔲
🚌 100m (110 yards) from Wanaka Visitor Information Office

STAYING

Planning

BEFORE YOU GO

TIME ZONES		
CITY	TIME DIFFERENCE IN HOURS	TIME AT 12 NOON IN NZ
Amsterdam	-11	1am
Berlin	-11	1am
Brussels	-11	1am
Cairo	-10	2am
Chicago	-18	6pm (previous day)
Dublin	-12	midnight
Johannesburg	-10	2am
London	-12	midnight
Madrid	-10	2am
Montréal	-17	7pm (previous day)
New York	-17	7pm (previous day)
Paris	-11	1am
Perth, Australia	-4	8am
San Francisco	-20	4pm (previous day)
Sydney	-2	10am
Tokyo	-3	9am

New Zealand is one of the first countries in the world to see the dawn. Standard time is 12 hours ahead of Greenwich Mean Time, and New Zealand Daylight Saving Time (summer time) runs from 2am on the first Sunday in October to 2am on the third Sunday in March. During this period clocks go forward one hour.

CLIMATE

New Zealand has what is called an ocean temperate climate—that is, generally agreeable. As the country is fairly elongated and lies at a north-to-south angle, the weather varies considerably. The north is consistently a few degrees warmer than the south; the warmest region is usually Northland and the coldest Southland. However, especially in recent years, uncommon weather patterns have seen the reverse to be true, sometimes for days on end.

● In Auckland average temperatures for winter (June–August) are 8°C to 15°C (46°F to 59°F) and for summer (December–March) 14°C to 23°C (57°F to 74°F).

● In Dunedin winter temperatures average at 4°C to 12°C (39°F to 53°F) and summer temperatures at 9°C to 19°C (48°F to 66°F). But this can be misleading. Inland from

Snow on the central volcanic peaks of the North Island

Dunedin, Alexandra is often the hottest spot in the country.

● Nelson and Marlborough, in the South Island, have won the competition for sunniest place for several years running. Next year, though, it could just as easily be Napier, on the relatively dry and sunny east coast of the North Island, or even Whakatane in the Bay of Plenty.

● Wellington and Auckland also boast a lot of sunshine, Auckland being far more humid and Wellington notoriously windier.

● The west coast and Fiordland also have extremes of wind and rain, but even in winter the rain in New Zealand doesn't last for long periods.

WHEN TO GO

The summer, or high season, lasts from November to March and is the busiest time, when New Zealanders are themselves taking a break. At these times, especially over Christmas and

WEATHER STATIONS

Auckland
6m
20ft

WELLINGTON
128m
420ft

Christchurch
34m
112ft

AUCKLAND
TEMPERATURE

Average temperature per day
per night

°C 30 20 10 0

°F 86 68 50 32

J F M A M J J A S O N D

RAINFALL

Average rainfall

mm 160 120 80 40 0

in 6 4.5 3 1.5 0

J F M A M J J A S O N D

CHRISTCHURCH
TEMPERATURE

Average temperature per day
per night

°C 30 20 10 0

°F 86 68 50 32

J F M A M J J A S O N D

RAINFALL

Average rainfall

mm 160 120 80 40 0

in 6 4.5 3 1.5 0

J F M A M J J A S O N D

WELLINGTON
TEMPERATURE

Average temperature per day
per night

°C 30 20 10 0

°F 86 68 50 32

J F M A M J J A S O N D

RAINFALL

Average rainfall

mm 160 120 80 40 0

in 6 4.5 3 1.5 0

J F M A M J J A S O N D

PLANNING

the whole of January, almost the entire country shuts up shop and heads for the beach or the mountains. Accommodation is at a premium and the roads to major resorts can be busy—though in some areas, particularly the remoter parts of the South Island, 'busy' can mean a car passing every five or ten minutes.

• The months of late spring (September–October) or early autumn (March–April) are good alternatives. At these times the weather is still pleasant, accommodation easier to find and prices lower. The winter, or low season, sits between April/May and August/September.

• Some places close in winter but generally New Zealand serves its visitors year-round. Places such as Queenstown, where skiing is a major activity, can be busier in winter than they are in summer.

NATURAL HAZARDS
Be aware that the sun in New Zealand is dangerous. Ozone depletion is heavy in the southern latitudes and the incidence of melanoma and other skin cancers is above average. Burn times, especially in summer, are greatly reduced: always wear a hat and appropriate sun block.

• If you are climbing, tramping or going into the bush, note that the weather is particularly changeable at higher elevations and can sometimes be deadly. Make sure you are properly clothed and shod and take maps, a first-aid kit and a compass. Above all, inform someone of your intentions.

• Major volcanic eruptions and earthquakes are rare but they do happen and can prove fatal. In

the event of an earthquake stand in a doorway, get under a table or, if you are in the open, get indoors or keep away from loose rock formations and trees.

• Advance weather reports and safety information can be found on the Department of Conservation's website, **www.doc.govt.nz**.

PASSPORTS AND VISAS
All visitors must be in possession of a passport that is valid for three months beyond the date of intended departure. Australian citizens or holders of an Australian returning resident visa do not need a visitor's visa and can stay in New Zealand indefinitely. Citizens of some countries, including the UK and the US, do not need visas for stays of up to three months (six months for UK citizens).

• For detailed visa information consult the Visiting section of the Immigration New Zealand (INZ) website, **www.immigration.govt.nz** or contact them at NZIS, Private Bag, Wellesley Street, Auckland (tel 09-914 4100/0508-558 855).

• Entry requirements can change: Always check before you travel.

LONGER STAYS/WORK VISAS
It is illegal to work on a visitor's permit. Non-residents (with the exception of Australian citizens)

New Zealand's exceptionally clear air makes for great photos but also certain health risks

must obtain a work visa, which allows entry to the country, and then a work permit, which allows the holder to work on arrival. Applications for both should be made well before arrival. The INZ website has details and application forms that can be downloaded.

• One exception to the rule is the working holiday visa, which is available for those aged 18 to 30 from countries including Argentina, Canada, Chile, Denmark, France, Germany, Hong Kong, Ireland, Italy, Japan, Korea, Malaysia, Netherlands, Singapore, Sweden, Taiwan, UK and Uruguay. This allows holders to work for 12 months.

• Student visas are needed for anyone (other than Australian citizens) planning to study a course of more than three months; anyone studying shorter courses will need a valid visitor's permit.

TRAVEL INSURANCE
Full travel insurance is recommended, covering at least medical care and personal effects.

• The New Zealand accident compensation scheme (ACC) covers visitors to New Zealand for personal injury by accident. Benefits include some emergency medical expenses, but do not include loss of earnings.

• Healthline gives free 24-hour health advice and tells you how best to access the New Zealand health system, tel 0800 611 116.

• There is a wide variety of policies from which to choose, so shop around. Always read the small print carefully and check

NEW ZEALAND EMBASSIES ABROAD		
COUNTRY	**ADDRESS**	**WEBSITE**
Australia	High Commission: Commonwealth Avenue, Canberra, ACT 2600, tel 02-6270 4211	www.nzembassy.com
Canada	High Commission: Suite 727, Metropolitan House, 99 Bank Street, Ottowa, Ont K1P 6G3, tel 613/238-5991	www.nzembassy.com
France	7ter, rue Leonard de Vinci, 75116 Paris, tel 01 45 01 43 43	www.nzembassy.com
Germany	Atrium, Friedrichstrasse 60, 10117, Berlin, tel 30 206 210	www.nzembassy.com
Ireland	Consulate, PO Box 999, Dublin 6, tel 01 660 4233	www.nzembassy.com
Netherlands	Carnegielaan 10, 2517 KH, Den Haag, tel 703 469324	www.nzembassy.com
UK	High Commission: New Zealand House, Haymarket, London SW1Y 4TQ, tel 020 7930 8422	www.nzembassy.com
USA	37 Observatory Circle NW, Washington DC 20008, tel 202/328-4800	www.nzembassy.com

that the policy covers any activities you may intend to pursue, such as white-water rafting or bungy jumping. Also check exactly what the medical cover includes—for example, ambulance, helicopter rescue or emergency flights home. You may have to pay before being reimbursed by the insurance company, so check the payment protocol.

WHAT TO TAKE

New Zealand is a well-developed nation and all you are likely to need, from pharmaceuticals to camping equipment, is readily available throughout the country.
● If you are backpacking, bring a good sleeping bag and a bed sheet, items which are not always provided in hostels and which are certainly not available in backcountry tramping huts.
● Other items to remember are a compatible electrical adaptor plug, binoculars, a sun hat, sunscreen, insect repellent and sunglasses.

CUSTOMS AND DUTY-FREE ALLOWANCES

New Zealand's environment and unique biodiversity have been decimated by non-native flora and fauna. Not surprisingly, therefore, the country has strict bio-security laws. You must not bring with you any fruit, animal or plant matter of any kind without prior permission. Heavy fines are imposed on those breaking the rules. Comprehensive advice for visitors is available on the New Zealand Customs Service website, **www**.customs.govt.nz.

If you are over 17 years of age you may import the following:

- 200 cigarettes or 250g of tobacco or 50 cigars or a combination of all three weighing no more than 250g
- 4.5 litres of wine or beer and one 1.125l bottle of spirits, liqueur or other alcoholic drink

Goods of value up to NZ$700 are duty- and tax-free.

PRACTICALITIES

ELECTRICITY
The New Zealand supply is 230/240 volts (50 hertz).
● Plugs are either two- or three-pronged with flat pins.
● North American appliances require both an adaptor and a transformer.
● UK appliances need an adaptor only, and Australian appliances are the same.
● Adaptors and transformers are available at local hardware stores or at the airport.

Laundromats are convenient if you're travelling widely

LAUNDRY
Most towns, villages and places to stay have laundry services.
● Washing and drying machines tend to operate with NZ$1 or NZ$2 coins.
● A full wash and dry costs about NZ$6.

MEASUREMENTS
New Zealand uses the metric system. Distances are measured and signed in kilometres and fuel is sold in litres. However, if you ask for a pint in a pub you will be understood.

PUBLIC TOILETS
Public toilets are readily available in towns and large villages and at major visitor attractions, urban parks and fuel stations. They are usually clean and well maintained. You may also be able to use conveniences at libraries or visitor offices.

CONVERSION CHART

FROM	TO	MULTIPLY BY
Inches	Centimetres	2.54
Centimetres	Inches	0.3937
Feet	Metres	0.3048
Metres	Feet	3.2810
Yards	Metres	0.9144
Metres	Yards	1.0940
Miles	Kilometres	1.6090
Kilometres	Miles	0.6214
Acres	Hectares	0.4047
Hectares	Acres	2.4710
Gallons	Litres	4.5460
Litres	Gallons	0.2200
Ounces	Grams	28.35
Grams	Ounces	0.0353
Pounds	Grams	453.6
Grams	Pounds	0.0022
Pounds	Kilograms	0.4536
Kilograms	Pounds	2.205
Tons	Tonnes	1.0160
Tonnes	Tons	0.9842

CLOTHING SIZES
The chart below shows how British, European and US clothing sizes differ.

UK	Europe	US	
36	46	36	SUITS
38	48	38	
40	50	40	
42	52	42	
44	54	44	
46	56	46	
48	58	48	
7	41	8	SHOES
7.5	42	8.5	
8.5	43	9.5	
9.5	44	10.5	
10.5	45	11.5	
11	46	12	
14.5	37	14.5	SHIRTS
15	38	15	
15.5	39/40	15.5	
16	41	16	
16.5	42	16.5	
17	43	17	
8	36	6	DRESSES
10	38	8	
12	40	10	
14	42	12	
16	44	14	
18	46	16	
20	46	18	
4.5	37.5	6	SHOES
5	38	6.5	
5.5	38.5	7	
6	39	7.5	
6.5	40	8	
7	41	8.5	

PLANNING

- Public toilets are usually free of charge and are run by local councils. Find out where they are located and when they open on **www.**govt.nz.
- Many toilets have two press-button flushes: one (usually marked with a circle) gives a full flush and the other (marked with a semi-circle) gives a half-flush to save water.

SMOKING REGULATIONS

New Zealand is increasingly smoke-free, and since December 2004, all bars, clubs, restaurants, cafés, casinos and gaming machine venues have been required to be entirely smoke-free indoors if they are work-places, serve alcohol or have a gambling licence.
- Budget Rent-a-Car have declared themselves a smoke-free company (0800-283 438, **www.**budget.co.nz).

VISITING WITH CHILDREN

Smelly springs, steaming vents, sandy beaches and a bewildering range of activities make New Zealand an excellent destination for children—not to speak of the set locations to be tracked down from the *Lord of the Rings* movies.
- There are discounts for children on public transport and at most attractions, and many offer family tickets as well. Most major attractions allow very young children free admission.
- Several companies specialise in organising trips and tours tailored for families: try **www.**familytravel.co.nz.
- A good source of information on family-based activities throughout New Zealand is **www.**familystophere.com.

Discounts for children are usually available

- Most hotels offer or can recommend a babysitting service, but don't be afraid to ask about the qualifications of the babysitter or the conditions applied to the service.
- Make sure children are well protected against the New Zealand sun, as their skin is more vulnerable than adult skin. Hats, sun-screen and long sleeved shirts can all help to avoid painful sunburn.
- Baby-on-the-Move is a company renting out and selling baby products to overseas visitors. Products include lightweight frames for prams or pushchairs (strollers), newborn and toddler seats for cars, detachable cots and child-carrying backpacks (tel 0800 222 966, **www.**babyonthemove.co.nz).

VISITORS WITH A DISABILITY

For visitors with disabilities New Zealand can be a frustrating place. While most public amenities are well equipped for wheelchair use, older hotels and some public transport systems (particularly rural buses) are not well adapted. However, it is now a requirement by law to have adequate facilities in new buildings.
- Larger airlines such as Air New Zealand and Qantas are well equipped and this applies both to international and to domestic flights.
- Visitors with disabilities usually receive discounts on travel and some admission charges, and parking concessions are also available, with temporary cards issued on receipt of a mobility card or medical certificate.
- Full details on local services are available from regional Disability Information Centres; a list of contacts can be obtained from the head office at PO Box 24-042, Royal Oak, Auckland (tel 09-625 8069/0800 693 342, **www.**weka.net.nz).
- Some tour operators specialise in providing itineraries and equipment for visitors with disabilities: for more details ▷ 54, On the Move: Visitors with a Disability.

PLACES OF WORSHIP

Most large urban centres in New Zealand have Anglican,

The oldest church in the country is at Russell and dates from 1835

Presbyterian, Baptist, Methodist and Catholic places of worship.
- Some useful websites are: **www.**baptist.org.nz **www.**rcnz.org.nz **www.**methodist.org.nz **www.**presbyterian.org.nz **www.**anglican.org.nz **www.**catholic.org.nz
- There are several mosques in Auckland, Hamilton, Palmerston North, Wellington, Christchurch and Dunedin. Full addresses are available on **www.**nzmuslim.net.
- There are synagogues in Auckland, Hamilton, Christchurch, Wellington and Dunedin; details of addresses are listed on the website **www.**haruth.com.
- The Auckland Buddhist Centre is run by the Western Buddhist Order and has a shrine room at 381 Richmond Road, Grey Lynn, Auckland (tel 09-378 1120, **www.** aucklandbuddhistcentre.org).
- The largest Maori religious movements are Ringatu and Ratana, now both regarded as Maori Christian churches. Ratana has more than 49,000 members and Ringatu over 8,000. The Ratana Church is based at Ratana, Taranaki province, in the North Island, and Ringatu membership is largely concentrated in the northern half of the island.

MONEY

BANKNOTES AND COINS

● The New Zealand currency is the dollar (NZ$), which is divided into 100 cents (c). Coins are in denominations of 10c, 20c, 50c, NZ$1 and NZ$2. Notes come in NZ$5, NZ$10, NZ$20, NZ$50 and NZ$100 denominations.

● Banknotes feature people important to New Zealand: Sir Edmund Hillary, conqueror of Everest (NZ$5); Kate Sheppard, pioneer of female emancipation (NZ$10); The Queen (NZ$20); Sir Apirana Ngata, Maori statesman (NZ$50); and Lord Rutherford, who split the atom (NZ$100).

CREDIT CARDS, ATMS AND EFTPOS

● All major credit cards (Visa, MasterCard, Amex, JCB, Diners)

ATMs are widely available

are widely accepted. New Zealand operates an EFTPOS (Electronic Funds Transfer at Point of Sale) system, which effectively means that there are mini-ATMs at points of sale throughout the country. Most hotels, shops, retail outlets and fuel stations have EFTPOS. Debit and credit cards may be used with the relevant PIN numbers.

● Standard ATMs are available in almost all towns and accept non-host bank cards, though there may be hidden fees. Some banks are linked internationally via such networks as Cirrus and Plus.

● New Zealand's banks include the ANZ National Bank, ASB Bank, Bank of New Zealand, Kiwibank, TSB Bank and Westpac. Most are represented in all main towns, and branches or ATMs operated by one or more of the banks can be found in smaller places. Internet banking facilities are also popular. For a full list see www.rbnz.govt.nz/nzbanks/.

● Bank opening hours are

CASH

The New Zealand currency is the dollar (NZ$), which is divided into 100 cents (c). Coins are in denominations of 10c, 20c, 50c, NZ$1 and NZ$2. Notes come in NZ$5, NZ$10, NZ$20, NZ$50 and NZ$100 denominations.

For further information on New Zealand currency, and how to tell whether a New Zealand note is genuine, please go to www.rbnz.govt.nz/currency/money/index.html.

All images shown are not to scale.

PLANNING

Relaxed café society has become a regular part of New Zealand life

10 EVERYDAY ITEMS AND HOW MUCH THEY COST	
Sandwich	NZ$4
50cl bottle of water	NZ$2
Cup of tea or coffee	NZ$3
Pint of beer	NZ$6–NZ$7
Glass of wine	NZ$5
Daily newspaper	NZ$1.20
Roll of camera film	NZ$7–NZ$14
20 cigarettes	NZ$10
Ice cream	NZ$2.50
Litre of fuel	NZ$1.50

LOST OR STOLEN CREDIT CARDS

Visa International
0800-443 019

MasterCard International
0800-449 140
or any bank displaying the VISA
or MasterCard trademark

American Express
0800-656 660
or any American Express
Travel Service Office

Monday to Friday 9–4.30; some city branches also open on Saturday until 12.30.
● Exchange offices such as Travelex and American Express sometimes stay open until 9pm in the cities.

TRAVELLERS' CHEQUES
The safest way to carry money is in travellers' cheques. These are available for a small commission from all major banks. American Express (Amex), Visa and Thomas Cook cheques are widely accepted.
● Most banks do not charge for changing travellers' cheques and they usually offer the best exchange rates.
● Be sure to keep a record of your cheque numbers and keep the cheques you have cashed separate from the cheques themselves, so that you can get a full refund of all uncashed cheques should you lose them.
● It is best to bring NZ$ cheques to avoid exchange costs.

WIRING MONEY
If you need money quickly or in an emergency, you can have it wired to you via any major bank with Western Union (through New Zealand Post, tel 0800-005 253) or via Travelex and moneygram (tel 0800-200 232, www.travelex.co.nz). This transfer can be completed in less than an hour or may take up to a week depending on how much is being wired and how much you are willing to pay (about NZ$30–NZ$80).

TAXES
A 12.5 per cent GST (Goods and Services Tax) is placed on almost every bought item in New Zealand. Prices quoted almost always include GST, but on bigger items or services it pays to check. On leaving New Zealand there is a departure charge of NZ$20–NZ$25, depending on which airport you use. This is not included in your ticket price.

TIPPING
Tipping is at the customer's discretion and is not generally expected in New Zealand.

Visitors can reclaim GST on more expensive items

HEALTH

VACCINATIONS

No vaccinations are officially required for entry into New Zealand. You are, however, advised to get a tetanus shot or ensure that your booster is up to date.

TREATMENT COSTS

If you are injured in an accident while in New Zealand you are covered for treatment, regardless of fault, under the national personal injury insurance scheme, run by the Accident Rehabilitation and Compensation Insurance Corporation (ACC): PO Box 242, Wellington (tel 04-918 7700/0800 101 996, www.acc.co.nz); there are also 31 branch offices spread all over the country—details are available on the website. The provider of your treatment will help you complete the appropriate form.

● If you see a doctor or another healthcare professional for treatment for a personal injury, you may be asked to pay part of the cost.

● ACC does not cover illness, so health insurance is highly recommended, as standard visits to the doctor cost about NZ$40 excluding prescription charges, and dental and hospital services are expensive. See also Before You Go, pages 292–294.

WHAT TO TAKE

● It's advisable to take photocopies of your insurance documents and to keep these separately from the originals, or scan them onto an e-mail address that can be reached from abroad, in case they are lost in an accident or stolen.

● If you are on unusual medication take supplies with you in case they are not easily available locally, and bring your prescription certificate in case of difficulties at customs.

● New Zealand's sun is dangerous due to ozone depletion, so be sure to bring a hat, sunglassess and the strongest possible sunblock to protect against the damage caused by ultraviolet rays. Be prepared to cover up, and be sure to wear this protection even on overcast days.

● Bring an insect repellent, especially to ward off the common and very annoying

---

HEALTHY FLYING

● Visitors to New Zealand from as far as the US, UK and other parts of Europe may be concerned about the effect of long-haul flights on their health. The most widely publicised concern is Deep Vein Thrombosis, or DVT. Misleadingly called 'economy class syndrome', DVT is the forming of a blood clot in the body's deep veins, particularly in the legs. The clot can move around the bloodstream and could be fatal.

● Those most at risk include the elderly, pregnant women, those using the contraceptive pill, smokers and the overweight. If you are at increased risk of DVT see your doctor before departing. Flying increases the likelihood of DVT because passengers are often seated in a cramped position for long periods of time and may become dehydrated.

To minimise risk:
Drink water (not alcohol)
Don't stay immobile for hours at a time
Stretch and exercise your legs periodically
Do wear elastic flight socks, which support veins and reduce the chances of a clot forming

EXERCISES

1 ANKLE ROTATIONS   **2 CALF STRETCHES**   **3 KNEE LIFTS**

Lift feet off the floor. Draw a circle with the toes, moving one foot clockwise and the other counterclockwise

Start with heel on the floor and point foot upward as high as you can. Then lift heels high, keeping balls of feet on the floor

Lift leg with knee bent while contracting your thigh muscle. Then straighten leg, pressing foot flat to the floor

Other health hazards for flyers are airborne diseases and bugs spread by the plane's air-conditioning system. These are largely unavoidable but if you have a serious medical condition seek advice from a doctor before flying.

Sun hats are essential wear, even on hazy days

sandflies. The size of a pinhead, they are found in some coastal and wetter inland areas, and their bite can produce unpleasant spots on the skin that may itch for weeks. Repellents come in two forms: chemical-based—which are toxic and should be used only in the lowest concentrations (5–10 per cent)—and natural. If you are unable to find natural repellent at home, New Zealand manufacturers offer a wide range of natural creams and oils using ingredients such as eucalyptus or citronella.

PLANNING

HAZARDS
● New Zealand is a great outdoors destination for visitors. Make sure you match your chosen activities to your level of fitness and skill, and that you are fully equipped for sudden changes in the weather.
● When tramping (hiking) be aware that water levels in streams and rivers can change swiftly. On coastal walks such as the Abel Tasman (▷ 108–110) be aware of local tides and their likely impact on your route and schedule.
● If you are planning a serious hike or an overnight trip, make sure someone knows your intentions and when to raise the alarm if you are missing. You can sign in at the start of your trip at a Department of Conservation (DoC) visitor centre—but make sure you remember to sign out again on your safe return. Unless you are very experienced, tramping alone on the more remote and quieter tracks is not advisable.
● There are very few dangerous creatures in New Zealand. One exception is the katipo spider, about 25mm (0.9in) from leg tip to leg tip and found on beaches, under stones and in driftwood throughout the North Island and

Watch out for falling rocks

in parts of the South. Its bite inflicts agonising localised pain and can be fatal. Antivenom is readily available in hospitals.
● Sharks are a common sight around New Zealand shores, but shark attacks on humans are rare. The last fatal attack occurred in Eastland in 1976.
● Giardia is a water-borne parasite which, if it enters your system, causes severe vomiting and diarrhoea and rapid weight loss. The best safeguard is not to drink water from lakes, ponds or rivers without boiling it first.
● Tap water is safe to drink throughout New Zealand; city supplies are chlorinated and most are also fluoridated.

HOSPITALS
● There are public hospitals throughout the North and South Islands of New Zealand. Most, but not all, of these have emergency facilities—details are in the front of every white pages telephone directory.

AMBULANCES
● In an emergency dial 111 anywhere in the country for an ambulance.
● Ambulances in most of the country are provided by organisations like St. John Ambulance, which charge patients for their use—this cost should be covered by medical insurance.
● The exception is Wellington, where the Wellington Free Ambulance makes no charge for its services, and is supported by public donations.
● In remoter areas and offshore islands, rescue helicopters and fixed-wing air ambulances are used where necessary.

DOCTORS
● There are about 10,000 doctors in New Zealand. The Medical Council of New Zealand supplies a list of registered doctors and updates it weekly: The Medical Council of New Zealand, Level 13, Mid City Tower, 139–143 Willis Street, PO Box 11 649, Wellington (tel 04-384 7635, **www.**mcnz.org.nz).
● Many cities and towns have private after-hours clinics and pharmacies, which treat non-emergency cases for a fee. Details are in the white pages telephone directory.

DENTISTS
● Emergency dentists can be found in the telephone directory Yellow Pages.

PHARMACIES
● New Zealand pharmacists are known as chemists, and their shops sell a selection of cosmetics and other products, as well as drugs.
● Chemist shops open during normal shopping hours, and in most large towns and cities

emergency dispensaries are open outside these hours as well. These are listed in the front of the phone book, under Hospitals.
● Some drugs sold over the counter in other countries may be available in New Zealand only with a prescription.

ALTERNATIVE MEDICINE
● The New Zealand Charter of Health Practitioners is the biggest organisation representing complementary and alternative health (CAM) practitioners in New Zealand. Members of its signatories must meet a set level of competence and are entitled to advertise as chartered health practitioners: New Zealand Charter of Health Practitioners, Private Box 302 305, North Harbour, Auckland, tel 09-414 5501, **www.**healthcharter.org.nz.
● The New Zealand Register of Complementary Health Professionals (NZRCHP) provides a directory of practitioners who have trained and qualified in their discipline and who abide by their field's code of ethics: NZRCHP, PO Box 337, Christchurch.

EMERGENCIES
● Contact details for hospital Accident and Emergency departments are listed in the front of the white pages telephone directory.
● In an emergency, dial 111 for an ambulance.

COMMUNICATION

National directory assistance
018
International directory assistance
0172
International operator
0170
Toll help desk
123

TELEPHONES

Payphones are readily available throughout the country and are colour-coded. Both coin (blue) and credit card (yellow) booths are available.

● Phone cards come in NZ$5, NZ$10, NZ$20 and NZ$50 denominations and can be bought from many retail outlets, post and visitor information offices, fuel stations and hostels. Do not use these cards for anything other than domestic calls within New Zealand.

● Coin phones take 10c, 20c, 50c, NZ$1 and NZ$2 coins.

● If you dial 013 (instead of 0) before the number the operator will call back after you have finished to let you know the cost of your call, but this service adds NZ$2.80 to the overall cost.

● Local non-business calls cost 50c from public telephones, but are free from residential telephones in New Zealand, so it should not cause offence if you

COUNTRY CODES FROM NEW ZEALAND	
Australia	00 61
Belgium	00 32
Canada	00 1
France	00 33
Germany	00 49
Greece	00 30
Ireland	00 353
Italy	00 39
Netherlands	00 31
Spain	00 34
Sweden	00 46
UK	00 44
USA	00 1
New Zealand international code: 00 64	

AREA CODES WITHIN NEW ZEALAND	
Auckland	09
Northland	09
Bay of Plenty	07
Coromandel	07
Taupo	07
Ruapehu	07
Waikato	07
Eastland	06
Hawkes Bay	06
Wanganui	06
Taranaki	06
Wellington	04
South Island	03

Internet cafés offer swift communication (top); public phone boxes (right) accept a variety of payment methods

POST SHOPS WITH POST RESTANTE PICK-UP POINTS		
CITY	**ADDRESS AND TELEPHONE**	**OPEN**
Auckland	24 Wellesley Street, Bledisloe Street, tel 09-379 6710	Mon–Fri 7.30–5.30
Christchurch	3 Cathedral Square, tel 03-377 5411	Mon–Fri 8–6, Sat 10–4
Dunedin	243 Princes Street, tel 03-477 3518	Mon–Fri 8.30–5.30
Nelson	Corner of Trafalgar and Halifax streets, tel 03-546 7818	Mon–Fri 7.45–5, Sat 9.30–12.30
Queenstown	15–19 Camp Street, tel 03-422 7670	Mon–Fri 8.30am–10pm, Sat 9–4
Wellington	43 Manners Street, tel 04-473 5922	Mon–Fri 8–5.30, Sat 10–1.30

PLANNING

ask to use a host's or a friend's domestic (non-business) telephone for that purpose.
• Toll-free numbers start with 0508 or 0800. 0900 numbers are usually very expensive.
• Cell phone numbers usually start with 027 (Telecom) or 021 (Vodafone).

INTERNATIONAL CALLS
There are now numerous inexpensive international calling cards and call centres, one of the best being E Phone, www.telstraclear.co.nz, a calling card that accesses the net through an 0800 number. The cards, which vary from NZ$10 to NZ$50, can be bought from shops displaying the E Phone flag sign. Cards come with simple instructions and can be used from any landline telephone. Voice instructions guide you through the process and tell you how much credit you have available before you make each call.
• Credit cards can be used directly in many public phones.

INTERNET AND E-MAIL
Internet cafés and terminals are everywhere in New Zealand and it is fairly easy to get email access. The major cities are well served with internet outlets and most towns have cafés or terminals, often in visitor information offices or libraries. These charge the standard rates of NZ$2–NZ$5 per hour.
• Speed of access varies considerably.

POSTAL SERVICES
Post offices, called Post Shops, typically open Monday to Friday 9–5, Saturday 9–12.30.
• Mail can also be sent to Post Restante, CPO (Chief Post Office) in the main cities, where it will be held for up to 30 days.

• If you are being sent mail make sure the sender marks your surname in capitals and underlines it.
• Within New Zealand standard post costs 45c for medium letters and postcards (two to three days); 80c for Fastpost (airmail) to domestic centres (one to two days); NZ$1.50 for airmail letters to Australia and NZ$2 for standard overseas airmail letters to Europe, North America and East Asia.
• When sending cards and letters overseas be sure to use the free blue 'air economy' stickers. Books of stamps are available in Post Shops, as are pre-paid envelopes and a range of purpose-made cardboard boxes. Stamps can also be bought in bookstores, fuel stations and supermarkets.
• Average international delivery times depend on the day of the week the item is posted, and can take anywhere from four to twelve days to the UK or North America.

INTERNET ACCESS POINTS		
CITY	**ADDRESS**	**TELEPHONE**
NORTH ISLAND		
Auckland	City Library, 44–46 Lorne Street	09-377 0209
	Cyberdate2, 320 Queen Street	09-377 0320
	Login 1, 1/12 Rialto Centre, 163 Broadway, Newmarket	09-522 9303
	Net Central Cybercafé, 5 Lorne Street	09-373 5186
	Net Zone, 4 Fort Street	09-377 3906
	Email access: Travellers Contact Point, 87 Queen Street	09-300 7197
Napier	Cybers, 98 Dickens Street	06-835 0125
Palmerston North	icafé, corner of the Square and Fitzherbert Avenue	06-353 7899
Rotorua	E-Funz, 1174 Huapapa Street	07-349 3789
	Cybershed, 1176 Pukuatua Street	07-349 4965
	Heavenley's Internet Bar and Café, 1195 Fenton Street	07-348 3288
Wellington	Cyber City, 99 Courtenay Place	04-384 3717
	Cyber Spot, Lambton Square, 180 Lambton Quay	04-473 0098
	Library, Victoria Street, Civic Square	04-801 4040
SOUTH ISLAND		
Christchurch	E Blah Blah, 53–57 Cathedral Square	03-377 2381
	Cyber Pass Internet Café, 27 Chancery Lane	03-365 9000
	Dungeon and Dragon, 705 Colombo Street	03-372 3450
Dunedin	Dunedin Cue Club and Cyber Café, 65 St. Andrew Street	03-477 3064
	Webrunner, 237 Moray Place	03-471 8182
Greymouth	Grey District Library, Mackay Street	03-768 5597
Nelson	Aurora Tech, 161 Trafalgar Street	03-546 6867
	Café Affair, 295 Trafalgar Street	03-548 8295
Queenstown	Internet Output, 27 Shotover Street	03-441 3018
	E Café, 50 Shotover Street	03-442 9888
	Internet Depot, 26 Shotover Street	03-442 8581

FINDING HELP

PERSONAL SECURITY

New Zealand has its fair share of crime, and while visitors are rarely targeted for anything other than petty crime, it pays to be careful.

● Theft is rife, especially in Auckland, and tourist hotels, hostels and other accommodation are not exempt.

● Cars and campervans and their contents are regularly targeted, and are especially vulnerable when left at isolated but well-known beauty spots. Carry all money and valuables with you, and lock anything else safe and out of sight in the boot (trunk). Keep your vehicle locked at all times, and make sure your insurance covers theft.

● Hitching is still quite heavily practised in New Zealand but is not entirely safe, and is inadvisable for those travelling alone. If you do decide to hitch, keep to the main highways and restrict your hitching to the daylight hours; and never take off a rucksack and put that or a bag in the car first.

EMERGENCY PHONE NUMBER
Police, Fire or Ambulance **111**

LOST PROPERTY

Report any lost property to the local police station; www.police.govt.nz has a list of all station addresses.

● See page 297 for numbers to contact regarding lost or stolen credit cards.

POLICE

The New Zealand police force is a national service responsible for enforcing criminal and traffic laws.

● Police wear light blue shirts with epaulettes and insignia on the arms; darker blue tie and trousers; and dark blue peaked caps with a chequerboard design around the band.

● The police organisation is divided into 12 districts, each of which has a central station. Contact details for some of the major stations are listed in the table below. For a list of all police stations, see www.police.govt.nz

WHAT TO DO IF YOU'RE ARRESTED

If you are taken to a police station because the police suspect you might have committed a crime, give your name, address, occupation and date and place of birth.

● The police have the right to search, fingerprint and photograph you, and you are

Police in New Zealand do not routinely carry firearms

entitled to see a lawyer privately without delay. There should be a list of lawyers at the station; ask for the list and pick one. If you use a lawyer from the roster it will not cost anything.

● For legal advice contact the local Citizens Advice Bureau. A full list of branches is available on www.cab.org.nz.

MAIN CITY CENTRAL POLICE STATIONS		
CITY	**ADDRESS**	**TELEPHONE**
Auckland	Corner of Cook and Vincent streets	09-302 6400
Christchurch	Corner of Hereford Street and Cambridge Terrace	03-363 7400
Dunedin	25 Great King Street	03-471 4800
Palmerston North	400 Church Street	06-351 3600
Wellington	Corner of Victoria and Harris streets	04-381 2000

EMBASSIES AND CONSULATES IN NEW ZEALAND		
COUNTRY	**ADDRESS**	**TELEPHONE**
Australia	72–78 Hobson Street, Wellington	04-473 6411
	7th Floor, 188 Quay Street, Auckland	09-921 8800
Canada	Level 11, 125 The Terrace, Wellington	04-473 9577
France	34–42 Manners Street, Wellington	04-384 2555
Germany	Private Bag 92-093, Auckland	09-375 8709
	90 Hobson Street, Wellington	04-473 6063
Ireland	7th Floor, Citibank Building, 23 Customs Street West, Auckland	09-977 2252
UK	IAG House, 151 Queen Street, Auckland	09-303 2973
	44 Hill Street, Wellington	04-924 2888
US	Level 3, Citibank Centre, 23 Customs Street East, Auckland	09-303 2724
	29 Fitzherbert Terrace, Thorndon, Wellington	04-462 6000

OPENING TIMES AND TICKETS

BANKS
Bank opening hours are Monday to Friday 9–4.30. Some branches in cities open Saturday until 12.30.

CHURCHES
City churches are generally open to visitors Monday to Saturday 9 or 10–5 and to worshippers during church services.

DOCTORS AND CHEMISTS
Pharmacies open Monday to Friday 9–5. Emergency services are provided outside these hours; dispensaries are listed under Hospitals in the front of the phone book.

Typical doctors' surgery hours are Monday to Friday 7.30–6.30, and Saturday 8–noon; each clinic will supply details and contact numbers for after-hours arrangements.

FUEL STATIONS
Fuel stations in more populous areas open until about 11pm, and some open 24 hours a day; expect earlier closure in rural areas. Many sell a substantial range of supermarket-type items.

MUSEUMS AND GALLERIES
Opening hours for museums and galleries vary widely according to their size and location. In major cities and resorts they may open any time between 8am and 10am and close some time between 4.30pm and 7pm during weekdays, and some have restricted hours during weekends or on Sunday. In remoter areas museums may open on a seasonal basis or by previous arrangement only; others close during weekends or for part of the week. See individual entries for details, and check ahead with the local visitor information centre if you are planning a special trip.

RESTAURANTS, CAFÉS, BARS
Opening hours vary and are often seasonal. Most cafés open for breakfast between 7am and 9am and remain open until at least 5pm. Many also remain open until late into the evening or into the small hours. This usually applies seven days a week, with special Sunday brunch hours.

Most mid-range restaurants open their doors daily for lunch (11–2) and dinner (from 6pm). The more exclusive establishments usually open for dinner at about 6pm and some have restricted days or hours, especially in winter.

Pubs and bars are generally open 11am–11.30pm. Many have extended licences and stay open until midnight or even 3am during weekends.

SHOPS AND OFFICES
Most shops and businesses open Monday to Friday 9–5. Many shops also open on Saturday and Sunday. Large malls open daily and have at least one late shopping night a week. Larger supermarket chains open most evenings, and New Zealand dairies—convenience stores, found on almost every main street—are often open until 10 or 11pm.

DISCOUNTS AND CONCESSIONS
Virtually all visitor attractions and transportation systems offer discounted entrance fees and fares to children, usually of school age, and many give free admission or travel to under 5s.

● Senior citizens are also offered discounts at most major attractions and on trains and buses. Savings can range from 30 per cent to 50 per cent of the full price.

● Many, though not all, attractions offer family tickets; the definition of 'family' varies from place to place. See individual attractions for details.

● Student discounts are not as widespread, but holders of YHA or VIP cards can save on accommodation and travel, and there are plenty of budget options for anyone backpacking around the country.

National museums, such as Te Papa in Wellington (▷ 96) have the longest opening times

PLANNING

NATIONAL HOLIDAYS		
Shops and banks shut on public holidays. During school vacations—particularly in January and February—you should book accommodation and activities well ahead. This also applies to the winter season at major ski resorts like Tongariro, Wanaka and Queenstown.	**1–2 January**	New Year
	6 February	Waitangi Day
	April (variable)	Good Friday;
		Easter Monday
	25 April	Anzac Day
	1st Mon in June	Queen's Birthday
	4th Mon in October	Labour Day
	25 December	Christmas Day
	26 December	Boxing Day

'Flightseeing' tours are just one of the adventures you can book at i-SITES

VISITOR OFFICES

The official New Zealand Visitor Information Network is made up of around 100 accredited visitor information centres, nationally known as i-Sites.

● National i-Sites are based in Auckland and Christchurch and main visitor resorts such as Rotorua and Queenstown. They open seven days a week and provide a comprehensive information service, including advance hotel reservation and domestic airline, bus and train tickets. Souvenir shops and occasionally other retail outlets, currency exchange and cafés may be attached.

● Regional i-Sites are found throughout the country; there may be more than one in each region. They provide a general information and reservation service, usually seven days a week, and there is also a huge amount of free material available.

● Local i-Sites can be found almost everywhere, providing local information as well as assistance in lodging and transport reservations. They open at least five days a week, but are subject to varying hours during weekends and in low season.

NATIONAL I-SITES

Auckland
Princes Wharf,
137 Quay Street,
tel 09-307 0612/
0800 AUCKLAND,
www.aucklandnz.com

Christchurch
Old Chief Post Office,
Cathedral Square, PO Box 2600,
tel 03-379 9629,
www.christchurchnz.net

Queenstown
Corner of Shotover and Camp streets,
tel 03-442 4100,
www.queenstown-vacation.com

Rotorua
1167 Fenton Street, tel 07-348 5179, www.rotoruanz.com

SELECTED REGIONAL AND LOCAL INFORMATION

North Island

Auckland
International Terminal,
Arrivals Lounge,
Auckland Airport,
tel 09-275 6467,
www.aucklandnz.com

SKYCITY, tel 09-363 7182,
www.aucklandnz.com

Bay of Islands
Marsden Road, Pahia, tel 09-402 7345, www.fndc.govt.nz/infocentre

Coromandel
355 Kapanga Road,
tel 07-866 8598,
www.coromandeltown.co.nz

Hamilton
Corner of Bryce and Anglesea streets, tel 07-839 3580,
www.waikatonz.com

Hastings
Russell Street North, tel 06-873 0080/ 0800 HASTINGS,
www.hastings.co.nz

Mount Maunganui
Salisbury Avenue, tel 07-575 5099,
www.bayofplentynz.com

Napier
100 Marine Parade, tel 06-834 1911, www.isitehawkesbaynz.co.nz

Palmerston North
The Square, tel 06-354 6593,
www.manawatunz.co.nz

Taupo
30 Tongariro Street, tel 07-376 0027, www.laketauponz

Thames
206 Pollen Street, tel 07-868 7284, www.thames-info.co.nz

Wanganui
101 Guyton Street, tel 06-349 0508, www.wanganui.com

Wellington
101 Wakefield Street, Civic Square, tel 04-802 4860,
www.wellingtonnz.com

Whakatane
Quay Street, tel 07-308 6058,
www.whakatane.com

Whangarei
Tarewa Park, 92 Otaika Road,
tel 09-438 1079,
www.whangareinz.org.nz

PLANNING

MAIN TOURISM NEW ZEALAND OFFICES OVERSEAS		
www.newzealand.com		
COUNTRY	**ADDRESS**	**TELEPHONE**
Australia	Suite 3, Level 24, 1 Albert Street, Sydney, NSW 2000	02-8220 9000
Canada	Suite 1200, 888 Dunsmuir Street, Vancouver BC V6C 3K4	604/634-2117
UK	New Zealand House, Haymarket, London SWIY 4QT	020 7930 1662
US	Suite 2510, 221 East 41st Street, New York, NY 10017	212/661-7088
	Suite 300, 501 Santa Monica Boulevard, Los Angeles, CA 90401	310/395-7480

South Island

Arthur's Pass
Main Road, tel 03-318 9211,
www.doc.govt.nz

Christchurch
Domestic Terminal, Christchurch
Airport, tel 03-353 7774,
www.travelinfo.co.nzz

Dunedin
48 The Octagon, tel 03-474
3300, www.cityofdunedin.com

Franz Josef
Main Road, tel 03-752 0796,
www.doc.govt.nz

Greymouth
Corner of Mackay and Herbert
streets, tel 03-768 5101,
www.greydistrict.co.nz

Haast
Main Road, tel 03-750 0809,
www.doc.govt.nz

Hanmer Springs
42 Amuri Avenue, tel 03-315
7128, www.hurunui.com

Hokitika
The Carnegie Building, tel 03-
755 6166, www.hokitika.org

Invercargill
Queens Park, 108 Gala Street,
tel 03-214 6243,
www.invercargill.org.nz

Kaikoura
Westend, tel 03-319 5641,
www.kaikoura.co.nz

Mount Cook
Bowen Drive, tel 03-435 1186,
www.doc.govt.nz

Nelson
Corner of Trafalgar and Halifax
streets, tel 03-548 2304,
www.nelsonnz.com

Picton
The Foreshore, tel 03-520 3113,
www.destinationmarlborough.com

Stewart Island/Rakiura
Halfmoon Bay, tel 03-219
0009, www.doc.govt.nz

Te Anau
Lakefront Drive, tel 03-249 8900,
www.fiordland.org.nz

Wanaka
Ardmore Street, tel 03-443
1233, www.lakewanaka.co.nz

Westport
1 Brougham Street, tel 03-789
6658, www.westport.org.nz

USEFUL WEBSITES

VISITOR INFORMATION
www.newzealand.com
Official New Zealand visitor
information website

ACCOMMODATION
www.purenz.com
National farmstay information

www.stayyha.com
Youth Hostals Association website

www.vip.co.nz
Backpacker organisation

www.backpack.co.nz
Budget Backpacker Hostels Ltd
website

www.doc.govt.nz
Information on Department of
Conservation (DoC) campsites
and huts

RESTAURANTS
www.vegsoc.wellington.net.nz
National list of vegetarian
restaurants

www.time2dine.co.nz
Online guide and reservation
facility

MAJOR SIGHTS
www.doc.govt.nz
Department of Conservation
(DoC) site with information on
national parks and walks

www.nzmuseums.co.nz
Guide to museums nationwide

www.tepapa.govt.nz
Te Papa-Museum of New Zealand

www.rotoruanz.com
Rotorua website

www.skycity.co.nz
Sky Tower, Auckland

www.mtcooknz.com
Mount Cook/Aoraki National Park

www.abeltasmangreenrush.co.nz
Motueka visitor office website,
with information on Abel Tasman
National Park

HISTORY
www.enzed.com
Links to history, from the arrival
of Maori

www.nzhistory.net.nz
National history resource

www.teara.govt.nz
The encyclopedia of New
Zealand

ENTERTAINMENT
www.nz-events.co.nz
NZ AA's online guide to New
Zealand

www.ticketek.co.nz
Listings of shows and events and
ticketing information

WEATHER AND CLIMATE
www.metservice.co.nz
Weather information and analysis

www.nzcity.co.nz
Regional news and weather
satellite picture

CULTURE AND SOCIETY
www.gaytravelnet.com/nz
www.gaynewzealand.com
Information for gay and
lesbian visitors

www.tpk.govt.nz
Maori life and culture

www.wwoof.co.nz
Organic farm work in return for
bed and board

**NEWS AND GENERAL
INTEREST**
http://tvnz.co.nz
National site with regional
news links

www.stuff.co.nz
Website of the *Dominion Post*,
The Press and sister newspapers

www.nzherald.co.nz
New Zealand's largest daily
newspaper; national and
international news

**INFORMATION ON
MAORI LIFE**

Te Puni Kokiri
(Ministry of Maori Development)
143 Lambton Quay, PO Box 3943,
Wellington, tel 04-819 6000,
www.tpk.govt.nz

PLANNING

MEDIA

MAGAZINES

Several national New Zealand magazines are particularly worth a look for visitors: *The Listener*, covering national issues, politics and the arts; *North and South*, a magazine covering a wide range of traditional and contemporary issues; *New Zealand Geographic*, the quality New Zealand equivalent of the American icon; and two glossy outdoor activity publications, *New Zealand Wilderness* and *New Zealand Outside*. All are widely available at bookshops or Post Shops.

Most mainstream international magazines and newspapers can be found at specialist outlets such as Magazzino in Auckland.

Major Magazine Retailers:
Auckland
Magascene
33 Hurstmere Road, Takapuna
tel 09-489 5953

Magazzino
123 Ponsonby Road
tel 09-376 6933

Maggazino
Extreme on Broadway
Newmarket
tel 09-524 0604

Magazine City
Westfield Shoppingtown
West City, Henderson
tel 09-978 6752,
www.nzmagazineshop.co.nz

Christchurch
Canterbury Magazines
246 High Street
tel 03-377 0991

Hamilton
Accent on Magazines
113 Alexandra Street
tel 07-838 0269

Nelson
Page & Blackmore Booksellers
254 Trafalgar Street
tel 03-548 9992
www.pageandblackmore.co.nz

New Plymouth
Wadsworth's Bookcentre Ltd
Shop 9, Centre City, Gill Street
tel 06-759 4350

Wellington
City Cards and Mags
112 Lambton Quay
tel 04-472 7448

Magnetix, Midland Park
Lambton Quay
tel 04-472 2820

Village Newsagent
6/142 Willis Street
tel 04-385 1230

NEWSPAPERS
The principal daily newspapers (except Sundays) are the *New Zealand Herald* (Auckland and upper North Island), the *Dominion Post* (Wellington and lower North Island), *The Press* (Christchurch and central South Island) and the *Otago Daily Times* (South Island).

Smaller local newspapers can be accessed online from www.stuff.co.nz and include the *Waikato Times*, the *Manawatu Standard*, *The Daily News*, *The Nelson Mail*, *The Marlborough Express*, *The Timaru Herald* and *The Southland Times*.

TELEVISION
The four terrestrial TV channels have very little to offer except news and current affairs programmes. The rest of the output chiefly consists of UK or US soaps, reality and quiz shows.

All four channels carry advertising, which is heavily repetitive, sometimes featuring the same commercial every 10 minutes for several days. TV One shows news, sports and current affairs; Channel Two mainly drama and light entertainment; both are state-owned. TV3 and TV4 combine news and entertainment and are privately owned. Maori Television broadcasts bilingually in Maori and English, with 90 per cent New Zealand content.

Many New Zealanders (and most hotels and bed-and-breakfasts) subscribe to Sky TV.

There are local TV stations in some cities and towns.

RADIO
State-owned radio stations include Radio New Zealand Concert (classical music) and Radio New Zealand National (news, drama, light entertainment, talk shows). These broadcast on medium wave and VHF nationwide. There are also several stations broadcasting to Maori audiences. Some areas outside the large centres of population receive only medium wave.
● Tourist Information FM broadcasts 24 hours a day and features items on New Zealand's history and culture, news for visitors and commercials for places to stay and eat. It transmits in English (88.2MHz), Japanese (100.8MHz) and German (100.4MHz).

Newspapers are well read, and contain a high proportion of local news

BOOKS, MAPS AND FILMS

BACKGROUND READING

Despite its forbidding extent (some 570 pages) *The Penguin History of New Zealand*, by Michael King (2003), is a very readable account of New Zealand's history. King has contributed other history books, including *Nga Iwi O Te Motu: 1,000 Years of Maori History*. *The Oxford Illustrated History of New Zealand*, by Keith Sinclair (1997), does it with pictures.

There are various anthologies of Maori mythology available—the *Reed Book of Maori Mythology*, by AW Reed (2004) is an update of an old favourite.

Old New Zealand Houses 1800–1940, by Jeremy Salmond (1986) is a beautifully illustrated account of the country's vernacular architecture, from early Maori dwellings to gingerbread villas, which also acts as a fascinating record of social history.

Two natural history guides are particularly recommended to make the most of what you see: Geoff Moon's *Reed Field Guide to New Zealand Birds* (2000), and the Collins *Field Guide to New Zealand Wildlife*, by Rod Morris and Terence Linsey.

GUIDES AND MAPS

If you're planning a tramping (trekking) holiday, the Moirs Guides, published by the New Zealand Alpine Club, are recommended, as is *New Zealand's Great Walks*, by Pearl Hewson. Bruce Ringer's *New Zealand by Bike* is a useful guide for cyclists, while skiers will want to obtain a copy of the annual *Ski and Snowboard* guide, which is available free from Brown Bear Publications, PO Box 31–207, Christchurch, tel 03-388 5331, www.brownbear.co.nz.

The NZ AA produces a road atlas, and an extensive listing guide to accommodation, updated annually. Wises and Minimaps are the major city and provincial town map companies, producing a range of handbooks and foldout city maps. Visitor information centres also stock free leaflet maps.

NEW ZEALAND IN FICTION

New Zealand literature is flourishing, with a wealth of new talent writing across all genres. A selective cross-section is suggested in the panel here, and you can find out more about the authors and their works on www.bookcouncil.org.nz.

The genre which New Zealand authors have made their own is the short story. Katherine Mansfield started it in 1906, writing in London but drawing on her Wellington childhood (▷ 33)—and her short stories are still widely available. Other names to look for are Frank Sargeson, Maurice Shadbolt and Owen Marshall. Witi Ihimaera's collection of short stories, *Pounamu, Pounamu* (1972), was the first fiction to be published by a Maori—he came to wider world attention when his novel *The Whale Rider* (1987) was filmed.

English artist and writer Samuel Butler, who farmed in Canterbury around 1860, was one of the first to describe the landscape of the high country in his famous satire *Erewhon* (1872). A better picture of New Zealand appears in his letters to his father, published as *A First Year in Canterbury Settlement* (1863).

Novelists flourished in the second half of the 20th century—look for authors such as Janet Frame, Maurice Gee, Maurice Shadbolt, C.K. Stead, Alan Duff and Dame Ngaio Marsh—the country's best known writer of detective fiction.

James K. Baxter is New Zealand's most celebrated poet, but a wealth of other names includes Fleur Adcock and Alan Curnow.

FILMS

The movie scene has been dominated in recent years by the success of Peter Jackson's filming of the *Lord of the Rings* trilogy against a New Zealand backdrop. Check out the locations with Ian Brodie's comprehensive *The Lord of the Rings Location Guide* (2000), complete with GPS references. The 13-year-old actress at the heart of *Whale Rider*, Keisha Castle-Hughes, was another New Zealand star in the Oscars firmament of 2004.

Jackson's earlier film *Heavenly Creatures*, based on the story of two schoolgirl murderers in Christchurch in the 1950s, was a popular success. Jane Campion's *The Piano* (1993) was the award-winning tale of a mute immigrant. Lee Tamahori's *Once Were Warriors* (1995) is the shockingly violent and highly praised film of Alan Duff's novel about a Maori family struggling with poverty in inner-city Auckland.

---

10 TOP NZ READS

The New Zealanders, by Maurice Shadbolt (1959): The author's first short stories, rarely out of print, reveal an emerging New Zealand identity.

A Good Keen Man, by Barry Crump (1960): The first in a series of tales of a rugged outdoor bloke by a Kiwi icon, who went on to sell over 1 million books in New Zealand alone.

A River Rules My Life, by Mona Anderson (1963): A classic account of life on an isolated high-country sheep station, Mount Algidus, in the mid-20th century.

To the Is-land, by Janet Frame (1982): The first volume of her autobiography tells of a remarkable childhood of poverty, tragedy and rich imagination.

The Bone People, by Keri Hulme (1984): Reality and dreams, past and present meld together in a Booker-winning novel about bi-culturality, identity, love and hurt.

All Visitors Ashore, by C.K. Stead (1984): A time-shot of a youthful bohemian community and its relationship with the outside world in the 1950s.

Potiki, by Patricia Grace (1986): A remarkable novel about life on a *marae* in a changing world, which reveals much about Maori ways and thoughts.

The Man Who Never Lived, by Kevin Ireland (1997): A hilarious novel of selfishness, self deception and families.

The Denniston Rose, by Jenny Pattrick (2003): A well-told historic tale of life, love and survival in a tough West Coast mining community.

Barking, by Joe Bennett (2003): Sharp, humorous articles composed originally for *The Press*, with a wry eye for the follies of daily life.

SPEAKING 'KIWI'

English is the common language of New Zealand, and in its written form generally follows British rather than US spelling conventions. There is little difference in pronunciation from one part of the country to another, although you may detect a burr in the southern half of the South Island and other locations where localised settlement was particularly strong. New Zealand has developed its own slang words and phrases, a selection of which are listed below.

bach holiday cottage (pronounced 'batch', originates from a shortened form of 'bachelor', referring to a dwelling fit for a single man)

Beehive the main government building in Wellington

bludge scrounge, borrow

bush forest, native woodland

BYO a café or restaurant that allows you to take your own beer or wine

chook chicken

cocky farmer (usually 'cow cocky')

chilly-bin portable cooler box for a picnic

crib holiday cottage (South Island)

crook sick, ill

cuppa cup of tea

dag a character, or entertaining person

dairy general grocery store

good as gold fine, OK

handle beer glass with a handle

jandals flip-flops, thongs

judder bars speed bumps in the road

morning tea mid-morning tea or coffee break

mozzie mosquito

Pakeha person of European descent

smoko tea or coffee break

she'll be right that's OK

shout a round pay for a round of drinks

togs swimwear

wopwops the back of beyond

wowser killjoy

MAORI WORDS AND PHRASES

Maori words and phrases are used throughout New Zealand and the Maori language is generally encouraged and spoken with pride within the *whanau* and *iwi* (Maori family and tribes). It is wise to be aware of a few basic rules before arriving in the country. The easiest way to say Maori words is to pronounce each syllable phonetically. Perhaps the most important feature is the pronunciation of 'wh' as the English 'f'. For example, *whanau* is pronounced 'fha-now' and Whangarei 'Fhongarei'. Vowels are pronounced openly, as in Italian, and all words end in a vowel.

ana cave

Aotearoa New Zealand

ara path, road

ariki tribal leader

atua spiritual being

au rain

awa river, valley

haere mai welcome

haera ra farewell

hangi Maori feast

hau wind

harakeke flax plant, leaves

Hawaiiki ancestral Polynesian homeland

hapu sub-tribe/to be pregnant

he ao a land or a world

he tangata the people

hei tiki carved figure worn round the neck, usually shortened to tiki

hoe paddle

hongi traditional greeting (pressing noses)

huka spray, snow

iti small

iwi tribe, bone

kahu blue

kai eat

Kaikaiawaro a dolphin (also known as Pelorus Jack) who cruised the Marlborough Sounds and became a guardian to *iwi*

kaitiaki protector, caretaker

kainga village

kapa haka group of Maori performers

kia ora welcome

kaumatua elders

kawa protocols

kete basket

kohu mist, fog

kowhaiwhai rafter patterns

ma stream, white

mana integrity, prestige, control

manawhenua people with tribal affiliations with the area

manu bird

Maori ordinary people

Maoritanga Maoriness

marae sacred courtyard or plaza

maunga mountain

mauri life essence

moana lake, sea

moko tattoo

motu island, or anything isolated

muka flax fibre

namu sandfly

Ngati people of

nui big, plenty

o of, the place of

one sand, beach, mud

pa fortified village

Pakeha foreigner, white person, European

papa broad, flat

poi ball attached to flax string

pounamu sacred greenstone

puke hill

puna spring of water

rangatira tribal leader	**te** the	**waka** canoe	
rangi sky	**Te Ika-a-Maui** North Island	**whakairo** carvings	
roa long	**tiki** see **hei tiki**	**whakapapa** origins or	
roto lake	**tipuna** ancestor	genealogy	

rangatira tribal leader	**te** the	**waka** canoe
rangi sky	**Te Ika-a-Maui** North Island	**whakairo** carvings
roa long	**tiki** see **hei tiki**	**whakapapa** origins or genealogy
roto lake	**tipuna** ancestor	
	tukutuku wall panels	**whanau** extended family/to give birth
taiaha a fighting staff		**whanga** bay, inlet
tangata people/person	**utu** cost, retribution	**whare** house
tangihanga death ritual		**whare runanga** meeting house
taonga treasure, prized object (often passed down by ancestors)	**wahakatauki** proverb or saying	**whenua** land
tapu sacred, out of bounds	**wai** water	**whero** red
	waiata song, flute music	
	wairua soul	

GLOSSARY FOR US VISITORS

A&E	emergency room (hospital department)	**lorry**	truck
anticlockwise	counterclockwise	**licensed**	a café or restaurant that has a license to serve alcohol
aubergine	eggplant	**lift**	elevator
bill	check (at restaurant)	**nappy**	diaper
biscuit	cookie	**note**	bill (when referring to money)
bonnet	hood (car)		
boot	trunk (car)	**pants**	underpants (men's)
busker	street musician	**pavement**	sidewalk
		petrol	gas
caravan	house trailer or RV	**plaster**	Band-Aid or bandage
car park	parking lot	**post**	mail
carriage	car (on a train)	**pudding**	dessert
chemist	pharmacy	**purse**	change purse
chips	french fries	**pushchair**	stroller
coach	long-distance bus		
corridor	hall	**return ticket**	roundtrip ticket
courgette	zucchini	**rocket**	arugula
crèche	day care	**roundabout**	traffic circle or rotary
dual carriageway	two-lane highway	**self-catering**	accommodation including a kitchen
en suite	a bedroom with its own private bathroom; may also just refer to the bathroom	**single ticket**	one-way ticket
		stalls	(in theatre) orchestra seats
		subway	underpass
		surgery	doctor's office
football	Rugby (sometimes soccer)	**tailback**	stalled line of traffic
full board	a hotel tariff that includes all meals	**takeaway**	takeout
		taxi rank	taxi stand
		ten-pin bowling	bowling
garden	yard (residential)	**T-junction**	an intersection where one road meets another at right angles (making a T shape)
GP	doctor		
half board	hotel tariff that includes breakfast and either lunch or dinner		
		toilets	restrooms
handbag	purse	**torch**	flashlight
high street	main street	**trolley**	cart
hire	rent	**trousers**	pants
jelly	Jello™	**way out**	exit
junction	intersection		
layby	rest stop; *also* payment of a deposit to secure an article		
level crossing	grade crossing		
loo	rest room		

TIMELINE

AD 800 Polynesian navigator Kupe lands at Hokianga, in Northland.

1000 Polynesians move south-east to Pacific Islands from Asia.

1300 Polynesian colonies established on North Island and some tribes are clearing bush and hunting in the South Island.

1642 Dutch explorer Abel Tasman, commissioned by East India Company, sights the land he calls Staten Landt, later renamed Nieuw Zeeland.

1769 British explorer Captain James Cook makes the first of three voyages to New Zealand on the *Endeavour*, claiming the country for King George III.

1773 Cook lands at Dusky Cove on the *Resolution* and returns to Ship Cove via the South Island's west coast.

1776 Cook returns to Ship Cove and the Sounds before sailing to Hawaii, where he is killed.

1791 The *William and Ann*, the first whaling vessel, anchors at Doubtless Bay, heralding a period of intensive whaling, sealing and timber- and flax-trading.

1814 British missionary Samuel Marsden establishes an Anglican mission station in the Bay of Islands.

1820–35 Maori Musket Wars: fierce inter-tribal warfare.

1833 Official British Resident James Busby arrives in Waitangi and encourages adoption of United Tribes flag.

1835 Declaration of Independence by United Tribes of New Zealand signed by 34 northern chiefs.

1839 Captain William Hobson appointed Lieutenant Governor with remit to transfer sovereignty of land from Maori Chiefs to British Crown.

1840 Treaty of Waitangi signed in the Bay of Islands, proclaiming British sovereignty. French settlers land at Akaroa.

1844 Chief Hone Heke cuts down British flagpole and instigates two-year War of the North.

1848 Dunedin founded as a Scottish Presbyterian colony.

1850 Christchurch founded as an Anglican colony.

1852 Constitution Act creates General Assembly and six provinces. Discovery of gold in the Coromandel.

1855 Earthquake changes the face of Wellington.

1858 Te Wherowhero installed as first Maori king, taking the name Potatau I.

1860s Gold boom attracts thousands of prospectors.

1865 Wellington becomes capital of New Zealand. Native Lands Act investigates Maori land ownership and distributes land titles.

1867 First Maori Members of Parliament elected.

1882 First refrigerator ship sails to London with a cargo of frozen lamb, heralding a new economic era.

1893 New Zealand is the first country in the world to give women the vote.

1907 New Zealand constituted as a British Dominion.

1914–18 New Zealand suffers the greatest casualties per head of population of any combat nation in World War I.

1931 Earthquake destroys Napier.

1938 Government lays basis of welfare state.

1939–45 New Zealand fights on the Allied side in World War II.

1945 New Zealand is one of the founding member states of the United Nations.

1947 New Zealand is declared an independent nation.

1952 Population tops 2 million.

1953 New Zealander Edmund Hillary conquers Mount Everest.

1966 International airport opens at Auckland.

1973 Preferential trade with Britain ends when the UK joins the Common Market, and a new economic era starts.

1980s Anti-nuclear policy is adopted. Deregulation of economy.

1985 Greenpeace vessel *Rainbow Warrior* is bombed by French Secret Service in Auckland harbour.

1987 Maori Language Act gives Maori language official status. The All Blacks win the first Rugby World Cup title.

1988 Unemployment exceeds 100,000.

1990 Dame Catherine Tizard becomes the first woman Governor-General.

1993 Referendum votes in favour of mixed-member proportional representation, giving each elector two votes and Maori retaining the choice of voting in a general or a Maori electorate.

1995 Peter Blake's *Black Magic* crew wins the hugely prestigious America's Cup, heralding a yachting revival based in Auckland.

1997 Jenny Shipley of the National Party becomes New Zealand's first woman prime minister.

1999 Peter Jackson, from Wellington, begins filming *The Lord of the Rings* trilogy by J. R. R. Tolkien, mainly around Queenstown, Otago.

2004 *The Return of the King*, last in the *Rings* trilogy, scoops 11 Oscars at the Academy Awards.

2008 New Zealand voters go to the polls once again to elect the government that will take them through the next three years.

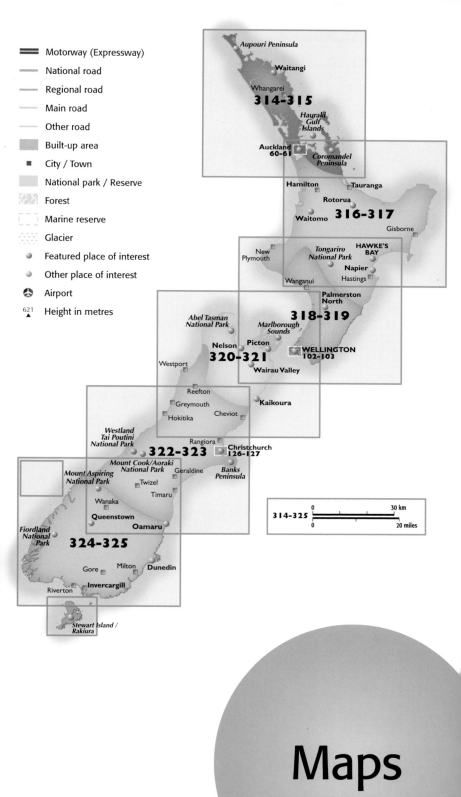

	Motorway (Expressway)
	National road
	Regional road
	Main road
	Other road
	Built-up area
■	City / Town
	National park / Reserve
	Forest
	Marine reserve
	Glacier
●	Featured place of interest
●	Other place of interest
✈	Airport
⁶²¹▲	Height in metres

Aupouri Peninsula

Waitangi

Whangarei

314–315

Hauraki Gulf Islands

Auckland
60–61

Coromandel Peninsula

Hamilton • Tauranga

Rotorua

Waitomo • **316–317**

Gisborne

New Plymouth

Tongariro National Park

HAWKE'S BAY

Napier

Wanganui • Hastings

Palmerston North

318–319

Abel Tasman National Park

Marlborough Sounds

Nelson • Picton

320–321

Westport

WELLINGTON 102–103

Wairau Valley

Reefton

Greymouth • **Kaikoura**

Hokitika • Cheviot

Westland Tai Poutini National Park

Rangiora

322–323

Christchurch **126–127**

Mount Cook/Aoraki National Park

Geraldine

Banks Peninsula

Mount Aspiring National Park

Twizel

Timaru

Wanaka

Queenstown

Oamaru

Fiordland National Park

324–325

Gore • Milton • **Dunedin**

Riverton • **Invercargill**

Stewart Island / Rakiura

	0	30 km
314–325		
	0	20 miles

Maps

Spirits
Bay
Cape Reinga
Lighthouse
Kapowairua
North Cape
Motuopao Island
Cape Maria Van Diemen
Whareana Bay
149
Te Paki
Paua
Scott Point
Parengarenga Harbour
Te Kao
Great Exhibition Bay
Aupouri Peninsula
Ngataki
Moturoa Islands
Cape Karikari
Pukenui
Karikari Peninsula
Rangaunu Bay
Knuckle Point
Ninety Mile Beach
Motutangi
Whatuwhiwhi
Subritzky / Wagener
Berghan Point
Homestead
Hukatere
Rangaunu Harbour
Gumdiggers Park
Doubtless Bay
Whangaroa Bay
Mahinepua
Waipapakauri Beach
Awanui
Taipa
Taupo Bay
Cavalli Islands
Ahipara Bay
315
Oruaiti
Otoroa
Matauri Bay
Kaitaia
Otangaroa
Takou Bay
Purerua Peninsula
Pamapuria
Kaeo
Te Tii
Ahipara
Mangapa
Te Whau
Bay of Isla
Tauroa Point
Takahue
Mangamuka
371
Kerikeri
Waitangi
Puketi
Paihia
Ra
Awaroa
Mohuiti
Russell
Rangiahua
Okaihau
Puketona
Opua
Whangape
603
Kohukohu
Lake Omapere
Pakaraka
Wai
Panguru
Rawene
Kaikohe
40
Mitimiti
Oue
Taheke
Tautoro
Kawakawa
Towai
Omapere
12
Opahi
Waipoua Kauri Forest
Mataraua
Whakapa
Waimamaku
Waipoua Forest Sanctuary
Kaikou
575
Twin Bridges
Otakairangi
Katui
Tutamoe
Moengawahine
Ka
770
Kaihu
Parakao
Whangar
Kai Iwi Lakes
Tutamoe
Maungatapere
Waihue
Waiotama
Oakl
Omamari
Pukehuia
Taur
Dargaville
14
Ruara
Manganui
Baylys Beach
Mititai
Okahu
Arar
Redhill
Whenuanui
Pa
12
Ruawai
Mata
Taingaehe
Huk
Rototuna
Wairoa
214
Pouto
10
North Head
South Head
South Head

H

J

Pukearuhe
Kotare
533
Taumarunui
Aukopae
Manu

Mount Damper
Waitara
43
632
Kirikau
Owha

New Plymouth
Okoki
Tahora
Retaruke
Ka

Sugar Loaf Island
Onaero
391
Waitara

Okato
Inglewood
Matau
Pohokura
Whanganui National Park
National

45
3A
Tarata
Strathmore
316

Newall
North Egmont
Tariki
Toko
43
Puniwhakau
Poka

2518
Mount Egmont
Strathford
Mangamingi
Tohunga Junction

Rahotu
Mount Egmont/ Mount Taranaki ▲
Mount Egmont National Park
Moeroa
Waitotara
Raetihi
Oha

Opunake
Awatuna
Eltham
Lake Rotorangi
Pipiriki
Ranana
Ka

45
Manaia
Ararata
Makakaho Junction

Oeo
Hawera
Ohangai
356
Orangimea
Whanganui National Park
Ka

Manutahi
Hurleyville
Mangawhio
Paparangi
Whakaihuwl

Patea
Waverley
Maxwell

Patea
Waitotara
3
Brunswick
Mangamahu
Upokongaro

Wanganui
Kuangaroa

Turakina
Mart

Koitiata
Santoft
Bulls

9
Tasman Sea
Tangimoana
Sans

Himatangi Beach
Glen Oro

Bainesse
Fox

Shann

Hokio Beach

Levin

Stephens Island

Cape Stephens
Patuki
Featherston

D'Urville Island
Rangitoto Islands
Kapiti Island Nature Reserve and Marine Reserve
Te Horo
Manakau

Haukawakawa
French Pass
Forsyth Island
Kapiti Island ▲
364
Waikanae
Otaki

Tasman Bay
Sauvage Point
Cape Jackson
Marlborough Sounds
Paraparaumu
Otaki Forks
Otaki Tara Fores

10
Cape Soucis
Okiwi Bay
1203
Endeavour Inlet
Cape Koamaru
Paekakariki
924
Cloustonville

Island
Delaware Bay
Tennyson Inlet
Mount Stokes
Te Rewarewa Point
Plimmerton
Pakuratahi
Greyt

ka
Pepin Island
Manaroa
Arapawa Island
Mana Island
Porirua
Upper Hutt
58

Wakapuaka
Rai Valley
Kenepuru Head
Perano Head
Tawa
Lower Hutt
Wainuiomata
Martinbor

pua
6
Queen Charlotte Sound
Ohariu Bay
Makara
Somes/ Matiu Island
Tuhitara

Nelson
Havelock
Pelorus Bridge
Cape Terawhiti
WELLINGTON
Ruakokoputun
Hauranga Forest Park

Richmond
1330
Picton
Robertson Point
Orongorongo
Lake Ferry

field
Okaramio
Tuamarina
Cloudy Bay
Turakirae Head
Palliser Bay
Putangiru Pinnacles

Mount Richmond Forest Park
Te Rou
Renwick
Blenheim
321
Cook Strait
Te Humenga Pt
Ngawihi
Hauranga Forest Park

Wairau
63
Wairau Valley
Seddon
Lake Grassmere
Clifford Bay
Cape Palliser
Kau

Hillersden
1579
Altimarloch
Cape Campbell

11
2009
Mount Horrible
Ward

318
Gladst
Peggioh

Langridge
H
Wharanui
J

2621

Rimutaka Range

Taranu Range

Wanganui

Whenuakura

Waitotara

Patea

Whanganui

ACKNOWLEDGMENTS

Abbreviations for the picture credits are as follows:
AA = AA World Travel Library, **t** (top), **b** (bottom), **c** (centre), **l** (left), **r** (right), **bg** (background)

UNDERSTANDING NEW ZEALAND

4 New Zealand Tourist Board; **5cl** Destination Lake Taupo/Marcel Tromp; **5c, 5cr, 5b** AA/P Kenward; **6tl** Destination Lake Taupo/Marcel Tromp; **6tr, 6bl, 6bc, 7** AA/P Kenward; **6ctl, 6cbl, 6br** AA/M Langford; **8tl, 8ctr, 8c, 8cb, 8b, 9tctl, 9tcl** AA/P Kenward; **8tr** Collingwood Homestead Lodge; **8tctr** SkyCity Auckland; **9tl** AA/A Belcher; **9tr** Hilton Hotel Auckland; **9bcl** International Antarctic Centre; **9bcbl** Te Papa, Wellington; **9b** Te Papa, Wellington; **10l, 10trt, 10cbr** AA/P Kenward; **10trbg, 10ctr** AA/A Belcher; **10cr** AA/M Langford; **10br** Destination Lake Taupo

LIVING NEW ZEALAND

11 AA/M Langford; **12/13bg, 13tl, 13clt** AA/A Belcher; **12tl** Photo by Simon Runting/Rex Features; **12tr, 12cl, 12b, 13tr** AA/M Langford; **12cr** Mountain Buggy; **13tc** Office of the Governor General of New Zealand; **13clb** Wingnut Productions; **13c** Office of the Prime Minister of New Zealand; **13cr** Oxford University Press; **14/15bg** AA/A Belcher; **14tl** Speight's Coast to Coast Race; **14tr, 15tl, 15cl** AA/A Reisinger & V Meduna; **14cl** Speight's Coast to Coast Race; **14clt, 14/15c, 15tr** AA/M Langford; **14b** © Simon Baker/Reuters/Corbis; **15cl, 15cr** AA/P Kenward; **15rcr** Burton Silver/Golf Cross; **16/17bg, 16tl, 16tc, 17tl** AA/A Belcher; **16tr, 16cr, 16cb, 16b, 17tr, 17cr** AA/M Langford; **16cl** New Zealand Film Commission/The Kobal Collection; **17cl** Brian Rasic/Rex Features; **17c** World of WearableArt; **18/19bg, 18tr** AA/P Kenward; **18tl, 18tc, 18c, 18b, 19tl, 19cl, 19c, 19cr** AA/M Langford; **19tr** AA/A Belcher; **20/21bg, 20tr, 20c, 20r, 21r, 21ii, 21iii** AA/M Langford; **20tl, 20cl, 21tc, 21i** AA/A Belcher; **20b, 21tl, 21iv** AA/P Kenward; **21tr** Latitude Nelson; **21cl** New Zealand Tourist Board; **21c** Kiwi Experience; **22bg** AA/P Kenward; **22tl, 22cl** AA/A Belcher; **22tr** Charles Royal/Kinaki Wild Herbs; **22c** AA/A Belcher; **22cr** Charles Royal/Kinaki Wild Herbs

THE STORY OF NEW ZEALAND

23 AA; **24/25bg, 24bl** AA/P Kenward; **24c** AA/M Langford; **24/25b** AA; **25c** © The Natural History Museum, London; **25cb** AA; **25bc** Mary Evans Picture Library; **25br** AA; **26/27bg** AA; **26cl** AA; **26cr** AA; **26cb** AA; **26bl** National Library of Australia, Canberra, Australia/Bridgeman Art Library; **26bc** AA/M Langford; **26/27b** The Signing of the Treaty of Waitangi, February 6th 1840. 1938, by Marcus King (library reference G-821-2)/Alexander Turnbull Library, Wellington, New Zealand/Bridgeman Art Library; **27c** AA; **27cr** AA; **27b** © The Natural History Museum, London; **28/29bg, 28cl** AA/P Kenward; **28c** Illustrated London News Picture Library; **28cr** AA; **28bl** Mary Evans Picture Library; **28/29** © Corbis; **29cl** Illustrated London News Picture Library; **29cr** AA/A Belcher; **29b** Mary Evans Picture Library; **30/31bg, 31b** AA/P Kenward; **30c** AA; **30bl** National Library of Australia, Canberra, Australia/Bridgeman Art Library; **30bc** AA; **30/31** Mary Evans Picture Library; **31cl, 31cb** AA/M Langford; **31cr** Mary Evans Picture Library; **32/33bg, 33cl, 33br** AA/P Kenward; **32c** Private Collection, Barbara Singer/Bridgeman Art Library. *We have been unable to trace the copyright holder of 'Together' by English School and would be grateful to receive any information as to their identity.* **32cr** Getty Images; **32bl** Illustrated London News Picture Library; **32/33b** Getty Images; **33c** Getty Images; **33bl** AA/M Langford; **34/35bg, 35cl** AA/P Kenward; **34c** ©Amos Nachoum/Corbis; **34bcl** Getty Images; **34bl** © Kevin Fleming/Corbis; **34/35** © Neil Rabinowitz/Corbis; **35cr** AA/P Aithie; **35bl** Rex Features; **35br** Getty Images; **35bg** AA/M Langford; **36c** Office of the Governor General of New Zealand; **36bl** © Guido Cantini/ACM; **36br** © Paul Hanna/Reuters/Corbis

ON THE MOVE

37 AA/M Langford; **38t** Digital Vision; **38b** AA/A Belcher; **39t** Digital Vision; **39b** AA/P Kenward; **39c** Auckland International Airport; **40t** Digital Vision; **40c** Air New Zealand; **40b** Britz New Zealand; **41** Britz New Zealand; **42t** Christchurch Tram; **42c** AA/M Langford; **43t** Christchurch Tram; **43c** Christchurch Tram; **44t** Digital Vision; **44c, 45c** AA/M Langford; **45t** Digital Vision; **46t** Digital Vision; **46c, 46b, 47cl, 47c, 47bcl** AA/M Langford; **47t** Digital Vision; **47cr** AA/P Kenward; **47bcr** AA/N Hanna; **48t** Digital Vision; **48c** AA/P Kenward; **48b, 49c, 49t** AA/M Langford; **49b** Magic Travellers Network; **49t** Digital Vision; **50t** Digital Vision; **50c, 50b** AA/M Langford; **51** Digital Vision; **52t, 53t, 53b** AA/A Belcher; **52c** Sounds Air New Zealand; **52b** AA/A Belcher; **53c** AA/M Langford; **54t** AA/N Sumner; **54c** AA/C Jones

THE SIGHTS

55 AA/P Kenward; **Sights background picture** AA/M Langford; **57t** Destination Northland (courtesy of Fullers BOI); **57cr** Destination Northland; **58c** SkyCity Auckland; **58c** AA/A Belcher; **59tr** SkyCity Auckland; **59br** AA/P Kenward; **62cl, 62c, 63cr** AA/A Belcher; **62cr** AA/M Langford; **63tl** SkyCity Auckland; **64tl** AA/P Kenward; **64/65cr, 64bl, 65b** AA/M Langford; **65cr** SkyCity Auckland; **66tc, 66cl, 66c, 66cr, 66bl, 67cl, 67cr** AA/M Langford; **68tl, 68b, 69tl** AA/A Belcher; **68tc** Destination Northland; **68tr** Destination Northland; **69tr** AA/P Kenward; **70t, 70cl, 70cr, 71c** AA/M Langford; **70c, 70b** AA/A Belcher; **71tr** AA/P Kenward; **72tl** Destination Northland; **72tr** Destination Northland; **73tl, 73b** AA/P Kenward; **73tr** AA/M Langford; **74t** AA/A Belcher; **74cl** AA/P Kenward; **75tl, 75tr** AA/M Langford; **77tl, 77tr** AA/M Langford; **78tl, 78tc, 78tr, 78br, 79cr** AA/M Langford; **79t** Hawkes Bay Tourism; **80tl, 80tr, 80b** AA/P Kenward; **81tl, 81tc, 81tr** AA/M Langford; **82t, 83cl** AA/P Kenward; **82cl, 82c, 82c, 82cr, 82b, 83cr, 83b** AA/M Langford; **84t, 84cl, 84cr** AA/A Belcher; **84c, 85t, 85cr** AA/M Langford; **86/87t, 87cr, 87br** AA/M Langford; **86cl** AA/A Belcher; **88t** AA/P Kenward; **88cl** AA/A Belcher; **88tr** Destination Lake Taupo; **88b** Destination Lake Taupo/Marcel Tromp; **89cl** AA/M Langford; **89c** Destination Lake Taupo; **89cr** Destination Lake Taupo; **90t, 90cr, 91bl** AA/M Langford; **90cl** AA; **90c** Waitomo Caves (Tourism Holdings Limited); **91br** Jean-Paul Ferrero/Auscape; **92tl** AA/A Belcher; **92c** AA/A Reisinger & V Meduna; **92tr** AA/M Langford; **94tl** Martinborough Wine Centre; **94tr** Steam Inc; **95tl** AA/M Langford; **95tr** Pukaha Mount Bruce National Wildlife Centre; **95b** Southward Car Museum; **96/97** Te Papa, Wellington; **96c** Te Papa, Wellington; **98cl** Te Papa, Wellington; **98c** Te Papa, Wellington; **98b** Te Papa, Wellington; **98/99t** Te Papa, Wellington; **98/99b** Worldwide Picture Library/Alamy; **99cl** Te Papa, Wellington; **100** AA/P Kenward; **101t, 101cl, 101c, 101cr** AA/A Belcher; **104cl** AA/P Kenward; **104c, 104cr** AA/A Belcher; **105** AA/M Langford; **106tl** Wairarapa Tourism; **106tr** AA/P Kenward; **106b** Paua Shell Factory, Carterton; **108, 109t, 109cl, 109c, 109cr, 109b** AA/M Langford; **110cr, 111tl, 111c** AA/M Langford; **110br** AA/P Kenward; **111tr** Nelson Tourism;

111b Nelson Tourism; 112tl, 112b AA/M Langford; 112tr, 113t, 113cr AA/P Kenward; 114t, 114cl, 114cl, 114cr, 114rcr, 114b, 115t, 115b AA/M Langford; 116t, 116cl, 117tr AA/M Langford; 117tl Nelson Tourism; 118tl, 118tr, 118b AA/M Langford; 119t Centrestage New Zealand; 119cr Centrestage New Zealand; 121tl, 121tr AA/A Belcher; 122t, 122cl, 122b AA/A Belcher; 123tl AA/P Kenward; 123tr, 123c AA/M Langford; 124t AA/M Birkitt; 124cl, 124c, 124cr, 124b, 125 AA/M Langford; 128cl, 128c, 128cr, 129t, 129b AA/M Langford; 130tl World Pictures; 130tr, 130b AA/P Kenward; 131t, 131tr, 131b AA/M Langford; 132tl, 132tr, 133tr, 133b AA/M Langford; 133tl AA/P Kenward; 134t, 134c, 134cr, 134b, 135 AA/A Belcher; 134cl AA/M Langford; 137tl AA/P Kenward; 137tc, 137tr, 137b AA/M Langford; 138t, 138cl, 138c, 138cr, 138b, 139 AA/A Belcher; 140, 141t, 141c AA/A Belcher; 141cl AA; 141cr AA/P Kenward; 142cl AA/A Belcher; 142c, 142cr, 142b, 143 AA/P Kenward; 144tl, 144tr AA/P Kenward; 144b, 145tl AA/M Langford; 145tr Nature Photographers; 146 AA/P Kenward; 147tl AA/A Reisinger & V Meduna; 147tr AA/M Langford; 147c Royal Albatross Centre; 148t, 148c, 149c AA/P Kenward; 148cl, 148cr AA/A Belcher; 148b AJ Hackett Bungy; 149t AJ Hackett Bungy; 150t, 150c AA/M Langford

WHAT TO DO

151 AA/M Langford; 152, 153 AA/M Langford; 154t, 155t AA/M Langford; 154cl AA/C Coe; 154cr AA/P Kenward; 155c Digital Vision; 155b AA/K Paterson; 156t, 157t, 157cl, 157cr AA/M Langford; 156c Speight's Coast to Coast Race; 158t, 158cr, 159t AA/M Langford; 158cl AA/A Reisinger & V Meduna; 159c Destination Lake Taupo; 160t, 161t, 161c AA/M Langford; 160cl Destination Lake Taupo/Marcel Tromp; 160cr AA/A Reisinger & V Meduna; 162t, 162c, 163 AA/M Langford; 164t Matana Confections; 164c AA/M Langford; 165t Matana Confections; 165c AA/A Belcher; 166t Matana Confections; 166c Auckland Fine Wine Tours; 167t Matana Confections; 167c AJ Hackett Bungy; 168t Matana Confections; 168c Matana Confections; 169t Matana Confections; 169c Pakiri Beach Horse Riding; 170t Matana Confections; 170c Kiwi Dundee Adventures; 171t Matana Confections; 171c Auckland Festival; 172t, 173t AA/A Belcher; 172c Destination Lake Taupo; 173c Hamilton Gardens; 174t, 175t AA/A Belcher; 174c Splash Planet; 175c AA/P Kenward; 176t, 177t, 177c AA/A Belcher; 176c Canoe Safari; 178t, 179 AA/A Belcher; 178c Kiwi360; 180t, 181t AA/C Sawyer; 180c Centrestage New Zealand; 181c Martinborough Wine Centre; 182t, 183t AA/C Sawyer; 182c Olivo; 183c Efil Doog Garden of Art; 184t, 185t AA/C Sawyer; 184c Sommerfields; 185c Embassy Theatre; 186t, 187 AA/C Sawyer; 186c Seal Coast Safari; 188t, 189t AA/P Kenward; 188c Latitude Nelson; 189c Marlborough Farmer's Markets; 190t, 191t AA/P Kenward; 190c Maori Tours; 191c Pomeroys Coffee and Tea Company; 192t, 193t AA/P Kenward; 192c Happy Valley Adventures; 193c Höglund Art Glass; 194 AA/P Kenward; 195t Addington Raceway; 195c Addington Raceway; 196t Addington Raceway; 196c Naturally Jade; 197t Addington Raceway; 197c Untouched World; 198t Addington Raceway; 198c Addington Raceway; 199t Addington Raceway; 199c AA/A Belcher; 200t Addington Raceway; 200c Barker's Berry Barn; 201t Addington Raceway; 201c Alpine Horse Safaris; 202t Addington Raceway; 202c AA/M Langford; 203 Addington Raceway; 204t Catlins Wildlife Trackers; 204c AA/M Langford; 205t Catlins Wildlife Trackers; 205c Catlins Wildlife Trackers; 206t Catlins Wildlife Trackers; 206c Speight's Brewery; 207t Catlins Wildlife Trackers; 207c Photodisc; 208t Catlins Wildlife Trackers; 208c Kingston Flyer; 209t Catlins Wildlife Trackers; 209c Wine Deli; 210t Catlins Wildlife Trackers; 210c Fly by Wire; 211t Catlins Wildlife Trackers; 211c Puzzling World; 212 Catlins Wildlife Trackers

OUT AND ABOUT

213 Destination Lake Taupo; 215 AA/M Langford; 216t, 216c, 216b, 217b AA/M Langford; 217c AA/P Kenward; 219t AA/P Kenward; 219ct, 219b AA/M Langford; 220, 221c AA/M Langford; 221t, 221b AA/P Kenward; 223tl, 223tr, 223b AA/M Langford; 224, 225tr, 225c, 225b AA/M Langford; 225tl AA/P Kenward; 227tl Destination Lake Taupo; 227tr Destination Lake Taupo; 227b Destination Lake Taupo; 228b AA/M Langford; 229t AA/P Kenward; 229b Waitomo Caves (Tourism Holdings Limited); 230, 231b AA/M Langford; 231t Latitude Nelson; 231c Apex News and Pictures Agency/Alamy; 232, 233tl, 233tr, 233ct, 233b AA/M Langford; 233cb AA/P Kenward; 234 Kaikoura Information and Tourism Inc.; 235tc D Parer & E Parer-Cook/Auscape; 235tr Kaikoura Information and Tourism Inc.; 235cl Ann Stonehouse; 235cr, 235bl AA/P Kenward; 235br Kaikoura Information and Tourism Inc.; 236 AA/A Belcher; 237t, 237c, 237b AA/M Langford; 238 AA/P Kenward; 239tl AA/M Langford; 239tr, 239c, 239bl, 239br AA/A Belcher; 240, 241t, 241ct, 241cb, 241b AA/M Langford; 242, 243c AA/M Langford; 243t, 243b AA/P Kenward; 244 AA/M Langford; 245t AA/P Kenward; 245c Royal Albatross Centre; 245b AA/A Belcher; 246 AA/A Reisinger & V Meduna

EATING AND STAYING

247 AA/M Langford; 248cl, 248cr, 249 AA/M Langford; 248c Matana Confections; 250cl Destination Lake Taupo; 250c Charles Royal/Kinaki Wild Herbs; 250cr AA/A Belcher; 250b, 251cl, 251c, 251cr AA/M Langford; 251b Destination Lake Taupo; 252c, 252cr, 253 AA/M Langford; 255 AA/M Langford; 257bt, 257bc, 257br AA/M Langford; 259c, 259cr, 259bl, 259br AA/M Langford; 260c, 260cr, 260br, 261 AA/M Langford; 262t, 263bl, 263bc, 263br AA/M Langford; 263b Mussel Inn; 264, 265cl, 265cr AA/M Langford; 266tl, 266bl, 266br, 267t, 267b AA/M Langford; 268c Gantleys; 268cr AA/M Langford; 270cl, 270cr AA/C Sawyer; 270c AA/M Langford; 273c, 273bl, 273br AA/M Langford; 273cr Hilton Hotel Auckland; 274 AA/M Langford; 275 Villa Toscana; 276cl Maungatautari Lodge; 276cr, 276b, 277 AA/M Langford; 278tl, 278b AA/M Langford; 279 Wharekauhau Country Estate; 280tr, 280bl, 281tl, 281r AA/M Langford; 282 AA/M Langford; 283 Fyffe Country Lodge; 284ct, 284c, 284b, 285t AA/M Langford; 286tl, 286tc, 286cl, AA/M Langford; 288t, 288bl, 289tl AA/M Langford; 288bc Corstorphine House Private Hotel; 289tr Larnach Lodge; 290c AA/M Langford; 290tr Fiordland Lodge; 290b Queenstown House

PLANNING

291 AA/M Langford; 292 Destination Lake Taupo/Craig Wilson; 293 Destination Lake Taupo; 294 AA/M Langford; 295t AA/P Kenward; 295b AA/A Belcher; 296t, 297b AA/M Langford; 296b courtesy of RBNZ; 297t AA/A Belcher; 298b AA/M Langford; 299bl AA/P Kenward; 299tr AA/C Sawyer; 300ct AA/A Belcher; 300b AA/M Langford; 301 AA/P Kenward; 302, 303c AA/A Belcher; 303b AA/P Kenward; 304 AA/P Kenward; 306 AA/M Langford

Project editor
Ann F Stonehouse

Design work
Kate Harling

Picture research
Vivien Little

Internal repro work
Susan Crowhurst, Ian Little, Michael Moody

Production
Helen Brown, Lyn Kirby

Mapping
Maps produced by the Cartography Department of AA Publishing

Main contributors
Mavis Airey, Jane Bellerby, Darroch Donald, Kathryn Fitzpatrick, Michael Mellor

Copy editors
Rebecca Snelling, Nia Williams

Updater
Michael Mellor

Revision management
Bookwork Creative Associates Ltd

Published by AA Publishing, a trading name of Automobile Association Developments Limited,
whose registered office is Fanum House, Basing View, Basingstoke, Hampshire, RG21 4EA, UK.
Registered number 1878835.

A CIP catalogue record for this book is available from the British Library.

ISBN-13: 978-0-7495-4630-4
ISBN-10: 0-7495-4630-1

Selected text supplied by Footprint Handbooks Limited © 2004

Key Guide is a registered trademark in Australia and is used under license.
Binding style with plastic section dividers by permission of AA Publishing.

Colour separation by Keenes
Printed and bound by Leo, China

Find out more about AA Publishing and the wide range of travel publications and services
the AA provides by visiting our website at www.theAA.com/travel

A03163
Maps in this title produced from map data:
© New Holland Publishing (South Africa) (PTY) Limited 2007
and © Footprint Handbooks Limited 2004

Administrative regions map © Crown copyright, Government of New Zealand
Relief map images supplied by Mountain High Maps® Copyright © 1993 Digital Wisdom, Inc
Weather chart statistics supplied by Weatherbase © Copyright 2004 Canty and Associates, LLC
Communicarta assistance with time chart gratefully acknowledged

We believe the contents of this book are correct at the time of printing.
However, some details, particularly prices, opening times and telephone numbers,
do change. We do not accept responsibility for any consequences arising from the use
of this book. This does not affect your statutory rights. We would be grateful if readers would
advise us of any inaccuracies they may encounter, or any suggestions they might like to make to
improve the book. There is a form provided at the back of the book for this purpose, or you can
email us at Keyguides@theaa.com

COVER PICTURE CREDITS

Front cover, top to bottom: AA/Paul Kenward; (inset) AA/Steve Day; AA/Mike Langford; AA/Mike Langford;
AA/Paul Kenward. Back cover, top to bottom: AA/Paul Kenward; AA/Paul Kenward; AA/Andy Belcher;
AA/Paul Kenward. Spine: AA/Paul Kenward; (inset) AA/Steve Day

Dear KeyGuide Reader

●

Thank you for buying this KeyGuide. Your comments and opinions are very important to us, so please help us to improve our travel guides by taking a few minutes to complete this questionnaire.

You do not need a stamp (unless posted outside the UK). If you do not want to cut this page from your guide, then photocopy it or write your answers on a plain sheet of paper.

Send to: KeyGuide Editor, AA World Travel Guides
FREEPOST SCE 4598, Basingstoke RG21 4GY

Find out more about AA Publishing and the wide range of
travel publications the AA provides by visiting our website at
www.theAA.com/travel

ABOUT THIS GUIDE

Which KeyGuide did you buy? _____

Where did you buy it?_____

When? _ _ month/ _ _ year

Why did you choose this AA KeyGuide?
- ❏ Price ❏ AA Publication
- ❏ Used this series before; title _____
- ❏ Cover ❏ Other (please state) _____

Please let us know how helpful the following features of the guide were to you by circling the appropriate category: very helpful (**VH**), helpful (**H**) or little help (**LH**)

Size	**VH**	**H**	**LH**
Layout	**VH**	**H**	**LH**
Photos	**VH**	**H**	**LH**
Excursions	**VH**	**H**	**LH**
Entertainment	**VH**	**H**	**LH**
Hotels	**VH**	**H**	**LH**
Maps	**VH**	**H**	**LH**
Practical info	**VH**	**H**	**LH**
Restaurants	**VH**	**H**	**LH**
Shopping	**VH**	**H**	**LH**
Walks	**VH**	**H**	**LH**
Sights	**VH**	**H**	**LH**
Transport info	**VH**	**H**	**LH**

What was your favourite sight, attraction or feature listed in the guide?

Page _____ Please give your reason _____

Which features in the guide could be changed or improved? Or are there any other comments you would like to make?

_____

_____